FREEDOM

Its History, Nature, and Varieties

FREEDOM

Its History, Nature, and Varieties

Robert E. Dewey
The University of Nebraska

James A. Gould
The University of South Florida

The Macmillan Company
Collier-Macmillan Limited, London

To **Charlie**, in memory of the days and nights of freedom.

J. A. G.

To **Ellen, Barb, and Chris**, in good hope of future days and nights of freedom.

R. E. D.

First Printing

Library of Congress catalog card number: 70-10369

THE MACMILLAN COMPANY
COLLIER-MACMILLAN CANADA, LTD., TORONTO, ONTARIO

PRINTED IN THE UNITED STATES OF AMERICA

ACKNOWLEDGMENTS

Herbert J. Muller: Freedom and Justice in History, from "Freedom and Justice in History" by Herbert Muller, reprinted from David Bidney, editor, THE CONCEPT OF FREEDOM IN ANTHROPOLOGY, The Hague: Mouton & Co., 1963. Copyright 1963 by The Wenner-Gren Foundation for Anthropological Research, Inc., New York. Reprinted by permission also of the author who drew his material from his forthcoming book, FREEDOM IN THE ANCIENT WORLD.

Harold J. Laski: The Changing Content of Freedom in History, from "Liberty" by Harold J. Laski, in the ENCYCLOPAEDIA OF SOCIAL SCIENCES, Seligman and Johnson, editors, Vol. IX, pp. 442-446. Copyright 1933, 1961 by The Macmillan Company, New York.

H. J. Pos: UNESCO Report on the Investigation Concerning Freedom, from the JOURNAL OF PHILOSOPHY, Vol. XLIX, No. 2, January 17, 1952, Columbia University, New York.

Mortimer J. Adler: Freedom as Natural, Acquired, and Circumstantial, from THE IDEA OF FREEDOM by Mortimer Adler. Copyright © 1958 by The Institute for Philosophical Research. Reprinted by permission of Doubleday & Co., Inc., New York.

Herbert J. Muller: Freedom as the Ability to Choose and Carry Out Purposes, from "The Meanings of Freedom" from ISSUES OF FREEDOM by Herbert J. Muller. Copyright © 1960 by Herbert J. Muller. Reprinted by permission of Harper & Row, Publishers, New York and the author.

Isaiah Berlin: Two Concepts of Liberty, from TWO CONCEPTS OF LIBERTY by Isaiah Berlin (Inaugural Lecture 1958; revised form reprinted in Isaiah Berlin's FOUR ESSAYS ON LIBERTY, Oxford University Press, London, 1969). Reprinted by permission of the Clarendon Press, Oxford, England.

PREFACE

In this book, we have sought to make available a set of readings treating the theme of human freedom. Since freedom is a topic of discussion in many fields and a subject of concern to all men who wish to understand themselves and the societies in which they live, appropriate readings cannot be confined to those provided by a given academic discipline, nor can they be confined to the realm of academic scholarship. If one is even to approach an understanding of freedom in the contemporary world, one must not only read the philosophers but listen to the Hippies, not only attend to historians but learn the programs of those who are now urging social reform and revolution, not only study the contributions of social scientists but understand the opinions of jurists. Accordingly, we have drawn our selections from a broad range of classical and contemporary sources and from the works of a wide variety of authors.

It would be presumptuous for us to suppose that this book contains a complete coverage of the many problems of freedom. It would be equally presumptuous for us to suppose that every important author and point of view are here represented. To comprehend the important literature on freedom from Western civilization alone is the task of a major library, not a single book. Our goal has been the more modest one of seeking readings that will highlight some of the central issues about freedom in the main areas where the subject is treated.

The basic organization of the book into five parts was determined by the fact that writings on freedom tend to fall into one of five categories. Some are concerned with the history of freedom; some seek to clarify the meaning of the various concepts of freedom; some focus upon the question whether man has free will; some concentrate upon characterizing the traits of personality possessed by a free man; and, finally, a vast literature deals with the problems faced by men in their quest for freedom in society.[1] While this division of the literature on freedom into five areas is helpful in bringing out the major focus of most writers, however, there is an element of arbitrariness in adopting any classification. Any given author is likely to have interests in, and write about, freedom in more than one area. Furthermore, it is difficult to write about one aspect of freedom without saying something about another aspect. Thus, most authors will put forward some view of the meaning of freedom even though their main concern may be to trace its history or to make suggestions about how to achieve freedom in society. Similarly, authors who emphasize the free will problem or who discuss the personality characteristics of free men are likely to make observations about the impact of social forces upon human freedom. Accordingly, the reader will find that selections in each part of the book will contain materials of relevance to the main topic of another part.

---

[1] In organizing the book in terms of these five areas of discussion, the editors are indebted to the classification of freedoms presented in *The Idea of Freedom* written by Mortimer J. Adler for the Institute for Philosophical Research (Garden City, N.Y.: Doubleday, Vol. I, 1958; Vol. II, 1961).

Although we have been aware from the outset of our work that we could not include all of the outstanding points of view and issues concerning freedom, we especially regret that space limitations did not permit us to draw more materials from poems, dramas, and novels. We were also reluctant to exclude such famous classics on freedom as those by Aquinas, Spinoza, Rousseau, and Hegel. With respect to contemporary social issues, the problems of freedom and their proposed solutions are both fascinating and endless. Thus, we could have devoted individual sections to problems of property and individual freedom, to problems of sexual freedom, to the New Left and their critics, and to problems of international order and freedom.

Despite these omissions, we are hopeful that the present volume has provided enough variety in points of view to stimulate thought, discussion, and further reading on the subject. We also hope that this volume will contribute to the growing recognition that an interdisciplinary approach is necessary when it comes to problems as fundamental as those of human freedom.

In the selection of materials we have been helped by the excellent comments and criticisms of Professor Vincent C. Punzo of St. Louis University and Professor Richard Taylor of the University of Rochester. In his capacity as editor at The Macmillan Company, Charles Smith has admirably performed the almost contradictory task of sympathetically understanding our other commitments while yet emphatically encouraging us to provide the finished manuscript. For the actual preparation of the manuscript, we especially acknowledge the patience and energy expended by Delma Alvarez, Charles Piatt, Julie Bovee, Joyce and Kay Felton, Fay Muth, Arlene Rash, Phyllis Schwartzman, and Vivian Trott.

R. E. D.
J. A. G.

CONTENTS

Introduction

The subject of human freedom is one which raises fundamental issues about the nature of man and his goals. Do men really wish to have a wide measure of freedom to choose and to determine their own lives? Would they not be happier without the burdens of such freedom? Can they be trusted to use such freedom wisely?

In the literature of Western civilization, Fyodor Dostoevsky has provided one of the most famous discussions of these basic questions. In a chapter of his novel The Brothers Karamazov, Dostoevsky narrates a conversation between two of the central characters, Ivan Karamazov and his younger brother, Alyosha. For the novel as a whole, Ivan and Alyosha represent contrasting types. Ivan is primarily an intellectual who portrays the problems of one who has become sceptical of traditional beliefs and faiths, whereas Alyosha is primarily a man of faith, training for a future career as a Christian priest. At the point in the novel from which the reading selection is taken, Ivan has written a story about the Grand Inquisitor and he proceeds to tell it to Alyosha.

Ivan sets the scene of his tale in Spain of the sixteenth century. He imagines Christ returning to earth and meeting a cardinal of the church, the Grand Inquisitor, who has been responsible for burning a hundred heretics on the day before. The Grand Inquisitor recognizes Christ, imprisons him, and then explains why Christ must also be sentenced to death by fire.

In the eyes of the Grand Inquisitor, Christ's heresy consists in the value which he placed upon man's freedom of choice and conscience. The Grand Inquisitor reviews Christ's three temptations and notes that in each case Christ could have chosen to enslave men and thereby make them happy but did not do so for the sake of leaving them free. When Christ, in the first temptation, would not turn stones into bread, he thwarted the desire of men to have some one to worship. When Christ next refused to prove he was the son of God by flinging himself from the top of a temple and being saved by angels, he rejected the needs of men for "miracle, mystery, and authority." Finally, when Christ would not take the kingdoms of the world, he turned down the opportunity to give men unity and peace on earth. For the Grand Inquisitor, men are weak by nature and the true lover of humanity must correct Christ's work by removing their freedom and giving them "all that man seeks on earth—that is, some one to worship, some one to keep his conscience, and some means of uniting all in one unanimous and harmonious ant-heap."

1

"THE GRAND INQUISITOR"

Fyodor Dostoevsky

"My story is laid in Spain, in Seville, in the most terrible time of the Inquisition, when fires were lighted every day to the glory of God, and 'in the splendid *auto da fé* the wicked heretics were burnt.' Oh, of course, this was not the coming in which He will appear according to His promise at the end of time in all His heavenly glory, and which will be sudden 'as lightning flashing from east to west.' No, He visited His children only for a moment, and there where the flames were crackling round the heretics. In His infinite mercy He came once more among men in that human shape in which He walked among men for three years fifteen centuries ago. He came down to the 'hot pavement' of the southern town in which on the day before almost a hundred heretics had, *ad majorem gloriam Dei*, been burnt by the cardinal, the Grand Inquisitor, in a magnificent *auto da fé*, in the presence of the king, the court, the knights, the cardinals, the most charming ladies of the court, and the whole population of Seville.

"He came softly, unobserved, and yet, strange to say, every one recognized Him. That might be one of the best passages in the poem. I mean, why they recognized Him. The people are irresistibly drawn to Him, they surround Him, they flock about Him, follow Him. He moves silently in their midst with a gentle smile of infinite compassion. The sun of love burns in His heart, light and power shine from His eyes, and their radiance, shed on the people, stirs their hearts with responsive love. He holds out his hands to them, blesses them, and a healing virtue comes from contact with Him, even with His garments. An old man in the crowd, blind from childhood, cries out, 'O Lord, heal me and I shall see Thee!' and, as it were, scales fall from his eyes and the blind man sees Him. The crowd weeps and kisses the earth under His feet. Children throw flowers before Him, sing, and cry hosannah. 'It is He—it is He!' all repeat. 'It must be He, it can be no one but Him!' He stops at the steps of the Seville cathedral at the moment when the weeping mourners are bringing in a little open white coffin. In it lies a child of seven, the only daughter of a prominent citizen. The dead child lies hidden in flowers. 'He will raise your child,' the crowd shouts to the weeping mother. The priest, coming to meet the coffin, looks perplexed, and frowns, but the mother of the dead child throws herself at His feet with a wail. 'If it is Thou, raise my child!' she cries, holding out her hands to Him. The procession halts, the coffin is laid on the steps at His feet. He looks with compassion, and His lips once more softly pronounce, 'Maiden, arise!' and the maiden arises. The little girl sits up in the coffin and looks around, smiling with wide-open wondering eyes, holding a bunch of white roses they had put in her hand.

"There are cries, sobs, confusion among the people, and at that moment the cardinal himself, the Grand Inquisitor, passes by the cathedral. He is an old man, almost ninety, tall and erect, with a withered face and sunken eyes, in which there is still a gleam of light. He is not dressed in his gorgeous cardinal's robes, as he was the day before, when he was burning the enemies of the Roman Church—at that moment he was wearing his coarse, old, monk's cassock. At a distance behind him come his gloomy assistants and slaves and the 'holy guard.' He stops at the sight of the crowd and watches it from a distance. He sees everything; he sees them set the coffin down at His feet, sees the child rise up, and his face darkens. He knits his thick grey brows and his eyes gleam with a sinister fire. He holds out his finger and bids the guards take Him. And such is his power, so completely are the people cowed into submission and trembling obedience to him, that the crowd immediately make way for the guards, and in the midst of deathlike silence they lay hands on Him and lead Him away. The crowd instantly bows down to the earth, like one man, before the old inquisitor. He blesses the people in silence and passes on. The guards lead their prisoner to the close, gloomy vaulted prison in the ancient palace of the Holy Inquisition and shut Him in it. The day passes and is followed by the dark, burning 'breathless' night of Seville. The air is 'fragrant with laurel and lemon.' In the pitch darkness the iron door of the prison is suddenly open and the Grand Inquisitor himself comes in with a light in his hand. He is alone; the door is closed at once behind him. He stands in the doorway and for a minute or two gazes into His face. At last he goes up slowly, sets the light on the table and speaks.

" 'Is it Thou? Thou?' but receiving no answer, he adds at once, 'Don't answer, be silent. What canst Thou say, indeed? I know too well what Thou wouldst say. And Thou hast no right to add anything to what Thou hadst said of old. Why, then, art Thou come to hinder us? For Thou hast come to hinder us, and Thou knowest that. But dost Thou know what will be tomorrow? I know not who Thou art and care not to know whether it is Thou or only a semblance of Him, but tomorrow I shall condemn Thee and burn Thee at the stake as the worst of heretics. And the very people who have today kissed Thy feet, tomorrow at the faintest sign from me will rush to heap up the embers of Thy fire. Knowest Thou that? Yes, maybe Thou knowest it,' he added with thoughtful penetration, never for a moment taking his eyes off the Prisoner."

"I don't quite understand, Ivan. What does it mean?" Alyosha, who has been listening in silence, said with a smile. "Is it simply a wild fantasy, or a mistake on the part of the old man—some impossible *quiproquo*?"

"Take it as the last," said Ivan, laughing, "if you are so corrupted by modern realism and can't stand anything fantastic. If you like it to be a case of mistaken identity, let it be so. It is true," he went on, laughing, "the old man was ninety; and he might well be crazy over his set idea. He might have been struck by the appearance of the Prisoner. It might, in fact, be simply his ravings, the delusion of an old man of ninety, over-excited by the *auto de fé* of a hundred heretics the day before. But does it matter to us after all whether it was a mistake of identity or a wild fantasy? All that matters is that the old man should speak out, should speak openly of what he has thought in silence for ninety years."

"And the Prisoner too is silent? Does He look at him and not say a word?"

"That's inevitable in any case," Ivan laughed again. "The old man has told Him He hasn't the right to add anything to what He has said of old. One may say it is the most fundamental feature of Roman Catholicism, in my opinion at least. 'All has been given by Thee to the Pope,' they say, 'and all, therefore, is still in the Pope's hands, and there is no need for Thee to come now at all. Thou must not meddle for the time, at least.' That's how they speak and write too—the Jesuits, at any rate. I have read it myself in the works of their theologians. 'Hast Thou the right to reveal to us one of the mysteries of that world from which thou hast come?' my old man asks Him, and answers the question for Him. 'No, Thou hast not: that Thou mayest not add to what has been said of old, and mayest not take from men the freedom which Thou didst exalt when Thou wast on earth. Whatsoever thou revealest anew will encroach on men's freedom of faith; for it will be manifest as a miracle, and the freedom of their faith was dearer to Thee than anything in those days fifteen hundred years ago. Didst Thou not often say then, "I will make you free"? But now Thou hast seen these "free" men,' the old man adds suddenly, with a pensive smile. 'Yes, we've paid dearly for it,' he goes on, looking sternly at Him, 'but at last we have completed that work in Thy name. For fifteen centuries we have been wrestling with Thy freedom, but now it is ended and over for good. Dost Thou not believe that it's over for good? Thou lookest meekly at me and deignest not even to be wroth with me. But let me tell Thee that now, today, people are more persuaded than ever that they have perfect freedom, yet they have brought their freedom to us and laid it humbly at our feet. But that has been our doing. Was this what Thou didst? Was this Thy freedom?' "

"I don't understand again," Alyosha broke in. "Is he ironical, is he jesting?"

"Not a bit of it! He claims it as a merit for himself and his Church that at last they have vanquished freedom and have done so to make men happy. 'For now' (he is speaking of the Inquisition, of course) 'for the first time it has become possible to think of the happiness of men. Man was created a rebel; and how can rebels be happy? Thou wast warned,' he says to Him. 'Thou has had no lack of admonitions and warnings, but Thou didst not listen to those warnings: Thou didst reject the only way by which men might be made happy. But, fortunately, departing Thou didst hand on the work to us. Thou hast promised, Thou has established by Thy word. Thou hast given to us the right to bind and to unbind, and now, of course, Thou canst not think of taking it away. Why, then, hast Thou come to hinder us?"

"And what's the meaning of 'no lack of admonitions and warnings'?" asked Alyosha.

"Why, that's the chief part of what the old man must say."

" 'The wise and dread spirit, the spirit of self-destruction and non-existence,' the old man goes on, 'the great spirit talked with Thee in the wilderness, and we are told in the books that he "tempted" Thee. Is that so? And could anything truer be said than what he revealed to Thee in three questions and what Thou didst reject, and what in the books is called "the temptation"? And yet if there has ever been on earth a real stupendous miracle, it took place on that day, on the day of the three temptations. The statement of those three questions was itself the miracle. If it were possible to imagine simply for the sake of argument that those three questions of the dread spirit has perished utterly from the books, and that we had to restore them and to invent them anew, and to do so had gathered together all the wise men of the earth—rulers, chief priests, learned men, philosophers, poets— and had set them the task to invent three questions, such as would not only fit the occasion, but express in three words, three human phrases, the whole future history of the world and of humanity—dost Thou believe that all the wisdom of the earth united could have invented anything in depth and force equal to the three questions which were actually put to Thee then by the wise and mighty spirit in the wilderness? From those questions alone, from the miracle of their statement, we can see that we have here to do not with the fleeting human intelligence, but with the absolute and eternal. For in those three questions the whole subsequent history of mankind is, as it were, brought together into one whole, and foretold, and in them are united all the unsolved historical contradictions of human nature. At the time it could not be so clear, since the future was unknown; but now that fifteen hundred years have passed, we see that everything in those three questions was so justly divined and foretold, and has been so truly fulfilled, that nothing can be added to them or taken from them.

" 'Judge Thyself who was right—Thou or he who questioned Thee then? Remember the first question; its meaning, in other words, was this: "Thou wouldst go into the world, and art going with empty hands, with some promise of freedom which men in their simplicity and their natural unruliness cannot even understand, which they fear and dread—for nothing has ever been more insupportable for a man and a human society than freedom. But seest Thou these stones in this parched and barren wilderness? Turn them into bread, and mankind will run after Thee like a flock of sheep, grateful and obedient, though for ever trembling, lest Thou withdraw Thy hand and deny them Thy bread." But Thou wouldst not deprive man of freedom and didst reject the offer, thinking, what is that freedom worth, if obedience is bought with bread? Thou didst reply that man lives not by bread alone. But dost Thou know that for the sake of that earthly bread the spirit of the earth will rise up against Thee and will strive with Thee and overcome Thee and all will follow him, crying, "Who can compare with this beast? He has given us fire from heaven!" Dost Thou know that the ages will pass, and humanity will proclaim by the lips of their sages that there is no crime, and therefore no sin; there is only hunger? "Feed men, and then ask of them virtue!" that's what they'll write on the banner, which they will raise against Thee, and with which they will destroy Thy temple. Where Thy temple stood will rise a new building; the terrible tower of Babel will be built again, and though, like the one of old, it will not be finished, yet Thou mightest have prevented that new tower and have cut short the sufferings of men for a thousand years; for they will come back to us after a thousand years of agony with their tower. They will seek us again, hidden underground in the catacombs, for we shall be again persecuted and tortured. They will find us and cry to us, "Feed us, for those who have promised us fire from heaven haven't given it!"

And then we shall finish building their tower, for he finishes the building who feeds them. And we alone shall feed them in Thy name, declaring falsely that it is in Thy name. Oh, never, never can they feed themselves without us! No science will give them bread so long as they remain free. In the end they will lay their freedom at our feet, and say to us, "Make us your slaves, but feed us." They will understand themselves, at last, that freedom and bread enough for all are inconceivable together, for never, never will they be able to share between them! They will be convinced, too, that they can never be free, for they are weak, vicious, worthless and rebellious. Thou didst promise them the bread of Heaven, but, I repeat again, can it compare with earthly bread in the eyes of the weak, ever sinful and ignoble race of men? And if for the sake of the bread of Heaven thousands and tens of thousands shall follow Thee, what is to become of the millions and tens of thousands of millions of creatures who will not have the strength to forego the earthly bread for the sake of the heavenly? Or dost Thou care only for the tens of thousands of the great and strong, while the millions, numerous as the sands of the sea, who are weak but love Thee, must exist only for the sake of the great and strong? No, we care for the weak too. They are sinful and rebellious, but in the end they too will become obedient. They will marvel at us and look on us as gods, because we are ready to endure the freedom which they have found so dreadful and to rule over them—so awful it will seem to them to be free. But we shall tell them that we are Thy servants and rule them in Thy name. We shall deceive them again, for we will not let Thee come to us again. That deception will be our suffering for we shall be forced to lie.

" 'This is the significance of the first question in the wilderness, and this is what Thou has rejected for the sake of that freedom which Thou hast exalted above everything. Yet in this question lies hid the great secret of this world. Choosing "bread," Thou wouldst have satisfied the universal and everlasting craving of humanity—to find some one to worship. So long as man remains free he strives for nothing so incessantly and so painfully as to find some one to worship. But man seeks to worship what is established beyond dispute, so that all men would agree at once to worship it. For these pitiful creatures are concerned not only to find what one or the other can worship, but to find something that all would believe in and worship; what is essential is that all may be *together* in it. This craving for *community* of worship is the chief misery of every man individually and of all humanity from the beginning of time. For the sake of common worship they've slain each other with the sword. They have set up gods and challenged one another, "Put away your gods and come and worship ours, or we will kill you and your gods!" And so it will be to the end of the world, even when gods disappear from the earth; they will fall down before idols just the same. Thou didst know, Thou couldst not but have known, this fundamental secret of human nature, but Thou didst reject the one infallible banner which was offered Thee to make all men bow down to Thee alone—the banner of earthly bread; and Thou hast rejected it for the sake of freedom and the bread of Heaven. Behold what Thou didst further. And all again in the name of Freedom! I tell Thee that man is tormented by no greater anxiety than to find some one quickly to whom he can hand over that gift of freedom with which the ill-fated creature is born. But only one who can appease their conscience can take over their freedom. In bread there was offered Thee an invincible banner; give bread, and man will worship Thee, for nothing is more certain than bread. But if some one else gains possession of his conscience—oh! then he will cast away Thy bread and follow after him who has ensnared his conscience. In that Thou wast right. For the secret of man's being is not only to live but to have something to live for. Without a stable conception of the object of life, man would not consent to go on living, and would rather destroy himself than remain on earth, though he had bread in abundance. That is true. But what happened? Instead of taking men's freedom from them, Thou didst make it greater than ever! Didst Thou forget that man prefers peace, and even death, to freedom of choice in the knowledge of good and evil? Nothing is more seductive for man than his freedom of conscience, but nothing is a greater cause of suffering. And behold, instead of giving a firm foundation for setting the conscience of man at rest for ever, Thou didst choose all that is exceptional, vague and enigmatic; Thou didst choose what was utterly beyond the strength of men, acting as though Thou didst not love them at all—Thou who didst come to give Thy life for them! Instead of taking possession of men's freedom, Thou didst increase it, and burdened the spiritual kingdom of mankind with its sufferings for ever. Thou didst desire man's free love, that he should follow Thee freely, enticed and taken captive by Thee. In place of the rigid ancient law, man must hereafter with free heart decide for himself what is good and what is evil, having only Thy image before him as his guide. But didst Thou not know he would at last reject even Thy image and Thy truth, if he is weighed down with the fearful burden of free choice? They will cry aloud at last that the truth is not in Thee, for they could not have been left in greater confusion and suffering than Thou hast caused, laying upon them so many cares and unanswerable problems.

" 'So that, in truth, Thou didst Thyself lay the foundation for the destruction of Thy kingdom, and no one is more to blame for it. Yet what was offered Thee? There are three powers, three powers alone, able to conquer and to hold captive for ever the conscience of these impotent rebels for their happiness—those forces are miracle, mystery and authority. Thou hast rejected all three and hast set the example for doing so. When the wise and dread spirit set Thee on the pinnacle of the temple and said to Thee, "If Thou wouldst know whether Thou art the Son of God then cast Thyself down, for it is written: the angels shall hold him up lest he fall and bruise himself, and Thou shalt know then whether Thou art the Son of God and shalt prove then how great is Thy faith in Thy Father." But Thou didst refuse and wouldst not cast Thyself down. Oh! of course, Thou didst proudly and well, like God; but the weak, unruly race of men, are they gods? Oh, Thou didst know then that in taking one step, in making one movement to cast Thyself down, Thou wouldst be tempting God and have lost all Thy faith in Him, and wouldst have been dashed to pieces against that earth which Thou didst come to save. And the wise spirit that tempted Thee would have rejoiced. But I ask again, are there many like Thee? And couldst Thou believe for one moment that men, too, could face such a temptation? Is the nature of men such, that they can reject miracle, and at the great moments of their life, the moments of their deepest, most agonising spiritual difficulties, cling only to the free verdict of the heart? Oh, Thou didst know that Thy deed would be recorded in books, would be handed down to remote times and the utmost ends of the earth, and Thou didst hope that man, following Thee, would cling to God and not ask for a miracle. But Thou didst not know that when man rejects miracle he rejects God too; for man seeks not so much God as the miraculous. And as man cannot bear to be without the miraculous, he will create new miracles of his own for himself, and will worship deeds of sorcery and witchcraft, though he might be a hundred times over a rebel, heretic and infidel. Thou didst not come down from the Cross when they shouted to Thee, mocking and reviling Thee, "Come down from the cross and we will believe that Thou art He." Thou didst not come down, for again Thou wouldst not enslave man by a miracle, and didst crave faith given freely, not based on miracle. Thou didst crave for free love and not the base raptures of the slave before the might that has overawed him for ever. But Thou didst think too highly of men therein, for they are slaves, of course, though rebellious by nature. Look round and judge; fifteen centuries have passed, look upon them. Whom hast Thou raised up to Thyself? I swear, man is weaker and baser by nature than Thou hast believed him! Can he, can he do what Thou didst? By showing him so much respect, Thou didst, as it were, cease to feel for him, for Thou didst ask far too much from him—Thou who hast loved him more than Thyself! Respecting him less, Thou wouldst have asked less of him. That would have been more like love, for his burden would have been lighter. He is weak and vile. What though he is everywhere now rebelling against our power, and proud of his rebellion? It is the pride of a child and a schoolboy. They are little children rioting and barring out the teacher at school. But their childish delight will end; it will cost them dear. They will cast down temples and drench the earth with blood. But they will see at last, the foolish children, that, though they are rebels, they are impotent rebels, unable to keep up their own rebellion. Bathed in their foolish tears, they will recognise at last that He who created them rebels must have meant to mock at them. They will say this in despair, and their utterance will be a blasphemy which will make them more unhappy still, for man's nature cannot bear blasphemy, and in the end always avenges it on itself. And so unrest, confusion and unhappiness—that is the present lot of man after Thou didst bear so much for their freedom! Thy great prophet tells in vision and in image, that he saw all those who took part in the first resurrection and that there were of each tribe twelve thousand. But if there were so many of them, they must have been not men but gods. They had borne Thy cross, they had endured scores of years in the barren, hungry wilderness, living upon locusts and roots—and Thou mayest indeed point with pride at those children of freedom, of free love, of free and splendid sacrifice for Thy name. But remember that they were only some thousands; and what of the rest? And how are the other weak ones to blame, because they could not endure what the strong have endured? How is the weak soul to blame that it is unable to receive such terrible gifts? Canst Thou have simply come to the elect and for the elect? But if so, it is a mystery and we cannot understand it. And if it is a mystery, we too have a right to preach a mystery, and to teach them that it's not the free judgment of their hearts, not love that matters, but a mystery which they must follow blindly, even against their conscience. So we have done. We have corrected Thy work and have founded it upon *miracle*, *mystery* and *authority*. And men rejoiced that they were again led like sheep, and that the terrible gift that had brought them such suffering, was, at last, lifted from their hearts. Were we right teaching them this? Speak! Did we not love mankind, so meekly acknowledging their feebleness, lovingly lightening their burden, and permitting their weak nature even sin with our sanction? Why hast Thou come now to hinder us? And why dost Thou look silently and searchingly at me with Thy mild eyes? Be angry. I don't want Thy love, for I love Thee not. And what use is it for me to hide anything from Thee? Don't I know to Whom I am speaking? All that I can say is known to Thee already. And is it for me to conceal from Thee our mystery? Perhaps it is Thy will to hear it from my lips. Listen, then. We are not working with Thee, but with *him*—that is our mystery. It's long—eight centuries—since we have been on *his* side and not on Thine. Just eight centuries ago, we took from him what Thou didst reject with scorn, that last gift he offered Thee, showing Thee all the kingdoms of the earth. We took from him Rome and the sword of Caesar, and proclaimed ourselves sole rulers of the earth, though hitherto we have not been able to complete our work. But whose fault is that? Oh, the work is only beginning, but it has begun. It has long to await completion and the earth has yet much to suffer, but we shall triumph and shall be Caesars, and then we shall plan the universal happiness of man. But Thou mightest have taken even then the sword of Caesar. Why didst Thou reject that last gift? Hadst Thou accepted that last counsel of the mighty spirit, Thou wouldst have accomplished all that man seeks on earth—that is, some one to worship, some one to keep his conscience, and some means of uniting all in one unanimous and harmonious ant-heap, for the craving for universal unity is the third and last anguish of men. Mankind as a whole has always striven to organise a universal state. There have been many great nations with great histories, but the more highly they were developed the more unhappy they were, for they felt more acutely than other people the craving for worldwide union. The great conquerors, Timours and Ghenghis-Khans, whirled like hurricanes over the face of the earth striving to subdue its people, and they too were but the unconscious expression of the same craving for universal unity. Hadst Thou taken the world and Caesar's purple, Thou wouldst have founded the universal state and have given universal peace. For who can rule men if not he who holds their conscience and their bread in his hands? We have taken the sword of Caesar, and in taking it, of course, have rejected Thee and followed *him*. Oh, ages are yet to come of the confusion of free thought, of their science and cannibalism. For having begun to build their tower of Babel without us, they will end, of course, with cannibalism. But then the beast will crawl to us and lick our feet and spatter them with tears of blood. And we shall sit upon the beast and raise the cup, and on it will be written, "Mystery." But then, and only then, the reign of peace and happiness will come for men. Thou art proud of Thine elect, but Thou hast only the elect, while we give rest to all. And besides, how many of those elect, those mighty ones who could become elect, have grown weary waiting for Thee, and have transferred and will transfer the powers of their spirit and the warmth of their heart to the other camp, and end by raising their *free* banner against Thee. Thou didst Thyself lift up that banner. But with us all will be happy and will no more rebel nor destroy one another as under Thy freedom. Oh, we shall persuade them that they will only become free when they renounce their freedom to us and submit to us. And shall we be right or shall we be lying? They will be convinced that we are right, for they will remember the horrors of slavery and confusion to which Thy freedom brought them. Freedom, free thought and science, will lead them into such straits and will bring them face to face with such marvels and insoluble mysteries, that some of them, the fierce and rebellious, will destroy themselves, others, rebellious but weak, will destroy one another, while the rest, weak and unhappy, will crawl fawning to our feet and whine to us: "Yes, you were right, you alone possess His mystery, and we come back to you, save us from ourselves!"

" 'Receiving bread from us, they will see clearly that we take the bread made by their hands from them, to give it to them, without any miracle. They will see that we do not change the stones to bread, but in truth they will be more thankful for taking it from our hands than for the bread itself! For they will remember only too well that in old days, without our help, even the bread they made turned to stones in their hands, while since they have come back to us, the very stones have turned to bread in their hands. Too, too well they know the value of complete submission! And until men know that, they will be unhappy. Who is most to blame for their not knowing it, speak? Who scattered the flock and sent it astray on unknown paths? But the flock will come together again and will submit once more, and then it will be once for all. Then we shall give them the quiet humble happiness of weak creatures such as they are by nature. Oh, we shall persuade them at last not to be proud, for Thou didst lift them up and thereby taught them to be proud. We shall show them that they are weak, that they are only pitiful children, but that childlike happiness is the sweetest of all. They will become timid and will look to us and huddle close to us in fear, as chicks to the hen. They will marvel at us and will be awe-stricken before us, and will be proud at our being so powerful and clever, that we have been able to subdue such a turbulent flock of thousands of millions. They will tremble impotently before our wrath, their minds will grow fearful, they will be quick to shed tears like women and children, but they will be just as ready at a sign from us to pass to laughter and rejoicing, to happy mirth and childish song. Yes, we shall set them to work, but in their leisure hours we shall make their life like a child's game, with children's songs and innocent dance. Oh, we shall allow them even sin, they are weak and helpless, and they will love us like children because we allow them to sin. We shall tell them that every sin will be expiated, if it is done with our permission, that we allow them to sin because we love them, and the punishment for these sins we take upon ourselves. And we shall take it upon ourselves, and they will adore us as their saviours, who have taken on themselves their sins before God. And they will have no secrets from us. We shall allow or forbid them to live with their wives and mistresses, to have or not to have children—according to whether they have been obedient or disobedient—and they will submit to us gladly and cheerfully. The most painful secrets of their conscience, all, all they will bring to us, and we shall have an answer for all. And they will be glad to believe our answer, for it will save them from the great anxiety and terrible agony they endure at present in making a free decision for themselves. And all will be happy, all the millions of creatures except the hundred thousand who rule over them. For only we, we who guard the mystery, shall be unhappy. There will be thousands of millions of happy babes, and a hundred thousand sufferers who have taken upon themselves the curse of the knowledge of good and evil. Peacefully they will die, peacefully they will expire in Thy name, and beyond the grave they will find nothing but death. But we shall keep the secret, and for our happiness we shall allure them with the reward of heaven and eternity. Though if there were anything in the other world, it certainly would not be for such as they. It is prophesied that Thou wilt come again in victory, Thou wilt come with Thy chosen, the proud and strong, but we will say that they have only saved themselves, but we have saved all. We are told that the harlot who sits upon the beast, and holds in her hands the *mystery*, shall be put to shame, that the weak will rise up again, and will rend her royal purple and will strip naked her loathsome body. But then I will stand up and point out to Thee the thousand millions of happy children who have known no sin. And we who have taken their sins upon us for their happiness will stand up before Thee and say: "Judge us if Thou canst and darest." Know that I fear Thee not, Know that I too have been in the wilderness, I too have lived on roots and locusts, I too prized the freedom with which Thou has blessed men, and I too was striving to stand among Thy elect, among the strong and powerful, thirsting "to make up the number." But I awakened and would not serve madness. I turned back and joined the ranks of those *who have corrected Thy work*. I left the proud and went back to the humble, for the happiness of the humble. What I say to Thee will come to pass, and our dominion will be built up. I repeat, tomorrow Thou shalt see that obedient flock who at a sign from me will hasten to heap up the hot cinders about the pile on which I shall burn Thee for coming to hinder us. For if any one has ever deserved our fires, it is Thou. Tomorrow I shall burn Thee. Dixi.'

". . . When the Inquisitor ceased speaking, he waited some time for his prisoner to answer him. His silence weighed down upon him. He saw that the prisoner had listened intently all the time, looking gently in his face and evidently not wishing to reply. The old man longed for Him to say something, however bitter and terrible. But he suddenly approached the old man in silence and softly kissed him on his bloodless aged lips. That was all his answer. The old man shuddered. His lips moved. He went to the door, opened it, and said to Him: 'Go, and come no more. . . . come not at all, never, never!' And he let Him out into the dark alleys of the town. The prisoner went away."

"And the old man?"

"The kiss glows in his heart, but the old man adheres to his idea."

"And you with him, you too?" cried Alyosha, mournfully.

Ivan laughed.

"Why, it's all nonsense, Alyosha. It's only a senseless poem of a senseless student, who could never write two lines of verse. Why do you take it so seriously? . . ."

1. The History of Freedom

It is important to realize that there are many freedoms—political, social, economic, and so on—and that these various freedoms have had histories. We have freedoms now that scarcely existed five hundred years ago or even one hundred years ago. A century from now new freedoms or aspects of freedoms will exist. These new freedoms, like the old ones, will probably have to be won through the blood of martyrs.

The three writers in this section, Muller, Lord Acton, and Laski, are aware of the history and emergence of freedoms. Each of them has conceptions of freedom (or "liberty"—the terms will be used interchangeably in this text). The conceptions of the three writers are not in complete accord, yet they have common agreement as to the existence and nonexistence of such freedoms as the political and the religious.

Muller goes further back into history than do the other two. After he begins his essay with a definition of freedom, "the condition of being able to choose and to carry out purposes" (which will be contrastingly analyzed with others in Part 2), his historical analysis starts as far back as the cave painters. These artists and those who followed were concerned with magical powers, a power which was readily claimed by the earliest type of political leaders, the sacred monarchists. These gave rise to the most ancient political ruler, the despot, under whom few if any freedoms existed.

The first great change came during the first millenium B.C. with the appearance and effect of such men as Buddha, Confucius, Amos, Homer, Solon, and Socrates. Their main contribution was the introduction of universal ethical ideals—i.e., "spiritual freedom" (selections dealing with this type of freedom will be found in Part 3). The Greek city-state government is said by Muller, Acton, and Laski to be the first significant government granting political freedom, via laws and elected legal officials.

Lord Acton, the devout Catholic, has a tolerant attitude about the contribution of religion to freedom, although he sees the history of freedom mainly in terms of the development of liberal political institutions. Muller and Laski contend that Western religions contributed little to the concept and institutions of freedom. In fact,

*Muller says that their belief in an exclusive, unique god created a fanaticism which
has had disastrous effects on the history of freedom. Muller sees freedom in terms
of positive means as well as the negative freedom of political liberalism. He argues
that freedom must be correlated with justice, a position similar to Laski's belief that
liberty (freedom) advances with the advance of equality. Of the three Laski alone
emphasizes the importance of economic freedom. He says freedom increases with an
improved economic condition. Muller and Laski view freedom democratically, in
contrast with Acton's distrust of democratic claims to power. Nevertheless, they all
are optimistic about the progressive increase of freedom in our world.*

"FREEDOM AND JUSTICE IN HISTORY"

Herbert J. Muller

For the purposes of a historian, I have sought a broad but relatively neutral,
objective definition of freedom, and settled on this one: the condition of being able to
choose and to carry out purposes. This involves both the primary dictionary
meaning, the absence of external constraints or the common idea of freedom *from*
coercion, and the idea of practicable purposes, an actual ability with available
means, or effective freedom *to* do what one wishes. With such ability it assumes a
power of conscious choice between known alternatives, or freedom *of* mind and
spirit, as the distinctive freedom that man is capable of, beyond the ability of other
animals to carry out their instinctive purposes. So defined, freedom means concretely freedoms of various kinds. But I am ruling out the various concepts of "true
freedom" that philosophers have been fond of: the notion that a person is "really"
free only when he is avoiding "license", acting virtuously, doing his duty to the
state, being wholly rational, serving God, or being his "true self". These concepts all
come down to the idea that freedom consists in doing what is right and good—by
the standards of the thinker; while thinkers remain notoriously unable to agree on
these standards, or on the nature of the alleged "true self". From this point of view
I mean by freedom a state in which a person may decide for himself what is right
and good, what to do with his freedom, what kind of self to become. I am
assuming that the question of freedom *for* what is always pertinent, in fact
inescapable, but that it may be discussed more profitably if we hold to a neutral
definition and distinguish the problem of the nature of freedom from the problem
of its proper uses or ends. We should all be able to agree that free men are not
necessarily virtuous or wise.

It follows that freedom is more than a political matter. Although men brought up
in a consciously free society generally assume, with good reason, that rights or civil
liberties guaranteed by law are its essential condition, I assume that a historian in

particular has to consider it in relation not only to government but to mores, technology, commerce, art, religion—the culture as a whole. Thus the rise of civilization made political power a major problem ever after, but it also widened the range of man's choices, gave freer rein to his creative powers, made possible a fuller realization of his potentialities, and eventually produced the higher religions, philosophy, and science, which cannot possibly be ignored in a history of freedom.

As for justice, which in our own society is often declared to be one and inseparable from freedom, I judge that it must be distinguished. All civilized societies have had codes of justice, but almost none have equated it with freedom. It took many centuries to abolish slavery, for example, because this was all the while a legal institution, defended as just by eminent philosophers and high churchmen. At the same time, I take for granted an intimate connection between these ideas. There can of course be no effective freedom in society without some principle of justice, rights assured by custom or law; and historically, conscious ideals of justice have in the long run clearly tended to promote freedom for the many, the poor and weak. The growth of freedom has in turn as clearly tended to promote the ideal of equity. Among other things, it has by now led to a general agreement among civilized men that the venerable institution of slavery is unjust.

Now, of the history of these very large subjects, I can of course present only the sketchiest outline here. In this outline I am merely introducing a number of themes, all of them controversial, as possible topics for discussion. So I should begin with a commonplace of Western thought, that man has a natural passion for freedom, and that his whole history has been an endless cry for justice and freedom. Charles Beard, for instance, wrote: "Since the beginning of civilization there has been a struggle between sheer force and humanity, between the few who have sought dominance by physical might and the many who have sought to protect and govern themselves under customs and rules of their own making." By contrast, there remains the thesis so memorably stated by Dostoyevsky's Grand Inquisitor in *The Brothers Karamazov:* the Spanish Inquisitor who recognized the true Christ, come back to earth, but sentences him to death again. Christ, he said, was offering men freedom of choice and conscience, and for the great masses of men such freedom is an intolerable burden; what they need first of all is bread, and then "miracle, mystery, and authority". On the historical record, I regret to say, the Grand Inquisitor seems closer to the truth. What most men in most societies have lived by, if not consciously sought, was miracle, mystery, and authority, often without enough bread; and they did not struggle for freedom. Folklore, I am told, gives little suggestion of a yearning for freedom.

More specifically, men very early became obsessed with magic. One of the basic paradoxes of human history, already apparent in the superb animal drawing of the prehistoric cavemen, is that as men achieved more mastery of their natural environment, more empirical knowledge or skill, more effective freedom through their own natural gifts, they became more devoted to magic, employed their natural gifts more painstakingly in the quest of supernatural power. The immediate question is whether their obsession with magic chiefly expressed fear or emancipated them from fear by giving them the illusion of power; thus Malinowski saw in it a recognition of

man's limitations, Freud a belief in "the omnipotence of thought". I should suppose
that it was ambivalent, and that the dominant feeling—of anxiety or confidence—
would depend on the culture and its fortunes. In any case, it forces the important
distinction between subjective and objective freedom, or feeling free and being free.
But whatever the feeling, the historical truth seems to be that as man approached
civilization he became more convinced of his utter dependence on supernatural
powers, now called gods. In Sumer the early cities were owned by a god, managed
by his priest, and dedicated primarily to his welfare or upkeep; in Egypt the whole
land was managed by Pharaoh, himself a god, and all Egyptians knew that their
welfare depended wholly upon him.

A related theme is the predominance of myth, or mythopoeic thought, in early
civilization. This raises more difficult issues, now that students of myth have
discounted the early scientific view of it as a mere aberration of thought, or
"disease of language", and students of society have recognized its abiding power or
need. In literary circles it is quite the fashion to celebrate the imaginative or poetic
truth of myth, or its "timeless truth"; Malinowski wrote that we should regard it as
not pre- but post-scientific, a necessary means of validating our cultural beliefs; Jung
finds in it an essential corrective of the extravagances of the conscious mind; etc.
Still, all this talk is highly self-conscious, and thinkers tend to forget an elementary
distinction between fact and fable that we now take for granted. Although men in
the early civilizations had a great deal of empirical knowledge, and showed some
capacity for rational or logical thought, the evidence suggests that they made no
clear, consistent distinction between fact and fable, or between natural and supernatural, empirical and magical means of dealing with nature. They never spoke or
thought of *myths*—they had no such word in their lexicon. They took their basic
myths literally, with entire seriousness, never considering them mere poetry or
allegory, never using them consciously to express lofty ideals or "mystic" truths.
They could imaginatively embroider, elaborate, multiply their myths, but they had
no rational means of translating, discounting, or criticizing them. We need not
"explode" the myth unless it is taken literally, or until it becomes as dangerous as
Hitler's racial mythology. They were simply unable to explode it; they took fable
for fact, and were stuck with it.

This basic mentality had much to do with the basic political pattern in all the
early civilizations—the sacred monarchy. Everywhere men were governed by an
absolute monarch, who was an agent of the gods when not himself a god, and who
was supported by the priesthood; the ruling principle in both religious and political
life was absolute obedience. Karl Wittfogel, who has made the closest study of this
basic pattern, summed it up as "Oriental despotism". And it remained the common
form of government in almost all later societies, and the longest-lived. It kept Egypt
going for almost three thousand years—a record approached only by China, under
its imperial "Son of Heaven".

Now, I should say that "despotism" is too strong a word for it. It was not so
pure an autocracy as Wittfogel insists; the god-king often met opposition from the
army, the priesthood, or especially the nobility. Moreover, it was not simple
tyranny, still less villainy, a brutal exploitation of the masses out of greed or lust

for power. All we know of early history suggests that kingship was generally a natural, an unforced, and on the whole a welcome development, out of the natural authority of the chieftain or war leader who clearly emerged in later neolithic society. It was not necessarily harsh, but often benevolent; it was a practical success, attested by the maintenance of law and order in large societies, the growth in population, and the general rise in standards of living; and it had much to do with the remarkable creative achievements of the early civilizations. Nor was it based on sheer force. It was legitimate, literally "sacred", because the natural way—however unpremeditated—of legitimatizing the authority of the monarch was to say that he got it from the gods; given the ruling mentality, this was almost a foregone conclusion. At any rate, it was generally accepted. The kings had no police force (the police is a modern institution) and did not use their armies to hold down the people; we hardly ever hear of popular uprising against the god-king—and never in Egypt. Essentially, "Oriental despotism" represented government by consent of the governed.

Yet Wittfogel's thesis seems to me essentially sound. At least he proposes a sound criterion: "A government is absolutist when its rule is not effectively checked by nongovernmental forces. The ruler of an absolutist regime is an autocrat when his decisions are not effectively checked by intragovernmental forces." The only apparent checks on the government or the king in the early sacred monarchies were sporadic, uncertain, unreasoned, commonly unprincipled. It seems clear that no class or group maintained a strong tradition of independence, or ever secured any constitutional right to oppose the monarch; none had inviolable rights to their rank or property. We hear of no Magna Cartas, no embattled champions or either ancient privileges or the public weal. Neither did men appeal over the king's head to a higher law or to the things that were God's. The correct posture in the royal presence everywhere remained the typical Oriental symbol of total submission—prostration.

Above all, the common people had no voice whatever in the government. At its best, the sacred monarchy gave them ample bread and beer, gave them psychological security, gave them the spiritual comforts of "miracle, mystery, and authority"; but it never gave them political freedom. They enjoyed somewhat less personal freedom than men had in neolithic society; as many were serfs, most were liable to periodic conscription for work on dykes, temple, or pyramid, and all were subject to an absolute power that they could not openly resist or hope to change. We must accordingly qualify the statement that the sacred monarchy represented government by consent of the governed. This was not a reasoned consent, a free choice among known alternatives, but essentially a blind obedience, in much the same spirit in which men accepted the weather. What freedom of thought and speech may have been permitted made little difference. There was no need of laws prohibiting fundamental criticism of the monarchy because there was little if any such subversive thought on principle; as a divinely ordained institution, it was immune to searching inquiry or criticism. There were no treatises whatever on political theory or public affairs. The rare adventurers in thought proclaimed no conscious ideal of adventure, of free inquiry, or of free criticism.

There were, however, some clear gains in justice. The prehistoric village, like primitive societies today, was presumably held together by unquestioned and unwritten custom, bound by taboo. With the rise of civilization, especially of the heterogeneous city, pure custom would no longer do, and we encounter conscious ideals of justice, formulated in law codes. The first recorded use of the word "freedom" was in Sumer in the 24th century B.C., when a scribe wrote that King Urukagina of Lagash—the first social reformer known to history—"established the freedom" of his subjects in decrees restoring their ancient rights, protecting them against "men of power". (I should add that there is evidence of popular assemblies in early Sumer before "kingship descended from the heavens".) Later kings repeatedly boasted of restoring justice. Law codes indicate positive advances toward ideals of justice, or more effective freedom for the many, by protecting them against the abuses of power and privilege. Thus Hammurabi announced in the preamble to his famous code that the gods had sent "me, Hammurabi, the obedient, god-fearing prince, to make manifest justice in the land, to destroy the wicked and the evildoer, that the strong harm not the weak".

Still, the repeated boasts of the kings reveal that justice was uncertain, the restorations generally did not last long. Always it depended on the monarch—on "me, Hammurabi". It recalls the social question raised by the increasing surplus of material wealth provided by the growth of civilization, the question who was to possess and enjoy this wealth, and the invariable answer: a privileged few. The poor have not always been with us—as a class they came with civilization. So did the new type of the slave. So did the most common of all types, the peasant: no longer preliterate, on a cultural par with his fellows, but illiterate, aware of the writing he did not know, and of his dependence on remote powers in the city; and as we now see him, most notable all through history for his own powers of passive endurance.

All this accordingly forces a drastic discount of some popular generalizations. Since all civilized societies may be divided into haves and have-nots, all history may look like what Marx called it—the history of class struggles; but there was no class struggle of the Marxist kind in the ancient East. We know little about the masses of have-nots if only because they did not actively struggle. At most there was some conflict within the upper class, usually in the form of intrigue or conspiracy, usually motivated by purely personal ambition. Class struggles have been conspicuous only in Western history, beginning with the Greeks, and appear to be chiefly a luxury of free societies. Likewise the middle class failed to play the rôle it has been assigned in much political theory, both democratic and Marxist. A considerable and growing commercial class in the early civilizations had little perceptible influence on either the political system or the basic structure of society; the evidence suggests that such a class has no manifest political destiny, as either friend or enemy of freedom, and is not by nature either dynamic or solid. Nor did private property exert either the wholesome or the baneful influence attributed to it in much Western theory. There was considerable such property in the early civilizations, with rights defined by law; yet it did not lead to political freedom or inspire a struggle to defend or extend freedom. Both the ideal value and the practical force of private property evidently depend less on any inherent sanctity or innate passion for it than on social custom and political system.

Finally, there was some social mobility in these civilizations, or measure of opportunity for the ambitious; but this led to no significant change either. Basically these were closed societies. While they had their ups and downs, soon experiencing the cycle of rise and fall that would recur ever after (as it does not in primitive societies), they kept returning to the same basic pattern. Their art, thought, and learning were always devoted primarily to the service of the gods and the god-kings. Their natural cultural fate was stagnation. In fact, almost all the great achievements of the early civilizations came in the early centuries of their history, long before the end of the third millennium B.C. Thereafter, and all through the second millenium, they contributed much less to either the spiritual life or the technological power of man. And this was to be the typical career of the Oriental sacred monarchy down through the Ottoman Empire: an early period of cultural achievement, more or less brilliant but usually brief, followed by a long period of stagnation or decline.

Finally, however, there did occur among some newer peoples in the first millenium B.C. the revolutionary change that Karl Jaspers has called the "Axial period". The change was marked immediately by the appearance of great names—no longer the names of kings and conquerors, and of their gods, but of great individuals of a very different kind: Zoroaster, Buddha, Confucius, and Lao-Tse; Amos, Jeremiah, and Isaiah; Homer, Thales, Solon, Aeschylus, Socrates, and a hundred other Greeks. Together they represent the most extraordinary creative era since the rise of civilization, distinguished in particular by the emergence of the higher religions and of philosophy and science. This era made a mark on every major society thereafter, and provided the standards by which we judge all previous societies. It seems more extraordinary because of the mysterious coincidence that the most influential of these pioneers all appeared in or about the sixth century B.C., independently, in widely separated lands, without any apparent influence on one another.

As I have used the word "mysterious", I pause to note the problem of causation, the question why this momentous change occurred at this time. I assume that we do not know, that we can point to some relevant conditions but cannot wholly explain it, and that a student of freedom should not be distressed thereby, since we could explain it only if history were completely governed by determinate laws. As it was, the Axial period did not affect most peoples of the time, and the mere fact that the creativity was extraordinary implies that it was not clearly determined by the common material conditions of life. I would suggest that it was perhaps the plainest demonstration of the power of genius, the difference that great men may make in history. And as I mentioned the word "judgment", implying the horrid idea of value-judgment, I should remark the still common assumption of historians, sociologists, and anthropologists that we have no scientific, logical, or moral right to pass judgment on the values of different cultures—the judgments that nevertheless we constantly do make, and I assume must make if we are seriously concerned about freedom and justice. I would suggest that although we cannot literally believe in all these "higher" religions, and many of us believe in none of them, still almost all of us at heart do believe that they deserve the name "higher"; and I think we have good enough grounds for this belief.

Thus all these religions moved away from the immemorial tribal gods and nature gods, toward more universal, spiritual conceptions of deity or the cosmic order.

Their primary concern was no longer the material success of the nation or the assurance of good crops, but the spiritual welfare of man. They offered visions of some Good beyond the flux of earthly life, rescuing man from his long obsession with food and phallus. They proposed different ways of treating the powers above, but ways alike more amenable to his ideal purposes. Their service of deity was far from mere servility, as far from any mere opium for the masses. And the advance represented by such loftier spirituality is as plain in terms of values of science, for it signified as well a growth of rationality. Thought was much freer, more conscious, and more critical. Above all, it was no longer governed by myth. In Buddha, Confucius, and the Greeks the emancipation was specifically philosophical; but prophets and philosophers alike repudiated the universal practice of magic, or any merely ritual way of dealing with nature or deity. The religious teachers in particular sought to educate man, enlighten him, elevate him by insisting on righteousness instead of rites, the ideal instead of the idol. They introduced universal ethical ideals, based on the tacit if not explicit assumption of the brotherhood of man. Although none preached a gospel of individualism, indirectly they did much to emancipate the individual too. By discrediting the external forms of ritual religion, they led the way to some inner relation with deity that might stir a consciousness of selfhood, or of personality. They conferred a spiritual independence and responsibility on the individual, a moral obligation to serve the god or to seek the good that was yet a free choice, up to him. While preaching the good will essential to the maintenance of any kind of social freedom and justice, they fostered a respect for the spirit in man that seeks truth and goodness, and that might therefore claim a right to freedom.

The prehistoric myth and magic came back, of course, and with them the ancient tribalism, or heavenly favoritism. One result of the higher religions was to create a much wider gap between the lofty spirits and the masses of simple worshippers, whose needs were tended or exploited by naturally conservative priesthoods, with vested interests in "miracle, mystery, and authority". (A surprising number of writers still overlook this elementary distinction between ideal and popular religion.) Also, almost all the societies that took to the higher religions, now and later, adhered to the basic pattern of the sacred monarchy. But this points to another significant theme that emerges from the Axial period—to my mind the most important for a student of freedom: the much abused theme of East and West.

None of the great Eastern societies became basically free societies, dedicated to any proposition of liberty and equality, or of government of and by the people. The higher religions they embraced—Hinduism, Buddhism, Taoism, Confucianism— fostered values that may be deemed higher or holier than freedom, in particular a peace of mind that many free men now yearn for (and in America apparently enjoy only with the help of tranquilizers); but none inspired a conscious ideal of freedom. The reason seems to me plainest in Buddhism and Hinduism, which alike held up ideals of non-attachment to life in the temporal, natural world, based on the assumption that it is evil or unimportant or even unreal, and which therefore offered men what is commonly called "spiritual freedom", but what remained essentially a freedom *from* desire to carry out all but the indispensable earthly purposes, or to realize the common garden varieties of freedom; they naturally bred an indifference to ideas of political freedom, or to energetic efforts at social reform. Thus there was not even a word for "freedom" in ancient Sanskrit. The issues raised by the essentially humanistic, worldly teaching of Confucius are more complicated, but it may be enough to mention here that by his own word he was primarily a conservative, that his primary objective was order and harmony, not freedom, and that to achieve it he stressed duties, not rights; there was no word for "rights" in ancient China, in which good Confucianists all accepted the idea of rule by the "Son of Heaven". The historical fact remains that the Western world has unquestionably made the major contributions to the theory and conscious practice of freedom as I define it.

In this view Judaism, as the basis of Christianity, was a major source of the distinctive Western tradition. Its most obvious contribution was the ideal of social justice preached by the great prophets, and their impassioned indignation at social injustice—an indignation unparalleled either in Greece or in other Eastern societies, and for that matter rare in Christian saints. (St. Thomas Aquinas could write very calmly about the naturalness of serfdom, while even gentle St. Francis stressed mainly the blessings of poverty—blessings that a saint may appreciate, but that few of the poor can.) Even godless revolutionaries have therefore paid tribute to the prophets as the first great social reformers, the creators of the social conscience of Western man. Their moral earnestness was intensified by a view of earthly life that we now take for granted, but that made much more earthly difference than we are likely to realize until we consider Hinduism and Buddhism. The prophets never doubted the reality or importance of the natural world—God's creation, which the God of Genesis had repeated seven times was "good"; and they took earthly time with entire seriousness, the more as they did not believe in an immortal soul or a life to come. Hence, too, their novel moral theory of history, in which they insisted that national success or failure was due wholly to human good or human evil, the service of a God who demanded righteousness; they accordingly called for ceaseless, strenuous moral effort, rejecting the fatalistic resignation common to other Eastern peoples. With the coming of the national disaster they introduced the novel, portentous idea of the Messiah, and visions of a millennium of universal peace and justice on earth—the germs of the dynamic idea of progress. Some writers have seen a "charter of human freedom" in the vision of Micah: "Neither shall they learn war any more. But they shall sit every man under his vine and under his fig tree." For all such reasons kingship in Israel was essentially different from the sacred monarchy. Although ordained by God, the king was in no sense divine or eligible for deification, and his power was not absolute; he was always subject to a higher law, not of his own making and not even his business to interpret; and he could be openly denounced on principle, as he often was by the prophets and even the high priests.

Nevertheless Israel was hardly devoted to ideals of freedom, beyond national independence. Judaism also had distinctive elements that made it illiberal on principle, and that in coming through Christianity constituted a major barrier to the growth of freedom. Most obvious was its exclusiveness, its service of a jealous God who would tolerate the worship of no other gods; however lofty this devotion, it meant a plain denial of religious freedom, and at worst led to its ugliest legacy— fanaticism; in Christianity this produced by far the bloodiest record of persecution in religious history. Linked with this claim to a monopoly on religious truth was an authoritarian insistence on faith rather than reason, on the primary duty of unquestioning obedience to a God who could seem pretty despotic or unreasonable, and in time on the literal, infallible truth of its Scriptures, which became a closed book, and under Christianity made the Bible a major bulwark of obscurantism, and of hostility alike to political, intellectual, and religious freedom. The prophets themselves did not consciously write any charters for freedom, because they simply were not concerned with such freedoms. Although they were radical innovators, clearly introducing new conceptions of God, as clearly they were not inquirers or philosophers, and proclaimed no ideal of free inquiry or rational criticism, no right to independent judgment or freedom of conscience; there is no word for conscience in the Old Testament. (Lord Acton, incidentally, regarded freedom of conscience as the very essence of freedom; and his unhappiness as at once an ardent liberal and a devout Catholic helps to explain why he never wrote the History of Freedom that he worked on almost all his life, and that has been called the greatest book that was never written.) The prophets simply laid down the law of God with a sublime, impassioned unreasoned conviction that in ordinary men might induce simple credulity or positive irrationality. Their image of the Messiah and an ideal future was scarcely drawn from historical or philosophical analysis, but came down to pure myth. And they exemplified the narrowness as well as the loftness of the Judaic legacy in their indifference to the natural sources of beauty, truth, and goodness, to art, philosophy, science—to almost all the values of civilization except the religious values. Altogether, it is impossible to calculate with any precision the dual effects of Judaism, or by simple addition and subtraction to come out with a definite sum; but there is little question, I believe, that the Western tradition of freedom owes much more to the Greek than to the Hebraic spirit.

I come to these Greeks somewhat wearily, as I have reviewed their familiar achievement in four books now; so I should add at once that on this last time through I became still more convinced of their supreme importance in the history of freedom. Of all the peoples who contributed to the spiritual ferment of the Axial period, they made the most radical break with the tradition of "miracle, mystery, and authority". They alone developed an open society in keeping with the new modes of thought. They alone set up a conscious ideal of freedom, and rose to political freedom.

Again I can merely touch on some considerations raised by the many-sided achievement of the Greeks. The chief immediate means to their rise in the world was commerce. They are perhaps the most conspicuous example of how much commerce may contribute to the growth of freedom, through the promotion of enterprise, initiative, rational calculation, cultural exchange, broadening of horizons, etc.; and by their uniqueness they make as plain that commerce or business enterprise does not necessarily, automatically, promote other freedoms, since other commercial peoples, such as the Babylonians and the Phoenicians, never approached the Greek achievement. The main clues to their distinctive spirit as I see them are pretty much the conventional ones—their humanism, rationalism, naturalism, individualism, or their discovery of Mind, Nature, and Man. These were apparent as early as Homer, notably in his basic realism and his remarkably free treatment of myth; though we cannot be certain just how seriously he took all the fables in his epics, the very uncertainty indicates that in effect he possessed the myth, was not possessed by it. The basic condition of their achievement was the *polis*: the little city-state in which they learned to govern themselves and to rationalize authority, and through class struggle consciously arrived at their essential idea of rule by law: man-made law based on public consent, binding on both rulers and ruled, denying any right to arbitrary rule in the name of any god. Later Greeks believed that the *polis* as they knew it had been established deliberately in order to secure justice.

In this *polis* they developed their exceptional freedom of mind and spirit, reflected in the unprecedented range as well as the brilliance of their creativity. Among its many distinctive signs was the growing autonomy of art, bent to civic purposes, no longer primarily to the service of gods and god-kings; the creation of lyric poetry, in which poets spoke out as individuals, expressing purely personal emotions; the creation of such other new forms as comedy and tragedy, the latter to me one of the profoundest, if most paradoxical expressions of a free spirit; the birth of history as a branch of inquiry, instead of royal annals or religious propaganda; and above all the birth of natural philosophy and science, the self-conscious, critical effort to explain the universe in natural rather than mythical terms, for rational rather than magical purposes, which led to the first clear realization of natural causes and natural law in the scientific sense, and more broadly to the first clear emergence of the scientific spirit, the disinterested pursuit of truth for its own sake, which at once emancipated and disciplined thought. There remains a significant exception in the unparalleled range and variety of their cultural achievement: the Greeks did not develop a higher religion. But this was another sign of the humanism and naturalism that were among the essential conditions of their achievement.

In Athens, finally, the Greeks developed a full-fledged democracy—the first important state of this kind in history. The Funeral Oration of Pericles is a major document in the history of freedom as the first manifesto of democracy: not only boasting of the freedoms of Athens, but asserting that democracy was what had made Athens great. In this century there also occurred about the most extraordinary burst of creativity in all history. I should not argue that democracy was the primary cause of this creativity—else we might expect all America to be abloom. But it does seem to me plainly one of the major conditions, and no coincidence that the freest city in Greece was also the most brilliant. Or that it produced Socrates, with whom the ideal of freedom of conscience begins to emerge—though the Greeks too as yet had no word for conscience.

This brings up, however, the disagreeable truth that Athens failed in the Peloponnesian War with totalitarian Sparta—the disastrous war that heralded the loss of Greek independence and signaled the failure of classical Greece, or of the first notable historic adventure in the life of freedom. The immediate reasons for the

failure seem plain enough, in particular the narrow, violent factionalism that prevented the Greeks from ever uniting; it should remind us that the Greeks were not,
of course, such clear-eyed rationalists or such devotees of the Apollonian ideal as
classical scholars long made out. There are also some plain enough excuses for their
failure, simply in that they were pioneers in the free, open society, a much riskier
enterprise than the settled societies of the ancient East, and that they had no
historic landmarks to guide them, no long tradition to steady them, no time-tested
institutions to support them. In particular the Athenian freedoms that Pericles
boasted of were mostly unsupported, as uncontrolled, by strong institutions, clear
principles, or deeply engrained habits of responsibility. But I should also emphasize
some specific shortcomings of Greek democracy by modern standards that help to
explain its failure, and in any case set off later developments in democratic theory.

One reason why their individualism was likely to become reckless and lawless, or
simply selfish, was that it was neither sanctioned nor disciplined by any explicit
political or religious principle. Athens had no Bill of Rights, no principle of
individual rights against the state, or freedom from it; in their intimate *polis* the
Greeks failed to distinguish clearly between state and society, or to wall off from
the state any major social domain, such as religion. Although their thought was on
the whole remarkably free, they had no declared principle of freedom of thought,
speech, or conscience; the execution of Socrates was entirely legal—as he himself
acknowledged. The classical Greeks lacked as well the Christian idea of the sanctity
of the person; their acceptance of slavery was only the clearest example. Their
inveterate factionalism, within as well as between the city-states, was the more
violent because they had little sense of strictly moral responsibility, or in particular
of altruism. They still had no clear conception of Humanity, or of Man apart from
the *polis*, and had as little idea of crimes against Humanity as of sins against God.
Thus the Funeral Oration of Pericles, which neglected to mention the gods, was no
paean to human dignity either. He never suggested that Athens had a mission to
defend democracy, much less to spread its blessings, and expressed nothing like the
sense of high dedication in Lincoln's comparable Gettysburg Address: dedication to
a supra-national cause of liberty and equality, that government of, by, and for the
people should not perish from the earth. All such limitations are understandable;
but simply in justice to the Greeks we need to keep in mind that the conditions of
their singular achievement included inexperience, immaturity, considerable ignorance, and an ancient legacy of violence, superstition, and dread, as well as the
inevitable costs of freedom.

The Hellenistic period that followed upon the conquests of Alexander the Great
has suffered somewhat from the too familiar idea of the cycle of growth and decay.
As by common consent the golden age of Athens was the peak of Greek culture, it
follows that the aftermath was necessarily a decline. Actually, the period was still
exceptionally creative, most notably in philosophy and science; in science the
Hellenistic Greeks far outstripped the achievements of the classical Greeks. The
Stoics transcended the little *polis* that was still the ideal of Plato and Aristotle,
introducing the ideal of *cosmopolis*, "one great City of gods and men": a universal
commonwealth based on "natural law", which embodied a principle of equality and

led some Stoics to criticize the almost universal institution of slavery, defended by Plato and Aristotle. Alexander the Great himself had had a vision of brotherhood when at a great banquet, during which Greeks and Asiatics drank from a common mixing bowl, he offered a prayer for *homonoia*, "a union of hearts". Thereby he gave the first clear political expression to the loftier ethical and religious ideals realized in the Axial period.

Yet Alexander also points to the reasons why the Hellenistic era unmistakably did end in decline. There was a clear loss of freedom, beginning with the return of kingship, nominally sacred; Alexander had ruled as an absolute monarch and had himself deified. Although the Greek *polis* retained considerable local autonomy and civic spirit, it was no longer independent, in command of its destiny. Rhetoric became the main subject of formal education and remained the rage until the end of the Greco-Roman world; it taught men to orate about anything or nothing, achieve an elegance the hollower because great public issues were no longer being debated. (One could write a depressing book on the historical influence of formal education, which has mostly tended to fetter thought, discourage independence and imaginativeness.) There was as plain a decline in creativity, in all fields of culture, very few works of importance being produced by the first century B.C. In philosophy there was a marked decline in rationality, a growing obsession with such superstitions as astrology, corresponding to the growing popularity of Oriental mystery cults—a decline that would eventually carry all the way back to the prehistoric myth and magic out of which Greek philosophy had arisen. The whole story may be summed up as a return to "miracle, mystery, and authority".

I would stress, however, an important qualification of the Grand Inquisitor's thesis. In taking to the mystery cults, the Hellenistic masses were not seeking an escape from the intolerable burden of freedom. Mostly very poor and illiterate, they had never enjoyed much effective freedom, had much real choice. The Grand Inquisitor spoke for the superior few who presumably were capable of freedom, above the vulgar needs; and the "failure of nerve" was most apparent in the Hellenistic elite. It was the thinkers and teachers who were succumbing to the need of miracle and mystery.

The story was much the same in the decline of the Roman Empire. The Romans had first made some important contributions, apart from their transmission of Greek culture. They had early begun learning something that the much brilliant Greeks never learned to do—to extend the rights of citizenship to other communities outside their *polis*; at length the Romans extended it to virtually all free men in the Empire. In this empire they approached a realization of the Stoic *cosmopolis*. In the ideal theory of the Principate established by Augustus, the state was a commonwealth, the property of the people, who were the source of all authority; the Emperor was a servant of the people, ruling by common consent, exercising only the authority they had delegated to him. This theory enshrined the basic principle of constitutional government, limited by law, that became a cornerstone in Western political tradition. Above all, the Romans developed their famous law, by all odds the most equitable, rational, and enlightened law that man had yet formulated, far transcending the hodgepodge of "God-given" laws in the Old Testament. They gradually evolved a *jus gentium*, or "law of nations", that was in effect a social revolution. It became a law of contract, applying to all men alike regardless of their tribal status; it made every citizen a *persona*, a man with private rights to life, liberty, and property. It embodied the Stoic concept of "natural law", a universal principle of justice, written in the constitution of the cosmos, immutable and everlasting, above all conventional law and the criterion of its rightness—a cloudy, ambiguous concept, which is obviously vulnerable to criticism and seems like simple nonsense to positivists, but which has obviously worked to promote the cause of freedom in the West, especially when men derived from it the doctrine of natural rights. It was written into the preamble of the American Declaration of Independence.

As for the famous decline and fall, I am wearier of that (having made the Roman Empire fall three times now), but at least need not here go into the fifty reasons for it. It is enough to remark that a loss of freedom was among them, as at least a symptom if not a cause. The Emperor in fact ruled as an absolute monarch, since the Romans never developed institutions, legislative or judicial, to make good their theory of constitutional, limited government. The many high-minded emperors, especially the series from Trajan through Hadrian and Antoninus Pius to Marcus Aurelius, are perhaps the best illustration of John Stuart Mill's thesis that benevolent despotism is in the long run likely to be more fatal than a brutal one. Harsh rule, he argued, may stir a struggle for liberty, whereas under a benevolent despotism men naturally tend to become passive, submissive, dependent; content to be ruled by others, without active participation in their government, they lose the habit of initiative, enterprise, and self-reliance in public life; and eventually they lose all capacity for self-rule. At any rate, both Romans and Greeks became helpless enough as citizens. Although the many cities in the Empire retained some autonomy, they had no voice whatever in the federal government, became increasingly dependent on the emperors, and dropped their popular assemblies. The emperors consistently banned all except the most harmless private associations, as potential menaces to the state, and periodically violated the customary civil liberties, exiling writers, banning philosophers, executing assorted subversives. The tradition of freedom remained just live enough to make some Romans, such as Tacitus, lament the loss of intellectual freedom. "Genius died by the same blow that ended public liberty", he wrote; and by his time a marked decline in creativity had set in. The Romans in turn took the Oriental mystery cults, in a feverish pursuit of private salvation. But again this was not clearly an escape from freedom—except in the elite; for the Roman masses had enjoyed very little freedom even before the end of the Republic. If we can never be certain that a really free citizenry would have saved the Roman Empire, there is no question that the Empire was weakened by a dispirited populace, lacking the energy, resolution, and self-reliance that freedom might have maintained.

The most vital force in the last centuries of Rome, of course, was Christianity. It had the potentialities for freedom inherited from Judaism, emphasized by the more insistent gospel of love and brotherhood preached by Jesus and spread to the Gentiles by St. Paul. They were supplemented by the one original idea that

Christianity added to the higher religions—that God himself had appeared on earth in order to redeem man. Christ gave a new meaning to history because he was a Person, not an impersonal Necessity, and his crucifixion a unique historical event, potentially a promise of a new and better life—not merely more of the same, as was implied by the gods of all the other mystery religions, who died annually, cyclically. How much difference this might make is clearer when we consider the prevailing classical view of history, the theory of endless cycles: a view that might offer the solace of resignation to the uniform, inevitable fate, as Marcus Aurelius insisted, but that was more likely to make history seem meaningless, pointless, as the melancholy of Marcus testified.

At the time, however, Christianity had little effect on freedom, except an adverse effect when it became the imperial religion. Christians then began oppressing pagans and Jews, and turned most violently on heretical fellow Christians; they repudiated freedom of religious thought and conscience with an explicitness and thoroughness never before known in history. Meanwhile their Church was supporting an imperial regime that was doing away with the remnants of political freedom, and still oppressing the many poor; in the nascent Byzantine Empire the Christian God was pressed into the service of another Oriental sacred monarchy. With its original doctrine of the Redeemer, Christianity had also introduced the doctrine of Original Sin, a possibly salutary teaching, but not one calculated to encourage an active effort to extend freedom; the Church Fathers used this doctrine to justify their acceptance of despotism and slavery, as conservatives would always use it to oppose social reform—any apparent social evils were natural for a naturally depraved creature. At the same time, a sense of sin and guilt became a hallmark of Christian spirituality: again a possible means to humility, but not conducive to freedom of mind or spirit. In the West, Christianity would not realize its potentialities for freedom until the rise of a new civilization, in the Middle Ages, when it also began recovering its classical heritage; though its repressive tendencies would then also become more pronounced. It is, I should say, the most profoundly ambiguous of the world's religions.

Of our own civilization, I should in this context emphasize primarily its obvious distinctiveness—so obvious that many overlook it. It has been by far the most dynamic, continuously creative of the great societies, and the most continuously given to radical or revolutionary change, from the Renaissance through the Protestant Reformation, the rise of the nation-state, the rise of capitalism, the rise of science, the Age of Enlightenment, the political revolutions, the Industrial Revolution, the world wars, the rise of Communism, and now the Atomic Age, or maybe the Interplanetary Age. Its dynamism has been intensified by its unique faith in progress, an optimism such as no previous society was given to. This has generally been a shallow, uncritical, unreasoned faith, but it has plainly made for more effective freedom; it helps to explain why Western civilization has given common men not only more rights but more opportunity then they ever enjoyed in the past. We are now more aware of the inescapable costs of all this adventure, the abuses of opportunity, the growing threats to freedom. I need not add that there is no assurance whatsoever of the ultimate triumph of the cause of freedom and justice as most of us conceive them. But in the perspective that I have tried to give I shall venture a few concluding observations, at the risk of sounding like a poor man's Toynbee, on the excuse of some popular tendencies in current thought.

One such tendency is the fashion of dwelling on analogies between our civilization and declining civilizations in the past, especially the Roman Empire. There are indeed some suggestive analogies, as well as the endless recurrences of the story of rise and fall, the themes of ambition, selfishness, greed, hate—the quite unoriginal expressions of what some thinkers now again prefer to call Original Sin. But otherwise the plainest fact remains the fundamental differences between our civilization and all previous ones. None before ours ever attempted large scale democracy with free education for all, none had anything like modern science and technology, none tried or could possibly have tried to establish a United Nations—in general, none had our immense potentialities, for better or for worse, or so vivid a sense of potentiality. We can of course still learn a great deal from the experience of the past (or so as a historian I must hope), but it still seems necessary to repeat that history cannot teach us the solutions to our unprecedented, literally extraordinary problems, and that the stagnation of the Roman Empire is no clue to the fate of a society furiously busy making hydrogen bombs, sputniks, and rockets to visit the moon.

Another popular theme is all that we can learn from the wisdom and spirituality of the East. This is perhaps what most needs to be said, in view of both the cultural conceit of the West and its evident failure to enjoy its blessings, its growing dependence on tranquilizers and happiness pills. But again the immediate fact—and the chief excuse for dwelling on the much abused theme of East and West—is that the East is astir with Western ideas and ideals. The last decade or so has seen the most astounding development, as virtually the whole world is now astir, and hundreds of millions of men are beginning to realize possibilities, demand opportunities, and cherish aspirations hitherto largely confined to a small minority of the human race: hopes and demands that their own native traditions have not prepared them to realize. Among the most pressing and difficult problems facing the Western democracies is how to convey the idea of freedom under law—an idea that seems elementary to us, but is alien to the traditions of most other peoples, including such highly civilized peoples as the Chinese.

This brings me back, finally, to the thesis of the Grand Inquisitor. It has lately come to seem more plausible, given all the pressures to conformity in an industrial mass civilization, the portents of Huxley's Brave New World, the symptoms of anxiety, the flight from freedom, and enough other reasons to fill the many volumes of alarm. But since I have emphasized that most of history has been on his side, or does not support the popular idea that all through history mankind has been struggling for freedom and justice, I should now remark that this idea at least reflects Western history in recent centuries, and lately the stir all over the world. Thus the principle of the Rights of Man—a revolutionary slogan a little more than a century ago—has come to be universally accepted in theory, however much violated in practice, as the "human rights" affirmed by the United Nations. It has even come to include the rights of women, who all along have made up half the human race (a fact slurred in most histories). It at least gives some reason to hope that the Grand Inquisitor may be wrong, and to believe that once men have known freedom, or known of it, they are disposed to cherish it and not knowingly to surrender it.

"THE HISTORY OF FREEDOM
IN ANCIENT AND MODERN EUROPE"

Lord Acton

Liberty, next to religion, has been the motive of good deeds and the common pretext of crime, from the sowing of the seed at Athens, two thousand four hundred and sixty years ago, until the ripened harvest was gathered by men of our race. It is the delicate fruit of a mature civilisation; and scarcely a century has passed since nations, that knew the meaning of the term, resolved to be free. In every age its progress has been beset by its natural enemies, by ignorance and superstition, by lust of conquest and by love of ease, by the strong man's craving for power, and the poor man's craving for food. During long intervals it has been utterly arrested, when nations were being rescued from barbarism and from the grasp of strangers, and when the perpetual struggle for existence, depriving men of all interest and understanding in politics, has made them eager to sell their birthright for a pottage, and ignorant of the treasure they resigned. At all times sincere friends of freedom have been rare, and its triumphs have been due to minorities, that have prevailed by associating themselves with auxiliaries whose objects often differed from their own; and this association, which is always dangerous, has been sometimes disastrous, by giving to opponents just grounds of opposition, and by kindling dispute over the spoils in the hour of success. No obstacle has been so constant, or so difficult to overcome, as uncertainty and confusion touching the nature of true liberty. If hostile interests have wrought much injury, false ideas have wrought still more; and its advance is recorded in the increase of knowledge, as much as in the improvement of laws. The history of institutions is often a history of deception and illusions; for their virtue depends on the ideas that produce and on the spirit that preserves them, and the form may remain unaltered when the substance has passed away. . .

By liberty I mean the assurance that every man shall be protected in doing what he believes his duty against the influence of authority and majorities, custom and opinion. The State is competent to assign duties and draw the line between good and evil only in its immediate sphere. Beyond the limits of things necessary for its well-being, it can only give indirect help to fight the battle of life by promoting the influences which prevail against temptation,—religion, education, and the distribution of wealth. In ancient times the State absorbed authorities not its own, and intruded on the domain of personal freedom. In the Middle Ages it possessed too little authority, and suffered others to intrude. Modern States fall habitually into both excesses. The most certain test by which we judge whether a country is really free is the amount of security enjoyed by minorities. Liberty, by this definition, is the essential condition and guardian of religion; and it is in the history of the Chosen People, accordingly, that the first illustrations of my subject are obtained. The government of the Israelites was a Federation, held together by no political authority, but by the unity of race and faith, and founded, not on physical force, but on a voluntary covenant. The principle of self-government was carried out not only in each tribe, but in every group of at least 120 families; and there was neither privilege of rank nor inequality before the law. Monarchy was so alien to the primitive spirit of the community that it was resisted by Samuel in that momentous protestation and warning which all the kingdoms of Asia and many of the kingdoms of Europe have unceasingly confirmed. The throne was erected on a compact; and the king was deprived of the right of legislation among a people that recognised no lawgiver but God, whose highest aim in politics was to restore the original purity of the constitution, and to make its government conform to the ideal type that was hallowed by the sanctions of heaven. The inspired men who rose in unfailing succession to prophesy against the usurper and the tyrant, constantly proclaimed that the laws, which were divine, were paramount over sinful rulers, and appealed from the established authorities, from the king, the priests, and the princes of the people, to the healing forces that slept in the uncorrupted consciences of the masses. Thus the example of the Hebrew nation laid down the parallel lines on which all freedom has been won—the doctrine of national tradition and the doctrine of the higher law; the principle that a constitution grows from a root by process of development, and not of essential change; and the principle that all political authorities must be tested and reformed according to a code which was not made by man. The operation of these principles, in unison, or in antagonism, occupies the whole of the space we are going over together.

The conflict between liberty under divine authority and the absolutism of human authorities ended disastrously. In the year 622 a supreme effort was made at Jerusalem to reform and preserve the State. The High Priest produced from the temple of Jehovah the book of the deserted and forgotten Law, and both king and people bound themselves by solemn oaths to observe it. But that early example of limited monarchy and of the supremacy of law neither lasted nor spread; and the forces by which freedom has conquered must be sought elsewhere. In the very year 586, in which the flood of Asiatic despotism closed over the city which had been, and was destined again to be, the sanctuary of freedom in the East, a new home was prepared for it in the West, where, guarded by the sea and the mountains, and by valiant hearts, that stately plant was reared under whose shade we dwell, and which is extending its invincible arms so slowly and yet so surely over the civilised world.

According to a famous saying of the most famous authoress of the Continent, liberty is ancient, and it is despotism that is new. It has been the pride of recent historians to vindicate the truth of that maxim. The heroic age of Greece confirms it, and it is still more conspicuously true of Teutonic Europe. Wherever we can trace the earlier life of the Aryan nations we discover germs which favouring circumstances and assiduous culture might have developed into free societies. They exhibit some sense of common interest in common concerns, little reverence for external authority, and an imperfect sense of the function and supremacy of the State. Where the division of property and labour is incomplete there is little division of classes and of power. Until societies are tried by the complex problems of civilisation they may escape despotism, as societies that are undisturbed by religious diversity avoid persecution. In general, the forms of the patriarchal age failed to resist the growth of absolute States when the difficulties and temptations of advancing life began to tell; and with one sovereign exception . . ., it is scarcely possible to trace their survival in the institutions of later times. Six hundred years before the birth of Christ absolutism held unbounded sway. Throughout the East it was propped by the unchanging influence of priests and armies. In the West, where there were no sacred books requiring trained interpreters, the priesthood acquired no preponderance, and when the kings were overthrown their powers passed to aristocracies of birth. What followed, during many generations, was the cruel domination of class over class, the oppression of the poor by the rich, and of the ignorant by the wise. The spirit of that domination found passionate utterance in the verses of the aristocratic poet Theognis, a man of genius and refinement, who avows that he longed to drink the blood of his political adversaries. From these oppressors the people of many cities sought deliverance in the less intolerable tyranny of revolutionary usurpers. The remedy gave new shape and energy to the evil. The tyrants were often men of surprising capacity and merit, like some of those who, in the fourteenth century, made themselves lords of Italian cities; but rights secured by equal laws and by sharing power existed nowhere.

From this universal degradation the world was rescued by the most gifted of the nations. Athens, which like other cities was distracted and oppressed by a privileged class, avoided violence and appointed Solon to revise its laws. It was the happiest choice that history records. Solon was not only the wisest man to be found in Athens, but the most profound political genius of antiquity; and the easy, bloodless, and pacific revolution by which he accomplished the deliverance of his country was the first step in a career which our age glories in pursuing, and instituted a power which has done more than anything, except revealed religion, for the regeneration of society. The upper class had possessed the right of making and administering the laws, and he left them in possession, only transferring to wealth what had been the privilege of birth. To the rich, who alone had the means of sustaining the burden of public service in taxation and war, Solon gave a share of power proportioned to the demands made on their resources. The poorest classes were exempt from direct taxes, but were excluded from office. Solon gave them a voice in electing magistrates from the classes above them, and the right of calling them to account. This concession, apparently so slender, was the beginning of a mighty change. It introduced the idea that a man ought to have a voice in selecting those to whose rectitude and wisdom he is compelled to trust his fortune, his family, and his life.

And this idea completely inverted the notion of human authority, for it inaugurated the reign of moral influence where all political power had depended on moral force. Government by consent superseded government by compulsion, and the pyramid which had stood on a point was made to stand upon its base. By making every citizen the guardian of his own interest Solon admitted the element of Democracy into the State. The greatest glory of a ruler, he said, is to create a popular government. Believing that no man can be entirely trusted, he subjected all who exercised power to the vigilant control of those for whom they acted.

The only resource against political disorders that had been known till then was the concentration of power. Solon undertook to effect the same object by the distribution of power. He gave to the common people as much influence as he thought them able to employ, that the State might be exempt from arbitrary government. It is the essence of Democracy, he said, to obey no master but the law. Solon recognised the principle that political forms are not final or inviolable, and must adapt themselves to facts; and he provided so well for the revision of his constitution, without breach of continuity or loss of stability, that for centuries after his death the Attic orators attributed to him, and quoted by his name, the whole structure of Athenian law. The direction of its growth was determined by the fundamental doctrine of Solon, that political power ought to be commensurate with public service. In the Persian war the services of the Democracy eclipsed those of the Patrician orders, for the fleet that swept the Asiatics from the Egean Sea was manned by the poorer Athenians. That class, whose valour had saved the State and had preserved European civilisation, had gained a title to increase of influence and privilege. The offices of State, which had been a monopoly of the rich, were thrown open to the poor, and in order to make sure that they should obtain their share, all but the highest commands were distributed by lot.

Whilst the ancient authorities were decaying, there was no accepted standard of moral and political right to make the framework of society fast in the midst of change. The instability that had seized on the forms threatened the very principles of government. The national beliefs were yielding to doubt, and doubt was not yet making way for knowledge. There had been a time when the obligations of public as well as private life were identified with the will of the gods. But that time had passed. Pallas, the ethereal goddess of the Athenians, and the Sun god whose oracles, delivered from the temple between the twin summits of Parnassus, did so much for the Greek nationality, aided in keeping up a lofty ideal of religion; but when the enlightened men of Greece learnt to apply their keen faculty of reasoning to the system of their inherited belief, they became quickly conscious that the conceptions of the gods corrupted the life and degraded the minds of the public. Popular morality could not be sustained by the popular religion. The moral instruction which was no longer supplied by the gods could not yet be found in books. There was no venerable code expounded by experts, no doctrine proclaimed by men of reputed sanctity like those teachers of the far East whose words still rule the fate of nearly half mankind. The effort to account for things by close observation and exact reasoning began by destroying. There came a time when the philosophers of the Porch and the Academy wrought the dictates of wisdom and virtue into a system so consistent and profound that it has vastly shortened the task of the Christian divines. But that time had not yet come.

The epoch of doubt and transition during which the Greeks passed from the dim fancies of mythology to the fierce light of science was the age of Pericles, and the endeavour to substitute certain truth for the prescriptions of impaired authorities, which was then beginning to absorb the energies of the Greek intellect, is the grandest movement in the profane annals of mankind, for to it we own, even after the immeasurable progress accomplished by Christianity, much of our philosophy and far the better part of the political knowledge we possess. Pericles, who was at the head of the Athenian Government, was the first statesman who encountered the problem which the rapid weakening of traditions forced on the political world. No authority in morals or in politics remained unshaken by the motion that was in the air. No guide could be confidently trusted; there was no available criterion to appeal to, for the means of controlling or denying convictions that prevailed among the people. The popular sentiment as to what was right might be mistaken, but it was subject to no test. The people were, for practical purposes, the seat of the knowledge of good and evil. The people, therefore, were the seat of power.

The political philosophy of Pericles consisted of this conclusion. He resolutely struck away all the props that still sustained the artificial preponderance of wealth. For the ancient doctrine that power goes with land, he introduced the idea that power ought to be so equitably diffused as to afford equal security to all. That one part of the community should govern the whole, or that one class should make laws for another, he declared to be tyrannical. The abolition of privilege would have served only to transfer the supremacy from the rich to the poor, if Pericles had not redressed the balance by restricting the right of citizenship to Athenians of pure descent. By this measure the class which formed what we should call the third estate was brought down to 14,000 citizens, and became about equal in numbers with the higher ranks. Pericles held that every Athenian who neglected to take his part in the public business inflicted an injury on the commonwealth. That none might be excluded by poverty, he caused the poor to be paid for their attendance out of the funds of the State; for his administration of the federal tribute had brought together a treasure of more than two million sterling. The instrument of his sway was the art of speaking. He governed by persuasion. Everything was decided by argument in open deliberation, and every influence bowed before the ascendency of mind. The idea that the object of constitutions is not to confirm the predominance of any interest, but to prevent it; to preserve with equal care the independence of labour and security of property; to make the rich safe against envy, and the poor against oppression, marks the highest level attained by the statesmanship of Greece. It hardly survived the great patriot who conceived it; and all history has been occupied with the endeavour to upset the balance of power by giving the advantage to money, land, or numbers. A generation followed that has never been equalled in talent—a generation of men whose works, in poetry and eloquence, are still the envy of the world, and in history, philosophy, and politics remain unsurpassed. But it produced no successor to Pericles, and no man was able to wield the sceptre that fell from his hand.

It was a momentous step in the progress of nations when the principle that every interest should have the right and the means of asserting itself was adopted by the Athenian Constitution. But for those who were beaten in the vote there was no redress. The law did not check the triumph of majorities or rescue the minority from the dire penalty of having been outnumbered. When the overwhelming influence of Pericles was removed, the conflict between classes raged without restraint, and the slaughter that befell the higher ranks in the Peloponnesian war gave an irresistible preponderance to the lower. The restless and inquiring spirit of the Athenians was prompt to unfold the reason of every institution and the consequences of every principle, and their Constitution ran its course from infancy to decrepitude with unexampled speed.

Two men's lives span the interval from the first admission of popular influence, under Solon, to the downfall of the State. Their history furnishes the classic example of the peril of Democracy under conditions singularly favourable. For the Athenians were not only brave and patriotic and capable of generous sacrifice, but they were the most religious of the Greeks. They venerated the Constitution which had given them prosperity, and equality, and freedom, and never questioned the fundamental laws which regulated the enormous power of the Assembly. They tolerated considerable variety of opinion and great licence of speech; and their humanity towards their slaves roused the indignation even of the most intelligent partisan of aristocracy. Thus they became the only people of antiquity that grew great by democratic institutions. But the possession of unlimited power, which corrodes the conscience, hardens the heart, and confounds the understanding of monarchs, exercised its demoralising influence on the illustrious democracy of Athens. It is bad to be oppressed by a minority, but it is worse to be oppressed by a majority. For there is a reserve of latent power in the masses which, if it is called into play, the minority can seldom resist. But from the absolute will of an entire people there is no appeal, no redemption, no refuge but treason. The humblest and most numerous class of the Athenians united the legislative, the judicial, and, in part, the executive power. The philosophy that was then in the ascendant taught them that there is no law superior to that of the State—the lawgiver is above the law.

It followed that the sovereign people had a right to do whatever was within its power, and was bound by no rule of right or wrong but its own judgment of expediency. On a memorable occasion the assembled Athenians declared it monstrous that they should be prevented from doing whatever they chose. No force that existed could restrain them; and they resolved that no duty should restrain them, and that they would be bound by no laws that were not of their own making. In this way the emancipated people of Athens became a tyrant; and their Government, the pioneer of European freedom, stands condemned with a terrible unanimity by all the wisest of the ancients. They ruined their city by attempting to conduct war by debate in the marketplace. Like the French Republic, they put their unsuccessful commanders to death. They treated their dependencies with such injustice that they lost their maritime Empire. They plundered the rich until the rich conspired with the public enemy, and they crowned their guilt by the martyrdom of Socrates.

When the absolute sway of numbers had endured for near a quarter of a century, nothing but bare existence was left for the State to lose; and the Athenians, wearied and despondent, confessed the true cause of their ruin. They understood that for liberty, justice, and equal laws, it is as necessary that Democracy should restrain itself as it had been that it should restrain the Oligarchy. They resolved to take their stand once more upon the ancient ways, and to restore the order of things which had subsisted when the monopoly of power had been taken from the rich and had not been acquired by the poor. After a first restoration had failed, which is only memorable because Thucydides, whose judgment in politics is never at fault, pronounced it the best Government Athens had enjoyed, the attempt was renewed with more experience and greater singleness of purpose. The hostile parties were reconciled, and proclaimed an amnesty, the first in history. They resolved to govern by concurrence. The laws, which had the sanction of tradition, were reduced to a code; and no act of the sovereign assembly was valid with which they might be found to disagree. Between the sacred lines of the Constitution which were to remain inviolate, and the decrees which met from time to time the needs and notions of the day, a broad distinction was drawn; and the fabric of a law which had been the work of generations was made independent of momentary variations in the popular will. The repentance of the Athenians came too late to save the Republic. But the lesson of their experience endures for all times, for it teaches that government by the whole people, being the government of the most numerous and most powerful class, is an evil of the same nature as unmixed monarchy, and requires, for nearly the same reasons, institutions that shall protect it against itself, and shall uphold the permanent reign of law against arbitrary revolutions of opinion.

Parallel with the rise and fall of Athenian freedom, Rome was employed in working out the same problems, with greater constructive sense, and greater temporary success, but ending at last in a far more terrible catastrophe. That which among the ingenious Athenians had been a development carried forward by the spell of plausible argument, was in Rome a conflict between rival forces. Speculative politics had no attraction for the grim and practical genius of the Romans. They did not consider what would be the cleverest way of getting over a difficulty, but what way was indicated by analogous cases; and they assigned less influence to the impulse and spirit of the moment, than to precedent and example. Their peculiar character prompted them to ascribe the origin of their laws to early times, and in their desire to justify the continuity of their institutions, and to get rid of the reproach of innovation, they imagined the legendary history of the kings of Rome. The energy of their adherence to traditions made their progress slow, they advanced only under compulsion of almost unavoidable neccessity, and the same questions recurred often, before they were settled. The constitutional history of the Republic turns on the endeavours of the aristocracy, who claimed to be the only true Romans, to retain in their hands the power they had wrested from the kings, and of the plebeians to get an equal share in it. And this controversy, which the eager and restless Athenians went through in one generation, lasted for more than two centuries, from a time when the *plebs* were excluded from the government of the city, and were taxed, and made to serve without pay, until, in the year 285, they were admitted to political equality. Then followed one hundred and fifty years of unexampled prosperity and glory; and then, out of the original conflict which had been compromised, if not theoretically settled, a new struggle arose which was without an issue.

The mass of poorer families, impoverished by incessant service in war, were reduced to dependence on an aristocracy of about two thousand wealthy men, who divided among themselves the immense domain of the State. When the need became intense the Gracchi tried to relieve it by inducing the richer classes to allot some share in the public lands to the common people. The old and famous aristocracy of birth and rank had made a stubborn resistance, but it knew the art of yielding. The later and more selfish aristocracy was unable to learn it. The character of the people was changed by the sterner motives of dispute. The fight for political power had been carried on with the moderation which is so honourable a quality of party contests in England. But the struggle for the objects of material existence grew to be as ferocious as civil controversies in France. Repulsed by the rich, after a struggle of twenty-two years, the people, three hundred and twenty thousand of whom depended on public rations for food, were ready to follow any man who promised to obtain for them by revolution what they could not obtain by law.

For a time the Senate, representing the ancient and threatened order of things, was strong enough to overcome every popular leader that arose, until Julius Caesar, supported by an army which he had led in an unparalleled career of conquest, and by the famished masses which he won by his lavish liberality, and skilled beyond all other men in the art of governing, converted the Republic into a Monarchy by a series of measures that were neither violent nor injurious.

The Empire preserved the Republican forms until the reign of Diocletian; but the will of the Emperors was as uncontrolled as that of the people had been after the victory of the Tribunes. Their power was arbitrary even when it was most wisely employed, and yet the Roman Empire rendered greater services to the cause of liberty than the Roman Republic. I do not mean by reason of the temporary accident that there were emperors who made good use of their immense opportunities, such as Nerva, of whom Tacitus says that he combined monarchy and liberty, things otherwise incompatible; or that the Empire was what its panegyrists declared it, the perfection of Democracy. In truth it was at best an ill-disguised and odious despotism. But Frederic the Great was a despot; yet he was a friend to toleration and free discussion. The Bonapartes were despotic; yet no liberal ruler was ever more acceptable to the masses of the people than the First Napoleon, after he had destroyed the Republic, in 1805, and the Third Napoleon at the height of his power in 1859. In the same way, the Roman Empire possessed merits which, at a distance, and especially at a great distance of time, concern men more deeply than the tragic tyranny which was felt in the neighbourhood of the Palace. The poor had what they had demanded in vain of the Republic. The rich fared better than during the Triumvirate. The rights of Roman citizens were extended to the people of the provinces. To the imperial epoch belong the better part of Roman literature and nearly the entire Civil Law; and it was the Empire that mitigated slavery, instituted religious toleration, made a beginning of the law of nations, and created a perfect system of the law of property. The Republic which Caesar overthrew had been anything but a free State. It provided admirable securities for the rights of citizens; it treated with savage disregard the rights of men; and allowed the free Roman to inflict atrocious wrongs on his children, on debtors and dependants, on prisoners and slaves. Those deeper ideas of right and duty, which are not found on the tables of municipal law, but with which the generous minds of Greece were conversant, were held of little account, and the philosophy which dealt with such speculations was repeatedly proscribed, as a teacher of sedition and impiety. . . .

If, drawing the limit in the second century, when the influence of Christianity becomes perceptible, we should form our judgment of the politics of antiquity by its actual legislation, our estimate would be low. The prevailing notions of freedom were imperfect, and the endeavours to realise them were wide of the mark. The ancients understood the regulation of power better than the regulation of liberty. They concentrated so many prerogatives in the State as to leave no footing from which a man could deny its jurisdiction or assign bounds to its activity. If I may employ an expressive anachronism, the vice of the classic State was that it was both Church and State in one. Morality was undistinguished from religion and politics from morals; and in religion, morality, and politics there was only one legislator and one authority. The State, while it did deplorably little for education, for practical science, for the indigent and helpless, or for the spiritual needs of man, nevertheless claimed the use of all his faculties and the determination of all his duties. Individuals and families, associations and dependencies were so much material that the sovereign power consumed for its own purposes. What the slave was in the hands of his master, the citizen was in the hands of the community. The most sacred obligations vanished before the public advantage. The passengers existed for the sake of the ship. By their disregard for private interests, and for the moral welfare and improvement of the people, both Greece and Rome destroyed the vital elements on which the prosperity of nations rests, and perished by the decay of families and the depopulation of the country. They survive not in their institutions, but in their ideas, and by their ideas, especially on the art of government, they are—

> The dead, but sceptred sovereigns, who still rule
> Our spirits from their urns.

. . . But, having sounded the depth of their errors, I should give you a very inadequate idea of the wisdom of the ancients if I allowed it to appear that their precepts were no better than their practice. While statesmen and senates and popular assemblies supplied examples of every description of blunder, a noble literature arose, in which a priceless treasure of political knowledge was stored, and in which the defects of the existing institutions were exposed with unsparing sagacity. The point on which the ancients were most nearly unanimous is the right of the people to govern, and their inability to govern alone. To meet this difficulty, to give to the popular element a full share without a monopoly of power, they adopted very generally the theory of a mixed Constitution. They differed from our notion of the same thing, because modern Constitutions have been a device for limiting monarchy; with them they were invented to curb democracy. The idea arose in the time of Plato—though he repelled it—when the early monarchies and oligarchies had vanished, and it continued to be cherished long after all democracies had been absorbed in the Roman Empire. But whereas a sovereign prince who surrenders part of his authority yields to the argument of superior force, a sovereign people relinquishing its own prerogative succumbs to the influence of reason. And it has in all times proved more easy to create limitations by the use of force than by persuasion.

The ancient writers saw very clearly that each principle of government standing alone is carried to excess and provokes a reaction. Monarchy hardens into despotism. Aristocracy contracts into oligarchy. Democracy expands into the supremacy of numbers. They therefore imagined that to restrain each element by combining it with the others would avert the natural process of self-destruction, and endow the State with perpetual youth. But this harmony of monarchy, aristocracy, and democracy blended together, which was the ideal of many writers, and which they supposed to be exhibited by Sparta, by Carthage, and by Rome, was a chimera of philosophers never realised by antiquity. . . .

If the topic of my address was the history of political science, the highest and the largest place would belong to Plato and Aristotle. The *Laws* of the one, the *Politics* of the other, are, if I may trust my own experience, the books from which we may learn the most about the principles of politics. The penetration with which those great masters of thought analysed the institutions of Greece, and exposed their vices, is not surpassed by anything in later literature; by Burke or Hamilton, the best political writers of the last century; by Tocqueville or Roscher, the most eminent of our own. But Plato and Aristotle were philosophers, studious not of unguided freedom, but of intelligent government. They saw the disastrous effects of ill-directed striving for liberty; and they resolved that it was better not to strive for it, but to be content with a strong administration, prudently adapted to make men prosperous and happy.

Now liberty and good government do not exclude each other; and there are excellent reasons why they should go together. Liberty is not a means to a higher political end. It is itself the highest political end. It is not for the sake of a good public administration that it is required, but for security in the pursuit of the highest objects of civil society, and of private life. Increase of freedom in the State may sometimes promote mediocrity, and give vitality to prejudice; it may even retard useful legislation, diminish the capacity for war, and restrict the boundaries of Empire. It might be plausibly argued that, if many things would be worse in England or Ireland under an intelligent despotism, some things would be managed better; that the Roman Government was more enlightened under Augustus and Antoninus than under the Senate, in the days of Marius or of Pompey. A generous spirit prefers that his country should be poor, and weak, and of no account, but free, rather than powerful, prosperous, and enslaved. It is better to be the citizen of a humble commonwealth in the Alps, without a prospect of influence beyond the narrow frontier, than a subject of the superb autocracy that overshadows half of

Asia and of Europe. But it may be urged, on the other side, that liberty is not the sum or the substitute of all the things men ought to live for; that to be real it must be circumscribed, and that the limits of circumscription vary; that advancing civilisation invests the State with increased rights and duties, and imposes increased burdens and constraint on the subject; that a highly instructed and intelligent community may perceive the benefit of compulsory obligations which, at a lower stage, would be thought unbearable; that liberal progress is not vague or indefinite, but aims at a point where the public is subject to no restrictions but those of which it feels the advantage; that a free country may be less capable of doing much for the advancement of religion, the prevention of vice, or the relief of suffering, than one that does not shrink from confronting great emergencies by some sacrifice of individual rights, and some concentration of power; and that the supreme political object ought to be sometimes postponed to still higher moral objects. My argument involves no collision with these qualifying reflections. We are dealing, not with the effects of freedom, but with its causes. We are seeking out the influences which brought arbitrary government under control, either by the diffusion of power, or by the appeal to an authority which transcends all government, and among those influences the greatest philosophers of Greece have no claim to be reckoned.

It is the Stoics who emancipated mankind from its subjugation to despotic rule, and whose enlightened and elevated views of life bridged the chasm that separates the ancient from the Christian state, and led the way to freedom. Seeing how little security there is that the laws of any land shall be wise or just, and that the unanimous will of a people and the assent of nations are liable to err, the Stoics looked beyond those narrow barriers, and above those inferior sanctions, for the principles that ought to regulate the lives of men and the existence of society. They made it known that there is a will superior to the collective will of man, and a law that overrules those of Solon and Lycurgus. Their test of good government is its conformity to principles that can be traced to a higher legislator. That which we must obey, that to which we are bound to reduce all civil authorities, and to sacrifice every earthly interest, is that immutable law which is perfect and eternal as God Himself, which proceeds from His nature, and reigns over heaven and earth and over all the nations.

The great question is to discover, not what governments prescribe, but what they ought to prescribe; for no prescription is valid against the conscience of mankind. Before God, there is neither Greek nor barbarian, neither rich nor poor, and the slave is as good as his master, for by birth all men are free; they are citizens of that universal commonwealth which embraces all the world, brethren of one family, and children of God. The true guide of our conduct is no outward authority, but the voice of God, who comes down to dwell in our souls, who knows all our thoughts, to whom are owing all the truth we know, and all the good we do; for vice is voluntary, and virtue comes from the grace of the heavenly spirit within.

What the teaching of that divine voice is, the philosophers who had imbibed the sublime ethics of the Porch went on to expound: It is not enough to act up to the written law, or to give all men their due; we ought to give them more than their due, to be generous and beneficent, to devote ourselves for the good of others, seeking our reward in self-denial and sacrifice, acting from the motive of sympathy and not of personal advantage. Therefore we must treat others as we wish to be treated by them, and must persist until death in doing good to our enemies, regardless of unworthiness and ingratitude. For we must be at war with evil, but at peace with men, and it is better to suffer than to commit injustice. True freedom, says the most eloquent of the Stoics, consists in obeying God. A State governed by such principles as these would have been free far beyond the measure of Greek, or Roman freedom; for they open a door to religious toleration, and close it against slavery. Neither conquest nor purchase, said Zeno, can make one man the property of another.

These doctrines were adopted and applied by the great jurists of the Empire. The law of nature, they said, is superior to the written law, and slavery contradicts the law of nature. Men have no right to do what they please with their own, or to make profit out of another's loss. Such is the political wisdom of the ancients, touching the foundations of liberty. . . .

II

. . . Diocletian's attempt to transform the Roman Government into a despotism of the Eastern type had brought on the last and most serious persecution of the Christians; and Constantine, in adopting their faith, intended neither to abandon his predecessor's scheme of policy nor to renounce the fascinations of arbitrary authority, but to strenghten his throne with the support of a religion which had astonished the world by its power of resistance, and to obtain that support absolutely and without a drawback he fixed the seat of his government in the East, with a patriarch of his own creation.

Nobody warned him that by promoting the Christian religion he was tying one of his hands, and surrendering the prerogative of the Caesars. As the acknowledged author of the liberty and superiority of the Church, he was appealed to as the guardian of her unity. He admitted the obligation; he accepted the trust; and the divisions that prevailed among the Christians supplied his successors with many opportunities of extending that protectorate, and preventing any reduction of the claims or of the resources of imperialism.

Constantine declared his own will equivalent to a canon of the Church. According to Justinian, the Roman people had formally transferred to the emperors the entire plenitude of its authority, and, therefore, the Emperor's pleasure, expressed by edict or by letter, had force of law. Even in the fervent age of its conversion the Empire employed its refined civilisation, the accumulated wisdom of ancient sages, the reasonableness and sublety of Roman law, and the entire inheritance of the Jewish, the Pagan, and the Christian world, to make the Church serve as a gilded crutch of absolutism. Neither an enlightened philosophy, nor all the political wisdom of Rome, nor even the faith and virtue of the Christians availed against the incorrigible tradition of antiquity. Something was wanted beyond all the gifts of reflection and experience—a faculty of self-government and self-control, developed like its language in the fibre of a nation, and growing with its growth. This vital element, which many centures of warfare, of anarchy, of oppression had extinguished in the countries that were still draped in the pomp of ancient civilisation, was deposited on the soil of Christendom by the fertilising stream of migration that overthrew the empire of the West. . . .

The spirit of immemorial paganism which had saturated ancient society could not be exorcised except by the combined influence of Church and State; and the universal sense that their union was necessary created the Byzantine despotism. The divines of the Empire who could not fancy Christianity flourishing beyond its borders, insisted that the State is not in the Church, but the Church in the State. This doctrine had scarcely been uttered when the rapid collapse of the Western Empire opened a wider horizon; and Salvianus, a priest at Marseilles, proclaimed that the social virtues, which were decaying amid the civilised Romans, existed in greater purity and promise among the Pagan invaders. They were converted with ease and rapidity; and their conversion was generally brought about by their kings.

Christianity, which in earlier times had addressed itself to the masses, and relied on the principle of liberty, now made its appeal to the rulers, and threw its mighty influence into the scale of authority. The barbarians, who possessed no books, no secular knowledge, no education, except in the schools of the clergy, and who had scarcely acquired the rudiments of religious instruction, turned with childlike attachment to men whose minds were stored with the knowledge of Scripture, of Cicero, of St. Augustine; and in the scanty world of their ideas, the Church was felt to be something infinitely vaster, stronger, holier than their newly founded States. The clergy supplied the means of conducting the new governments, and were made exempt from taxation, from the jurisdiction of the civil magistrate, and of the political administrator. They taught that power ought to be conferred by election; and the Councils of Toledo furnished the framework of the Parliamentary system of Spain, which is, by a long interval, the oldest in the world. But the monarchy of the Goths in Spain, as well as that of the Saxons in England, in both of which the nobles and the prelates surrounded the throne with the semblance of free institutions, passed away; and the people that prospered and overshadowed the rest were the Franks, who had no native nobility, whose law of succession to the Crown became for one thousand years the fixed object of an unchanging superstition, and under whom the feudal system was developed to excess.

Feudalism made land the measure and the master of all things. Having no other source of wealth than the produce of the soil, men depended on the landlord for the means of escaping starvation; and thus his power became paramount over the liberty of the subject and the authority of the State. Every baron, said the French maxim, is sovereign in his own domain. The nations of the West lay between the competing tyrannies of local magnates and of absolute monarchs, when a force was brought upon the scene which proved for a time superior alike to the vassal and his lord.

In the days of the Conquest, when the Normans destroyed the liberties of England, the rude institutions which had come with the Saxons, the Goths, and the Franks from the forests of Germany were suffering decay, and the new element of popular government afterwards supplied by the rise of towns and the formation of a middle class was not yet active. The only influence capable of resisting the feudal hierarchy was the ecclesiastical hierarchy; and they came into collision, when the process of feudalism threatened the independence of the Church by subjecting the prelates severally to that form of personal dependence on the kings which was peculiar to the Teutonic state.

To that conflict of four hundred years we owe the rise of civil liberty. If the Church had continued to buttress the thrones of the king whom it anointed, or if the struggle had terminated speedily in an undivided victory, all Europe would have sunk down under a Byzantine or Muscovite despotism. For the aim of both contending parties was absolute authority. But although liberty was not the end for which they strove, it was the means by which the temporal and the spiritual power called the nations to their aid. The towns of Italy and Germany won their franchises, France got her States-General, and England her Parliament out of the alternate phases of the contest; and as long as it lasted it prevented the rise of divine right. A disposition existed to regard the crown as an estate descending under the law of real property in the family that possessed it. But the authority of religion, and especially of the papacy, was thrown on the side that denied the indefeasible title of kings. In France what was afterwards called the Gallican theory maintained that the reigning house was above the law, and that the sceptre was not to pass away from it as long as there should be princes of the royal blood of St. Louis. But in other countries the oath of fidelity itself attested that it was conditional, and should be kept only during good behavior; and it was in conformity with the public law to which all monarchs were held subject, that King John was declared a rebel against the barons, and that the men who raised Edward III. to the throne from which they had deposed his father invoked the maxim *Vox populi Vox Dei.*

And this doctrine of the divine right of the people to raise up and pull down princes, after obtaining the sanctions of religion, was made to stand on broader grounds, and was strong enough to resist both Church and king. . . .

Looking back over the space of a thousand years, which we call the Middle Ages, to get an estimate of the work they had done, if not towards perfection in their institutions, at least towards attaining the knowledge of political truth, this is what we find: Representative government, which was unknown to the ancients, was almost universal. The methods of election were crude; but the principle that no tax was lawful that was not granted by the class that paid it—that is, that taxation was inseparable from representation—was recognised, not as the privilege of certain countries, but as the right of all. Not a prince in the world, said Philip de Commines, can levy a penny without the consent of the people. Slavery was almost everywhere extinct; and absolute power was deemed more intolerable and more criminal than slavery. The right of insurrection was not only admitted but defined, as a duty sanctioned by religion. Even the principles of the Habeas Corpus Act, and the method of the Income Tax, were already known. The issue of ancient politics was an absolute state planted on slavery. The political produce of the Middle Ages was a system of states in which authority was restricted by the representation of powerful classes, by privileged associations, and by the acknowledgment of duties superior to those which are imposed by man. . . .

The tide was running fast when the Reformation began at Wittenberg, and it was to be expected that Luther's influence would stem the flood of absolutism. For he was confronted everywhere by the compact alliance of the Church with the State; and a great part of his country was governed by hostile potentates who were prelates of the Court of Rome. He had, indeed, more to fear from temporal than from spiritual foes. The leading German bishops wished that the Protestant demands should be conceded; and the Pope himself vainly urged on the Emperor a conciliatory policy. But Charles V. had outlawed Luther, and attempted to waylay him; . . . whilst the democracy of the towns generally took his side. But the dread of revolution was the deepest of his political sentiments; . . . the substance of his political teaching was eminently conservative, the Lutheran States became the stronghold of rigid immobility. . . .

. . . Calvin, although a Republican, judged that the people are unfit to govern themselves, and declared the popular assembly an abuse that ought to be abolished. He desired an aristocracy of the elect, armed with the means of punishing not only crime but vice and error. For he thought that the severity of the mediaeval laws was insufficient for the need of the times; and he favoured the most irresistible weapon which the inquisitorial procedure put into the hand of the Government, the right of subjecting prisoners to intolerable torture, not because they were guilty, but because their guilt could not be proved. His teaching, though not calculated to promote popular institutions, was so adverse to the authority of the surrounding monarchs, that he softened down the expression of his political views in the French edition of his *Institutes*.

The direct political influence of the Reformation effected less than has been supposed. Most States were strong enough to control it. Some, by intense exertion, shut out the pouring flood. Others, with consummate skill, diverted it to their own uses. The Polish Government alone at that time left it to its course. Scotland was the only kingdom in which the Reformation triumphed over the resistance of the State; and Ireland was the only instance where it failed, in spite of Government support. But in almost every other case, both the princes that spread their canvas to the gale and those that faced it, employed the zeal, the alarm, the passions it aroused as instruments for the increase of power. Nations eagerly invested their rulers with every prerogative needed to preserve their faith, and all the care to keep Church and State asunder, and to prevent the confusion of their powers, which had been the work of ages, was renounced in the intensity of the crisis. Atrocious deeds were done, in which religious passion was often the instrument, but policy was the motive. . . .

All through the religious conflict policy kept the upper hand. When the last of the Reformers died, religion, instead of emancipating the nations, had become an excuse for the criminal art of despots. Calvin preached and Bellarmine lectured, but Machiavelli reigned. Before the close of the century three events occurred which mark the beginning of a momentous change. The massacre of St. Bartholomew convinced the bulk of Calvinists of the lawfulness of rebellion against tyrants, and they became advocates of that doctrine in which the Bishop of Winchester had led the way, and which Knox and Buchanan had received, through their master at Paris, straight from the mediaeval schools. Adopted out of aversion to the King of France, it was soon put in practice against the King of Spain. The revolted Netherlands, by a solemn Act, deposed Philip II., and made themselves independent under the Prince of Orange, who had been, and continued to be, styled his Lieutenant. Their example was important, not only because subjects of one religion deposed a monarch of another, for that had been seen in Scotland, but because, moreover, it put a republic in the place of a monarchy, and forced the public law of Europe to recognise the accomplished revolution. At the same time, the French Catholics, rising against Henry III., who was the most contemptible of tyrants, and against his heir, Henry of Navarre, who, as a Protestant, repelled the majority of the nation, fought for the same principles with sword and pen. . . .

The Bourbons, who had snatched the crown from a rebellious democracy, the Stuarts, who had come in as usurpers, set up the doctrine that States are formed by the valour, the policy, and the appropriate marriages of the royal family; that the king is consequently anterior to the people, that he is its maker rather than its handiwork, and reigns independently of consent. Theology followed up divine right with passive obedience. In the golden age of religious science, Archbishop Ussher, the most learned of Anglican prelates, and Bossuet, the ablest of the French, declared that resistance to kings is a crime, and that they may lawfully employ compulsion against the faith of their subjects. The philosophers heartily supported the divines. Bacon fixed his hope of all human progress on the strong hand of kings. Descartes advised them to crush all those who might be able to resist their power. Hobbes taught that authority is always in the right. Pascal considered it absurd to reform laws, or to set up an ideal justice against actual force. Even Spinoza, who was a Republican and a Jew, assigned to the State the absolute control of religion.

Monarchy exerted a charm over the imagination, so unlike the unceremonious spirit of the Middle Ages, that, on learning the execution of Charles I., men died of the shock; and the same thing occurred at the death of Louis XVI. and of the Duke of Enghien. The classic land of absolute monarchy was France. Richelieu held that it would be impossible to keep the people down if they were suffered to be well off. The Chancellor affirmed that France could not be governed without the right of arbitrary arrest and exile; and that in case of danger to the State it may be well that a hundred innocent men should perish. The Minister of Finance called it sedition to demand that the Crown should keep faith. One who lived on intimate terms with Louis XIV. says that even the slightest disobedience to the royal will is a crime to be punished with death. Louis employed these precepts to their fullest extent. He candidly avows that kings are no more bound by the terms of a treaty than by the words of a compliment; and that there is nothing in the possession of their subjects which they may not lawfully take from them. In obedience to this principle, when Marshal Vauban, appalled by the misery of the people, proposed that all existing imposts should be repealed for a single tax that would be less onerous, the King took his advice, but retained all the old taxes whilst he imposed the new. With half the present population, he maintained an army of 450,000 men; nearly twice as large as that which the late Emperor Napoleon assembled to attack Germany. Meanwhile the people starved on grass. France, said Fénelon, is one enormous hospital. French historians believe that in a single generation six millions of people died of want. It would be easy to find tyrants more violent, more malignant, more odious than Louis XIV., but there was not one who ever used his power to inflict greater suffering or greater wrong; and the admiration with which he inspired the most illustrious men of his time denotes the lowest depth to which the turpitude of absolutism has ever degraded the conscience of Europe. . . .

Religious liberty had been the dream of great Christian writers in the age of Constantine and Valentinian, a dream never wholly realised in the Empire, and rudely dispelled when the barbarians found that it exceeded the resources of their art to govern civilised populations of another religion, and unity of worship was imposed by laws of blood and by theories more cruel than the laws. But from St. Athanasius and St. Ambrose down to Erasmus and More, each age heard the protest of earnest men in behalf of the liberty of conscience, and the peaceful days before the Reformation were full of promise that it would prevail.

In the commotion that followed, men were glad to get tolerated themselves by way of privilege and compromise, and willingly renounced the wider application of the principle. Socinus was the first who, on the ground that Church and State ought to be separated, required universal toleration. But Socinus disarmed his own theory, for he was a strict advocate of passive obedience.

The idea that religious liberty is the generating principle of civil, and that civil liberty is the necessary condition of religious, was a discovery reserved for the seventeenth century. Many years before the names of Milton and Taylor, of Baxter and Locke were made illustrious by their partial condemnation of intolerance, there were men among the Independent congregations who grasped with vigour and sincerity the principle that it is only by abridging the authority of States that the liberty of Churches can be assured. That great political idea, sanctifying freedom and consecrating it to God, teaching men to treasure the liberties of others as their own, and to defend them for the love of justice and charity more than as a claim of right, has been the soul of what is great and good in the progress of the last two hundred years. The cause of religion, even under the unregenerate influence of worldly passion, had as much to do as any clear notions of policy in making this country the foremost of the free. . . .

By arresting the preponderance of France, the Revolution of 1688 struck the first real blow at Continental despotism. At home it relieved Dissent, purified justice, developed the national energies and resources, and ultimately, by the Act of Settlement, placed the crown in the gift of the people. But it neither introduced nor determined any important principle, and, that both parties might be able to work together, it left untouched the fundamental question between Whig and Tory. For the divine right of kings it established, in the words of Defoe, the divine right of freeholders; and their domination extended for seventy years, under the authority of John Locke, the philosopher of government by the gentry. Even Hume did not enlarge the bounds of his ideas; and his narrow materialistic belief in the connection between liberty and property captivated even the bolder mind of Fox.

By his idea that the powers of government ought to be divided according to their nature, and not according to the division of classes, which Montesquieu took up and developed with consummate talent, Locke is the originator of the long reign of

English institutions in foreign lands. And his doctrine of resistance, or, as he finally termed it, the appeal to Heaven, ruled the judgment of Chatham at a moment of solemn transition in the history of the world. Our Parliamentary system, managed by the great revolution families, was a contrivance by which electors were compelled, and legislators were induced to vote against their convictions; and the intimidation of the constituencies was rewarded by the corruption of their representatives. About the year 1770 things had been brought back, by indirect ways, nearly to the condition which the Revolution had been designed to remedy for ever. Europe seemed incapable of becoming the home of free States. It was from America that the plain ideas that men ought to mind their own business, and that the nation is responsible to Heaven for the acts of the State,—ideas long locked in the breast of solitary thinkers, and hidden among Latin folios,—burst forth like a conqueror upon the world they were destined to transform, under the title of the Rights of Man. . . .

But I have reached the end of my time, and have hardly come to the beginning of my task. In the ages of which I have spoken, the history of freedom was the history of the thing that was not. But since the Declaration of Independence, or, to speak more justly, since the Spaniards, deprived of their king, made a new government for themselves, the only known forms of liberty, Republics and Constitutional Monarchy, have made their way over the world. It would have been interesting to trace the reaction of America on the Monarchies that achieved its independence; to see how the sudden rise of political economy suggested the idea of applying the methods of science to the art of government; how Louis XVI., after confessing that despotism was useless, even to make men happy by compulsion, appealed to the nation to do what was beyond his skill, and thereby resigned his sceptre to the middle class, and the intelligent men of France, shuddering at the awful recollections of their own experience, struggled to shut out the past, that they might deliver their children from the prince of the world and rescue the living from the clutch of the dead, until the finest opportunity ever given to the world was thrown away, because the passion for equality made vain the hope of freedom.

And I should have wished to show you that the same deliberate rejection of the moral code which smoothed the paths of absolute monarchy and of oligarchy, signalised the advent of the democratic claim to unlimited power,—that one of its leading champions avowed the design of corrupting the moral sense of men, in order to destroy the influence of religion, and a famous apostle of enlightenment and toleration wished that the last king might be strangled with the entrails of the last priest. I would have tried to explain the connection between the doctrine of Adam Smith, that labour is the original source of all wealth, and the conclusion that the producers of wealth virtually compose the nation, by which Sieyes subverted historic France; and to show that Rousseau's definition of the social compact as a voluntary association of equal partners conducted Marat, by short and unavoidable stages, to declare that the poorer classes were absolved, by the law of self-preservation, from the conditions of a contract which awarded to them misery and death; that they were at war with society, and had a right to all they could get by exterminating the rich, and that their inflexible theory of equality, the chief legacy of the Revolution, together with the avowed inadequacy of economic science to grapple with problems of the poor, revived the idea of renovating society on the principle of self-sacrifice, which had been the generous aspiration of the Essenes and the early Christians, of Fathers and Canonists and Friars; of Erasmus, the most celebrated precursor of the Reformation; of Sir Thomas More, its most illustrious victim; and of Fénelon, the most popular of bishops, but which, during the forty years of its revival, has been associated with envy and hatred and bloodshed, and is now the most dangerous enemy lurking in our path.

Last, and most of all, having told so much of the unwisdom of our ancestors, having exposed the sterility of the convulsion that burned what they adored, and made the sins of the Republic mount up as high as those of the monarchy, having shown that Legitimacy, which repudiated the Revolution, and Imperialism, which crowned it, were but disguises of the same element of violence and wrong, I should have wished, in order that my address might not break off without a meaning or a moral, to relate by whom, and in what connection, the true law of the formation of free States was recognised, and how that discovery, closely akin to those which, under the names of development, evolution, and continuity, have given a new and deeper method to other sciences, solved the ancient problem between stability and change, and determined the authority of tradition on the progress of thought; how that theory, which Sir James Mackintosh expressed by saying that Constitutions are not made, but grow; the theory that custom and the national qualities of the governed, and not the will of the government, are the makers of the law; and therefore that the nation, which is the source of its own organic institutions, should be charged with the perpetual custody of their integrity, and with the duty of bringing the form into harmony with the spirit, was made, by the singular co-operation of the purest Conservative intellect with red-handed revolution, of Niebuhr with Mazzini, to yield the idea of nationality, which, far more than the idea of liberty, has governed the movement of the present age.

I do not like to conclude without inviting attention to the impressive fact that so much of the hard fighting, the thinking, the enduring that has contributed to the deliverance of man from the power of man, has been the work of our countrymen, and of their descendants in other lands. We have had to contend, as much as any people, against monarchs of strong will and of resources secured by their foreign possession, against men of rare capacity, against whole dynasties of born tyrants. And yet that proud prerogative stands out on the background of our history. Within a generation of the Conquest, the Normans were compelled to recognise, in some grudging measure, the claims of the English people. When the struggle between Church and State extended to England, our Churchmen learned to associate themselves with the popular cause; and, with few exceptions, neither the hierarchical spirit of the foreign divines, nor the monarchical bias peculiar to the French, characterised the writers of the English school. The Civil Law, transmitted from the degenerate Empire to be the common prop of absolute power, was excluded from England. The Canon Law was restrained, and this country never admitted the Inquisition, nor fully accepted the use of torture which invested Continental royalty with so many terrors. At the end of the Middle Ages foreign writers acknowledged our superiority, and pointed to these causes. After that, our gentry maintained the means of local self-government such as no other country possessed. Divisions in religion forced toleration. The confusion of the common law taught the people that their best safeguard was the independence and the integrity of the judges.

All these explanations lie on the surface, and are as visible as the protecting ocean; but they can only be successive effects of a constant cause which must lie in the same native qualities of perseverance, moderation, individuality, and the manly sense of duty, which give to the English race its supremacy in the stern art of labour, which has enabled it to thrive as no other can on inhospitable shores, and which (although no great people has less of the bloodthirsty craving for glory and an army of 50,000 English soldiers has never been seen in battle) caused Napoleon to exclaim, as he rode away from Waterloo, "It has always been the same since Crecy."

Therefore, if there is reason for pride in the past, there is more for hope in the time to come. Our advantages increase, while other nations fear their neighbours or covet their neighbours' goods. Anomalies and defects there are, fewer and less intolerable, if not less flagrant than of old.

But I have fixed my eyes on the spaces that Heaven's light illuminates, that I may not lay too heavy a strain on the indulgence with which you have accompanied me over the dreary and heart-breaking course by which men have passed to freedom; and because the light that has guided us is still unquenched, and the causes that have carried us so far in the van of free nations have not spent their power; because the story of the future is written in the past, and that which hath been is the same thing that shall be.

"THE CHANGING CONTENT OF FREEDOM IN HISTORY"

Harold J. Laski

The basic idea of liberty as a part of the armory of human ideals goes back to the Greeks and is born, as the funeral oration of Pericles makes abundantly clear, of two notions: the first is the protection of the group from attack, the second is the ambition of the group to realize itself as fully as possible. In such an organic society the concept of individual liberty was virtually unknown. But when the city-state was absorbed by the idea of empire, new elements came into play. Stoicism especially gave birth to the idea of the individual and made his self-realization the main objective of human endeavor. Christianity added little to this notion by way of substantial content; but it added to its force the impetus of a religious sanction, not improbably the more powerful because Christianity was in its original phase essentially a society of the disinherited, to whom the idea of the eminent dignity of human personality as such would necessarily make an urgent appeal. In this stage it is difficult to dissociate the idea of liberty from that of equality, with which it is frequently intertwined. But as Christianity became the triumphant religion of the western world, the idea of equality became largely relegated to the theoretical sphere; and the liberty in which the church became interested was that of ecclesiastical groups seeking immunity from invasion at the hands of the secular power. In this aspect the liberty it sought was in essence indistinct from the liberty claimed by other groups in the mediaeval community. For until the end of the fifteenth century, roughly, the defense of particular liberties against invasion by external authority was the work of a functional group, such as the barons of Runnymede or the merchants of London. In this period liberty may be said to have resolved itself into a system of liberties or customary negative rights which were bought and sold between the parties for hard cash. Custom became codified into law, and the invasion of custom came to be taken as a denial of liberty. There is little that is universal about such a conception of liberty; the group is largely defending itself from attack without undue regard to the interest of other groups. Thus in mediaeval England liberty had no meaning for the villein; and it is hardly illegitimate to argue that those who fought for liberty when they wrung Magna Carta from King John were good syndicalists whose minds were largely bounded by the narrow demands of a small group within the realm. Liberty has been as often the rallying cry of a selfish interest intent upon privilege for itself as it has been the basis for a demand which sought the realization of a good wider than that by which it was itself affected. It is therefore not unfair to describe the mediaeval idea of liberty as a system of corporate privileges wrung or purchased from the dominant power and affecting the individual less as himself than as a member of some group in whom those privileges cohere.

Philosophically no doubt restraint upon freedom of behavior has always been resented as an invasion of individual personality. But historically the best way of regarding the substance of liberty in the modern period as well as in the mediaeval is to realize that the new elements which enter into its composition at any given time have almost invariably been rationalizations of particular demands from some class or race of creed which have sought a place in the sun denied to them. Thus the history of religious liberty has been the demand for toleration by group after group of dissidents from recognized creeds, few of which have been willing to admit the claims of their rivals to toleration. So again the history of the franchise has been the demand of men for the right to share in political power, while many of those to whom the right has been granted have had no difficulty in urging that it was unwise or unjust to admit the next claimants to their place; Macaulay, who urged with passion the enfranchisement of the middle class, opposed not less urgently the grant of universal suffrage on the ground that it would necessarily dissolve the fabric of society.

The Reformation may be said to have been the most important factor in revitalizing the stoic doctrine of the primacy of the individual and in giving a new emphasis to individual rights as a separate and distinct subject of liberty. The breakdown of the *republica christiana* gave birth to new religions; these by demanding toleration gave birth, even if painfully and in doubt, to the idea of liberty of conscience. The centralization of monarchical power consequent upon the break-down of feudalism made political liberty more abstract and general than it had previously been; and the discovery of the printing press gave to the idea of freedom of expression within the general concept of political liberty a valuable concreteness which it had never before possessed. Nor is this all. The voyages of discovery synchronized with the emergence of a capitalist economy, and the importance given by the character of this economy to the individual entrepreneur made the problems of civil and economic liberty take on a new sharpness of form. By the time of Locke the idea of the individual as the embodiment of certain natural and impre-scriptible rights which authority is not entitled to invade had become a common-place of political speculation.

In a sense the emergence of the Reformation state on the ruins of the mediaeval commonwealth meant the substitution of the idea of the nation for the idea of the group; and it would not be illegitimate to argue that until the maturity of capitalism in the nineteenth century the struggle for national liberty proceeds along parallel lines with that of individual liberty. The two become until the threshold of our own day the two supreme embodiments of that passion for self-realization which has always lain at the root of the idea of liberty. The nation rejects the subordination of itself to an external authority just as the individual seeks to define for himself spheres of conduct into which external authority is not entitled to enter. Each seeks to make its claims as absolute as possible. The one for that end assumes the panoply of a sovereign state, thereby recognizing no superior; the other attempts to define the limits of governmental interference in terms of wants he discovers as brooking no denial. The history of the search for national liberty resulted in a chaos of sovereignties which stood in sharp contrast to that unified economic life made possible by scientific discovery; and it was clear that the history of the twentieth century would be largely occupied in bringing order into the anarchy to which the struggle for national liberty had given birth.

Something not dissimilar occurred in the history of individual liberty. So long as it was conceived as a body of absolute rights inherent in the individual and entitled to be exerted without regard to their social consequences, liberty was divorced from the ideas of both equality and justice. The individual became the antithesis of the state; and liberty itself became, as with Herbert Spencer, a principle of anarchy rather than a body of claims to be read in the context of the social process. The reason for this evolution is clear. The body of ideas we call liberalism emphasized the undesirability of restraint, because those who gave it birth had mainly experi-enced the state as an organization interfering with the behavior they regarded as necessary to self-realization. Because of this they sought to reduce the state to the role of a mere guardian of order, keeping the ring in a vast competition of individual strivings of men who received in the social process the reward to which their effort and ability entitled them. Laissez faire was assumed at once to max-imize self-realization on the one hand and on the other to serve the state by selecting the fittest for survival. Historic experience and biological principle seemed to the Victorian age to canonize the classic antithesis of individual and state.

The conception of an individual whose liberty was a function—the maintenance of order apart—of the weakness of the state was intelligible enough in its period. It failed to take account of the fact that the differences between men are too great under such conditions to make self-realization possible for more than a few. Liberty in a laissez faire society is attainable only by those who have the wealth or opportunity to purchase it; and these are always a negligible minority. Experience accordingly drove the state to interfere; and the liberal state of the nineteenth century was gradually replaced by the social service state of the twentieth. This may be desribed by saying that it again joins the ideal of liberty to that of equality, and this in the name of social justice. As the claims of liberty broke down the privileges of birth and creed, so with obvious logic they began an assault upon the claims of wealth also. The state was increasingly driven to widen its functions to mitigate the consequences of that social inequality to which the system of absolute liberty gave rise. Education, public health, provision against unemployment, housing, public parks and libraries are only a few of the outstanding services it was driven to organize in the interest of those who could not be expected to help themselves. Democratic agitation, which from 1600 to about 1870 had been occupied with the removal of barriers upon individual action, after 1870 began to press for the deliberate creation of equalitarian conditions. It has become clear, in a word, that the idea of liberty depends upon the results of the social process at any given time; *theme* and it is against that background that its essential elements require analysis.

Liberty may be defined as the affirmation by an individual or group of his or its own essence. It seems to require the presence of three factors. It seeks in the first place a certain harmonious balance of personality; it requires on the negative side the absence of restraint upon the exercise of that affirmation; and it demands on the positive the organization of opportunities for the exercise of a continuous initiative. The problem of liberty has always been the prevention of those restraints, upon the one hand, that men at any given period are not prepared to tolerate and, upon the other, the organization of those opportunities the denial of which results in that sense of frustration which when widely felt leads to imminent or actual disorder.

So regarded, two things are clear about liberty. While its large outlines may have a fairly permanent character, its particular content is always changing with the conditions of time and place. To one age the demand for liberty may express itself in an insistence upon religious toleration; to another political enfranchisement may be its essential expression. This serves to remind us that liberty is always inherent in a social process and is unintelligible apart from it. Liberty therefore must always be conceived, if its philosophy is to be an adequate one, as related to law. It can never be absolute; some restraints are inevitable, some opportunities must be denied, simply because men have to live with one another and move differently to the attainment of antithetic desires. So closely moreover is this network interwoven that we cannot ever seek permanently to define a sphere of conduct within which freedom of action may be defined as liberty. For while we may claim, to take an obvious example, that there is unlikely to be liberty in any community in which there is no legal right to freedom of speech, we cannot maintain that an absolute right to say what he pleases is or should be inherent in any person; it is not, as Mr.

Justice Holmes has said, a denial of freedom of speech when a man is prohibited from crying "Fire!" in a crowded theater.

Liberty, in a word, has to be reconciled with the necessities of the social process; it has to find terms upon which to live with authority. Those terms have never been absolute or unchanging; they have always been a function of the historic environment in some given time and place. And that environment has always given birth to its own system of ideas, to which it has contributed some special emphasis in the notion of liberty, born of its peculiar conditions. That emphasis is always seeking its translation into an idea of law, whether by way of negation or affirmation; and the relation of authority to the substance of this idea is usually dependent upon what those who exercise authority consider will be the effect of the translation upon the order they seek to maintain. Trade unions demand the right to combine; authority admits that right or stigmatizes it as conspiracy, according to whether it considers the admission compatible with the way of life it seeks to uphold. A religious group demands the removal of the barriers upon the admission of its members to citizenship; the action of authority will turn upon its judgment of the consequences of the demand. Usually it will be found that the action of authority turns upon its estimate of the power possessed by those who make the demand and the way in which they will use their power; that is the truth embodied in Royer-Collard's great aphorism that liberty is the courage to resist.

The history of liberty since the Reformation has largely passed through two great periods. In the one the essence of the struggle for its realization has been to free the individual from subordination to a position, religious, political or economic, in which he has been placed by an authority external to himself. The effort has been the conferment upon him of rights—that is, of claims recognized by the law—which he is to enjoy without regard to the groups to which he may belong. This may be called the period of personal emancipation, and its classic expression is in the program of the French Revolution. The conception of society involved in it is that of an aggregate of persons; and it is argued that the fewer the restraints upon the free play of personality, the greater will be the liberty attained. Social effort is devoted to the destruction of privileges which inhere in some specially favored groups. It is generally conceived that the more men are let alone, the less positive the action of the state, the more likely is the individual to be free. In this period liberty is related to justice and equality in a negative way. My relation to my neighbor is deemed socially adequate if the state does not positively intervene to confer benefits upon him which I do not enjoy. Religious privilege, political privilege, privileges of birth or sex or race, little by little go by the board.

But in the period which roughly synchronizes with the growth of the modern proletariat it is rapidly discovered that the merely negative liberty to do what one can does not give freedom to the masses. We then enter upon the period of social emancipation. Government becomes increasingly paternalistic. It regulates the behavior of individuals and groups in the interest of an increasing complexion of equality in their lives. The size of the community tends to make the individual less and less significant. He has to obtain his liberty in concert with others similarly placed in the society to which be belongs. In this period the emphasis of liberty is predom-

inantly in the economic sphere. Men become increasingly aware that grave inequalities in property mean grave differences in access to liberty. The struggle for
freedom is largely transferred from the plane of political to that of economic rights.
Men become less interested in the abstract fragment of political power an individual
can secure than in the use of massed pressure of the groups to which they belong to
secure an increasing share of the social product. Individualism gives way before
socialism. The roots of liberty are held to be in the ownership and control of the
instruments of production by the state, the latter using its power to distribute the
results of its regulation with increasing approximation to equality. So long as there
is inequality, it is argued, there cannot be liberty.

The historic inevitability of this evolution was seen a century ago by de
Tocqueville. It is interesting to compare his insistence that the democratization of
political power meant equality and that its absence would be regarded by the
masses as oppression with the argument of Lord Acton that liberty and equality are
antitheses. To the latter liberty was essentially an autocratic ideal; democracy
destroyed individuality, which was the very pith of liberty, by seeking identity of
conditions. The modern emphasis is rather toward the principle that material
equality is growing inescapable and that the affirmation of personality must be
effective upon an immaterial plane. It is found that doing as one likes, subject only
to the demands of peace, is incompatible with either international or municipal
necessities. We pass from contract to relation, as we have passed from status to
contract. Men are so involved in intricate networks of relations that the place for
their liberty is in a sphere where their behavior does not impinge upon that
self-affirmation of others which is liberty.

In short, the problems of liberty in a pluralistic world are extraordinarily complex. The individual who seeks self-realization finds himself confronted by a network of protective relationships which restrain him at every turn. Trade unions,
professional and employers' associations, statutory controls of every kind, limit his
power of choice by standardizing the manner of his effort. He has to adjust himself
to an atmosphere in which there is hardly an aspect of his life not suffused at least
partially with social regulation. To do anything he must be one with other men; for
it is only by union with his fellows that he can hope to make an impact upon his
environment. And even outside the realm in which the state defines the contours of
his effort he finds himself surrounded by a complex of social customs and habits
which force him despite himself into conventional modes of behavior. The scale of
the great society is definitely unfavorable to the individuality of an earlier period.

One other aspect of this position is notable. The history of liberty has been the
growth of a tendency to take for granted certain constituent elements in its
substance. There is certainly greater religious freedom, for example, than at any
previous time. But when the causes of this change are analyzed, it will be found
that the growth of religious freedom is a function of the growth of religious
indifference. The battle of liberty is not won but merely transferred to another
portion of the field. As the contest over the place of individual property in the
state becomes more sharp, the state limits freedom of expression and association in
those matters which seem to it dangerous to the principles it seeks to impose. Social

instability and liberty are antithetic terms. A society is tolerant when men do not challenge the foundations upon which it rests. Wherever these are in question, it moves rapidly to the conditions of dictatorship; and the elements of liberty are unattainable until a new and acceptable equilibrium has been reached.

It is therefore relatively easy to say what things go to make up liberty; it is extraordinarily difficult to say how its atmosphere can be guaranteed. Liberty can be resolved into a system of liberties: of speech, of association, of the right to share fully in political power, of religious belief, of full and undifferentiated protection by the law. But the question of giving to these separate liberties factual realization turns upon the objects to which they are devoted in any particular society at a given time. No doubt in Soviet Russia a Communist has a full sense of liberty; no doubt also he has a keen sense that liberty is denied him in Fascist Italy. Liberty in fact always means in practise liberty within law, and law is the body of regulations enacted in a particular society for its protection. Their color for the most part depends upon its economic character. The main object of law is not the fulfilment of abstract justice but the conference of security upon a way of life which is deemed satisfactory by those who dominate the machinery of the state. Wherever my exercise of my liberty threatens this security, I shall always find that it is denied; and in an economically unequal society an effort on the part of the poor to alter in a radical way the property rights of the rich at once throws the whole scheme of liberties into jeopardy. In the last resort liberty is always a function of power.

It is no doubt true that men have endeavored to set the conditions upon which liberty depends beyond the reach of peradventure. Locke sought to do so by his conception of a limited liability state; but experience has grimly shown that in times of crisis the limits of the liability cannot be maintained. Montesquieu argued that liberty is born of the separation of powers in a state; but the truth of his argument is at bottom the very partial one that men are unlikely to be free unless the judicial authority is largely independent of executive and legislature. The constitutions of many modern states have sought to make the alterations of certain fundamentals a matter of special difficulty in order to protect the liberty of their subjects from invasion. Experience suggests that the technique is not without its value; but, as war and dictatorship have shown, it is an expedient for fair weather, always liable to fundamental neglect in times of crisis. It seemed to de Tocqueville that large local liberties were the secret of a general free atmosphere; liberty, he thought, is born of the wide distribution of power. But this appears to be true only when an equal society can take such advantage of the distribution as to make its benefits unbiased in their incidence; and in the struggle for such a society not the most unlikely thing is the rapid disappearance of this characteristic. The great idealist school of political philosophy has found the essence of freedom in obedience to the general will of the state; but it cannot be said that it has made clear, save to its own votaries, either the nature of a general will or the conditions under which a general will, if it exists, may be said to be in effective operation. An important school of modern publicists has sought to find the essential condition of liberty in a supply of truthful news, since in its absence no rational judgment is possible. But it is clear that the supply of truthful news depends upon men being equally interested in the results which the impact of news may make upon opinion; and no such equal interest exists, above all in an economically unequal society.

Generally it may be argued that the existence of liberty depends upon our willingness to build the foundations of society upon the basis of rational justice and to adjust them to changing conditions in terms of reasoned discussion and not of violence. But if that be the case, the existence of liberty depends upon the attainment of a society in which men are recognized to have an equal claim upon the results of social effort and the general admission that if differences are to obtain these must be proved desirable in terms of rational justice also. In this background, as Aristotle saw at the very dawn of political science, liberty is unattainable until the passion for equality has been satisfied. For the failure to satisfy that passion in an adequate way prevents the emergence of equilibrium in the state. Its foundations are then in jeopardy because men are disputing about fundamentals. In such circumstances proscription and persecution are inevitable, since the community will lack that unified outlook upon the principles of its life of which liberty is the consequence. Men who differ upon ultimate matters, particularly in the realm of economic affairs, are rarely prepared to risk the prospect of defeat by submitting their disagreement to the arbitrament of reason. And when reason is at a discount, liberty has never had a serious prospect of survival.

FURTHER READINGS FOR PART 1

Bainton, Roland H., *The Travail of Religious Liberty: Nine Biographical Studies* (Philadelphia: Westminster, 1951). A study of the development of religious liberty through the biographies of nine men who lived in the period between the late fifteenth and the late seventeenth centuries.

Bury, J. B., *A History of Freedom of Thought* (New York: Holt, 1913). Covers the history of freedom of thought from ancient Greece and Rome through the nineteenth century; concludes with a general justification of liberty of thought.

Girvetz, Harry K., *The Evolution of Liberalism* (New York: Collier Books, 1963). Analyzes the basic beliefs held by the classical liberals of the eighteenth and nineteenth centuries; then characterizes the new set of beliefs which contemporary liberals have developed in response to historical changes.

Handlin, Oscar and Mary, *The Dimensions of Liberty* (Cambridge, Mass.: Harvard U.P., 1961). Using the ability of the individual to take action as a working measure of the extent of liberty at any time, the Handlins identify and describe the factors that have had an important effect on American freedom since colonial days.

Kamen, Henry, *The Rise of Toleration* (New York: McGraw-Hill, 1967). A study of the development of religious toleration in early modern Europe.

Krieger, Leonard, "Stages in the History of Political Freedom," in C. J. Friedrich (ed.), *Nomos IV: Liberty* (New York: Atherton, 1962), pp. 1—28. Traces the changing role of political freedom from the sixteenth century to the present.

Laski, Harold J., *The Rise of European Liberalism: An Essay in Interpretation* (London: George Allen and Unwin, 1936). Beginning with the Renaissance and the Reformation, traces the development of liberalism to the French Revolution; special attention is paid to the relation between the growth of liberalism and economic developments.

Muller, Herbert J., *Freedom in the Ancient World* (New York: Harper, 1961). A history of freedom from prehistoric times through the fall of Rome.

———, *Freedom in the Western World: From the Dark Ages to the Rise of Democracy* (New York: Harper, 1963). A history of freedom from the fall of Rome to 1800.

———, *Freedom in the Modern World* (New York: Harper, 1966). A history of freedom from 1800 to the present.

———, *Religion and Freedom in the Modern World* (Chicago: Chicago U.P., 1963). A study of the role of religion, especially Christianity, in both furthering and impeding the development of free societies in Western civilization. Considerable attention is devoted to the twentieth century.

Plamenatz, John, "In What Sense Is Freedom a Western Idea?" in *Current Law and Social Problems* (Toronto: Toronto U. P., 1960), pp. 3—18. Discusses how the idea of freedom has arisen in Western civilization as a response to problems of bureaucratic government, ecclesiastical authority, industrialization, and social mobility.

Pohlenz, Max, *Freedom in Greek Life and Thought: The History of an Ideal*, trans. by Carl Lofmark (New York: Humanities, 1966). Describes freedom as conceived by the ancient Greeks and traces its development in their history.

Shotwell, James T., *The Long Way to Freedom* (Indianapolis: Bobbs—Merrill, 1960). A history of the development of freedom from primitive society to the present.

Watkins, Frederick, *The Political Traditions of the West: A Study of the Development of Modern Liberalism* (Cambridge, Mass.: Harvard U. P., 1948). Traces the history of liberalism from its origins in Ancient Greece and Rome through World War II.

2. General Concepts of Freedom

On the surface, "freedom" is a strange and puzzling concept, for it has application in radically different contexts. As we have seen in the preceding part, the history of human freedom can be traced to the beginnings of civilization and encompasses struggles for liberty in virtually every sphere of human activity. The call for "freedom" can be a denunciation of existing religious institutions; it can be a plea for changes in governments and laws; it can be a demand for economic reform or for a revolution in the entire organization of society. In Part 5, we shall see still further the complexity of phenomena covered by "freedom" as various authors present their views of what is important in man's search for freedom in society. Some will attend to the general influence of culture upon the individual; some will stress political and economic factors; and some will emphasize the subtle influence of social organization.

Despite the diversity of factors thought to be relevant to a discussion of man's freedom in relationship to the institutions of his community, use of the term "freedom" is not exhausted by these applications. The concept of freedom is employed in a central way by authors whose primary concern is quite different. Thus, in Part 3, the subject of discussion will be whether man possesses free will. In Part 4, another dimension of freedom will appear as the authors seek to characterize the traits of a "free" personality.

Given this broad-ranging use of the term "freedom," it is natural to ask whether there is any genuine unity in the concept. What, after all, does "freedom" mean? Do we have one concept or many? And, if it should be necessary to distinguish several concepts of freedom, is it possible to enumerate them and thereby make clear to ourselves the various subjects which have occasioned so much discussion? In the reading selections which follow, the authors are concerned with these questions. As one might expect, they are not in agreement with one another. Yet each presents a synoptic view of freedom which can be helpful to the reader not only in placing the various essays of this volume in perspective but also in clarifying his own thinking.

The first article, by H. J. Pos, reports the results of a research project done by the International Federation of Philosophical Societies. This research was undertaken in 1950 at the request of the United Nations Educational, Scientific, and Cultural Organization (UNESCO). At that time, members of UNESCO, recognizing both the importance of the concept of freedom and the wide differences of opinion concerning the concept, urged that research be conducted to accomplish the following objectives: "(1) to analyze and define the principal meanings that the concept of freedom has assumed in the history of political philosophy and in philosophy of law, (2) to determine the present effect of this concept, (3) to evaluate the importance of the role that this concept may play in current ideological conflicts, (4) to give suitable publicity to the results of this project." As the then President of the International Federation of Philosophical Societies, Professor Pos of the University of Amsterdam responded to this request from UNESCO by sending a questionnaire to outstanding thinkers in Europe and the Americas. Fifty-eight persons responded. Pos then synthesized the results, presenting them in the report which is here reprinted. As the reader will note, the materials are organized somewhat loosely under what seemed to be the recurring topics of concern to those who replied to the questionnaire. The report does not provide a very systematic or precise analysis of the various meanings of freedom. Nevertheless, Pos's work does indicate the wealth of considerations which must be taken into account by anyone who would do justice to the many dimensions of freedom regarded as important by contemporary thinkers.

A more systematic account of the various concepts of freedom is provided by Mortimer J. Adler. In the selection which follows, Adler summarizes the results of research on the subject of freedom done by more than twenty scholars at the Institute for Philosophical Research over a five-year period in the 1950's. These results were obtained by having the scholars read the major authors in Western thought who have written on freedom. Reports were then presented which summarized the conceptions of freedom discussed by each of the authors. These reports were then examined in the effort to probe beyond differences of terminology to learn how many basic conceptions of freedom are actually treated in the literature. As a result, three basic conceptions of freedom were distinguished. First, there is a circumstantial freedom of self-realization, described as "a freedom which is possessed by any individual who, under favorable circumstances, is able to act as he wishes for his own good as he sees it." Typically, some version of this conception is under consideration when authors are discussing man's freedom in society. Second, there is an acquired freedom of self-perfection, conceived as "a freedom which is possessed only by those men who, through acquired virtue or wisdom, are able to will or live as they ought in conformity to the moral law or an ideal befitting human nature." When authors discuss the traits of personality possessed by a free man, their conceptions of freedom are usually variants of this acquired freedom of self-perfection. Finally, there is a natural freedom of self-determination defined as "a freedom which is possessed by all men, in virtue of a power inherent in human nature, whereby a man is able to change his own character creatively by deciding for himself what he shall do or shall become." Authors concerned with the question whether man possesses free will ordinarily are dealing with some form of this conception. *After distinguishing these three basic conceptions of human freedom, Adler asks whether it is possible to provide a formulation of what is common to them. He then concludes by suggesting that the following statement expresses what is common to all conceptions of human freedom: "A man is free who has in himself the ability or power to make what he does his own action and what he achieves his own property."*

Writing from the point of view of a historian who has devoted much of his life to research on the development of freedom in Western civilization, Herbert J. Muller also finds that there is a relatively neutral, objective definition of freedom which provides a unity of conception to the many concrete freedoms discussed and sought by men. For him, freedom means "the condition of being able to choose and to carry out purposes." He notes that according to this definition, freedom implies (1) the absence of external constraints, (2) the possession of an actual ability with available means to do what one wishes, and (3) the power of conscious choice between significant known alternatives. As partial confirmation of the adequacy of his definition, Muller explicitly considers the conceptions of freedom discriminated by Adler and observes that his own definition comprehends them.

In the essay "Two Concepts of Liberty," Isaiah Berlin does not seek to provide definitions of what is common to the many meanings of freedom recorded by historians of ideas. Rather, he proposes to examine what he finds to be the two central senses of political liberty. On the one hand, he finds that a significant group of political theorists hold a negative notion of freedom. For them, a man is free to the extent that no other human being interferes with his activity. On the other hand, there is an equally significant group of writers who hold a positive notion of freedom. For them, a man is free to the extent that he is master of himself. While at first it may seem that "negative" and "positive" freedom are but two ways of saying the same thing, Berlin notes that these notions of freedom historically developed in different directions until they came into direct conflict. For many of those who held the positive notion of freedom, it was a relatively easy step to distinguish within the individual a "higher" self as opposed to a "lower" self. A man's positive freedom came to be identified not with what the individual in fact wanted but with what he would want if he were under the control of his "higher" self. With this conception of freedom, it then became possible to urge that some men have the right to interfere and direct the lives of other men with the aim of increasing their positive freedom by making them do what their "higher" selves would really want to do if those individuals only knew better. From the standpoint of those committed to preserving man's freedom in the negative sense, such views merely provided an excuse for tyrants to create the very opposite of a free society while invoking the ideal of positive freedom to justify their dictates. Berlin concludes by observing that while tyranny may also be justified by those who hold the negative notion of freedom, the lesson of history is that tyranny is more likely to result when power is in the hands of those who would make men free in the positive sense.

In the final selection of this part, P. H. Partridge reviews several conceptions of freedom which have been influential in recent social thought. He begins by noting that the conception of freedom central in the tradition of European individualism

*and liberalism is one that takes freedom as primarily a negative notion. By this
tradition, a man is said to be free when he is not coerced or constrained by other
persons. Partridge then discusses the views of those who urge that a man's freedom
requires not simply the absence of interference from other persons but possession of
the power to achieve what is wanted. He also comments upon conceptions of
freedom which emphasize the positive aspects of being free to choose and act on
one's own initiative in behalf of an individual's important interests. Finally, he
suggests that one may do justice to the important aspects of freedom stressed by
these differing conceptions if one takes the essential condition of freedom to be
giving individuals the possibility of making meaningful choices.*

"UNESCO REPORT ON THE
INVESTIGATION CONCERNING FREEDOM"

H. J. Pos

(A) M. Émile Bréhier sent us valuable remarks on the successive meanings
assumed by the term "liberty" in the history of Western thought. Here follows a
brief summary of his account: The idea of liberty appeared in Greece, and its *first*
meaning was purely political and social. Understood thus, it designates that complex
of attributes included in the epithet "liberal." During the period of political
decadence which followed the reign of Alexander, liberty acquired an inner and
spiritual meaning. It signified the liberation from the passions and the emotions. It
described the independence of the wise man. Christianity brought an entirely
different meaning, namely, *free will*, i.e., the liberty to choose between good and
evil. This idea allows acts to be imputed to agents and makes men responsible
individually. M. Bréhier asserts that free will can have no meaning outside of a
Christian theology or one that derives its inspiration from similar sources. Yet the
Stoic meaning survives in the Christian world and exists side by side with the
theological meaning. The social complexities of our age have posed the problem in a
new form. Should the modern state aim at the emancipation of the individual or
should it lead to a new form of slavery, in which the individual will exist only as an
instrument of society? In any case, liberty is neither an organ nor a thing; it is
always the object of a desire and of a reasonable will, and it must be won and
preserved continually. "Men often reason as if the fundamental liberties could be
decreed like a law: yet, while it is possible to force man to respect the freedom of
his fellows, it is impossible to force him to be free."

(B) Professor Richard McKeon, whose work and whose active participation in the preceding UNESCO investigations are well known, has sent us a substantial answer which, because of its extent and especially because of the exactness of its information and its powers of synthesis, also deserves, in our opinion, to be summarized briefly at the beginning of this report. It is to be hoped that this treatise will eventually be published *in extenso*.

In his introduction to *Philosophical Differences and the Issues of Freedom*, the author reminds us how difficult it has proved to come to an agreement about the philosophic bases of the rights of man. The search for eventual principles consisting either in inalienable rights based on human nature or in the evolution of society which, under specific circumstances, determines rights that are actually claimed, has led merely to the elaboration and to the strengthening of contradictory philosophic principles. On the other hand, no difficulty arose in the way of an agreement on a list of rights and on a plan designed to coördinate them. It was therefore concluded that the philosophic problem consists, not in reaching a doctrinal agreement, but rather in obtaining an agreement on the rights themselves and in setting up the defense of these rights on the basis of very different principles. The report on the rights of man did not seek, therefore, to reduce their interpretation to a single formula. The members of the Committee decided to reach a "working formula."

The investigation concerning Democracy faced a similar problem. The author finds that in contemporary society there are no democracies and no anti-democracies, since all parties invoke the same democratic ideal; within this common agreement, however, differences subsist. They have to do chiefly with the questions of liberty and of tolerance toward dissenting opinions. The biggest problem confronting the UNESCO Committee was the relation between the traditional democratic rights and the social and economic rights newly proclaimed in the XIXth and the XXth century. The list of rights is split into two rigorously distinct parts: on the one hand such rights as freedom of religion and freedom of speech which guarantee the individual's independence, and on the other such rights as liberation from poverty and fear, which require the active participation of other human beings and depend, in the long run upon a world organization. . . .

Marx teaches that true freedom will have been achieved when men have learned to regulate material production for the satisfaction of their needs. Karl Mannheim recognizes several stages in social evolution. The first of these was to accept social conditions as fate (fatalism). In the second, man rises above his fate (ethics of conscience). In the third, social relations no longer escape investigation, they even become predictable. Politics is replaced by administration. . . .

After having defined the doctrines of St. Augustine, Rousseau, and Kant, the author goes back to Plato and to the Stoics. He quotes a famous passage from Cicero's *Paradoxa Stoicorum*: "Indeed, what is liberty? The ability to live as one desires. But who lives as he desires, excepting the man who follows the rules of equity, is happy to do his duty, . . . who does not obey the laws out of fear, but observes them and respects them because he judges this conduct to be more salutary, . . . to whom Fortune, whose power is said to be supreme, submits if, as the wise poet said, every one models his destiny on his own behavior?"

Noting that the English language possesses two terms for the word *Liberté*,

Freedom and *Liberty*, the author quotes R. B. Perry's definition: "By freedom I mean enlightened choice.... Liberty has to do with the action of circumstances upon man. *I recognize the fact that freedom and liberty interact upon each other.*"...

This investigation reveals itself, upon further reflection, to be quite complex. Its numerous and complicated aspects are reflected in the answers that we received. In order to avoid a disorganized enumeration, it has seemed preferable to us to offer a systematic scheme of the chief problems raised by the term "liberty." The answers received will be fitted into this scheme as illustrations. The reader will find in this report the main trends emerging in the answers. We shall take the liberty to insist on some aspects that did not receive, on the part of the authors, all the attention which they seemed to deserve. This appears all the more necessary since most of the authors make a personal choice among the problems concerning freedom, and center them on the deepest concerns of their own thinking. Such a selection is completely natural, since the term "liberty" covers fields that differ widely. We shall first establish the fundamental meanings in which the term is used, and then proceed to outline the relationships that connect them. The prime difficulty in examining the various concepts of freedom lies in the fact that all the senses of the term base themselves on inner experiences which language does not find it easy to express.

I. Physical and vital liberty. The terms "free" and "freedom" may be used in the case of certain inanimate phenomena. It is said that a spring is not free enough, and that a gas frees itself. These expressions are, of course, metaphors. They teach us nothing about the real nature of the phenomena involved, but merely refer back to the human experiences that constitute their point of departure. Man and, generally speaking, all living beings experience psychosomatic states of oppression and discomfort from which they tend to free themselves. These states can be determined by external factors, such as lack of air, certain odors, excessive noise, the presence of undesirable individuals, as well as by factors conditioned by the body itself. One may feel uncomfortable owing to an empty or a heavy stomach, to a wrinkle in the sheet on which one is lying, or to a garment that has become too tight, and one will try to free oneself from these conditions by means of actions leading to a feeling of comfort and tranquillity. In all these cases—and they are extremely varied—one will speak of liberation from inconvenience or pain when one succeeds in eliminating the physical or the psychosomatic disturbance.

Several of those who sent us answers set apart this "external" freedom which consists, negatively speaking, in the urge to free oneself from factors causing inconvenience or pain, and, positively, in the exercising of the natural function of behaving as one pleases and, more generally, of being "free as a bird in the air." For man is a being endowed with inclinations to self-preservation and to the enjoyment of pleasures. Therefore the first liberty to which, impelled by nature, he aspires, is of a psychophysical order.

II. The freedom of compromise. Besides the elementary tendencies toward freedom, man is endowed with tendencies that drive him to meet his fellow men, whether he consider them as obstacles to the fulfillment of his desires or as means to satisfy them. In the pursuit of material goods, a certain amount of compromise becomes necessary. One person will always own at the expense of others who own less, one will exercise power only if there are fellow men who submit, one will attain honors only on condition that there be others to admit their inferiority in talent or in accomplishments. To come into one's own on this plane, one needs the community; and the community in turn reduces one's satisfactions to construct a framework allowing the simultaneous existence of several tendencies aiming at the same goal. The reciprocal pressure of those who vie with each other for the conquest of economic or civic power, for domination and honors, necessarily creates a state of inequality which, although it tends to stabilize itself, will remain a permanent source of tension. In this state of affairs, respect for the rights of others, which induces the individual to curb his personal desires, assumes the character of a constraint complied with by calculation. The individual, measuring his forces against those which oppose him most, chooses the wisest course. His freedom consists in accomplishing the utmost within a network of forces opposing each other.

III. Moral freedom. The social order and the relative stability to which the struggle for power and domination leads, may impress the individual as a makeshift so long as he has not renounced his selfish tendencies. He will obey the laws out of fear. His freedom will be a relative one. However, another form of liberty arises: that of the honest and wise men who voluntarily accept the laws and, by this very acceptance, find a surer and higher freedom than the freedom of compromise. Socrates formulated this moral freedom when he said that the philosopher is the man who observes the laws for their own sake, independently of any thought of reward or punishment. During classical antiquity, moral liberty first consisted in obedience to the laws, which were conceived as being watched over by the gods. After the Sophists' critique, it consisted in voluntary obedience to the laws. Socrates was the initiator of that inner liberty which was to be preached later by the Stoics and which has remained an essential element of the notion of freedom in Western civilization. We shall return to this aspect of liberty in § V, in which the different analyses of moral freedom will be outlined. There too, we shall discuss the relation between moral and economic freedom.

IV. Freedom of conscience. It seems necessary to distinguish between moral liberty, which finds the material for its realization in the laws of society, and the freedom of a more individualized conscience, which finds its ultimate norm within itself and hence may come into conflict with the laws. For society may make demands on the individual which have weight for a conscience formally ready to forsake the pursuit of its personal interests, but but which are, materially, judged by the same conscience to be objectionable. The same Socrates who, in the *Crito*, professes toward the laws an attachment that goes so far as to dissuade him from saving his life by fleeing, refuses to obey when he must execute a command that goes against his conscience.

Although Greek philosophy, while maintaining the general principle of the agreement between moral liberty and the demands of the laws, already recognized problems of conscience, Christianity has singularly strengthened the role of the latter by teaching that one must "obey God before men." To the present day,

Christianity has inspired acts of resistance against tyrannical and criminal governments and upheld the rights of the religious conscience by contempt for suffering
and for death. In so doing, it has demonstrated how thoroughly wrong is the theory
of Hegel which asserts that "the state is the substance of morality."

V. *The struggle for moral and social freedom.* Greco-Roman humanism and
Christianity handed down to Western civilization the struggle for moral liberty. The
humanist is an optimist who believes in the liberation of man and the
spiritualization of his existence through will-power, which is the principle regulating
the instincts and the impulses. Christianity in its Roman form teaches that divine
Grace must needs concur with the will, whereas Protestantism is decidedly pessimistic. Despite these fundamentally divergent evaluations, humanism and
Christianity together have reared Western society in the knowledge of a moral law
which is to rule over egotistical tendencies and thus to enable the community of
men to live together in justice. Yet the ideals of justice and of universal peace are
far from being realized, and the last few centuries of Western history show greater
injustice in the distribution of earthly goods and bloodier wars than have ever been
known before. This state of affairs has made the problem of liberty, in all its
meanings, particularly complex.

Man today, if he lives in a large city, constantly sees his vital liberty impeded by
the narrowness of his environment, by noises of all kinds, and by a very noticeable
dependence on those who cater to his primary needs for food, clothing, etc.
Discomforts of this sort might still be overcome by training the will, which would
teach individuals to be indifferent, while maintaining and upholding the moral law,
the fulfillment of which gives promise of a higher freedom. However, the uneasiness
has spread to the moral law itself, and it too has become problematic. There are
consciences that revolt against all wars, even defensive. They note with despair that
the sacrifices which this attitude entails do not in any way prevent the preparation
of new wars, and that the moral conscience of the immense majority of men
accepts the notion that mankind must pass through bloody struggles in order to
reach its apogee at last. Does national defense respect the individual's right to
liberty when it calls young men to arms? Do the authorities that set the armies into
motion ask the soldiers whether they approve the reasons for which war has been
declared? Of course not, and thus it happens that millions of men, every one of
whom, taken individually, is convinced of the inhuman and criminal character of
war, as a group obey orders, and in so doing renounce the freedom of their
conscience. There exist, in the structure of contemporary life, other hindrances that
seem to paralyze the exercise of moral liberty. Life in past centuries has known
forms of economic dependence that lent themselves to grave injustices, such as
serfdom and slavery. Since the industrial revolution, a corresponding form of
domination and slavery has arisen, unknown in former centuries: a concentration of
economic power transcending the frontiers of nations in time of peace, and even in
time of war, and an industrial proletariat. . . .

A good many of the answers received show concerns that gravitate around
problems of this order. Most of the writers, it is true, treat of moral liberty and of

the struggle of man with himself, and imply that, in the last resort, all problems concerning liberty are of a personal order. The orientation of several of our correspondents, however, is decidedly political and economic. They do not try to solve the complicated knot in which the notions of responsibility and determinism, of liberty and fatality, intertwine; if they can be said to solve it, in a sense, it is because they turn outward, away from the microcosm of the personal struggle, toward the macrocosm of social realities that essentially determine the life of individuals: one must investigate and know these realities so that one may free oneself from them.

Along this line, one writer notes "Europe's pessimism, hemmed in between communism and totalitarian fascism," while another, having in mind the communist menace, exclaims: "if freedom were to die in the world, neither equality, nor security, nor prosperity would mean anything any longer." On this subject, the most diverse voices are heard. They seem to reflect the picture of a humanity striving for unity, but still grievously torn. One author, after expressing his preference for social love, already preached by Saint Paul in the *Epistle to the Galatians*, asks the question: "whether it is permissible to achieve supreme moral freedom by suppressing the existing freedom, even if it is the freedom of a dominant minority?" He then answers in the affirmative.

In the field of politics, the word "liberty" sometimes becomes the rallying cry for an attitude of defense in behalf of all that one wishes to preserve. Thus it happens that the defenders of economic freedom appear as champions of moral or spiritual freedom threatened by the regimentation of the modern state. The majority of those who mention economic freedom explicitly underline its dangers. Indeed it seems to us that to limit the desire for material gain is entirely compatible with, not to say the logical consequence of, moral liberty. A few voices, however, raise themselves in defense of economic freedom. Let us quote a French thinker who, under certain conditions, cautiously defends it, invoking arguments of a moral and a psychological nature: "Does not leaving it to the state to provide for you mean that you have renounced your responsibility? ... Do we not risk a disappearance of all restlessness that would spread to our very spiritual life?"

The concern of the great majority of authors is realistic. How could it be otherwise, in a world where one feels that the yearning for liberties is hampered by forces that are in no way ideal or unreal? Nevertheless, a distant echo of the old, idealistic intellectualism is heard in the case of one author, who declares that the problem of liberty is "of a purely speculative nature," and that the problem is to liberate conscience by means of thought, "whereupon the two great perspectives, liberalism and socialism," will fit in automatically.

Next to the description of bourgeois democracy as "an outdated society that prepares the socialist revolution," we note the numerous apologies for Western democracy as the most adequate expression of liberty. A British thinker defines the essence of democracy thus: man is not only a means, but an end in himself. The same writer declares himself in favor of preserving private ownership of personal belongings, while the state should control the means of production.

An answer coming from Switzerland frankly and vehemently criticizes liberalism, which has always defended economic liberty in close connection with the autonomy of the individual. The writer asks us "not to cling to liberal hypocrisies," and insists on the maintenance of the distinction between metaphysical liberty (the freedom of the act) and economic liberty.

The problem of economic order may seem very distant from the metaphysical interpretation of liberty. Yet the fact that this external and material aspect holds the attention of the many metaphysicians who wrote us, seems to indicate to what an extent, in our time, economic factors enter into the struggle. A clergyman's answer contains the following sentence: "The primary need of our age is for an economic and social order effectively promoting freedom for all." In our opinion, this is a most remarkable statement. It might serve as a basis for quite different orientations of thought. An Anglo-Saxon writer proposes the free discussion of communism in non-communist countries; an American, in turn, tells us that "Russians and Occidentals should get to know each other better." When another American reminds us that "democracy is a form of freedom, but not the only one," such a statement seems to indicate a desire for an understanding that would break through the usual limits of political distrust and isolation. One should not underestimate the value of this tendency toward an agreement both philosophic and practical, an agreement stopping at no boundaries, since it seeks to englobe all of mankind.

We note also that some writers started from their own country's history in their attempt to throw light on the contemporary problems of mankind. A Frenchman reminds us of the great values proclaimed by the Revolution of 1789. In his opinion, these universal values have not always been realized in the right proportions; too much emphasis has been placed upon Liberty, to the detriment of Equality and Fraternity. Comparing modern France and modern Russia, he believes that "the seeds of fraternity should be sowed among us, whereas the seeds of liberty should be planted among the Russians, who, up to the present, have been concerned mainly with equality." A Swiss writer, treating the problem from the point of view of the jurist, proclaims that "Switzerland has chosen freedom," and that "the experience of it requires a dignity of living and the scrupulousness of the magistrates. . . . One must deserve it." Another Swiss writer reminds us of the need for organized freedom, based on respect for the freedom of others. It should be noted that the notion of duty is vitally connected with that of liberty.

It would be interesting to study systematically each country's contribution to Western civilization. Such a study would show, in our opinion, that each country has realized in exemplary fashion one or more of the values which, taken together, constitute the common patrimony of our civilization. Through ever more close contact, these values should become "denationalized," in order to prepare the united civilization toward which mankind is tending.

VI. Freedom and determinism. In the innermost reaches of his being, man feels himself free. He feels himself determined to act with regard to external circumstances. Freedom is not a faculty, but an act. These facts of experience are recognized by thinkers of very different outlooks. The problem of determinism arises when one passes from experience to reflection, from the immediate to its objectification. Reflection then comes up against experienced freedom, or rather against the way in which the latter interprets itself. The memory of freedom experienced in deed seems to object to being integrated into the context of reality in the form required by theoretical reflection.

Among the authors who concerned themselves with the theory of freedom and determinism, the following trends may be noted:

1. the religious and metaphysical outlook,
2. the psychological outlook.

A Canadian thinker revives the old thesis that "Reason sees the good clearly and necessarily induces the will to follow her. The free will stems from the self, which remains autonomous with regard to external determinations. To negate the spirit inevitably leads to materialism and to atheism." Another, following in the footsteps of Aristotle and the Scholastics, asserts that the innermost motivation of liberty is the pursuit of happiness, and that freedom, human and imperfect, tends toward the perfection which lies in God. Still another believes that there can be no freedom without transcendence. Most of the writers refuse to admit determinism. Some categorically condemn it, affirming that "in a deterministic perspective, all moral notions disappear."

One writer explains the relation of determinism to liberty in terms of the relation of realism to idealism. Another apologist of liberty agrees with Nicolai Hartmann in saying: "it is sufficient that, among the many heteronomous determinations of liberty, there be one autonomous determinant"; and he agrees with Saint Thomas in saying that man is determined in nature, which does not contradict the freedom residing in the individual. Another writer, after having emphasized "the painful experiences we have when we behave freely," urges us to "dispel the negative illusions of freedom." A psychiatrist draws attention to the fact that "determinism does not oppose freedom, but free will." Free will has indeed fewer apologists than freedom. A philosopher of science reminds us that physical determinism involves the intervention of the human will to induce or prevent phenomena. "There exists, in the direction of the future, an availability of the universe, hence there is a place for liberty." An epistemologist defines the liberty that is implied in knowledge: "To be able to observe a fact, one must be free to think that it might not occur. . . . There exists at least one kind of freedom, so deeply ingrained in our being that one could not suppress it without cutting the very thread of our fate."

In the psychological studies of liberty, we note the idea that "the great enemy of freedom is fear, and that religion is capable of delivering us from it." Another writer declares that "only goodness of heart can lead to a true and to a social life." A few people underline "the essentially Christian origin of liberty."

"Moral freedom could not exercise itself without a certain amount of constraint." In fact, the word "constraint" is ambivalent: it means both an obstacle to liberty and a condition stimulating conduct. It is in the first sense that one writer uses it when he defines liberty as "a state of the conscious individual escaping all influences tending to force his behavior into channels chosen by others." Another uses it in the second sense when he speaks of "the discipline of freedom, which imposes normative restrictions." In the same line of thought a third writer states that liberty gains a positive character when it is limited by other persons. Determinism cannot be total, since there exist in every human being a spark of originality, a drive toward fulfillment, and a choice in favor of the higher and harder urge. He who engages himself is free; freedom and responsibility are therefore intimately connected.

Conclusions. Does the diversity of the statements received in answer to the questionnaire allow us to draw general conclusions? Here are some common features that, in our opinion, stand out:

1. Liberty, in the sense of absence of constraint, is a blessing.

2. There exists a moral liberty consisting in the fulfillment of personality. It displays the double character of an effort and of an impulse. In it resides man's dignity.

3. Although moral liberty rests exclusively upon the energy with which the individual achieves it within himself,—and in this sense the truly free man does not depend on external circumstances—, the conscience of today accepts the evidence that the exercise of liberty is conditioned by circumstances. This evidence inspires all social and humanitarian movements.

4. While agreement exists over the social principle implied by the individual's moral liberty, namely, that he is bound to help his fellow men and to create for them the conditions favorable to their fulfillment, there is disagreement on the subject of the role played in man's liberation by present economic systems. Adherents of the two great contrasting systems cast the same reproaches at each other. The one party considers economic freedom as one of the fundamental rights of the individual, and believes that it is in fact the very condition upon which the material and the moral health of a society depends. Therefore it denounces economic planning as a form of tyranny which must be fought against in the name of the sacred value of liberty. The other party asserts that the liberation of individuals can be guaranteed only by an economic structure devoid of the faults of individual profit-seeking. . . .

"FREEDOM AS NATURAL, ACQUIRED, AND CIRCUMSTANTIAL"

Mortimer J. Adler

I. Five Subjects of Controversy

We have used the words "circumstantial," "acquired," and "natural" to identify a freedom according to the way in which it is possessed by men. To complete the identification of freedoms that are distinct subjects of discussion, we have used the words "self-realization," "self-perfection," and "self-determination" to signify the mode of self in which a freedom consists.

In Book II we presented evidence for the identification of three main subjects of controversy: (i) a circumstantial freedom of self-realization, (ii) an acquired freedom of self-perfection, and (iii) a natural freedom of self-determination. In addition, we identified two other subjects which, while distinct from these three, are not co-ordinate with them, for each is a special variant of one of the principal subjects: (iv) political liberty, a special variant of circumstantial self-realization, and (v) collective freedom, a special variant of acquired self-perfection.

Each of these five subjects is discussed in the literature on freedom under a variety of conceptions which have enough in common to be grouped together. To enumerate the common traits of each is simply another way of stating the descriptive formula for identifying the freedom which is defined in different ways by the divergent conceptions in each group. Even though the authors who hold these divergent conceptions disagree about how that freedom should be defined, they agree implicitly on the descriptive formula by which we identify the subject of their disagreement. Such agreement about the identification of a subject of discussion—or disagreement—we have called a "minimal topical agreement."

What follows is a recapitulation of the minimal topical agreements for which we presented documentary evidence in Book II. For each of the five subjects that we have identified we shall state the brief descriptive formula which we have used to summarize our identification. We shall then list in alphabetical order the major authors who were shown in Book II to hold conceptions of the freedom named and who affirm it either as man's only human freedom or as, in some way, one of the freedoms man enjoys, or at least as a distinguishable aspect of human freedom. Finally, we shall comment briefly on the points in each topical agreement which constitute the understanding of freedom that is common to a given family of conceptions and which serve to distinguish it from the others.

CIRCUMSTANTIAL FREEDOM OF SELF-REALIZATION

Descriptive formula: a freedom which is possessed by any individual who, under favorable circumstances, is able to act as he wishes for his own good as he sees it.

Major authors: Aquinas, Ayer, Bentham, Burke, Dewey, Edwards, Freud, Hale, Hayek, N. Hartmann, Hobbes, Hobhouse, Hume, Kelsen, Knight, Laski, Locke, Macmurray, Malinowski, Mannheim, Maritain, J.S. Mill, Montesquieu, Nowell-Smith, Pareto, Priestley, B. Russell, Schlick, Yves Simon, Spencer, Adam Smith, Stevenson, Tawney, Voltaire.

Comment: The foregoing authors are in topical agreement on the following points about the freedom named:

(a)   that it is a freedom which the individual possesses *only* under favorable circumstances, i.e., circumstances which do not prevent him from acting as he wishes or do not coerce him into behavior contrary to his wishes;

(b)   that the circumstantial character of such freedom lies in the fact that the individual's ability to carry out his wishes, plans, or desires is a *circumstantial ability*, i.e., an ability wholly or partly dependent on propitious circumstances;

(c)   that "acting as one wishes" or "doing as one pleases" expresses the meaning of self-realization only when two conditions are fulfilled: first, *execution*, whereby the individual's wish is translated into action; and second, *individual fulfillment*, wherein the individual's own good, as he sees it, is achieved by the action performed.

ACQUIRED FREEDOM OF SELF-PERFECTION

Descriptive formula: a freedom which is possessed only by those men who, through acquired virtue or wisdom, are able to will or live as they ought in conformity to the moral law or an ideal befitting human nature.

Major authors: Ambrose, Anselm, Aquinas, Augustine, Marcus Aurelius, Barth, Bellarmine, Boethius, Bosanquet, Bradley, Calvin, Cicero, Dewey, Duns Scotus, Epictetus, Epicurus, Fouillée, Freud, Green, Hegal, Kant, Leibniz, Locke, Luther, Maimonides, Marcel, Maritain, Montesquieu, Philo, Plotinus, Rousseau, B. Russell, Santayana, Seneca, Yves Simon, Spinoza, Suarez, Tillich, Whitehead.

Comment: The foregoing authors are in topical agreement on the following points about the freedom named:

(a)   that it is a freedom which, even under circumstances most favorable to the execution of what a man wills, is possessed only by those men whose state of mind or character enables them to will as they ought;

(b)   that the acquired character of such freedom lies in the fact that the individual's ability to live in conformity to an ideal befitting human nature, or to obey the moral law willingly, is an *acquired ability*; i.e., an ability which represents a relatively stable change in the constitution, make-up, or inner workings of a human being;

(c)   that "willing or living as one ought" expresses the meaning of self-perfection only when three conditions are present: first, the *objectivity and universality of the moral standards or goals* which determine what ought to be willed; second, the *autonomy of the individual* insofar as the moral standards, goals, or laws to which he conforms become, through acquired virtue or wisdom, to some extent his own rather than wholly external impositions; and third, the *spontaneity of his voluntary compliance* with such moral standards, goals, or laws.

NATURAL FREEDOM OF SELF-DETERMINATION

Descriptive formula: a freedom which is possessed by all men, in virtue of a power inherent in human nature, whereby a man is able to change his own character creatively by deciding for himself what he shall do or shall become.

Major authors: Anselm, Aquinas, Aristotle, Augustine, Barth, Bellarmine, Bergson, Berkeley, Boethius, Burke, Calvin, Cicero, Descartes, Dewey, Duns Scotus, Epicurus, Fichte, Fouillée, Green, N. Hartmann, Hegel, William James, Kant, Knight, Leibniz, Locke, Lucretius, Luther, Maimonides, Marcel, Maritain, Montesquieu, Philo, Renouvier, Rousseau, Santayana, Sartre, Secrétan, Yves Simon, Adam Smith, Suarez, Tillich, Weiss, Whitehead.

Comment: The foregoing authors are in topical agreement on the following points about the freedom named:

(a)   that it is a freedom which all men possess because every man, simply in virtue of being a man, always has the power to decide for himself what he wishes to do or to become;

(b)   that the natural character of such freedom lies in the fact that the aforesaid power is a *natural ability*, i.e., an ability inherent in the native constitution or make-up of the members of the human species;

(c)   that "deciding what one wishes to do or to become" expresses the meaning of self-determination only when at least two of the three following conditions obtain: (i) the decision is *intrinsically unpredictable*, i.e., given perfect knowledge of all relevant causes, it cannot be foreseen with certitude; (ii) the decision is *not necessitated*, i.e., it is always one of a number of alternative possible decisions any one of which it was within the power of the self to cause, no matter what other antecedent or concurrent factors exercise a causal influence on the making of the decision; (iii) the decision flows from the *causal initiative* of the self, i.e., on the plane of natural causes, the self is the *uncaused cause* of the decision it makes.[1]

Before we attempt to summarize the topical agreements about the two remaining subjects—political liberty and collective freedom—it may be useful to recall certain contrasts which we have found helpful in distinguishing the three freedoms we have so far considered.

It is distinctive of authors who affirm a circumstantial freedom of self-realization that they advocate social reforms or changes in the environment as ways of increasing or decreasing the amount of freedom men enjoy or the number of men who enjoy it. In contrast, authors who affirm an acquired freedom of self-perfection look to the moral improvement of men, rather than to alterations in the institutions

---

[1] Most of the authors who affirm man's natural freedom of self-determination hold conceptions of it that involve all three of the conditions stated above. A few authors, notably Bergson, Dewey, and Weiss, hold conceptions that involve the first two conditions but not the third. (See Vol. I, pp. 492-94.) The conceptions to be found in Aquinas, Hegel, and Fouillée do not require the first two conditions to be present in all cases of self-determination; but for Aquinas they are normally present, and for Hegel and Fouillée they are present at imperfect stages of self-determination. (See Vol. I, pp. 531-39 and pp. 551-55.) Leibniz is the one author for whom self-determination involves only the third of the three conditions stated above. (See Vol I, pp. 539-45 and pp. 549-51.)

under which they live. For them, freedom is a development in the inner life of the individual.

Another point of contrast between these two groups of conceptions lies in the positions their exponents take on the relation of liberty to law. For those who affirm a circumstantial freedom of self-realization, it is not the individual's state of mind or character, but the amount of legal regulation or the compatibility of particular laws with what the individual wishes to do that affects the degree of his freedom. But for those who affirm an acquired freedom of self-perfection, freedom under law rests wholly on the harmony between the rightness of what the law requires and the rectitude of the individual's will, making his compliance with the law a voluntary act of obedience.

As contrasted with both of the foregoing, authors who affirm man's natural freedom of self-determination attribute it to power which is inherent in human nature and does not depend upon any alterable conditions whatsoever, neither upon the individual's external circumstances of life nor upon his moral state.

These contrasts can be stated in another way by reference to the typical questions that one would ask to discover whether a man exercised one or another of these freedoms in a particular act. In the case of self-realization, one would ask whether a man's behavior is uncoerced or unconstrained, whether it proceeds from his own wish or desire, and so on. In the case of self-perfection, one would ask whether an act is morally right and whether it is done through wisdom or virtuous inclination, and thus done willingly. But in the case of self-determination, one would ask whether the act is intrinsically unpredictable, whether it flows from the causal initiative of the agent, or whether the individual could have chosen to act otherwise, since he was under no necessity to make the choice he did.

We turn now to a summary of the topical agreements about political liberty and collective freedom, and to the contrasts which we have found helpful in distinguishing them from self-realization and self-perfection, of which they are, respectively, the variants.

POLITICAL LIBERTY

Descriptive formula: a freedom which is possessed only by citizens who, through the right of suffrage and the right of juridical appeal against the abuses of government, are able to participate in making the positive law under which they live and to alter the political institutions of their society.

Major authors: Aquinas, Aristotle, Hobhouse, Kant, Locke, Maritain, Montesquieu, Yves Simon.

Comment: The foregoing authors are in topical agreement on the following points about the freedom named:

   (a)   that it is a freedom which is conferred on men by constitutional government and which is possessed only by those who are citizens with suffrage, i.e., those who through their constitutionally granted political rights and privileges are full-fledged and active members of a self-governing community;

(b) that the political character of such freedom lies in the fact that the individual's ability to participate in making laws and shaping political institutions is a power conferred on him by the *political status* he enjoys, together with all the rights and privileges which appertain thereto;

(c) that "self-government" expresses the meaning of political liberty only when two conditions obtain: (i) the public or legislative will to which the individual is subject is *not a will wholly alien to his own*, but one to the formation of which he, as a citizen, has contributed through his suffrage; and (ii) the individual as a citizen has the opportunity and power to say what is for the common good *from the point of view of his own particular interests.*

That political liberty is a variant of circumstantial rather than of acquired freedom is evident from the fact that it is possessed only by individuals who are favored by certain circumstances, regardless of their moral condition. The citizen with suffrage has political liberty whether or not, in exercising it, his will is directed by acquired virtue or wisdom.

That political liberty, while circumstantial, is not identical with the freedom of self-realization is equally clear from the fact that those who lack political liberty (i.e., all disfranchised persons) may have in varying degrees the circumstantial ability to act as they wish, while, on the other hand, those who have political liberty (i.e., enfranchised citizens) may be subject to coercions or constraints which eliminate their freedom of self-realization, but not their political liberty.

As we have seen, authors who affirm a circumstantial freedom of self-realization see in the amount of legal regulation to which an individual is subject or in the compatibility of particular laws with his individual wishes two conditions that affect the degree of his freedom. In sharp contrast, neither of these conditions is regarded as having any effect on political liberty by those who affirm it as a distinct freedom. Political liberty, they maintain, does not consist in obeying oneself alone or in not being subject to the will of others. It suffices for political liberty that the public will, by which the law is made, represents each citizen's own will together with that of every other citizen who has exercised his suffrage. So long as the law is made with his consent through constitutional processes in which he participates, the citizen remains politically free whether he is in the minority or the majority.

COLLECTIVE FREEDOM

Descriptive formula: a freedom which will be possessed by humanity or the human race in the future when, through the social use of the knowledge of both natural and social necessities, men achieve the ideal mode of association that is the goal of mankind's development and are able to direct their communal life in accordance with such necessities.

Major authors: Bakunin, Comte, Engels, Marx.

Comment: The foregoing authors are in topical agreement on the following points about the freedom named:

(a)   that it is a freedom which will be acquired by mankind only when human life and social organization are directed by man's knowledge of natural and social necessities, and do not involve man-made rules or coercive force of any sort;

(b)   that the collective character of such freedom lies in the fact that it accrues to the individual only when it is *acquired by mankind*, and will be enjoyed by him as a member of the human race only when men have *collectively achieved* an ideal form of association;

(c)   that "being subject to scientifically established necessities and to these alone" expresses the meaning of collective freedom only if it is understood that mankind has reached that point in its development where, through putting to social use its knowledge of the inviolable laws of nature and of society, it directs all human affairs solely by reference to these acknowledged necessities.

Like the freedom of self-perfection, collective freedom is acquired, but, unlike the freedom of self-perfection, it is acquired by the human race in the course of its historical development, not by the human person in the course of his individual life. In addition to being acquired, collective freedom is akin to the freedom of self-perfection in that it involves compliance with law or necessity. But it is precisely at this point that they also differ.

According to the self-perfection authors, the moral laws or obligations to which a man should be able to conform in order to be free are *violable*. Since he can either obey or disobey them, his freedom is thought to lie in his being able to comply with them *willingly rather than against his will*; and such voluntary compliance is thought to stem from his acquired virtue or wisdom. In contrast, according to theories of collective freedom, the scientifically discovered laws of nature and society are *inviolable*. They cannot be disobeyed, but they *can be put to beneficial social use or not*. It is when men, through achieving an ideal form of association, come to govern themselves solely by reference to these acknowledged necessities that they become collectively free. . . .

II. A Unified Set of Controversies

. . .The diverse theories we have classified cannot be regarded as offering conflicting views about the kinds of freedom unless the five subjects, each of which may be defended or challenged as a *kind*, have something more in common than the name "freedom.". . .

"What is that generic meaning or general understanding which is common to all the authors who write about a subject they call 'freedom' and whose theories involve one or more of the subjects we have been able to identify?"

Self and *other*, we found, are the basic common terms in the general understanding of freedom. These terms are present in the understanding of self-realization, self-perfection, and self-determination, as well as in the understanding of political liberty as a variant of self-realization and collective freedom as a variant of self-perfection. But in each of these, *self* and *other* are differently specified: each involves a different mode of *self* and a different *other* as the opponent of its freedom. In each the *ability to act in a certain way*, which is present in all conceptions of freedom, is differently specified as the power whereby *the self is exempt from the power of another*.

In every conception of freedom, we pointed out, the free act is that which proceeds from the self, in contrast to such behavior on a man's part which is somehow the product of another. It is *his own act* and the result it achieves is a *property of his self*—the realization of his self, the perfection of his self, the determination or creation of his self. A man lacks freedom to whatever extent he is passively affected, or subject to an alien power, the power of another rather than his own. In every conception of freedom, the self is the principle of freedom through possessing the power to be actively the source of whatever kind of activity is thought to manifest human freedom.

Let us recall the descriptive formulas by which we identified the three freedoms that are the main subjects of controversy. What is common to all conceptions of the freedom of self-realization can be expressed as follows: *a man is free who is able, under favorable circumstances, to act as he wishes for his own individual good as he sees it*. What is common to all conceptions of the freedom of self-perfection can be expressed as follows: *a man is free who is able, through acquired virtue or wisdom, to will or live as he ought in conformity to the moral law or an ideal befitting human nature*. What is common to all conceptions of the freedom of self-determination can be expressed as follows: *a man is free who is able, by a power inherent in human nature, to change his own character creatively by deciding for himself what he shall do or become*.

A descriptive formula for identifying freedom in general would obviously have to be indeterminate enough to allow for all the specifications introduced by the foregoing identifications of self-realization, self-perfection, and self-determination; and it would also have to be determinate enough to express what is common to all conceptions of human freedom. The required formulation can be stated as follows: *a man is free who has in himself the ability or power to make what he does his own action and what he achieves his own property*.

"FREEDOM AS THE ABILITY TO CHOOSE
AND CARRY OUT PURPOSES"

Herbert J. Muller

To the ordinary man, freedom means the feeling of being able to do as he likes, act at his own sweet pleasure. We all know and like this feeling; it always enters consciousness as "Free, hurrah!" But we also know that the good feeling never lasts. Presently, restless or discontent, we realize the truism that man never is free to do just what he pleases or only what he pleases. Then we may ask what freedom "really" means—only to get really confused. As a hurrah word, it has meant different things to different men, the more because of its liaisons with other good feelings. Mortimer Adler and a team of scholars spent several years analyzing the meanings it has had for Western thinkers, and the ordinary man might be dismayed by the report of their findings in *The Idea of Freedom*, a digest that takes up more than six hundred pages. Here it appears that philosophers have usually meant by freedom the very opposite of our sweet pleasure. "True freedom," most of them have agreed, consists in doing one's duty, being virtuous and wise, being one's "true self." They thereby confirm the popular idea that freedom is a good thing, but they do not clear up the confusion. They have never agreed on what duty and wisdom consist in or on how to recognize one's true self, tell whether it is the inner voice that cries no or the voice that cries yes. They too are talking about different things.

Common sense may now rebel, declaring that these are only verbal complications—we all know what freedom really is even if we can't put it into words. But then let us ask a natural, sensible question. America has been known all over the world as a free country, though recently some people have had doubts; and are Americans today more free or less free than they were a generation ago, before the New Deal? Or than their ancestors were a century ago on the frontier, in their rude cabins? Or than the ancient Athenians were, in a society without time clocks and stop signals? The most sensible answer might seem to be another question: Who can say?

Now, I do not assume that the confusion can be dispelled by logical or semantic rigor. We cannot give an utterly precise meaning to so broad and rich a concept as freedom, at least without arbitrarily excluding a great deal of its vital historical meaning. Neither can we hope to sterilize it, stop it from touching off hurrahs. Yet we must be able to give meaningful answers to such pertinent questions about the state of freedom if we are going to talk about the subject at all. Short of exactitude, we can aim at a relatively neutral, objective, operational definition: one that refers to roughly observable conditions, permits roughly verifiable statements about them, and so makes theoretically possible a rough agreement. In giving us pause, the questions also give us cues. They make plain that *freedom* means concretely *freedoms*, of various kinds. We cannot make out any such thing as "true" freedom in the abstract, but we can distinguish some common garden varieties, can specify in what respects some men are more or less free than others.

As the only true meanings of a word, strictly speaking, are dictionary meanings, we might at least begin by accepting common usage, based on common experience. It is remarkable, indeed, how much confusion we can avoid by clinging to the simple idea that freedom means first of all being *free* in the ordinary sense—unconfined, unfettered, unconstrained—and not necessarily dutiful, virtuous, or wise. We can never positively demonstrate that Americans are better or worse men than they used to be, but we can point to positive ways in which they are more or less confined and constrained. Then we might hope to discuss more profitably the further question of the uses and abuses of freedom, its relation to other goods.

In formal terms, *freedom* in this work will mean "the condition of being able to choose and to carry out purposes." This definition has three immediate implications: (1) the primary dictionary meaning—the absence of external constraints; (2) practicable purposes, or an actual ability with available means; and (3) a power of conscious choice, between significant, known alternatives. It accordingly involves the common ideas of freedom *from*, freedom *to*, and freedom *of*, but it leaves open the question of freedom *for* what. In simple words, a man is free in so far as he can do something or choose not to do it, can make up his own mind, can say yes or no to any given question or command, can decide for himself the matter of duty or *for* what. He is not free in so far as he is prohibited from following his inclinations or is obliged to do something against his own volition, whether by direct coercion or by fear of consequences, even though it might be better for him than his heart's desire. Granted that such statements may ring bells, they are none the less meaningful and refer objectively to a recognizable condition—a condition that feels good but may not produce further good, may lead to folly, sin, or unhappiness.

All these statements must of course be qualified. Man is always constrained by physical necessities, subject to natural law, and as he lives with his fellows he must always submit to further social constraints. Freedom is restricted only when the constraints appear to be arbitrary—unaccustomed, unnecessary, unreasonable, or unjust. The primary historical source of such restriction has been political power, the subjection of most men to the will of one or a few. Since these subjects have generally accepted as natural what seems to us arbitrary rule, we cannot readily set up a universal criterion for deciding what constraints are unreasonable or unjust. But we can begin by determining the actual constraints, by whom and on whom. We can state it as a fact that freedom is broadened in so far as arbitrary power is limited, rule is constrained by the recognition of rights, and rights are extended to all members of a society, guaranteed by law.[1] In this respect Americans today are certainly freer than the overwhelming majority of men ever were in the past, or than Germans were under Hitler. In recent years they have as certainly been subjected to unaccustomed constraints by security regulations and peacetime draft; though most of them have accepted these as reasonable.

The absence of external constraints has little meaning, however, until it is coupled with the positive idea of "actual ability with available means." A child dropped in the middle of a desert is freed from constraints—he no longer has to go to school, eat spinach, do chores; but he is free only to starve. As nominal was the freedom of

---

[1] In the form of civil liberties, such rights have led some thinkers to make fine distinctions between *freedom* and *liberty*, but in common usage the terms are virtually interchangeable. The French have got along with only one word, *liberté*. While making no real distinction, I have preferred *freedom* because it has an adjective to go with it, as *liberty* does not. *Liberal* has a specialized meaning, and may further confuse the issues because to many Americans it is a bad word.

many children who once had only a choice of factories in which to work twelve hours a day, or of the many poor who were "just as free as the rich to sleep under bridges." Effective freedom requires opportunities as well as rights. From this point of view, the major historical barrier has been not merely political oppression but poverty and ignorance. All other things equal, a man with money is freer than a man without it, an educated man freer than an illiterate. In this respect too Americans have plainly been much freer in their land of opportunity than were the masses of the past, including ordinary Athenians, and today are on the whole better off than their ancestors. They have been made so by free public education, more recently by social security and unemployment relief—by measures that have created new problems, involving threats to freedom, but that have nevertheless given most Americans more opportunity, more power to carry out their purposes.

Most important—and most troublesome—is the intimately related power of conscious choice, through intelligence and knowledge. Other animals are able to carry out their instinctive purposes, and may seem so unhampered that men sometimes envy them, saying that they would like to be free as birds. Actually, of course, birds are not simply free to fly and sing—they *have* to fly and sing. Man also has to go through many motions in order to go on living, but he is the only animal that can deliberately choose and change his purposes, even to deciding not to go on living. Over the last five thousand years of his history he has enormously widened the range of his choices. In this view, freedom has been limited by stupidity and ignorance but more specifically by social constraints, the power of custom and convention. These induce *internal* constraints, which may appear as dutifulness or reverence, but may owe chiefly to inertia, superstition, insecurity, anxiety, or dread. We must therefore qualify the apparent freedom of primitive societies, which civilized men are also wont to envy in their harried or sentimental moods. The most easygoing primitives (such as the Stone Age Eskimos described by Stefansson) are free to consider relatively few possibilities and do relatively few things, but the great majority are hidebound by tribal custom. All have a severely limited range of self-determination, or power to decide for themselves what kind of selves they would like to be or become.

An immediate difficulty here is that internal constraints, as states of mind, are more intangible, elusive, and ambiguous than external constraints or positive abilities. To minimize this difficulty, some social analysts prefer Bertrand Russell's negative definition of freedom as "the absence of obstacles to the realization of desires," ruling out consideration of the nature of these desires. I am assuming that we may waive for the time being the question of the propriety or wisdom of the desires, but that we should take into consideration the range and openness of choice, the awareness of different possibilities, the desire to make choices—the *presence* of conditions helping to refine, extend, and enrich consciousness—as essential to the distinctive freedom that man is capable of, even though this gets him (and the analyst) into more trouble. Considering only "the absence of obstacles," no creature is freer than a well-fed, castrated household cat, and the freest man is the perfectly conditioned inhabitant of Huxley's Brave New World. A civilized man is conscious of richer possibilities than a South Seas islander, and as he seeks them is bound to face more obstacles; yet he alone is able to make his desires and his choices really his own. If he is a Shakespeare or a Beethoven, he may become aware of still more obstacles, lay himself wide open to frustration, but in his creativity he may know a godlike freedom. And for ordinary mortals this matter of the power and the range of conscious choice becomes more important as we approach our own society. An immense increase in power over the natural environment has created a multiplicity of choices, a wealth of means and opportunities for the realization of desire—and as many more potential obstacles, opportunities for waste, blunder, and frustration.

On this count ordinary Americans are again much freer than the masses of men throughout history, and potentially freer than ordinary Athenians in ancient Greece, than their ancestors on the rude frontier, or than their fathers in the strait-laced small town. But here we may not be at all sure. One reason is the growing conformism, the popular ideal of being "well adjusted" at any cost, with little idea of the possible costs. The conformism is due immediately to the constraints upon those seeking economic and social success, but it is due as well to consensus, a willing acceptance of such constraints. In their prosperity, many Americans seem content to think and to want what others tell them to. They display little desire to realize their own purposes, make individual choices beyond choices in the latest models. In the absence of serious obstacles to the realization of paltry desires, they may feel free because they feel complacent.

They bring up another complication—the basic distinction between subjective and objective freedom, or between *feeling* free and *being* free. It is not an absolute distinction. One who does not feel free is liable to impotence, however great his latent abilities and wide his actual opportunities; one who does feel free may exercise his powers more fully and effectively, however limited they be. Feelings are no less real for being subjective or scientifically disreputable, and they cannot be simply disregarded, since they influence the capacity to choose and carry out purposes. They are among the chief threats to freedom in the modern world, in which a vast collective power and mass have dwarfed the individual, and ever bigger organizations make men feel ever smaller.

Nevertheless I assume that we should look first to objective freedom—to the roughly observable conditions and powers rather than the infinite subjective experiences that flow from them. We can hope to answer with some assurance the question how free peoples actually were in the past. We might find it very hard to say how free they felt. And in any case feelings are not a trustworthy index to the state of freedom as I define it. Primitives may consider themselves free, or more precisely not feel unfree, because they are unconscious of the constraints we perceive. Although we cannot be sure of the state of mind of the illiterate peasant masses throughout history, their usual passivity suggests that they generally took their subjection for granted and did not feel deprived of the freedoms we take for granted; folklore gives little indication of a yearning for such freedom. When feelings are written into the record by civilized peoples, they as often lend themselves to an ironic as to a compassionate contemplation. Scribes proclaim the deathless glory and felicity of rotten empires on the verge of collapse. Priests give thanks to false gods for blessings won by human effort. Today the many Americans who get red in the face over the "creeping socialism that is destroying our freedom" remain as free as ever to voice their complaints, to vote the rascals out, to go about their increasingly profitable business, and to enjoy the highest standard of living in all history; while in pursuing success they may look to outsiders like the veriest slaves to business, and in enjoying it may respond like puppets to advertisers and publicity men.

Such ambiguities accentuate the complexity of the social condition, the tangle of variable, immeasurable factors that make it impossible to specify with precision the kinds and degrees of freedom. The awareness of such ambiguities also indicates the possibility of at least a partial detachment, a reasonably objective view of the conditions that make men feel as they do, and make it necessary to discount and supplement their feelings. And immediately it spots a primary source of confusion—the inveterate tendency to identify freedom with other goods. One seeking to adhere to a neutral, operational definition is obliged to spell out what he does *not* mean by freedom.

Dreaming of his beloved, the imprisoned poet sang:

> Stone walls do not a prison make,
> Nor iron bars a cage.

We may rejoice that he felt so; but then we must add prosaically that iron bars do make a cage, that only a poet who had known freedom could write this, and that he will be freer when he is outside the stone walls. As an ardent lover, he might then run afoul of John Milton:

> License they mean when they cry liberty,
> For who loves that must first be good and wise.

Prizing liberty, we may relish this lofty sentiment too; but again we must first acknowledge that liberty can be loved by sinners and fools, can run into "license." We must face up to such historical actualities as republican Florence in the Renaissance—the freest, most brilliantly creative city of the age, and one of the most licentious. To identify freedom and virtue promotes the understanding of neither.

As high-minded, and often as arbitrary, is the concept of "rational freedom" that philosophers have been fond of. "A free man," wrote Spinoza out of a tradition dating back to Plato, "is one who lives according to the dictate of reason alone." Human freedom does require a measure of rationality; a man governed by impulse or passion is obviously limited in his ability to choose his purposes; and it may be argued that no kind of freedom is more important than freedom from bondage to unconscious or irrational desire. Yet Spinoza was strictly defining a *wise* man—or more strictly a monster. Free men and free countries have never been governed by the dictate of reason alone. Philosophers have never agreed on the content of this dictate. Spinoza himself might be called a slave to his passion for utter rationality.

The endless disagreement among the wise men may not clinch the right to be wrong, but at least it gives good reason to question any prescribed form of rationality. "If only rational freedom be allowed," Edgar Sheffield Brightman observed, "freedom ceases to be free and rationality ceases to be rational."

Another practical objection to such definitions is that they have commonly encouraged an indifference to seemingly unreasonable external constraints, in particular the condition of the masses of men. The last word in "rational freedom" is the Stoic ideal of freedom from all desire. "If once you swerve from this course," Epictetus warned, "you are a slave, you are a subject, you have become liable to hindrance and to compulsion." So indeed you have—freedom is always a risky business. The way of the Stoics could afford more tranquillity, to men in any condition of life; it was a "freedom" that even slaves could enjoy. But this is precisely the objection to it. A slave is not actually free, no matter how indifferent he may be to his chains. In spite of their ideal of universal brotherhood, most Stoics were content to accept the institution of slavery, though most slaves were not. Prizing above all the power to accept any lot, to "choose" whatever happened, the Stoics could ignore all constraints except desire itself, or their own desire to be imperturbable at any cost.

For similar reasons one may question the more common and atractive idea of "spiritual freedom," or specifically the Christian teaching, "In God's service is perfect freedom." This service can promote freedom in the ordinary sense of the word—*if* it is a free, conscious choice, and service of a God who encourages purposeful activity on earth, including free inquiry into his own purposes. Historically, however, the service of God has not always made for such freedom. Most men have served him out of unthinking habit, when not compulsion or fear. Those who seemed to be most intimately acquainted with his will gave different accounts of it, but typically they permitted men little latitude in choice. Martin Luther, who preached so eloquently the "spiritual liberty" of Christians, was as fiercely hostile to religious, intellectual, or political freedom. Only in recent centuries has God blessed the idea of political freedom, and more doubtfully of intellectual freedom. At its best, "spiritual freedom" is essentially subjective, the feeling of emancipation that may come through religious experience. A more precise word for it is peace of mind. If it brings freedom from anxiety, its essence is still service: obedience, submission, renunciation—"Not mine but Thy will be done." Such holiness may not be wholesome, but may come down to a surrender of human powers and purposes for the sake of freedom *from* freedom.

In general, the proponents of both rational and spiritual freedom have been inclined to agree that it means only the freedom to do what is right and good, by their own standards. What I mean by it is a state in which the individual may decide for himself what is right and good. It includes freedom of conscience, a kind of freedom that appeared late and intermittently in history, and that Lord Acton (himself a devout Catholic) made the very essence of freedom: "the assurance that every man shall be protected in doing what he believes to be his duty against the influence of authority and majorities, custom and opinion." And I have been stressing these objections to "true freedom" because those who know what it is naturally assume that all other good men will think and feel as they do, want the same good that they call freedom. At best, they confuse the actual social problem, which arises from the different kinds of freedom desired by different men, and the need of accommodating and adjusting these different desires. At worst, they tend to impose their standards of the right and good, and so to deny men actual freedom in thought and deed.

Western history is an endless illustration of such confusion and coercion. In Western thought a celebrated example is Hegel's pronouncement that "positive freedom" is achieved by an "utter obedience or complete abnegation of one's own opinion and reasonings," which meant specifically an utter obedience to the Prussian state. Only in being what the state wills us to be, added his English disciple Bosanquet, can we find freedom; and he concluded, "Thus it is that we can speak, without a contradiction, of being forced to be free." It is gratifying to a dialectician to be able to speak so, but it therefore becomes necessary to insist that this *is* a contradiction, compulsion is *not* freedom. For such philosophical double talk comes down to a hoary linguistic trick that today is a means of systematic, high-powered fraud—the trick of exploiting the emotional value of a word in order to sell some other idea. Insensibly it leads to the "Newspeak" of George Orwell: "Freedom is slavery."

All this is by no means to deny the intimate connection of freedom with questions of what is right and good. The power to choose one's own purposes leads naturally to the ideal of sovereignty over oneself, mastery of mean, irrational, self-defeating desires. When men claim the *right* to freedom, moreover, they must logically assume the moral obligation to respect the rights of others and the claims of the whole community, else there can be no effective freedom. They become more deeply indebted to the many other men, living and dead, who have upheld the ideal of freedom as an ethical principle. The very growth of freedom forces the questions of what is right and good, which ordinarily do not trouble primitive societies or most men in closed societies. Hence no student of freedom can ignore these questions, no matter how conscientiously he tries to refrain from moral judgment. He is obliged to consider its relation to such social needs as order and security, to such social ideals as justice and equality, to cultural or spiritual values in general. In the modern democracies, where common men have been freer to do as they please, he has to consider the questions raised by what they please to do; for the popular ends of freedom react upon the institutional means, and may confuse or obstruct the processes of democracy. I am merely assuming, once more, that one may hope to get a clearer view of such problems if one keeps one's eye on objective freedom, in the relatively neutral sense of my definition, and distinguishes the question of its nature from the question of its proper uses or ends.

Lest this definition seem arbitrary, I conclude with a restatement in terms of the categories made out by Mortimer Adler and his associates, from their exhaustive analysis of twenty-five centuries of thought on the idea of freedom. They found that all conceptions of it came down to variants on three basic definitions: *circumstantial* freedom of self-realization, or the ability of a man under favorable circumstances to act as he wishes for his own good as he sees it; *acquired* freedom of self-perfection, or the ability of a man through acquired virtue or wisdom to will or live as he ought in conformity to the moral law or an ideal befitting human nature; and *natural* freedom of self-determination, or the ability of a man to change his own character creatively by deciding for himself what he shall do or become. (The wording is Adler's.) Common to all the definitions are the idea of a positive ability and the idea of the "self" contrasted with some other, exempt from the power of others. Adler summarizes the underlying agreement as follows: "A man is free who has in himself the ability or power whereby he can make what he does his own action and what he achieves his own property."

Now I have emphasized this ability or power as distinctive of human freedom, beyond the ability of animals to carry out their instinctive purposes. My definition accordingly includes the idea of "natural" freedom, latent in all men by virtue of their powers of mind; but unlike many thinkers who have regarded such freedom as primary, I hold that the realization of the power of self-determination depends on circumstance or culture. My definition also includes the concept of "acquired" freedom, though in a broader sense and with important qualifications; for in most definitions this is the "rational" or "spiritual" freedom popular with philosophers. I believe it essential to conceive freedom as something that has been achieved and that can be increased, diminished, or lost. For similar reasons I object to definitions that limit it to a particular mode of self-perfection, and that slight when they do not exclude the common garden varieties of freedom. As Adler makes clear, most proponents of "acquired" freedom have held that it could be acquired only by a superior few. As he perhaps does not make clear enough, most have been indifferent to social and political conditions that made it difficult or impossible for ordinary men to become masters of their faculties, to make their actions their own, or to achieve any perfection beyond complete obedience.

For a historian, the most important freedom is "circumstantial." It forces attention to the whole culture by which the self is molded, and thought about freedom is conditioned. One variant of it is political freedom, a major theme in Western history. Allied with this was the characteristic Western effort at social reform, the deliberate alteration of circumstance. But apart from such efforts I assume that for a society at large "circumstantial" freedom is essential to the other freedoms. However "natural," the freedom of self-determination has been rare or negligible in primitive societies, and among the illiterate masses of most civilized societies. If the "acquired" freedom of self-perfection may make a man superior to circumstance, its attainment initially requires the favorable circumstance of a high level of culture. The philosophers and saints who have preached such freedom had to preach it because it was beyond the ken of most men. The circumstances of civilization made possible their lofty ideal, and in most societies also made it attractive because there was little if any hope of more "circumstantial" freedom.[2]

---

[2] Adler has confined his study to Western thought, for reasons possibly parochial but still legitimate. In Eastern thought, from ancient Egypt to India and China, there has been little specific concern with freedom or effort to define it. Many of the wise and holy men never used the word. But Adler could find a great deal of Eastern thought to illustrate the concept of acquired freedom of self-perfection.

And so I think it may be well to stress at the end that the noble ideal of freedom involves the possibly ignoble idea of doing as one pleases, the irresponsible idea of doing things just for fun. As the old ex-slave said, he liked freedom because "there's a kind of looseness about it." Most of us cherish this looseness. As we acknowledge our obligations and our immense indebtedness to our fellows, recognize that "no man is an island," we still want an island of privacy, where we can sprawl and indulge our own sweet pleasure. If we are depressed by the growing conformism, we might cherish as well the stubbornness, even the cussedness of the ordinary man in resisting his superiors who are so sure that they know better than he what is good for him. "It is man's inherent willfulness that I would preserve," Learned Hand declared, "and in which I wish to set the stronghold of that Liberty I prize; that stone which social reformers have always rejected I would make the head of the corner." This willfulness can be very dangerous, needless to add. Still, it is in fact of the essence of human freedom. If it is ever extinguished in man, he may at last become a contented, well-behaved animal; but he will no longer be a free one.

"TWO CONCEPTS OF LIBERTY"

Isaiah Berlin

To coerce a man is to deprive him of freedom—freedom from what? Almost every moralist in human history has praised freedom. Like happiness and goodness, like nature and reality, the meaning of this term is so porous that there is little interpretation that it seems able to resist. I do not propose to discuss either the history or the more than two hundred senses of this protean word recorded by historians of ideas. I propose to examine no more than two of these senses—but those central ones, with a great deal of human history behind them, and, I dare say, still to come. The first of these political senses of freedom or liberty (I shall use both words to mean the same), which (following much precedent) I shall call the 'negative' sense, is involved in the answer to the question 'What is the area within which the subject—a person or group of persons—is or should be left to do or be what he is able to do or be, without interference by other persons?' The second, which I shall call the positive sense, is involved in the answer to the question 'What, or who, is the source of control or interference that can determine someone to do, or be, this rather than that?' The two questions are clearly different, even though the answers to them may overlap.

The Notion of 'Negative' Freedom

I am normally said to be free to the degree to which no man or body of men interferes with my activity. Political liberty in this sense is simply the area within which a man can act unobstructed by others. If I am prevented by others from doing what I could otherwise do, I am to that degree unfree; and if this area is contracted by other men beyond a certain minimum, I can be described as being coerced, or, it may be, enslaved. Coercion is not, however, a term that covers every form of inability. If I say that I am unable to jump more than ten feet in the air, or cannot read because I am blind, or cannot understand the darker pages of Hegel, it would be eccentric to say that I am to that degree enslaved or coerced. Coercion implies the deliberate interference of other human beings within the area in which I could otherwise act. You lack political liberty or freedom only if you are prevented from attaining a goal by human beings.[1] Mere incapacity to attain a goal is not lack of political freedom.[2] This is brought out by the use of such modern expressions as 'economic freedom' and its counterpart, 'economic slavery'. It is argued, very plausibly, that if a man is too poor to afford something on which there is no legal ban—a loaf of bread, a journey round the world, recourse to the law courts—he is as little free to have it as he would be if it were forbidden him by law. If my poverty were a kind of disease, which prevented me from buying bread, or paying for the journey round the world or getting my case heard, as lameness prevents me from running, this inability would not naturally be described as a lack of freedom, least of all political freedom. It is only because I believe that my inability to get a given thing is due to the fact that other human beings have made arrangements whereby I am, whereas others are not, prevented from having enough money with which to pay for it, that I think myself a victim of coercion or slavery. In other words, this use of the term depends on a particular social and economic theory about the causes of my poverty or weakness. If my lack of material means is due to my lack of mental or physical capacity, then I begin to speak of being deprived of freedom (and not simply about poverty) only if I accept the theory.[3] If, in addition, I believe that I am being kept in want by a specific arrangement which I consider unjust or unfair, I speak of economic slavery or oppression. 'The nature of things does not madden us, only ill will does', said Rousseau. The criterion of oppression is the part that I believe to be played by other human beings, directly or indirectly, with or without the intention of doing so in frustrating my wishes. By being free in this sense I mean not being interfered with by others. The wider the area of non-interference the wider my freedom.

This is what the classical English political philosophers meant when they used this word.[4] They disagreed about how wide the area could or should be. They supposed

---

[1] I do not, of course, mean to imply the truth of the converse.

[2] Helvétius made this point very clearly: 'The free man is the man who is not in irons, nor imprisoned in a gaol, nor terrorized like a slave by the fear of punishment . . . it is not lack of freedom not to fly like an eagle or swim like a whale.'

[3] The Marxist conception of social laws is, of course, the best-known version of this theory, but it forms a large element in some Christian and utilitarian, and all socialist, doctrines.

[4] 'A free man', said Hobbes, 'is he that . . . is not hindered to do what he hath the will to do.' Law is always a 'fetter', even if it protects you from being bound in chains that are heavier than those of the law, say, some more repressive law or custom, or arbitrary despotism or chaos. Bentham says much the same.

that it could not, as things were, be unlimited, because if it were, it would entail a
state in which all men could boundlessly interfere with all other men; and this kind
of 'natural' freedom would lead to social chaos in which men's minimum needs
would not be satisfied; or else the liberties of the weak would be suppressed by the
strong. Because they perceived that human purposes and activities do not automatically harmonize with one another, and because (whatever their official doctrines)
they put high value on other goals, such as justice, or happiness, or culture, or
security, or varying degrees of equality, they were prepared to curtail freedom in
the interests of other values and, indeed, of freedom itself. For, without this, it was
impossible to create the kind of association that they thought desirable. Consequently, it is assumed by these thinkers that the area of men's free action must be
limited by law. But equally it is assumed, especially by such libertarians as Locke
and Mill in England, and Constant and Tocqueville in France, that there ought to
exist a certain minimum area of personal freedom which must on no account be
violated; for if it is overstepped, the individual will find himself in an area too
narrow for even that minimum development of his natural faculties which alone
makes it possible to pursue, and even to conceive, the various ends which men hold
good or right or sacred. It follows that a frontier must be drawn between the area
of private life and that of public authority. Where it is to be drawn is a matter of
argument, indeed of haggling. Men are largely interdependent, and no man's activity
is so completely private as never to obstruct the lives of others in any way.
'Freedom for the pike is death for the minnows'; the liberty of some must depend
on the restraint of others. 'Freedom for an Oxford don', others have been known to
add, 'is a very different thing from freedom for an Egyptian peasant.'

This proposition derives its force from something that is both true and important,
but the phrase itself remains a piece of political claptrap. It is true that to offer
political rights, or safeguards against intervention by the state, to men who are
half-naked, illiterate, underfed, and diseased is to mock their condition; they need
medical help or education before they can understand, or make use of, an increase
in their freedom. What is freedom to those who cannot make use of it? Without
adequate conditions for the use of freedom, what is the value of freedom? First
things come first: there are situations, as a nineteenth-century Russian radical writer
declared, in which boots are superior to the works of Shakespeare; individual
freedom is not everyone's primary need. For freedom is not the mere absence of
frustration of whatever kind; this would inflate the meaning of the word until it
meant too much or too little. The Egyptian peasant needs clothes or medicine
before, and more than, personal liberty, but the minimum freedom that he needs
today, and the greater degree of freedom that he may need tomorrow, is not some
species of freedom peculiar to him, but identical with that of professors, artists, and
millionaires.

What troubles the consciences of Western liberals is not, I think, the belief that
the freedom that men seek differs according to their social or economic conditions,
but that the minority who possess it have gained it by exploiting, or, at least,
averting their gaze from, the vast majority who do not. They believe, with good
reason, that if individual liberty is an ultimate end for human beings, none should

be deprived of it by others; least of all that 'some should enjoy it at the expense of others. Equality of liberty; not to treat others as I should not wish them to treat me; repayment of my debt to those who alone have made possible my liberty or prosperity or enlightenment; justice, in its simplest and most universal sense—these are the foundations of liberal morality. Liberty is not the only goal of men. I can, like the Russian critic Belinsky, say that if others are to be deprived of it—if my brothers are to remain in poverty, squalor, and chains—then I do not want it for myself, I reject it with both hands and infinitely prefer to share their fate. But nothing is gained by a confusion of terms. To avoid glaring inequality or widespread misery I am ready to sacrifice some, or all, of my freedom: I may do so willingly and freely: but it is freedom that I am giving up for the sake of justice or equality or the love of my fellow men. I should be guilt-stricken, and rightly so, if I were not, in some circumstances, ready to make this sacrifice. But a sacrifice is not an increase in what is being sacrificed, namely freedom, however great the moral need or the compensation for it. Everything is what it is: liberty is liberty, not equality or fairness or justice or culture, or human happiness or a quiet conscience. If the liberty of myself or my class or nation depends on the misery of a number of other human beings, the system which promotes this is unjust and immoral. But if I curtail or lose my freedom, in order to lessen the shame of such inequality, and do not thereby materially increase the individual liberty of others, an absolute loss of liberty occurs. This may be compensated for by a gain in justice or in happiness or in peace, but the loss remains, and it is a confusion of values to say that although my 'liberal', individual freedom may go by the board, some other kind of free-dom—'social' or 'economic'—is increased. Yet it remains true that the freedom of some must at times be curtailed to secure the freedom of others. Upon what principle should this be done? If freedom is a sacred, untouchable value, there can be no such principle. One or other of these conflicting rules or principles must, at any rate in practice, yield: not always for reasons which can be clearly stated, let alone generalized into rules or universal maxims.

Still, a practical compromise has to be found.

Philosophers with an optimistic view of human nature and a belief in the possibility of harmonizing human interests, such as Locke or Adam Smith and, in some moods, Mill, believed that social harmony and progress were compatible with reserving a large area for private life over which neither the state nor any other authority must be allowed to trespass. Hobbes, and those who agreed with him, especially conservative or reactionary thinkers, argued that if men were to be prevented from destroying one another and making social life a jungle or a wilderness, greater safeguards must be instituted to keep them in their places; he wished correspondingly to increase the area of centralized control and decrease that of the individual. But both sides agreed that some portion of human existence must remain independent of the sphere of social control. To invade that preserve, however small, would be despotism. The most eloquent of all defenders of freedom and privacy, Benjamin Constant, who had not forgotten the Jacobin dictatorship, declared that at the very least the liberty of religion, opinion, expression, property, must be guaranteed against arbitrary invasion. Jefferson, Burke, Paine, Mill, compiled different catalogues of individual liberties, but the argument for keeping authority at bay is always substantially the same. We must preserve a minimum area of personal freedom if we are not to 'degrade or deny our nature'. We cannot remain absolutely free, and must give up some of our liberty to preserve the rest. But total self-surrender is self-defeating. What then must the minimum be? That which a man cannot give up without offending against the essence of his human nature. What is this essence? What are the standards which it entails? This has been, and perhaps always will be, a matter of infinite debate. But whatever the principle in terms of which the area of non-interference is to be drawn, whether it is that of natural law or natural rights, or of utility or the pronouncements of a categorical imperative, or the sanctity of the social contract, or any other concept with which men have sought to clarify and justify their convictions, liberty in this sense means liberty *from*; absence of interference beyond the shifting, but always recognizable, frontier. 'The only freedom which deserves the name is that of pursuing our own good in our own way', said the most celebrated of its champions. If this is so, is compulsion ever justified? Mill had no doubt that it was. Since justice demands that all individuals be entitled to a minimum of freedom, all other individuals were of necessity to be restrained, if need be by force, from depriving anyone of it. Indeed, the whole function of law was the prevention of just such collisions: the state was reduced to what Lassalle contemptuously described as the functions of a night-watchman or traffic policeman.

What made the protection of individual liberty so sacred to Mill? In his famous essay he declares that, unless men are left to live as they wish 'in the path which merely concerns themselves', civilization cannot advance; the truth will not, for lack of a free market in ideas, come to light; there will be no scope for spontaneity, originality, genius, for mental energy, for moral courage. Society will be crushed by the weight of 'collective mediocrity'. Whatever is rich and diversified will be crushed by the weight of custom, by men's constant tendency to conformity, which breeds only 'withered capacities', 'pinched and hidebound', 'cramped and warped' human beings. 'Pagan self-assertion is as worthy as Christian self-denial.' 'All the errors which a man is likely to commit against advice and warning are far outweighed by the evil of allowing others to constrain him to what they deem is good.' The defence of liberty consists in the 'negative' goal of warding off interference. To threaten a man with persecution unless he submits to a life in which he exercises no choices of his goals; to block before him every door but one, no matter how noble the prospect upon which it opens, or how benevolent the motives of those who arrange this, is to sin against the truth that he is a man, a being with a life of his own to live. This is liberty as it has been conceived by liberals in the modern world from the days of Erasmus (some would say of Occam) to our own. Every plea for civil liberties and individual rights, every protest against exploitation and humilia-tion, against the encroachment of public authority, or the mass hypnosis of custom or organized propaganda, springs from this individualistic, and much disputed, conception of man.

Three facts about this position may be noted. In the first place Mill confuses two distinct notions. One is that all coercion is, in so far as it frustrates human desires, bad as such, although it may have to be applied to prevent other, greater evils; while non-interference, which is the opposite of coercion, is good as such, although it is not the only good. This is the 'negative' conception of liberty in its classical form. The other is that men should seek to discover the truth, or to develop a certain type of character of which Mill approved—fearless, original. imaginative, independent, non-conforming to the point of eccentricity, and so on—and that truth can be found, and such character can be bred, only in conditions of freedom. Both these are liberal views, but they are not identical, and the connexion between them is, at best, empirical. No one would argue that truth or freedom of self-expression could flourish where dogma crushes all thought. But the evidence of history tends to show (as, indeed, was argued by James Stephen in his formidable attack on Mill in his *Liberty, Equality, Fraternity*) that integrity, love of truth, and fiery individualism grow at least as often in severely disciplined communities among, for example, the puritan Calvinists of Scotland or New England, or under military discipline, as in more tolerant or indifferent societies; and if this is so, Mill's argument for liberty as a necessary condition for the growth of human genius falls to the ground. If his two goals proved incompatible, Mill would be faced with a cruel dilemma, quite apart from the further difficulties created by the inconsistency of his doctrines with strict utilitarianism, even in his own humane version of it.[5]

In the second place, the doctrine is comparatively modern. There seems to be scarcely any discussion of individual liberty as a conscious political ideal (as opposed to its actual existence) in the ancient world. Condorcet had already remarked that the notion of individual rights was absent from the legal conceptions of the Romans and Greeks; this seems to hold equally of the Jewish, Chinese, and all other ancient civilizations that have since come to light.[6] The domination of this ideal has been the exception rather than the rule, even in the recent history of the West. Nor has liberty in this sense often formed a rallying cry for the great masses of mankind. The desire not to be impinged upon, to be left to oneself, has been a mark of high civilization both on the part of individuals and communities. The sense of privacy itself, of the area of personal relationships as something sacred in its own right, derives from a conception of freedom which, for all its religious roots, is scarcely older, in its developed state, than the Renaissance or the Reformation.[7] Yet its decline would mark the death of a civilization, of an entire moral outlook.

The third characteristic of this notion of liberty is of greater importance. It is that liberty in this sense is not incompatible with some kinds of autocracy, or at any

[5] This is but another illustration of the natural tendency of all but a very few thinkers to believe that all the things they hold good must be intimately connected, or at least compatible, with one another. The history of thought, like the history of nations, is strewn with examples of inconsistent, or at least disparate, elements artificially yoked together in a despotic system, or held together by the danger of some common enemy. In due course the danger passes, and conflicts between the allies arise, which often disrupt the system, sometimes to the great benefit of mankind.

[6] See the valuable discussion of this in Michel Villey, *Leçons d'histoire de la philosophie du droit*, who traces the embryo of the notion of subjective rights to Occam.

[7] Christian (and Jewish or Moslem) belief in the absolute authority of divine or natural laws, or in the equality of all men in the sight of God, is very different from belief in freedom to live as one prefers.

rate with the absence of self-government. Liberty in this sense is principally concerned with the area of control, not with its source. Just as a democracy may, in fact, deprive the individual citizen of a great many liberties which he might have in some other form of society, so it is perfectly conceivable that a liberal-minded despot would allow his subjects a large measure of personal freedom. The despot who leaves his subjects a wide area of liberty may be unjust, or encourage the wildest inequalities, care little for order, or virtue, or knowledge; but provided he does not curb their liberty, or at least curbs it less than many other régimes, he meets with Mill's specification.[8] Freedom in this sense is not, at any rate logically, connected with democracy or self-government. Self-government may, on the whole, provide a better guarantee of the preservation of civil liberties than other régimes, and has been defended as such by libertarians. But there is no necessary connexion between individual liberty and democratic rule. The answer to the question 'Who governs me?' is logically distinct from the question 'How far does government interfere with me?' It is in this difference that the great contrast between the two concepts of negative and positive liberty, in the end, consists.[9] For the 'positive' sense of liberty comes to light if we try to answer the question, not 'What am I free to do or be?', but 'By whom an I ruled?' or 'Who is to say what I am, and what I am not, to be or do?' The connexion between democracy and individual liberty is a good deal more tenuous than it seemed to many advocates of both. The desire to be governed by myself, or at any rate to participate in the process by which my life

[8] Indeed, it is arguable that in the Prussia of Frederick the Great or in the Austria of Josef II, men of imagination, originality, and creative genius, and, indeed, minorities of all kinds, were less persecuted and felt the pressure, both of institutions and custom, less heavy upon them than in many an earlier or later democracy.

[9] 'Negative liberty' is something the extent of which, in a given case, it is difficult to estimate. It might, prima facie, seem to depend simply on the power to choose between at any rate two alternatives. Nevertheless, not all choices are equally free, or free at all. If in a totalitarian state I betray my friend under threat of torture, perhaps even if I act from fear of losing my job, I can reasonably say that I did not act freely. Nevertheless, I did, of course, make a choice, and could, at any rate in theory, have chosen to be killed or tortured or imprisoned. The mere existence of alternatives is not, therefore, enough to make my action free (although it may be voluntary) in the normal sense of the word. The extent of my freedom seems to depend on (a) how many possibilities are open to me (although the method of counting these can never be more than impressionistic. Possibilities of action are not discrete entities like apples, which can be exhaustively enumerated); (b) how easy or difficult each of these possibilities is to actualize; (c) how important in my plan of life, given my character and circumstances, these possibilities are when compared with each other; (d) how far they are closed and opened by deliberate human acts; (e) what value not merely the agent, but the general sentiment of the society in which he lives, puts on the various possibilities. All these magnitudes must be 'integrated', and a conclusion, necessarily never precise, or indisputable, drawn from this process. It may well be that there are many incommensurable kinds and degrees of freedom, and that they cannot be drawn up on any single scale of magnitude. Moreover, in the case of societies, we are faced by such (logically absurd) questions as 'Would arrangement X increase the liberty of Mr. A more than it would that of Messrs. B, C, and D between them, added together?' The same difficulties arise in applying utilitarian criteria. Nevertheless, provided we do not demand precise measurement, we can give valid reasons for saying that the average subject of the King of Sweden is, on the whole, a good deal freer today than the average citizen of Spain or Albania. Total patterns of life must be compared directly as wholes, although the method by which we make the comparison, and the truth of the conclusions, are difficult or impossible to demonstrate. But the vagueness of the concepts, and the multiplicity of the criteria involved, is an attribute of the subject-matter itself, not of our imperfect methods of measurement, or incapacity for precise thought.

is to be controlled, may be as deep a wish as that of a free area for action, and perhaps historically older. But it is not a desire for the same thing. So different is it, indeed, as to have led in the end to the great clash of ideologies that dominates our world. For it is this—the 'positive' conception of liberty: not freedom from, but freedom to—to lead one prescribed form of life—which the adherents of the 'negative' notion represent as being, at times, no better than a specious disguise for brutal tyranny.

The Notion of Positive Freedom

The 'positive' sense of the word 'liberty' derives from the wish on the part of the individual to be his own master. I wish my life and decisions to depend on myself, not on external forces of whatever kind. I wish to be the instrument of my own, not of other men's, acts of will. I wish to be a subject, not an object; to be moved by reasons, by conscious purposes, which are my own, not by causes which affect me, as it were, from outside. I wish to be somebody, not nobody; a doer—deciding, not being decided for, self-directed and not acted upon by external nature or by other men as if I were a thing, or an animal, or a slave incapable of playing a human role, that is, of conceiving goals and policies of my own and realizing them. This is at least part of what I mean when I say that I am rational, and that it is my reason that distinguishes me as a human being from the rest of the world. I wish, above all, to be conscious of myself as a thinking, willing, active being, bearing responsibility for my choices and able to explain them by references to my own ideas and purposes. I feel free to the degree that I believe this to be true, and enslaved to the degree that I am made to realize that it is not.

The freedom which consists in being one's own master, and the freedom which consists in not being prevented from choosing as I do by other men, may, on the face of it, seem concepts at no great logical distance from each other—no more than negative and positive ways of saying much the same thing. Yet the 'positive' and 'negative' notions of freedom historically developed in divergent directions not always by logically reputable steps, until, in the end, they came into direct conflict with each other.

One way of making this clear is in terms of the independent momentum which the, initially perhaps quite harmless, metaphor of self-mastery acquired. 'I am my own master'; 'I am slave to no man'; but may I not as Platonists or Hegelians tend to say be a slave to nature? Or to my own 'unbridled' passions? Are these not so many species of the identical genus 'slave'—some political or legal, others moral or spiritual? Have not men had the experience of liberating themselves from spiritual slavery, or slavery to nature, and do they not in the course of it become aware, on the one hand, of a self which dominates, and, on the other, of something in them which is brought to heel? This dominant self is then variously identified with reason, with my 'higher nature', with the self which calculates and aims at what will satisfy it in the long run, with my 'real', or 'ideal', or 'autonomous' self, or with my self 'at its best'; which is then contrasted with irrational impulse, uncontrolled desires, my 'lower' nature, the pursuit of immediate pleasures, my 'empirical' or 'heteronomous' self, swept by every gust of desire and passion, needing to be rigidly disciplined if it is ever to rise to the full height of its 'real' nature. Presently the two selves may be represented as divided by an even larger gap: the real self may be conceived as something wider than the individual (as the term is normally understood), as a social 'whole' of which the individual is an element or aspect: a tribe, a race, a church, a state, the great society of the living and the dead and the yet unborn. This entity is then identified as being the 'true' self which, by imposing its collective, or 'organic', single will upon its recalcitrant 'members', achieves its own, and therefore their, 'higher' freedom. The perils of using organic metaphors to justify the coercion of some men by others in order to raise them to a 'higher' level of freedom have often been pointed out. But what gives such plausibility as it has to this kind of language is that we recognize that it is possible, and at times justifiable, to coerce men in the name of some goal (let us say, justice or public health) which they would, if they were more enlightened, themselves pursue, but do not, because they are blind or ignorant or corrupt. This renders it easy for me to conceive of myself as coercing others for their own sake, in their, not my, interest. I am then claiming that I know what they truly need better than they know it themselves. What, at most, this entails is that they would not resist me if they were rational and as wise as I and understood their interests as I do. But I may go on to claim a good deal more than this. I may declare that they are actually aiming at what in their benighted state they consciously resist, because there exists within them an occult entity—their latent rational will, or their 'true' purpose—and that this entity, although it is belied by all that they overtly feel and do and say, is their 'real' self, of which the poor empirical self in space and time may know nothing or little; and that this inner spirit is the only self that deserves to have its wishes taken into account.[10] Once I take this view, I am in a position to ignore the actual wishes of men or societies, to bully, oppress, torture them in the name, and on behalf, of their 'real' selves, in the secure knowledge that whatever is the true goal of man (happiness, fulfilment of duty, wisdom, a just society, self-fulfilment) must be identical with his freedom—the free choice of his 'true', albeit often submerged and inarticulate, self.

This paradox has been often exposed. It is one thing to say that I know what is good for X, while he himself does not; and even to ignore his wishes for its—and his—sake; and a very different one to say that he has *eo ipso* chosen it, not indeed consciously, not as he seems in everyday life, but in his role as a rational self which his empirical self may not know—the 'real' self which discerns the good, and cannot help choosing it once it is revealed. This monstrous impersonation, which consists in equating what X would choose if he were something he is not, or at least not yet, with what X actually seeks and chooses, is at the heart of all political theories of self-realization. It is one thing to say that I may be coerced for my own good which I am too blind to see: this may, on occasion, be for my benefit; indeed it may

---

[10] 'The ideal of true freedom is the maximum of power for all the members of human society alike to make the best of themselves', said T. H. Green in 1881. Apart from the confusion of freedom with equality, this entails that if a man chose some immediate pleasure—which (in whose view?) would not enable him to make the best of himself (what self?)—what he was exercising was not 'true' freedom: and if deprived of it, would not lose anything that mattered. Green was a genuine liberal: but many a tyrant could use this formula to justify his worst acts of oppression.

enlarge the scope of my liberty. It is another to say that if it is my good, then I am not being coerced, for I have willed it, whether I know this or not, and am free or 'truly' free even while my poor earthly body and foolish mind bitterly reject it, and struggle against those who seek however benevolently to impose it, with the greatest desperation.

This magical transformation, or sleight of hand (for which William James so justly mocked the Hegelians), can no doubt be perpetrated just as easily with the 'negative' concept of freedom, where the self that should not be interfered with is no longer the individual with his actual wishes and needs as they are normally conceived, but the 'real' man within, identified with the pursuit of some ideal purpose not dreamed of by his empirical self. And, as in the case of the 'postively' free self, this entity may be inflated into some super-personal entity—a state, a class, a nation, or the march of history itself, regarded as a more 'real' subject of attributes than the empirical self. But the 'positive' conception of freedom as self-mastery, with its suggestion of a man divided against himself, has, in fact, and as a matter of history, of doctrine and of practice, lent itself more easily to this splitting of personality into two: the transcendent, dominant controller, and the empirical bundle of desires and passions to be disciplined and brought to heel. It is this historical fact that has been influential. This demonstrates (if demonstration of so obvious a truth is needed) that conceptions of freedom directly derive from views of what constitutes a self, a person, a man. Enough manipulation with the definition of man, and freedom can be made to mean whatever the manipulator wishes. Recent history has made it only too clear that the issue is not merely academic. . . .

"FREEDOM AS THE POSSIBILITY OF MEANINGFUL CHOICE"

P. H. Partridge

In the history of philosophical and social thought "freedom" has a specific use as a moral and a social concept—to refer either to circumstances which arise in the relations of man to man or to specific conditions of social life. Even when so restricted, important differences of usage are possible, and most of the political or philosophical argument about the meaning or the nature of freedom is concerned with the legitimacy or convenience of particular applications of the term.

Absence of Constraint or Coercion. It is best to start from a conception of freedom that has been central in the tradition of European individualism and liberalism. According to this conception, freedom refers primarily to a condition characterized by the absence of coercion or constraint imposed by another person; a man is said to be free to the extent that he can choose his own goals or course of conduct, can choose between alternatives available to him, and is not compelled to act as he would not himself choose to act, or prevented from acting as he would otherwise choose to act, by the will of another man, of the state, or of any other authority. Freedom in the sense of not being coerced or constrained by another is sometimes called negative freedom (or "freedom from"); it refers to an area of conduct within which each man chooses his own course and is protected from compulsion or restraint. J. S. Mill's essay *On Liberty* is perhaps the best-known expression in English of this outstanding individualistic and liberal conception of freedom.

Some writers take the view that the absence of coercion is the sufficient and necessary condition for defining freedom; so long as a man acts of his own volition and is not coerced in what he does, he is free. Other writers wish to widen the concept in one or both of two ways. They argue that natural conditions, and not only the will or the power of other men, impose obstructions and restraints on our capacity to choose between alternatives and that therefore the growth of knowledge or anything else that increases our capacity to employ natural conditions for the achievement of our purposes *ipso facto* enlarges our freedom. They also sometimes argue that whether or not it is the will of other men or natural obstacles that are considered as limiting or constraining our actions, we cannot truly be said to be free to choose some preferred alternative unless we have the means or the power to achieve it, and thus the absence of means or power to do X is equivalent to absence of freedom to do it. For those who take this view the necessary conditions for the existence of freedom would be (*a*) the absence of human coercion or restraint preventing one from choosing alternatives he would wish to choose; (*b*) the absence of natural conditions preventing one from achieving a chosen objective; (*c*) the possession of the means or the power to achieve the objective one chooses of one's own volition. Many of the assertions frequently made about liberty in recent political thought assume that possession of the means or power to realize preferred objectives is part of what it means to be free. For example, the contention that men who suffer from poverty or have a low level of education cannot really be free, or that they cannot be as free as the well-to-do and the well educated, relies on the assumption that "to be free to do X" includes within its meaning "to be able," "to have the means," and "to have the power" to do X.

What are the objections to thus connecting "being free to" with "having the capacity or the power to?" It can be said that, at least in many cases, equating freedom with possession of power will involve a distortion of ordinary language. If I ask, "Am I free to walk into the Pentagon?" the question will be clearly understood; but if I ask, "Am I free to walk across the Atlantic Ocean?" the appropriate answer will be "You are free to, if you can." This suggests the main argument: The linking of "being free to" with "having the capacity or power" deprives the word "free" of its essential and unequivocal function, which is to refer to a situation or state of affairs in which a man's choice of how he acts is not deliberately forced or restrained by another man. As de Jouvenel points out, if we say that to be free to achieve chosen ends requires the possession of the power and the social means necessary for their achievement, then the problem of freedom coincides with (or becomes confused with) the quite different problem of how satisfactions are to be maximized. It may be true to say that the poor man is as free to spend his holidays in Monte Carlo as the rich man is, and true also to say that he cannot afford to do so. These two statements, it is argued, refer to two distinct states of affairs, and nothing is gained by amalgamating them.

Meaning of "Coercion." Even if we confine ourselves to saying that a man is free insofar as his action is not coerced by another, it is evident that the concept of coercion itself requires some consideration. An important point may be made by examining Betrand Russell's often-quoted sentence: "Freedom in general may be defined as the absence of obstacles to the realization of desires." This hardly goes far enough. Let us imagine an authoritarian society in which rulers have for years been so successful in controlling and manipulating what members of the community read and what views they encounter, and in which the educators have been able so subtly and skillfully to mold the minds and dispositions of the very young, that almost all citizens naturally desire what their rulers desire them to desire, without its ever occurring to them that there are alternatives to what they are accustomed to or that their freedom to choose has been in any way circumscribed. They are not conscious of any obstructions to the satisfaction of desire and, indeed, no obstructions may exist to the satisfaction of any desires they experience. This is a limiting case, but it points to conditions which exist more or less in all societies. We would scarcely concede that the members of such a society enjoyed any or much freedom. The society described many be one in which coercion in the usual sense does not occur and has in fact become unnecessary.

Two important points follow from this. First, if absence of coercion is a necessary condition of being free, coercion must be understood as including not only the direct forms—commands or prohibitions backed by sanctions or superior power—but also the many indirect forms—molding and manipulation or, more generally, forms of control which are indirect because they involve control by certain persons of the conditions that determine or affect the alternatives available to others. This is an important extension of the notion of coercion. Second, if liberty means the right of individual choice between alternatives, then this right in turn implies that the alternatives can be known by those who are to choose; that individuals have the opportunity to understand the character of available alternatives and can make a deliberate or informed choice. The freedom that members of a society enjoy will be connected, therefore, with the extent to which competing opinions, objectives, modes of behavior, ways of living, and so on are, so to speak, on display; on how freely they can be recommended, criticized and examined; and thus on the ease with which men can make a deliberate choice between them.

For this reason, since literacy or education enlarges the capacity or faculty of choice and decision, it is an important precondition of the existence of freedom: knowledge extends the capacity for acting freely. Similarly, not only suppression but also distortion and misrepresentation, any kind of dishonest propaganda which gains its effect from privileged control over sources of publicity, may restrict the freedom of others; insofar as it succeeds in concealing or misrepresenting the character of certain of the available alternatives, it will tend to restrict or manipulate the range of choice no less effectively than direct coercion or constraint may; and thus it will also tend to limit the exercise of freedom in a particular society. It is not sufficient to consider only the presence or absence of coercion in the more literal and direct sense. Freedom in its positive aspect is the activity or process of choosing for oneself and acting on one's own initiative, and choice can be manipulated as readily as it can be coerced.

Does it follow from this that the extent of freedom is related to the number of available alternatives, in that the more alternatives there are for choice, the freer a man is? Clearly there can be no simple or direct relationship between the range of available alternatives and the extent of freedom. However numerous the alternatives between which a man may choose, he will not admit himself to be free if the one alternative that he would most prefer is the one which is excluded. In a society that forbids the preaching of Catholic doctrine and the practice of Catholic forms of worship, Catholics will not concede that they are free just because they are still free to be either Anglicans, Methodists, or Buddhists. In certain circumstances the extent of the range of available alternatives may be relevant to a judgment of the extent of freedom; but in general we can talk profitably about both the existence and the extent of freedom in a particular society only by taking into account the individual and social interests, the capacities, the modes of behavior, and the ways of living on behalf of which freedom is claimed.

Kinds of Freedom. When men speak of their being free or claim freedom for themselves, they are referring not only to the absence of coercion and restraint imposed by others (freedom *from*) but also to that on behalf of which freedom is being claimed (what they are claiming freedom *for*). This is another sense in which we can speak about a positive aspect of freedom. In political and social discussion a claim to freedom is almost invariably (albeit usually implicitly) a claim to a particular liberty, a claim to freedom for or in the exercise of some particular interest or form of activity. Although Russell says that freedom is the absence of obstacles to the satisfaction of desire, probably no serious philosophical or social thinker has defended freedom in the sense of absence of obstacles to the satisfaction of *any* desire; what has been defended, and what freedom has been identified with, is the absence of obstacles to the exercise and satisfaction of specific interests and forms of activity which are accepted as possessing especial moral and social significance.

Thus, freedom in the abstract is a class comprising many species—freedom of thought and speech, freedom of association, freedom of assembly, freedom of worship, freedom of movement, freedom in the use or disposal of one's property, freedom in the choice of one's employer or occupation, and so on. In every case there is, of course, a reference to the absence of coercion or interference and to an area within which one can choose or act on one's own initiative; not to an abstract or indeterminate possibility of choosing but instead to a specific sphere of individual or social activity within which the right to make one's own choices and decisions, to follow one's own course, is regarded as being of particular importance in the moral life of the individual. This seems to be one way in which positive notions of freedom (as contrasted with the more abstract idea of bare immunity from coercion or interference by others) have emerged, namely, in the attempt to identify (and thus to identify with freedom) those specific spheres of human activity within which what Mill calls individuality, the right and capacity for individual choice and initiative, really' matter.

Some of the particular freedoms which have been much emphasized in recent times (freedom from want and freedom from fear are important examples) seem at first sight to refer neither to the absence of coercion nor to any specific interest or form of activity for which freedom is being claimed. It might appear that what *is* being claimed is, rather, the institution of political and economic arrangements by means of which men may be made immune from feelings and circumstances which they find to be evil. If this is all that is meant, then this is to employ freedom in a sense different from the one we have been discussing; this is shown by the fact that freedom from want and fear could conceivably be attained by the setting up of political and social arrangements under which the amplitude of choice within important spheres of activity would be drastically restricted and under which there might be a considerable measure of coercion and constraint; in other words, freedom from want and freedom from fear might well be compatible with a very authoritarian regime, just as in contemporary China freedom from flies is said to have been achieved by very authoritarian methods. Thus, if "freedom from want" and "freedom from fear" are taken simply in that way, the freedom involved is logically and socially distinct from that which has so far been taken as being central and fundamental in the tradition of liberal thinking. However, this may be to interpret these two freedoms superficially. For a more sympathetic interpretation we must return to what has been said about manipulation.

Freedom and Power. In modern societies manipulation in various forms is at least as important as the process we normally identify as coercive. It is well known that, within a society, a group of men may enjoy such control over property or the means of production, or over an educational system or the media of communication, that they are able to determine within a fairly narrow range the alternatives between which their fellow citizens can choose. It is not only true that less privileged men often lack the means or the power to attain their preferred alternative but also that others can exploit their lack of power in order to prevent them from attaining what they would wish to attain; sometimes the less powerful can even be prevented from knowing what alternatives there are and from knowing that some of them might be capable or worthy of being pursued. It is this argument which can justify notions like "freedom from want" or "freedom from economic insecurity" and which links them with what has been taken to be the central sense of freedom, the absence of constraint. Even though we refuse to conclude that the mere absence of the means or the power to attain a preferred alternative goal is equivalent to not being *free* to pursue it, it is a different situation when means and power are controlled and manipulated by others in order to secure compliance with their demands. Thus, if "want" and "insecurity" describe a condition in which there is unequal control over the means and conditions of choice and action, in consequence of which some men can manipulate the range of choice available to others, then freedom from want and insecurity belongs with freedom from coercion; in that case, freedom from want and insecurity is the condition of the ability to act on one's own initiative, which is the positive side of liberty.

There is, then, this connection between freedom and power: When there is conflict between individuals and groups for possession or control of scarce means and conditions of action, control over means is a condition of the availability of alternatives, and hence of choice and freedom. It follows, therefore, that when men have unequal power, this will often mean that they will also be unequal with respect to the freedom they enjoy—not merely in the sense that the man who is better off has the means to choose more widely and live more abundantly than his poorer brother (although this is also true) but in the more relevant sense that the more powerful man can restrict the range of choice and the freedom of the less powerful in order to satisfy his own interests more fully. Obviously this relation between inequality of power and inequality of freedom provides one of the connections that exist between liberty and democracy. If we define democracy as being a form of political organization in which all adult members of the community share in making decisions about the common arrangements of the society (including those decisions about the use and distribution of the resources which affect the choices of acting available to men), then the right to participate in the making of these decisions is a liberty that will affect (or at least may very substantially affect) the range and character of the alternatives that are available in very important areas of social and private life.

Political Participation. Thus, we may say that political participation, or sharing in the process of government, will enter into the meaning of "liberty" in society in at least two different ways. First, political activity and participation in government is an interest and mode of activity to which many men attach great importance, and thus the existence of the right and opportunity to engage in this form of activity is one of the liberties that some men cherish highly. Second, it is in addition a liberty that forms part of a wider structure of liberties because the extent to which this liberty is accorded and exercised will usually also affect the extent to which liberty is available in other areas of social life. This is not to say, of course, that the more democratic a society is (the less men are restrained or restricted in their participation in the activity of government), the more freedom there will be in other areas of social life; it is possible for democracies to be exceptionally coercive, restrictive, or intolerant in certain areas of living and, apart from this, it is also true that expansion of particular liberties (or of liberty in particular areas) often entails the curtailment of others. The point is, rather, that political liberty in the sense specified forms part of a more complex system of liberties in any developed society; both logically and causally, political liberty is connected with the liberties that are established in other spheres of individual activity.

Freedom and Choice. We have seen that liberty has its negative and its positive sides—"negative" referring to the absence of obstructions, interference, coercion, or indirect control; "positive," to the processes of choosing and acting on one's own initiative, and more concretely and less formally to the general types of human interests or forms of activity for the expression and exercise of which liberty is claimed. Some writers, concentrating particularly on the positive aspect, have been inclined to assert that a man is being free only when he is actually choosing, exercising initiative, and acting deliberately or responsibly. Mill, in what he says in *On Liberty* about "individuality," "individual spontaneity," the "despotism of custom," and related matters, comes very close to asserting this, although he never quite does so. The same kind of view is hinted at in Graham Wallas' "Freedom is the capacity for continuous initiative," but it would be difficult to accept this as a general position. For the devotee of a religious faith, the religious freedom he claims and he believes himself to enjoy may be no more than the freedom to practice unmolested a form of worship he has inherited and which he has never felt the faintest temptation to question; in such a case it is a fiction to speak of a process of choice. The same can be said of the man who is content to follow narrowly, uncritically, and unadventurously the established customs and conventions of his society. Even though there may be a sense in which we can intelligibly talk of such men as being slaves to customs, habits, or orthodoxies, it would still be straining the point to maintain that they are not free.

On the other hand, the man who has been so molded and manipulated that he always wants what his ruler or superior wants him to want is scarcely free. This case suggests that freedom will exist only where there exists the *possibility* of choice, and the possibility of choice in turn implies not only the absence of direct coercion and compulsion but also that the availability and the characteristics of alternatives must be capable of being known. Thus, whatever the situation of any particular individual may be, it is most likely that there will be a large measure of individual freedom within a society when there exists what Mill calls a variety of conditions— where a wide variety of beliefs are in fact expressed and where there is a considerable diversity of tastes and pursuits, customs and codes of conduct, ways and styles of living. And, because of the connection between inequality of power and inequality with respect to the enjoyment of freedom, a society in which power is widely distributed is also likely to be the one characterized by the existence of wide possibilities for choice and individual initiative.

FURTHER READINGS FOR PART 2

Anthologies

Actes du IVe Congrès des Sociétés de Philosophie do Langue Française, *La Liberté* (Neuchâtel: Baconnière, 1949). A collection of seventy papers on the meanings and problems of freedom.

Anshen, Ruth Nanda (ed.), *Freedom: Its Meaning* (New York: Harcourt, 1940). Forty-two essays by outstanding persons in a variety of fields on topics concerned with the history, meanings, and conditions of freedom.

Bryson, Lyman, Louis Finkelstein, R. M. MacIver, and Richard McKeon (eds.), *Freedom and Authority in Our Time*: Twelfth Symposium of the Conference on Science, Philosophy, and Religion (New York: Harper, 1953). A collection of fifty-seven papers on various aspects of freedom and authority, together with comments on the papers from other participants in the symposium.

Fédération Internationale des Sociétés de Philosophie, *Enquête Sur la Liberté*, Publié avec le concourse de l'UNESCO (Paris: Hermann, 1953). Contains the response of forty-seven authors to a questionnaire about freedom sent out by the International Federation of Philosophical Societies for UNESCO. For a summary of some of the results, see the reading selection by H. J. Pos in this text.

Grindel, Carl W. (ed.), *Concept of Freedom* (Chicago: Regnery, 1955). A collection of eleven papers on the concept of freedom and on various aspects of individual and social freedom.

Kallen, Horace M. (ed.), *Freedom in the Modern World* (New York: Coward–McCann, 1928). Eleven essays dealing with the meanings and conditions of freedom.

Individual Works

Adler, Mortimer J., "Freedom: A Study of the Development of the Concept in the English and American Traditions of Philosophy," *Review of Metaphysics*, XI (1958), pp. 380-410. Describes the main concepts of freedom in Western thought, attends particularly to the development of these concepts in English and American philosophy, and seeks to assess the extent of real disagreement between the English and American traditions.

———, *The Idea of Freedom*, 2 Vols. (Garden City, N. Y.: Doubleday, 1958-1961). Summarizes the results of research done by the staff of the Institute for Philosophical Research. Vol. I examines conceptions of freedom. Vol. II examines controversies about freedom.

Bay, Christian, *The Structure of Freedom* (Stanford, Calif.: Stanford U.P., 1958). A comprehensive study of the major forms of freedom and the conditions of achieving them.

Cranston, Maurice, *Freedom: A New Analysis* (London: Longmans, Green, 1953). A three-part study dealing with the meaning of freedom, the ambiguity of liberalism, and the freedom of the will.

Dobzhansky, Theodosius, *The Biological Basis of Human Freedom* (New York: Columbia U.P., 1956). Maintains that man's ability to choose freely between ideas and acts is one of the fundamental characteristics of his biological and cultural evolution.

Fuller, Lon L., "Freedom–A Suggested Analysis," *Harvard Law Review*, LXVIII (1955), pp. 1305-1325. Distinguishes two meanings of freedom, "freedom from" and "freedom to"; then discusses the forms of order needed to realize these freedoms.

Knight, Frank H., "The Meaning of Freedom," in C. M. Perry (ed.), *The Philosophy of American Democracy* (Chicago: Chicago U.P., 1943). Distinguishes three main concepts of freedom corresponding to the religious, the romantic, and the modern liberal views of life.

MacCallum, Gerald C., Jr., "Negative and Positive Freedom," *Philosophical Review*, LXXVI (1967), pp. 312-334. A general discussion of the meaning of freedom. Disputes the view, held by persons such as Isaiah Berlin in the article contained in this text, that the distinction between positive and negative freedom is an important distinction.

Muller, Herbert J., *Issues of Freedom: Paradoxes and Promises* (New York: Harper, 1960). Concerned with the meanings of freedom, the assumptions made in holding a view of freedom, and the basic cultural factors relevant to freedom.

Oppenheim, Felix E., *Dimensions of Freedom: An Analysis* (New York: St. Martin's, 1961). Provides a conceptual framework of freedom, explicating not only the concept of freedom but such related concepts as influence, constraint, and power.

——, "Freedom," in D. L. Sills, (ed.), *International Encyclopedia of the Social Sciences*, Vol. 5 (New York: Macmillan, 1968), pp. 554-559. Gives an analysis of several meanings of freedom.

Perry, Ralph Barton, "What Does It Mean to Be Free?" *Pacific Spectator*, VII (1953), pp. 124-141. Defines freedom as "effective choice"; then discusses some of the conditions of its achievement.

Petrović, Gajo, "What Is Freedom?" in *Marx in the Mid-twentieth Century* (Garden City, N.Y.: Doubleday, 1967), pp. 115-134. A contemporary Yugoslavian Marxist's view of freedom.

3. Freedom of the Will

In discussions of human freedom, few problems have occasioned more debate than the problem of free will. The major question at issue is whether all human choices and actions are wholly determined by past causes. The importance of this question stems from the fact that as we try to answer it, some of our most fundamental beliefs seem to come into conflict.

On the one hand, there is much evidence which suggests that man has a power to choose among alternatives and to act upon his choices. There is, for example, the testimony of our own direct experience in making choices and acting upon them. When we order a meal in a restaurant, when we decide what to wear in the morning, when we choose a career, we seem to be directly aware of our freedom to choose and to pursue alternatives other than those we have selected. Furthermore, the assumption that men are free in their choices and actions seems to be necessary if we are to justify many of our ordinary feelings and beliefs. Thus, we feel obligations to perform various moral duties; we feel regret when we perform wrong actions; we believe that other persons are responsible for at least some of their actions; and we believe that it is proper at times to praise and blame, or to reward and punish, men for their actions. In each of these cases, it is difficult to see how we can justify our feelings and beliefs if human choice and action are wholly determined by past causes.

On the other hand, the progress of the sciences in coming to understand human behavior suggests that there are definite causes for every human choice and action. It would appear that if we could learn all the scientific laws which govern human behavior, we would be able to predict in detail every future choice and action of any given individual. Should this be so, we seem forced to conclude that freedom of choice and action are illusions. Moreover, one's religious beliefs may easily reinforce this conclusion. If one believes that God knows everything which will happen in the history of the world, it would appear that at least He can predict every human choice and action and that man does not really possess any freedom of the will.

In the first of our selections, St. Augustine considers the problem of free will in relation to his own religious belief that God does have foreknowledge of everything. Taking Cicero as a representative of those who hold that a belief in God's foreknowledge cannot be reconciled with a belief in free will, St. Augustine argues that Cicero has made a fundamental mistake. Cicero has failed to recognize that free will itself is one of the causes of human choice and action. Thus, although God knows in advance the causes and effects of every human action, such knowledge is consistent with man's possession of free will because the operation of free will is among the causes.

Baron Holbach puts forward a traditional case for determinism in the second selection. Accepting the view that human behavior is wholly determined by past causes, Holbach does not hesitate to draw the conclusion that man is not a free agent and is totally under the influence of causes over which he has no control. Holbach acknowledges that men believe themselves to be free agents in making choices but explains this belief as stemming from their ignorance of the causes which produce their choices and actions.

The third author, David Hume, holds that the entire dispute between free-willists and determinists is misguided. According to him, the dispute arises because the debating parties have failed to define the key terms involved. When we carefully explain what we mean when we say that an action is "necessitated" and what we mean by "liberty" when the term is applied to voluntary actions, we shall see that our possession of "liberty" is consistent with our actions being "necessitated." In other words, Hume urges that to believe a man is free in his actions is consistent with the belief that his actions are thoroughly caused. When this situation is recognized, any further dispute about the matter is idle. Hume also argues that our moral experience of rewarding and punishing or praising and blaming makes sense only if actions are caused.

In sharp disagreement with the position stated by Hume, the fourth author, Campbell, argues that we cannot reconcile our belief in man's free agency with a belief that man's actions are necessitated. Campbell calls attention to the fact that we do hold men morally responsible for at least some of their actions. He argues that such judgments of moral responsibility assume that men are free in a stronger sense than Hume's position permits. For Campbell, two conditions must be met before we can properly say that a free act has been performed: (1) the man must be the sole *cause of the act, and (2) it must be possible that the man could have acted otherwise than he did.*

The concluding selection by the French existentialist Sartre provides yet another approach to the problem of man's freedom of choice. For Sartre, the crucial question is not whether our decisions have causes but whether we determine what causes are to be operative in our choices. He draws a distinction between two types of being. There is, first, being-in-itself, which is the realm of brute fact. A physical object, such as a rock, has being-in-itself. It is simply what it is. But there is another type of being in the world, being-for-itself. This type of being exists in man insofar as he is conscious. By virtue of being conscious, man is able to transcend whatever he has been, or is now, and make himself something different. Through consciousness (the for-itself), man determines what causes are to function in his decisions. Thus, when a man decides to grow a beard to express his personality, he is determining for himself that the motive (or cause) of expressing his personality is to govern his future behavior. Furthermore, because he is a conscious being, he can at any time determine that another motive (or cause) shall take priority in his behavior. Perhaps he will determine for himself that pleasing another person by being clean-shaven is more important than expressing his personality. In this case, he will transcend what he is and determine himself in another direction. What the individual cannot do is shirk the responsibility for being what he is, since it is always open to him to change. Accordingly, for Sartre, man is a radically free being, continuously able to rise above his past and his present to remake himself in the future.

"FREE WILL AND GOD'S FOREKNOWLEDGE"

St. Augustine

The manner in which Cicero addresses himself to the task of refuting the Stoics, shows that he did not think he could effect anything against them in argument unless he had first demolished divination.[1] And this he attempts to accomplish by denying that there is any knowledge of future things, and maintains with all his might that there is no such knowledge either in God or man, and that there is no prediction of events. Thus he both denies the foreknowledge of God, and attempts by vain arguments, and by opposing to himself certain oracles very easy to be refuted, to overthrow all prophecy, even such as is clearer than the light (though even these oracles are not refuted by him).

But, in refuting these conjectures of the mathematicians, his argument is triumphant, because truly these are such as destroy and refute themselves. Nevertheless, they are far more tolerable who assert the fatal influence of the start than they who deny the foreknowledge of future events. For, to confess that God exists, and at the same time to deny that He has foreknowledge of future things, is the most manifest folly. This Cicero himself saw, and therefore attempted to assert the doctrine embodied in the words of Scripture, "The fool hath said in his heart, There is no God."[2] That, however, he did not do in his own person, for he saw how odious and offensive such an opinion would be; and, therefore in his book on the nature of the gods,[3] he makes Cotta dispute concerning this against the Stoics, and preferred to give his own opinion in favour of Lucilius Balbus, to whom he assigned the defense of the Stoical position, rather than in favour of Cotta, who

[1] *De Divinat.* ii.
[2] Ps. xiv. 1.
[3] Bk. iii.

maintained that no divinity exists. However, in his book on divination, he in his own person most openly opposes the doctrine of the prescience of future things. But all this he seems to do in order that he may not grant the doctrine of fate, and by so doing destroy free will. For he thinks that, the knowledge of future things being once conceded, fate follows as so necessary a consequence that it cannot be denied.

But, let these perplexing debatings and disputations of the philosophers go on as they may, we, in order that we may confess the most high and true God Himself, do confess His will, supreme power, and prescience. Neither let us be afraid lest, after all, we do not do by will that which we do by will, because He, whose foreknowledge is infallible, foreknew that we would do it. It was this which Cicero was afraid of, and therefore opposed foreknowledge. The Stoics also maintained that all things do not come to pass by necessity, although they contended that all things happen according to destiny. What is it, then, that Cicero feared in the prescience of future things? Doubtless it was this,—that if all future things have been foreknown, they will happen in the order in which they have been foreknown; and if they come to pass in this order, there is a certain order of things foreknown by God; and if a certain order of things, then a certain order of causes, for nothing can happen which is not preceded by some efficient cause. But if there is a certain order of causes according to which everything happens which does happen, then by fate, says he, all things happen which do happen. But if this be so, then is there nothing in our own power, and there is no such thing as freedom of will; and if we grant that, says he, the whole economy of human life is subverted. In vain are laws enacted. In vain are reproaches, praises, chidings, exhortations had recourse to; and there is no justice whatever in the appointment of rewards for the good, and punishments for the wicked. And that consequences so disgraceful, and absurd, and pernicious to humanity may not follow, Cicero chooses to reject the foreknowledge of future things, and shuts up the religious mind to this alternative, to make choice between two things, either that something is in our own power, or that there is foreknowledge,—both of which cannot be true; but if the one is affirmed, the other is thereby denied. He therefore, like a truly great and wise man, and one who consulted very much and very skilfully for the good of humanity, of those two choose the freedom of the will, to confirm which he denied the foreknowledge of future things; and thus, wishing to make men free, he makes them sacrilegious. But the religious mind chooses both, confesses both, and maintains both by the faith of piety. But how so? says Cicero; for the knowledge of future things being granted, there follows a chain of consequences which ends in this, that there can be nothing depending on our own free wills. And further, if there is anything depending on our wills, we must go backwards by the same steps of reasoning till we arrive at the conclusion that there is no foreknowledge of future things. For we go backwards through all the steps in the following order:—If there is free will, all things do not happen according to fate; if all things do not happen according to fate, there is not a certain order of causes; and if there is not a certain order of causes, neither is there a certain order of things foreknown by God,—for things cannot come to pass except they are preceded by efficient causes,—but, if there is no fixed and certain order of causes foreknown by God, all things cannot be said to happen according as He foreknew that they would happen. And further, if it is not true that all things happen just as they have been foreknown by Him, there is not, says he, in God any foreknowledge of future events.

Now, against the sacrilegious and impious darings of reason, we assert both that God knows all things before they come to pass, and that we do by our free will whatsoever we know and feel to be done by us only because we will it. But that all things come to pass by fate, we do not say; nay we affirm that nothing comes to pass by fate; for we demonstrate that the name of fate, as it is wont to be used by those who speak of fate, meaning thereby the position of the stars at the time of each one's conception or birth, is an unmeaning word, for astrology itself is a delusion. But an order of causes in which the highest efficiency is attributed to the will of God, we neither deny nor do we designate it by the name of fate, unless, perhaps, we may understand fate to mean that which is spoken, deriving it from *fari*, to speak; for we cannot deny that it is written in the sacred Scriptures, "God hath spoken once; these two things have I heard, that power belongeth unto God. Also unto Thee, O God, belongeth mercy: for Thou wilt render unto every man according to his works."[4] Now the expression, "Once hath He spoken," is to be understood as meaning "immovably," that is, unchangeably hath He spoken, inasmuch as He knows unchangeably all things which shall be, and all things which He will do. We might, then, use the word fate in the sense it bears when derived from *fari*, to speak, had it not already come to be understood in another sense, into which I am unwilling that the hearts of men should unconsciously slide. But it does not follow that, though there is for God a certain order of all causes, there must therefore be nothing depending on the free exercise of our own wills, for our wills themselves are included in that order of causes which is certain to God, and is embraced by His foreknowledge, for human wills are also causes of human actions; and He who foreknew all the causes of things would certainly among those causes not have been ignorant of our wills. For even that very concession which Cicero himself makes is enough to refute him in this argument. For what does it help him to say that nothing takes place without a cause, but that every cause is not fatal, there being a fortuitous cause, a natural cause, and a voluntary cause? It is sufficient that he confesses that whatever happens must be preceded by a cause. For we say that those causes which are called fortuitous are not a mere name for the absence of causes, but are only latent, and we attribute them either to the will of the true God, or to that of spirits of some kind or other. And as to natural causes, we by no means separate them from the will of Him who is the author and framer of all nature. But now as to voluntary causes. They are referable either to God, or to angels, or to men, or to animals of whatever description, if indeed those instinctive movements of animals devoid of reason, by which, in accordance with their own nature, they seek or shun various things, are to be called wills. And when I speak of the wills of angels, I mean either the wills of good angels, whom we call the angels of God, or of the wicked angels, whom we call the angels of the devil, or demons. Also by the wills of men I mean the wills either of the good or of the wicked. And

[4] Ps. lxii. 11, 12.

from this we conclude that there are no efficient causes of all things which come to pass unless voluntary causes, that is, such as belong to that nature which is the spirit of life. For the air or wind is called spirit, but, inasmuch as it is a body, it is not the spirit of life. The spirit of life, therefore, which quickens all things, and is the creator of every body, and of every created spirit, is God Himself, the uncreated spirit. In His supreme will resides the power which acts on the wills of all created spirits, helping the good, judging the evil, controlling all, granting power to some, not granting it to others. For, as He is the creator of all natures, so also is He the bestower of all powers, not of all wills; for wicked wills are not from Him, being contrary to nature, which is from Him. As to bodies, they are more subject to wills: some to our wills, by which I mean the wills of all living mortal creatures, but more to the wills of men than of beasts. But all of them are most of all subject to the will of God, to whom all wills also are subject, since they have no power except what He has bestowed upon them. The cause of things, therefore, which makes but is not made, is God; but all other causes both make and are made. Such are all created spirits, and especially the rational. Material causes, therefore, which may rather be said to be made than to make, are not to be reckoned among efficient causes, because they can only do what the wills of spirits do by them. How, then, does an order of causes which is certain to the foreknowledge of God necessitate that there should be nothing which is dependent on our wills, when our wills themselves have a very important place in the order of causes? Cicero, then, contends with those who call this order of causes fatal, or rather designate this order itself by the name of fate; to which we have an abhorrence, especially on account of the word, which men have become accustomed to understand as meaning what is not true. But, whereas he denies that the order of all causes is most certain, and perfectly clear to the prescience of God, we detest his opinion more than the Stoics do. For he either denies that God exists,—which, indeed, in an assumed personage, he has laboured to do, in his book *De Natura Deorum,*—or if he confesses that He exists, but denies that He is prescient of future things, what is that but just "the fool saying in his heart there is no God"? For one who is not prescient of all future things is not God. Wherefore our wills also have just so much power as God willed and foreknew that they should have; and therefore whatever power they have, they have it within most certain limits; and whatever they are to do, they are most assuredly to do, for He whose foreknowledge is infallible foreknew that they would have the power to do it, and would do it. Wherefore, if I should choose to apply the name of fate to anything at all, I should rather say that fate belongs to the weaker of two parties, will to the stronger, who has the other in his power, than that the freedom of our will is excluded by that order of causes, which, by an unusual application of the word peculiar to themselves, the Stoics call *Fate.*

Wherefore, neither is that necessity to be feared, for dread of which the Stoics laboured to make such distinctions among the causes of things as should enable them to rescue certain things from the dominion of necessity, and to subject others to it. Among those things which they wished not to be subject to necessity they placed our wills, knowing that they would not be free if subjected to necessity. For

if that is to be called *our necessity* which is not in our power, but even though we
be unwilling, effects what it can effect,—as, for instance, the necessity of death,—it
is manifest that our wills by which we live uprightly or wickedly are not under such
a necessity; for we do many things which, if we were not willing, we should
certainly not do. This is primarily true of the act of willing itself,—for if we will, it
is; if we will not, it *is* not,—for we should not will if we were unwilling. But if we
define necessity to be that according to which we say that it is necessary that
anything be of such or such a nature, or be done in such and such a manner, I
know not why we should have any dread of that necessity taking away the freedom
of our will. For we do not put the life of God or the foreknowledge of God under
necessity if we should say that it is necessary that God should live for ever, and
foreknow all things; as neither is His power diminished when we say that He cannot
die or fall into error,—for this is in such a way impossible to Him, that if it were
possible for Him, He would be of less power. But assuredly He is rightly called
omnipotent on account of His doing what He wills, not on account of His suffering
what He wills not; for if that should befall Him, He would by no means be
omnipotent. Wherefore, He cannot do some things for the very reason that He is
omnipotent. So also, when we say that it is necessary that, when we will, we will
by free choice, in so saying we both affirm what is true beyond doubt, and do not
still subject our wills thereby to a necessity which destroys liberty. Our wills,
therefore, *exist* as *wills*, and do themselves whatever we do by willing, and which
would not be done if we were unwilling. But when any one suffers anything, being
unwilling, by the will of another, even in that case will retains its essential
validity,—we do not mean the will of the party who inflicts the suffering, for we
resolve it into the power of God. For if a will should simply exist, but not be able
to do what it wills, it would be overborne by a more powerful will. Nor would this
be the case unless there had existed will, and that not the will of the other party,
but the will of him who willed, but was not able to accomplish what he willed.
Therefore, whatsoever a man suffers contrary to his own will, he ought not to
attribute to the will of men, or of angels, or of any created spirit, but rather to His
will who gives power to wills. It is not the case, therefore, that because God
foreknew what would be in the power of our wills, there is for that reason nothing
in the power of our wills. For he who foreknew this did not foreknow nothing.
Moreover, if He who foreknew what would be in the power of our wills did not
foreknow nothing, but something, assuredly, even though He did foreknow, there is
something in the power of our wills. Therefore we are by no means compelled,
either retaining the prescience of God, to take away the freedom of the will, or,
retaining the freedom of the will, to deny that He is prescient of future things,
which is impious. But we embrace both. We faithfully and sincerely confess both.
The former, that we may believe well; the latter, that we may live well. For he lives
ill who does not believe well concerning God. Wherefore, be it far from us, in order
to maintain our freedom, to deny the prescience of Him by whose help we are or
shall be free. Consequently, it is not in vain that laws are enacted, and that
reproaches, exhortations, praises, and vituperations are had recourse to; for these
also He foreknew, and they are of great avail, even as great as He foreknew that

they would be of. Prayers, also, are of avail to procure those things which He foreknew that He would grant to those who offered them; and with justice have rewards been appointed for good deeds, and punishments for sins. For a man does not therefore sin because God foreknew that he would sin. Nay, it cannot be doubted but that it is the man himself who sins when he does sin, because He, whose foreknowledge is infallible, foreknew not that fate, or fortune, or something else would sin, but that the man himself would sin, who, if he wills not, sins not. But if he shall not will to sin, even this did God foreknow.

"DETERMINISM"

Baron Holbach

Motives and the Determination of the Will. In whatever manner man is considered, he is connected to universal nature, and submitted to the necessary and immutable laws that she imposes on all the beings she contains, according to their peculiar essences or to the respective properties with which, without consulting them, she endows each particular species. Man's life is a line that nature commands him to describe upon the surface of the earth, without his ever being able to swerve from it, even for an instant. He is born without his own consent; his organization does in nowise depend upon himself; his ideas come to him involuntarily; his habits are in the power of those who cause him to contract them; he is unceasingly modified by causes, whether visible or concealed, over which he has no control, which necessarily regulate his mode of existence, give the hue to his way of thinking, and determine his manner of acting. He is good or bad, happy or miserable, wise or foolish, reasonable or irrational, without his will being for anything in these various states. Nevertheless, in spite of the shackles by which he is bound, it is pretended he is a free agent, or that independent of the causes by which he is moved, he determines his own will, and regulates his own condition.

However slender the foundation of this opinion, of which everything ought to point out to him the error, it is current at this day and passes for an incontestable truth with a great number of people, otherwise extremely enlightened; it is the basis of religion, which, supposing relations between man and the unknown being she has placed above nature, has been incapable of imagining how man could merit reward or deserve punishment from this being, if he was not a free agent. Society has been believed interested in this system; because an idea has gone abroad, that if all the actions of man were to be contemplated as necessary, the right of punishing those who injure their associates would no longer exist. At length human vanity accommodated itself to a hypothesis which, unquestionably, appears to distinguish man from all other physical beings, by assigning to him the special privilege of a total independence of all other causes, but of which a very little reflection would have shown him the impossibility. . . .

The will, as we have elsewhere said, is a modification of the brain, by which it is disposed to action, or prepared to give play to the organs. This will is necessarily determined by the qualities, good or bad, agreeable or painful, of the object or the motive that acts upon his senses, or of which the idea remains with him, and is resuscitated by his memory. In consequence, he acts necessarily, his action is the result of the impulse he receives either from the motive, from the object, or from the idea which has modified his brain, or disposed his will. When he does not act according to this impulse, it is because there comes some new cause, some new motive, some new idea, which modifies his brain in a different manner, gives him a new impulse, determines his will in another way, by which the action of the former impulse is suspended: thus, the sight of an agreeable object, or its idea, determines his will to set him in action to procure it; but if a new object or a new idea more powerfully attracts him, it gives a new direction to his will, annihilates the effect of the former, and prevents the action by which it was to be procured. This is the mode in which reflection, experience, reason, necessarily arrests or suspends the action of man's will: without this he would of necessity have followed the anterior impulse which carried him towards a then desirable object. In all this he always acts according to necessary laws from which he has no means of emancipating himself.

If when tormented with violent thirst, he figures to himself in idea, or really perceives a fountain, whose limpid streams might cool his feverish want, is he sufficient master of himself to desire or not to desire the object competent to satisfy so lively a want? It will no doubt be conceded, that it is impossible he should not be desirous to satisfy it; but it will be said—if at this moment it is announced to him that the water he so ardently desires is poisoned, he will, notwithstanding his vehement thirst, abstain from drinking it: and it has, therefore, been falsely concluded that he is a free agent. The fact, however, is, that the motive in either case is exactly the same: his own conservation. The same necessity that determined him to drink before he knew the water was deleterious upon this new discovery equally determined him not to drink; the desire of conserving himself either annihilates or suspends the former impulse; the second motive becomes stronger than the preceding, that is, the fear of death, or the desire of preserving himself, necessarily prevails over the painful sensation caused by his eagerness to drink: but, it will be said, if the thirst is very parching, an inconsiderate man without regarding the danger will risk swallowing the water. Nothing is gained by this remark: in this case, the anterior impulse only regains the ascendency; he is persuaded that life may possibly be longer preserved, or that he shall derive a greater good by drinking the poisoned water than by enduring the torment, which, to his mind, threatens instant dissolution; thus the first becomes the strongest and necessarily urges him on to action. Nevertheless, in either case, whether he partakes of the water, or whether he does not, the two actions will be equally necessary; they will be the effect of that motive which finds itself most puissant; which consequently acts in the most coercive manner upon his will.

This example will serve to explain the whole phenomena of the human will. This will, or rather the brain, finds itself in the same situation as a bowl, which, although it has received an impulse that drives it forward in a straight line, is deranged in its course whenever a force superior to the first obliges it to change its direction. The man who drinks the poisoned water appears a madman; but the actions of fools are as necessary as those of the most prudent individuals. The motives that determine the voluptuary and the debauchee to risk their health, are as powerful, and their actions are as necessary, as those which decide the wise man to manage his. But, it will be insisted, the debauchee may be prevailed on to change his conduct: this does not imply that he is a free agent; but that motives may be found sufficiently powerful to annihilate the effect of those that previously acted upon him; then these new motives determine his will to the new mode of conduct he may adopt as necessarily as the former did to the old mode. . . .

The errors of philosophers on the free agency of man, have arisen from their regarding his will as the *primum mobile*, the original motive of his actions; for want of recurring back, they have not perceived the multiplied, the complicated causes which, independently of him, give motion to the will itself; or which dispose and modify his brain, whilst he himself is purely passive in the motion he receives. Is he the master of desiring or not desiring an object that appears desirable to him? Without doubt it will be answered, no: but he is the master of resisting his desire, if he reflects on the consequences. But, I ask, is he capable of reflecting on these consequences, when his soul is hurried along by a very lively passion, which entirely depends upon his natural organization, and the causes by which he is modified? Is it in his power to add to these consequences all the weight necessary to counterbalance his desire? Is he the master of preventing the qualities which render an object desirable from residing in it? I shall be told: he ought to have learned to resist his passions; to contract a habit of putting a curb on his desires. I agree to it without any difficulty. But in reply, I again ask, is his nature susceptible of this modification? Does his boiling blood, his unruly imagination, the igneous fluid that circulates in his veins, permit him to make, enable him to apply true experience in the moment when it is wanted? And even when his temperament has capacitated him, has his education, the examples set before him, the ideas with which he has been inspired in early life, been suitable to make him contract this habit of repressing his desires? Have not all these things rather contributed to induce him to seek with avidity, to make him actually desire those objects which you say he ought to resist?

The *ambitious man* cries out: you will have me resist my passion; but have they not unceasingly repeated to me that rank, honours, power, are the most desirable advantages in life? Have I not seen my fellow citizens envy them, the nobles of my country sacrifice every thing to obtain them? In the society in which I live, am I not obliged to feel, that if I am deprived of these advantages, I must expect to languish in contempt; to cringe under the rod of oppression?

The *miser* says: you forbid me to love money, to seek after the means of acquiring it: alas! does not every thing tell me that, in this world, money is the greatest blessing; that it is amply sufficient to render me happy? In the country I inhabit, do I not see all my fellow citizens covetous of riches? but do I not also witness that they are little scrupulous in the means of obtaining wealth? As soon as they are enriched by the means which you censure, are they not cherished, considered and respected? By what authority, then, do you defend me from amassing treasure? What right have you to prevent my using means, which, although you call them sordid and criminal, I see approved by the sovereign? Will you have me renounce my happiness?

The *voluptuary* argues: you pretend that I should resist my desires; but was I the maker of my own temperament, which unceasingly invites me to pleasure? You call my pleasures disgraceful; but in the country in which I live, do I not witness the most dissipated men enjoying the most distinguished rank? Do I not behold that no one is ashamed of adultery but the husband it has outraged? Do not I see men making trophies of their debaucheries, boasting of their libertinism, rewarded with applause?

The *choleric man* vociferates: you advise me to put a curb on my passions, and to resist the desire of avenging myself: but can I conquer my nature? Can I alter the received opinions of the world? Shall I not be forever disgraced, infallibly dishonoured in society, if I do not wash out in the blood of my fellow creatures the injuries I have received?

The *zealous enthusiast* exclaims: you recommend me mildness; you advise me to be tolerant; to be indulgent to the opinions of my fellow men; but is not my temperament violent? Do I not ardently love my God? Do they not assure me, that zeal is pleasing to him; that sanguinary inhuman persecutors have been his friends? As I wish to render myself acceptable in his sight, I therefore adopt the same means.

In short, the actions of man are never free; they are always the necessary consequence of his temperament, of the received ideas, and of the notions, either true or false, which he has formed to himself of happiness; of his opinions, strengthened by example, by education, and by daily experience. So many crimes are witnessed on the earth only because every thing conspires to render man vicious and criminal; the religion he has adopted, his government, his education, the examples set before him, irresistibly drive him on to evil: under these circumstances, morality preaches virtue to him in vain. In those societies where vice is esteemed, where crime is crowned, where venality is constantly recompensed, where the most dreadful disorders are punished only in those who are too weak to enjoy the privilege of committing them with impunity, the practice of virtue is considered nothing more than a painful sacrifice of happiness. Such societies chastise, in the lower orders, those excesses which they respect in the higher ranks; and frequently have the injustice to condemn those in the penalty of death, whom public prejudices, maintained by constant example, have rendered criminal.

Man, then, is not a free agent in any one instant of his life; he is necessarily guided in each step by those advantages, whether real or fictitious, that he attaches to the objects by which his passions are roused: these passions themselves are necessary in a being who unceasingly tends towards his own happiness; their energy is necessary, since that depends on his temperament; his temperament is necessary, because it depends on the physical elements which enter into his composition; the modification of this temperament is necessary, as it is the infallible and inevitable consequence of the impulse he receives from the incessant action of moral and physical beings.

Choice Does Not Prove Freedom. In spite of these proofs of the want of free agency in man, so clear to unprejudiced minds, it will, perhaps be insisted upon with no small feeling of triumph, that if it be proposed to any one, to move or not to move his hand, an action in the number of those called indifferent, he evidently appears to be the master of choosing; from which it is concluded that evidence has been offered of free agency. The reply is, this example is perfectly simple; man in performing some action which he is resolved on doing, does not by any means prove his free agency: the very desire of displaying this quality, excited by the dispute, becomes a necessary motive, which decides his will either for the one or the other of these actions: What deludes him in this instance, or that which persuades him he is a free agent at this moment, is, that he does not discern the true motive which sets him in action, namely, the desire of convincing his opponent: if in the heat of the dispute he insists and asks, "Am I not the master of throwing myself out of the window?" I shall answer him, no; that whilst he preserves his reason there is no probability that the desire of proving his free agency, will become a motive sufficiently powerful to make him sacrifice his life to the attempt: if, notwithstanding this, to prove he is a free agent, he should actually precipitate himself from the window, it would not be a sufficient warranty to conclude he acted freely, but rather that it was the violence of his temperament which spurred him on to this folly. Madness is a state, that depends upon the heat of the blood, not upon the will. A fanatic or a hero, braves death as necessarily as a more phlegmatic man or coward flies from it.

There is, in point of fact, no difference between the man that is cast out of the window by another, and the man who throws himself out of it, except that the impulse in the first instance comes immediately from without whilst that which determines the fall in the second case, springs from within his own peculiar machine, having its more remote cause also exterior. When Mutius Scaevola held his hand in the fire, he was as much acting under the influence of necessity (caused by interior motives) that urged him to this strange action, as if his arm had been held by strong men: pride, despair, the desire of braving his enemy, a wish to astonish him, and anxiety to intimidate him, etc., were the invisible chains that held his hand bound to the fire. The love of glory, enthusiasm for their country, in like manner caused Codrus and Decius to devote themselves for their fellow-citizens. The Indian Colanus and the philosopher Peregrinus were equally obliged to burn themselves, by desire of exciting the astonishment of the Grecian assembly.

It is said that free agency is the absence of those obstacles competent to oppose themselves to the actions of man, or to the exercise of his faculties: it is pretended that he is a free agent whenever, making use of these faculties, he produces the effect he has proposed to himself. In reply to this reasoning, it is sufficient to consider that it in nowise depends upon himself to place or remove the obstacles that either determine or resist him; the motive that causes his action is no more in his own power than the obstacle that impedes him, whether this obstacle or motive be within his own machine or exterior of his person: he is not master of the thought presented to his mind, which determines his will; this thought is excited by some cause independent of himself.

To be undeceived on the system of his free agency, man has simply to recur to the motive by which his will is determined; he will always find this motive is out of his own control. It is said: that in consequence of an idea to which the mind gives birth, man acts freely if he encounters no obstacle. But the question is, what gives birth to this idea in his brain? was he the master either to prevent it from presenting itself, or from renewing itself in his brain? Does not this idea depend either upon objects that strike him exteriorly and in despite of himself, or upon causes, that without his knowledge, act within himself and modify his brain? Can he prevent his eyes, cast without design upon any object whatever, from giving him an idea of this object, and from moving his brain? He is not more master of the obstacles; they are the necessary effects of either interior or exterior causes, which always act according to their given properties. A man insults a coward; this necessarily irritates him against his insulter; but his will cannot vanquish the obstacle that cowardice places to the object of his desire, because his natural conformation, which does not depend upon himself, prevents his having courage. In this case, the coward is insulted in spite of himself; and against his will is obliged patiently to brook the insult he has received.

Absence of Restraint Is Not Absence of Necessity. The partisans of the system of free agency appear ever to have confounded constraint with necessity. Man believes he acts as a free agent, every time he does not see any thing that places obstacles to his actions; he does not perceive that the motive which causes him to will, is always necessary and independent of himself. A prisoner loaded with chains is compelled to remain in prison; but he is not a free agent in the desire to emancipate himself; his chains prevent him from acting, but they do not prevent him from willing; he would save himself if they would loose his fetters; but he would not save himself as a free agent; fear or the idea of punishment would be sufficient motives for his action.

Man may, therefore, cease to be restrained, without, for that reason, becoming a free agent: in whatever manner he acts, he will act necessarily, according to motives by which he shall be determined. He may be compared to a heavy body that finds itself arrested in its descent by any obstacle whatever: take away this obstacle, it will gravitate or continue to fall; but who shall say this dense body is free to fall or not? Is not its descent the necessary effect of its own specific gravity? The virtuous Socrates submitted to the laws of his country, although they were unjust; and though the doors of his jail were left open to him, he would not save himself; but in this he did not act as a free agent: the invisible chains of opinion, the secret love of decorum, the inward respect for the laws, even when they were iniquitous, the fear of tarnishing his glory, kept him in his prison; they were motives sufficiently powerful with this enthusiast for virtue, to induce him to wait death with tranquility; it was not in his power to save himself, because he could find no potential motive to bring him to depart, even for an instant, from those principles to which his mind was accustomed.

Man, it is said, frequently acts against his inclination, from whence it is falsely concluded he is a free agent; but when he appears to act contrary to his inclination, he is always determined to it by some motive sufficiently efficacious to vanquish this inclination. A sick man, with a view to his cure, arrives at conquering his repugnance to the most disgusting remedies: the fear of pain, or the dread of death, then become necessary motives; consequently this sick man cannot be said to act freely.

When it is said, that man is not a free agent, it is not pretended to compare him to a body moved by a simple impulsive cause: he contains within himself causes inherent to his existence; he is moved by an interior organ, which has its own peculiar laws, and is itself necessarily determined in consequence of ideas formed from perception resulting from sensation which it receives from exterior objects. As the mechanism of these sensations, of these perceptions, and the manner they engrave ideas on the brain of man, are not known to him; because he is unable to unravel all these motions; because he cannot perceive the chain of operations in his soul, or the motive principle that acts within him, he supposes himself a free agent; which literally translated, signifies, that he moves himself by himself; that he determines himself without cause: when he rather ought to say, that he is ignorant how or why he acts in the manner he does. It is true the soul enjoys an activity peculiar to itself: but it is equally certain that this activity would never be displayed, if some motive or some cause did not put it in a condition to exercise itself: at least it will not be pretended that the soul is able either to love or to hate without being moved, without knowing the objects, without having some idea of their qualities. Gunpowder has unquestionably a particular activity, but this activity will never display itself, unless fire be applied to it; this, however, immediately sets it in motion.

The Complexity of Human Conduct and the Illusion of Free Agency. It is the great complication of motion in man, it is the variety of his action, it is the multiplicity of causes that move him, whether simultaneously or in continual succession, that persuades him he is a free agent: if all his motions were simple, if the causes that move him did not confound themselves with each other, if they were distinct, if his machine were less complicated, he would perceive that all his actions were necessary, because he would be enabled to recur instantly to the cause that made him act. A man who should be always obliged to go towards the west, would always go on that side; but he would feel that, in so going, he was not a free agent: if he had another sense, as his actions or his motion, augmented by a sixth, would be still more varied and much more complicated, he would believe himself still more a free agent than he does with his five senses.

It is, then, for want of recurring to the causes that move him; for want of being able to analyze, from not being competent to decompose the complicated motion of his machine, that man believes himself a free agent: it is only upon his own ignorance that he founds the profound yet deceitful notion he has of his free agency; that he builds those opinions which he brings forward as a striking proof of his pretended freedom of action. If, for a short time, each man was willing to examine his own peculiar actions, search out their true motives to discover their concatenation, he would remain convinced that the sentiment he has of his natural free agency, is a chimera that must speedily be destroyed by experience.

Nevertheless it must be acknowledged that the multiplicity and diversity of the causes which continually act upon man, frequently without even his knowledge, render it impossible, or at least extremely difficult for him to recur to the true principles of his own peculiar actions, much less the actions of others: they frequently depend upon causes so fugitive, so remote from their effects, and which, superficially examined, appear to have so little analogy, so slender a relation with them, that it requires singular sagacity to bring them into light. This is what renders the study of the moral man a task of such difficulty; this is the reason why his heart is an abyss, of which it is frequently impossible for him to fathom the depth. . . .

If he understood the play of his organs, if he were able to recall to himself all the impulsions they have received, all the modifications they have undergone, all the effects they have produced, he would perceive that all his actions are submitted to that fatality, which regulates his own particular system, as it does the entire system of the universe: no one effect in him, any more than in nature, produces itself by chance; this, as has been before proved, is word void of sense. All that passes in him; all that is done by him; as well as all that happens in nature, or that is attributed to her, is derived from necessary causes, which act according to necessary laws, and which produce necessary effects from whence necessarily flow others.

Fatality, is the eternal, the immutable, the necessary order, established in nature; or the indispensable connexion of causes that act, with the effects they operate. Conforming to this order, heavy bodies fall: light bodies rise; that which is analogous in matter reciprocally attracts; that which is heterogeneous mutually repels; man congregates himself in society, modifies each his fellow; becomes either virtuous or wicked; either contributes to his mutual happiness, or reciprocates his misery; either loves his neighbour, or hates his companion necessarily, according to the manner in which the one acts upon the other. From whence it may be seen, that the same necessity which regulates the physical, also regulates the moral world, in which every thing is in consequence submitted to fatality. Man, in running over, frequently without his own knowledge, often in spite of himself, the route which nature has marked out for him, resembles a swimmer who is obliged to follow the current that carries him along: he believes himself a free agent, because he some-times consents, sometimes does not consent, to glide with the stream, which, notwithstanding, always hurries him forward; he believes himself the master of his condition, because he is obliged to use his arms under the fear of sinking. . . .

"THE RECONCILIATION OF
LIBERTY AND NECESSITY"

David Hume
Part I

It might reasonably be expected, in questions which have been canvassed and disputed with great eagerness since the first origin of science and philosophy, that the meaning of all the terms, at least, should have been agreed upon among the disputants, and our inquiries, in the course of two thousand years, been able to pass from words to the true and real subject of the controversy. For how easy may it seem to give exact definitions of the terms employed in reasoning, and make these definitions, not the mere sound of works, the object of future scrutiny and examination? But if we consider the matter more narrowly, we shall be apt to draw a quite opposite conclusion. From this circumstance alone, that a controversy has been long kept on foot and remains still undecided, we may presume that there is some ambiguity in the expression, and that the disputants affix different ideas to the terms employed in the controversy. For as the faculties of the mind are supposed to be naturally alike in every individual—otherwise nothing could be more fruitless than to reason or dispute together—it were impossible, if men affix the same ideas to their terms, that they could so long form different opinions of the same subject, especially when they communicate their views and each party turn themselves on all sides in search of arguments which may give them the victory over their antagonists. It is true, if men attempt the discussion of questions which lie entirely beyond the reach of human capacity, such as those concerning the origin of worlds or the economy of the intellectual system or region of spirits, they may long beat the air in their fruitless contests and never arrive at any determinate conclusion. But if the question regard any subject of common life and experience, nothing, one would think, could preserve the dispute so long undecided, but some ambiguous expressions which keep the antagonists still at a distance and hinder them from grappling with each other.

This has been the case in the long-disputed question concerning liberty and necessity, and to so remarkable a degree that, if I be not much mistaken, we shall find that all mankind, both learned and ignorant, have always been of the same opinion with regard to this subject, and that a few intelligible definitions would immediately have put an end to the whole controversy. I own that this dispute has been so much canvassed on all hands, and has led philosophers into such a labyrinth of obscure sophistry, that it is no wonder if a sensible reader indulge his ease so far as to turn a deaf ear to the proposal of such a question from which he can expect neither instruction nor entertainment. But the state of the argument here proposed may, perhaps, serve to renew his attention, as it has more novelty, promises at least some decision of the controversy, and will not much disturb his ease by any intricate or obscure reasoning.

I hope, therefore, to make it appear that all men have ever agreed in the doctrine both of necessity and of liberty, according to any reasonable sense which can be put on these terms, and that the whole controversy has hitherto turned merely upon words. We shall begin with examining the doctrine of necessity.

It is universally allowed that matter, in all its operations, is actuated by a necessary force, and that every natural effect is so precisely determined by the energy of its cause that no other effect, in such particular circumstances, could possibly have resulted from it. The degree and direction of every motion is, by the laws of nature, prescribed with such exactness that a living creature may as soon arise from the shock of two bodies, as motion, in any other degree or direction than what is actually produced by it. Would we, therefore, form a just and precise idea of *necessity*, we must consider whence that idea arises when we apply it to the operation of bodies.

It seems evident that, if all the scenes of nature were continually shifted in such a manner that no two events bore any resemblance to each other, but every object was entirely new, without any similitude to whatever had been seen before, we should never, in that case, have attained the least idea of necessity or of a connection among these objects. We might say, upon such a supposition, that one object or event has followed another, not that one was produced by the other. The relation of cause and effect must be utterly unknown to mankind. Inference and reasoning concerning the operations of nature would, from that moment, be at an end; and the memory and senses remain the only canals by which the knowledge of any real existence could possibly have access to the mind. Our idea, therefore, of necessity and causation arises entirely from the uniformity observable in the operations of nature, where similar objects are constantly conjoined together, and the mind is determined by custom to infer the one from the appearance of the other. These two circumstances form the whole of that necessity which we ascribe to matter. Beyond the constant *conjunction* of similar objects and the consequent *inference* from one to the other, we have no notion of any necessity of connection.

If it appear, therefore, that all mankind have ever allowed, without any doubt or hesitation, that these two circumstances take place in the voluntary actions of men and in the operations of mind, it must follow that all mankind have ever agreed in the doctrine of necessity, and that they have hitherto disputed merely for not understanding each other.

As to the first circumstance, the constant and regular conjunction of similar events, we may possibly satisfy ourselves by the following considerations. It is universally acknowledged that there is a great uniformity among the actions of men, in all nations and ages, and that human nature remains still the same in its principles and operations. The same motives always produce the same actions; the same events follow from the same causes. Ambition, avarice, self-love, vanity, friendship, generosity, public spirit—these passions, mixed in various degrees and distributed through society, have been, from the beginning of the world, and still are, the source of all the actions and enterprises which have ever been observed among mankind. Would you know the sentiments, inclinations, and course of life of the Greeks and Romans? Study well the temper and actions of the French and English: you cannot be much mistaken in transferring to the former *most* of the observations which you have made with regard to the latter. Mankind are so much the same, in all times and places, that history informs us of nothing new or strange in the particular. Its chief use is only to discover the constant and universal principles of human nature by showing men in all varieties of circumstances and situations, and furnishing us with materials from which we may form our observations and become acquainted with the regular springs of human action and behavior. These records of wars, intrigues, factions, and revolutions are so many collections of experiments by which the politician or moral philosopher fixes the principles of his science, in the same manner as the physician or natural philosopher becomes acquainted with the nature of plants, minerals, and other external objects, by the experiments which he forms concerning them. Nor are the earth, water, and other elements examined by Aristotle and Hippocrates more like to those which at present lie under our observation than the men described by Polybius and Tacitus are to those who now govern the world.

Should a traveler, returning from a far country, bring us an account of men wholly different from any with whom we were ever acquainted, men who were entirely divested of avarice, ambition, or revenge, who knew no pleasure but friendship, generosity, and public spirit, we should immediately, from these circumstances, detect the falsehood and prove him a liar with the same certainty as if he had stuffed his narration with stories of centaurs and dragons, miracles and prodigies. And if we would explode any forgery in history, we cannot make use of a more convincing argument than to prove that the actions ascribed to any person are directly contrary to the course of nature, and that no human motives, in such circumstances, could ever induce him to such a conduct. The veracity of Quintus Curtius is as much to be suspected when he describes the supernatural courage of Alexander by which he was hurried on singly to attack multitudes, as when he describes his supernatural force and activity by which he was able to resist them. So readily and universally do we acknowledge a uniformity in human motives and actions as well as in the operations of body.

Hence, likewise, the benefit of that experience acquired by long life and a variety of business and company, in order to instruct us in the principles of human nature and regulate our future conduct as well as speculation. By means of this guide we mount up to the knowledge of men's inclinations and motives from their actions, expressions, and even gestures, and again descend to the interpretation of their actions from our knowledge of their motives and inclinations. The general observations, treasured up by a course of experience, give us the clue of human nature and teach us to unravel all its intricacies. Pretexts and appearances no longer deceive us. Public declarations pass for the specious coloring of a cause. And though virtue and honor be allowed their proper weight and authority, that perfect disinterestedness, so often pretended to, is never expected in multitudes and parties, seldom in their leaders, and scarcely even in individuals of any rank or station. But were there no uniformity in human actions, and were every experiment which we could form of this kind irregular and anomalous, it were impossible to collect any general observations concerning mankind, and no experience, however accurately digested by reflection, would ever serve to any purpose. Why is the aged husbandman more skillful in his calling than the young beginner, but because there is a certain uniformity in the operation of the sun, rain, and earth toward the production of vegetables, and experience teaches the old practitioner the rules by which this operation is governed and directed?

We must not, however, expect that this uniformity of human actions should be carried to such a length as that all men, in the same circumstances, will always act precisely in the same manner, without making any allowance for the diversity of characters, prejudices, and opinions. Such a uniformity, in every particular, is found in no part of nature. On the contrary, from observing the variety of conduct in different men we are enabled to form a greater variety of maxims which still suppose a degree of uniformity and regularity.

Are the manners of men different in different ages and countries? We learn thence the great force of custom and education, which mold the human mind from its infancy and form it into a fixed and established character. Is the behavior and conduct of the one sex very unlike that of the other? It is thence we become acquainted with the different characters which nature has impressed upon the sexes, and which she preserves with constancy and regularity. Are the actions of the same person much diversified in the different periods of his life from infancy to old age? This affords room for many general observations concerning the gradual change of our sentiments and inclinations, and the different maxims which prevail in the different ages of human creatures. Even the characters which are peculiar to each individual have a uniformity in their influence, otherwise our acquaintance with the persons, and our observations of their conduct, could never teach us their dispositions or serve to direct our behavior with regard to them.

I grant it possible to find actions which seem to have no regular connection with any known motives and are exceptions to all the measures of conduct which have ever been established for the government of men. But if we could willingly know what judgment should be formed of such irregular and extraordinary actions, we may consider the sentiments commonly entertained with regard to those irregular events which appear in the course of nature and the operations of eternal objects. All causes are not conjoined to their usual effects with like uniformity. An artificer who handles only dead matter may be disappointed of his aim, as well as the politician who directs the conduct of sensible and intelligent agents.

The vulgar, who take things according to their first appearance, attribute the uncertainty of events to such an uncertainty in the causes as makes the latter often fail of their usual influence, though they meet with no impediment in their operation. But philosophers, observing that almost in every part of nature there is contained a vast variety of springs and principles which are hid by reason of their minuteness or remoteness, find that it is at least possible the contrariety of events may not proceed from any contingency in the cause but from the secret operation of contrary causes. This possibility is converted into certainty by further observation, when they remark that, upon an exact scrutiny, a contrariety of effects always betrays a contrariety of causes and proceeds from their mutual opposition. A peasant can give no better reason for the stopping of any clock or watch than to say that it does not commonly go right. But an artist easily perceives that the same force in the spring or pendulum has always the same influence on the wheels, but fails of its usual effect perhaps by reason of a grain of dust which puts a stop to the whole movement. From the observation of several parallel instances philosophers form a maxim that the connection between all causes and effects is equally necessary, and that its seeming uncertainty in some instances proceeds from the secret opposition of contrary causes.

Thus, for instance, in the human body, when the usual symptoms of health or sickness disappoint our expectation, when medicines operate not with their wonted powers, when irregular events follow from any particular cause, the philosopher and physician are not surprised at the matter, nor are ever tempted to deny, in general, the necessity and uniformity of those principles by which the animal economy is conducted. They know that a human body is a mighty complicated machine, that many secret powers lurk in it which are altogether beyond our comprehension, that to us it must often appear very uncertain in its operations, and that, therefore, the irregular events which outwardly discover themslves can be no proof that the laws of nature are not observed with the greatest regularity in its internal operations.

The philosopher, if he be consistent, must apply the same reasonings to the actions and volitions of intelligent agents. The most irregular and unexpected resolutions of men may frequently be accounted for by those who know every particular circumstance of their character and situation. A person of an obliging disposition gives a peevish answer; but he has the toothache, or has not dined. A stupid fellow discovers an uncommon alacrity in his carriage; but he has met with a sudden piece of good fortune. Or even when an action, as sometimes happens, cannot be particularly accounted for, either by the person himself or by others, we know, in general, that the characters of men are to a certain degree inconstant and irregular. This is, in a manner, the constant character of human nature, though it be applicable, in a more particular manner, to some persons who have no fixed rule for their conduct, but proceed in a continual course of caprice and inconstancy. The internal principles and motives may operate in a uniform manner, notwithstanding these seeming irregularities—in the same manner as the winds, rains, clouds, and other variations of the weather are supposed to be governed by steady principles, though not easily discoverable by human sagacity and inquiry.

Thus it appears not only that the conjunction between motives and voluntary actions is as regular and uniform as that between the cause and effect in any part of nature, but also that this regular conjunction has been universally acknowledged among mankind and has never been the subject of dispute either in philosophy or common life. Now, as it is from past experience that we draw all inferences concerning the future, and as we conclude that objects will always be conjoined together which we find to have always been conjoined, it may seem superfluous to prove that this experienced uniformity in human actions is a source when we draw *inferences* concerning them. But in order to throw the argument into a greater variety of lights, we shall also insist, though briefly, on this latter topic.

The mutual dependence of men is so great in all societies that scarce any human action is entirely complete in itself or is performed without some reference to the actions of others, which are requisite to make it answer fully the intention of the agent. The poorest artificer who labors alone expects at least the protection of the magistrate to insure him thy enjoyment of the fruits of his labor. He also expects that when he carries his goods to market and offers them at a reasonable price, he shall find purchasers and shall be able, by the money he acquires, to engage others to supply him with those commodities which are requisite for his subsistence. In porportion as men extend their dealings and render their intercourse with others more complicated, they always comprehend in their schemes of life a greater variety of voluntary actions which they expect, from the proper motives, to co-operate with their own. In all these conclusions they take their measures from past experience, in the same manner as in their reasonings concerning external objects, and firmly believe that men, as well as all the elements, are to continue in their operations the same that they have ever found them. A manufacturer reckons upon the labor of his servants for the execution of any work as much as upon the tools which he employs, and would be equally surprised were his expectations disappointed. In short, this experimental inference and reasoning concerning the actions of others enters so much into human life that no man, while awake, is ever a moment without employing it. Have we not reason, therefore, to affirm that all mankind have always agreed in the doctrine of necessity, according to the foregoing definition and explication of it?

Nor have philosophers ever entertained a different opinion from the people in this particular. For, not to mention that almost every action of their life supposes that opinion, there are even few of the speculative parts of learning to which it is not essential. What would become of *history* had we not a dependence on the veracity of the historian according to the experience which we have had of mankind? How could *politics* be a science if laws and forms of government had not a uniform influence upon society? Where would be the foundation of *morals* if particular characters had no certain or determinate power to produce particular sentiments, and if these sentiments had no constant operation on actions? And with what pretense could we employ our *criticism* upon any poet or polite author if we could not pronounce the conduct and sentiments of his actors either natural or unnatural to such characters and in such circumstances? It seems almost impossible, therefore, to engage either in science or action of any kind without acknowledging the doctrine of necessity, and this *inference* from motives to voluntary action, from characters to conduct.

And, indeed, when we consider how aptly *natural* and *moral* evidence link together and form only one chain of argument, we shall make no scruple to allow that they are of the same nature and derived from the same principles. A prisoner who has neither money nor interest discovers the impossibility of his escape as well when he considers the obstinacy of the jailer as the walls and bars with which he is surrounded, and in all attempts for his freedom chooses rather to work upon the stone and iron of the one than upon the inflexible nature of the other. The same prisoner, when conducted to the scaffold, foresees his death as certainly from the constancy and fidelity of his guards as from the operation of the ax or wheel. His mind runs along a certain train of ideas: the refusal of the soldiers to consent to his escape; the action of the executioner; the separation of the head and body; bleeding, convulsive motions, and death. Here is a connected chain of natural causes and voluntary actions, but the mind feels no difference between them in passing from one link to another, nor is less certain of the future event than if it were connected with the objects present to the memory or senses by a train of causes cemented together by what we are pleased to call a "physical" necessity. The same experienced union has the same effect on the mind, whether the united objects be motives, volition, and actions, or figure and motion. We may change the names of things, but their nature and their operation on the understanding never change.

Were a man whom I know to be honest and opulent, and with whom I lived in intimate friendship, to come into my house, where I am surrounded with my servants, I rest assured that he is not to stab me before he leaves it in order to rob me of my silver standish; and I no more suspect this event than the falling of the house itself, which is new and solidly built and founded.—*But he may have been seized with a sudden and unknown frenzy.*—So may a sudden earthquake arise, and shake and tumble my house about my ears. I shall, therefore, change the suppositions. I shall say that I know with certainty that he is not to put his hand into the fire and hold it there till it be consumed. And this event I think I can foretell with the same assurance as that, if he throw himself out of the window and meet with no obstruction, he will not remain a moment suspended in the air. No suspicion of an unknown frenzy can give the least possibility to the former event which is so contrary to all the known principles of human nature. A man who at noon leaves his purse full of gold on the pavement at Charing Cross may as well expect that it will fly away like a feather as that he will find it untouched an hour after. Above one-half of human reasonings contain inferences of a similar nature, attended with more or less degrees of certainty, proportioned to our experience of the usual conduct of mankind in such particular situations.

I have frequently considered what could possibly be the reason why all mankind, though they have ever, without hesitation, acknowledged the doctrine of necessity in their whole practice and reasoning, have yet discovered such a reluctance to acknowledge it in words, and have rather shown a propensity, in all ages, to profess the contrary opinion. The matter, I think, may be accounted for after the following manner. If we examine the operations of body and the production of effects from their causes, we shall find that all our faculties can never carry us further in our knowledge of this relation than barely to observe that particular objects are *constantly conjoined* together, and that the mind is carried, by a *customary transition*, from the appearance of the one to the belief of the other. But though this conclusion concerning human ignorance be the result of the strictest scrutiny of this subject, men still entertain a strong propensity to believe that they penetrate further into the powers of nature and perceive something like a necessary connection between the cause and the effect. When, again, they turn their reflections toward the operations of their own minds and *feel* no such connection of the motive and the action, they are thence apt to suppose that there is a difference between the effects which result from material force and those which arise from thought and intelligence. But being once convinced that we know nothing further of causation of any kind than merely the *constant conjunction* of objects and the consequent *inference* of the mind from one to another, and finding that these two circumstances are universally allowed to have place in voluntary actions, we may be more easily led to own the same necessity common to all causes. And though this reasoning may contradict the systems of many philosophers in ascribing necessity to the determinations of the will, we shall find, upon reflection, that they dissent from it in words only, not in their real sentiments. Necessity, according to the sense in which it is here taken, has never yet been rejected, nor can ever, I think, be rejected by any philosopher. It may only, perhaps, be pretended that the mind can perceive in the operations of matter some further connection between the cause and effect, and a connection that has not place in the voluntary actions of intelligent beings. Now, whether it be so or not can only appear upon examination, and it is incumbent on these philosophers to make good their assertion by defining or describing that necessity and pointing it out to us in the operations of material causes.

It would seem, indeed, that men begin at the wrong end of this question concerning liberty and necessity when they enter upon it by examining the faculties of the soul, the influence of the understanding, and the operations of the will. Let them first discuss a more simple question, namely, the question of body and brute unintelligent matter, and try whether they can there form any idea of causation and necessity, except that of a constant conjunction of objects and subsequent inference of the mind from one to another. If these circumstances form, in reality, the whole of that necessity which we conceive in matter, and if these circumstances be also universally acknowledged to take place in the operations of the mind, the dispute is at an end; at least, must be owned to be thenceforth merely verbal. But as long as we will rashly suppose that we have some further idea of necessity and causation in the operations of external objects, at the same time that we can find nothing further in the voluntary actions of the mind, there is no possibility of bringing the question to any determinate issue while we proceed upon so erroneous a supposition. The only method of undeceiving us is to mount up higher, to examine the narrow extent of science when applied to material causes, and to convince ourselves that all we know of them is the constant conjunction and inference above mentioned. We may, perhaps, find that it is with difficulty we are induced to fix such narrow limits to human understanding, but we can afterwards find no difficulty when we come to apply this doctrine to the actions of the will. For as it is evident that these have a regular conjunction with motives and circumstances and character, and as we always draw inferences from one to the other, we must be obliged to acknowledge in words that necessity which we have already avowed in every deliberation of our lives and in every step of our conduct and behavior.[1]

[1] The prevalence of the doctrine of liberty may be accounted for from another cause, viz., a false sensation, or seeming experience, which we have, or may have, of liberty or indifference in many of our actions. The necessity of any action, whether of matter or of mind, is not,

But to proceed in this reconciling project with regard to the question of liberty and necessity—the most contentious question of metaphysics, the most contentious science—it will not require many words to prove that all mankind have ever agreed in the doctrine of liberty as well as in that of necessity, and that the whole dispute, in this respect also, has been hitherto merely verbal. For what is meant by liberty when applied to voluntary actions? We cannot surely mean that actions have so little connection with motives, inclinations, and circumstances that one does not follow with a certain degree of uniformity from the other, and that one affords no inference by which we can conclude the existence of the other. For these are plain and acknowledged matters of fact. By liberty, then, we can only mean *a power of acting or not acting according to the determinations of the will*; that is, if we choose to remain at rest, we may; if we choose to move, we also may. Now this hypothetical liberty is universally allowed to belong to everyone who is not a prisoner and in chains. Here then is no subject of dispute.

Whatever definition we may give of liberty, we should be careful to observe two requisite circumstances: *first*, that it be consistent with plain matter of fact; *secondly*, that it be consistent with itself. If we observe these circumstances and render our definition intelligible, I am persuaded that all mankind will be found of one opinion with regard to it.

It is universally allowed that nothing exists without a cause of its existence, and that chance, when strictly examined, is a mere negative word and means not any real power which has anywhere a being in nature. But it is pretended that some causes are necessary, some not necessary. Here then is the advantage of definitions. Let anyone *define* a cause without comprehending, as a part of the definition, a *necessary connection* with its effect, and let him show distinctly the origin of the idea expressed by the definition, and I shall readily give up the whole controversy. But if the foregoing explication of the matter be received, this must be absolutely impracticable. Had not objects a regular conjunction with each other, we should

properly speaking, a quality in the agent but in any thinking or intelligent being who may consider the action; and it consists chiefly in the determination of his thoughts to infer the existence of that action from some preceding objects; as liberty, when opposed to necessity, is nothing but the want of that determination, and a certain looseness or indifference which we feel in passing, or not passing, from the idea of one object to that of any succeeding one. Now we may observe that though, in *reflecting* on human actions, we seldom feel such a looseness or indifference, but are commonly able to infer them with considerable certainty from their motives, and from the disposition of the agent; yet it frequently happens that, in *performing* the actions themselves, we are sensible of something like it; and as all resembling objects are readily taken for each other, this has been employed as a demonstrative and even intuitive proof of human liberty. We feel that our actions are subject to our will on most occasions, and imagine we feel that the will itself is subject to nothing, because, when by a denial of it we are provoked to try, we feel that it moves easily every way, and produces an image of itself (or a "velleity," as it is called in the schools), even on that side on which it did not settle. This image, or faint motion, we persuade ourselves, could at that time have been completed into the thing itself, because, should that be denied, we find upon a second trial that at present it can. We consider not that the fantastical desire of showing liberty is here the motive of our actions. And it seems certain that however we may imagine we feel a liberty within ourselves, a spectator can commonly infer our actions from our motives and character; and even where he cannot, he concludes in general that he might, were he perfectly acquainted with every circumstance of our situation and temper, and the most secret springs of our complexion and disposition. Now this is the very essence of necessity, according to the foregoing doctrine.

never have entertained any notion of cause and effect; and this regular conjunction produces that inference of the understanding which is the only connection that we can have any comprehension of. Whoever attempts a definition of cause exclusive of these circumstances will be obliged either to employ unintelligible terms or such as are synonymous to the term which he endeavors to define.[2] And if the definition above mentioned be admitted, liberty, when opposed to necessity, not to constraint, is the same thing with chance, which is universally allowed to have no existence.

Part II

There is no method of reasoning more common, and yet none more blamable, than in philosophical disputes to endeavor the refutation of any hypothesis by a pretense of its dangerous consquences to religion and morality. When any opinion leads to absurdity, it is certainly false; but it is not certain that an opinion is false because it is of dangerous consequence. Such topics, therefore, ought entirely to be forborne as serving nothing to the discovery of truth, but only to make the person of an antagonist odious. This I observe in general, without pretending to draw any advantage from it. I frankly submit to an examination of this kind, and shall venture to affirm that the doctrines both of necessity and liberty, as above explained, are not only consistent with morality, but are absolutely essential to its support.

Necessity may be defined two ways, conformably to the two definitions of *cause* of which it makes an essential part. It consists either in the constant conjunction of like objects or in the inference of the understanding from one object to another. Now necessity, in both these senses (which, indeed, are at bottom the same), has universally, though tacitly, in the schools, in the pulpit, and in common life been allowed to belong to the will of man, and no one has ever pretended to deny that we can draw inferences concerning human actions, and that those inferences are founded on the experienced union of like actions, with like motives, inclinations, and circumstances. The only particular in which anyone can differ is that either perhaps he will refuse to give the name of necessity to this property of human actions—but as long as the meaning is understood I hope the word can do no harm—or that he will maintain it possible to discover something further in the operations of matter. But this, it must be acknowledged, can be of no consquence to morality or religion, whatever it may be to natural philosophy or metaphysics. We may here be mistaken in asserting that there is no idea of any other necessity or connection in the actions of the body, but surely we ascribe nothing to the actions of the mind but what everyone does and must readily allow of. We change no circumstance in the received orthodox system with regard to the will, but only in that with regard to material objects and causes. Nothing, therefore, can be more innocent at least than this doctrine.

---

[2] Thus, if a cause be defined, *that which produces anything*, it is easy to observe that *producing* is synonymous to *causing*. In like manner, if a cause be defined, *that by which anything exists*, this is liable to the same objection. For what is meant by these words, *"by which"*? Had it been said that a cause is *that* after which *anything constantly exists*, we should have understood the terms. For this is, indeed, all we know of the matter. And this constancy forms the very essence of necessity, nor have we any other idea of it.

All laws being founded on rewards and punishments, it is supposed, as a fundamental principle, that these motives have a regular and uniform influence on the mind and both produce the good and prevent the evil actions. We may give to this influence what name we please; but as it is usually conjoined with the action, it must be esteemed a *cause* and be looked upon as an instance of that necessity which we would here establish.

The only proper object of hatred or vengeance is a person or creature endowed with thought and consciousness; and when any criminal or injurious actions excite that passion, it is only by their relation to the person, or connection with him. Actions are, by their very nature, temporary and perishing; and where they proceed not from some *cause* in the character and disposition of the person who performed them, they can neither redound to his honor if good, nor infamy if evil. The actions themselves may be blamable; they may be contrary to all the rules of morality and religion; but the person is not answerable for them and, as they proceeded from nothing in him that is durable and constant and leave nothing of that nature behind them, it is impossible he can, upon their account, become the object of punishment or vengeance. According to the principle, therefore, which denies necessity and, consequently, causes, a man is as pure and untainted, after having committed the most horrid crime, as at the first moment of his birth, nor is his character anywise concerned in his actions, since they are not derived from it; and the wickedness of the one can never be used as a proof of the depravity of the other.

Men are not blamed for such actions as they perform ignorantly and casually, whatever may be the consequences. Why? But because the principles of these actions are only momentary and terminate in them alone. Men are less blamed for such actions as they perform hastily and unpremeditately than for such as proceed from deliberation. For what reason? But because a hasty temper, though a constant cause or principle in the mind, operates only by intervals and infects not the whole character. Again, repentance wipes off every crime if attended with a reformation of life and manners. How is this to be accounted for? But by asserting that actions render a person criminal merely as they are proofs of criminal principles in the mind; and when, by an alteration of these principles, they cease to be just proofs, they likewise cease to be criminal. But, except upon the doctrine of necessity, they never were just proofs, and consequently never were criminal.

It will be equally easy to prove, and from the same arguments, that *liberty*, according to that definition above mentioned, in which all men agree, is also essential to morality, and that no human actions, where it is wanting, are susceptible of any moral qualities or can be the objects of approbation or dislike. For as actions are objects of our moral sentiment so far only as they are indications of the internal character, passions, and affections, it is impossible that they can give rise either to praise or blame where they proceed not from these principles, but are derived altogether from external violence.

I pretend not to have obviated or removed all objections to this theory with regard to necessity and liberty. I can forsee other objections derived from topics which have not here been treated of. It may be said, for instance, that if voluntary actions be subjected to the same laws of necessity with the operations of matter, there is a continued chain of necessary causes, preordained and predetermined, reaching from the Original Cause of all to every single volition of every human creature. No contingency anywhere in the universe, no indifference, no liberty. While we act, we are at the same time acted upon. The ultimate Author of all our volitions is the Creator of the world, who first bestowed motion on this immense machine and placed all beings in that particular position whence every subsequent event, by an inevitable necessity, must result. Human actions, therefore, either can have no moral turpitude at all, as proceeding from so good a cause, or if they have any turpitude, they must involve our Creator in the same guilt, while he is acknowledged to be their ultimate cause and Author. For as a man who fired a mine is answerable for all the consequences, whether the train he employed be long or short, so, wherever a continued chain of necessary causes is fixed, that Being, either finite or infinite, who produces the first is likewise the author of all the rest and must both bear the blame and acquire the praise which belong to them. Our clear and unalterable ideas of morality establish this rule upon unquestionable reasons when we examine the consequences of any human action; and these reasons must still have greater force when applied to the volitions and intentions of a Being infinitely wise and powerful. Ignorance or impotence may be pleaded for so limited a creature as man, but those imperfections have no place in our Creator. He foresaw, he ordained, he intended all those actions of men which we so rashly pronounce criminal. And we must, therefore, conclude either that they are not criminal or that the Deity, not man, is accountable for them. But as either of these positions is absurd and impious, it follows that the doctrine from which they are deduced cannot possibly be true, as being liable to all the same objections. An absurd consequence, if necessary, proves the original doctrine to be absurd in the same manner as criminal actions render criminal the original cause if the connection between them be necessary and inevitable.

This objection consists of two parts, which we shall examine separately:

First, that if human actions can be traced up, by a necessary chain, to the Deity, they can never be criminal, on account of the infinite perfection of that Being from whom they are derived, and who can intend nothing but what is altogether good and laudable. Or, *secondly*, if they be criminal, we must retract the attribute of perfection which we ascribe to the Deity and must acknowledge him to be the ultimate author of guilt and moral turpitude in all his creatures.

The answer to the first objection seems obvious and convincing. There are many philosophers who, after an exact scrutiny of the phenomena of nature, conclude that the WHOLE, considered as one system, is, in every period of its existence, ordered with perfect benevolence; and that the utmost possible happiness will, in the end, result to all created beings without any mixture of positive or absolute ill and misery. Every physical ill, say they, makes an essential part of this benevolent system, and could not possibly be removed, by even the Deity himself, considered as a wise agent, without giving entrance to greater ill or excluding greater good which will result from it. From this theory some philosophers, and the ancient Stoics among the rest, derived a topic of consolation under all afflictions, while they taught their pupils that those ills under which they labored were in reality goods to the universe, and that to an enlarged view which could comprehend the whole system of nature every event became an object of joy and exultation. But though this topic be specious and sublime, it was soon found in practice weak and ineffectual. You would surely more irritate than appease a man lying under the racking pains of the gout by preaching up to him the rectitude of those general laws which produced the malignant humors in his body and led them through the proper canals to the sinews and nerves, where they now excite such acute torments. These enlarged views may, for a moment, please the imagination of a speculative man who is placed in ease and security, but neither can they dwell with constancy on his mind, even though undisturbed by the emotions of pain or passion, much less can they maintain their ground when attacked by such powerful antagonists. The affections take a narrower and more natural survey of their object and, by an economy more suitable to the infirmity of human minds, regard alone the beings around us, and are actuated by such events as appear good or ill to the private system.

The case is the same with *moral* as with *physical* ill. It cannot reasonably be supposed that those remote considerations which are found of so little efficacy with regard to the one will have a more powerful influence with regard to the other. The mind of man is so formed by nature that, upon the appearance of certain characters, dispositions, and actions, it immediately feels the sentiment of approbation or blame; nor are there any emotions more essential to its frame and constitution. The characters which engage our approbation are chiefly such as contribute to the peace and security of human society, as the characters which excite blame are chiefly such as tend to public detriment and disturbance; whence it may reasonably be presumed that the moral sentiments arise, either mediately or immediately, from a reflection on these opposite interests. What though philosophical meditations establish a different opinion or conjecture that everything is right with regard to the whole, and that the qualities which disturb society are, in the main, as beneficial, and are as suitable to the primary intention of nature, as those which more directly promote its happiness and welfare? Are such remote and uncertain speculations able to counterbalance the sentiments which arise from the natural and immediate view of the objects? A man who is robbed of a considerable sum, does he find his vexation for the loss anywise diminished by these sublime reflections? Why, then, should his moral resentment against the crime be supposed incompatible with them? Or why should not the acknowledgment of a real distinction between vice and virtue be reconcilable to all speculative systems of philosophy, as well as that of a real distinction between personal beauty and deformity? Both these distinctions are founded in the natural sentiments of the human mind; and these sentiments are not to be controlled or altered by any philosophical theory or speculation whatsoever.

The *second* objection admits not of so easy and satisfactory an answer, nor is it possible to explain distinctly how the Deity can be the immediate cause of all the actions of men without being the author of sin and moral turpitude. These are mysteries which mere natural and unassisted reason is very unfit to handle; and whatever system she embraces, she must find herself involved in inextricable difficulties, and even contradictions, at every step which she takes with regard to such subjects. To reconcile the indifference and contingency of human actions with prescience or to defend absolute decrees, and yet free the Deity from being the author of sin, has been found hitherto to exceed all the power of philosophy. Happy, if she be thence sensible of her temerity, when she pries into these sublime mysteries, and, leaving a scene so full of obscurities and perplexities, return with suitable modesty to her true and proper province, the examination of common life, where she will find difficulties enough to employ her inquiries without launching into so boundless an ocean of doubt, uncertainty, and contradiction.

"A DEFENCE OF FREE WILL"

C. Arthur Campbell

In casting about for a suitable topic upon which to address you to-day, I have naturally borne in mind that an inaugural lecture of this sort should be devoted to some theme of much more than merely esoteric import: to some theme, for preference, sufficiently central in character to have challenged the attention of all who possess a speculative interest in the nature of the universe and man's place within it. That is a principal reason why I have chosen to-day to speak on free will. Mighty issues turn, and turn directly, on the solution of the free will problem. It is in no way surprising that for centuries past it has exercised a fascination for thinkers both within and without the ranks of the professional philosophers that is probably not paralleled in the case of any of the other great problems of metaphysics.

There are, however, other considerations also which have governed my choice of subject. More particularly, I have been influenced by a conviction that the present state of philosophical opinion on free will is, for certain definitely assignable reasons, profoundly unsatisfactory. In my judgment, a thoroughly perverse attitude to the whole problem has been created by the almost universal acquiescence in the view that free will in what is often called the 'vulgar' sense is too obviously nonsensical a notion to deserve serious discussion. Free will in a more 'refined' sense—which is apt to mean free will purged of all elements that may cause embarrassment to a Deterministic psychology or a Deterministic metaphysics—is, it is understood, a conception which may be defended by the philosopher without loss of caste. But in its 'vulgar' sense, as maintained, for example, by the plain man, who clings to a belief in genuinely open possibilities, it is (we are told) a wild and even obnoxious delusion, long ago discredited for sober thinkers.

Now, as it happens, I myself firmly believe that free will, in something extremely like the 'vulgar' sense, is a fact. And I am anxious to-day to do what I can, within the limits of a single lecture, to justify that belief. I propose therefore to develop a statement of the Libertarian's position which will try to make clear why he finds himself obliged to hold what he does hold, and to follow this up with a critical examination of the grounds most in vogue among philosophers for impugning this position. Considerations of time will, I fear, compel a somewhat close economy in my treatment of objections. But I shall hope to say enough to instigate a doubt in some minds concerning the validity of certain very fashionable objections whose authority is often taken to be virtually final. And if no other good purpose is served, it will at least be of advantage if I can offer, in my positive statement, a target for the missiles of the critics more truly representative of Libertarianism than the targets at which they sometimes direct their fire—targets, I may add, upon which even the clumsiest of marksmen could hardly fail to register bull's-eyes.

Let us begin by noting that the problem of free will gets its urgency for the ordinary educated man by reason of its close connection with the conception of moral responsibility. When we regard a man as morally responsible for an act, we regard him as a legitimate object of moral praise or blame in respect of it. But it seems plain that a man cannot be a legitimate object of moral praise or blame for an act unless in willing the act he is in some important sense a 'free' agent. Evidently free will in some sense, therefore, is a pre-condition of moral responsibility. Without doubt it is the realization that any threat to freedom is thus a threat to moral responsibility—with all that that implies—combined with the knowledge that there are a variety of considerations, philosophic, scientific, and theological, tending to place freedom in jeopardy, that gives to the problem of free will its perennial and universal appeal. And it is therefore in close connection with the question of the conditions of moral responsibility that any discussion of the problem must proceed, if it is not to be academic in the worst sense of the term.

We raise the question at once, therefore, what are the conditions, in respect of freedom, which must attach to an act in order to make it a morally responsible act? It seems to me that the fundamental conditions are two. I shall state them with all possible brevity, for we have a long road to travel.

The first condition is the universally recognised one that the act must be *self*-caused, *self*-determined. But it is important to accept this condition in its full rigour. The agent must be not merely *a* cause but the *sole* cause of that for which he is deemed morally responsible. If entities other than the self have also a causal influence upon an act, then that act is not one for which we can say without qualification that the *self* is morally responsible. If in respect of it we hold the self responsible at all, it can only be for some feature of the act—assuming the possibility of disengaging such a feature—of which the self *is* the sole cause. I do not see how this conclusion can be evaded. But it has awkward implications which have led not a few people to abandon the notion of individual moral responsibility altogether.

This first condition, however, is quite clearly not sufficient. It is possible to conceive an act of which the agent is the sole cause, but which is at the same time an act *necessitated* by the agent's nature. Some philosophers have contended, for example, that the act of Divine creation is an act which issues necessarily from the

Divine nature. In the case of such an act, where the agent could not do otherwise than he did, we must all agree, I think, that it would be inept to say that he *ought* to have done otherwise and is thus morally blameworthy, or *ought not* to have done otherwise and is thus morally praiseworthy. It is perfectly true that we do sometimes hold a person morally responsible for an act, even when we believe that he, being what he now is, virtually could not do otherwise. But underlying that judgment is always the assumption that the person has *come* to be what he now is in virtue of past acts of will in which he *was* confronted by real alternatives, by genuinely open possibilities: and, strictly speaking, it is in respect of these *past* acts of his that we praise or blame the agent *now*. For ultimate analysis, the agent's power of alternative action would seem to be an inexpugnable condition of his liability to moral praise or blame, i.e. of his moral responsibility.

We may lay down, therefore, that an act is a 'free' act in the sense required for moral responsibility only if the agent (*a*) is the sole cause of the act; and (*b*) could exert his causality in alternative ways. And it may be pointed out in passing that the acceptance of condition (*b*) implies the recognition of the inadequacy for moral freedom of mere 'self-determination'. The doctrine called 'Self-determinism' is often contrasted by its advocates with mere Determinism on the one hand and Indeterminism on the other, and pronounced to be the one true gospel. I must insist, however, that if 'Self-determinism' rejects condition (*b*), it cannot claim to be a doctrine of free will in the sense required to vindicate moral responsibility. The doctrine which demands, and asserts, the fulfilment of both conditions is the doctrine we call 'Libertarianism'. And it would in my opinion minister greatly to clarity if it were more widely recognized that for any doctrine which is not a species of Libertarianism to pose as a doctrine of 'free will' is mere masquerade.

And now, the conditions of free will being defined in these general terms, we have to ask whether human beings are in fact capable of performing free acts; and if so, where precisely such acts are to be found. In order to prepare the way for an answer, it is desirable, I think, that we should get clear at once about the significance of a certain very familiar, but none the less formidable, criticism of free will which the Self-determinist as well as the Libertarian has to meet. This is the criticism which bases itself upon the facts of heredity on the one hand and of environment on the other. I may briefly summarize the criticism as follows.

Every historic self has an hereditary nature consisting of a group of inborn propensities, in range more or less common to the race, but specific to the individual in their respective strengths. With this equipment the self just *happens* to be born. Strictly speaking, it antedates the existence of the self proper, i.e. the existence of the self-conscious subject, and it is itself the effect of a series of causes leading back to indefinitely remote antiquity. It follows, therefore, that any of the self's choices that manifests the influence of his hereditary nature is not a choice of which *he*, the actual historic self, is the sole cause. The choice is determined, at least in part, by factors external to the self. The same thing holds good of 'environment'. Every self is born and bred in a particular physical and social environment, not of his own choosing, which plays upon him in innumerable ways, encouraging this propensity, discouraging that, and so on. Clearly any of the self's

choices that manifests the influence of environmental factors is likewise a choice
which is determined, at least in part, by factors external to the self. But if we thus
grant, as seems inevitable, that heredity and environment are external influences,
where shall we find a choice in the whole history of a self that is not subject to
external influence? Surely we must admit that every particular act of choice bears
the marks of the agent's hereditary nature and environmental nurture; in which case
a free act, in the sense of an act determined solely by the self, must be dismissed as
a mere chimaera.

To this line of criticism the Self-determinist—T. H. Green is a typical example—has
a stock reply. He urges that these factors, heredity and environment, are not, in so
far as their operation in willing (and therefore in conduct proper) is concerned,
'external' to the self at all. For the act of willing, when we analyse it, reveals itself
to be in its nature such that no end can be willed save in so far as it is conceived
by the self as a good for the self. A 'native propensity' cannot function *as such* in
willing. It can function only in so far as the self conceives its object as a good for
the self. It follows that the self in willing is essentially *self*-determining; not moved
from the outside, but moved always by its own conception of its own good.
Inherited nature and environmental circumstance do play their part; but not as
factors external to the self. They can function only in so far as their suggestions
are, as it were, incorporated by the self in its conception of its own good.
Consequently—so we are told—the threat to self-determination from the side of
inheritance and environment disappears on an adequate analysis of the act of
willing.

I am afraid, however, that this argument, though it contains important truth,
cannot bear the heavy weight that is here imposed upon it. Let us grant that
inheritance and environment can operate in willing only in the medium of the self's
conception of its own good. But then let us ask, how is the self's conception of its
own good constituted? Self-consciousness is required, of course: but mere self-
conscious reflection *in vacuo* will not furnish the self with any conception of a
personal good whatsoever. Obviously to answer the question in regard to any agent
we are obliged to make reference to certain sheer external facts; viz., to the quality
and strength of that person's inherited propensities, and to the nature of the
influences that are brought to bear upon him from the side of environment. It
seems certain, then, that the self's conception of its own good is influenced directly
by its particular inheritance and environment. But to admit this surely involves the
admission that external determination enters into choices. It may be true that the
self's choices are always determined by its conception of its own good. But if what
it conceives to be its own good is always dependent, at least partly, upon inheritance and environment, as external facts, then it is idle to deny that the self's
choices are externally influenced likewise.

Indeed I cannot but regard the attempt to save self-determination by denying the
externality of the influence of heredity and environment as a quite desperate
expedient. It is significant that nobody really believes it in practice. The externality
of these influences is taken for granted in our reflective practical judgments upon
persons. On those occasions when we are in real earnest about giving a critical and

considered estimate of a man's moral calibre—as, e.g., in any serious biographical study—we impose upon ourselves as a matter of course the duty of enquiring with scrupulous care into his hereditary propensities and environmental circumstances, with a view to discovering how far his conduct is influenced by these factors. And having traced these influences, we certainly do not regard the result as having no bearing on the question of the man's moral responsibility for his conduct. On the contrary, the very purpose of the enquiry is to enable us, by due appreciation of the *external* influences that affect his conduct, to gain as accurate a view as possible of that which can justly be attributed to the man's own *self*-determination. The allowances that we all of us do in practice make for hereditary and environmental influences in passing judgment on our fellows would be meaningless if we did not suppose these influences to be in a real sense 'external' to the self.

Now the recognition of this externality is, of course, just as serious a matter for the Libertarian as for the Self-determinist. For the Libertarian, as we saw, accepts condition (*a*) no less wholeheartedly than the Self-determinist does: i.e. that an act is free only if it is determined by the self and nothing but the self. But though we have not been *directly* advancing our course by these recent considerations, we have been doing so indirectly, by narrowing and sharpening the issue. We know now that condition (*a*) is not fulfilled by any act in respect of which inheritance or environment exerts a causal influence. For that type of influence has been shown to be in a real sense external to the self. The free act of which we are in search has therefore got to be one into which influences of this kind do not enter at all.

Moreover, one encouraging portent has emerged in the course of our brief discussion. For we noticed that our reflective practical judgments on persons, while fully recognizing the externality of the influence of heredity and environment, do nevertheless presuppose throughout that there *is something* in conduct which is genuinely self-determined; something which the agent contributes solely on his own initiative, unaffected by external influences; something for which, accordingly, he may justly be held morally responsible. That conviction may, of course, be a false one. But the fact of its widespread existence can hardly be without significance for our problem.

Let us proceed, then, by following up this clue. Let us ask, why do human beings so obstinately persist in believing that there is an indissoluble core of purely *self*-originated activity which even heredity and environment are powerless to affect? There can be little doubt, I think, of the answer in general terms. They do so, at bottom, because they feel certain of the existence of such activity from their immediate practical experience of themselves. Nor can there be in the end much doubt, I think, in what function of the self that activity is to be located. There seems to me to be one, and only one, function of the self with respect to which the agent can even pretend to have an assurance of that absolute self-origination which is here at issue. But to render precise the nature of that function is obviously of quite paramount importance: and we can do so, I think, only by way of a somewhat thorough analysis—which I now propose to attempt—of the experiential situation in which it occurs, viz., the situation of 'moral temptation'.

It is characteristic of that situation that in it I am aware of an end A which I believe to be morally right, and also of an end B, incompatible with A, towards which, in virtue of that system of conative dispositions which constitutes my 'character' as so far formed, I entertain a strong desire. There may be, and perhaps must be, desiring elements in my nature which are directed to A also. But what gives to the situation its specific character as one of moral temptation is that the urge of our desiring nature towards the right end, A, is felt to be *relatively* weak. We are sure that if our desiring nature is permitted to issue directly in action, it is end B that we shall choose. That is what is meant by saying, as William James does, that end B is 'in the line of least resistance' relatively to our conative dispositions. The expression is, of course, a metaphorical one, but it serves to describe, graphically enough, a situation of which we all have frequent experience, viz., where we recognize a specific end as that towards which the 'set' of our desiring nature most strongly inclines us, and which we shall indubitably choose if no inhibiting factor intervenes.

But inhibiting factors, we should most of us say, *may* intervene: and that in two totally different ways which it is vital to distinguish clearly. The inhibiting factor may be of the nature of another desire (or aversion), which operates by changing the balance of the desiring situation. Though at one stage I desire B, which I believe to be wrong, more strongly than I desire A, which I believe to be right, it may happen that before action is taken I become aware of certain hitherto undiscerned consequences of A which I strongly desire, and the result may be that now not *B* but *A* presents itself to me as the end in the line of least resistance. Moral temptation is here overcome by the simple process of ceasing to be a moral temptation.

That is one way, and probably by far the commoner way, in which an inhibiting factor intervenes. But it is certainly not regarded by the self who is confronted by moral temptation as the *only* way. In such situations we all believe, rightly or wrongly, that even although B *continues* to be in the line of least resistance, even although, in other words, the situation remains one with the characteristic marks of moral temptation, we *can* nevertheless align ourselves with A. We can do so, we believe, because we have the power to introduce a new energy, to make what we call an 'effort of will', whereby we are able to act contrary to the felt balance of mere desire, and to achieve the higher end despite the fact that it continues to be in the line of greater resistance relatively to our desiring nature. The self in practice believes that it has this power; and believes, moreover, that the decision rests solely with its self, here and now, whether this power be exerted or not.

Now the objective validity or otherwise of this belief is not at the moment in question. I am here merely pointing to its existence as a psychological fact. No amount of introspective analysis, so far as I can see, even tends to disprove that we do as a matter of fact believe, in situations of moral temptation, that it rests with our self absolutely to decide whether we exert the effort of will which will enable us to rise to duty, or whether we shall allow our desiring nature to take its course.

I have now to point out, further, how this act of moral decision, at least in the significance which it has for the agent himself, fulfils in full the two conditions which we found it necessary to lay down at the beginning for the kind of 'free' act which moral responsibility presupposes.

For obviously it is, in the first place, an act which the agent believes he could perform in alternative ways. He believes that it is genuinely open to him to put forth effort—in varying degrees, if the situations admits of that—or withhold it altogether. And when he *has* decided—in whatever way—he remains convinced that these alternative courses were really open to him.

It is perhaps a little less obvious, but, I think, equally certain, that the agent believes the second condition to be fulfilled likewise, i.e. that the act of decision is determined *solely* by his self. It appears less obvious, because we all realize that formed character has a great deal to do with the choices that we make; and formed character is, without a doubt, partly dependent on the external factors of heredity and environment. But it is crucial here that we should not misunderstand the precise nature of the influence which formed character brings to bear upon the choices that constitute conduct. No one denies that it determines, at least largely, what things we desire, and again how greatly we desire them. It may thus fairly be said to determine the felt balance of desires in the situation of moral temptation. But all that that amounts to is that formed character prescribes the nature of the situation *within* which the act of moral decision takes place. It does not in the least follow that it has any influence whatsoever in determining the act of decision itself—the decision as to whether we shall exert effort or take the easy course of following the bent of our desiring nature: take, that is to say, the course which, in virtue of the determining influence of our character as so far formed, we feel to be in the line of least resistance.

When one appreciates this, one is perhaps better prepared to recognize the fact that the agent himself in the situation of moral temptation does not, and indeed could not, regard his formed character as having any influence whatever upon his act of decision as such. For the very nature of that decision, as it presents itself to him, is as to whether he will or will not permit his formed character to dictate his action. In other words, the agent distinguishes sharply between the self which makes the decision, and the self which, as formed character, determines not the decision but the situation within which the decision takes place. Rightly or wrongly, the agent believes that through his act of decision he can oppose and transcend his own formed character in the interest of duty. We are therefore obliged to say, I think, that the agent *cannot* regard his formed character as in any sense a determinant of the act of decision as such. The act is felt to be a genuinely creative act, originated by the self *ad hoc*, and by the self alone.

Here then, if my analysis is correct, in the function of moral decision in situations of moral temptation, we have an act of the self which at least *appears to the agent* to satisfy both of the conditions of freedom which we laid down at the beginning. The vital question now is, is this 'appearance' true or false? Is the act of decision really what it appears to the agent to be, determined solely by the self, and capable of alternative forms of expression? If it is, then we have here a free act which serves as an adequate basis for moral responsibility. We shall be entitled to regard the agent as morally praiseworthy or morally blameworthy according as he decides to put forth effort or to let his desiring nature have its way. We shall be entitled, in short, to judge the agent as he most certainly judges himself in the situation of moral temptation. If, on the other hand, there is good reason to believe that the agent is the victim of illusion in supposing his act of decision to bear this character, then in my opinion the whole conception of moral responsibility must be jettisoned altogether. For it seems to me certain that there is no other function of the self that even looks as though it satisfied the required conditions of the free act.

Now in considering the claim to truth of this belief of our practical consciousness, we should begin by noting that the onus of proof rests upon the critic who rejects this belief. Until cogent evidence to the contrary is adduced, we are entitled to put our trust in a belief which is so deeply embedded in our experience as practical beings as to be, I venture to say, ineradicable from it. Anyone who doubts whether it is ineradicable may be invited to think himself imaginatively into a situation of moral temptation as we have above described it, and then to ask himself whether in that situation he finds it possible to *disbelieve* that his act of decision has the characteristics in question. I have no misgivings about the answer. It is possible to disbelieve only when we are thinking abstractly about the situation; not when we are living through it, either actually or in imagination. This fact certainly establishes a strong prima facie presumption in favour of the Libertarian position. Nevertheless I agree that we shall have to weigh carefully several criticisms of high authority before we can feel justified in asserting free will as an ultimate and unqualified truth.

Fortunately for our purpose, however, there are some lines of criticism which, although extremely influential in the recent past, may at the present time be legitimately ignored. We are not to-day confronted, for example, by any widely accepted system of metaphysic with implications directly hostile to free will. Only a decade or two ago one could hardly hope to gain a sympathetic hearing for a view which assigned an ultimate initiative to finite selves, unless one were prepared first to show reason for rejecting the dominant metaphyscial doctrine that all things in the universe are the expression of a single Mind or Spirit. But the challenge so lately offered by monistic Idealism has in the present age little more significance than the challenge once offered by monistic Materialism.

Much the same thing holds good of the challenge from the side of physical science. Libertarianism is certainly inconsistent with a rigidly determinist theory of the physical world. It is idle to pretend that there can be open possibilities for psychical decision, while at the same time holding that the physical events in which such decisions manifest themselves are determined in accordance with irrevocable law. But whereas until a few years ago the weight of scientific authority was thrown overwhelmingly on the side of a universal determinism of physical phenomena, the situation has, as everybody knows, profoundly altered during the present century more especially since the advent of Planck's Quantum Theory and Heisenberg's Principle of Uncertainty. Very few scientists to-day would seek to impugn free will on the ground of any supposed implications of the aims or achievements of physical science. I am not myself, I should perhaps add in passing, disposed to rest any part of the case against a universal physical determinism upon these recent dramatic developments of physical science. In my view there never were in the established results of physical science cogent reasons for believing that the apparently universal determinism of inorganic processes holds good also of the processes of the human body. The only inference I here wish to draw from the trend of present-day science is that it removes from any *contemporary* urgency the problem of meeting one particular type of objection to free will. And it is with the contemporary situation that I am in this paper anxious to deal.

I may turn at once, therefore, to lines of argument which do still enjoy a wide currency among anti-Libertarians. And I shall begin with one which, though it is a simple matter to show its irrelevance to the Libertarian doctrine as I have stated it, is so extremely popular that it cannot safely be ignored.

The charge made is that the Libertarian view is incompatible with the *predictability* of human conduct. For we do make rough predictions of people's conduct, on the basis of what we know of their character, every day of our lives, and there can be no doubt that the practice, within certain limits, is amply justified by results. Indeed if it were not so, social life would be reduced to sheer chaos. The close relationship between character and conduct which prediction postulates really seems to be about as certain as anything can be. But the Libertarian view, it is urged, by ascribing to the self a mysterious power of decision uncontrolled by character, and capable of issuing in acts inconsistent with character, denies that continuity between character and conduct upon which prediction depends. If Libertarianism is true, prediction is impossible. But prediction *is* possible, therefore Libertarianism is untrue.

My answer is that the Libertarian view is perfectly compatible with prediction within certain limits, and that there is no empirical evidence at all that prediction is in fact possible beyond these limits. The following considerations will, I think, make the point abundantly clear.

(1) There is no question, on our view, of a free will that can will just anything at all. The range of possible choices is limited by the agent's character in every case; for nothing can be an object of possible choice which is not suggested by either the agent's desires or his moral ideals, and these depend on 'character' for us just as much as for our opponents. We have, indeed explicitly recognized at an earlier stage that character determines the situation within which the act of moral decision takes place, although not the act of moral decision itself. This consideration obviously furnishes a broad basis for at least approximate predictions.

(2) There is *one* experiential situation, and *one only*, on our view, in which there is any possibility of the act of will not being in accordance with character; viz. the situation in which the course which formed character prescribes is a course in conflict with the agent's moral ideal: in other words, the situation of moral temptation. Now this is a situation of comparative rarity. Yet with respect to all other situations in life we are in full agreement with those who hold that conduct is the response of the agent's formed character to the given situation. Why should it not be so? There could be no reason, on our view any more than on another, for the agent even to consider deviating from the course which his formed character

prescribes and he most strongly desires, *unless* that course is believed by him to be incompatible with what is right.

(3) Even within that one situation which is relevant to free will, our view can still recognize a certain basis for prediction. In that situation our character as so far formed prescribes a course opposed to duty, and an effort of will is required if we are to deviate from that course. But of course we are all aware that a greater effort of will is required in proportion to the degree in which we have to transcend our formed character in order to will the right. Such action is, as we say, 'harder'. But if action is 'harder' in proportion as it involves deviation from formed character, it seems reasonable to suppose that, on the whole, action will be of rarer occurrence in that same proportion: though perhaps we may not say that at any level of deviation it becomes flatly impossible. It follows that even with respect to situations of moral temptation we may usefully employ our knowledge of the agent's character as a clue to prediction. It will be a clue of limited, but of by no means negligible, value. It will warrant us in predicting, e.g., of a person who has become enslaved to alcohol, that he is unlikely, even if fully aware of the moral evil of such slavery, to be successful immediately and completely in throwing off its shackles. Predictions of this kind we all make often enough in practice. And there seems no reason at all why a Libertarian doctrine should wish to question their validity.

Now when these three considerations are borne in mind, it becomes quite clear that the doctrine we are defending is compatible with a very substantial measure of predictability indeed. And I submit that there is not a jot of empirical evidence that any larger measure than this obtains in fact.

Let us pass on then to consider a much more interesting and, I think, more plausible criticism. It is constantly objected against the Libertarian doctrine that it is fundamentally *unintelligible.* Libertarianism holds that the act of moral decision is the *self's* act, and yet insists at the same time that it is not influenced by any of those determinate features in the self's nature which go to constitute its 'character'. But, it is asked, do not these two propositions contradict one another? Surely a *self*-determination which is determination by something other than the self's *character* is a contradiction in terms? What meaning is there in the conception of a 'self' in abstraction from its 'character'? If you really wish to maintain, it is urged, that the act of decision is not determined by the self's character, you ought to admit frankly that it is not determined by the *self* at all. But in that case, of course, you will not be advocating a freedom which lends any kind of support to moral responsibility; indeed very much the reverse.

Now this criticism, and all of its kind, seem to me to be the product of a simple, but extraordinarily pervasive, error: the error of confining one's self to the categories of the external observer in dealing with the actions of human agents. Let me explain.

It is perfectly true that the standpoint of the external observer, which we are obliged to adopt in dealing with physical processes, does not furnish us with even a glimmering of a notion of what can be meant by an entity which acts causally and yet not through any of the determinate features of its character. So far as we confine ourselves to external observation, I agree that this notion must seem to us pure nonsense. But then we are *not* obliged to confine ourselves to external observation in dealing with the human agent. Here, though here alone, we have the inestimable advantage of being able to apprehend operations from the *inside*, from the standpoint of *living experience*. But if we do adopt this internal standpoint— surely a proper standpoint, and one which we should be only too glad to adopt if we could in the case of other entities—the situation is entirely changed. We find that we not merely can, but constantly do, attach meaning to a causation which is the self's causation but is yet not exercised by the self's character. We have seen as much already in our analysis of the situation of moral temptation. When confronted by such a situation, we saw, we are certain that it lies with our *self* to decide whether we shall let our character as so far formed dictate our action or whether we shall by effort oppose its dictates and rise to duty. We are certain, in other words, that the act is *not* determined by our *character*, while we remain equally certain that the act *is* determined by our *self.*

Or look, for a further illustration (since the point we have to make here is of the very first importance for the whole free will controversy), to the experience of effortful willing itself, where the act of decision has found expression in the will to rise to duty. In such an experience we are certain that it is our self which makes the effort. But we are equally certain that the effort does not flow from that system of conative dispositions which we call our formed character; for the very function that the effort has for us is to enable us to act against the 'line of least resistance', i.e. to act in a way *contrary* to that to which our formed character inclines us.

I conclude, therefore, that those who find the Libertarian doctrine of the self's causality in moral decision inherently unintelligible find it so simply because they restrict themselves, quite arbitrarily, to an inadequate standpoint: a standpoint from which, indeed, a genuinely creative activity, if it existed, never *could* be appre- hended.

It will be understood, of course, that it is no part of my purpose to deny that the act of moral decision is in *one* sense 'unintelligible'. If by the 'intelligibility' of an act we mean that it is capable, at least in principle, of being inferred as a consequence of a given ground, then naturally my view is that the act in question is *'un*intelligible'. But that, presumably, is not the meaning of 'intelligibility' in the critic's mind when he says that the Libertarian holds an 'unintelligible' doctrine. If it were all he meant, he would merely be pointing out that Libertarianism is not compatible with Determinism! And that tautologous pronouncement would hardly deserve the title of 'criticism'. Yet, strangely enough, not all of the critics seem to be quite clear on this matter. The Libertarian often has the experience of being challenged by the critic to tell him *why*, on his view, the agent now decides to put forth moral effort and now decides not to, with the obviously intended implication that if the Libertarian cannot say 'why' he should give up his theory. Such critics apparently fail to see that if the Libertarian *could* say why he would already have given up his theory! Obviously to demand 'intelligibility' in this sense is simply to prejudge the whole issue in favour of Determinism. The sense in which the critic is entitled to demand intelligibility of our doctrine is simply this; he may demand that the kind of action which our doctrine imputes to human selves should not be, for ultimate analysis, meaningless. And in that sense, as I have already argued, our doctrine is perfectly intelligible.

Let us suppose, then, that the Determinist, confronted by the plain evidence of our practical self-consciousness, now recognizes his obligation to give up the position that the Libertarian doctrine is without qualification 'meaningless', and concedes that from the standpoint of our practical self-consciousness at any rate it is 'meaningful'. And let us ask what will be his next move. So far as I can see, his most likely move now will be to attack the value of that 'internal' standpoint, contrasting it unfavourably, in respect of its claim to truth, with the rational, objective, standpoint of 'pure philosophy'. 'I admit,' he may tell us, 'that there is begotten in the self, in the practical experience you refer to, a belief in a self-causality which is yet not a causality exercised through the self's character. But surely this must weigh but lightly in the balance against the proposition, which appeals to our reason with axiomatic certainty, that an act cannot be caused by a self if it has no ground in the determinate nature of that self. If the choice lies between either disbelieving that rational proposition, or dismissing the evidence of practical self-consciousness as illusion, it is the latter alternative which in my opinion any sane philosophy is bound to adopt.'

But a very little reflection suffices to show that this position is in reality no improvement at all on that from which the critic has just fallen back. For it is evident that the proposition alleged to be axiomatic is axiomatic, at most, only to a reason which knows nothing of acts or events save as they present themselves to an external observer. It obviously is *not* axiomatic to a reason whose field of apprehension is broadened to include the data furnished by the direct experience of acting. In short, the proposition is axiomatic, at most, only to reason functioning *abstractly*; which most certainly cannot be identified with reason functioning *philosophically*.

What is required of the critic, of course, if he is to make good his case, is a reasoned justification of his cavalier attitude towards the testimony of practical self-consciousness. That is the primary desideratum. And the lack of it in the bulk of Determinist literature is in my opinion something of a scandal. Without it, the criticism we have just been examining is sheer dogmatism. It is, indeed, dogmatism of a peculiarly perverse kind. For the situation is, in effect, as follows. From our practical self-consciousness we gain a notion of a genuinely creative act—which might be defined as an act which nothing determines save the agent's doing of it. Of such a character is the act of moral decision as we experience it. But the critic says 'No! This sort of thing cannot be. A person cannot without affront to reason be conceived to be the author of an act which bears, *ex hypothesi*, no intelligible relation to his character. A mere intuition of practical self-consciousness is the solitary prop of this fantastic notion, and surely that is quite incapable of bearing the weight that you would thrust upon it.' Now observe the perversity! The critic says, excluding the evidence of practical self-consciousness, the notion makes nonsense. In other words, excluding the only evidence there ever *could* be for such a notion, the notion makes nonsense! For, of course, if there should be such a thing as creative activity, there is absolutely no other way save an intuition of practical self-consciousness in which we could become aware of it. Only from the inside, from the standpoint of the agent's living experience, can 'activity' possibly be apprehended. So that what the critic is really doing is to condemn a notion as nonsensical on the ground that the only evidence for it is the only evidence there ever could be for it.

Up to the present I have deemed it advisable, in order better to cover the ground, to deal with typical rather than with individual criticisms of the Libertarian position. I wish, however, to depart from that precedent in one instance before I conclude. I am anxious to come to somewhat closer grips with the criticism which Professor C. D. Broad makes in an inaugural lecture published under the title 'Determinism, Indeterminism, and Libertarianism': a work which, short as it is, seems to me to offer incomparably the best elucidation of the problem of freedom that we have. Mr. Broad's criticism does not, as I shall try to show, raise any really new point of principle. But its author's pre-eminence in contemporary philosophy, combined with the recency of this pronouncement, makes it desirable to give a rather particular attention to his views.

The business of elucidation—with which by far the greater part of his lecture is concerned—is in my opinion executed almost to perfection. I acquiesce with especial pleasure in the position Mr. Broad adopts on three important aspects of the problem. (1) He takes as his starting-point the conditions implied in moral obli-gability; the only starting-point, as I believe, which will ensure that the freedom to be discussed will be the freedom which constitutes the real problem. (2) He is entirely clear that the freedom implied in moral obligability is a freedom in which there are genuinely open possibilities before the self: a freedom in which, to use Mr. Broad's terminology, our volition is not merely 'conditionally' but 'categorically' substitutable: i.e. a freedom in which the agent 'could have done otherwise than he did' even though the whole set of conditions environing his decision remained constant. And (3) his analysis culminates in the frank recognition of what he calls the 'effortful factor' in willing as the crux of the whole problem. It is by reference to this that the Libertarian position has got to be defined. What the Libertarian wants to say, he tells us, is that where an effort of will is put forth to reinforce my desire for a course A, 'it is logically consistent with all the nomic, occurrent, dispositional, and background facts that no effort should have been made, or that it should have been directed towards reinforcing the desire for B instead of the desire for A, or that it should have been put forth more or less strongly than it actually was in favour of the desire for A'; and that, nevertheless, the putting forth of the effort was no mere *accident*, but was 'in a unique and peculiar way' determined '*by the agent or self*'.

Now up to this point, p. 43 of a book of less than fifty pages, I am, with only a few relatively unimportant reservations, in almost verbal agreement with what Mr. Broad says. Yet I doubt whether even those who, unlike myself, are in sympathy also with Mr. Broad's ultimate verdict will escape disappointment from the re-maining few pages. The problem of free will has at this juncture been no more than stated. But for Mr. Broad, apparently, the mere statement is virtually tantamount to a Determinist solution. In one single paragraph he now proceeds to offer his reasons for rejecting the Libertarian position as certainly false. Let me quote from it the passage on which this summary dismissal turns. 'The putting forth of an effort', he says, 'of a certain intensity, in a certain direction, at a certain moment, for a certain duration, is quite clearly an event or process, however unique and peculiar it may be in other respects. It is therefore subject to any conditions which self-evidently apply to every event, as such. Now it is surely quite evident that, if the beginning of a certain process at a certain time is determined at all, its total cause *must* contain as an essential factor another event or process which *enters into* the moment from which the determined event or process *issues*. I see no prima facie objection to there being events that are not completely determined. But, in so far as an event *is* determined, an essential factor in its total cause must be other events' (p. 44).

I wish to suggest, with all respect, that we have here merely another manifestation of the cardinal fallacy of anti-Libertarian criticism, the fallacy of bringing to the interpretation of human action categories derived solely from the stand point of the external observer.

For consider. 'It is surely quite evident', says Mr. Broad, 'that if the beginning of a certain process at a certain time is determined at all, its total cause *must* contain as an essential factor another event or process which *enters into* the moment from which the determined event or process *issues*.' On this contention his whole argument rests. On this, and this alone, depends his conclusion that the act of moral decision is preconditioned, and therefore not, as Libertarianism holds, creative. But *is* this contention evident? It may seem evident with respect to those events to which we stand in the relation solely of external observer. But that is not the only relation in which we can stand to events. If the decision to put forth or forbear from putting forth effort in the situation of moral temptation is an event—and I agree that from one point of view it may rightly be called so—it is an event which we can know from within. And, as known from within, it is the *reverse* of evident that its total cause must contain another event which enters into the moment from which the determined event issues. On the contrary, from the internal standpoint of the experiment himself, it is evident that while the event which is the moral decision is determined, in that the self is recognized as its author, there is no *other* event concerned in the matter at all. What determines my 'deed', in the act of moral decision, is felt to be nothing but my doing of it. And this 'doing' is of course not some other event antecedent to the deed itself. It is just the deed (or decision) as *act*, which is the other side of the deed (or decision) as *event*. It seems to me perfectly clear, therefore, that the proposition which Mr. Broad says is 'quite evident' must in fact appear to be a false proposition to any moral agent engaged in the actual function of moral decision.

It will be seen, then, that my objection to Mr. Broad's criticism is identical in principle with the general objection which I urged earlier. Mr. Broad is not entitled to say that certain conditions of the occurrence of an event as such are 'self-evidently' necessary, if that 'self-evidence' is achieved only by ignoring the testimony of our practical self-consciousness. This holds good, it seems to me, irrespective of any question as to the ultimate value of that testimony. The point is that if that testimony is relevant to the problem at all—and if it is not, I should very much like to know *why* it is not—then it *cannot* be 'self-evident' that the conditions Mr. Broad alleges are necessary conditions. It may possibly be the case, though I do not believe it to be so, that Mr. Broad's ultimate verdict is the correct one: that Libertarianism is a false theory, and the notion of 'categorical obligability' in consequence a delusive notion. But it is not the case that, in Mr. Broad's words, 'Libertarianism is self-evidently impossible'. Mr. Broad has helped enormously towards the solution of the free will problem by his masterly statement of the issues involved. But, if I am right, much laborious analysis and deliberation upon *pros* and *cons* (which to Mr. Broad, for the reasons we have seen, appears as a work of mere supererogation) must ensue before we can possibly be in a position to say that the problem is 'solved' one way or the other.

And here, to my regret, my own too brief discussion must terminate. There is much more that I should have liked to say: much more, in my opinion, that badly requires to be said. I should have liked, perhaps above all, to have been able to give more space to an analysis of the experience we call 'effort of will', and to have attempted to expose the fallacies which seem to me to underlie all attempts to explain away that experience by resolving it into something other than itself. That, however, is a matter with which I have partially dealt on a previous occasion, and to which I propose to return under conditions more appropriate to the full-length treatment which can alone be of much service on a difficult psychological theme of this kind. Meantime I can only hope that the little I have been able to say may do something towards regaining for free will in the 'vulgar' sense a place in serious philosophical discussion: that it may do something—to use language of an appropriate vulgarity—towards putting Libertarianism 'on the map' once more. It is not, in my opinion, 'on the map' at all at present. It cannot be, when critics are so often content to make slogans and shibboleths do the work of analysis and argument; when a few satirical references to the 'mysterious fiat' of a 'pure ego' are regarded in so many quarters as a sufficient rejoinder to the Libertarian's claims. Prejudicial phrases like these have certainly a good deal of power. They are evocative of an acutely hostile emotional atmosphere. But, unless accompanied by the most careful analysis, they seem to me to stand for bad habits rather than for good reasons. And it would be no disservice to philosophy if they were extruded from the literature of the free will problem altogether.

"AN EXISTENTIALIST'S VIEW OF FREEDOM"

Jean-Paul Sartre

It is strange that philosophers have been able to argue endlessly about determinism and free-will, to cite examples in favor of one or the other thesis without ever attempting first to make explicit the structures contained in the very idea of *action*. The concept of an act contains, in fact, numerous subordinate notions which we shall have to organize and arrange in a hierarchy: to act is to modify the *shape* of the world; it is to arrange means in view of an end; it is to produce an organized instrumental complex such that by a series of concatenations and connections the modification effected on one of the links causes modifications throughout the whole series and finally produces an anticipated result. But this is not what is important for us here. We should observe first that an action is on principle *intentional*. The careless smoker who has through negligence caused the explosion of a powder magazine has not *acted*. On the other hand the worker who is charged with dynamiting a quarry and who obeys the given orders has acted when he has produced the expected explosion; he knew what he was doing or, if you prefer, he intentionally realized a conscious project.

This does not mean, of course, that one must foresee all the consequences of his act. The emperor Constantine when he established himself at Byzantium, did not foresee that he would create a center of Greek culture and language, the appearance of which would ultimately provoke a schism in the Christian Church and which would contribute to weakening the Roman Empire. Yet he performed an act just in so far as he realized his project of creating a new residence for emperors in the Orient. Equating the result with the intention is here sufficient for us to be able to speak of action. But if this is the case, we establish that the action necessarily implies as its condition the recognition of a "desideratum"; that is, of an objective lack or again of a *négatité*. The intention of providing a rival for Rome can come to Constantine only through the apprehension of an objective lack: Rome lacks a counterweight; to this still profoundly pagan city ought to be opposed a Christian city which at the moment *is missing*. Creating Constantinople is understood as an act only if first the conception of a new city has preceded the action itself or at least if this conception serves as an organizing theme for all later steps. But this conception cannot be the pure representation of the city as *possible*. It apprehends the city in its essential characteristic, which is to be a *desirable* and not yet realized possible.

This means that from the moment of the first conception of the act, consciousness has been able to withdraw itself from the full world of which it is consciousness and to leave the level of being in order frankly to approach that of non-being. Consciousness in so far as it is considered exclusively in its being, is perpetually referred from being to being and can not find in being any motive for revealing non-being. The imperial system with Rome as its capital functions positively and in a certain real way which can be easily discovered. Will someone say that the taxes are collected badly, that Rome is not secure from invasions, that it does not have the geographical location which is suitable for the capital of a Mediterranean empire which is threatened by barbarians, that its corrupt morals make the spread of the Christian religion difficult? How can anyone fail to see that all these considerations are *negative*; that is, that they aim at what is not, not at what is. To say that sixty per cent of the anticipated taxes have been collected can pass, if need be for a positive appreciation of the situation *such as it is*. To say that they are *badly* collected is to consider the situation across a situation which is posited as an absolute end but which precisely *is not*. To say that the corrupt morals at Rome hinder the spread of Christianity is not to consider this diffusion for what it is; that is, for a propagation at a rate which the reports of the clergy can enable us to determine. It is to posit the diffusion in itself as insufficient; that is, as suffering from a secret nothingness. But it appears as such only if it is surpassed toward a limiting-situation posited *a priori* as a value (for example, toward a certain rate of religious conversions, toward a certain mass morality). This limiting-situation can not be conceived in terms of the simple consideration of the real state of things; for the most beautiful girl in the world can offer only what she *has*, and in the same way the most miserable situation can by itself be designated only as it *is* without any reference to an ideal nothingness.

In so far as man is immersed in the historical situation, he does not even succeed in conceiving of the failures and lacks in a political organization or determined economy; this is not, as is stupidly said, because he "is accustomed to it," but because he apprehends it in its plentiude of being and because he can not even imagine that he can exist in it otherwise. For it is necessary here to reverse common opinion and on the basis of what it is not, to acknowledge the harshness of a situation or the sufferings which it imposes, both of which are motives for conceiving of another state of affairs in which things would be better for everybody. It is on the day that we can conceive of a different state of affairs that a new light falls on our troubles and our suffering and that we *decide* that these are unbearable. A worker in 1830 is capable of revolting if his salary is lowered, for he easily conceives of a situation in which his wretched standard of living would be not as low as the one which is about to be imposed on him. But he does not represent his sufferings to himself as unbearable; he adapts himself to them not through resignation but because he lacks the education and reflection necessary for him to conceive of a social state in which these sufferings would not exist. Consequently *he* does not act. Masters of Lyon following a riot, the workers at Croix-Rousse do not know what to do with their victory; they return home bewildered, and the regular army has no trouble in overcoming them. Their misfortunes do not appear to them "habitual" but rather *natural*; they *are*, that is all, and they constitute the worker's condition. They are not detached; they are not seen in the clear light of day, and consequently they are integrated by the worker with his being. He suffers without considering his suffering and without conferring value upon it. To suffer and to *be* are one and the same for him. His suffering is the pure affective tenor of his non-positional consciousness, but he does not contemplate it. Therefore this suffering can not be in itself a *motive*[1] for his acts. Quite the contrary, it is after he has formed the project of changing the situation that it will appear intolerable to

---

[1] In this and following sections Sartre makes a sharp distinction between *motif* and *mobile*. The English word "motive" expresses sufficiently adequately the French *mobile*, which refers to an inner subjective fact or attitude. For *motif* there is no true equivalent. Since it refers to an external fact or situation, I am translating it by "cause." The reader must remember, however, that this carries with it no idea of determinism. Sartre emphatically denies the existence of any cause in the usual deterministic sense. Tr.

him. This means that he will have had to give himself room, to withdraw in relation
to it, and will have to have effected a double nihilation: on the one hand, he must
posit an ideal state of affairs as a pure *present* nothingness; on the other hand, he
must posit the actual situation as nothingness in relation to this state of affairs. He
will have to conceive of a happiness attached to his class as a pure possible—that is,
presently as a certain nothingness—and on the other hand, he will return to the
present situation in order to illuminate it in the light of this nothingness and in
order to nihilate it in turn by declaring: "I *am not* happy."

Two important consequences result. (1) No factual state whatever it may be (the
political and economic structure of society, the psychological "state," *etc.*) is
capable by itself of motivating any act whatsoever. For an act is a projection of the
for-itself toward what is not, and what is can in no way determine by itself what is
not. (2) No factual state can determine consciousness to apprehend it as a *négatité*
or as a lack. Better yet no factual state can determine consciousness to define it and
to circumscribe it since, as we have seen, Spinoza's statement, "Omnis determinatio
est negatio," remains profoundly true. Now every action has for its express condition not only the discovery of a state of affairs as "lacking in—," *i.e.*, as a
négatité—but also, and before all else, the constitution of the state of things under
consideration into an isolated system. There is a factual state—satisfying or not—
only by means of the nihilating power of the for-itself. But this power of nihilation
can not be limited to realizing a simple *withdrawal* in relation to the world. In fact
in so far as consciousness is "invested" by being, in so far as it simply suffers what
is, it must be included in being. It is the organized form—worker-finding-
his-suffering-natural—which must be surmounted and denied in order for it to be
able to form the object of a revealing contemplation. This means evidently that it is
by a pure wrenching away from himself and the world that the worker can posit his
suffering as unbearable suffering and consequently can *make of it the motive* for his
revolutionary action. This implies for consciousness the permanent possibility of
effecting a rupture with its own past, of wrenching itself away from its past so as to
be able to consider it in the light of a non-being and so as to be able to confer on
it the meaning which *it has* in terms of the project of a meaning which it *does not
have*. Under no circumstances can the past in any way by itself produce *an act*; that
is, the positing of an end which turns back upon itself so as to illuminate it. This is
what Hegel caught sight of when he wrote that "the mind is the negative," although
he seems not to have remembered this when he came to presenting his own theory
of action and of freedom. In fact as soon as one attributes to consciousness this
negative power with respect to the world and itself, as soon as the nihilation forms
an integral part of the *positing* of an end, we must recognize that the indispensable
and fundamental condition of all action is the freedom of the acting being.

Thus at the outset we can see what is lacking in those tedious discussions between
determinists and the proponents of free will. The latter are concerned to find cases
of decision for which there exists no prior cause, or deliberations concerning two
opposed acts which are equally possible and possess causes (and motives) of exactly
the same weight. To which the determinists may easily reply that there is no action
without a *cause* and that the most insignificant gesture (raising the right hand rather

than the left hand, *etc.*) refers to causes and motives which confer its meaning upon it. Indeed the case could not be otherwise since every action must be *intentional*; each action must, in fact, have an end, and the end in turn is referred to a cause. Such indeed is the unity of the three temporal ekstases; the end or temporalization of my future implies a cause (or motive); that is, it points toward my past, and the present is the upsurge of the act. To speak of an act without a cause is to speak of an act which would lack the intentional structure of every act; and the proponents of free will by searching for it on the level of the act which is in the process of being performed can only end up by rendering the act absurd. But the determinists in turn are weighing the scale by stopping their investigation with the mere designation of the cause and motive. The essential question in fact lies beyond the complex organization "cause-intention-act-end"; indeed we ought to ask how a cause (or motive) can be constituted as such.

Now we have just seen that if there is not act without a cause, this is not in the sense that we can say that there is no phenomenon without a cause. In order to be a *cause*, the *cause* must be *experienced* as such. Of course this does not mean that it is to be thematically conceived and made explicit as in the case of deliberation. But at the very least it means that the for-itself must confer on it its value as cause or motive. And, as we have seen, this constitution of the cause as such can not refer to another real and positive existence; that is, to a prior cause. For otherwise the very nature of the act as engaged intentionally in non-being would disappear. The motive is understood only by the end; that is, by the non-existent. It is therefore in itself a *négatité*. If I accept a niggardly salary it is doubtless because of fear; and fear is a motive. But it is *fear of dying from starvation*; that is, this fear has meaning only outside itself in an end ideally posited, which is the preservation of a life which I apprehend as "in danger." And this fear is understood in turn only in relation to the *value which I* implicitly give to this life; that is, it is referred to that hierarchal system of ideal objects which are values. Thus the motive makes itself understood as what it is by means of the ensemble of beings which "are not," by ideal existences, and by the future. Just as the future turns back upon the present and the past in order to elucidate them, so it is the ensemble of my projects which turns back in order to confer upon the *motive* its structure as a motive. It is only because I escape the in-itself by nihilating myself toward my possibilities that this in-itself can take on value as cause or motive. Causes and motives have meaning only inside a projected ensemble which is precisely an ensemble of non-existents. And this ensemble is ultimately myself as transcendence; it is Me in so far as I have to be myself outside of myself.

If we recall the principle which we established earlier—namely that it is the apprehension of a revolution as possible which gives to the workman's suffering its value as a motive—we must thereby conclude that it is by fleeing a situation toward our possibility of changing it that we organize this situation into complexes of causes and motives. The nihilation by which we achieve a withdrawal in relation to the situation is the same as the ekstasis by which we project ourselves toward a modification of this situation. The result is that it is in fact impossible to find an act without a motive but that this does not mean that we must conclude that the motive causes the act; the motive is an integral part of the act. For as the resolute project toward a change is not distinct from the act, the motive, the act, and the end are all constituted in a single upsurge. Each of these three structures claims the two others as its meaning. But the organized totality of the three is no longer explained by any particular structure, and its upsurge as the pure temporalizing nihilation of the in-itself is one with freedom. It is the act which decides its ends and its motives, and the act is the expression of freedom. . . .

In our attempt to reach to the heart of freedom we may be helped by the few observations which we have made on the subject in the course of this work and which we must summarize here . . . we established the fact that if negation comes into the world through human-reality, the latter must be a being who can realize a nihilating rupture with the world and with himself; and we established that the permanent possibility of this rupture is the same as freedom. But on the other hand, we stated that this permanent possibility of nihilating what I am in the form of "having-been" implies for man a particular type of existence. We were able then to determine by means of analyses like that of bad faith that human reality is its own nothingness. For the for-itself, to be is to nihilate the in-itself which it is. Under these conditions freedom can be nothing other than this nihilation. It is through this that the for-itself escapes its being as its essence; it is through this that the for-itself is always something other than what can be said of it. For in the final analysis the for-itself is the one which escapes this very denomination, the one which is already beyond the name which is given to it, beyond the property which is recognized in it. To say that the for-itself has to be what it is, to say that it is what it is not while not being what it is, to say that in it existence precedes and conditions essence or inversely according to Hegel, that for it "Wesen ist was gewesen ist"—all this is to say one and the same thing: to be aware that man is free. Indeed by the sole fact that I am conscious of the causes which inspire my action, these causes are already transcendent objects for my consciousness; they are outside. In vain shall I seek to catch hold of them; I escape them by my very existence. I am condemned to exist forever beyond my essence, beyond the causes and motives of my act. I am condemned to be free. This means that no limits to my freedom can be found except freedom itself or, if you prefer, that we are not free to cease being free. To the extent that the for-itself wishes to hide its own nothingness from itself and to incorporate the in-itself as its true mode of being, it is trying also to hide its freedom from itself.

The ultimate meaning of determinism is to establish within us an unbroken continuity of existence in itself. The motive conceived as a psychic fact—*i.e.*, as a full and given reality—is, in the deterministic view, articulated without any break with the decision and the act, both of which are equally conceived as psychic givens. The in-itself has got hold of all these "data"; the motive provokes the act as the physical cause its effect; everything is real, everything is full. Thus the refusal of freedom can be conceived only as an attempt to apprehend oneself as being-in-itself; it amounts to the same thing. Human reality may be defined as a being such that in its being its freedom is at stake because human reality perpetually tries to refuse to recognize its freedom. Psychologically in each one of us this amounts to trying to take the causes and motives as *things*. We try to confer permanence upon them. We attempt to hide from ourselves that their nature and their weight depend each moment on the meaning which I give to them; we take them for constants. This amounts to considering the meaning which I gave to them just now or yesterday— which is irremediable because it is *past*—and extrapolating from it a character fixed still in the present. I attempt to persuade myself that the cause *is* as it was. Thus it would pass whole and untouched from my past consciousness to my present consciousness. It would inhabit my consciousness. This amounts to trying to give an essence to the for-itself. In the same way people will posit ends as transcendences, which is not an error. But instead of seeing that the transcendences there posited are maintained in their being by my own transcendence, people will assume that I encounter them upon my surging up in the world; they come from God, from nature, from "my" nature, from society. These ends ready made and pre-human will therefore define the meaning of my act even before I conceive it, just as causes as pure psychic givens will produce it without my even being aware of them.

Cause, act, and end constitute a *continuum*, a *plenum*. These abortive attempts to stifle freedom under the weight of being (they collapse with the sudden upsurge of anguish before freedom) show sufficiently that freedom in its foundation coincides with the nothingness which is at the heart of man. Human-reality is free because it *is not enough*. It is free because it is perpetually wrenched away from itself and because it has been separated by a nothingness from what it is and from what it will be. It is free, finally, because its present being is itself a nothingness in the form of the "reflection-reflecting." Man is free because he is not himself but presence to himself. The being which is what it is can not be free. Freedom is precisely the nothingness which *is made-to-be* at the heart of man and which forces human-reality *to make itself* instead of to be. As we have seen, for human reality, to be is to *choose oneself*; nothing comes to it either from the outside or from within which it can *receive or accept*. Without any help whatsoever, it is entirely abandoned to the intolerable necessity of making itself be—down to the slightest detail. Thus freedom is not *a* being; it is *the being* of man—*i.e.*, his nothingness of being. If we start by conceiving of man as a plenum, it is absurd to try to find in him afterwards moments or psychic regions in which he would be free. As well look for emptiness in a container which one has filled beforehand up to the brim! Man can not be sometimes slave and sometimes free; he is wholly and forever free or he is not free at all.

These observations can lead us, if we know how to use them, to new discoveries. They will enable us first to bring to light the relations between freedom and what we call the "will." There is a fairly common tendency to seek to identify free acts with voluntary acts and to restrict the deterministic explanation to the world of the passions. In short the point of view of Descartes. The Cartesian will is free, but there are "passions of the soul." Again Descartes will attempt a physiological interpretation of these passions. Later there will be an attempt to instate a purely psychological determinism. Intellectualistic analyses such as Proust, for example, attempts with respect to jealousy or snobbery can serve as illustrations for this concept of the passional "mechanism." In this case it would be necessary to conceive of man as simultaneously free and determined, and the essential problem would be that of the relations between this unconditioned freedom and the determined processes of the psychic life: how will it master the passions, how will it utilize them for its own benefit? A wisdom which comes from ancient times—the wisdom of the Stoics—will teach us to come to terms with these passions so as to master them; in short it will counsel us how to conduct ourselves with regard to affectivity as man does with respect to nature in general when he obeys it in order better to control it. Human reality therefore appears as a free power besieged by an ensemble of determined processes. One will distinguish wholly free acts, determined processes over which the free will has power, and processes which on principle escape the human-will.

It is clear that we shall not be able to accept such a conception. But let us try better to understand the reasons for our refusal. There is one objection which is obvious and which we shall not waste time in developing; this is that such a trenchant duality is inconceivable at the heart of the psychic unity. How in fact could we conceive of a being which could be *one* and which nevertheless on the one hand would be constituted as a series of facts determined by one another—hence existents in exteriority—and which on the other hand would be constituted as a spontaneity determining itself to be and revealing only itself? *A priori* this spontaneity would be capable of no action on a determinism already *constituted.* On what could it act? On the object itself (the present psychic fact)? But how could it modify an in-itself which by definition is and can be only what it is? On the actual law of the process? This is self-contradictory. On the antecedents of the process? But it amounts to the same thing whether we act on the present psychic fact in order to modify it in itself or act upon it in order to modify its consequences. And in each case we encounter the same impossibility which we pointed out earlier. Moreover, what instrument would this spontaneity have at its disposal? If the hand can clasp, it is because it can be clasped. Spontaneity, since by definition it is *beyond reach* can not in turn *reach*; it can produce only itself. And if it could dispose of a special instrument, it would then be necessary to conceive of this as of an intermediary nature between free will and determined passions—which is not admissible. For different reasons the passions could get no hold upon the will. Indeed it is impossible for a determined process to act upon a spontaneity, exactly as it is impossible for objects to act upon consciousness. Thus any synthesis of two types of existents is impossible; they are not homogeneous; they will remain each one in its incommunicable solitude. The only bond which a nihilating spontaneity could maintain with mechanical processes would be the fact that it *produces itself by an internal negation directed toward these existents.* But then the spontaneity will exist precisely only in so far as it denies concerning itself that it is these passions. Henceforth the ensemble of the determined πάθος will of necessity be apprehended by spontaneity as a pure transcendent; that is, as what is necessarily *outside*, as what *is* not it.[2] This internal negation would therefore have for its effect

---

[2]*I.e.*, is not spontaneity. Tr.

only the dissolution of the πάθος in the world, and the πάθος would exist as some sort of object in the midst of the world for a free spontaneity which would be simultaneously will and consciousness. This discussion shows that two solutions and only two are possible: either man is wholly determined (which is inadmissible, especially because a determined consciousness—*i.e.*, a consciousness externally motivated—becomes itself pure exteriority and ceases to be consciousness) or else man is wholly free. . . .

But this is not all: the will, far from being the unique or at least the privileged manifestation of freedom, actually—like every event of the for-itself—must presuppose the foundation of an original freedom in order to be able to constitute itself as will. The will in fact is posited as a reflective decision in relation to certain ends. But it does not create these ends. It is rather a mode of being in relation to them: it decrees that the pursuit of these ends will be reflective and deliberative. Passion can posit the same ends. For example, if I am threatened, I can run away at top speed because of my fear of dying. This passional fact nevertheless posits implicitly as a supreme end the value of life. Another person in the same situation will, on the contrary, understand that he must remain at his post even if resistance at first appears more dangerous than flight; he "will stand firm." But his goal, although better understood and explicitly posited, remains the same as in the case of the emotional reaction. It is simply that the methods of attaining it are more clearly conceived; certain of them are rejected as dubious or inefficacious, others are more solidly organized. The difference here depends on the choice of means and on the degree of reflection and of making explicit, not on the end. Yet the one who flees is said to be "passionate," and we reserve the term "voluntary" for the man who resists. Therefore the question is of a difference of subjective attitude in relation to a transcendent end. But if we wish to avoid the error which we denounced earlier and not consider these transcendent ends as pre-human and as an *a priori* limit to our transcendence, then we are indeed compelled to recognize that they are the temporalizing projection of our freedom. Human reality can not receive its ends, as we have seen, either from outside or from a so-called inner "nature." It chooses them and by this very choice confers upon them a transcendent existence as the external limit of its projects. From this point of view—and if it is understood that the existence of the *Dasein* precedes and commands its essence—human reality in and through its very upsurge decides to define its own being by its ends. It is therefore the positing of my ultimate ends which characterizes my being and which is identical with the sudden thrust of the freedom which is mine. And this thrust is an *existence*; it has nothing to do with an essence or with a property of a being which would be engendered conjointly with an idea.

Thus since freedom is identical with my existence, it is the foundation of ends which I shall attempt to attain either by the will or by passionate efforts. Therefore it can not be limited to voluntary acts. Volitions, on the contrary, like passions are certain subjective attitudes by which we attempt to attain the ends posited by original freedom. By original freedom, of course, we should not understand a freedom which would be *prior* to the voluntary or passionate act but rather a foundation which is strictly contemporary with the will or the passion and which these *manifest*, each in its own way. Neither should we oppose freedom to the will or to passion as the "profound self" of Bergson is opposed to the superficial self; the for-itself is wholly selfness and can not have a "profound self," unless by this we mean certain transcendent structures of the psyche. Freedom is nothing but the *existence* of our will or of our passions in so far as this existence is the nihilation of facticity; that is, the existence of being which is its being in the mode of having to be it. We shall return to this point. In any case let us remember that the will is determined within the compass of motives and ends already posited by the for-itself in a transcendent projection of itself toward its possibles. If this were not so, how could we understand deliberation, which is an evaluation of means in relation to already existing ends?

If these ends are already posited, then what remains to be decided at each moment is the way in which I shall conduct myself with respect to them; in other words, the attitude which I shall assume. Shall I act by volition or by passion? Who can decide except me? In fact, if we admit that circumstances decide for me (for example, I can act by volition when faced with a minor danger but if the peril increases, I shall fall into passion), we thereby suppress all freedom. It would indeed be absurd to declare that the will is autonomous when it appears but that external circumstances strictly determine the moment of its appearance. But, on the other hand, how can it be maintained that a will which does not yet exist can suddenly decide to shatter the chain of the passions and suddenly stand forth on the fragments of these chains? Such a conception would lead us to consider the will as a *power* which sometimes would manifest itself to consciousness and at other times would remain hidden, but which would in any case possess the permanence and the existence "in-itself" of a property. This is precisely what is inadmissible. It is, however, certain that common opinion conceives of the moral life as a struggle between a will-thing and passion-substances. There is here a sort of psychological Manichaeism which is absolutely insupportable.

Actually it is not enough to will; it is necessary to will to will. Take, for example, a given situation: I can react to it emotionally. We have shown elsewhere that emotion is not a physiological tempest;[3] it is a reply adapted to the situation; it is a type of conduct, the meaning and form of which are the object of an intention of consciousness which aims at attaining a particular end by particular means. In fear, fainting and cataplexie[4] aim at suppressing the danger by suppressing the consciousness of the danger. There is an *intention* of losing consciousness in order to do away with the formidable world in which consciousness is engaged and which comes into being through consciousness. Therefore we have to do with magical behavior provoking the symbolic satisfactions of our desires and revealing by the same stroke a magical stratum of the world. In contrast to this conduct voluntary and rational

[3] *Esquisse d'une théorie phénoménologique des émotions*, Hermann, 1939. In English, *The Emotions: Outline of a Theory*. Tr. by Bernard Frechtman. Philosophical Library, 1948.

[4] A word invented by Preyer to refer to a sudden inhibiting numbness produced by any shock. Tr.

conduct will consider the situation scientifically, will reject the magical, and will apply itself to realizing determined series and instrumental complexes which will enable us to resolve the problems. It will organize a system of means by taking its stand on instrumental determinism. Suddenly it will reveal a technical world; that is, a world in which each instrumental-complex refers to another larger complex and so on. But what will make me decide to choose the magical aspect or the technical aspect of the world? It can not be the world itself, for this in order to be manifested waits to be discovered. Therefore it is necessary that the for-itself in its project must choose being the one by whom the world is revealed as magical or rational; that is, the for-itself must as a free project of itself give to itself magical or rational existence. It is responsible for either one, for the for-itself can *be* only if it has chosen itself. Therefore the for-itself appears as the free foundation of its emotions as of its volitions. My fear *is* free and manifests my freedom; I have put all my freedom into my fear, and I have chosen myself as fearful in this or that circumstance. Under other circumstances I shall exist as deliberate and courageous, and I shall have put all my freedom into my courage. In relation to freedom there is no privileged psychic phenomenon. All my "modes of being" manifest freedom equally since they are all ways of being my own nothingness. . . .

Yet if the motive is transcendent, if it is only the irremediable being which we have to be in the mode of the "was," if like all our past it is separated from us by a breadth of nothingness, then it can act only if it is *recovered*; in itself it is without force. It is therefore by the very thrust of the engaged consciousness that a value and a weight will be conferred on motives and on prior causes. What they have been does not depend on consciousness, but consciousness has the duty of maintaining them in their existence in the past. I have willed this or that: here is what remains irremediable and which even constitutes my essence, since my essence is what I have been. But the meaning held for me by this desire, this fear, these objective considerations of the world when presently I project myself toward my futures—this must be decided by me alone. I determine them precisely and only by the very act by which I project myself toward my ends. The recovery of former motives—or the rejection or new appreciation of them—is not distinct from the project by which I assign new ends to myself and by which in the light of these ends I apprehend myself as discovering a supporting cause in the world. Past motives, past causes, present motives and causes, future ends, all are organized in an indissoluble unity by the very upsurge of a freedom which is beyond causes, motives, and ends.

The result is that a voluntary deliberation is always a deception. How can I evaluate causes and motives on which I myself confer their value before all deliberation and by the very choice which I make of myself? The illusion here stems from the fact that we endeavor to take causes and motives for entirely transcendent things which I balance in my hands like weights and which possess a weight as a permanent property. Yet on the other hand we try to view them as contents of consciousness, and this is self-contradictory. Actually causes and motives have only the weight which my project—*i.e.*, the free production of the end and of the known act to be realized—confers upon them. When I deliberate, the chips are down.[5] And if I am brought to the point of deliberating, this is simply because it is a part of my original project to realize motives by means of *deliberation* rather than by some other form of discovery (by passion, for example, or simply by action, which reveals to me the organized ensemble of causes and of ends as my language informs me of my thought). There is therefore a choice of deliberation as a procedure which will make known to me what I project and consequently what I am. And *the choice* of deliberation is organized with the ensemble motives-causes and end by free spontaneity. When the will intervenes, the decision is taken, and it has no other value than that of making the announcement. . . .

The essential consequence of our earlier remarks is that man being condemned to be free carries the weight of the whole world on his shoulders; he is responsible for the world and for himself as a way of being. We are taking the word "responsibility" in its ordinary sense as "consciousness (of) being the incontestable author of an event or of an object." In this sense the responsibility of the for-itself is overwhelming since he[6] is the one by whom it happens that there is a world; since he is also the one who makes himself be, then whatever may be the situation in which he finds himself, the for-itself must wholly assume this situation with its peculiar coefficient of adversity, even though it be insupportable. He must assume the situation with the proud consciousness of being the author of it, for the very worst disadvantages or the worst threats which can endanger my person have meaning only in and through my project; and it is on the ground of the engagement which I am that they appear. It is therefore senseless to think of complaining since nothing foreign has decided what we feel, what we live, or what we are.

Furthermore this absolute responsibility is not resignation; it is simply the logical requirement of the consequences of our freedom. What happens to me happens through me, and I can neither affect myself with it nor revolt against it nor resign myself to it. Moreover everything which happens to me is *mine*. By this we must understand first of all that I am always equal to what happens to me *qua* man, for what happens to a man through other men and through himself can be only human. The most terrible situations of war, the worst tortures do not create a non-human state of things; there is no non-human situation. It is only through fear, flight, and recourse to magical types of conduct that I shall decide on the non-human, but this decision is human, and I shall carry the entire responsibility for it. But in addition the situation is *mine* because it is the image of my free choice of myself, and everything which it presents to me is *mine* in that this represents me and symbolizes me. Is it not I who decide the coefficient of adversity in things and even their unpredictability by deciding myself?

Thus there are no *accidents* in a life; a community event which suddenly bursts

[5] *Les jeux sont faits.* Sartre has written a novel by this title. Tr.

[6] I am shifting to the personal pronoun here since Sartre is describing the for-itself in concrete personal terms rather than as a metaphysical entity. Strictly speaking, of course, this is his position throughout, and the French "il" is indifferently "he" or "it." Tr.

forth and involves me in it does not come from the outside. If I am mobilized in a war, this war is *my* war; it is in my image and I deserve it. I deserve it first because I could always get out of it by suicide or by desertion; these ultimate possibles are those which must always be present for us when there is a question of envisaging a situation. For lack of getting out of it, I have *chosen* it. This can be due to inertia, to cowardice in the face of public opinion, or because I prefer certain other values to the value of the refusal to join in the war (the good opinion of my relatives, the honor of my family, etc.). Anyway you look at it, it is a matter of a choice. This choice will be repeated later on again and again without a break until the end of the war. Therefore we must agree with the statement by J. Romains, "In war there are no innocent victims."[7] If therefore I have preferred war to death or to dishonor, everything takes place as if I bore the entire responsibility for this war. Of course others have declared it, and one might be tempted perhaps to consider me as a simple accomplice. But this notion of complicity has only a juridical sense, and it does not hold here. For it depended on me that for me and by me this war should not exist, and I have decided that it does exist. There was no compulsion here, for the compulsion could have got no hold on a freedom. I did not have any excuse; for as we have said repeatedly in this book, the peculiar character of human-reality is that it is without excuse. Therefore it remains for me only to lay claim to this war.

But in addition the war is *mine* because by the sole fact that it arises in a situation which I cause to be and that I can discover it there only by engaging myself for or against it, I can no longer distinguish at present the choice which I make of myself from the choice which I make of the war. To live this war is to choose myself through it and to choose it through my choice of myself. There can be no question of considering it as "four years of vacation" or as a "reprieve," as a "recess," the essential part of my responsibilities being elsewhere in my married, family, or professional life. In this war which I have chosen I choose myself from day to day, and I make it mine by making myself. If it is going to be four empty years, then it is I who bear the responsibility for this.

Finally, as we pointed out earlier, each person is an absolute choice of self from the standpoint of a world of knowledges and of techniques which this choice both assumes and illumines; each person is an absolute upsurge at an absolute date and is perfectly unthinkable at another date. It is therefore a waste of time to ask what I should have been if this war had not broken out, for I have chosen myself as one of the possible meanings of the epoch which imperceptibly led to war. I am not distinct from this same epoch; I could not be transported to another epoch without contradiction. Thus *I am* this war which restricts and limits and makes comprehensible the period which preceded it. In this sense we may define more precisely the responsibility of the for-itself if to the earlier quoted statement, "There are no innocent victims," we add the words, "We have the war we deserve." Thus, totally free, undistinguishable from the period for which I have chosen to be the meaning, as profoundly responsible for the war as if I had myself declared it, unable to live

[7]J. Romains: *Les hommes de bonne volonté*; "Prélude à Verdun."

without integrating it in *my* situation, engaging myself in it wholly and stamping it with my seal, I must be without remorse or regrets as I am without excuse; for from the instant of my upsurge into being, I carry the weight of the world by myself alone without anything or any person being able to lighten it.

Yet this responsibility is of a very particular type. Someone will say, "I did not ask to be born." This is a naive way of throwing greater emphasis on our facticity. I am responsible for everything, in fact, except for my very responsibility, for I am not the foundation of my being. Therefore everything takes place as if I were compelled to be responsible. I am *abandoned* in the world, not in the sense that I might remain abandoned and passive in a hostile universe like a board floating on the water, but rather in the sense that I find myself alone and without help, engaged in a world for which I bear the whole responsibility without being able, whatever I do, to tear myself away from this responsibility for an instant. For I am responsible for my very desire of fleeing responsibilities. To make myself passive in the world, to refuse to act upon things and upon others is still to choose myself, and suicide is one mode among others of being-in-the-world. Yet I find an absolute responsibility for the fact that my facticity (here the fact of my birth) is directly inapprehensible and even inconceivable, for this fact of my birth never appears as a brute fact but always across a projective reconstruction of my for-itself. I am ashamed of being born or I am astonished at it or I rejoice over it, or in attempting to get rid of my life I affirm that I live and I assume this life as bad. Thus in a certain sense I *choose* being born. This choice itself is integrally affected with facticity since I am not able not to choose, but this facticity in turn will appear only in so far as I surpass it toward my ends. Thus facticity is everywhere but inapprehensible; I never encounter anything except my responsibility. That is why I can not ask, "*Why* was I born?" or curse the day of my birth or declare that I did not ask to be born, for these various attitudes toward my birth—*i.e.*, toward the *fact* that I realize a presence in the world—are absolutely nothing else but ways of assuming this birth in full responsibility and of making it *mine*. Here again I encounter only myself and my projects so that finally my abandonment—*i.e.*, my facticity—consists simple in the fact that I am condemned to be wholly responsible for myself. I am the being which is in such a way that in its being its being is in question. And this "is" of my being *is* as present and inapprehensible.

Under these conditions since every event in the world can be revealed to me only as an *opportunity* (an opportunity made use of, lacked, neglected, *etc.*), or better yet since everything which happens to us can be considered as a *chance* (*i.e.*, can appear to us only as a way of realizing this being which is in question in our being) and since others as transcendences-transcended are themselves only *opportunities* and *chances*, the responsibility of the for-itself extends to the entire world as a peopled-world. It is precisely thus that the for-itself apprehends itself in anguish; that is, as a being which is neither the foundation of its own being nor of the Other's being nor of the in-itselfs which form the world, but a being which is compelled to decide the meaning of being—within it and everywhere outside of it. The one who realizes in anguish his condition as *being* thrown into a responsibility which extends to his very abandonment has no longer either remorse or regret or excuse; he is no longer anything but a freedom which perfectly reveals itself and whose being resides in this very revelation. But as we pointed out at the beginning of this work, most of the time we flee anguish in bad faith.

FURTHER READINGS FOR PART 3

Anthologies

Berofsky, Bernard (ed.), *Free Will and Determinism* (New York: Harper, 1966). Twenty essays, mostly by contemporary authors, arranged in such a way that proponents and opponents debate various issues about free will and determinism.

Enteman, Willard F., *The Problem of Free Will: Selected Readings* (New York: Scribner, 1967). Seventeen articles by classical and contemporary authors organized to bring out different points of view on issues involved in the problem of free will.

Hook, Sidney (ed.), *Determinism and Freedom in the Age of Modern Science* (New York: New York U.P., 1958). Twenty-seven contemporaries contribute papers concerning freedom and determinism.

Lehrer, Keith (ed.), *Freedom and Determinism* (New York: Random House, 1966). Seven essays by contemporary American philosophers on problems involved in the debate between free-willists and determinists.

Morgenbesser, Sidney, and James Walsh (eds.), *Free Will* (Englewood Cliffs, N.J.: Prentice-Hall, 1962). Twelve selections from classical and contemporary sources arranged to present different views on some of the key issues concerning free will.

Pears, D. F., *Freedom and the Will* (New York: St. Martin's, 1963). Seven essays by contemporary British philosophers on the nature of the will and its freedom. Most of the essays originated as talks in the Third Programme of the B.B.C., in which there was a direct exchange of views between the participants.

Determinism

Clemens, Samuel, "What Is Man?" in *What Is Man? And Other Essays* (New York: Harper, 1917). With typical touches of humor, Mark Twain argues in this essay that man is a machine totally determined by outside influences.

Darrow, Clarence, *Plea in Defense of Loeb and Leopold* (Gerard, Kan.: Little Blue Books, 1926), pp. 40-43. A famous lawyer, in the course of defending two killers, argues that determinism is true and therefore man is not responsible for his actions.

Freud, Sigmund, *Psychopathology of Everyday Life*, Chap. XII, in A. A. Brill (trans. and ed.), *Basic Writings of Sigmund Freud* (New York: Modern Library, 1938), pp. 150-178. Argues that there is a complete psychic determinism and that the feeling of free will arises from our unawareness of unconscious motivation.

Spinoza, Benedict de, *Ethics*, esp. Part I, Appendix, and Part III, Prop. II. A classic statement of determinism; contends that men think themselves free only because they are ignorant of the causes of their behavior.

Wood, Ledger, "The Free-Will Controversy," *Philosophy*, XVI (1941), pp. 386-397. Highly readable statement of arguments in behalf of determinism and against libertarianism.

Reconciliationism

Ayer, A. J., "Freedom and Necessity," in *Philosophical Essays* (London: Macmillan, 1954), pp. 271-284. A clearly written article in behalf of the view that freedom is compatible with determinism.

Hobart, R. E., "Free Will as Involving Determination and Inconceivable Without It," *Mind*, XLIII (1934), pp. 1-27. Argues that free will involves determinism and that a belief in moral responsibility and moral desert is consistent with a belief in determinism.

Nowell-Smith, P. H., "Freewill and Moral Responsibility," *Mind*, LVII (1948), pp. 45-61. Argues against the libertarian position and for the view that both free will and moral responsibility are compatible with determinism.

Schlick, Moritz, *Problems of Ethics*, (New York: Prentice-Hall, 1939), Chap. VII. Argues that the problem of free will is a false problem, urging that freedom is the opposite of compulsion rather than casual determination.

Stevenson, Charles L., *Ethics and Language* (New Haven: Yale U.P., 1944), Chap. XIV. Urges that in order to make ethical judgments about actions, we need only assume that the actions were avoidable. Since an avoidable action might be fully determined, the traditional controversy about free will is irrelevant to ethics.

Libertarianism

Aquinas, Thomas, *Summa Theologica*, trans. by Fathers of the English Dominican Province (2d. and rev. ed., London: Burns, Oates and Washbourne, 1922), Part I, Ques. LXXXIII, "Of Free-Will." A classic statement of the libertarian position in which the author states objections to his own position and replies to them.

———, *Truth*, Vol. III, trans. by Robert W. Schmidt, S.J. (Chicago: Regnery, 1954), Question 24, "Free Choice." A similar but somewhat more comprehensive statement of the author's position than is provided in the *Summa Theologica*.

Campbell, C. A., "Is 'Free Will' a Pseudo-Problem?" *Mind*, LX (1951), pp. 446-465. Criticizes the reconciliationist position, especially in the way it is put forward by Nowell-Smith, Schlick, and Stevenson in the writings cited above.

Carritt, E. F., *Ethical and Political Thinking* (Oxford: Clarendon, 1947), Chap. XII. Gives arguments both against determinism and in behalf of man's possessing freedom of choice.

Cranston, Maurice, *Freedom: A New Analysis* (London: Longmans, Green, 1953), Part III. Surveys various positions about free will, ending on the side of the libertarians but with some doubts.

Lehrer, Keith, "Can We Know That We Have Free Will by Introspection?" *Journal of Philosophy*, LVII (1960), pp. 145-157. Argues that we can know that we have free will by introspection.

Special Problems

Foot, Philippa, "Free Will as Involving Determinism," *Philosophical Review*, LXVI (1957), pp. 439-450. A critic of the view that free will is compatible with determinism. Explicitly mentions Ayer, Hobart, Hume, and Nowell-Smith as opponents.

Mabbott, J. D., "Freewill and Punishment," in H. D. Lewis (ed.), in *Contemporary British Philosophy*, Third Series (New York: Macmillan, 1956), pp. 289-309. Discusses the relations between free choice, moral responsibility, and punishment. Argues for a type of libertarian position.

Pike, Nelson, "Divine Omniscience and Voluntary Action," *Philosophical Review*, LXXIV (1965), pp. 27-46. Analyzes arguments which contend that if God is omniscient, then no human action is voluntary.

Rowe, William L., "Augustine on Foreknowledge and Free Will," *Review of Metaphysics*, XVIII (1964), pp. 356-363. Explains and criticizes Augustine's reasoning in rejecting the view that God's foreknowledge is incompatible with free will; then offers an alternative way of arguing in behalf of such a rejection.

Stout, A. K., "Free Will and Responsibility," *Proceedings of the Aristotelian Society*, XXXVII (1936-7), pp. 213-230. Offers a view of free will, without removing volition from the casual order, which will satisfy ethical needs and provide an account of moral responsibility.

Taylor, Richard, "Deliberation and Foreknowledge," *American Philosophical Quarterly*, I (1964), pp. 73-80. Argues that foreknowledge is not compatible with deliberation. Can be viewed as a critic of the position put forward by St. Augustine in this text.

Workman, Rollin W., "Is Indeterminism Supported by Quantum Theory?" *Philosophy of Science*, XXVI (1959), pp. 251-259. Argues that it is doubtful that quantum mechanics supports indeterminism, though quantum mechanics may show that the concepts of "determined" and "indetermined" are inapplicable to the world.

4. The Free Personality

The preceding discussion of human freedom has been concerned with the question whether man possesses the freedom to choose and to act. Generally speaking, answers to this question have been given by the authors in terms which either affirm or deny that all men have such freedom. As traditionally posed, the issue is whether the evidence does or does not support the belief that man by nature possesses free will.

In Part 4, we turn to a different type of freedom—a freedom which concerns a man's total personality, rather than his individual choices and actions, a freedom that is not given by nature but is acquired by men as they achieve virtue or wisdom. For the authors in this section, the problem is to characterize the state of mind, or the personality traits, that an individual must possess in order to be free from external pressures and internal motives which threaten to enslave him.

At first sight, it may appear that this type of freedom differs so radically from the type of freedom under discussion in the previous section that the term "freedom" no longer has a common meaning. Without wishing to take sides on the complex issues raised in Part 2 about the meaning of "freedom," we may note that there is agreement that freedom involves some kind of self-determination, as opposed to determination by factors external to the self. Thus, the debate over free will focuses upon the influence of causes external to the individual and an individual is regarded as "free" if his choices are not wholly determined by them. In Part 4, the authors are also concerned with self-determination but their attention is directed to the features of personality which genuinely express selfhood as opposed to those features of personality which characterize men in bondage. Differences among them arise according to the way they construe the nature of the "self." For religious writers, the "self" is typically identified with the type of person who has acquired habits of virtue. In this view, the man of vice is the one in bondage, enslaved by forces alien to his true self. For other authors, man is truly "himself" when he develops and expresses his rational nature, rather than being enslaved by his passions. There can thus be as many conceptions of a free personality as there are conceptions of what constitutes man's true selfhood; yet each author will agree with the others and with those who are concerned with free will that "freedom" involves some type of self-determination.

Despite this common thread of meaning, it should be noted that discussions about free will and about the characteristics of a free personality can be quite independent of one another. One might suppose that an author who believes that men can achieve self-determination as a personality trait will automatically be an author who believes that men have free choice. Such is not the case. When one has decided what constitutes man's true self, it is possible to believe that men become free persons not by any decisions of their own but by the operation of forces beyond their control. For instance, Luther believes that it is only the grace of God which can make men free; the question of whether men have free will is not relevant to whether they achieve Christian liberty. Other authors, disagreeing with Luther, contend that any freedom which the individual himself has not achieved through his own free choice is not properly "freedom" at all. Accordingly, the connection between freedom of choice and freedom of personality is itself debatable, and one cannot conclude from the fact that an author believes in freedom of personality that he is necessarily on the free-willist side of the issues treated in Part 3.

In the first of the specific readings, Epictetus expresses a point of view about human freedom which is typical of the Stoic school of philosophy. Telling us that "he is free who lives as he wishes to live," Epictetus observes that we are free only as we acquire self-mastery. Self-mastery is attained when we have acquired the ability to accept without frustration what is not in our power. Thus, the man who bemoans the loss of his wealth, or who is upset by the criticism of others, or who grieves at the death of a loved one displays the fact that his personality is not his own but is at the mercy of these external things. In contrast, the free man recognizes that such things are not in his power. He lives as he wishes to live because he has achieved a state of mind which can willingly accept whatever happens.

Luther discusses human freedom from the standpoint of his Christian outlook. For him, man is by nature sinful. Only through faith and the grace of God can man become free. Given grace, the Christian man is then "a perfectly free lord of all." His freedom is such that no circumstances—poverty, ill health, or any other misfortune—can dominate or injure the spiritual nature which constitutes his true selfhood. Moreover, he is free in yet other ways: he is free from domination by the sinful side of his nature; and, by spontaneously doing what is right, he is free from constraints imposed by external and internal laws of obligation. Yet there is a paradox, for the Christian man is also "a perfectly dutiful servant of all." He is one who does good works, not because he is constrained to do them for salvation, but because he is a good man who freely does service.

Kant, Germany's outstanding philosopher in the eighteenth century, also links achieving freedom to acquiring the power to be moral. In contrast to Luther, however, Kant places the responsibility for becoming virtuous upon man himself. Noting that internal freedom requires that a man be master of himself in a given case and that he have control of his emotions and passions, Kant finds that both freedom and virtue require that a man's powers and inclinations become subordinate *to the rule of reason. In the earlier part of the selection included here, Kant describes in terms of "good will" and "duty" what it means to follow the rule of reason. To do so, he tells us, a person must always act out of respect for the moral law—a law that requires that the principles a man adopts for his behavior be of such a type that he could also will that those principles become universal laws.*

Bosanquet, a British philosopher writing at the turn of the twentieth century, adds yet another dimension, the State to the discussion of the nature of a free personality. For him, a man is free insofar as he affirms his "real" or "rational" self. To affirm such a self requires that an individual find a stable purpose and satisfying object capable of unifying his partial impulses and providing him with something to do and to care for. Such a purpose and object is provided by the State, conceived as including all the institutions of social life from the family to the Church when these are organized in one system working for the common good. Furthermore, since the path of real self-affirmation (or freedom) lies in dedication to the common good, and since individuals may out of indolence or selfishness seek a private good at the expense of the common good, we must recognize the rightful use of force by the State to correct such individuals. In short, for Bosanquet, there is a legitimate sense in which the State may force men to be free.

With John Dewey, whose thought dominated much of American philosophy in the first half of the twentieth century, an unusual conception of human freedom is put forward which synthesizes materials concerning free choice, man's freedom in society, and what it means to be a free person. Refusing to confine his attention to one aspect of man's freedom, Dewey notes that traditional discussions have tended to emphasize either the importance of choice as an element of freedom or the importance of the power to act in accordance with choice—a power which varies according to the opportunities provided by political and economic institutions. He then offers a unifying conception of freedom as growth. For him, the key to growth lies in an individual's capacity to make intelligent decisions—decisions made in the light of his best knowledge about his preferences and the consequences of acting upon them. By acting upon such decisions, the individual learns more about what he can and cannot do, thereby increasing his power to act. Accordingly, a continuous growth cycle is made possible as intelligent choices increase the individual's power to act and as his exercise of that power brings additional information to render choices more intelligent in the future.

Influenced by his training as a psychoanalyst, Erich Fromm begins by identifying freedom as realizing one's self and then offers a more specific description of what this means for modern men who have lost the security of older traditions. For Fromm, men must seek "positive freedom," which "consists in the spontaneous activity of the total, integrated personality." Such spontaneity is contrasted to the compulsive behavior of persons who act simply to escape feelings of isolation and powerlessness. He then suggests that the two primary components of spontaneity are to be found in love of others and in creative work.

Each of the authors mentioned thus far has his intellectual roots in Western civilization. In the last selection of Part 4, we move to an Oriental philosophy, as Daisetz Suzuki seeks to explain the Zen Buddhist conception of freedom and how it is to be achieved. Defining freedom in terms which remind one of Fromm, Suzuki tells us that, for Zen, freedom means "giving free play to all the creative and benevolent impulses inherently lying in our hearts." It is ignorance of our own capacities to be happy and loving which prevents us from achieving freedom. What Zen seeks to do is to dispel this ignorance by appealing to facts of experience. By noting the deepening of character which can come from suffering, by calling attention to the ego-centered character of our lives which prevents genuine love, and by shaking us away from relying upon purely intellectual solutions to our problems of living, Zen tries to point the way for the individual to experience the life of freedom for himself.

"FREEDOM AS SELF-MASTERY"

Epictetus

He is free who lives as he wishes to live; who is neither subject to compulsion nor to hindrance, nor to force; whose movements to action are not impeded, whose desires attain their purpose, and who does not fall into that which he would avoid. Who then chooses to live in error? No man. Who choose to live deceived, liable to mistake, unjust, unrestrained, discontented, mean? No man. Not one then of the bad lives as he wishes; nor is he then free. And who chooses to live in sorrow, fear, envy, pity, desiring and failing in his desires, attempting to avoid something and falling into it? Not one. Do we then find any of the bad free from sorrow, free from fear, who does not fall into that which he would avoid, and does not obtain that which he wishes? Not one; nor then do we find any bad man free.

If then a man who has been twice consul should hear this, if you add, But you are a wise man; this is nothing to you: he will pardon you. But if you tell him the truth, and say, You differ not at all from those who have been thrice sold as to being yourself not a slave, what else ought you to expect than blows? For he says, What, I a slave, I whose father was free, whose mother was free, I whom no man can purchase: I am also of senatorial rank, and a friend of Caesar, and I have been a consul, and I own many slaves.—In the first place, most excellent senatorial man, perhaps your father was a slave in the same kind of servitude, and your mother, and your grandfather and all your ancestors in an ascending series. But even if they were as free as it is possible, what is this to you? What if they were of a noble nature, and you of a mean nature; if they were fearless, and you a coward; if they had the power of self-restraint, and you are not able to exercise it.

And what, you may say, has this to do with being a slave? Does it seem to you to be nothing to do a thing unwillingly, with compulsion, with groans, has this nothing to do with being a slave? It is something, you say: but who is able to compel me, except the lord of all, Caesar? Then even you yourself have admitted that you have one master. But that he is the common master of all, as you say, let not this console you at all: but know that you are a slave in a great family. So also the people of Nicopolis are used to exclaim, By the fortune of Caesar, we are free.

However, if you please, let us not speak of Caesar at present. But tell me this: did you never love any person, a young girl, or slave, or free? What then is this with respect to being a slave or free? Were you never commanded by the person beloved to do something which you did not wish to do? have you never flattered your little slave? have you never kissed her feet? And yet if any man compelled you to kiss Caesar's feet, you would think it an insult and excessive tyranny. What else then if slavery? Did you never go out by night to some place whither you did not wish to go, did you not expend what you did not wish to expend, did you not utter words with sighs and groans, did you not submit to abuse and to be excluded? But if you are ashamed to confess your own acts, see what Thrasonides says and does, who having seen so much military service as perhaps not even you have, first of all went out by night, when Geta (a slave) does not venture out, but if he were compelled by his master, would have cried out much and would have gone out lamenting his bitter slavery. Next, what does Thrasonides say? A worthless girl has enslaved me, me whom no enemy ever did. Unhappy man, who are the slave even of a girl, and a worthless girl. Why then do you still call yourself free? and why do you talk of your service in the army? Then he calls for a sword and is angry with him who out of kindness refuses it; and he sends presents to her who hates him, and intreats and weeps, and on the other hand having had a little success he is elated. But even then how? was he free enough neither to desire nor to fear?

Now consider in the case of animals, how we employ the notion of liberty. Men keep tame lions shut up, and feed them, and some take them about; and who will say that this lion is free? Is it not the fact that the more he lives at his ease, so much the more he is in a slavish condition? and who if he had perception and reason would wish to be one of these lions? Well, these birds when they are caught and are kept shut up, how much do they suffer in their attempts to escape? and some of them die of hunger rather than submit to such a kind of life. And as many of them as live, hardly live and with suffering pine away; and if they ever find any opening, they make their escape. So much do they desire their natural liberty, and to be independent and free from hindrance. And what harm to you in this? What do you say? I am formed by nature to fly where I choose, to live in the open air, to sing when I choose: you deprive me of all this, and say, what harm is it to you? For this reason we shall say that those animals only are free, which cannot endure capture, but as soon as they are caught, escape from captivity by death. So Diogenes also somewhere says that there is only one way to freedom, and that is to die content: and he writes to the Persian king, You cannot enslave the Athenian state any more than you can enslave fishes. How is that? cannot I catch them? If you catch them, says Diogenes, they will immediately leave you, as fishes do: for if you catch a fish, it dies; and if these men that are caught shall die, of what use to you is the preparation for war? These are the words of a free man who had carefully examined the thing, and, as was natural, had discovered it. But if you look for it in a different place from where it is, what wonder if you never find it? . . .

Further than answer me this question also, does freedom seem to you to be something great and noble and valuable?—How should it not seem so? Is is possible then when a man obtains anything so great and valuable and noble to be mean?—It is not possible—When then you see any man subject to another or flattering him contrary to his own opinion, confidently affirm that this man also is not free; and not only if he do this for a bit of supper, but also if he does it for a government (province) or a consulship: and call these men little slaves who for the sake of little matters do these things, and those who do so for the sake of great things call great slaves, as they deserve to be.—This is admitted also—Do you think that freedom is a thing independent and self governing?—Certainly—Whomsoever then it is in the power of another to hinder and compel, declare that he is not free. And do not look, I intreat you, after his grandfathers and great grandfathers, or inquire about his being bought or sold; but if you hear him saying from his heart and with feeling, 'Master,' even if the twelve fasces precede him (as consul), call him slave. And if you hear him say, 'Wretch that I am, how much I suffer,' call him a slave. If finally you see him lamenting, complaining, unhappy, call him a slave though he wears a praetexta. If then he is doing nothing of this kind, do not yet say that he is free, but learn his opinions, whether they are subject to compulsion, or may produce hindrance, or to bad fortune; and if you find him such, call him a slave who has a holiday in the Saturnalia: say that his master is from home: he will return soon, and you will know what he suffers. Who will return? Whoever has in himself the power over anything which is desired by the man, either to give it to him or to take it away? Thus then have we many masters? We have: for we have circumstances as masters prior to our present masters; and these circumstances are many. Therefore it must of necessity be that those who have the power over any of these circumstances must be our masters. For no man fears Caesar himself, but he fears death, banishment, deprivation of his property, prison and disgrace. Nor does any man love Caesar, unless Caesar is a person of great merit, but he loves wealth, the office of tribune, praetor or consul. When we love, and hate and fear these things, it must be that those who have the power over them must be our masters. Therefore we adore them even as gods; for we think that what possesses the power of conferring the greatest advantage on us is divine. Then we wrongly assume that a certain person has the power of conferring the greatest advantages; therefore he is something divine. For if we wrongly assume that a certain person has the power of conferring the greatest advantages, it is a necessary consequence that the conclusion from these premises must be false.

What then is that which makes a man free from hindrance and makes him his own master? For wealth does not do it, nor consulship, nor provincial government, nor royal power; but something else must be discovered. What then is that which when we write makes us free from hindrance and unimpeded? The knowledge of the art of writing. What then is it in playing the lute? The science of playing the lute. Therefore in life also it is the science of life. You have then heard in a general way: but examine the thing also in the several parts. Is it possible that he who desires any of the things which depends on others can be free from hindrance? No—Is it possible for him to be impeded? No—Therefore he cannot be free. Consider then: whether we have nothing which is in our own power only, or whether we have all things, or whether some things are in our own power, and others in the power of others.—What do you mean?—When you wish the body to be entire (sound), is it in your power or not?—It is not in my power—When you wish it to be healthy? Neither is this in my power.—When you wish it to be handsome?—Nor is this—Life or death?—Neither is this in my power.—Your body then is another's, subject to every man who is stronger than yourself—It is—But your estate, is it in your power to have it when you please, and as long as you please, and such as you please?—No —And your slaves?—No—And your clothes?—No—And your house?—No—And your horses?—Not one of these things—And if you wish by all means your children to live, or your wife, or your brother, or your friends, is it in your power?—This also is not in my power.

Whether then have you nothing which is in your own power, which depends on yourself only and cannot be taken from you, or have you any thing of the kind?—I know not—Look at the thing thus, and examine it. Is any man able to make you assent to that which is false?—No man—In the matter of assent then you are free from hindrance and obstruction.—Granted—Well; and can a man force you to desire to move towards that to which you do not choose?—He can, for when he threatens me with death or bonds, he compels me to desire to move towards it. If then, you despise death and bonds, do you still pay any regard to him?—No—Is then the despising of death an act of your own or is it not yours?—It is my act—It is your own act then also to desire to move towards a thing; or is it not so?—It is my own act—But to desire to move away from a thing, whose act is that? This also is your act—What then if I have attempted to walk, suppose another should hinder me— What part of you does he hinder? does he hinder the faculty of assent?—No: but my poor body—Yes, as he would do with a stone—Granted; but I no longer walk—And who told you that walking is your own act free from hindrance? for I said that this only was free from hindrance, to desire to move: but where there is need of body and its co-operation, you have heard long ago that nothing is your own.—Granted this also—And who can compel you to desire what you do not wish?—No man—And to propose or intend, or in short to make use of the appearances which present themselves, can any man compel you?—He cannot do this: but he will hinder me when I desire from obtaining what I desire.—If you desire any thing which is your own, and one of the things which cannot be hindered, how will he hinder you?—He cannot in any way—Who then tells that he who desires the things that belong to another is free from hindrance?

Must I then not desire health? By no means, nor any thing else that belongs to another; for what is not in your power to acquire or to keep when you please, this belongs to another. Keep then far from it not only your hands, but more than that, even your desires. If you do not, you have surrendered yourself as a slave; you have subjected your neck, if you admire any thing not your own, to every thing that is dependent on the power of others and perishable, to which you have conceived a liking.—Is not my hand my own?—It is a part of your own body; but it is by nature earth, subject to hindrance, compulsion, and the slave of every thing which is stronger. And why do I say your hand? You ought to possess your whole body as a poor ass loaded, as long as it is possible, as long as you are allowed. But if there be a press, and a soldier should lay hold of it, let it go, do not resist, nor murmur; if you do, you will receive blows, and never the less you will also lose the ass. But when you ought to feel thus with respect to the body, consider what remains to be done about all the rest, which is provided for the sake of the body. When the body is an ass, all the other things are bits belonging to the ass, pack-saddles, shoes, barley, fodder. Let these also go: get rid of them quicker and more readily than of the ass.

When you have made this preparation, and have practised this discipline, to distinguish that which belongs to another from that which is your own, the things which are subject to hindrance from those which are not, to consider the things free from hindrance to concern yourself, and those which are not free not to concern yourself, to keep your desire steadily fixed to the things which do concern yourself, and turned from the things which do not concern yourself; do you still fear any man? No one. For about what will you be afraid? about the things which are your own, in which consists the nature of good and evil? and who has power over these things? who can take them away? who can impede them? No man can, no more than he can impede God. But will you be afraid about your body and your possessions, about things which are not yours, about things which in no way concern you? and what else have you been studying from the beginning than to distinguish between your own and not your own, the things which are in your power and not in your power, the things subject to hindrance and not subject? and why have you come to the philosophers? was it that you may never the less be unfortunate and unhappy? You will then in this way, as I have supposed you to have done, be without fear and disturbance. And what is grief to you? for fear comes from what you expect, but grief from that which is present. But what further will you desire? For of the things which are within the power of the will, as being good and present, you have a proper and regulated desire: but of the things which are not in the power of the will you do not desire any one, and so you do not allow any place to that which is irrational, and impatient, and above measure hasty.

When then you are thus affected towards things, what man can any longer be formidable to you? For what has a man which is formidable to another, either when you see him or speak to him or finally are conversant with him? Not more than one horse has with respect to another, or one dog to another, or one bee to another bee. Things indeed are formidable to every man; and when any man is able to confer these things on another or to take them away, then he too becomes formidable. . . .

This study you ought to practice from morning to evening, beginning with the smallest things and those most liable to damage, with an earthen pot, with a cup. Then proceed in this way to a tunic, to a little dog, to a horse, to a small estate in land: then to yourself, to your body, to the parts of your body, to your children,

to your wife, to your brothers. Look all round and throw these things from you
(which are not yours). Purge your opinions, so that nothing cleave to you of the
things which are not your own, that nothing grow to you, that nothing give you
pain which is torn from you; and say, while you are daily exercising yourself as you
do there (in the school), not that you are philosophizing, for this is an arrogant
(offensive) expression, but that you are presenting an asserter of freedom; for this is
really freedom. To this freedom Diogenes was called by Antisthenes, and he said
that he could no longer be enslaved by any man. For this reason when he was taken
prisoner, how did he behave to the pirates? Did he call any of them master? and I
do not speak of the name, for I am not afraid of the word but of the state of
mind, by which the word is produced. How did he reprove them for feeding badly
their captives? How was he sold? Did he seek a master? no; but a slave. And when
he was sold how did he behave to his master? Immediately he disputed with him
and said to his master that he ought not to be dressed as he was, nor shaved in such
a manner; and about the children he told him how he ought to bring them up. And
what was strange in this? for if his master had bought an exercise master, would he
have employed him in the exercises of the palaestra as a servant or as a master? and
so if he had bought a physician or an architect. And so in every matter, it is
absolutely necessary that he who has skill must be the superior of him who has not.
Whoever then generally possesses the science of life, what else must he be than
master? For who is master in a ship? The men who govern the helm? Why? Because
he who will not obey him suffers for it. But a master can give me stripes. Can he
do it then without suffering for it? So I also used to think. But because he cannot
do it without suffering for it, for this reason it is not in his power: and no man can
do what is unjust without suffering for it. And what is the penalty for him who
puts his own slave in chains? what do you think that is? The fact of putting the
slave in chains:—and you also will admit this, if you choose to maintain the truth,
that man is not a wild beast, but a tame animal. For when is a vine doing badly?
When it is in a condition contrary to its nature. When is a cock? Just the same.
Therefore a man also is so. What then is a man's nature? To bite, to kick, and to
throw into prison and to behead? No; but to do good, to co-operate with others, to
wish them well. At that time then he is in a bad condition, whether you choose to
admit it or not, when he is acting foolishly.

Socrates then did not fare badly?—No; but his judges and his accusers did. . . .

Well then let us recapitulate the things which have been agreed on. The man who
is not under restraint is free, to whom things are exactly in that state in which he
wishes them to be; but he who can be restrained or compelled or hindered, or
thrown into any circumstances against his will, is a slave. But who is fiee from
restraint? He who desires nothing that belongs to others? And what are the things
which belong to others? Those which are not in our power either to have or not to
have, or to have of a certain kind or in a certain manner. Therefore the body
belongs to another, the parts of the body belongs to another, possession (property)
belongs to another. If then you are attached to any of these things as your own,
you will pay the penalty which it is proper for him to pay who desires what

belongs to another. This road leads to freedom, this is the only way of escaping from slavery, to be able to say at last with all your soul

> Lead me, O Zeus, and thou O destiny,
> The way that I am bid by you to go.

... Diogenes was free. How was he free?—not because he war born of free parents, but because he was himself free, because he had cast off all the handles of slavery, and it was not possible for any man to approach him, nor had any man the means of laying hold of him to enslave him. He had everything easily loosed, everything only hanging to him. If you laid hold of his property, he would have rather let it go and be yours, than he would have followed you for it: if you had laid hold of his leg, he would have let go his leg; if of all his body, all his poor body; his intimates, friends, country, just the same. For he knew from whence he had them, and from whom, and on what conditions. His true parents indeed, the Gods, and his real country he would never have deserted, nor would he have yielded to any man in obedience to them and to their orders, nor would any man have died for his country more readily. For he was not used to inquire when he should be considered to have done anything on behalf of the whole of things (the universe, or all the world), but he remembered that every thing which is done comes from thence and is done on behalf of that country and is commanded by him who administers it. Therefore see what Diogenes himself says and writes:—"For this reason, he says, Diogenes, it is in your power to speak both with the King of the Persians and with Aarchidamus the king of the Lacedaemonians as you please." Was it because he was born of free parents? I suppose all the Athenians and all the Lacedaemonians because they were born of slaves, could not talk with them (these kings) as they wished, but feared and paid court to them. Why then does he say that it is in his power? Because I do not consider the poor body to be my own, because I want nothing, because law is every thing to me, and nothing else is. These were the things which permitted him to be free.

And that you may not think that I show you the example of a man who is a solitary person, who has neither wife nor children, nor country, nor friends nor kinsmen, by whom he could be bent and drawn in various directions, take Socrates and observe that he had a wife and children, but he did not consider them as his own; that he had a country, so long as it was fit to have one, and in such a manner as was fit; friends and kinsmen also, but he held all in subjection to law and to the obedience due to it. For this reason he was the first to go out as a soldier, when it was necessary, and in war he exposed himself to danger most unsparingly; and when he was sent by the tyrants to seize Leon, he did not even deliberate about the matter, because he thought it was a base action, and he knew he must die (for his refusal), if it so happened. And what difference did that make to him? for he intended to preserve something else, not his poor flesh, but his fidelity, his honourable character. These are things which could not be assailed nor brought into subjection. Then when he was obliged to speak in defence of his life, did he behave like a man who had children, who had a wife? No, but he behaved like a man who has neither. And what did he do when he was (ordered) to drink the poison, and when he had the power of escaping from prison, and when Crito said to him, Escape for the sake of your children, what did Socrates say? did he consider the power of escape as an unexpected gain? By no means: he considered what was fit and proper; but the rest he did not even look at or take into the reckoning. For he did not choose, he said, to save his poor body, but to save that which is increased and saved by doing what is just, and is impaired and destroyed by doing what is unjust. Socrates will not save his life by a base act; he who would not put the Athenians to the vote when they clamoured that he should do so, he who refused to obey the tyrants, he who discoursed in such a manner about virtue and right behaviour. It is not possible to save such a man's life by base acts, but he is saved by dying, not by running away. For the good actor also preserves his character by stopping when he ought to stop, better than when he goes on acting beyond the proper time. What then shall the children of Socrates do? "If," said Socrates, "I had gone off to Thessaly, would you have taken care of them; and if I depart to the world below, will there be no man to take care of them?" See how he gives to death a gentle name and mocks it. But if you and I had been in his place, we should have immediately answered as philosophers that those who act unjustly must be repaid in the same way, and we should have added, "I shall be useful to many, if my life is saved, and if I die, I shall be useful to no man." For, if it had been necessary, we should have made our escape by slipping through a small hole. And how in that case should we have been useful to any man? for where would they have been then staying? or if we were useful to men while we were alive, should we not have been much more useful to them by dying when we ought to die, and as we ought? And now Socrates being dead, no less useful to men, and even more useful, is the remembrance of that which he did or said when he was alive.

Think of these things, these opinions, these words: look to these examples, if you would be free, if you desire the thing according to its worth. And what is the wonder if you buy so great a thing at the price of things so many and so great? For the sake of this which is called liberty, some hang themselves, others throw themselves down precipices, and sometimes even whole cities have perished: and will you not for the sake of the true and unassailable and secure liberty give back to God when he demands them the things which he has given? Will you not, as Plato says, study not to die only, but also to endure torture, and exile, and scourging and in a word to give up all which is not your own? If you will not, you will be a slave among slaves, even if you be ten thousand times a consul; and if you make your way up to the Palace (Caesar's residence), you will no less be a slave; and you will feel, that perhaps philosophers utter words which are contrary to common opinion (paradoxes), as Cleanthes also said, but not words contrary to reason. For you will know by experience that the words are true, and that there is no profit from the things which are valued and eagerly sought to those who have obtained them; and to those who have not yet obtained them there is an imagination, that when these things are come, all that is good will come with them; then, when they are come, the feverish feeling is the same, the tossing to and fro is the same, the satiety, the desire of things which are not present; for freedom is acquired not by the full possession of the things which are desired, but by removing the desire. And that you may know that this is true, as you have laboured for those things, so transfer your labour to these; be vigilant for the purpose of acquiring an opinion which will make you free; pay court to a philosopher instead of to a rich old man: be seen about a philosopher's doors: you will not disgrace yourself by being seen; you will not go away empty nor without profit, if you go to the philosopher as you ought, and if not (if you do not succeed), try at least: the attempt is not disgraceful.

"CHRISTIAN LIBERTY"

Martin Luther

That I may make the way easier for the unlearned—for only such do I serve—I set down first these two propositions concerning the liberty and the bondage of the spirit:

A Christian man is a perfectly free lord of all, subject to none.

A Christian man is a perfectly dutiful servant of all, subject to all.

Although these two theses seem to contradict each other, yet, if they should be found to fit together they would serve our purpose beautifully. For they are both Paul's own, who says, in 1 Corinthians 9, "Whereas I was free, I made myself the servant of all," and Romans 8, "Owe no man anything, but to love one another." Now love by its very nature is ready to serve and to be subject to him who is loved. So Christ, although Lord of all, was made of a woman, made under the law, and hence was at the same time free and a servant, at the same time in the form of God and in the form of a servant.

Let us start, however, with something more remote from our subject, but more obvious. Man has a twofold nature, a spiritual and a bodily. According to the spiritual nature, which men call the soul, he is called a spiritual, or inner, or new man; according to the bodily nature, which men call the flesh, he is called a carnal, or outward, or old man, of whom the Apostle writes, in 2 Corinthians 4, "Though our outward man is corrupted, yet the inward man is renewed day by day." Because of this diversity of nature the Scriptures assert contradictory things of the same man, since these two men in the same man contradict each other, since the flesh lusteth against the spirit and the spirit against the flesh (Galatians 5).

First, let us contemplate the inward man, to see how a righteous, free, and truly Christian man, that is, a new, spiritual, inward man, comes into being. It is evident that no external thing, whatsoever it be, has any influence whatever in producing Christian righteousness or liberty, nor in producing unrighteousness or bondage. A simple argument will furnish the proof. What can it profit the soul if the body fare well, be free and active, eat, drink, and do as it pleases? For in these things even the most godless slaves of all the vices fare well. On the other hand, how will ill health or imprisonment or hunger or thirst or any other external misfortune hurt the soul? With these things even the most godly men are afflicted, and those who because of a clear conscience are most free. None of these things touch either the liberty or the bondage of the soul. The soul receives no benefit if the body is adorned with the sacred robes of the priesthood, or dwells in sacred places, or is occupied with sacred duties, or prays, fasts, abstains from certain kinds of food, or does any work whatsoever that can be done by the body and in the body. The righteousness and the freedom of the soul demand something far different, since the things which have been mentioned could be done by any wicked man, and such works produce nothing but hypocrites. On the other hand, it will not hurt the soul if the body is clothed in secular dress, dwells in unconsecrated places, eats and drinks as others do, does not pray aloud, and neglects to do all the things mentioned above, which hypocrites can do.

Further, to put aside all manner of works, even contemplation, meditation, and all that the soul can do, avail nothing. One thing and one only is necessary for Christian life, righteousness, and liberty. That one thing is the most holy Word of God, the Gospel of Christ, as he says, John 11, "I am the resurrection and the life: he that believeth in me shall not die forever"; and John 8, "If the Son shall make you free, you shall be free indeed"; and Matthew 4, "Not in bread alone doth man live; but in every word that proceedeth from the mouth of God." Let us then consider it certain and conclusively established that the soul can do without all things except the Word of God, and that where this is not there is no help for the soul in anything else whatever. But if it has the Word it is rich and lacks nothing, since this Word is the Word of life, of truth, of light, of peace, of righteousness, of salvation, of joy, of liberty, of wisdom, of power, of grace, of glory, and of every blessing beyond our power to estimate. This is why the prophet in the entire One Hundred and Nineteenth Psalm, and in many other places of Scripture, with so many sighs yearns after the Word of God and applies so many names to it. On the other hand, there is no more terrible plague with which the wrath of God can smite men than a famine of the hearing of His Word, as He says in Amos, just as there is no greater mercy than when He sends forth His Word, as we read in Psalm 107, "He sent His word and healed them, and delivered them from their destructions." Nor was Christ sent into the world for any other ministry but that of the Word, and the whole spiritual estate, apostles, bishops and all the priests, has been called and instituted only for the ministry of the Word.

You ask, "What then is this Word of God, and how shall it be used, since there are so many words of God?" I answer, the Apostle explains that in Romans 1. The Word is the Gospel of God concerning His Son, who was made flesh, suffered, rose from the dead, and was glorified through the Spirit who sanctifies. For to preach Christ means to feed the soul, to make it righteous, to set it free, and to save it, if it believe the preaching. For faith alone is the saving and efficacious use of the Word of God, Romans 10, "If thou confess with thy mouth that Jesus is Lord, and believe with thy heart that God hath raised Him up from the dead, thou shalt be saved"; and again, "The end of the law is Christ, unto righteousness to everyone that believeth"; and, in Romans 1, "The just shall live by his faith." The Word of God cannot be received and cherished by any works whatever, but only by faith. Hence it is clear that, as the soul needs only the Word for its life and righteousness, so it is justified by faith alone and not by any works; for if it could be justified by anything else, it would not need the Word, and therefore it would not need faith. But this faith cannot at all exist in connection with works, that is to say, if you at the same time claim to be justified by works, whatever their character; for that would be to halt between two sides, to worship Baal and to kiss the hand, which as Job says, is a very great iniquity. Therefore the moment you begin to believe, you learn that all things in you are altogether blameworthy, sinful, and damnable, as Romans 3 says, "For all have sinned and lack the glory of God"; and again, "There is none just, there is none that doeth good, all have turned out of the way: they are become unprofitable together." When you have learned this, you will know that you need Christ, who suffered and rose again for you, that, believing in Him, you may through this faith become a new man, in that all your sins are forgiven, and you are justified by the merits of another, namely, of Christ alone.

Since, therefore, this faith can rule only in the inward man, as Romans 10 says, "With the heart we believe unto righteousness"; and since faith alone justifies, it is clear that the inward man cannot be justified, made free, and be saved by any outward work or dealing whatsoever, and that works, whatever their character, have nothing to do with this inward man. On the other hand, only ungodliness and unbelief of heart, and no outward work, make him guilty and a damnable servant of sin. Wherefore it ought to be the first concern of every Christian to lay aside all trust in works, and more and more to strengthen faith alone, and through faith to grow in the knowledge, not of works, but of Christ Jesus, who suffered and rose for him, as Peter teaches, in the last chapter of his first Epistle; since no other work makes a Christian. Thus when the Jews asked Christ, John 6, what they should do that they might work the works of God, He brushed aside the multitude of works in which He saw that they abounded, and enjoined upon them a single work, saying, "This is the work of God, that you believe in Him whom He hath sent. For him hath God the Father sealed."

Hence true faith in Christ is a treasure beyond comparison, which brings with it all salvation and saves from every evil, as Christ says in the last chapter of Mark, "He that believeth and is baptized, shall be saved; but he that believeth not, shall be condemmed." This treasure Isaiah beheld and foretold in Chapter 10, "The Lord shall make an abridged and consuming word upon the land, and the consumption abridged shall overflow with righteousness"; as if he said, "Faith, which is a brief and perfect fulfillment of the law, shall fill believers with so great righteousness that they shall need nothing more for their righteousness." So also Paul says, Romans 10, "With the heart we believe unto righteousness."

Should you ask how it comes that faith alone justifies and without works offers us such a treasury of great benefits, when so many works, ceremonies, and laws are prescribed in the Scriptures, I answer: First of all, remember what has been said: faith alone, without works, justifies, makes free and saves, as we shall later make still more clear. Here we must point out that all the Scriptures of God are divided into two parts—commands and promises. The commands indeed teach things that are good, but the things taught are not done as soon as taught; for the commands show us what we ought to do, but do not give us the power to do it; they are intended to teach a man to know himself, that through them he may recognize his inability to do good and may despair of his powers. That is why they are called and are the Old Testament. For example: "Thou shalt not covet" is a command which convicts us all of being sinners, since no one is able to avoid coveting, however much he may struggle against it. Therefore, in order not to covet, and to fulfill the command, a man is compelled to despair of himself, and to seek elsewhere and from someone else the help which he does not find in himself, as is said in Hosea, "Destruction is thy own, O Israel: thy help is only in Me." And as we fare with this one command, so we fare with all; for it is equally impossible for us to keep any of them.

But when a man through the commands has learned to know his weakness, and has become troubled as to how he may satisfy the law, since the law must be fulfilled so that not a jot or tittle shall perish, otherwise man will be condemned without hope; then, being truly humbled and reduced to nothing in his own eyes, he finds in himself no means of justification and salvation. Here the second part of the Scriptures stands ready—the promises of God, which declare the glory of God and say, "If you wish to fulfill the law, and not to covet, as the law demands, come, believe in Christ, in whom grace, righteousness, peace, liberty and all things are promised you; if you believe you shall have all, if you believe not you shall lack all." For what is impossible for you in all the works of the law, many as they are, but all useless, you will accomplish in a short and easy way through faith. For God our Father has made all things depend on faith, so that whoever has faith, shall have all, and whoever has it not, shall have nothing. "For He has concluded all under unbelief, that He might have mercy on all," Romans 11. Thus the promises of God give what the commands of God ask, and fulfill what the law prescribes, that all things may be of God alone, both the commands and the fulfilling of the commands. He alone commands, He also alone fulfills. Therefore the promises of God belong to the New Testament, nay, they are the New Testament.

And since these promises of God are holy, true, righteous, free and peaceful words, full of all goodness, it comes to pass that the soul which clings to them with a firm faith is so united with them, nay, altogether taken up into them, that it not only shares in all their power, but is saturated and made drunken with it. For if a touch of Christ healed, how much more will this most tender touch in the spirit, rather this absorbing of the Word, communicate to the soul all things that are the Word's. This, then, is how through faith alone without works the soul is justified by the Word of God, sanctified, made true and peaceful and free, filled with every blessing and made truly a child of God, as John 1 says, "To them gave he power to become the sons of God, even to them that believe on his name."

From what has been said it is easily seen whence faith has such great power, and why no good work nor all good works together can equal it: no work can cling to the Word of God nor be in the soul; in the soul faith alone and the Word have sway. As the Word is, so it makes the soul, as heated iron glows like fire because of the union of fire with it. It is clear then that a Christian man has in his faith all that he needs, and needs no works to justify him. And if he has no need of works, neither does he need the law; and if he has no need of the law, surely he is free from the law, and it is true, "the law is not made for a righteous man." And this is that Christian liberty, even our faith, which does not indeed cause us to live in idleness or in wickedness, but makes the law and works unnecessary for any man's righteousness and salvation. . . .

Let this suffice concerning the inward man, his liberty and its source, the righteousness of faith, which needs neither laws nor good works, nay, is rather injured by them, if a man trusts that he is justified by them.

Now let us turn to the second part, to the outward man. Here we shall answer all those who, misled by the word "faith" and by all that has been said, now say: "If faith does all things and is alone sufficient unto righteousness, why then are good works commanded? We will take our ease and do no works, and be content with faith." I answer, Not so, ye wicked men, not so. That would indeed be proper, if we were wholly inward and perfectly spiritual men; but such we shall be only at the last day, the day of the resurrection of the dead. As long as we live in the flesh we only begin and make some progress in that which shall be perfected in the future life. For this reason the Apostle, in Romans 8, calls all that we attain in this life "the first fruits" of the spirit, because, forsooth, we shall receive the greater portion, even the fullness of the spirit, in the future. This is the place for that which was said above, that a Christian man is the servant of all and made subject to all. For in so far as he is free he does no works, but in so far as he is a servant he does all manner of works. How this is possible we shall see.

Although, as I have said, a man is abundantly justified by faith inwardly, in his spirit, and so has all that he ought to have, except in so far as this faith and riches must grow from day to day even unto the future life: yet he remains in this mortal life on earth, and in this life he must needs govern his own body and have dealings with men. Here the works begin; here a man cannot take his ease; here he must, indeed, take care to discipline his body by fastings, watchings, labors, and other reasonable discipline, and to make it subject to the spirit so that it will obey and conform to the inward man and to faith, and not revolt against faith and hinder the inward man, as it is the body's nature to do if it be not held in check. For the inward man, who by faith is created in the likeness of God, is both joyful and happy because of Christ in whom so many benefits are conferred upon him, and therefore it is his one occupation to serve God joyfully and for naught, in love that is not constrained.

While he is doing this, lo, he meets a contrary will in his own flesh, which strives to serve the world and to seek its own advantage. This the spirit of faith cannot tolerate, and with joyful zeal it attempts to put the body under and to hold it in check, as Paul says in Romans 7, "I delight in the law of God after the inward man; but I see another law in my members, warring against the law of my mind, and bringing me into captivity to the law of sin"; and, in another place, "I keep under my body, and bring it into subjection: lest by any means, when I have preached to others, I myself should be a castaway," and in Galatians, "They that are Christ's have crucified the flesh with its lusts."

In doing these works, however, we must not think that a man is justified before God by them: for that erroneous opinion faith, which alone is righteousness before God, cannot endure; but we must think that these works reduce the body to subjection and purify it of its evil lusts, and our whole purpose is to be directed only toward the driving out of lusts. For since by faith the soul is cleansed and made a lover of God, it desires that all things, and especially its own body, shall be pure as itself, so that all things may join with it in loving and praising God. Hence a man cannot be idle, because the need of his body drives him and he is compelled to do many good works to reduce it to subjection. Nevertheless the works themselves do not justify him before God, but he does the works out of spontaneous love in obedience to God, and considers nothing except the approval of God, whom he would in all things most scrupulously obey. . . .

The Christian, who is consecrated by his faith, does good works, but the works do not make him more holy or more Christian; for that is the work of faith alone, and if a man were not first a believer and a Christian, all his works would amount to nothing at all and would be truly wicked and damnable sins.

These two sayings, therefore, are true: "Good works do not make a good man, but a good man does good works; evil works do not make a wicked man, but a wicked man does evil works"; so that it is always necessary that the "substance" or person itself be good before there can be any good works, and that good works follow and proceed from the good person, as Christ also says, "A corrupt tree does not bring forth good fruit, a good tree does not bring forth evil fruit." It is clear that the fruits do not bear the tree, nor does the tree grow on the fruits, but, on the contrary, the trees bear the fruits and the fruits grow on the trees. As it is necessary, therefore, that the trees must exist before their fruits, and the fruits do not make trees either good or corrupt, but rather as the trees are so are the fruits they bear; so the person of a man must needs first be good or wicked before he does a good or wicked work, and his works do not make him good or wicked, but he himself makes his works either good or wicked. . . .

Let this suffice concerning works in general, and at the same time concerning the works which a Christian does for his own body. Lastly, we will also speak of the things which he does toward his neighbor. A man does not live for himself alone in this mortal body, so as to work for it alone, but he lives also for all men on earth, nay, rather, he lives only for others and not for himself. And to this end he brings his body into subjection, that he may the more sincerely and freely serve others, as Paul says in Romans 14, "No one lives to himself, and no man dies to himself. For he that liveth, liveth unto the Lord, and he that dieth, dieth unto the Lord." Therefore, it is impossible that he should ever in this life be idle and without works toward his neighbors. For of necessity he will speak, deal with and converse with men, as Christ also, being made in the likeness of men, was found in form as a man, and conversed with men, as Baruch 3 says.

But none of these things does a man need for his righteousness and salvation. Therefore, in all his works he should be guided by this thought and look to this one thing alone, that he may serve and benefit others in all that he does, having regard to nothing except the need and the advantage of his neighbor. Thus, the Apostle commands us to work with our hands that we may give to him who is in need, although he might have said that we should work to support ourselves; he says, however, "that he may have to give to him that needeth." And this is what makes it a Christian work to care for the body, that through its health and comfort we may be able to work, to acquire and to lay by funds with which to aid those who are in need, that in this way the strong member may serve the weaker, and we may be sons of God, each caring for and working for the other, bearing one another's burdens, and so fulfilling the law of Christ. Lo, this is a truly Christian life, here faith is truly effectual through love; that is, it issues in works of the freest service cheerfully and lovingly done, with which a man willingly serves another without hope of reward, and for himself is satisfied with the fullness and wealth of his faith.

So Paul after teaching the Philippians how rich they were made through faith in Christ, in which they obtained all things, proceeds immediately to teach them further, saying, "If there be any consolation in Christ, if any comfort of love, if any fellowship of the Spirit, fulfill ye my joy, that ye be like-minded, having the same love, being of one accord, thinking nothing through strife or vainglory, but in lowliness each esteeming the other better than themselves; looking not every man on his own things, but on the things of others." Here we see clearly that the Apostle has prescribed this rule for the life of Christians—that we should devote all our works to the welfare of others, since each has such abundant riches in his faith, that all his other works and his whole life are a surplus with which he can by voluntary benevolence serve and do good to his neighbor.

As an example of such a life the Apostle cites Christ, saying, "Let this mind be in you, which was also in Christ Jesus, who, being in the form of God, thought it not robbery to be equal with God: but made himself of no reputation, and took upon him the form of a servant, and was made in the likeness of men: and being found in fashion as a man, he became obedient unto death." This salutary word of the Apostle has been obscured for us by those who have not at all understood the Apostle's words, "form of God," "form of a servant," "fashion," "likeness of men," and have applied them to the divine and the human nature. Paul means this: Although Christ was filled with the form of God and rich in all good things, so that He needed no work and no suffering to make Him righteous and saved (for He had all this always from the beginning), yet He was not puffed up by them, nor did He lift Himself up above us and assume power over us, although He could rightly have done so; but, on the contrary, He so lived, labored, worked, suffered and died, that He might be like other men, and in fashion and in actions be nothing else than a man, just as if He had need of all these things and had nothing of the form of God. But He did all this for our sake, that He might serve us, and that all things He accomplished in this form of a servant might become ours.

So a Christian, like Christ, his Head, is filled and made rich by faith, and should be content with this form of God which he has obtained by faith; only, as I have said, he ought to increase this faith until it be made perfect. For this faith is his life, his righteousness, and his salvation: it saves him and makes him acceptable, and bestows upon him all things that are Christ's as has been said above, and as Paul asserts in Galatians 2, when he says, "And the life which I now live in the flesh, I live by the faith of the Son of God." Although the Christian is thus free from all works, he ought in this liberty to empty himself, to take upon himself the form of a servant, to be made in the likeness of men, to be found in fashion as a man, and to serve, help and in every way deal with his neighbor as he sees that God through Christ has dealt and still deals with himself. And this he should do freely, having regard to nothing except the divine approval. He ought to think: "Though I am an unworthy and condemmed man, my God has given me in Christ all the riches of righteousness and salvation without any merit on my part, out of pure, free mercy, so that henceforth I need nothing whatever except faith which believes that this is true. Why should I not therefore freely, joyfully, with all my heart, and with an eager will, do all things which I know are pleasing and acceptable to such a Father, who has overwhelmed me with His inestimable riches? I will therefore give myself as a Christ to my neighbor, just as Christ offered Himself to me; I will do nothing in this life except what I see is necessary, profitable and salutary to my neighbor, since through faith I have an abundance of all good things in Christ.". . .

We conclude, therefore, that a Christian man lives not in himself, but in Christ and in his neighbor. Otherwise he is not a Christian. He lives in Christ through faith, in his neighbor through love; by faith he is caught up beyond himself into God, by love he sinks down beneath himself into his neighbor; yet he always remains in God and in His love, as Christ says in John 1, "Verily, I say unto you, Hereafter ye shall see heaven open, and the angels of God ascending and descending upon the Son of man."

Enough now of liberty. As you see, it is a spiritual and true liberty, and makes our hearts free from all sins, laws and mandates, as Paul says, 1 Timothy 1, "The law is not made for a righteous man." It is more excellent than all other liberty which is external, as heaven is more excellent than earth. This liberty may Christ grant us both to understand and to preserve. Amen. . . .

"FREEDOM THROUGH THE MORAL LAW"

Immanuel Kant

Nothing can possibly be conceived in the world, or even out of it, which can be called good, without qualification, except a Good Will. Intelligence, wit, judgment, and the other *talents* of the mind, however they may be named, or courage, resolution, perseverance, as qualities of temperament, are undoubtedly good and desirable in many respects; but these gifts of nature may also become extremely bad and mischievous if the will which is to make use of them, and which, therefore, constitutes what is called *character*, is not good. It is the same with the *gifts of fortune.* Power, riches, honour, even health, and the general well-being and contentment with one's condition which is called *happiness*, inspire pride, and often presumption, if there is not a good will to correct the influence of these on the mind, and with this also to rectify the whole principle of acting, and adapt it to its end. The sight of a being who is not adorned with a single feature of a pure and good will, enjoying unbroken prosperity, can never give pleasure to an impartial rational spectator. Thus a good will appears to constitute the indispensable condition even of being worthy of happiness.

There are even some qualities which are of service to this good will itself, and may facilitate its action, yet which have no intrinsic unconditional value, but always presuppose a good will, and this qualifies the esteem that we justly have for them, and does not permit us to regard them as absolutely good. Moderation in the affections and passions, self-control, and calm deliberation are not only good in many respects, but even seem to constitute part of the intrinsic worth of the person; but they are far from deserving to be called good without qualification, although they have been so unconditionally praised by the ancients. For without the principles of a good will, they may become extremely bad; and the coolness of a villain not only makes him far more dangerous, but also directly makes him more abominable in our eyes than he would have been without it.

A good will is good not because of what it performs or effects, not by its aptness for the attainment of some proposed end, but simply by virtue of the volition, that is, it is good in itself, and considered by itself is to be esteemed much higher than all that can be brought about by it in favour of any inclination, nay, even of the sum-total of all inclinations. Even if it should happen that, owing to special disfavour of fortune, or the niggardly provision of a step-motherly nature, this will should wholly lack power to accomplish its purpose, if with its greatest efforts it should yet achieve nothing, and there should remain only the good will (not, to be sure, a mere wish, but the summoning of all means in our power), then, like a jewel, it would still shine by its own light, as a thing which has its whole value in itself. Its usefulness or fruitlessness can neither add to nor take away anything from this value. It would be, as it were, only the setting to enable us to handle it the more conveniently in common commerce, or to attract to it the attention of those who are not yet connoisseurs, but not to recommend it to true connoisseurs, or to determine its value.

There is, however, something so strange in this idea of the absolute value of the mere will, in which no account is taken of its utility, that notwithstanding the thorough assent of even common reason to the idea, yet a suspicion must arise that it may perhaps really be the product of mere high-flown fancy, and that we may have misunderstood the purpose of nature in assigning reason as the governor of our will. Therefore we will examine this idea from this point of view.

In the physical constitution of an organized being, that is, a being adapted suitably to the purposes of life, we assume it as a fundamental principle that no organ for any purpose will be found but what is also the fittest and best adapted for that purpose. Now in a being which has reason and a will, if the proper object of nature were its *conservation*, its *welfare*, in a word, its *happiness*, then nature would have hit upon a very bad arrangement in selecting the reason for the creature to carry out this purpose. For all the actions which the creature has to perform with a view to this purpose, and the whole rule of its conduct, would be far more surely prescribed to it by instinct, and that end would have been attained thereby much more certainly than it ever can be by reason. Should reason have been communicated to this favoured creature over and above, it must only have served it to contemplate the happy constitution of its nature, to admire it, to congratulate itself thereon, and to feel thankful for it to the beneficent cause, but not that it should subject its desires to that weak and delusive guidance, and meddle bunglingly with the purpose of nature. In a word, nature would have taken care that reason should not break forth into *practical exercise*, nor have the presumption, with its weak insight, to think out for itself the plan of happiness, and of the means of attaining it. Nature would not only have taken on herself the choice of the ends, but also of the means, and with wise foresight would have entrusted both to instinct.

And, in fact, we find that the more a cultivated reason applies itself with deliberate purpose to the enjoyment of life and happiness, so much the more does the man fail of true satisfaction. And from this circumstance there arises in many, if they are candid enough to confess it, a certain degree of *misology*, that is, hatred of reason, especially in the case of those who are most experienced in the use of it, because after calculating all the advantages they derive, I do not say from the invention of all the arts of common luxury, but even from the sciences (which seem to them to be after all only a luxury of the understanding), they find that they have, in fact, only brought more trouble on their shoulders, rather than gained in happiness; and they end by envying, rather than despising, the more common stamp of men who keep closer to the guidance of mere instinct, and do not allow their reason much influence on their conduct. And this we must admit, that the judgment of those who would very much lower the lofty eulogies of the advantages which reason gives us in regard to the happiness and satisfaction of life, or who would even reduce them below zero, is by no means morose or ungrateful to the goodness with which the world is governed, but that there lies at the root of these judgments the idea that our existence has a different and far nobler end, for which, and not for happiness, reason is properly intended, and which must, therefore, be regarded as the supreme condition to which the private ends of man must, for the most part, be postponed.

For as reason is not competent to guide the will with certainty in regard to its objects and the satisfaction of all our wants (which it to some extent even multiplies), this being an end to which an implanted instinct would have led with much greater certainty; and since, nevertheless, reason is imparted to us as a practical faculty, *i.e.* as one which is to have influence on the *will*, therefore, admitting that nature generally in the distribution of her capacities has adapted the means to the end, its true destination must be to produce a *will*, not merely good as a *means* to something else, but *good in itself*, for which reason was absolutely necessary. This will then, though not indeed the sole and complete good, must be the supreme good and the condition of every other, even of the desire of happiness. Under these circumstances, there is nothing inconsistent with the wisdom of nature in the fact that the cultivation of the reason, which is requisite for the first and unconditional purpose, does in many ways interfere, at least in this life, with the attainment of the second, which is always conditional, namely, happiness. Nay, it may even reduce it to nothing, without nature thereby failing of her purpose. For reason recognizes the establishment of a good will as its highest practical destination, and in attaining this purpose is capable only of a satisfaction of its own proper kind, namely, that from the attainment of an end, which end again is determined by reason only, notwithstanding that this may involve many a disappointment to the ends of inclination.

We have then to develop the notion of a will which deserves to be highly esteemed for itself, and is good without a view to anything further, a notion which exists already in the sound natural understanding, requiring rather to be cleared up than to be taught, and which in estimating the value of our actions always takes the first place, and constitutes the condition of all the rest. In order to do this, we will take the notion of duty, which includes that of a good will, although implying certain subjective restrictions and hindrances. These, however, far from concealing it, or rendering it unrecognizable, rather bring it out by contrast, and make it shine forth so much the brighter.

I omit here all actions which are already recognized as inconsistent with duty, although they may be useful for this or that purpose, for with these the question whether they are done *from duty* cannot arise at all, since they even conflict with it. I also set aside those actions which really conform to duty, but to which men have *no* direct *inclination*, performing them because they are impelled thereto by some other inclination. For in this case we can readily distinguish whether the action which agrees with duty is done *from duty*, or from a selfish view. It is much harder to make this distinction when the action accords with duty, and the subject has besides a *direct* inclination to it. For example, it is always a matter of duty that a dealer should not overcharge an inexperienced purchaser; and wherever there is much commerce the prudent tradesman does not overcharge, but keeps a fixed price for everyone, so that a child buys of him as well as any other. Men are thus *honestly* served; but this is not enough to make us believe that the tradesman has so acted from duty and from principles of honesty: his own advantage required it; it is out of the question in this case to suppose that he might besides have a direct inclination in favour of the buyers, so that, as it were, from love he should give no advantage to one over another. Accordingly the action was done neither from duty nor from direct inclination, but merely with a selfish view.

On the other hand, it is a duty to maintain one's life; and, in addition, everyone has also a direct inclination to do so. But on this account the often anxious care which most men take for it has no intrinsic worth, and their maxim has no moral import. They preserve their life *as duty requires*, no doubt, but not *because duty requires*. On the other hand, if adversity and hopeless sorrow have completely taken away the relish for life; if the unfortunate one, strong in mind, indignant at his fate rather than desponding or dejected, wishes for death, and yet preserves his life without loving it—not from inclination or fear, but from duty—then his maxim has a moral worth.

To be beneficent when we can is a duty; and besides this, there are many minds so sympathetically constituted that, without any other motive of vanity or self-interest, they find a pleasure in spreading joy around them, and can take delight in the satisfaction of others so far as it is their own work. But I maintain that in such a case an action of this kind, however proper, however amiable it may be, has nevertheless no true moral worth, but is on a level with other inclinations, *e.g.* the inclination to honour, which, if it is happily directed to that which is in fact of public utility and accordant with duty, and consequently honourable, deserves praise and encouragement, but not esteem. For the maxim lacks the moral import, namely, that such actions be done *from duty*, not from inclination. Put the case that the mind of that philanthropist was clouded by sorrow of his own, extinguishing all sympathy with the lot of others, and that while he still has the power to benefit others in distress, he is not touched by their trouble because he is absorbed with his own; and now suppose that he tears himself out of this dead insensibility, and performs the action without any inclination to it, but simply from duty, then first has his action its genuine moral worth. Further still; if nature has put little sympathy in the heart of this or that man; if he, supposed to be an upright man, is by temperament cold and indifferent to the sufferings of others, perhaps because in respect of his own he is provided with the special gift of patience and fortitude, and supposes, or even requires, that others should have the same—and such a man would certainly not be the meanest product of nature—but if nature had not specially framed him for a philanthropist, would he not still find in himself a source from whence to give himself a far higher worth than that of a good-natured temperament could be? Unquestionably. It is just in this that the moral worth of the character is brought out which is incomparably the highest of all, namely, that he is beneficent, not from inclination, but from duty.

To secure one's own happiness is a duty, at least indirectly; for discontent with one's condition, under a pressure of many anxieties and amidst unsatisfied wants, might easily become a great *temptation to transgression of duty*. But here again, without looking to duty, all men have already the strongest and most intimate inclination to happiness, because it is just in this idea that all inclinations are combined in one total. But the precept of happiness is often of such a sort that it greatly interferes with some inclinations, and yet a man cannot form any definite and certain conception of the sum of satisfaction of all of them which is called happiness. It is not then to be wondered at that a single inclination, definite both as to what it promises and as to the time within which it can be gratified, is often able to overcome such a fluctuating idea, and that a gouty patient, for instance, can choose to enjoy what he likes, and to suffer what he may, since, according to his calculation, on this occasion at least, he has [only] not sacrificed the enjoyment of the present moment to a possibly mistaken expectation of a happiness which is supposed to be found in health. But even in this case, if the general desire for happiness did not influence his will, and supposing that in his particular case health was not a necessary element in this calculation, there yet remains in this, as in all other cases, this law, namely, that he should promote his happiness not from inclination but from duty, and by this would his conduct first acquire true moral worth.

It is in this manner, undoubtedly, that we are to understand those passages of Scripture also in which we are commanded to love our neighbour, even our enemy. For love, as an affection, cannot be commanded, but beneficence for duty's sake may; even though we are not impelled to it by any inclination—nay, are even repelled by a natural and unconquerable aversion. This is *practical* love, and not *pathological*—a love which is seated in the will, and not in the propensions of sense—in principles of action and not of tender sympathy; and it is this love alone which can be commanded.

The second[1] proposition is: That an action done from duty derives its moral worth, *not from the purpose* which is to be attained by it, but from the maxim by which it is determined, and therefore does not depend on the realization of the object of the action, but merely on the *principle of volition* by which the action has taken place, without regard to any object of desire. It is clear from what precedes that the purposes which we may have in view in our actions, or their effects regarded as ends and springs of the will, cannot give to actions any unconditional or moral worth. In what, then, can their worth lie, if it is not to consist in the will and in reference to its expected effect? It cannot lie anywhere but in the *principle of the will* without regard to the ends which can be attained by the action. For the will stands between its *à priori* principle, which is formal, and its *à posteriori* spring, which is material, as between two roads, and as it must be determined by something, it follows that it must be determined by the formal principle of volition when an action is done from duty, in which case every material principle has been withdrawn from it.

The third proposition, which is a consequence of the two preceding, I would express thus: *Duty is the necessity of acting from respect for the law.* I may have *inclination* for an object as the effect of my proposed action, but I cannot have *respect* for it, just for this reason, that it is an effect and not an energy of will. Similarly, I cannot have respect for inclination, whether my own or another's; I can at most, if my own, approve it; if another's, sometimes even love it; *i.e.* look on it as favourable to my own interest. It is only what is connected with my will as a principle, by no means as an effect—what does not subserve my inclination, but overpowers it, or at least in case of choice excludes it from its calculation—in other words, simply the law of itself, which can be an object of respect, and hence a command. Now an action done from duty must wholly exclude the influence of inclination, and with it every object of the will, so that nothing remains which can determine the will except objectively the *law*, and subjectively *pure respect* for this practical law, and consequently the maxim that I should follow this law even to the thwarting of all my inclinations.

---

[1] The first proposition was that to have moral worth an action must be done from duty.

Thus the moral worth of an action does not lie in the effect expected from it, nor in any principle of action which requires to borrow its motive from this expected effect. For all these effects—agreeableness of one's condition, and even the promotion of the happiness of others—could have been also brought about by other causes, so that for this there would have been no need of the will of a rational being; whereas it is in this alone that the supreme and unconditional good can be found. The pre-eminent good which we call moral can therefore consist in nothing else than *the conception of law* in itself, *which certainly is only possible in a rational being*, in so far as this conception, and not the expected effect, determines the will. This is a good which is already present in the person who acts accordingly, and we have not to wait for it to appear first in the result.

But what sort of law can that be, the conception of which must determine the will, even without paying any regard to the effect expected from it, in order that this will may be called good absolutely and without qualification? As I have deprived the will of every impulse which could arise to it from obedience to any law, there remains nothing but the universal conformity of its actions to law in general, which alone is to serve the will as a principle, *i.e.* I am never to act otherwise than so *that I could also will that my maxim should become a universal law.* Here, now, it is the simple conformity to law in general, without assuming any particular law applicable to certain actions, that serves the will as its principle, and must so serve it, if duty is not to be a vain delusion and a chimerical notion. The common reason of men in its practical judgments perfectly coincides with this, and always has in view the principle here suggested. Let the question be, for example: May I when in distress make a promise with the intention not to keep it? I readily distinguish here between the two significations which the question may have: Whether it is prudent, or whether it is right, to make a false promise? The former may undoubtedly often be the case. I see clearly indeed that it is not enough to extricate myself from a present difficulty by means of this subterfuge, but it must be well considered whether there may not hereafter spring from this lie much greater inconvenience than that from which I now free myself, and as, with all my supposed *cunning*, the consequences cannot be so easily foreseen but that credit once lost may be much more injurious to me than any mischief which I seek to avoid at present, it should be considered whether it would not be more *prudent* to act herein according to a universal maxim, and to make it a habit to promise nothing except with the intention of keeping it. But it is soon clear to me that such a maxim will still only be based on the fear of consequences. Now it is a wholly different thing to be truthful from duty, and to be so from apprehension of injurious consequences. In the first case, the very notion of the action already implies a law for me; in the second case, I must first look about elsewhere to see what results may be combined with it which would affect myself. For to deviate from the principle of duty is beyond all doubt wicked; but to be unfaithful to my maxim of prudence may often be very advantageous to me, although to abide by it is certainly safer. The shortest way, however, and an unerring one, to discover the answer to this question whether a lying promise is consistent with duty, is to ask myself, Should I be content that my maxim (to extricate myself from difficulty by a false promise) should hold good as a universal law, for myself as well as for others? and should I be able to say to myself, "Every one may make a deceitful promise when he finds himself in a difficulty from which he cannot otherwise extricate himself"? Then I presently become aware that while I can will the lie, I can by no means will that lying should be a universal law. For with such a law there would be no promises at all, since it would be in vain to allege my intention in regard to my future actions to those who would not believe this allegation, or if they over-hastily did so, would pay me back in my own coin. Hence my maxim, as soon as it should be made a universal law, would necessarily destroy itself.

I do not, therefore, need any far-reaching penetration to discern what I have to do in order that my will may be morally good. Inexperienced in the course of the world, incapable of being prepared for all its contingencies, I only ask myself: Canst thou also will that thy maxim should be a universal law? If not, then it must be rejected, and that not because of a disadvantage accruing from it to myself or even to others, but because it cannot enter as a principle into a possible universal legislation, and reason extorts from me immediate respect for such legislation. I do not indeed as yet *discern* on what this respect is based (this the philosopher may inquire), but at least I understand this, that it is an estimation of the worth which far outweighs all worth of what is recommended by inclination, and that the necessity of acting from *pure* respect for the practical law is what constitutes duty, to which every other motive must give place, because it is the condition of a will being good *in itself*, and the worth of such a will is above everything. . . .

Of Virtue in General

Virtue signifies a moral strength of Will. But this does not exhaust the notion; for such strength might also belong to a *holy* (superhuman) being, in whom no opposing impulse counteracts the law of his rational Will; who therefore willingly does everything in accordance with the law. Virtue then is the moral strength of a *man's* Will in his obedience to *duty*; and this is a moral *necessitation* by his own law giving reason, inasmuch as this constitutes itself a power *executing* the law. It is not itself a duty, nor is it a duty to possess it (otherwise we should be in duty bound to have a duty), but it commands, and accompanies its command with a moral constraint (one possible by laws of internal freedom). But since this should be irresistible, strength is requisite, and the degree of this strength can be estimated only by the magnitude of the hindrances which man creates for himself by his inclinations. Vices, the brood of unlawful dispositions, are the monsters that he has to combat; wherefore this moral strength as *fortitude* constitutes the greatest and only true martial glory of man; it is also called the true *wisdom*, namely, the practical, because it makes the *ultimate end* [= final cause] of the existence of man on earth its own end. Its possession alone makes man free, healthy, rich, a king, &c., nor can either chance or fate deprive him of this, since he possesses himself, and the virtuous cannot lose his virtue.

All the encomiums bestowed on the ideal of humanity in its moral perfection can lose nothing of their practical reality by the examples of what men now are, have been, or will probably be hereafter; *Anthropology* which proceeds from mere

empirical knowledge cannot impair *anthroponomy* which is erected by the unconditionally legislating reason; and although virtue may now and then be called meritori-
ous (in relation to men, not to the law), and be worthy of reward, yet in itself, as
it is its own end, so also it must be regarded as its own reward.

Virtue considered in its complete perfection is therefore regarded not as if man
possessed virtue, but as if virtue possessed the man, since in the former case it
would appear as though he had still had the choice (for which he would then
require another virtue, in order to select virtue from all other wares offered to him).
To conceive a plurality of virtues (as we unavoidably must) is nothing else but to
conceive various moral objects to which the (rational) will is led by the single
principle of virtue; and it is the same with the opposite vices. The expression which
personifies both is a contrivance for affecting the sensibility, pointing, however, to a
moral sense. Hence it follows that an Aesthetic of Morals is not a part, but a
subjective exposition, of the Metaphysic of Morals, in which the emotions that
accompany the necessitating force of the moral law make the efficiency of that
force to be felt; for example: disgust, horror, &c., which give a sensible form to the
moral aversion in order to gain the precedence from the *merely* sensible incitement.

Of the Principle on Which Ethics Is
Separated from Jurisprudence

This separation on which the subdivision of *moral philosophy* in general rests, is
founded on this: that the notion of *Freedom* which is common to both, makes it
necessary to divide duties into those of external and those of internal freedom; the
latter of which alone are ethical. Hence this internal freedom which is the condition
of all *ethical duty* must be discussed as a preliminary, just as above the doctrine of
conscience was discussed as the condition of all duty.

Of the Doctrine of Virtue on the
Principle of Internal Freedom

Habit is a facility of action and a subjective perfection of the *elective will*. But
not every such *facility* is a *free habit*; for if it is *custom*, that is, a uniformity of
action which, by frequent repetition, has become a *necessity*, then it is not a habit
proceeding from freedom, and therefore not a moral habit. Virtue therefore cannot
be *defined* as a habit of free law-abiding actions, unless indeed we add "determining
itself in its action by the idea of the law"; and then this habit is not a property of
the elective will, but of the *Rational Will*, which is a faculty that in adopting a rule
also declares it to be a universal law, and it is only such a habit that can be
reckoned as virtue. Two things are required for internal freedom: to be *master* of
oneself in a given case, and to have *command* over onself, that is to *subdue* his
emotions and to *govern* his passions. With these conditions the *character* is *noble*; in
the opposite case it is ignoble.

Virtue Requires First of All,
Command over Oneself

Emotions and *Passions* are essentially distinct; the former belong to *feeling* in so
far as this coming before reflection makes it more difficult or even impossible.

Hence emotion is called *hasty*. And reason declares through the notion of virtue that a man should *collect* himself; but this weakness in the life of one's understanding, joined with the strength of a mental excitement, is only a *lack of virtue*, and as it were a weak and childish thing, which may very well consist with the best will, and has further this one good thing in it, that this storm soon subsides. A propensity to emotion is therefore not so closely related to vice as passion is. *Passion*, on the other hand, is the sensible *appetite* grown into a permanent inclination (ex. gr. *hatred* in contrast to *resentment*). The calmness with which one indulges it leaves room for reflection and allows the mind to frame principles thereon for itself; and thus when the inclination falls upon what contradicts the law, to brood on it, to allow it to root itself deeply, and thereby to take up evil (as of set purpose) into one's maxim; and this is then specifically evil, that is, it is a true *vice*.

Virtue therefore, in so far as it is based on internal freedom, contains a positive command for man, namely, that he should bring all his powers and inclinations under his rule (that of reason); and this is a positive precept of command over himself which is additional to the prohibition, namely, that he should not allow himself to be governed by his feelings and inclinations (the duty of *apathy*); since, unless reason takes the reins of government into its own hands, the feelings and inclinations play the master over the man.

"PERSONAL FREEDOM THROUGH THE STATE"

Bernard Bosanquet

Liberty, no doubt, is as Rousseau has told us, so far agreeing with Mill, the essential quality of human life. It is so, we understood, because it is the condition of our being ourselves. But now that it has occurred to us that in order to be ourselves we must be always becoming something which we are not, or in other words, we must always recognise that we are something more than we have become, liberty, as the condition of our being ourselves, cannot simply be something which we have, still less something which we have always had—a *status quo* to be maintained. It must be a condition relevant to our continued struggle to assert the control of something in us, which we recognise as imperative upon us or as our real self, but which we only obey in a very imperfect degree. Thus it is that we can speak, without a contradiction, of being forced to be free. It is possible for us to acquiesce, as rational beings, in a law and order which on the whole makes for the possibility of asserting our true or universal selves, at the very moment when this law and order is constraining our particular private wills in a way which we resent, or even condemn. Such a law and order, maintained by force, which we recognise as on the whole the instrument of our greatest self-affirmation, is a system of rights; and our liberty, or to use a good old expression, our liberties, may be identified with such a system considered as the condition and guarantee of our becoming the best that we have it in us to be, that is, of becoming ourselves. And because such an order is the embodiment up to a certain point of a self or system of will which we recognise as what ought to be, as against the indolence, ignorance, or rebellion of our casual private selves, we may rightly call it a system of self-government or free government; a system, that is to say, in which ourselves, in one sense, govern ourselves in another sense; not as Mill has said, by each one of us being subject to all the "others" (taking "others" in the same sense in which each of us is "one"), but by all of us, as casual private units, being subject to an order which expresses, up to a certain point, the rational self or will which, as rational beings, we may be assumed[1] to recognise as imperative. . . .

In the simple ideal of liberty, as equivalent to the absence of all government—for we must not forget that it *is* an ideal, obtained by neglecting the facts of life which run counter to it—there is clearly embodied a claim which commands our respect. The claim is so self-evident and so convincing to average human feeling—Mr. Spencer would indeed say, with some truth, to animal feeling in general—that its precise nature is seldom stated in distinct language. We have assumed above that the root of it lies in the claim to be ourselves. But it is safer to take it in the shape which it actually has for the average consciousness, and this is the negative shape, as a claim to be free from constraint.[2] If we ask, "What is constraint?" the answer is founded on the current distinction between myself and others as different minds attached to different bodies. It is constraint when my mind is interfered with in its control of my body either by actual or by threatening physical violence under the direction of another mind. A permanent and settled condition of such constraint, by which I become in effect the instrument of another mind, is slavery. And it will not lead us far wrong if we assume that the value put upon liberty and its erection into something like an ideal comes from the contrast with slavery. The ideal of positive political freedom presupposes more complex experiences. But Homer already knows that "Zeus deprives a man of half his manhood when he becomes a slave."

This, then, we may take as the practical starting-point in the notion of freedom. It is what, with reference to a formed society, we may call a status; the position of a freeman as opposed to a slave; that is, of one who, whatever oppression he may meet with *de facto* from time to time, or whatever specified services he may be bound to render, normally regards himself and is regarded by others as, on the whole, at his own disposal, and not the mere instrument of another mind.

Thus the juristic meaning of the term "liberty," based on the normal distinction between one self-determining person and another, we may set down as its literal meaning, and so far the English writers, of whom Seeley is the latest type, are on

---

[1] In principle, actual individual assent is not needed. The question when the assumption breaks down belongs to the subject of the duty of rebellion and the significance of punishment.

[2] We must assume, I suppose, that in Seeley's sentence "Government"="Constraint," or its *vraisemblance* is lost.

solid ground when they define liberty as the absence of restraint, or perfect liberty as the absence of all government (in the sense of habitual constraint by others).

It is obvious that the above definition would be wholly inadequate to the simplest facts respecting the demands which have through all history been asserted and achieved under the name of political liberty. A man may be a long way more than a slave and yet a long way less than a citizen. If, as Seeley says, the English writer of the verses, "Ah, Freedom is a noble thing," only meant by Freedom, being out of prison, it is certain that he meant much less than the Greek historian who two thousand years before used almost the same words. "The right of equal speech," he wrote, "demonstrates itself in every way as a noble thing."[3] By this, as his words and their occasion make plain, he meant a certain determinate security for the positive exercise of activities affecting the welfare of the social whole, and some such security is always understood to be involved in the notion of political liberty. But we will content ourselves at this point with noting the distinction and connection between the negative or juristic, and the varyingly positive or political conception of liberty. For the latter is, in its degree, a case of that fuller freedom which we are about to trace to its embodiment in the state; and the phenomena of political liberty are covered, of course, by the point of view which we shall take in indicating the state as the main organ and condition of the fuller liberty.

The connection, we said, between juristic and political liberty should be observed at this point. It is merely an example of what we shall find throughout, that the apparently negative has its roots and its meaning in the positive, and, in proportion as its true nature becomes evident, its positive aspects become explicit. There is no true security for juristic liberty apart from political liberty; and it has constantly been the infraction of juristic liberty that has been the origin of the demand for a share in highly positive political duties and functions. Mere protection for person and property may seem an easy thing to define and maintain with just a little goodwill; but the questions when, how, and in what sense it is to be maintained involve the positive character of the political system, and there is no ultimate security unless that system is moulded by the whole compass of individuality which society contains.

Recurring then to the literal or elementary sense of liberty, as the absence of constraint exercised by one upon others, we may admit that, in going beyond it, we are more or less making use of a metaphor.[4] We are passing from the idea of non-constraint pure and simple to the idea of more or less moulding and selection within the powers and activities of the self. It is true, indeed, and must be maintained as a fundamental principle, that the "higher" liberty is also in fact the "larger" liberty, presenting the greater area to activity and the more extensive choice to self-determination.[5] But this larger development remains within a positive general character, and if more alternatives are open, there are also, by that very

[3] H.D.T., v. 78.

[4] In this and the following section I have made great use of Green's discussion in the first chapter of the *Principles of Political Obligation*.

[5] Perhaps I may refer on this head to "Liberty and Legislation" in my *Civilisation of Christendom* (Sonnenschein).

fact, more which are closed. We cannot wholly exhaust the new meaning of liberty as applied to the law-abiding and moral life of a conscientious citizen even by changing the negative into the positive, and saying that, whereas mere juristic freedom was only freedom *from* constraint, political freedom means freedom *to* act. The higher sense of liberty, like the lower, involves freedom *from* some things as well as freedom *to* others. And that which we are freed from is, in this case, not the constraint of those whom we commonly regard as others, but the constraint of what we commonly regard as a part of ourself. Here is the reason for saying that, when we speak of liberty in the higher sense, we must be admitted to be speaking metaphorically.

In the straightforward sense of the word, we saw, I am free when I am not made the instrument of another person's will through physical violence or the threat of it. The subtle questions which may arise with regard to due or undue degrees of influence, by which I may become the instrument of another's mind, with more or less willingness on the part of my own, are here disregarded. I am assumed to be acting freely so long as I follow the inclination of my mind, apart from any painful conflict forced upon it by the prospect of physical interference with its belongings.

But from the earliest ages of ethical reflection, a further sense has been ascribed to the term "liberty." It has been pointed out by moralists and philosophers—first, perhaps by Socrates and Plato—that the condition of man as to being himself is fundamentally affected not only by the power to do what he likes without constraint, but by the nature of that which he likes to do. The human mind, it is explained, is never wholly at one with itself, and the common phrases "self-mastery" or "self-control" are adduced by way of presenting what we spoke of above as the ethical paradox of self-government. The mind, then, is treated by a metaphor as if it were two or more persons; and the term "liberty," which applies *prima facie* to the non-constraint of one person by another, is applied to the non-constraint of something within an individual mind by something else within it. Now, apart from further scrutiny, it does not appear why the term "liberty," when thus applied, should mean anything of ethical value. As Plato observed, in a passage[6] from which the current use of all these phrases is probably derived, it seems absurd at first sight to speak of self-control as a distinctive predicate of certain states of mind. For surely, within the mind, that which is controlled must be of the nature of self no less than that which controls it, so that, in saying that I have self-control, I am saying that I am self-indulgent; in saying that my mind is free, I am at the same time saying that it is a slave. Within certain limits this paradox represents a truth, and the ethical rank of the elements which coerce and are coerced may be quite oppositely estimated. We may think fit to call ourselves free either when love conquers reason or when reason triumphs over love. Still, as Plato proceeds to point out, the general adoption of the metaphor, the fact that we think and call ourselves "free" or "self-controlled" or "fully ourselves" in some cases and not in others; and that we do not in each of these cases regard the opposite attribution "slave," "self-indulgent," "not ourselves" as equally true with

[6]*Republic*, 430 E.

the former, indicates that some substantial fact is forcing itself upon us through the metaphor in question. It is the same problem as that which Professor James has wittily stated when he points out that "the sluggard, the drunkard, the coward never talk of their conduct in that way (*i.e.* as 'conquering' their impulses and temptations) or say they resist their energy, overcome their sobriety, conquer their courage, and so forth."[7]

It is most important, we may venture to observe in passing, not to understand the substantive fact, or Plato's presentation of it, as if it lay in an alternative between two psychological factors, say intelligence and desire, the one of which was to be preferred and the other to be repudiated, through some quasi-ethical conception of rank, such as the supposed affinity of the one factor with divine or of the other with animal life. We are speaking of the sense in which it can be asserted that the human self is, comparatively speaking, free in one kind of life and unfree in another, both being assumed to be chosen, in the absence of constraint by an external will. It is plain that the only ground on which such an assertion can really be sustained is that the one life more than the other gives effect to the self as a whole, or removes its contradictions and so makes it most fully what it is able to be, or what, by the implied nature of each and all of its wants, it may be said really to want to be. The claims of intelligence and desire in their various phases must be criticised according to this principle, and not advocated upon presuppositions drawn from external comparisons.

But our question at the present moment is not as to the deeper nature of that which we call the self *par excellence*, but as to the bearing of the metaphor by which the assertion of such a self is identified with liberty or absence of constraint. And the point is plainly this:[8] that in the conflict between that which stands for the self *par excellence* and that which, at any time, stands opposed to it, we have the clear experience that we are capable of being determined by a will within our minds which nevertheless we repudiate and disown,[9] and therefore we feel ourselves to be like a slave as compared with a freeman if we yield, but like a freeman compared with a slave if we conquer. We may be determined by something which not only is not ourself—for in the greatest moments of life, when our being touches its maximum, we, in a sense, feel an impulse which is not ourself—but it is not ourself as something which has got hold of us by force, and operates upon us by conflict and violence, without having the kind of power needed to carry us away and sweep our whole self harmoniously into its current. That we can be determined by a will in us which neither is ourself nor represents it at a higher level, and which we loathe and disown, is the experience on which

[7] *Principles of Psychology*, ii. 548.
[8] See Green's *Principles of Political Obligation*, p. I.

[9] This remains substantially true, even if we agree with Socrates that it is impossible to know the better and prefer the worse at a given moment. Our normal self will repudiate the view we took at some moment.

the metaphor of freedom and slavery is based, when applied to the life of man considered apart from external constraint.[10]

The metaphorical application of the term "liberty" to a state of the individual mind has both its danger and its justification. The state of mind in question, we repeat, is that in which the impulse towards self-satisfaction sets itself upon an object which represents the nature of the self as a whole, as free from contradiction or as at its maximum of being, and triumphs over the alien and partial will, the tendency to narrower tracks of indulgence, when entangled in which it feels itself oppressed and constrained by a foreign influence. When the mind does what, as a whole, it wills, as Plato implies,[11] it feels free. When it cannot be said to will anything as a whole, but is distracted among aims which cannot satisfy it, then there is no sense in which it can be said to do what *it* wills, and it feels itself under constraint and a slave.

The metaphor has this danger. The contrast between whole and part is too readily transformed, in popular theory, into the contrast between an empty generality and everything in particular. The claim to be free then involves the separation between mind as a general faculty of volition, and every particular object. Mind is then said to be free as an undetermined faculty, but as filled and moulded by any object or idea, (the passive participles "filled" and "moulded" imply a relation which is not real, but, as assumed, is the ground of the fallacy in question), it has lost its freedom and become a slave. But if we retain the conception that mind has reality only as a whole of determinate character, self-determined through its power of being a self, but not through any power of creating particulars out of nothing, we shall avoid this caricature of the higher freedom.

But it is far more important to note the justification of the metaphor. We saw that, from Homer downwards, the conviction has been ineradicable that liberty is the true nature of man. And we now observe that the metaphor, through which the deepest sense of this quality has expressed itself, depends upon the same principle as the literal usage from which it is drawn. In the case of Liberty, conceived as a condition of the mind, just as in the case of Liberty, conceived as the absence of physical menace or coercion on the part of other persons, the root of the matter is the claim to be determined only by ourselves. But, in the literal case, what we mean by ourself is the given self, the group of will and wishes, of feelings and ideas, associated from time to time with my particular body; in short, the actual uncriticised "mind," as we experience it all day and every day. In the metaphorical case, we have made so much progress in self-criticism as to know at least that our "self" is something of a problem. We know that the given self, the mind from day to day, is not satisfactory; and we throw the centre of gravity outside it, and place the true self in something which we rather want to be than actually are; although, at the

---

[10]There is something worthy of Dante in Rousseau's observation (*Contrat Social*, Bk. IV., ch. ii., n.) that the convicts in the galleys at Genoa had "Liberty" stamped on their chains. The fetters of the bad self are the symbol of freedom. Rousseau turns his remark to commonplace, after his fashion, by referring it to the mere liberation of society from malefactors.

[11]*Republic*, ix. 577 E.

same time, it is clear that to some extent we are this something or we should not want to be it. We realise, indeed, that to be ourselves is a principle at once of distinction or position among others, and of thorough transition into and unity with the life which is at the root of theirs. And it is for this reason that we feel so confident, in proportion as we at all lay hold upon a life which can thus distinguish and identify us, that we have here the grasp of what is in its nature our true self. Here then, as in the literal case of liberty from personal constraint, we are putting in act the principle of "being determined only by ourself."

And thus Liberty as understood by "theorists of the first look," or by those who in all ages have resisted arbitrary tyranny, belongs after all to the same principle with the civil or moral liberty of the philosopher. The claim to obey only yourself is a claim essential to humanity; and the further significance of it rests upon what you mean by "yourself." Now if it is true that resistance to arbitrary aggression is a condition of obeying only ourselves, it is more deeply true, when man is in any degree civilised, that, in order to obey yourself as you want to be, you must obey something very different from yourself as you are. And it has been well pointed out[12] that the consciousness of civilised peoples is deeply alive to this significance of liberty, so that any work of self-improvement may be most effectively presented to a popular audience as an effort to attain freedom by breaking the bondage of drink, for example, or of ignorance, or of pauperism. In spite of the objection that Freedom as thus represented is a mere metaphor, "the feeling[13] of oppression, which always goes with the consciousness of unfulfilled possibilities, will always give meaning to the representation of the effort after any kind of self-improvement as a demand for 'freedom.' "

We have followed the usual course of English thought, and the example of a writer whose caution equalled his enthusiasm, in admitting that the lower sense of the term "liberty" is the literal sense, and that the deeper meaning may be treated as metaphorical. It is worth while to observe that the justice of this way of looking at the matter is very doubtful. It is because we know, however indefinitely, that our self has a reach beyond its daily needs, that arbitrary oppression becomes a thing to be resisted at the price of life itself. Herbert Spencer draws attention to the struggles of an animal which we try to confine, as a proof of the innate feeling of liberty. But the domesticated animal is the highest animal, or at any rate not the lowest; while the man domesticated on similar terms is what we call a slave, because he has sold his liberty for his life. It is therefore in truth the sense of the higher liberty—the greatness and unity of life—that has communicated uncontrollable force to the claim for the lower; and if the fuller meaning is the reality and the lesser the symbol, it would be nearer the truth to say that the reality is the liberty of a moral being whose will finds adequate expression in its life, of which liberty the absence of external constraint is only an elementary type or symbol. . . .

The ideal thus implied may be further explained by help of the philosophical expression, "The free will is the will that wills itself." We have already seen, by

---

[12] Green's *Principles*, p. 18.
[13] *Loc. cit.*

implication, the meaning of this. If we are asked, "But does not our will always will itself?" we have the answer ready, that in one sense it does, but in another it does not. We always want what we will, but what we will is not always what would satisfy our want. A will that willed itself would be a will that in willing had before it an object that would satisfy its whole want, and nothing but its want. Its desires would not be narrow and partial desires, in the fulfilment of which a man feels choked and oppressed like one lost in a blind alley which grows narrower and narrower. They would not be artificial desires stimulated and elaborated into a tyranny of the machinery of life by the self which gropes for more and cannot find the "more" which it needs. That is to say, the volitions of the self would have undergone a process just such as is undergone by a casual sensuous observation as it passes into a great scientific theory. As the observation stands it is inadequate to itself; for it poses as a truth, and is manifestly a false connection. So it is supplemented on the one hand and purged away on the other; conditions and qualifications are inserted into it to harmonise it with other knowledge, until it makes some approach to being an expression of experience fit to occupy a permanent place in man's conception of the world. This, the adjustment of a partial element to unity with the whole, is the essence of criticism. And it is just such another process by which the experience of life fills up and purifies the objects presented to the casual volition. That is to say, the nature of the process may be represented by considering it as having an effect of this kind on an unharmonised will; and relatively at any given moment such a process is in some degree going on. But we must bear in mind that we are not to think of the sensuous individual as totally prior in time to the social consciousness, and as a pre-existing matter, upon which such an effect is to be thought of as super-induced. That would be precisely the fallacy with which Rousseau struggles so hard, and the escape from which we are attempting to illustrate; none the worse, perhaps, if our own language betrays how very difficult it is to throw it off altogether. We really know the sensuous individual as such, the will in its impure and uncriticised form, only in our experience, constant as that is, of failure, error, and forgetfulness, in adhering to the rational life, which, on the whole, is inherent in the very nature of our rational being, and which we only desert in the same way and to the same extent as we make mistakes in intellectual matters. We go wrong by narrowness and confusion, by erroneous abstractions out of the whole, in a way only possible for a social and intellectual being, and not prior to our entire social and intellectual character....

Take, as we said above, the actual casual will of any individual at any given moment, especially if it is of a nature which, within the context of civilised life, we commonly pronounce to be wrong. Let it be, for example, an impulse of sensual passion. It is a commonplace that in such impulses the self can find no abiding satisfaction. They pass and leave him empty. They bring with them no opening out of fresh possibilities, no greater stability to the mind. Yet they have their meaning, and belong to human nature. They imply a need for union, and an attraction outside the immediate self. If we compare them with the objects and affections of a happy and devoted family, we see the difference between a less adequate and a more adequate will. The impulse, in passing into family affection, has become both less and more. It is both disciplined and expanded. The object presented to the will is transformed in character. Lawlessness is excluded; but, in place of a passing pleasure, a whole world of affections and interests, extending beyond the individual life, is offered as a purpose and a stimulus to the self. In short—for it is idle to expatiate upon what everybody recognises at once—you can make a life out of the one, and you cannot out of the other. In the family at its best the will has an object which is real and stable, and which corresponds to a great part of its own possibilities and capacities. In willing this object, it is, relatively speaking, willing itself. We might compare in the same way the mere will to earn our daily bread with the horizon of a great intellectual profession; or the routine of an industry or profession vacantly and formally pursued with the very same routine conscientiously followed in a spirit of enlightenment. In every case we are led up to the contrast of the actual indolent or selfish will, and the will, in as far as it comes to be what its nature implies, namely that which we have spoken of as the real or rational will embodied in objects which have power to make a life worth living for the self that wills them.

Now, our nature as rational beings implies the imperative claim upon us of a will which is thus real or rational. Recognised or unrecognised, it is rooted in our own wills, as the claim to be true is rooted in our assertions. Any system of institutions which represents to us, on the whole, the conditions essential to affirming such a will, in objects of action such as to constitute a tolerably complete life, has an imperative claim upon our loyalty and obedience as the embodiment of our liberty. The only question that can arise is whether the system is that which it pretends to be. But even if rebellion is a duty, it can only be so because the imperative obligation, as we recognise it, is irreconcilable with the particular system which claims our obedience in its name. The imperative claim of the will that wills itself is our own inmost nature, and we cannot throw it off. This is the ultimate root of political obligation.

It is such a "real" or rational will that thinkers after Rousseau have identified with the State. In this theory they are following the principles of Plato and Aristotle, no less than the indications which Rousseau furnished by his theory of the general will in connection with the work of the legislator. The State, when thus regarded, is to the general life of the individual much as we saw the family to be with regard to certain of his impulses. The idea is that in it, or by its help, we find at once discipline and expansion, the transfiguration of partial impulses, and something to do and to care for, such as the nature of a human self demands. If, that is to say, you start with a human being as he is in fact, and try to devise what will furnish him with an outlet and a stable purpose capable of doing justice to his capacities—a satisfying object of life—you will be driven on by the necessity of the facts at least as far as the State, and perhaps further. Two points may be insisted on to make this conception less paradoxical to the English mind.

The State, as thus conceived, is not merely the political fabric. The term "State" accents indeed the political aspect of the whole, and is opposed to the notion of an anarchical society. But it includes the entire hierarchy of institutions by which life is determined, from the family to the trade, and from the trade to the Church and the University. It includes all of them, not as the mere collection of the growths of the country, but as the structure which gives life and meaning to the political whole, while receiving from it mutual adjustment, and therefore expansion and a more liberal air. The State, it might be said, is thus conceived as the operative criticism of all institutions—the modification and adjustment by which they are capable of playing a rational part in the object of human will. And criticism, in this sense, is the life of institutions. As exclusive objects, they are a prey to stagnation and disease—think of the temper which lives solely for the family or solely for the Church; it is only as taken up into the movement and circulation of the State that they are living spiritual beings. It follows that the State, in this sense, is, above all things, not a number of persons, but a working conception of life. It is, as Plato has taught us, the conception by the guidance of which every living member of the commonwealth is enabled to perform his function. If we ask whether this means that a complete conception of the aims and possibilities of the common life exists even in the minds of statesmen, not to speak of ordinary citizens, the question answers itself in the negative. And yet the State can only live and work in as far as such a conception, in however fragmentary, one-sided shapes, pervades the general mind. It is not there mostly in reflective shape; and in so far as it is in reflective shape it is according to ultimate standards contradictory and incomplete. But everyone who has a fair judgment of what his own place demands from him, has, at his own angle, so to speak, a working insight into the end of the State; and, of course, practical contradictions would be fewer if such conceptions were completer and more covered by each other. But a complete reflective conception of the end of the State, comprehensive and free from contradiction, would mean a complete idea of the realisation of all human capacity, without waste or failure. Such a conception is impossible owing to the gradual character of the process by which the end of life, the nature of the good, is determined for man. The Real Will, as represented by the State, is only a partial embodiment of it.

The State, as the operative criticism of all institutions, is necessarily force; and in the last resort, it is the only recognised and justified force. It seems important to observe that force is inherent in the State, and no true ideal points in the direction of destroying it. For the force of the State proceeds essentially from its character of being our own mind extended, so to speak, beyond our immediate consciousness. Not only is the conduct of life as a whole beyond the powers of the average individual at its average level, but it is beyond the powers of all the average individuals in a society taken together at their average level. We make a great mistake in thinking of the force exercised by the State as limited to the restraint of disorderly persons by the police and the punishment of intentional lawbreakers. The State is the fly-wheel of our life. Its system is constantly reminding us of duties, from sanitation to the incidents of trusteeship, which we have not the least desire to neglect, but which we are either too ignorant or too indolent to carry out apart from instruction and authoritative suggestion. We profit at every turn by institutions, rules, traditions, researches, made by minds at their best, which, through State action are now in a form to operate as extensions of our own minds. It is not merely the contrast between the limited activity of one individual and the greater achievement of millions put together. It is the contrast between individuals working in the order and armed with the laws, customs, writings, and institutions devised by ages, and the same individuals considered as their daily average selves, with a varying but always limited range of immediate consciousness. For at any given moment, no judge knows all the law; no author knows all his own books, not to mention those of others; no official of an institution has the whole logic and meaning of the institution before his mind. All individuals are continually reinforced and carried on, beyond their average immediate consciousness, by the knowledge, resources, and energy which surround them in the social order, with its inheritance, of which the order itself is the greater part. And the return of this greater self, forming a system adjusted to unity, upon their isolated minds, as an expansion and stimulus to them, necessarily takes the shape of force, in as far as their minds are inert. And this must always be the case, not merely so long as wills are straightforwardly rebellious against the common good, but so long as the knowledge and energy of the average mind are unequal to dealing, on its own initiative and out of its own resources, with all possible conjunctions in which necessary conditions of the common good are to be maintained. In other words, there must be inertia to overcome, as long as the limitations of our animal nature[14] exist at all. The State is, as Plato told us, the individual mind writ large, or, as we have said, our mind reinforced by capacities which are of its own nature, but which supplement its defects. And this being so, the less complete must clearly submit to find itself in the more complete, and be carried along with it so far as the latter is able to advance. It is very important to note, however, that our mind at its best is very different from our mind at its average; and it has understood and approved, when at its best, a great deal which in its average moments comes upon it as force or custom from the outside. Thus, there is no abrupt division between our conscious mind and the social system of suggestion, custom, and force, which supports and extends and amends it. The two are related much as the focus of consciousness is related to the sub-conscious and automatic habits by which daily life is rendered possible. It is no more conceivable that social life should go on without force and authoritative custom, because the end of social life is reflected in the varying intelligence of individuals, then that individual life should go on without sub-consciousness and automatism, because it is ultimately relative to the ends which appear as ideas in the shifting focus of the mind. The inherent limitations of State action will be dealt with in a later chapter. We have thus far been attempting to make clear what is meant by the identification of the State with the Real Will of the Individual in which he wills his own nature as a rational being; in which identification we find the only true account of political obligation.

[14]Not "of our individuality." Individuality is not, in principle, a limitation which makes us unequal to our part in the whole.

"FREEDOM AS PERSONAL GROWTH"

John Dewey

I do not think there is any doubt that freedom is a word applied to many things of varied plumage and that it owes much of its magic to association with a variety of different causes. It has assumed various forms as needs have varied; its "utility" has been its service in helping men deal with many predicaments.

Primary among the needs it has been employed to meet and the interests it has served to promote is the moral. A good deal is assumed in asserting that the center of this moral need and cause is the fact of choice. The desire to dignify choice, to account for its significance in human affairs, to magnify that significance by making it the center of man's moral struggles and achievements has been reflected in the idea of freedom. There is an inexpugnable feeling that choice *is* freedom and that man without choice is a puppet, and that man then has no acts which he can call his very own. Without genuine choice, choice that when expressed in action makes things different from what they otherwise would be, men are but passive vehicles through which external forces operate. This feeling is neither self-explanatory nor self-justificatory. But at least it contributes an element in the statement of the problem of freedom. Choice is one of the things that demands examination. . . .

The discussion thus far has turned about the fact of choice alone. And such an exclusive emphasis may well render some readers impatient. It may seem to set forth an idea of freedom which is too individual, too "subjective." What has this affair to do with the freedom for which men have fought, bled and died: freedom from oppression and despotism, freedom of institutions and laws? This question at once brings to mind a philosophy of freedom which shifts the issue from choice to action, action in an overt and public sense. This philosophy is sufficiently well presented for our purposes in the idea of John Locke, the author, one may say, of the philosophy of Liberalism in its classic sense. Freedom is *power to act* in accordance with choice. It is actual ability to carry desire and purpose into operation, to *execute* choices when they are made. Experience shows that certain laws and institutions prevent such operation and execution. This obstruction and interference constitutes what we call oppression, enslavement. Freedom, in fact, the freedom worth fighting for, is secured by abolition of these oppressive measures, tyrannical laws and modes of government. It is liberation, emancipation; the posses-sion and active manifestation of *rights*, the right to self-determination in action. To many minds, the emphasis which has been put upon the formation of choice in connection with freedom will appear an evasion, a trifling with metaphysical futilities, in comparison with this form of freedom, a desire for which has caused revolutions, overthrown dynasties, and which as it is attained supplies the measure of human progress in freedom. . . .

We now face what is admittedly the crucial difficulty in framing a philosophy of freedom: What is the connection or lack of connection between freedom defined in terms of choice and freedom defined in terms of power in action? Do the two ways of conceiving freedom have anything but the name in common? The difficulty is the greater because we have so little material to guide us in dealing with it. Each type of philosophy has been upon the whole developed with little consideration of the point of view of the other. Yet it would seem that there must be some connection. Choice would hardly be significant if it did not take effect in outward action, and if it did not, when expressed in deeds, make a difference in things. Action as power would hardly be prized if it were power like that of an avalanche or an earthquake. The power, the ability to command issues and consequences, that forms freedom must, it should seem, have some connection with that something in personality that is expressed in choice. At all events, the essential problem of freedom, it seems to me, is the problem of the relation of choice and unimpeded effective action to each other.

I shall first give the solution to this problem that commends itself to me, and then trust to the further discussion not indeed to prove it but to indicate the reasons for holding it. There is an intrinsic connection between choice as freedom and power of action as freedom. A choice which intelligently manifests individuality enlarges the range of action, and this enlargement in turn confers upon our desires greater insight and foresight, and makes choice more intelligent. There is a circle, but an enlarging circle, or, if you please, a widening spiral. This statement is of course only a formula. We may perhaps supply it with meaning by first considering the matter negatively. Take for example an act following from a blind preference, from an impulse not reflected upon. It will be a matter of luck if the resulting action does not get the one who acts into conflict with surrounding conditions. Conditions go against the realization of his preference; they cut across it, obstruct it, deflect its course, get him into new and perhaps more serious entanglements. Luck may be on his side. Circumstances may happen to be propitious or he may be endowed with native force that enables him to brush aside obstructions and sweep away resistances. He thus gets a certain freedom, judged from the side of power-to-do. But this result is a matter of favor, of grace, of luck; it is not due to anything in himself. Sooner or later he is likely to find his deeds at odds with conditions; an accidental success may only reinforce a foolhardy impulsiveness that renders a man's future subjection the more probable. Enduringly lucky persons are exceptions.

Suppose, on the other hand, our hero's act exhibits a choice expressing a preference formed after consideration of consequences, an intelligent preference. Consequences depend upon an interaction of what he starts to perform with his environment, so he must take the latter into account. No one can foresee all consequences because no one can be aware of all the conditions that enter into their production. Every person builds better or worse than he knows. Good fortune or the favorable co-operation of environment is still necessary. Even with his best thought, a man's proposed course of action may be defeated. But in as far as his act is truly a manifestation of intelligent choice, he learns something: as in a scientific experiment an inquirer may learn through his experimentation, his intelligently directed action, quite as much or even more from a failure than from a success. He finds out at least a little as to what was the matter with his prior choice. He can choose better and *do* better next time; "better choice" meaning a more reflective one, and "better doing" meaning one better co-ordinated with the conditions that are involved in realizing purpose. Such control or power is never complete; luck or fortune, the propitious support of circumstances not foreseeable is always involved. But at least such a person forms the habit of choosing and acting with conscious regard to the grain of circumstance, the run of affairs. And what is more to the point, such a man becomes able to turn frustration and failure to account in his further choices and purposes. Everything in so far serves his purpose—to be an intelligent human being. This gain in power or freedom can be nullified by no amount of external defeats.

In a phrase just used, it was implied that intelligent choice may operate on different levels or in different areas. A man may, so to speak, specialize in intelligent choices in the region of economic or political affairs; he may be shrewd, politic, within the limit of these conditions, and in so far attain power in action or be free. Moralists have always held that such success is not success, such power not power, such freedom not freedom, in the ultimate sense.

One does not need to enter upon hortatory moralization in order to employ this contention of the great moral teachers for the sake of eliciting two points. The first is that there are various areas of freedom, because there is a plural diversity of conditions in our environment; and choice, intelligent choice, may select the special area formed by one special set of conditions—familial and domestic, industrial, pecuniary, political, charitable, scientific, ecclesiastic, artistic, etc. I do not mean, of course, that these areas are sharply delimited or that there is not something artificial in their segregation. But within limits, conditions are such that specialized types of choice and kinds of power or freedom develop. The second (and this is the one emphasized by moral teachers in drawing a line between true and false power and freedom), is that there *may* be—these moral idealists insist there *is*—one area in which freedom and power are always attainable by any one, no matter how much he may be blocked in other fields. This of course is the area they call *moral* in a distinctive sense. To put it roughly but more concretely: Any one can be kind, helpful to others, just and temperate in his choices, and in so far be sure of achievement and power in action. It would take more rashness than I possess to assert that there is not an observation of reality in this insight of the great teachers of the race. But without taking up that point, one may venture with confidence upon a hypothetical statement. If and in as far as this idea is correct, there is one way in which the force of fortunate circumstance and lucky original endowment is reduced in comparison with the force of the factor supplied by personal individuality itself. Success, power, freedom in *special* fields is in a maximum degree relatively at the mercy of external conditions. But against kindness and justice there is no law: that is, no counteracting grain of things nor run of affairs. With respect to such choices, there may be freedom and power, no matter what the frustrations and failures in other modes of action. Such is the virtual claim of moral prophets.

An illustration drawn from the denial of the idea that there is an intimate connection of the two modes of freedom, namely, intelligent choice and power in action, may aid in clearing up the idea. The attitude and acts of other persons is of course one of the most important parts of the conditions involved in bringing the manifestation of preference to impotency or to power in action. Take the case of a child in a family where the environment formed by others is such as to humor all his choices. It is made easy for him to do what he pleases. He meets a minimum of resistance; upon the whole others co-operate with him in bringing his preferences to fulfilment. Within this region he seems to have free power of action. By description he is unimpeded, even aided. But it is obvious that as far as he is concerned, this is a matter of luck. He is "free" merely because his surrounding conditions happen to be of the kind they are, a mere happening or accident as far as his make-up and his preferences are concerned. It is evident in such a case that there is *no growth* in the intelligent exercise of preferences. There is rather a conversion of blind impulse into regular habits. Hence his attained freedom is such only in appearance: it disappears as he moves into other social conditions.

Now consider the opposite case. A child is balked, inhibited, interfered with and nagged pretty continuously in the manifestation of his spontaneous preferences. He is constantly "disciplined" by circumstances adverse to his preferences—as discipline is not infrequently conceived. Does it follow then that he develops in "inner" freedom, in thoughtful preference and purpose? The question answers itself. Rather is some pathological condition the outcome. "Discipline" is indeed necessary as a preliminary to any freedom that is more than unrestrained outward power. But our dominant conception of discipline is a travesty; there is only one genuine discipline, namely, that which takes effect in producing habits of observation and judgment that insure intelligent desires. In short, while men do not think about and gain freedom in conduct unless they run during action against conditions that resist their original impulses, the secret of education consists in having that blend of check and favor which influences thought and foresight, and that takes effect in outward action through this modification of disposition and outlook.

I have borrowed the illustration from the life of a child at home or in school, because the problem is familiar and easily recognizable in those settings. But there is no difference when we consider the adult in industrial, political and ecclesiastic life. When social conditions are such as to prepare a prosperous career for a man's spontaneous preferences in advance, when things are made easy by institutions and by habits of admiration and approval, there is precisely the same kind of outward freedom, of relatively unimpeded action, as in the case of the spoiled child. But there is hardly more of freedom on the side of varied and flexible capacity of choice; preferences are restricted to the one line laid down, and in the end the individual becomes the slave of his successes. Others, vastly more in number, are in the state of the "disciplined" child. There is hard sledding for their spontaneous preferences; the grain of the environment, especially of existing economic arrangements, runs against them. But the check, the inhibition, to the immediate operation of their native preferences no more confers on them the quality of intelligent choice than it does with the child who never gets a fair chance to try himself out. There is only a crushing that results in apathy and indifference; a deflection into evasion and deceit; a compensatory over-responsiveness to such occasions as permit untrained preferences to run riot—and all the other consequences which the literature of mental and moral pathology has made familiar.

I hope these illustrations have rendered reasonably clear what is intended by our formula; by the idea that freedom consists in a trend of conduct that causes choices to be more diversified and flexible, more plastic and more cognizant of their own meaning, while it enlarges their range of unimpeded operation. . . .

In other words, freedom in its practical and moral sense (whatever is to be said about it in some metaphysical sense) is connected with possibility of growth, learning and modification of character. . . . The chief reason we do not think of a stone as free is because it is not capable of changing its mode of conduct, of purposely readapting itself to new conditions. An animal such as a dog shows plasticity; it acquires new habits under the tutelage of others. But the dog plays a passive rôle in this change; he does not initiate and direct it; he does not become interested in it on its own account. A human being, on the other hand, even a young child, not only learns but is capable of being interested in learning, interested in acquiring new attitudes and dispositions. As we mature we usually acquire habits that are settled to the point of routine. But unless and until we get completely fossilized, we can break old habits and form new ones. No argument about causation can affect the fact, verified constantly in experience, that we can and do learn, and that the learning is not limited to acquisition of additional information but extends to remaking old tendencies. As far as a person becomes a different self or character he develops different desires and choices. Freedom in the practical sense develops when one is aware of this possibility and takes an interest in converting it into a reality. Potentiality of freedom is a native gift or part of our constitution in that we have *capacity* for growth and for being actively concerned in the process and the direction it takes. Actual or positive freedom is not a native gift or endowment but is acquired. In the degree in which we become aware of possibilities of development and actively concerned to keep the avenues of growth open, in the degree in which we fight against induration and fixity, and thereby realize the possibilities of recreation of our selves, we are actually free.

Except as the outcome of arrested development, there is no such thing as a fixed, ready-made, finished self. Every living self causes acts and is itself caused in return by what it does. All voluntary action is a remaking of self, since it creates new desires, instigates to new modes of endeavor, brings to light new conditions which institute new ends. Our personal identity is found in the thread of continuous development which binds together these changes. In the strictest sense, it is impossible for the self to stand still; it is becoming, and becoming for the better or the worse. It is in the *quality* of becoming that virtue resides. We set up this and that end to be reached, but *the* end is growth itself. To make an end a final goal is but to arrest growth. Many a person gets morally discouraged because he has not attained the object upon which he set his resolution, but in fact his moral status is determined by his movement in that direction, not by his possession. If such a person would set his thought and desire upon the *process* of evolution instead of upon some ulterior goal, he would find a new freedom and happiness. It is the next step which lies within our power.

It follows that at each point there is a distinction between an old, an accomplished self, and a new and moving self, between the static and the dynamic self. The former aspect is constituted by habits already formed. Habit gives facility, and there is always a tendency to rest on our oars, to fall back on what we have already achieved. For that is the easy course; we are at home and feel comfortable in lines of action that run in the tracks of habits already established and mastered. Hence, the old, the habitual self, is likely to be treated as if it were *the* self; as if new conditions and new demands were something foreign and hostile. We become uneasy at the idea of initiating new courses; we are repelled by the difficulties that attend entering upon them; we dodge assuming a new responsibility. We tend to favor the old self and to make its perpetuation the standard of our valuations and the end of our conduct. In this way, we withdraw from actual conditions and their requirements and opportunities; we contract and harden the self.

The growing, enlarging, liberated self, on the other hand, goes forth to meet new demands and occasions, and readapts and remakes itself in the process. It welcomes untried situations. The necessity for choice between the interests of the old and of the forming, moving, self is recurrent. It is found at every stage of civilization and every period of life. The civilized man meets it as well as the savage; the dweller in the slums as well as the person in cultivated surroundings; the "good" person as well as the "bad." For everywhere there is an opportunity and a need to go beyond what one has been, beyond "himself," if the self is identified with the body of desires, affections, and habits which has been potent in the past. Indeed, we may say that the good person is precisely the one who is most conscious of the alternative, and is the most concerned to find openings for the newly forming or growing self; since no matter how "good" he has been, he becomes "bad" (even though acting upon a relatively high plane of attainment) as soon as he fails to respond to the demand for growth. Any other basis for judging the moral status of the self is conventional. In reality, direction of movement, not the plane of attainment and rest, determines moral quality.

Practically all moralists have made much of a distinction between a lower and a higher self, speaking of the carnal and spiritual, the animal and the truly human, the sensuous and the rational, selves which exist side by side in man and which war with one another. Moralists have often supposed that the line between the two selves could be drawn once for all and upon the basis of definite qualities and traits belonging respectively to one and the other. The only distinction, however, that can be drawn without reducing morals to conventionality, self-righteous complacency, or a hopeless and harsh struggle for the unattainable, is that between the attained static, and the moving, dynamic self. When there is talk of the lower animal self, and so on, it is always by *contrast*, not on the basis of fixed material. A self that was truly moral under a set of former conditions may become a sensuous, appetitive self when it is confronted with a painful need for developing new attitudes and devoting itself to new and difficult objectives. And, contrariwise, the higher self is that formed by the step in advance of one who *has* been living on a low plane. As he takes the step he enters into an experience of freedom. If we state the moral law as the injunction to each self on every possible occasion to identify the self with a new growth that is possible, then obedience to law is one with moral freedom.

"FREEDOM AS SPONTANEITY"

Erich Fromm

So far this book has dealt with one aspect of freedom: the powerlessness and insecurity of the isolated individual in modern society who has become free from all bonds that once gave meaning and security to life. We have seen that the individual cannot bear this isolation; as an isolated being he is utterly helpless in comparison with the world outside and therefore deeply afraid of it; and because of his isolation, the unity of the world has broken down for him and he has lost any point of orientation. He is therefore overcome by doubts concerning himself, the meaning of life, and eventually any principle according to which he can direct his actions. Both helplessness and doubt paralyze life, and in order to live man tries to escape from freedom, negative freedom. He is driven into new bondage. This bondage is different from the primary bonds, from which, though dominated by authorities or the social group, he was not entirely separated. The escape does not restore his lost security, but only helps him to forget his self as a separate entity. He finds new and fragile security at the expense of sacrificing the integrity of his individual self. He chooses to lose his self since he cannot bear to be alone. Thus freedom—as freedom from—leads into new bondage.

Does our analysis lend itself to the conclusion that there is an inevitable circle that leads from freedom into new dependence? Does freedom from all primary ties make the individual so alone and isolated that inevitably he must escape into new bondage? Are *independence* and freedom identical with *isolation* and fear? Or is there a state of positive freedom in which the individual exists as an independent self and yet is not isolated but united with the world, with other men, and nature?

We believe that there is a positive answer, that the process of growing freedom does not constitute a vicious circle, and that man can be free and yet not alone, critical and yet not filled with doubts, independent and yet an integral part of mankind. This freedom man can attain by the realization of his self, by being himself. What is realization of the self? Idealistic philosophers have believed that self-realization can be achieved by intellectual insight alone. They have insisted upon splitting human personality, so that man's nature may be suppressed and guarded by his reason. The result of this split, however, has been that not only the emotional life of man but also his intellectual faculties have been crippled. Reason, by becoming a guard set to watch its prisoner, nature, has become a prisoner itself; and thus both sides of human personality, reason and emotion, were crippled. We believe that the realization of the self is accomplished not only by an act of thinking but also by the realization of man's total personality, by the active expression of his emotional and intellectual potentialities. These potentialities are present in everybody; they become real only to the extent to which they are expressed. In other words, *positive freedom consists in the spontaneous activity of the total, integrated personality.*

We approach here one of the most difficult problems of psychology: the problem of spontaneity. An attempt to discuss this problem adequately would require another volume. However, on the basis of what we have said so far, it is possible to arrive at an understanding of the essential quality of spontaneous activity by means of contrast. Spontaneous activity is not compulsive activity, to which the individual is driven by his isolation and powerlessness; it is not the activity of the automaton, which is the uncritical adoption of patterns suggested from the outside. Spontaneous activity is free activity of the self and implies, psychologically, what the Latin root of the word, *sponte* means literally: of one's free will. By activity we do not mean "doing something," but the quality of creative activity that can operate in one's emotional, intellectual, and sensuous experiences and in one's will as well. One premise for this spontaneity is the acceptance of the total personality and the elimination of the split between "reason" and "nature"; for only if man does not repress essential parts of his self, only if he has become transparent to himself, and only if the different spheres of life have reached a fundamental integration, is spontaneous activity possible.

While spontaneity is a relatively rare phenomenon in our culture, we are not entirely devoid of it. In order to help in the understanding of this point, I should like to remind the reader of some instances where we all catch a glimpse of spontaneity.

In the first place, we know of individuals who are—or have been—spontaneous, whose thinking, feeling, and acting were the expression of their selves and not of an automaton. These individuals are mostly known to us as artists. As a matter of fact, the artist can be defined as an individual who can express himself spontaneously. If this were the definition of an artist—Balzac defined him just in that way—then certain philosophers and scientists have to be called artists too, while others are as different from them as an old-fashioned photographer from a creative painter. There are other individuals who, though lacking the ability—or perhaps merely the training—for expressing themselves in an objective medium as the artist does, possess the same spontaneity. The position of the artist is vulnerable, though, for it is really only the successful artist whose individuality or spontaneity is respected; if he does not succeed in selling his art, he remains to his contemporaries a crank, a "neurotic." The artist in this matter is in a similar position to that of the revolutionary throughout history. The successful revolutionary is a statesman, the unsuccessful one a criminal.

Small children offer another instance of spontaneity. They have an ability to feel and think that which is really *theirs*; this spontaneity shows in what they say and think, in the feelings that are expressed in their faces. If one asks what makes for the attraction small children have for most people I believe that, aside from sentimental and conventional reasons, the answer must be that it is this very quality of spontaneity. It appeals profoundly to everyone who is not so dead himself that he has lost the ability to perceive it. As a matter of fact, there is nothing more attractive and convincing than spontaneity whether it is to be found in a child, in an artist, or in those individuals who cannot thus be grouped according to age or profession.

Most of us can observe at least moments of our own spontaneity which are at the same time moments of genuine happiness. Whether it be the fresh and spontaneous perception of a landscape, or the dawning of some truth as the result of our thinking, or a sensuous pleasure that is not stereotyped, or the welling up of love for another person—in these moments we all know what a spontaneous act is and may have some vision of what human life could be if these experiences were not such rare and uncultivated occurrences.

Why is spontaneous activity the answer to the problem of freedom? We have said that negative freedom by itself makes the individual an isolated being, whose relationship to the world is distant and distrustful and whose self is weak and constantly threatened. Spontaneous activity is the one way in which man can overcome the terror of aloneness without sacrificing the integrity of his self; for in the spontaneous realization of the self man unites himself anew with the world— with man, nature, and himself. Love is the foremost component of such sponta- neity; not love as the dissolution of the self in another person, not love as the possession of another person, but love as spontaneous affirmation of others, as the union of the individual with others on the basis of the preservation of the individual self. The dynamic quality of love lies in this very polarity: that it springs from the need of overcoming separateness, that it leads to oneness—and yet that individuality is not eliminated. Work is the other component; not work as a compulsive activity in order to escape aloneness, not work as a relationship to nature which is partly one of dominating her, partly one of worship of and enslavement by the very products of man's hands, but work as creation in which man becomes one with nature in the act of creation. What holds true of love and work holds true of all spontaneous action, whether it be the realization of sensuous pleasure or participa- tion in the political life of the community. It affirms the individuality of the self and at the same time it unites the self with man and nature. The basic dichotomy that is inherent in freedom—the birth of individuality and the pain of aloneness—is dissolved on a higher plane by man's spontaneous action.

In all spontaneous activity the individual embraces the world. Not only does his individual self remain intact; it becomes stronger and more solidified. *For the self is as strong as it is active.* There is no genuine strength in possession as such, neither of material property nor of mental qualities like emotions or thoughts. There is also no strength in use and manipulation of objects; what we use is not ours simply because we use it. Ours is only that to which we are genuinely related by our creative activity, be it a person or an inanimate object. Only those qualities that result from our spontaneous activity give strength to the self and thereby form the basis of its integrity. The inability to act spontaneously, to express what one genuinely feels and thinks, and the resulting necessity to present a pseudo self to others and oneself, are the root of the feeling of inferiority and weakness. Whether or not we are aware of it, there is nothing of which we are more ashamed than of not being ourselves, and there is nothing that gives us greater pride and happiness than to think, to feel, and to say what is ours.

This implies that what matters is the activity as such, the process and not the result. In our culture the emphasis is just the reverse. We produce not for a concrete satisfaction but for the abstract purpose of selling our commodity; we feel that we can acquire everything material or immaterial by buying it, and thus things become ours independently of any creative effort of our own in relation to them. In the same way we regard our personal qualities and the result of our efforts as commodities that can be sold for money, prestige, and power. The emphasis thus shifts from the present satisfaction of creative activity to the value of the finished product. Thereby man misses the only satisfaction that can give him real happiness—the experience of the activity of the present moment—and chases after a phantom that leaves him disappointed as soon as he believes he has caught it—the illusory happiness called success.

If the individual realizes his self by spontaneous activity and thus relates himself to the world, he ceases to be an isolated atom; he and the world become part of one structuralized whole; he has his rightful place, and thereby his doubt concerning himself and the meaning of life disappears. This doubt sprang from his separateness and from the thwarting of life; when he can live, neither compulsively nor automatically but spontaneously, the doubt disappears. He is aware of himself as an active and creative individual and recognizes that *there is only one meaning of life: the act of living itself.*

"THE LIFE OF FREEDOM IN ZEN"

Daisetz Suzuki

Zen in its essence is the art of seeing into the nature of one's own being, and it points the way from bondage to freedom. By making us drink right from the fountain of life, it liberates us from all the yokes under which we finite beings are usually suffering in this world. We can say that Zen liberates all the energies properly and naturally stored in each of us, which are in ordinary circumstances cramped and distorted so that they find no adequate channel for activity.

This body of ours is something like an electric battery in which a mysterious power latently lies. When this power is not properly brought into operation, it either grows moldy and withers away or is warped and expresses itself abnormally. It is the object of Zen, therefore, to save us from going mad or being crippled. This is what I mean by freedom, giving free play to all the creative and benevolent impulses inherently lying in our hearts. Generally, we are blind to the fact that we are in possession of all the necessary faculties to make us happy and loving toward one another. All the struggles we see around us come from this ignorance. Zen, therefore, wants us to open a "third eye," as Buddhists call it, to the hitherto, undreamed-of region shut away from us through our own ignorance. When the cloud of ignorance disappears, the infinity of the heavens is manifested, where we see for the first time into the nature of our own being. We then know the signification of life, it is no longer blind striving, nor is it a mere display of brutal forces. While we know not definitely the ultimate purport of life, there is something in it that makes us feel infinitely blessed in the living of it and remain quite rested with it in all its evolution, without raising questions or entertaining pessimistic doubts.

When we are still full of vitality and not yet awakened to the knowledge of life, the seriousness of life's conflicts is for the moment in a state of quiescence. But sooner or later the time will come to face life squarely and solve its most perplexing and pressing riddles. Says Confucius, "At fifteen my mind was directed to study, and at thirty I knew where to stand." This is one of the wisest sayings by the Chinese sage. Psychologists will agree to this statement of his; for, generally, fifteen is about the age youth begins to look around in earnest and inquire into the meaning of life. All the spiritual powers hitherto securely hidden in the subconscious part of the mind break out almost simultaneously. When this breaking out is too precipitous and violent, the mind often loses its balance; in fact, many cases of nervous prostration reported during adolescence are chiefly due to this loss of the mental equilibrium. Usually the effect is not grave and the crisis may pass without leaving deep markings. In some characters, either through their inherent tendencies or the influence of environment upon their plastic constitution, the spiritual awakening stirs them to the very depths of their personality. This is the time they will be asked to choose between the "Everlasting No" and the "Everlasting Yea." This choosing is what Confucius means by "study"—the deeply delving into the mysteries of life.

Normally, the outcome of the struggle is the "Everlasting Yea," or "Let thy will be done"; for life is, after all, a form of affirmation, however negatively it might be conceived by the pessimists. Nevertheless, there are times in life when our too sensitive minds turn in the other direction and make us exclaim with Andréyev in *The Life of Man*: "I curse everything that you have given. I curse the day on which I was born. I curse the day on which I shall die. I curse the whole of my life. I fling everything back at your cruel face, senseless Fate! Be accursed, be forever accursed! With my curses I conquer you. What else can you do to me? . . . With my last thought I will shout into your asinine ears: Be accursed, be accursed!" This is a terrible indictment of life, it is a complete negation of life, it is a most dismal picture of the destiny of man on earth. Buddhists aptly speak of "Leaving no trace," for we know nothing of our future except that we all die away, including the very earth from which we have come. There are certainly things justifying pessimism.

Life, as most of us live it, is a struggle. As long as life is a form of struggle, it cannot be anything but suffering. Does not a struggle mean the impact of two conflicting forces, each trying to get the upper hand of the other? If life's battle is lost, the outcome is death, and death is the fearsomest thing in the world. Even when death be conquered, one is left alone, and the loneliness is more unbearable than the struggle itself. There is no turning away. One may not be conscious of this, and may go on indulging in momentary pleasures that are afforded by the senses. But this being unconscious does not in the least alter the facts of life. However insistently the blind may deny the existence of the sun, they cannot annihilate it.

The first of Buddha's "Fourfold Noble Truths" states that life is pain. Did not everyone of us come to this world screaming and in a way protesting? To be ejected from a warm, soft womb into cold and prohibitive surroundings was surely a painful incident, to say the least. Growth is always attended with pain. Teething is a painful process. Puberty is accompanied by a mental as well as physical disturbance. The growth of the organism called society is as well marked with painful cataclysms, and we are constantly witnessing its birth throes. We may calmly reason that this is all inevitable, that inasmuch as every reconstruction means the destruction of the old regime, we cannot help going through a painful operation. But cold, intellectual analysis does not alleviate the harrowing feelings we undergo. The pain inflicted on our nerves is ineradicable.

This process, however, is providential. For the more you suffer the deeper grows your character, and with the deepening of your character you read the more penetratingly into the secrets of life. Great artists, religious leaders, and social reformers have come out of the intensest struggles which they fought bravely, frequently in tears and with bleeding hearts. Unless you eat your bread in sorrow, you cannot taste of real life. Mencius says that when Heaven wants to perfect a great man it tries him in every possible way until he comes out triumphantly from all his painful experiences.

To me Oscar Wilde seems always posing or striving for an effect, and though he is considered an artist of standing, there is something about him that repels me. Yet even he exclaims in his *De Profundis*: "During the last few months I have, after terrible difficulties and struggles, been able to comprehend some of the lessons hidden in the heart of pain. Clergymen and people who use phrases without wisdom sometimes talk of suffering as a mystery. It is really a revelation. One discerns things one never discerned before. One approaches the whole of history from a different standpoint." You can observe what sanctifying effects his prison life produced on his character. Had he gone through a similar trial in the beginning of his career, he might have produced far greater works than those we have of him at present.

We are too ego-centered. The ego shell in which we live is the hardest thing to outgrow. We seem to carry it all the time from childhood up to the time we die. We are, however, given chances to break through this shell, and the first and greatest of them is when we reach adolescence. This is the first time the ego comes to recognize the "other," or the awakening of sexual love. An ego, entire and undivided, now begins to feel a split in itself. Love hitherto dormant lifts its head and causes a great commotion. For the love now stirred demands at once the assertion and the annihilation of the ego. Love makes the ego lose itself in the object it loves, and yet at the same time it wants to have the object as its own. This is a contradiction, and a struggle that is a tragedy of life. This elemental feeling must be one of the divine agencies whereby man is urged to advance in his upward walk. God gives tragedies to perfect man. The greatest bulk of literature ever produced in this world is but the harping on the same string of love, and we never seem to grow weary of it. But this is not what we are concerned with here. I want to emphasize that through the awakening of love we get a glimpse into the infinity of things, and that this glimpse urges youth to Romanticism or to Rationalism according to his temperament and environment and education.

When the ego shell is broken and the "other" is taken into its own body, we can say that the ego has denied itself or that the ego has taken its first steps toward the infinite. Religiously, here ensues an intense struggle between the finite and the infinite, between the intellect and a higher power, or, more plainly, between the flesh and the spirit. This is the problem of problems that has driven many a youth into the hands of Satan. The struggle to be fought in sincerity may go on up to the age of thirty, when Confucius "knew where to stand." The religious consciousness is then fully awakened, and all the possible ways of escaping from the struggle or bringing it to an end are most earnestly sought in every direction. Books are read, lectures are attended, sermons are greedily taken in, and various religious exercises or disciplines are tried.

How does Zen solve the problem of problems?

In the first place, it proposes the solution by directly appealing to facts of personal experience and not to book knowledge. The nature of one's own being where apparently rages the struggle between the finite and the infinite is to be grasped by a faculty beyond the intellect. For Zen says it is the latter that first made us raise the question which it could not answer by itself, and that therefore it is to be put aside to make room for something higher and more enlightening. The intellect has a peculiarly disquieting quality about it. Though it raises questions to disturb the serenity of the mind, it is too frequently unable to give ultimate answers to them. It upsets the blissful peace of ignorance and yet it does not restore the former state of rest. Because it points out ignorance, it is often considered illuminating, whereas the fact is that it disturbs, not always bringing light on its path. It is not final, it waits for something higher than itself for the solution of the questions it raises regardless of consequences. Were it able to bring rest and order for us settling the matter once for all, an Aristotle or a Hegel would have sufficed with a single system of philosophy. But the history of thought proves that each new structure raised even by a man of extraordinary intellect is sure to be torn down by the succeeding ones. This constant tearing down and building up are all right as far as philosophy itself is concerned, for the inherent nature of the intellect demands this kind of activity. But when it comes to the question of life itself we cannot wait for the ultimate solution to be offered by the intellect. We cannot suspend even for a moment our life activity in order that philosophy may unravel its mysteries. Mysteries or no, live we must. The hungry cannot wait until a complete analysis of food is obtained and the nourishing value of each element is determined. Scientific knowledge of food for the dead will be of no use whatever. Zen therefore does not rely on the intellect for the solution of its deepest problems.

By personal experience it is meant to plunge right into the fact firsthand and not to come to it through an intermediary. Its favorite analogy is: to point at the moon a finger is needed, but woe to those who take the finger for the moon; a basket is welcome to carry our fish home, but when the fish are safely on the table why should we eternally bother ourselves with the basket? Here stands the fact, and let us grasp it with naked hands lest it should slip away—this is what Zen proposes to do. As nature abhors a vacuum, Zen abhors anything coming between the fact and ourselves. According to Zen, there is no struggle in the fact itself such as between the finite and the infinite, between the flesh and the spirit. These are idle distinctions fictitiously designed by the intellect for its own interest. Those who take them seriously or those who try to read them into the very fact of life are those who take the finger for the moon. When we are hungry we eat; when we are sleepy we lay ourselves down; and where does the infinite or the finite come in here? Are not we complete in ourselves and each in himself? Life as it is lived suffices. It is only when the disquieting intellect steps in and tries to murder it that we stop living and imagine ourselves to be short of or in something. The intellect has its usefulness in its proper sphere, but it must not interfere with the flowing of the life stream. The fact of flowing must under no circumstances be arrested or meddled with; for the moment your hands are dipped into it, its transparency is disturbed, it ceases to reflect your image which you have had all the time and will continue to have to the end of time.

Almost corresponding to the "Four Maxims" of the Nichiren Sect, Zen has its own four statements:

> A special transmission outside the Scripture;
> No dependence on words or letters;
> Direct pointing at the Mind of man;
> Seeing into one's Nature and the attainment of Buddhahood.

This sums up all that is claimed by Zen as religion. Of course we must not forget that there is a historical background to this bold pronunciamento. At the time of the introduction of Zen into China, most of the Buddhists were addicted to the discussion of highly metaphysical questions, contented with merely observing the ethical precepts laid down by the Buddha and leading a lethargic life entirely absorbed in the contemplation of the evanescence of things worldly. They missed apprehending the great fact of life itself, which flows altogether outside of these vain exercises of the intellect or of the imagination. Bodhidharma and his successors recognized this pitiful state of affairs. Hence their proclamation as above cited. In a word, they mean that Zen has its way of pointing to the nature of one's own being, and that when this is done one attains to Buddhahood, in which all the contradictions and disturbances caused by the intellect are entirely harmonized in a unity of higher order.

For this reason Zen never explains but indicates, it does not appeal to circumlocution nor generalization. It always deals with facts, concrete and tangible. Seen from the world of logic, Zen may be full of contradictions and repetitions. But as it stands above all things, it goes serenely on its own way. As a Zen master aptly puts it, "carrying his homemade cane on the shoulder, he goes right among the mountains." It does not challenge logic, it simply walks its path of facts, leaving all the rest to their own fates. It is only when logic forgetting its place and functions tries to step into the track of Zen that it loudly proclaims its principles and forcibly drives out the intruder. The intellect is not despised for it is often utilized for the cause of Zen itself. To show some examples of Zen's direct dealing with the fundamental facts of existence, the following are selected:

Rinzai once delivered a sermon, saying: "Over a mass of reddish flesh there sits a true man who has no title; he is all the time coming in and out from your sense organs. If you have not yet testified to the fact, Look! Look!" A monk came forward and asked, "Who is this true man of no title?" Rinzai came right down from his straw chair and taking hold of the monk exclaimed: "Speak! Speak!" The monk remained irresolute, not knowing what to say, whereupon the master, letting him go, remarked, "What worthless stuff is this true man of no title!" Rinzai then went straight back to his room.

Rinzai was noted for his "rough" and direct treatment of his disciples. He never liked the roundabout dealings which characterized the methods of a lukewarm master. He must have inherited this directness from his own teacher Ōbaku, by whom he was struck three times for asking what the fundamental principle of Buddhism was. It goes without saying that Zen has nothing to do with mere striking or roughly shaking the questioner. If you take this as constituting the essentials of Zen, you would commit the same gross error as one who took the finger for the moon. As in everything else, but most particularly in Zen, all its outward manifestations or demonstrations must never be regarded as final. They just indicate the way where to look for the facts. Therefore, these indicators are important, we cannot do well without them. But once caught in them unawares, they are like entangling meshes, we are doomed; for Zen can never thus be comprehended. Zen does not try to ensnare you in the net of logic or of words. What Zen warns is not to be caught in them. Therefore, Rinzai grasps with his naked hands what is directly presented to us all. If a third eye of ours is opened undimmed, we shall know in an unmistakable manner where Rinzai is driving us. We have first to get right into the very spirit of the master and interview the inner man. No amount of wordy explanations will ever lead us into the nature of our own selves. The more you explain, the further astray it goes. It is like trying to catch your own shadow. You run after it and it runs with you at an identical pace. When you realize it, you read deep into the spirit of Rinzai or Ōbaku, and their kindheartedness will begin to be appreciated.

Ummon the great master had to lose one of his legs in order to get an insight into the life principle from which the whole universe takes rise, including his own humble existence. He visited his teacher Bokujū, who was a senior disciple of Rinzai under Ōbaku, three times before he was admitted to see him. The master asked, "Who are you?" "I am Bun-en,"[1] answered the monk. When the truth-seeking monk was allowed to go inside the gate, the master took hold of him by the collar and demanded: "Speak! Speak!" Ummon hesitated, whereupon the master pushed him out of the gate, saying, "Oh, you good-for-nothing fellow!"[2] While the gate was hastily shut, one of Ummon's legs was caught and broken. The intense pain resulting from this apparently awakened the poor fellow to the greatest fact of life. He was no more a solicitous, pity-begging monk; the realization now gained paid more than enough for the loss of his leg. Says Confucius, "If a man understands the Tao in the morning, it is well with him even when he dies in the evening." Some would feel indeed that truth is of more value than mere vegetative or animal living. But, alas, there are so many living corpses wallowing in the mud of ignorance and sensuality.

This is where Zen is most difficult to understand. Why this sarcastic vituperation? Why this seeming heartlessness? What fault had Ummon to deserve the loss of his leg? He was a poor truth-seeking monk, earnestly anxious to be enlightened by the master. Was it really necessary for the master to shut him out three times, and when the gate was half opened to close it again so violently, so inhumanly? Was this the truth of Buddhism Ummon was so eager to get? But the outcome of all this singularly was what was desired by both of them. As to the master, he was satisfied to see the disciple attain an insight into the secrets of his being; and as regards the disciple he was most grateful for what was done to him. Evidently, Zen is the most irrational, inconceivable thing in the world. And this is why Zen is not subject to logical analysis or to intellectual treatment. It is to be directly and personally experienced by each of us in his inner being. Just as two stainless mirrors reflect each other, the fact and our own spirits must stand facing each other with no intervening agents. When this is done we are able to seize upon the living, pulsating fact itself.

Freedom is an empty word until this happens. The first object was to escape the bondage in which all finite beings find themselves, but if we do not cut asunder the very chain of ignorance that binds us hands and feet, where shall we look for deliverance? And this chain of ignorance is wrought of nothing else but the intellect and sensuous infatuation, which cling tightly to every thought we may have, to every feeling we may entertain. They are hard to get rid of, they are like wet clothes as is aptly expressed by the Zen masters. "We are born free and equal."

---

[1] His name. Ummon is the monastery where he later became a master.
[2] Literally, "an old clumsy gimlet of the Ch'in dynasty."

Whatever this may mean socially or politically, Zen maintains that it is absolutely true in the spiritual domain, and that all the fetters and manacles we seem to be carrying about us are put on later through ignorance of the true condition of existence. All the treatments, sometimes literary and sometimes physical, which are liberally and kindheartedly given by the masters to inquiring souls, are intended to regain the original state of freedom. And this is never really realized until we once personally experience it through our own efforts, independent of any ideational representation. The ultimate standpoint of Zen is that we have been led astray through ignorance to find a split in our own being, that there was from the very beginning no need for a struggle between the finite and the infinite, that the peace we seek so eagerly has been here all the time. Sotōba (Su Tung-p'o), the noted Chinese poet and statesman, expresses the idea in the following verse:

> Misty rain on Mount Lu,
> And waves surging in Chê-chiang;
> When you have not yet been there,
> Many a regret surely you have;
> But once there and homeward you wend,
> And how matter-of-fact things look!
> Misty rain on Mount Lu,
> And waves surging in Chê-chiang.

Seigen Ishin also asserts, "Before a man studies Zen, to him mountains are mountains and waters are waters; after he gets an insight into the truth of Zen through the instruction of a good master, mountains are not mountains and waters are not waters; but after this when he really attains to the abode of rest, mountains are once more mountains and waters are waters."

Bokujū was once asked, "We have to dress and eat every day, and how can we escape from all that?"

The master replied, "We dress, we eat."

"I do not understand you," said the questioner.

"If you don't understand put your dress on and eat your food."

Zen thus deals in concrete facts and does not indulge in generalization. I do not wish to add legs to a painted snake, but if I may add my philosophical comments on Bokujū's, I say this. We are all finite, we cannot live out of time and space; inasmuch as we are earth-created, there is no way to grasp the infinite, how can we deliver ourselves from the limitations of existence? This is perhaps the idea put in the first question of the monk, to which the master replies: Salvation must be sought in the finite itself, there is nothing infinite apart from finite things; if you seek something transcendental, that will cut you off from this world of relativity, which is the same thing as the annihilation of yourself. Salvation cannot be had at the cost of your own existence. If so, put your dress on and eat your food, and find your way of freedom in this dressing and eating. This was too much for the questioner, who, therefore, confessed himself as not understanding the meaning of the master. Therefore, the latter continued: Whether you understand or not, just the same go on living in the finite, with the finite; for you die if you stop eating and keeping yourself warm on account of your aspiration for the infinite. No matter how you struggle, *nirvāna* is to be sought in the midst of *samsāra* (birth-and-death). Whether an enlightened Zen master or an ignoramus neither can escape the so-called laws of nature. When the stomach is empty, both are hungry; when it snows, both have to put on an extra flannel. I do not, however, mean that they are both material existences, they are what they are, regardless of their conditions of spiritual development. As the Buddhist scriptures have it, the darkness of the cave itself turns into enlightenment when a torch of spiritual insight burns. It is not that a thing called darkness is first taken out and another thing known by the name of enlightenment is carried in later, but that enlightenment and darkness are substantially one and the same thing from the very beginning; the change from the one to the other has taken place inwardly or subjectively. Therefore the finite is the infinite, and vice versa. These are not two separate things, though we are compelled to conceive them intellectually. This is the idea, logically interpreted, contained in Bokujū's answer given to the monk. The mistake consists in our splitting into two what is really and absolutely one. Is not life one as we live it, before we apply the murderous knife of intellect to it?

On being requested by the monks to deliver a sermon, Hyakujō Nehan told them to work on the farm, after which he would give them a talk on the great subject of Buddhism. They did as they were told, and came to the master for a sermon, when the latter, without saying a word, merely extended his open arms toward the monks. Perhaps there is after all nothing mysterious in Zen. Everything is open to your full view. If you eat your food and keep yourself cleanly dressed and work on the farm to raise your rice or vegetables, you are doing all that is required of you on this earth, and the infinte is realized in you. How realized? When Bokujū was asked what Zen was he recited a Sanskrit phrase from a sutra, "Mahā-prajñāpāramitā!" The inquirer acknowledged his inability to understand the purport of the strange phrase, and the master put a comment on it, saying:

> My robe is all worn out after so many years' usage.
> And parts of it in shreds loosely hanging have been
>   blown away to the clouds.

Is the infinite after all such a poverty-stricken mendicant?

One thing in this connection we cannot afford to lose sight of—that is, the peace of poverty (for peace is only possible in poverty) is obtained after a fierce battle with the entire strength of your personality. A complacency gleaned from idleness or from a *laissez-faire* attitude of mind is a thing most to be abhorred. There is no Zen in this, but sloth and mere vegetation. The battle must rage in its full vigor and masculinity. Without this, whatever peace obtains is a simulacrum, and it has no deep foundation, the first storm encountered will dash it to the ground. Zen is quite emphatic about this. The moral virility found in Zen, apart from its mystic flight, comes from the fighting of the battle of life courageously and undauntedly.

From the ethical point of view, therefore, Zen may be considered a discipline aiming at the reconstruction of character. Our ordinary life only touches the fringe of personality, it does not cause a commotion in the deepest parts of the soul. Even when the religious consciousness is awakened, most of us lightly pass it over. We thus live on the superficiality of things. We may be clever and bright but what we produce lacks depth and sincerity, and does not appeal to the inmost feelings. Some are utterly unable to create anything except makeshifts or imitations betraying their shallowness of character and want of spiritual experience. While Zen is primarily religious, it also molds our moral character. It may be better to say that a deep spiritual experience is bound to effect a change in the moral structure of one's personality.

How is this so?

The truth of Zen is such that when we want to comprehend it penetratingly we must undergo a great struggle, sometimes a long and exacting constant vigilance. To be disciplined in Zen is no easy task. A Zen master once remarked that the life of a monk can be attained only by a man of great moral strength, and that even a minister of the state may not be expected to become a successful monk. A minister of the state in China was considered to be the greatest achievement a man could ever hope for in this world. Not that a monkish life requires the austere practice of asceticism, but that it implies the raising of one's spiritual powers to their highest notch. The utterances and activities of the great Zen masters have come from this elevation. They are not intended to be enigmatic or driving us to confusion. They are the overflowing of a soul filled with deep experiences. Therefore, unless we are ourselves elevated to the same height as the masters, we cannot gain the same commanding views of life.

Says Ruskin:

And be sure also, if the author is worth anything, that you will not get at his meaning all at once—nay, that at his whole meaning you will not for a long time arrive in any wise. Not that he does not say what he means, and in strong words, too; but he cannot say it all and what is more strange, will not, but in a hidden way and in parable, in order that he may be sure you want it. I cannot see quite the reason of this, nor analyze that cruel reticence in the breasts of wise men which makes them always hide their deeper thought. They do not give it to you by way of help, but of reward, and will make themselves sure that you deserve it before they allow you to reach it.

And this key to the royal treasury of wisdom is given us only after patient and painful moral struggle.

The mind is ordinarily chock full with all kinds of intellectual nonsense and passional rubbish. They are of course useful in their own ways in our daily life. There is no denying that. But it is chiefly because of these accumulations that we are made miserable and groan under the feeling of bondage. Each time we want to make a movement, they fetter us, they choke us, and cast a heavy veil over our spiritual horizon. We feel as if we are constantly living under restraint. We long for naturalness and freedom, yet we do not seem to attain them. The Zen masters know this, for they too have gone through the same experiences. They want to have us rid ourselves of these wearisome burdens which we really do not have to carry in order to live a life of truth and enlightenment. Thus they utter a few words and demonstrate with action that, when rightly comprehended, will deliver us from the oppression and tyranny of these intellectual accumulations. But the comprehension does not come to us so easily. Being so long accustomed to the oppression, the mental inertia becomes hard to remove. In fact it has gone down deep into the roots of our own being, and the whole structure of personality is often to be overturned. The process of reconstruction is stained with tears and blood. But the height the great masters have climbed cannot otherwise be reached; the truth of Zen can never be attained unless it is attacked with the full force of one's being. The passage is strewn with thistles and brambles, and the climb is slippery in the extreme. It is no pastime but the most serious task in life; no idlers will ever dare attempt it. It is indeed a moral anvil on which your character is tempered. To the question, "What is Zen?" a master gave this answer, "Boiling oil over a blazing fire." This scorching experience we have to go through before Zen smiles on us and says, "Welcome home."

One of these utterances by the Zen masters that will stir a revolution in our minds is this: Hō-koji, formerly a Confucian, asked Baso, "What kind of man is he who does not keep company with any thing?" Replied the master, "I will tell you when you have swallowed up in one draught all the waters in the West River." What an irrelevant reply to the most serious question one can ever raise in the history of thought! It sounds almost sacrilegious when we know how many souls there are who go down under the weight of this question. But Baso's earnestness leaves no room for doubt, as is quite well known to all the students of Zen. In fact, the rise of Zen after the sixth patriarch, Enō, was due to the brilliant career of Baso, under whom there arose more than eighty fully-qualified masters, and Hō-koji, who was one of the foremost lay disciples of Zen, earned a well-deserved reputation as the Vimalakīrti of Chinese Buddhism. A talk between two such veteran Zen masters could not be an idle sport. However easy and even careless it may appear, there is hidden in it a most precious gem in the literature of Zen. We cannot tell how many students of Zen were made to sweat and weep because of the inscrutability of Baso's statement.

To give another instance: a monk asked the master Keishin of Chōsha, "Where has Nansen gone after his death?"

Replied the master, "When Sekitō was still in the order of young novitiates, he saw the sixth patriarch."

"I am not asking about the young novitiate. What I wish to know is, where is Nansen gone after his death?"

"As to that," said the master, "it makes one think."

The immortality of the soul is another big question. The history of religion is built upon this one question, one may almost say. Everybody wants to know about life after death. Where do we go when we pass away from this earth? Is there really another life? or is the end of this the end of all? While there may be many who do not worry themselves as to the ultimate significance of the solitary, "companionless" One, there are none perhaps who have not once at least in their lives asked themselves concerning their destiny after death. Whether Sekitō when young saw the sixth patriarch or not does not seem to have any inherent connection with the departure of Nansen. The latter was the teacher of Chōsha, and naturally the monk asked him whither the teacher finally passed. Chōsha's answer is no answer from the ordinary rules of logic. Hence the second question, but still a sort of equivocation from the lips of the master. What does this "making one think" explain? From this it is apparent that Zen is one thing and logic another. When we fail to make this distinction and expect of Zen to give us something logically consistent and intellectually illuminating, we altogether misinterpret the signification of Zen. Did I not state in the beginning that Zen deals with facts and not with generalizations? This is the very point where Zen goes straight to the foundations of personality. The intellect does not lead us there; for we do not live in the intellect, but in the Will. Brother Lawrence says (*The Practice of the Presence of God*) "that we ought to make a great difference between the acts of the understanding and those of the will: that the first were comparatively of little value, and the others, all."

Zen literature is brim full of such statements, which seem to have been uttered casually and innocently, but those who know will testify to the fact that all these utterances dropped so naturally from the lips of the masters are as potent as deadly poisons, that when they are once taken in they cause such violent pain as to make one's intestines wriggle nine times and more, as the Chinese would express it. But it is only after pain and turbulence that all the internal impurities are purged and one is reborn with a new outlook on life. It is strange that Zen grows intelligible only when these mental struggles are gone through. But the fact is that Zen is an experience actual and personal, and not a knowledge to be gained by mere analysis or comparison. "Do not talk poetry except to a poet; only the sick know how to sympathize with the sick." This explains the whole situation. Our minds are to be matured to be in tune with those of the masters. Let this be accomplished, and when one note is struck, the whole symphony is born. And what Zen does for us is to prepare our minds to be yielding and appreciative recipients of old masters. Psychologically, Zen thus releases whatever energies we may have in store, of which we are not conscious in ordinary circumstances.

FURTHER READINGS FOR PART 4

Ambrose, *Letters*, Trans. by Sister Mary Melchior Beyenke, in Vol. 26, *Fathers of the Church* (New York: Fathers of the Church, 1954), pp. 286-303. In a famous letter to Simplicianus, Ambrose puts forward his view that foolishness makes the slave, whereas learning and wisdom make a man free.

Bradley, F. H., *Ethical Studies* (2d ed., Oxford: Clarendon, 1927), Essay I. Argues that freedom is not merely doing what we wish to do, which might make us the slaves of our appetites; rather, man is free insofar as he realizes his true self. See, especially, Note C to Essay I, "Freedom."

Calvin, John, *Institutes of the Christian Religion*, Book III, Chap. XIX. A classic statement on Christian liberty.

Epicurus, *Letter to Menoeceus*, trans. by C. Bailey, in W. J. Oates (ed.), *The Stoic and Epicurean Philosophers* (New York: Random House, 1940), pp. 30–33. Taking pleasure to be the end of man, Epicurus states that the life of blessedness involves a state of mind in which the soul has achieved freedom from disturbance.

Green, Thomas Hill, *Lectures on the Principles of Political Obligation* (New York: Longmans, Green, 1895), pp. 2-27. Discusses different senses of "freedom" and defends the view that man's full freedom consists in the virtuous man's ability to will as he ought.

Hampshire, Stuart, *Spinoza* (Hammondsworth, Middlesex: Penguin, 1951), Chap. IV. A helpful and clarifying statement of Spinoza's conception of freedom and morality.

Hegel, Georg Wilhelm Friedrich, *The Philosophy of History*, trans. by J. Sibree (New York: Willey, 1944), esp. Intro., pp. 1-79. Rejects view that men are free when they can do as they wish. Holds that man's freedom consists in self-perfection—a perfection which is possible only by willingly subordinating one's private will to the laws of the state.

Hobhouse, L. T., *The Elements of Social Justice*, (New York: Holt, 1922), Chap. III. Conceives of man's freedom as self-determination—an internal state which is achieved insofar as the various interests of the self are brought into harmony.

Kubie, Lawrence S., "Psychiatry in Relation to Authority and Freedom," in L. Bryson, L. Finkelstein, R. M. MacIver, and R. McKeon (eds.), *Freedom and Authority in Our Time*: Twelfth Symposium of the Conference on Science, Philosophy and Religion (New York: Harper, 1953), pp. 385-391. Urges that we must recognize that one of the most important of man's freedoms is freedom from the tyranny of unconscious compulsions and unconscious fears.

Maritain, Jacques, *Freedom in the Modern World*, trans. by Richard O'Sullivan (New York: Scribner, 1936), pp. 3-73. Basing his view on the philosophy of St. Thomas Aquinas, Maritain expounds a philosophy of freedom which includes both free will and "freedom of autonomy." "Freedom of autonomy" is the perfect spontaneity of a spiritual nature—a property of persons who have achieved self-realization, best exemplified in the Saint.

Miyamoto, Shoson, "Freedom, Independence, and Peace in Buddhism," *Philosophy East and West*, I (Jan. 1952), pp. 30-40, and II (Oct. 1952), pp. 208-225. In this two-part article, Miyamoto expounds the views of Buddhism on the subjects of freedom, independence, and peace.

Philo, *Every Good Man Is Free*, in Vol. IX, *Philo*, trans. by F. H. Colson, Loeb Classical Library (Cambridge, Mass.: Harvard U. P. 1941). Argues that the wise man alone is free, for he is free from domination by the passions.

Plotinus, *The Enneads*, 5 Vols., trans. by Stephen McKenna (London: Philip Lee Warner, 1917-1930), *Sixth Ennead*, Tractate VIII, "On Free Will and the Will of the One." Maintains that freedom comes to the virtuous man insofar as he tames his passions and appetites.

Spinoza, Benedict de, *Ethics*, Parts IV and V. A difficult but classic statement on the power of the intellect to free men from the bondage of their passions. A useful exposition of Spinoza's view of freedom is to be found in the work by Hampshire cited above.

White, David, "Mokṣa as Value and Experience," *Philosophy East and West*, IX (Oct. 1959, Jan. 1960), pp. 145-161. An exposition of the meaning of *"mokṣa"* (liberation) in Indian philosophy.

5. Freedom In Society

As one surveys the crises and confrontations which mark the problems of men in the twentieth century, one may note a recurring theme. In the unrest of students in colleges and universities and in the turmoil of populations struggling for independence, in the insistence of young persons upon the right to experiment with new modes of dress and behavior and in the demands of minorities for rights denied them by established organizations, in the difficulties experienced by those with power in regulating and planning the economic life of nations and in the frustrations of governmental authorities in seeking law and order, the underlying problem is one of reconciling the claims of individuals to freedom with the requirements of institutionalized social life.

The particular issues that arise as part of this general problem are as various as the demands of individuals for change in any of the established traditions, laws, and institutions. In whatever direction individuals feel constraint and limitation, freedom becomes an issue. Men may feel restraint in the customs of their society regulating the relationship between the sexes; they may feel oppressed by laws restricting their economic activities; they may feel enslaved by the entire technological organization of modern society. As a consequence, the particular problems of freedom in this area tend to be as many-sided and numerous as are the limits upon individual activity which life in society involves.

Despite this complexity, discussions of man's freedom in society can be loosely classified as concerned with three types of limitation upon the individual's power to act: political, economic, and social. The readings which follow are organized in accordance with these three major areas of concern. While this classification has some merit in highlighting the type of topic under discussion, there is in fact no genuine separation of issues. The considerations relevant to man's political, economic, and social freedom overlap and interrelate in such a way that it is frequently arbitrary to place an author's view in one category rather than another. Moreover, *the logic of argumentation put forward in one area of discussion often has direct applicability to problems of man's freedom in another area. As a result, the following sections should be read with the awareness that what is said on any given topic may be helpful in thinking about the others.*

Political Freedom

Because government and laws play such a large role in regulating the lives of men, there is much concern in the literature on freedom with the proper limits of the state's power to rule and to legislate.

In the first group of selections, John Locke, Thomas Jefferson, and Harold J. Laski discuss two of the most fundamental questions which can be raised about the power of the state: Is rebellion ever justified? Who has the right to make such a decision? Each author agrees, as did the signers of the Declaration of Independence, that under some circumstances rebellion is justified. Locke would leave the decision to the majority; Jefferson points out that rebellion even by a wrongly informed but discontented minority is a sign of health in a free society; and Laski urges that each individual must decide for himself in the light of his own conscience.

While rebellion raises basic questions concerning the general authority of a given state to rule its citizens, every legislative act provides some kind of limitation on the behavior of those subject to the law. As a result, debate concerning the proper balance of individual freedom and regulation may arise at any point without necessarily touching such fundamental issues as those which cause rebellion. Men can, and do, feel their freedoms to be infringed when legislatures pass laws controlling the sale of guns, or establishing new taxes, or regulating the conduct of business affairs. It is difficult to say which area of legislation is the most important in its effect upon individual freedom, but there is general agreement that laws which seek to limit the rights of citizens to freedom of expression can easily become fundamental threats to other freedoms as well. Accordingly, we have chosen to illustrate the kind of subordinate controversies which can develop with respect to political freedom by including selections which discuss the two most difficult issues of our time involving freedom of speech.

The first of these issues centers in the question of whether a government can justifiably tolerate speeches which advocate the overthrow of that government by force or violence. In Dennis v. United States, *the Supreme Court in 1951 upheld the conviction of eleven Communist Party leaders for conspiracy under the Smith Act. Delivering the opinion of the Court, Chief Justice Vinson supports the view that revolutionary party speeches must be prohibited. A dissenting opinion by Justice Douglas in the same case argues that such speeches must be allowed.*

The second issue involves the question whether free speech is consistent with obscenity tests. In 1966, the Supreme Court faced this issue in the case of Ginzburg v. United States. Ginzburg had been convicted in 1963 for sending three allegedly obscene publications through the mails in violation of the federal obscenity law. The three publications were (1) Eros, *a quarterly magazine "devoted to the subjects of love and sex," in one issue of which a white female and a Negro male, both naked, were shown in various embraces; (2)* Liaison, *a biweekly newsletter dedicated to "keeping sex an art and preventing it from becoming a service," which argued in favor of the broadest possible license in sexual relations; and (3)* The Housewife's Handbook on Selective Promiscuity, *a woman's sexual autobiography. The federal district judge sentenced Ginzburg to five years imprisonment and fined him $28,000. Upholding the decision of the federal district judge, Justice Brennan delivered the opinion of the Court, arguing that free speech is consistent with obscenity tests. In their dissents, Justices Black and Stewart give reasons for their opposition to such tests.*

"THE MAJORITY HAVE A RIGHT TO REBEL"

John Locke

Perhaps it will be said that, the people being ignorant and always discontented, to lay the foundation of government in the unsteady opinion and uncertain humor of the people is to expose it to certain ruin; and no government will be able long to subsist if the people may set up a new legislative whenever they take offense at the old one. To this I answer: Quite the contrary. People are not so easily got out of their old forms as some are apt to suggest. They are hardly to be prevailed with to amend the acknowledged faults in the frame they have been accustomed to. And if there be any original defects, or adventitious ones introduced by time or corruption, it is not an easy thing to get them changed, even when all the world sees there is an opportunity for it. This slowness and aversion in the people to quit their old constitutions has, in the many revolutions which have been seen in this kingdom, in this and former ages still kept us to, or after some interval of fruitless attempts still brought us back again to, our old legislative of Kings, Lords, and Commons. And whatever provacations have made the crown be taken from some of our princes' heads, they never carried the people so far as to place it in another line.

But it will be said, this hypothesis lays a ferment for frequent rebellion. To which I answer:

First, no more than any other hypotheses. For when the people are made miserable, and find themselves exposed to the ill-usage of arbitrary power, cry up their governors as much as you will for sons of Jupiter, let them be sacred and divine, descended, or authorized from heaven, give them out for whom or what you please, the same will happen. The people generally ill-treated, and contrary to right, will be ready upon any occasion to ease themselves of a burden that sits heavy upon them. They will wish and seek for the opportunity, which in the change, weakness, and accidents of human affairs seldom delays long to offer itself. He must have lived but a little while in the world who has not seen examples of this in his time, and he must have read very little who cannot produce examples of it in all sorts of governments in the world.

Secondly, I answer, such revolutions happen not upon every little mismanagement in public affairs. Great mistakes in the ruling part, many wrong and inconvenient laws, and all the slips of human frailty will be borne by the people without mutiny or murmur. But if a long train of abuses, prevarications and artifices, all tending the same way, make the design visible to the people—and they cannot but feel what they lie under, and see whither they are going—it is not to be wondered that they should then rouse themselves and endeavor to put the rule into such hands which may secure to them the ends for which government was at first erected, and without which ancient names and specious forms are so far from being better that they are much worse than the state of nature or pure anarchy; the inconveniences being all as great and as near, but the remedy farther off and more difficult.

Thirdly, I answer that this power in the people of providing for their safety anew by a new legislative when their legislators have acted contrary to their trust by invading their property, is the best fence against rebellion, and the probablest means to hinder it. For rebellion being an opposition, not to persons, but authority, which if founded only in the constitutions and laws of the government, those whoever they be who by force break through, and by force justify their violations of them, are truly and properly rebels. For when men by entering into society and civil government have excluded force, and introduced laws for the preservation of property, peace, and unity amongst themselves, those who set up force again in opposition to the laws do *rebellare*—that is, bring back again the state of war—and are properly rebels; which they who are in power (by the pretense they have to authority, the temptation of force they have in their hands, and the flattery of those about them) being likeliest to do, the properest way to prevent the evil is to show them the danger and injustice of it who are under the greatest temptation to run into it.

In both the forementioned cases, when either the legislative is changed or the legislators act contrary to the end for which they were constituted, those who are guilty are guilty of rebellion. For if anyone by force takes away the established legislative of any society, and the laws by them made pursuant to their trust, he thereby takes away the umpirage which everyone had consented to for a peaceable decision of all their controversies, and a bar to the state of war amongst them. They who remove or change the legislative, take away his decisive power, which nobody can have by the appointment and consent of the people, and so destroying the authority which the people did, and nobody else can, set up; and introducing a power which the people hath not authorized, actually introduce a state of war which is that of force without authority. And thus by removing the legislative established by the society (in whose decisions the people acquiesced and united as to that of their own will), they untie the knot and expose the people anew to the state of war. And if those who by force take away the legislative are rebels, the legislators themselves, as has been shown, can be less esteemed so, when they who were set up for the protection and preservation of the people, their liberties and properties, shall by force invade and endeavor to take them away; and so they, putting themselves into a state of war with those who made them the protectors and guardians of their peace, are properly and with the greatest aggravation *rebellantes* (rebels).

But if they who say it lays a foundation for rebellion mean that it may occasion civil wars or intestine broils, to tell the people they are absolved from obedience when illegal attempts are made upon their liberties or properties, and may oppose the unlawful violence of those who were their magistrates when they invade their properties contrary to the trust put in them and that therefore this doctrine is not to be allowed, being so destructive to the peace of the world: they may as well say upon the same ground that honest men may not oppose robbers or pirates because this may occasion disorder or bloodshed. If any mischief come in such cases, it is not to be charged upon him who defends his own right, but on him that invades his neighbor's. If the innocent honest man must quietly quit all he has for peace's sake to him who will lay violent hands upon it, I desire it may be considered what a kind of peace there will be in the world which consists only in violence and rapine, and which is to be maintained only for the benefit of robbers and oppressors. Who would not think it an admirable peace betwixt the mighty and the mean when the lamb without resistance yielded his throat to be torn by the imperious wolf? Polyphemus's den gives us a perfect pattern of such a peace and such a government, wherein Ulysses and his companions had nothing to do but quietly to suffer themselves to be devoured. And no doubt Ulysses, who was a prudent man, preached up passive obedience, and exhorted them to a quiet submission by representing to them of what concernment peace was to mankind, and by showing the inconveniences which might happen if they should offer to resist Polyphemus, who had now the power over them.

The end of government is the good of mankind, and which is best for mankind, that the people should be always exposed to the boundless will of tyranny, or that the rulers should be sometimes liable to be opposed when they grow exorbitant in the use of their power, and employ it for the destruction and not the preservation of the properties of their people?

Nor let anyone say that mischief can arise from hence as often as it shall please a busy head or turbulent spirit to desire the alteration of the government. It is true such men may stir whenever they please, but it will be only to their own just ruin and perdition. For till the mischief be grown general, and the ill designs of the rulers become visible, or their attempts sensible to the greater part, the people, who are more disposed to suffer than right themselves by resistance, are not apt to stir.

The examples of particular injustice or oppression of here and there an unfortunate man moves them not. But if they universally have a persuasion grounded upon manifest evidence that designs are carrying on against their liberties, and the general course and tendency of things cannot but give them strong suspicions of the evil intention of their governors, who is to be blamed for it? Who can help it if they, who might avoid it, bring themselves into this suspicion? Are the people to be blamed if they have the sense of rational creatures, and can think of things no otherwise than as they find and feel them? And is it not rather their fault who put things in such a posture that they would not have them thought as they are? I grant that the pride, ambition, and turbulency of private men have sometimes caused great disorders in commonwealths, and factions have been fatal to states and kingdoms. But whether the mischief hath oftener begun in the people's wantonness, and a desire to cast off the lawful authority of their rulers, or in the rulers' insolence and endeavors to get and exercise an arbitrary power over their people, whether oppression or disobedience gave the first rise to the disorder, I leave it to impartial history to determine. This I am sure, whoever, either ruler or subject, by force goes about to invade the rights of either prince or people, and lays the foundation for overturning the constitution and frame of any just government, he is guilty of the greatest crime I think a man is capable of, being to answer for all those mischiefs of blood, rapine, and desolation, which the breaking to pieces of governments bring on a country; and he who does it is justly to be esteemed the common enemy and pest of mankind, and is to be treated accordingly.

THE DECLARATION OF INDEPENDENCE

When in the Course of human events, it becomes necessary for one people to dissolve the political bands which have connected them with another, and to assume among the Powers of the earth, the separate and equal station to which the Laws of Nature and of Nature's God entitle them, a decent respect to the opinions of mankind requires that they should declare the causes which impel them to the separation.

We hold these truths to be self-evident, that all men are created equal, that they are endowed by their Creator with certain unalienable Rights, that among these are Life, Liberty and the pursuit of Happiness. That to secure these rights, Governments are instituted among Men, deriving their just powers from the consent of the governed. That whenever any Form of Government becomes destructive of these ends, it is the Right of the People to alter or to abolish it, and to institute new

Government, laying its foundation on such principles and organizing its powers in such form, as to them shall seem most likely to effect their Safety and Happiness. Prudence, indeed, will dictate that Governments long established should not be changed for light and transient causes; and accordingly all experience hath shown, that mankind are more disposed to suffer, while evils are sufferable, than to right themselves by abolishing the forms to which they are accustomed. But when a long train of abuses and usurpations, pursuing invariably the same Object evinces a design to reduce them under absolute Despotism, it is their right, it is their duty, to throw off such Government, and to provide new Guards for their future security. Such has been the patient sufferance of these Colonies; and such is now the necessity which constrains them to alter their former Systems of Government.

"THE NEED FOR REBELLION"

Thomas Jefferson

The British ministry have so long hired their gazetteers to repeat and model into every form lies about our being in anarchy, that the world has at length believed them, the English nation has believed them, the ministers themselves have come to believe them, and what is more wonderful, we have believed them ourselves. Yet where does this anarchy exist? Where did it ever exist, except in the single instance of Massachusetts? And can history produce an instance of rebellion so honourably conducted? I say nothing of its motives. They were founded in ignorance, not wickedness. God forbid we should ever be twenty years without such a rebellion. The people cannot be all, and always, well informed. The part which is wrong will be discontented in proportion to the importance of the facts they misconceive. If they remain quiet under such misconceptions it is a lethargy, the forerunner of death to the public liberty. We have had thirteen states independent for eleven years. There has been one rebellion. That comes to one rebellion in a century and a half, for each state. What country before ever existed a century and a half without a rebellion? And what country can preserve its liberties if their rulers are not warned from time to time that their people preserve the spirit of resistance? Let them take arms. The remedy is to set them right as to facts, pardon and pacify them. What signify a few lives lost in a century or two? The tree of liberty must be refreshed from time to time with the blood of patriots and tyrants. It is its natural manure.

"EACH INDIVIDUAL HAS A RIGHT TO REBEL"

Harold J. Laski

There is, outside the purely formal realm, no obligation to obey the actual state. Our obedience is, and can only be, a function of our judgment upon its performance. That judgment, moreover, is never one which each citizen can make upon the same postulates, intellectual or emotional. What he decides will be the product of the place he occupies in the state, and the relation of that place to his view of what he ought to attain. He may be wrong in the view he takes; but he has never any rational alternative to action in the light of his own certainties. Upon this attitude there hinges a view of law the implications of which are important. It regards the validity of law as unrelated to the source from which it comes. Law becomes law as it goes into application; it is made law by being accepted. That is not to say that accepted law is right law; for law may be accepted by the might which is behind it. We have, in fact, to distinguish between three different senses in which the idea of law can be used. There is the formal juristic sense, which is no more than an announcement, ultimately dependent upon the sovereign authority, of the will to enforce certain decisions. There is the political sense, in which the formal announcement is validated by the acceptance of it by those to whom it applies. There is, finally, the ethical sense in which the decision announced ought to be obeyed, because it is morally right that what it proposes should be done.

Now it is clear that in the first two of these three senses the citizen has no inherent duty to obey. Few people would seriously claim that the juristic sense is always to be equated with the ethical; certainly, to take an obvious example, no Quaker could admit that a state whose government ordered its citizens to make war had, for this purpose, a title to their obedience. Nor can it, I think, be seriously claimed, either, that the political and ethical senses are identical; the commands of the Hitlerite state on June 30, 1934, were law in the sense that they went into effective operation, and were accepted by the population over whom it ruled; but most people in a position to make an independent judgment would, I suggest, regard them as ethically outrageous. Might, however profound, does not make right; effective operation of law still leaves undecided the question of ethical adequacy.

Neither formal competence, then, nor political power can confer a just title to obedience. With what are we left? Only, I think, with the insistence that law to be ethically valid must conform with the requirements of the system of rights the purposes of which the state exists to maintain. And since law is a command seeking to control my behaviour in some particular way, I must judge that conformity for myself as the test of its ethical adequacy. The roots of valid law, that is, are, and can only be, within the individual conscience. I make law legal, so to say, by giving to its operation the consent of my conscience.

If it is said that such a view, by justifying refusal to obey, opens the door to anarchy, the answer is that the accusation is true. But it is not a serious accusation. In the life of states the door to anarchy is always open because men are never willing to admit the unconditional conference of power. If, further, it be said that the individual conscience is at least as likely to be wrong as the consciences of those who rule the state, the answer, again, is that while this may be true, the citizen who yields his conviction on the ground that he may be mistaken will soon cease, in any meaning sense, to be a citizen at all. There is no way of making a state active in the fulfilment of its function except the knowledge that men will refuse to obey its commands where they regard them as a violation of that function. That was the truth that Pericles saw when he told the citizens of Athens that the secret of liberty was courage. Unless men are prepared to act by the insights they have, even when these insights are erroneous, they are bound to become no more than the passive recipients of orders to whose moral quality they are indifferent. When they do that, they poison the foundations of the state. For they then cease to be moral beings in any sense of the word that has meaning. They associate truth and justice and right automatically with the possession of physical power. No people prepared in that fashion to abdicate its humanity is likely to be long capable of creative achievement. For so to abdicate the duty of moral judgment is to sell oneself into slavery.

It is said that the individual is powerless, and that he wastes his energy by acting upon his judgment. But there are at least two answers to this view. A moral obligation is not less compelling because it may end in failure. To adopt that canon of effort is to accept the view that justice is the will of the stronger—a doctrine against which, as I have pointed out, the whole history of humanity is a protest. And to argue, secondly, that the individual is powerless is, on the record, quite untrue. He is powerless only when his perceptions are so completely unshared that he fails to arouse any note of response among his fellow-citizens; and he has always to remember that the shift of events may cause them to be shared at a later stage. The early Christians must have appeared singularly futile to their own generation when they challenged the majesty of Rome; but their steadfastness conquered the Western world. Luther's recalcitrance must have appeared akin to madness to a church which remembered its successful emergence from the stresses of the Conciliar revolt; but he changed the history of the world by his courage. Even so liberal a mind as Emerson could write of the American abolitionists that they were "narrow, self-pleasing, conceited men, and affect us as the insane do";[1] but it was hardly a generation afterwards that so respectable an observer as Oliver Wendell Holmes, not given to extreme views, could say of his friend's judgment that "it would have taken a long time to get rid of slavery if some of Emerson's teachings had been accepted as the whole gospel of liberty."[2]

[1] Quoted in V. F. Calverton, *The Liberalism of American Literature* (1932), p. 330.
[2] *Ibid.*, p. 331.

History, indeed, abounds with such instances. The individual who protests against the law he deems unjust is far less alone than he is likely to imagine. He is acting in a mental climate in which the experience borne in upon him is likely to be shared by others; and the gesture he makes may awaken others to the understanding of their obligations. No one who looks back upon their history can doubt that the suffragettes who, for eight years, defied the law awakened the British government to a sense that their claims were serious in a way that altered the whole perspective of those claims. No one can doubt either that the unbreakable will of Lenin was central to the success of the Bolshevik Revolution in 1917. That we must fight for our philosophy if we believe in it, seems to me the inescapable implication of the record.

Against this view two considerations are urged, in both of which there is, unquestionably, considerable force. It is said that to challenge the government is to weaken the authority of all law, and that to do so is to open the flood-gates to chaos. It was the sense of this danger which made T. H. Green, who admitted, in the last resort, the right to revolution, insist that we must approach the state in fear and trembling. But it is surely not less important to realise that respect for law must always mean respect for what the law does; and if the individual, whether alone or in concert with others, judges what the law does to be ethically intolerable, he must act upon the basis of his judgment. To decide otherwise is to argue that the highest duty of the individual is to maintain order, without regard to the quality of the order that is maintained. I do not find this argument compatible with the notion of the individual as a moral being.

It is said, secondly, that this view admits the right of any doctrine to support itself by force, if it can. Men have only to announce that they are moved by some profound conviction to be justified in using violence to attain their ends. Such an attitude, it is argued, is utterly destructive of the foundations of social well-being.

But the answer is surely that no doctrine, however evil, moves to the use of force unless it is rooted in profound grievance which it sees no other way to remedy. We may believe the Bolshevik Revolution to have been wholly evil; but it is clear that the previous conditions of the Russian state alone account for its origin and methods. We may argue, with the Communists, that Hitler has been no more than the agent of finance-capitalism in Germany;[3] but it is also clear that his victory was built upon the profound grievances of millions of Germans who saw no adequate redress for them in the habits of the Weimar republic. The truth is that men in general are so accustomed to obey that their departure from the normal canons of political behaviour is always an index to grave disease in the state. They have, as Burke said, "no interest in disorder; where they do wrong it is their error and not their crime." We need not argue that a doctrine which arms itself is wise or right to do so. But, on the facts, we have to argue that no doctrine ever does successfully arm itself unless the government it attacks has failed to deal with the grievances it expresses in a reasonable way.

That is, I think, apparent in the history of most revolutions. Certainly the student

3 Cf. E. Henri, *Hitler Over Europe* (1933).

of the English civil wars, of the revolutions of France and of Russia, will note as not the least remarkable of their features, the patient efforts of the common people to await reform before they turned to violence. And in any society violence is unlikely if the conviction is widespread that the state is seriously attempting to fulfil its obligations. Violence comes when the facts persuade men to believe that the bona-fides of their rulers is no longer to be trusted.

THE DENNIS CASE: "REVOLUTIONARY
PARTY SPEECHES MUST BE PROHIBITED"

Chief Justice Fred Vinson

Mr. Chief Justice Vinson:

Petitioners were indicted in July, 1948, for violation of the conspiracy provisions of the Smith Act, 54 Stat. 671, 18 U.S.C. (1946 ed.) § 11, during the period of April, 1945, to July, 1948. . . . A verdict of guilty as to all the petitioners was returned by the jury on October 14, 1949. The Court of Appeals affirmed the convictions. . . . We granted certiorari. . . . limited to the following two questions: (1) Whether either § 2 or § 3 of the Smith Act, inherently or as construed and applied in the instant case, violates the First Amendment and other provisions of the Bill of Rights; (2) whether either § 2 or § 3 of the Act, inherently or as construed and applied in the instant case, violates the First and Fifth Amendments because of indefiniteness.

Sections 2 and 3 of the Smith Act provide as follows:

Sec. 2

(a) it shall be unlawful for any person—

(1) to knowingly or willfully advocate, abet, advise, or teach the duty, necessity, desirability, or propriety of overthrowing or destroying any government in the United States by force or violence, or by the assassination of any officer of any such government;

(2) with the intent to cause the overthrow or destruction of any government in the United States, to print, publish, edit, issue, circulate, sell, distribute, or publicly display any written or printed matter advocating, advising, or teaching the duty, necessity, desirability, or propriety of overthrowing or destroying any government in the United States by force or violence;

(3) to organize or help to organize any society, group, or assembly of persons who teach, advocate, or encourage the overthrow or destruction of any government in the United States by force or violence; or to be or become a member of, or affiliate with, any such society, group, or assembly of persons, knowing the purposes thereof.

(b) For the purposes of this section, the term "government in the United States" means the Government of the United States, the government of any State, Territory, or possession of the United States, the government of the District of Columbia, or the government of any political sub-division of any of them.

Sec. 3. It shall be unlawful for any person to attempt to commit, or to consipre to commit, any of the acts prohibited by the provisions of . . . this title.

The indictment charged the petitioners with wilfully and knowingly conspiring (1) to organize as the Communist Party of the United States of America a society, group and assembly of persons who teach and advocate the overthrow and destruction of the Government of the United States by force and violence, and (2) knowingly and wilfully to advocate and teach the duty and necessity of overthrowing and destroying the Government of the United States by force and violence. The indictment further alleged that § 2 of the Smith Act proscribes these acts and that any conspiracy to take such action is a violation of § 3 of the Act.

The trial of the case extended over nine months, six of which were devoted to the taking of evidence, resulting in a record of 16,000 pages. Our limited grant of the writ of certiorari has removed from our consideration any question as to the sufficiency of the evidence to support the jury's determination that petitioners are guilty of the offense charged. Whether on this record petitioners did in fact advocate the overthrow of the Government by force and violence is not before us, and we must base any discussion of this point upon the conclusions stated in the opinion of the Court of Appeals, which treated the issue in great detail. That court held that the record in this case amply supports the necessary finding of the jury that petitioners, the leaders of the Communist Party in this country, were unwilling to work within our framework of democracy, but intended to initiate a violent revolution whenever the propitious occasion appeared. Petitioners dispute the meaning to be drawn from the evidence, contending that the Marxist-Leninist doctrine they advocated taught that force and violence to achieve a Communist form of government in an existing democratic state would be necessary only because the ruling classes of that state would never permit the transformation to be accomplished peacefully, but would use force and violence to defeat any peaceful political and economic gain the Communists could achieve. But the Court of Appeals held that the record supports the following broad conclusions: By virtue of their control over the political apparatus of the Communist Political Association, petitioners were able to transform that organization into the Communist Party; that the policies of the Association were changed from peaceful cooperation with the United States and its economic and political structure to a policy which had existed before the United States and the Soviet Union were fighting a common enemy, namely, a policy which worked for the overthrow of the Government by force and violence; that the Communist Party is a highly disciplined organization, adept at infiltration into strategic positions, use of aliases, and double-meaning language; that the Party is rigidly controlled; that Communists, unlike other political parties, tolerate no dissension from the policy laid down by the guiding forces, but that the approved program is slavishly followed by the members of the Party; that the literature of the Party and the statements and activities of its leaders ... advocate, and the general goal of the Party was, during the period in question, to achieve a successful overthrow of the existing order by force and violence. . . .

The structure and purpose of the statute demand the inclusion of intent as an element of the crime. Congress was concerned with those who advocate and organize for the overthrow of the Government. Certainly those who recruit and combine for the purpose of advocating overthrow intend to bring about that overthrow. We hold that the statute requires as an essential element of the crime proof of the intent of those who are charged with its violation to overthrow the Government by force and violence. . . .

Nor does the fact that there must be an investigation of a state of mind under this interpretation afford any basis for rejection of that meaning. A survey of Title 18 of the U.S. Code indicates that the vast majority of the crimes designated by that Title require, by express language, proof of the existence of a certain mental state in words such as "knowingly," "maliciously," "wilfully," "with the purpose of," "with intent to," or combinations or permutations of these and synonymous terms. The existence of a *mens rea* is the rule of, rather than the exception to, the principles of Anglo-American criminal jurisprudence. . . .

The obvious purpose of the statute is to protect existing Government, not from change by peaceable, lawful and constitutional means, but from change by violence, revolution and terrorism. That it is within the *power* of the Congress to protect the Government of the United States from armed rebellion is a proposition which requires little discussion. Whatever theoretical merit there may be to the argument that there is a "right" to rebellion against dictatorial governments is without force where the existing structure of the government provides for peaceful and orderly change. We reject any principle of governmental helplessness in the face of preparation for revolution, which principle, carried to its logical conclusion, must lead to anarchy. No one could conceive that it is not within the power of Congress to prohibit acts intended to overthrow the Government by force and violence. The question with which we are concerned here is not whether Congress has such *power*, but whether the *means* which it has employed conflict with the First and Fifth Amendments to the Constitution.

One of the bases for the contention that the means which Congress has employed are invalid takes the form of an attack on the face of the statute on the grounds that by its terms it prohibits academic discussion of the merits of Marxism-Leninism, that it stifles ideas and is contrary to all concepts of a free speech and a free press. . . .

The very language of the Smith Act negates the interpretation which petitioners would have us impose on that Act. It is directed at advocacy, not discussion. Thus, the trial judge properly charged the jury that they could not convict if they found that petitioners did "no more than pursue peaceful studies and discussions or teaching and advocacy in the realm of ideas." He further charged that it was not unlawful "to conduct in an American college and university a course explaining the philosophical theories set forth in the books which have been placed in evidence." Such a charge is in strict accord with the statutory language, and illustrates the meaning to be placed on those words. Congress did not intend to eradicate the free discussion of political theories, to destroy the traditional rights of Americans to discuss and evaluate ideas without fear of governmental sanction. Rather Congress was concerned with the very kind of activity in which the evidence showed these petitioners engaged. . . .

The basis of the First Amendment is the hypothesis that speech can rebut speech, propaganda will answer propaganda, free debate of ideas will result in the wisest governmental policies. It is for this reason that this Court has recognized the inherent value of free discourse. An analysis of the leading cases in this Court which have involved direct limitations on speech, however, will demonstrate that both the majority of the Court and the dissenters in particular cases have recognized that this is not an unlimited, unqualified right, but that the societal value of speech must, on occasion, be subordinated to other values and considerations. . . .

The rule we deduce from these cases is that where an offense is specified by a statute in nonspeech or nonpress terms, a conviction relying upon speech or press as evidence of violation may be sustained only when the speech or publication created a "clear and present danger" of attempting or accomplishing the prohibited crime, e.g., interference with enlistment. . . .

Neither Justice Holmes nor Justice Brandeis ever envisioned that a shorthand phrase should be crystallized into a rigid rule to be applied inflexibly without regard to the circumstances of each case. Speech is not an absolute, above and beyond control by the legislature when its judgment, subject to review here, is that certain kinds of speech are so undesirable as to warrant criminal sanction. Nothing is more certain in modern society than the principle that there are no absolutes, that a name, a phrase, a standard has meaning only when associated with the considerations which gave birth to the nomenclature. . . . To those who would paralyze our Government in the face of impending threat by encasing it in a semantic straitjacket we must reply that all concepts are relative. . . .

In this case we are squarely presented with the application of the "clear and present danger" test, and must decide what that phrase imports. We first note that many of the cases in which this Court has reversed convictions by use of this or similar tests have been based on the fact that the interest which the State was attempting to protect was itself too insubstantial to warrant restriction of speech. . . . Overthrow of the Government by force and violence is certainly a substantial enough interest for the Government to limit speech. Indeed, this is the ultimate value of any society, for if a society cannot protect its very structure from armed internal attack, it must follow that no subordinate value can be protected. If, then, this interest may be protected, the literal problem which is presented is what has been meant by the use of the phrase "clear and present danger" of the utterances bringing about the evil within the power of Congress to punish. . . .

Obviously, the words cannot mean that before the Government may act, it must wait until the *putsch* is about to be executed, the plans have been laid and the signal is awaited. If Government is aware that a group aiming at its overthrow is attempting to indoctrinate its members and to commit them to a course whereby they will strike when the leaders feel the circumstances permit, action by the

Government is required. The argument that there is no need for Government to concern itself, for Government is strong, it possesses ample powers to put down a rebellion, it may defeat the revolution with ease needs no answer. For that is not the question. Certainly an attempt to overthrow the Government by force, even though doomed from the outset because of inadequate numbers or power of the revolutionists, is a sufficient evil for Congress to prevent. The damage which such attempts create both physically and politically to a nation makes it impossible to measure the validity in terms of the probability of success, or the immediacy of a successful attempt. In the instant case the trial judge charged the jury that they could not convict unless they found that petitioners intended to overthrow the Government "as speedily as circumstances would permit." This does not mean, and could not properly mean, that they would not strike until there was certainty of success. What was meant was that the revolutionists would strike when they thought the time was ripe. We must therefore reject the contention that success or probability of success is the criterion. . . .

Chief Judge Learned Hand, writing for the majority below, interpreted the phrase as follows: "in each case [courts] must ask whether the gravity of the 'evil,' discounted by its improbability, justifies such invasion of free speech as is necessary to avoid the danger." . . . We adopt this statement of the rule. As articulated by Chief Judge Hand, it is as succinct and inclusive as any other we might devise at this time. It takes into consideration those factors which we deem relevant, and relates their significances. More we cannot expect from words. . . .

Likewise, we are in accord with the court below, which affirmed the trial court's finding that the requisite danger existed. The mere fact that from the period 1945 to 1948 petitioners' activities did not result in an attempt to overthrow the Government by force and violence is of course no answer to the fact that there was a group that was ready to make the attempt. The formation by petitioners of such a highly organized conspiracy, with rigidly disciplined members subject to call when the leaders, these petitioners, felt that the time had come for action, coupled with the inflammable nature of world conditions, similar uprisings in other countries, and the touch-and-go nature of our relations with countries with whom petitioners were in the very least ideologically attuned, convince us that their convictions were justified on this score. And this analysis disposes of the contention that a conspiracy to advocate, as distinguished from the advocacy itself, cannot be constitutionally restrained, because it comprises only the preparation. It is the existence of the conspiracy which creates the danger. . . . If the ingredients of the reaction are present, we cannot bind the Government to wait until the catalyst is added. . . .

Although we have concluded that the finding that there was a sufficient danger to warrant the application of the statute was justified on the merits, there remains the problem of whether the trial judge's treatment of the issue was correct. He charged the jury, in relevant part, as follows: . . .

If you are satisfied that the evidence establishes beyond a reasonable doubt that the defendants, or any of them, are guilty of a violation of the statute as I have interpreted it to you, I find as a matter of law that there is sufficient danger of a substantive evil that the Congress has a right to prevent to justify the application of the statute under the First Amendment of the Constitution.

This is matter of law about which you have no concern. It is a finding on a matter of law which I deem essential to support my ruling that the case should be submitted to you to pass upon the guilt or innocence of the defendants. . . .

It is thus clear that he reserved the question of the existence of the danger for his own determination, and the question becomes whether the issue is of such a nature that it should have been submitted to the jury. . . .

The argument that the action of the trial court is erroneous, in declaring as a matter of law that such violation shows sufficient danger to justify the punishment despite the First Amendment, rests on the theory that a jury must decide a question of the application of the First Amendment. We do not agree. . . .

The question in this case is whether the statute which the legislature has enacted may be constitutionally applied. In other words, the Court must examine judicially the application of the statute to the particular situation, to ascertain if the Constitution prohibits the conviction. We hold that the statute may be applied where there is a "clear and present danger" of the substantive evil which the legislature had the right to prevent. Bearing, as it does, the marks of a "question of law," the issue is properly one for the judge to decide.

There remains to be discussed the question of vagueness—whether the statute as we have interpreted it is too vague, not sufficiently advising those who would speak of the limitations upon their activity. It is urged that such vagueness contravenes the First and Fifth Amendments. . . .

We agree that the standard as defined is not a neat, mathematical formulary. Like all verbalizations it is subject to criticism on the score of indefiniteness. But petitioners themselves contend that the verbalization, "clear and present danger," is the proper standard. We see no difference from the standpoint of vagueness, whether the standard of "clear and present danger" is one contained in *haec verba* within the statute, or whether it is the judicial measure of constitutional applicability. We have shown the indeterminate standard the phrase necessarily connotes. We do not think we have rendered that standard any more indefinite by our attempt to sum up the factors which are included within its scope. We think it well serves to indicate to those who would advocate constitutionally prohibited conduct that there is a line beyond which they may not go—a line, which they, in full knowledge of what they intend and the circumstances in which their activity takes place, will well appreciate and understand. . . .

We hold that § § 2(a) (1), 2(a) (3) and 3 of the Smith Act, do not inherently, or as construed or applied in the instant case, violate the First Amendment and other provisions of the Bill of Rights, or the First and Fifth Amendments because of indefiniteness. Petitioners intended to overthrow the Government of the United States as speedily as the circumstances would permit. Their conspiracy to organize the Communist Party and to teach and advocate the overthrow of the Government of the United States by force and violence created a "clear and present danger" of an attempt to overthrow the Government by force and violence. They were properly and constitutionally convicted for violation of the Smith Act. The judgments of conviction are affirmed.

THE DENNIS CASE: "REVOLUTIONARY
PARTY SPEECHES MUST BE ALLOWED"

Justice William O. Douglas

Mr. Justice Douglas, dissenting:

If this were a case where those who claimed protection under the First Amendment were teaching the techniques of sabotage, the assassination of the President, the filching of documents from public files, the planting of bombs, the art of street warfare, and the like, I would have no doubts. The freedom to speak is not absolute; the teaching of methods of terror and other seditious conduct should be beyond the pale along with obscenity and immorality. This case was argued as if those were the facts. The argument imported much seditious conduct into the record. That is easy and it has popular appeal, for the activities of Communists in plotting and scheming against the free world are common knowledge. But the fact is that no such evidence was introduced at the trial. There is a statute which makes a seditious conspiracy unlawful. Petitioners, however, were not charged with a "conspiracy to overthrow" the Government. They were charged with a conspiracy to form a party and groups and assemblies of people who teach and advocate the overthrow of our Government by force or violence and with a conspiracy to advocate and teach its overthrow by force and violence. It may well be that indoctrination in the techniques of terror to destroy the Government would be indictable under either statute. But the teaching which is condemned here is of a different character.

So far as the present record is concerned, what petitioners did was to organize people to teach and themselves teach the Marxist-Leninist doctrine contained chiefly in four books: *Foundations of Leninism* by Stalin (1924), *The Communist Manifesto* by Marx and Engels (1848), *State and Revolution* by Lenin (1917), *History of the Communist Party of the Soviet Union* (1939).

Those books are to Soviet Communism what *Mein Kampf* was to Nazism. If they are understood, the ugliness of Communism is revealed, its deceit and cunning are exposed, the nature of its activities becomes apparent, and the chances of its success less likely. That is not, of course, the reason why petitioners chose these books for their classrooms. They are fervent Communists to whom these volumes are gospel. They preached the creed with the hope that some day it would be acted upon.

The opinion of the Court does not outlaw these texts nor condemn them to the fire, as the Communists do literature offensive to their creed. But if the books themselves are not outlawed, if they can lawfully remain on library shelves, by what reasoning does their use in a classroom become a crime? It would not be a crime under the Act to introduce these books to a class, though that would be teaching what the creed of violent overthrow of the government is. The Act, as construed, requires the element of intent—that those who teach the creed believe in it. The crime then depends not on what is taught but on who the teacher is. That is to make freedom of speech turn not on *what is said*, but on the *intent* with which it is said. Once we start down that road we enter territory dangerous to the liberties of every citizen.

There was a time in England when the concept of constructive treason flourished. Men were punished not for raising a hand against the king but for thinking murderous thoughts about him. The Framers of the Constitution were alive to that abuse and took steps to see that the practice would not flourish here. Treason was defined to require overt acts—the evolution of a plot against the country into an actual project. The present case is not one of treason. But the analogy is close when the illegality is made to turn on intent, not on the nature of the act. We then start probing men's minds for motive and purpose; they become entangled in the law not for what they did but *for what they thought; they* get convicted not for what they said but for the purpose with which they said it.

Intent, of course, often makes the difference in the law. An act otherwise excusable or carrying minor penalties may grow to an abhorrent thing if the evil intent is present. We deal here, however, not with ordinary acts but with speech, to which the Constitution has given a special sanction.

The vice of treating speech as the equivalent of overt acts of a treasonable or seditious character is emphasized by a concurring opinion, which by invoking the law of conspiracy makes speech do service for deeds which are dangerous to society. The doctrine of conspiracy has served divers and oppressive purposes and in its broad reach can be made to do great evil. But never until today has anyone seriously thought that the ancient law of conspiracy could constitutionally be used to turn speech into seditious conduct. Yet that is precisely what is suggested. I repeat that we deal here with speech alone, not with speech *plus* acts of sabotage or unlawful conduct. Not a single seditious act is charged in the indictment. To make a lawful speech unlawful because two men conceive it is to raise the law of conspiracy to appalling proportions. That course is to make a radical break with the past and to violate one of the cardinal principles of our constitutional scheme.

Free speech has occupied an exalted position because of the high service it has given our society. Its protection is essential to the very existence of a democracy. The airing of ideas releases pressures which otherwise might become destructive. When ideas compete in the market for acceptance, full and free discussion exposes the false and they gain few adherents. Full and free discussion even of ideas we hate encourages the testing of our own prejudices and preconceptions. Full and free discussion keeps a society from becoming stagnant and unprepared for the stresses and strains that work to tear all civilizations apart.

Full and free discussion has indeed been the first article of our faith. We have founded our political system on it. It has been the safeguard of every religious, political, philosophical, economic, and racial group amongst us. We have counted on it to keep us from embracing what is cheap and false; we have trusted the common sense of our people to choose the doctrine true to our genius and to reject the rest. This has been the one single outstanding tenet that has made our institutions the symbol of freedom and equality. We have deemed it more costly to liberty to suppress a despised minority than to let them vent their spleen. We have above all else feared the political censor. We have wanted a land where our people can be exposed to all the diverse creeds and cultures of the world.

There comes a time when even speech loses its constitutional immunity. Speech innocuous one year may at another time fan such destructive flames that it must be halted in the interests of the safety of the Republic. That is the meaning of the clear and present danger test. When conditions are so critical that there will be no time to avoid the evil that the speech threatens, it is time to call a halt. Otherwise, free speech which is the strength of the Nation will be the cause of its destruction.

Yet free speech is the rule, not the exception. The restraint to be constitutional must be based on more than fear, on more than passionate opposition against the speech, on more than a revolted dislike for its contents. There must be some immediate injury to society that is likely if speech is allowed. The classic statement of these conditions was made by Mr. Justice Brandeis in his concurring opinion in *Whitney v. California*, 274 U.S. 357.

Fear of serious injury cannot alone justify suppression of free speech and assembly. Men feared witches and burnt women. It is the function of speech to free men from the bondage of irrational fears. To justify suppression of free speech there must be reasonable ground to fear that serious evil will result if free speech is practiced. There must be reasonable ground to believe that the danger apprehended is imminent. There must be reasonable ground to believe that the evil to be prevented is a serious one. Every denunciation of existing law tends in some measure to increase the probability that there will be violation of it. Condonation of a breach enhances the probability. Expressions of approval add to the probability. Propagation of the criminal state of mind by teaching syndicalism increases it. Advocacy of law-breaking heightens it still further. But even advocacy of violation, however reprehensible morally, is not a justification for denying free speech where the advocacy falls short of incitement and there is nothing to indicate that the advocacy would be immediately acted on. The wide difference between advocacy and incitement, between preparation and attempt, between assembling and conspiracy, must be borne in mind. In order to support a finding of clear and present danger it must be shown either that immediate serious violence was to be expected or was advocated, or that the past conduct furnished reason to believe that such advocacy was then contemplated.

Those who won our independence by revolution were not cowards. They did not fear political change. They did not exalt order at the cost of liberty. To courageous self-reliant men, with confidence in the power of free and fearless reasoning applied through the processes of popular government, no danger flowing from speech can be deemed clear and present, unless the incidence of the evil apprehended is so imminent that it may befall before there is opportunity for full discussion. *If there be time to expose through discussion the falsehood and fallacies, to avert the evil by the processes of education, the remedy to be applied is more speech, not enforced silence.* (Italics added.)

I had assumed that the question of the clear and present danger, being so critical an issue in the case, would be a matter for submission to the jury. It was squarely held in *Pierce* v. *United States*, 252 U.S. 239, to be a jury question. Mr. Justice Pitney, speaking for the Court, said, "Whether the statements contained in the pamphlet had a natural tendency to produce the forbidden consequences, as alleged, was a question to be determined, not upon demurrer, but by the jury at the trial." That is the only time the Court has passed on the issue. None of our other decisions is contrary. Nothing said in any of the nonjury cases has detracted from that ruling. The statement in *Pierce* v. *United States* states the law as it has been and as it should be. The Court, I think, errs when it treats the question as one of law.

Yet, whether the question is one for the Court or the jury, there should be evidence of record on the issue. This record, however, contains no evidence whatsoever showing that the acts charged *viz.*, the teaching of the Soviet theory of revolution with the hope that it will be realized, have created any clear and present danger to the Nation. The Court, however, rules to the contrary. It says, "The formation by petitioners of such a highly organized conspiracy, with rigidly disciplined members subject to call when the leaders, these petitioners, felt that the time had come for action, coupled with the inflammable nature of world conditions, similar uprisings in other countries, and the touch-and-go nature of our relations with countries with whom petitioners were in the very least ideologically attuned, convince us that their convictions were justified on this score."

That ruling is in my view not responsive to the issue in the case. We might as well say that the speech of petitioners is outlawed because Soviet Russia and her Red Army are a threat to world peace.

The nature of Communism as a force on the world scene would, of course, be relevant to the issue of clear and present danger of petitioners' advocacy within the United States. But the primary consideration is the strength and tactical position of petitioners and their converts in this country. On that there is no evidence in the record. If we are to take judicial notice of the threat of Communists within the nation, it should not be difficult to conclude that *as a political party* they are of little consequence. Communists in this country have never made a respectable or serious showing in any election. I would doubt that there is a village, let alone a city or county or state which the Communists could carry. Communism in the world scene is no bogey-man; but Communists as a political faction or party in this country plainly is. Communism has been so thoroughly exposed in this country that it has been crippled as a political force. Free speech has destroyed it as an effective political party. It is inconceivable that those who went up and down this country preaching the doctrine of revolution which petitioners espouse would have any success. In days of trouble and confusion when bread lines were long, when the unemployed walked the streets, when people were starving the advocates of a short-cut by revolution might have a chance to gain adherents. But today there are no such conditions. The country is not in despair; the people know Soviet Communism; the doctrine of Soviet revolution is exposed in all of its ugliness and the American people want none of it.

How it can be said that there is a clear and present danger that this advocacy will succeed is, therefore, a mystery. Some nations less resilient than the United States, where illiteracy is high and where democratic traditions are only budding, might have to take drastic steps and jail these men for merely speaking their creed. But in America they are miserable merchants of unwanted ideas; their wares remain unsold. The fact that their ideas are abhorrent does not make them powerful.

The political impotence of the Communists in this country does not, of course, dispose of the problem. Their numbers; their positions in industry and government; the extent to which they have in fact infiltrated the police, the armed services, transportation, stevedoring, power plants, munitions works, and other critical places —these facts all bear on the likelihood that their advocacy of the Soviet theory of revolution will endanger the Republic. But the record is silent on these facts. If we are to proceed on the basis of judicial notice, it is impossible for me to say that the Communists in this country are so potent or so strategically deployed that they must be suppressed for their speech. I could not so hold unless I were willing to conclude that the activities in recent years of committees of Congress, of the Attorney General, of labor unions, of state legislatures, and of Loyalty Boards were so futile as to leave the country on the edge of grave peril. To believe that petitioners and their following are placed in such critical positions as to endanger the Nation is to believe the incredible. It is safe to say that the followers of the creed of Soviet Communism are known to the F.B.I.; that in case of war with Russia they will be picked up overnight as were all prospective saboteurs at the commencement of World War II; that the invisible army of petitioners is the best known, the most beset, and the least thriving of any fifth column in history. Only those held by fear and panic could think otherwise.

This is my view if we are to act on the basis of judicial notice. But the mere statement of the opposing views indicates how important it is that we know the facts before we act. Neither prejudice nor hate nor senseless fear should be the basis of this solemn act. Free speech—the glory of our system of government—should not be sacrificed on anything less than plain and objective proof of danger that the evil advocated is imminent. On this record no one can say that petitioners and their converts are in such a strategic position as to have even the slightest chance of achieving their aims.

The First Amendment provides that "Congress shall make no law ... abridging the freedom of speech." The Constitution provides no exception. This does not mean, however, that the Nation need hold its hand until it is in such weakened condition that there is no time to protect itself from incitement to revolution. Seditious conduct can always be punished. But the command of the First Amendment is so clear that we should not allow Congress to call a halt to free speech except in the extreme case of peril from the speech itself. The First Amendment makes confidence in the common sense of our people and in their maturity of judgment the great postulate of our democracy. Its philosophy is that violence is rarely, if ever, stopped by denying civil liberties to those advocating resort to force. The First Amendment reflects the philosophy of Jefferson "that it is time enough for the rightful purposes of civil government for its officers to interfere when principles break out into overt acts against peace and good order." The political censor has no place in our public debates. Unless and until extreme and necessitous circumstances are shown our aim should be to keep speech unfettered and to allow the processes of law to be invoked only when the provocateurs among us move from speech to action.

Vishinsky wrote in 1948 in *The Law of the Soviet State*, "In our state, naturally there can be no place for freedom of speech, press, and so on for the foes of socialism."

Our concern should be that we accept no such standard for the United States. Our faith should be that our people will never give support to these advocates of revolution, so long as we remain loyal to the purposes for which our Nation was founded. . . .

THE GINZBURG CASE: "FREE SPEECH IS CONSISTENT WITH OBSCENITY TESTS"

Justice William Brennan

Mr. Justice Brennan:

In the cases in which this Court has decided obscenity questions since *Roth [Roth v. United States]* it has regarded the materials as sufficient in themselves for the determination of the question. In the present case, however, the prosecution charged the offense in the context of the circumstances of production, sale, and publicity and assumed that, standing alone, the publications themselves might not be obscene. We agree that the question of obscenity may include consideration of the setting in which the publications were presented as an aid to determining the question of obscenity, and assume without deciding that the prosecution could not have succeeded otherwise. . . . [W]e view the publications against a background of commercial exploitation of erotica solely for the sake of their prurient appeal. The record in that regard amply supports the decision of the trial judge that the mailing of all three publications offended the statute. . . .

Besides testimony as to the merit of the material, there was abundant evidence to show that each of the accused publications was originated or sold as stock in the trade of the sordid business of pandering—"the business of purveying textual or graphic matter openly advertised to appeal to the erotic interest of their cus-tomers." *Eros* early sought mailing privileges from the postmasters of Intercourse and Blue Ball, Pennsylvania. The trial court found the obvious, that these hamlets were chosen only for the value their names would have in furthering petitioners' efforts to sell their publications on the basis of salacious appeal; the facilities of the post offices were inadequate to handle the anticipated volume of mail, and the privileges were denied. Mailing privileges were then obtained from the postmaster of Middlesex, New Jersey. *Eros* and *Liaison* thereafter mailed several million circulars soliciting subscriptions from that post office; over 5,500 copies of the *Handbook* were mailed.

The "leer of the sensualist" also permeates the advertising for the three publica-tions. The circulars sent for *Eros* and *Liaison* stressed the sexual candor of the respective publications, and openly boasted that the publishers would take full advantage of what they regarded as an unrestricted license allowed by law in the expression of sex and sexual matters. The advertising for the *Handbook*, apparently mailed from New York, consisted almost entirely of a reproduction of the introduc-tion of the book, written by one Dr. Albert Ellis. Although he alludes to the book's informational value and its putative therapeutic usefulness, his remarks are pre-occupied with the book's sexual imagery. The solicitation was indiscriminate, not limited to those, such as physicians or psychiatrists, who might independently discern the book's therapeutic worth. Inserted in each advertisement was a slip labeled "GUARANTEE" and reading, "Documentary Books, Inc. unconditionally guarantees full refund of the price of *The Housewife's Handbook on Selective Promiscuity* if the book fails to reach you because of U.S. Post Office censorship interference." Similar slips appeared in the advertising for *Eros* and *Liaison*; they highlighted the gloss petitioners put on the publications, eliminating any doubt what the purchaser was being asked to buy.

This evidence, in our view, was relevant in determining the ultimate question of obscenity and, in the context of this record, serves to resolve all ambiguity and doubt. The deliberate representation of petitioners' publications as erotically arousing, for example, stimulated the reader to accept them as prurient; he looks for titillation, not for saving intellectual content. Similarly, such representation would tend to force public confrontation with the potentially offensive aspects of the work; the brazenness of such an appeal heightens the offensiveness of the publications to those who are offended by such material. And the circumstances of presentation and dissemination of material are equally relevant to determining whether social importance claimed for material in the courtroom was, in the circumstances, pretense or reality—whether it was the basis upon which it was traded in the marketplace or a spurious claim for litigation purposes. Where the purveyor's sole emphasis is on the sexually provocative aspects of his publications, that fact may be decisive in the determination of obscenity. Certainly in a prosecu-tion which, as here, does not necessarily imply suppression of the materials in-volved, the fact that they originate or are used as a subject of pandering is relevant to the application of the *Roth* case. . . . *Eros* was created, represented and sold solely as a claimed instrument of the sexual stimulation it would bring. Like the other publications, its pervasive treatment of sex and sexual matters rendered it available to exploitation by those who would make a business of pandering to "the widespread weakness for titillation by pornography." Petitioners' own expert agreed, correctly we think, that "[i] f the object [of a work] is material gain for the creator through an appeal to the sexual curiosity and appetite," the work is pornographic. In other words, by animating sensual detail to give the publication a salacious cast, petitioners reinforced what is conceded by the Government to be an otherwise debatable conclusion.

A similar analysis applies to the judgment regarding the *Handbook.* The bulk of the proofs directed to social importance concerned this publication. Before selling publication rights to petitioners, its author had printed it privately; she sent circulars to persons whose names appeared on membership lists of medical and psychiatric associations, asserting its value as an adjunct in therapy. Over 12,000 sales resulted from this solicitation, and a number of witnesses testified that they found the work useful in their professional practice. The Government does not seriously contest the claim that the book has worth in such a controlled, or even neutral, environment. Petitioners, however, did not sell the book to such a limited audience, or focus their claims for it on its supposed therapeutic or educational value; rather, they deliberately emphasized the sexually provocative aspects of the work, in order to catch the salaciously disposed. They proclaimed its obscenity; and we cannot conclude that the court below erred in taking their own evaluation at its face value and declaring the book as a whole obscene despite the other evidence. . . .

We perceive no threat to First Amendment guarantees in thus holding that in close cases evidence of pandering may be probative with respect to the nature of the material in question and thus satisfy the *Roth* test. No weight is ascribed to the fact that petitioners have profited from the sale of publications which we have assumed but do not hold cannot themselves be adjudged obscene in the abstract; to sanction consideration of this fact might indeed induce self-censorship, and offend the frequently stated principle that commercial activity, in itself, is no justification for narrowing the protection of expression secured by the First Amendment. Rather, the fact that each of these publications was created or exploited entirely on the basis of its appeal to prurient interests strengthens the conclusion that the transactions here were sales of illicit merchandise, not sale of constitutionally protected matter. A conviction for mailing obscene publications, but explained in part by the presence of this element, does not necessarily suppress the materials in question, nor chill their proper distribution for a proper use. Nor should it inhibit the enterprise of others seeking through serious endeavor to advance human knowledge or understanding in science, literature, or art. All that will have been determined is that questionable publications are obscene in a context which brands them as obscene as that term is defined in *Roth*—a use inconsistent with any claim to the shelter of the First Amendment. . . .

Where an exploitation of interests in titillation by pornography is shown with respect to material lending itself to such exploitation through pervasive treatment or description of sexual matters, such evidence may support the determination that the material is obscene even though in other contexts the material would escape such condemnation. . . .

THE GINZBURG CASE: "FREE SPEECH IS
NOT CONSISTENT WITH OBSCENITY TESTS"

Justice Hugo Black

Mr. Justice Black, dissenting:

Only one stark fact emerges with clarity out of the confusing welter of opinions and thousands of words written in this and two other cases today. That fact is that Ginzburg, petitioner here, is now finally and authoritatively condemned to serve five years in prison for distributing printed matter about sex which neither Ginzburg nor anyone else could possibly have known to be criminal. Since, as I have said many times, I believe the Federal Government is without any power whatever under the Constitution to put any type of burden on speech and expression of ideas of any kind (as distinguished from conduct), . . . and I would reverse Ginzburg's conviction on this ground alone. . . .

Criminal punishment by government, although universally recognized as a necessity in limited areas of conduct, is an exercise of one of government's most awesome and dangerous powers. Consequently, wise and good governments make all possible efforts to hedge this dangerous power by restricting it within easily identifiable boundaries. Experience, and wisdom flowing out of that experience, long ago led to the belief that agents of government should not be vested with power and discretion to define and punish as criminal past conduct which had not been clearly defined as a crime in advance. . . . .

I agree with my Brother Harlan that the Court has in effect rewritten the federal obscenity statute and thereby imposed on Ginzburg standards and criteria that Congress never thought about, or if it did think about them certainly did not adopt them. Consequently, Ginzburg is, as I see it, having his conviction and sentence affirmed upon the basis of a statute amended by this Court for violation of which amended statute he was not charged in the courts below. Such an affirmance we have said violates due process. . . . Quite apart from this vice in the affirmance, I think that the criteria declared by a majority of the Court today as guidelines for a court or jury to determine whether Ginzburg or anyone else can be punished as a common criminal for publishing or circulating obscene material are so vague and meaningless that they practically leave the fate of a person charged with violating censorship statutes to the unbridled discretion, whim and caprice of the judge or jury which tries him. I shall separately discuss the three elements which a majority of the Court seems to consider material in proving obscenity.

The first element considered necessary for determining obscenity is that the dominant theme of the material taken as a whole must appeal to the prurient interest in sex. It seems quite apparent to me that human beings, serving either as judges or jurors, could not be expected to give any sort of decision on this element which would even remotely promise any kind of uniformity in the enforcement of this law. What conclusion an individual, be he judge or juror, would reach about whether the material appeals to "prurient interest in sex" would depend largely in the long run not upon testimony of witnesses such as can be given in ordinary criminal cases where conduct is under scrutiny, but would depend to a large extent upon the judge's or juror's personality, habits, inclinations, attitudes and other individual characteristics. In one community or in one courthouse a matter would be condemned as obscene under this so-called criterion but in another community, maybe only a few miles away, or in another courthouse in the same community, the material could be given a clean bill of health. In the final analysis the submission of such an issue as this to a judge or jury amounts to practically nothing more than a request for the judge or juror to assert his own personal beliefs about whether the matter should be allowed to be legally distributed. Upon this subjective determination the law becomes certain for the first and last time.

The second element for determining obscenity . . . is that the material must be "patently offensive because it affronts contemporary community standards relating to the description or representation of sexual matters. . . ." Nothing that I see in any position adopted by a majority of the Court today and nothing that has been said in previous opinions for the Court leaves me with any kind of certainty as to whether the "community standards" referred to are world-wide, nation-wide, section-wide, state-wide, country-wide, precinct-wide or township-wide. But even if some definite areas were mentioned, who is capable of assessing "community standards" on such a subject? Could one expect the same application of standards by jurors in Mississippi as in New York City, in Vermont as in California? So here again the guilt or innocence of a defendant charged with obscenity must depend in the final analysis upon the personal judgment and attitudes of particular individuals and the place where the trial is held. And one must remember that the Federal Government has the power to try a man for mailing obscene matter in a court 3,000 miles from his home.

A third element which three of my Brethren think is required to establish obscenity is that the material must be "utterly without redeeming social value." This element seems to me to be as uncertain, if not even more uncertain, than is the unknown substance of the Milky Way. If we are to have a free society as contemplated by the Bill of Rights, then I can find little defense for leaving the liberty of American individuals subject to the judgment of a judge or jury as to whether material that provokes thought or stimulates desire is "utterly without redeeming social value. . . ." Whether a particular treatment of a particular subject is with or without social value in this evolving, dynamic society of ours is a question upon which no uniform agreement could possibly be reached among politicians, statesmen, professors, philosophers, scientists, religious groups or any other type of group. A case-by-case assessment of social values by individual judges and jurors is, I think, a dangerous technique for government to utilize in determining whether a man stays in or out of the penitentiary.

My conclusion is that certainly after the fourteen separate opinions handed down in these three cases today no person, not even the most learned judge much less a layman, is capable of knowing in advance of an ultimate decision in his particular case by this Court whether certain material comes within the area of "obscenity" as that term is confused by the Court today. . . . I think the First Amendment forbids any kind or type or nature of governmental censorship over views as distinguished from conduct. . . .

It is obvious that the effect of the Court's decisions in the three obscenity cases handed down today is to make it exceedingly dangerous for people to discuss either orally or in writing anything about sex. Sex is a fact of life. Its pervasive influence is felt throughout the world and it cannot be ignored. Like all other facts of life it can lead to difficulty and trouble and sorrow and pain. But while it may lead to abuses, and has in many instances, no words need be spoken in order for people to know that the subject is one pleasantly interwoven in all human activities and involves the very substance of the creation of life itself. It is a subject which people are bound to consider and discuss whatever laws are passed by any government to try to suppress it. Though I do not suggest any way to solve the problems that may arise from sex or discussions about sex, of one thing I am confident, and that is that federal censorship is not the answer to these problems. I find it difficult to see how talk about sex can be placed under the kind of censorship the Court here approves without subjecting our society to more dangers than we can anticipate at the moment. It was to avoid exactly such dangers that the First Amendment was written and adopted. For myself I would follow the course which I believe is required by the First Amendment, that is, recognize that sex at least as any other aspect of life is so much a part of our society that its discussion should not be made a crime. . . .

THE GINZBURG CASE: "FREE SPEECH IS NOT CONSISTENT WITH OBSCENITY TESTS"

Justice Potter Stewart

Mr. Justice Stewart, dissenting:
Ralph Ginzburg has been sentenced to five years in prison for sending through the mail copies of a magazine, a pamphlet, and a book. There was testimony at his trial

that these publications possess artistic and social merit. Personally, I have a hard time discerning any. Most of the material strikes me as both vulgar and unedifying. But if the First Amendment means anything, it means that a man cannot be sent to prison merely for distributing publications which offend a judge's esthetic sensibilities, mine or any other's.

Censorship reflects a society's lack of confidence in itself. It is a hallmark of an authoritarian regime. Long ago those who wrote our First Amendment charted a different course. They believed a society can be truly strong only when it is truly free. In the realm of expression they put their faith, for better or for worse, in the enlightened choice of the people, free from the interference of policeman's intrusive thumb or a judge's heavy hand. So it is that the Constitution protects coarse expression as well as refined, and vulgarity no less than elegance. A book worthless to me may convey something of value to my neighbor. In the free society to which our Constitution has committed us, it is for each to choose for himself. . . .

The Court today appears to concede that the materials Ginzburg mailed were themselves protected by the First Amendment. But, the Court says, Ginzburg can still be sentenced to five years in prison for mailing them. Why? Because, says the Court, he was guilty of "commercial exploitation," of "pandering," and of "titillation." But Ginzburg was not charged with "commercial exploitation"; he was not charged with "pandering"; he was not charged with "titillation." Therefore to affirm his conviction now on any of those grounds, even if otherwise valid, is to deny him due process of law. . . . But those grounds are *not*, of course, otherwise valid. Neither the statute under which Ginzburg was convicted nor any other federal statute I know of makes "commercial exploitation" or "pandering" or "titillation" a criminal offense. And any criminal law that sought to do so in the terms so elusively defined by the Court would, of course, be unconstitutionally vague and therefore void. . . .

There is another aspect of the Court's opinion in this case that is even more regrettable. Today the Court assumes the power to deny Ralph Ginzburg the protection of the First Amendment because it disapproves of his "sordid business." That is a power the Court does not possess. For the First Amendment protects us all with an even hand. It applies to Ralph Ginzburg with no less completeness and force than to G. P. Putnam's Sons [publishers of Fanny Hill]. In upholding and enforcing the Bill of Rights, this Court has not power to pick or to choose. When we lose sight of that fixed star of constitutional adjudication, we lose our way. For then we forsake a government of law and are left with government by Big Brother.

Economic Freedom

Despite large variation in views concerning the extent to which man is an economic animal, there is widespread agreement that the way in which a society organizes its economic activities is of fundamental importance to the freedom of its members. Since the industrial revolution, the issue in this area that has divided men most sharply is the extent to which it is necessary for national governments to enter into the planning of the production and distribution of goods.

Friedrich Hayek, in the first of the readings for this section, makes clear the high value which he places upon individual freedom. He then considers the implications for this value if a society seeks by central planning to control its economic system. He believes that such planning, despite the best of intentions, will inevitably lead to dictatorship. Moreover, when economic power is combined with the coercive political power already possessed by governments, the centralized authority will control all human ends and the position of each individual in the society. When that time comes, individual freedom will have been lost and the "road to serfdom" will have been traversed.

Disagreeing with Hayek, Richard Tawney, in equal dedication to individual freedom, calls attention to the existing concentration of economic power in private hands. For him, the key question is whether concentrated economic power is to be used to protect the freedom and benefits of the minority who possess that power or whether the power should be transferred to some agency representing the public interest. Arguing that planning in a democracy need not lead to the dictatorship envisioned by Hayek, Tawney concludes that the authority to plan and direct the major economic activities must be transferred from private to public hands if economic freedom is to be achieved in modern industrial societies.

In the concluding selection, Friedrich Engels, the friend and collaborator of Karl Marx, provides what has now become one of the classic statements of Marxist doctrine. Describing his position as "scientific socialism," he states clearly at the outset his view that the ultimate causes of all social changes and political revolutions are economic. He then contends that the industrial revolution has so changed the economic order of society that the capitalist system of private ownership has become outmoded. He concludes by calling upon society to seize the means of production and institute a planned economic order. Only then will man become free by virtue of mastering for the first time in history his own social organization.

"MAN IS ONLY FREE
IN AN UNPLANNED SOCIETY"

Friedrich A. Hayek

The common features of all collectivist systems may be described, in a phrase ever dear to socialists of all schools, as the deliberate organization of the labors of society for a definite social goal. That our present society lacks such "conscious" direction toward a single aim, that its activities are guided by the whims and fancies of irresponsible individuals, has always been one of the main complaints of its socialist critics.

In many ways this puts the basic issue very clearly. And it directs us at once to the point where the conflict arises between individual freedom and collectivism. The various kinds of collectivism, communism, fascism, etc., differ among themselves in the nature of the goal toward which they want to direct the efforts of society. But they all differ from liberalism and individualism in wanting to organize the whole of society and all its resources for this unitary end and in refusing to recognize autonomous spheres in which the ends of the individuals are supreme. In short, they are totalitarian in the true sense of this new word which we have adopted to describe the unexpected but nevertheless inseparable manifestations of what in theory we call collectivism.

The "social goal," or "common purpose," for which society is to be organized is usually vaguely described as the "common good," the "general welfare," or the "general interest." It does not need much reflection to see that these terms have no sufficiently definite meaning to determine a particular course of action. The welfare and the happiness of millions cannot be measured on a single scale of less and more. The welfare of a people, like the happiness of a man, depends on a great many things that can be provided in an infinite variety of combinations. It cannot be adequately expressed as a single end, but only as a hierarchy of ends, a comprehensive scale of values in which every need of every person is given its place. To direct all our activities according to a single plan presupposes that every one of our needs is given its rank in an order of values which must be complete enough to make it possible to decide among all the different courses which the planner has to choose. It presupposes, in short, the existence of a complete ethical code in which all the different human values are allotted their due place.

The conception of a complete ethical code is unfamiliar, and it requires some effort of imagination to see what it involves. We are not in the habit of thinking of moral codes as more or less complete. The fact that we are constantly choosing between different values without a social code prescribing how we ought to choose does not surprise us and does not suggest to us that our moral code is incomplete.
In our society there is neither occasion nor reason why people should develop common views about what should be done in such situations. But where all the means to be used are the property of society and are to be used in the name of society according to a unitary plan, a "social" view about what ought to be done must guide all decisions. In such a world we should soon find that our moral code is full of gaps.

We are not concerned here with the question whether it would be desirable to have such a complete ethical code. It may merely be pointed out that up to the present the growth of civilization has been accompanied by a steady diminution of the sphere in which individual actions are bound by fixed rules. The rules of which our common moral code consists have progressively become fewer and more general in character. From the primitive man, who was bound by an elaborate ritual in almost every one of his daily activities, who was limited by innumerable taboos, and who could scarcely conceive of doing things in a way different from his fellows, morals have more and more tended to become merely limits circumscribing the sphere within which the individual could behave as he liked. The adoption of a common ethical code comprehensive enough to determine a unitary economic plan would mean a complete reversal of this tendency.

The essential point for us is that no such complete ethical code exists. The attempt to direct all economic activity according to a single plan would raise innumerable questions to which the answer could be provided only by a moral rule, but to which existing morals have no answer and where there exists no agreed view on what ought to be done. People will have either no definite views or conflicting views on such questions, because in the free society in which we have lived there has been no occasion to think about them and still less to form common opinions about them.

Not only do we not possess such an all-inclusive scale of values: it would be impossible for any mind to comprehend the infinite variety of different needs of different people which compete for the available resources and to attach a definite weight to each. For our problem it is of minor importance whether the ends for which any person cares comprehend only his own individual needs, or whether they include the needs of his closer or even those of his more distant fellows—that is, whether he is egoistic or altruistic in the ordinary senses of these words. The point which is so important is the basic fact that it is impossible for any man to survey more than a limited field, to be aware of the urgency of more than a limited number of needs. Whether his interests center round his own physical needs, or whether he takes a warm interest in the welfare of every human being he knows, the ends about which he can be concerned will always be only an infinitesimal fraction of the needs of all men.

This is the fundamental fact on which the whole philosophy of individualism is based. It does not assume, as is often asserted, that man is egoistic or selfish or ought to be. It merely starts from the indisputable fact that the limits of our powers of imagination make it impossible to include in our scale of values more than a sector of the needs of the whole society, and that, since, strictly speaking, scales of value can exist only in individual minds, nothing but partial scales of values exist—scales which are inevitably different and often inconsistent with each other. From this the individualist concludes that the individuals should be allowed, within defined limits, to follow their own values and preferences rather than somebody else's; that within these spheres the individual's system of ends should be supreme and not subject to any dictation by others. It is this recognition of the individual as the ultimate judge of his ends, the belief that as far as possible his own views ought to govern his actions, that forms the essence of the individualist position.

This view does not, of course, exclude the recognition of social ends, or rather of a coincidence of individual ends which makes it advisable for men to combine for their pursuit. But it limits such common action to the instances where individual views coincide; what are called "social ends" are for it merely identical ends of many individuals—or ends to the achievement of which individuals are willing to contribute in return for the assistance they receive in the satisfaction of their own desires. Common action is thus limited to the fields where people agree on common ends. Very frequently these common ends will not be ultimate ends to the individuals but means which different persons can use for different purposes. In fact, people are most likely to agree on common action where the common end is not an ultimate end to them but a means capable of serving a great variety of purposes.

When individuals combine in a joint effort to realize ends they have in common, the organizations, like the state, that they form for this purpose are given their own system of ends and their own means. But any organization thus formed remains one "person" among others, in the case of the state much more powerful than any of the others, it is true, yet still with its separate and limited sphere in which alone its ends are supreme. The limits of this sphere are determined by the extent to which the individuals agree on particular ends; and the probability that they will agree on a particular course of action necessarily decreases as the scope of such action extends. There are certain functions of the state on the exercise of which there will be practical unanimity among its citizens; there will be others on which there will be agreement of a substantial majority; and so on, until we come to fields where, although each individual might wish the state to act in some way, there will be almost as many views about what the government should do as there are different people.

We can rely on voluntary agreement to guide the action of the state only so long as it is confined to spheres where agreement exists. But not only when the state undertakes direct control in fields where there is no such agreement is it bound to suppress individual freedom. We can unfortunately not indefinitely extend the sphere of common action and still leave the individual free in his own sphere. Once the communal sector, in which the state controls all the means, exceeds a certain proportion of the whole, the effects of its actions dominate the whole system. Although the state controls directly the use of only a large part of the available resources, the effects of its decisions on the remaining part of the economic system become so great that indirectly it controls almost everything. Where, as was, for example, true in Germany as early as 1928, the central and local authorities directly control the use of more than half the national income (according to an official German estimate then, 53 per cent), they control indirectly almost the whole economic life of the nation. There is, then, scarcely an individual end which is not dependent for its achievement on the action of the state, and the "social scale of values" which guides the state's action must embrace practically all individual ends.

It is not difficult to see what must be the consequences when democracy embarks upon a course of planning which in its execution requires more agreement than in fact exists. The people may have agreed on adopting a system of directed economy because they have been convinced that it will produce great prosperity. In the discussions leading to the decision, the goal of planning will have been described by some such term as "common welfare," which only conceals the absence of real agreement on the ends of planning. Agreement will in fact exist only on the mechanism to be used. But it is a mechanism which can be used only for a common end; and the question of the precise goal toward which all activity is to be directed will arise as soon as the executive power has to translate the demand for a single plan into a particular plan. Then it will appear that the agreement on the desirability of planning is not supported by agreement on the ends the plan is to serve. The effect of the people's agreeing that there must be central planning, without agreeing on the ends, will be rather as if a group of people were to commit themselves to take a journey together without agreeing where they want to go: with the result that they may all have to make a journey which most of them do not want at all. That planning creates a situation in which it is necessary for us to agree on a much larger number of topics than we have been used to, and that in a planned system we cannot confine collective action to the tasks on which we can agree but are forced to produce agreement on everything in order that any action can be taken at all, is one of the features which contributes more than most to determining the character of a planned system.

It may be the unanimously expressed will of the people that its parliament should prepare a comprehensive economic plan, yet neither the people nor its representatives need therefore be able to agree on any particular plan. The inability of democratic assemblies to carry out what seems to be a clear mandate of the people will inevitably cause dissatisfaction with democratic institutions. Parliaments come to be regarded as ineffective "talking shops," unable or incompetent to carry out the tasks for which they have been chosen. The conviction grows that if efficient planning is to be done, the direction must be "taken out of politics" and placed in the hands of experts—permanent officials or independent autonomous bodies.

The difficulty is well known to socialists. It will soon be half a century since the Webbs began to complain of "the increased incapacity of the House of Commons to cope with its work."[1] More recently, Professor Laski has elaborated the argument:

It is common ground that the present parliamentary machine is quite unsuited to pass rapidly a great body of complicated legislation. The National Government, indeed, has in substance admitted this by implementing its economy and tariff measures not by detailed debate in the House of Commons but by a wholesale system of delegated legislation. A Labour Government would, I presume, build upon the amplitude of this precedent. It would confine the House of Commons to the two functions it can properly perform: the ventilation of grievances and the discussion of general principles of its measures. Its Bills would take the form of general formulae conferring wide powers on the appropriate government departments; and those powers would be exercised by Order in Council which could, if desired, be attacked in the House by means of a vote of no confidence. The necessity and value of delegated legislation has recently been strongly reaffirmed by the Donoughmore Committee; and its extension is inevitable if the process of socialisation is not to be wrecked by the normal methods of obstruction which existing parliamentary procedure sanctions.

[1] Sidney and Beatrice Webb, *Industrial Democracy* (1897), p. 800n.

And to make it quite clear that a socialist government must not allow itself to be too much fettered by democratic procedure, Professor Laski at the end of the same article raised the question "whether in a period of transition to Socialism, a Labour Government can risk the overthrow of its measures as a result of the next general election"—and left it significantly unanswered.[2]

It is important clearly to see the causes of this admitted ineffectiveness of parliaments when it comes to a detailed administration of the economic affairs of a nation. The fault is neither with the individual representatives nor with parliamentary institutions as such but with the contradictions inherent in the task with which they are charged. They are not asked to act where they can agree, but to produce agreement on everything—the whole direction of the resources of the nation. For such a task the system of majority decision is, however, not suited. Majorities will be found where it is a choice between limited alternatives; but it is a superstition to believe that there must be a majority view on everything. There is no reason why there should be a majority in favor of any one of the different possible courses of positive action if their number is legion. Every member of the legislative assembly might prefer some particular plan for the direction of economic activity to no plan, yet no one plan may appear preferable to a majority to no plan at all.

Nor can a coherent plan be achieved by breaking it up into parts and voting on particular issues. A democratic assembly voting and amending a comprehensive economic plan clause by clause, as it deliberates on an ordinary bill, makes nonsense. An economic plan, to deserve the name, must have a unitary conception. Even if a parliament could, proceeding step by step, agree on some scheme, it would certainly in the end satisfy nobody. A complex whole in which all the parts must be most carefully adjusted to each other cannot be achieved through a compromise between conflicting views. To draw up an economic plan in this fashion is even less possible than, for example, successfully to plan a military campaign by democratic procedure. As in strategy it would become inevitable to delegate the task to the experts.

Yet the difference is that, while the general who is put in charge of a campaign is given a single end to which, for the duration of the campaign, all the means under his control have to be exclusively devoted, there can be no such single goal given to the economic planner, and no similar limitation of the means imposed upon him. The general has not got to balance different independent aims against each other; there is for him only one supreme goal. But the ends of an economic plan, or of

[2] H. J. Laski, "Labour and the Constitution.," *New Statesman and Nation*, No. 81 (new ser.), September 10, 1932, p. 277. In a book (*Democracy in Crisis* [1933], particularly p. 87) in which Professor Laski later elaborated these ideas, his determination that parlimentary democracy must not be allowed to form an obstacle to the realization of socialism is even more plainly expressed: not only would a socialist government "take vast powers and legislate under them by ordinance and decree" and "suspend the classic formulae of normal opposition" but the "continuance of parliamentary government would depend on its [i.e., the Labour government's] possession of guarantees from the Conservative party that its work of transformation would not be disrupted by repeal in the event of its defeat at the polls"!

As Professor Laski invokes the authority of the Donoughmore Committee, it may be worth recalling that Professor Laski was a member of that committee and presumably one of the authors of its report.

any part of it, cannot be defined apart from the particular plan. It is the essence of the economic problem that the making of an economic plan involves the choice between conflicting or competing ends—different needs of different people. But which ends do so conflict, which will have to be sacrificed if we want to achieve certain others, in short, which are the alternatives between which we must choose, can only be known to those who know all the facts; and only they, the experts, are in a position to decide which of the different ends are to be given preference. It is inevitable that they should impose their scale of preferences on the community for which they plan. . . .

It is the price of democracy that the possibilities of conscious control are restricted to the fields where true agreement exists and that in some fields things must be left to chance. But in a society which for its functioning depends on central planning this control cannot be made dependent on a majority's being able to agree; it will often be necessary that the will of a small minority be imposed upon the people, because this minority will be the largest group able to agree among themselves on the question at issue. Democratic government has worked successfully where, and so long as, the functions of government were, by a widely accepted creed, restricted to fields where agreement among a majority could be achieved by free discussion; and it is the great merit of the liberal creed that it reduced the range of subjects on which agreement was necessary to one in which it was likely to exist in a society of free men. It is now often said that democracy will not tolerate "capitalism." If "capitalism" means here a competitive system based on free disposal over private property, it is far more important to realize that only within this system is democracy possible. When it becomes dominated by a collectivist creed, democracy will inevitably destroy itself.

We have no intention, however, of making a fetish of democracy. It may well be true that our generation talks and thinks too much of democracy and too little of the values which it serves. It cannot be said of democracy, as Lord Acton truly said of liberty, that it "is not a means to a higher political end. It is itself the highest political end. It is not for the sake of a good public administration that it is required, but for the security in the pursuit of the highest objects of civil society, and of private life." Democracy is essentially a means, a utilitarian device for safeguarding internal peace and individual freedom. As such it is by no means infallible or certain. Nor must we forget that there has often been much more cultural and spiritual freedom under an autocratic rule than under some democracies—and it is at least conceivable that under the government of a very homogeneous and doctrinaire majority democratic government might be as oppressive as the worst dictartorship. Our point, however, is not that dictatorship must inevitably extirpate freedom but rather that planning leads to dictatorship because dictatorship is the most effective instrument of coercion and the enforcement of ideals and, as such, essential if central planning on a large scale is to be possible. The clash between planning and democracy arises simply from the fact that the latter is an obstacle to the suppression of freedom which the direction of economic activity requires. But in so far as democracy ceases to be a guaranty of individual freedom, it may well persist in some form under a totalitarian regime. A true "dictatorship of the proletariat," even if democratic in form, if it undertook centrally to direct the economic system, would probably destroy personal freedom as completely as any autocracy has ever done.

The fashionable concentration on democracy as the main value threatened is not without danger. It is largely responsible for the misleading and unfounded belief that, so long as the ultimate source of power is the will of the majority, the power cannot be arbitrary. The false assurance which many people derive from this belief is an important cause of the general unawareness of the dangers which we face. There is no justification for the belief that, so long as power is conferred by democratic procedure, it cannot be arbitrary; the contrast suggested by this statement is altogether false: it is not the source but the limitation of power which prevents it from being arbitrary. Democratic control *may* prevent power from becoming arbitrary, but it does not do so by its mere existence. If democracy resolves on a task which necessarily involves the use of power which cannot be guided by fixed rules, it must become arbitrary power. . . .

Economic Control and Totalitarianism. Our freedom of choice in a competitive society rests on the fact that, if one person refuses to satisfy our wishes, we can turn to another. But if we face a monopolist we are at his mercy. And an authority directing the whole economic system would be the most powerful monopolist conceivable. While we need probably not be afraid that such an authority would exploit this power in the manner in which a private monopolist would do so, while its purpose would presumably not be the extortion of maximum financial gain, it would have complete power to decide what we are to be given and on what terms. It would not only decide what commodities and services were to be available and in what quantities; it would be able to direct their distribution between districts and groups and could, if it wished, discriminate between persons to any degree it liked. If we remember why planning is advocated by most people, can there be much doubt that this power would be used for the ends of which the authority approves and to prevent the pursuits of ends which it disapproves?

The power conferred by the control of production and prices is almost unlimited. In a competitive society the prices we have to pay for a thing, the rate at which we can get one thing for another, depend on the quantities of other things of which by taking one, we deprive the other members of society. This price is not determined by the conscious will of anybody. And if one way of achieving our ends proves too expensive for us, we are free to try other ways. The obstacles in our path are not due to someone's disapproving of our ends but to the fact that the same means are also wanted elsewhere. In a directed economy, where the authority watches over the ends pursued, it is certain that it would use its powers to assist some ends and to prevent the realization of others. Not our own view, but somebody else's, of what we ought to like or dislike would determine what we should get. And since the authority would have the power to thwart any efforts to elude its guidance, it would control what we consume almost as effectively as if it directly told us how to spend our income. . . .

Who, Whom? We have already seen that the close interdependence of all economic phenomena makes it difficult to stop planning just where we wish and that, once the free working of the market is impeded beyond a certain degree, the planner will be forced to extend his controls until they become all-comprehensive. These economic considerations, which explain why it is impossible to stop deliberate control just where we should wish, are strongly reinforced by certain social or political tendencies whose strength makes itself increasingly felt as planning extends.

Once it becomes increasingly true, and is generally recognized, that the position of the individual is determined not by impersonal forces, not as a result of the competitive effort of many, but by the deliberate decision of authority, the attitude of the people toward their position in the social order necessarily changes. There will always exist inequalities which will appear unjust to those who suffer from them, disappointments which will appear unmerited, and strokes of misfortune which those hit have not deserved. But when these things occur in a society which is consciously directed, the way in which people will react will be very different from what it is when they are nobody's conscious choice.

Inequality is undoubtedly more readily borne, and affects the dignity of the person much less, if it is determined by impersonal forces than when it is due to design. In a competitive society it is no slight to a person, no offense to his dignity, to be told by any particular firm that it has no need for his services or that it cannot offer him a better job. It is true that in periods of prolonged mass unemployment the effect on many may be very similar. But there are other and better methods to prevent that scourge than central direction. But the unemployment or the loss of income which will always affect some in any society is certainly less degrading if it is the result of misfortune and not deliberately imposed by authority. However bitter the experience, it would be very much worse in a planned society. There individuals will have to decide not whether a person is needed for a particular job but whether he is of use for anything, and how useful he is. His position in life must be assigned to him by somebody else.

While people will submit to suffering which may hit anyone, they will not so easily submit to suffering which is the result of the decision of authority. It may be bad to be just a cog in an impersonal machine; but it is infinitely worse if we can no longer leave it, if we are tied to our place and to the superiors who have been chosen for us. Dissatisfaction of everybody with his lot will inevitably grow with the consciousness that it is the result of deliberate human decision.

Once government has embarked upon planning for the sake of justice, it cannot refuse responsibility for anybody's fate or position. In a planned society we shall all know that we are better or worse off than others, not because of circumstances which nobody controls, and which it is impossible to foresee with certainty, but because some authority wills it. And all our efforts directed toward improving our position will have to aim, not at foreseeing and preparing as well as we can for the circumstances over which we have no control, but at influencing in our favor the authority which has all the power. The nightmare of English nineteenth-century political thinkers, the state in which "no avenue to wealth and honor would exist save through the government,"[3] would be realized in a completeness which they

---

[3] The actual words are those of the young Disraeli.

never imagined—though familiar enough in some countries which have since passed to totalitarianism.

As soon as the state takes upon itself the task of planning the whole economic life, the problem of the due station of the different individuals and groups must indeed inevitably become the central political problem. As the coercive power of the state will alone decide who is to have what, the only power worth having will be a share in the exercise of this directing power. There will be no economic or social questions that would not be political questions in the sense that their solution will depend exclusively on who wields the coercive power, on whose are the views that will prevail on all occasions.

I believe it was Lenin himself who introduced to Russia, the famous phrase "who, whom?"—during the early years of Soviet rule the byword in which the people summed up the universal problem of a socialist society.[4] Who plans whom, who directs and dominates whom, who assigns to other people their station in life, and who is to have his due allotted by others? These become necessarily the central issues to be decided solely by the supreme power.

More recently an American student of politics has enlarged upon Lenin's phrase and asserted that the problem of all government is "who gets what, when, and how." In a way this is not untrue. That all government affects the relative position of different people and that there is under any system scarcely an aspect of our lives which may not be affected by government action is certainly true. In so far as government does anything at all, its action will always have some effect on "who gets what, when, and how."

There are, however, two fundamental distinctions to be made. First, particular measures may be taken without the possibility of knowing how they will affect particular individuals and therefore without aiming at such particular effects. This point we have already discussed. Second, it is the extent of the activities of the government which decides whether everything that any person gets any time depends on the government, or whether its influence is confined to whether some people will get some things in some way at some time. Here lies the whole difference between a free and a totalitarian system.

The contrast between a liberal and a totally planned system is characteristically illustrated by the common complaints of Nazis and socialists of the "artificial separations of economics and politics" and by their equally common demand for the dominance of politics over economics. These phrases presumably mean not only that economic forces are now allowed to work for ends which are not part of the policy of the government but also that economic power can be used independently of government direction and for ends of which the government may not approve. But the alternative is not merely that there should be only one power but that this single power, the ruling group, should have control over all human ends and particularly that it should have complete power over the position of each individual in society.

[4]Cf. M. Muggeridge, *Winter in Moscow* (1934); Arthur Feiler, *The Experiment of Bolshevism* (1930).

"MAN CAN BE FREE IN THE
SOCIALIST PLANNED SOCIETY"

Richard H. Tawney

There is no such thing as freedom in the abstract, divorced from the realities of a specific time and place. Whatever else it may or may not imply, it involves a power of choice between alternatives—a choice which is real, not merely nominal, between alternatives which exist in fact, not only on paper. It means, in short, the ability to do—or refrain from doing—definite things, at a definite moment, in definite circumstances, or it means nothing at all. Because a man is most a man when he thinks, wills, and acts, freedom deserves the sublime things which poets have said about it; but, as part of the prose of everyday life, it is quite practical and realistic. Every individual possesses certain requirements—ranging from the material necessities of existence to the need to express himself in speech and writing, to share in the conduct of affairs of common interest, and to worship God in his own way or to refrain from worshipping Him—the satisfaction of which is necessary to his welfare. Reduced to its barest essentials, his freedom consists in the opportunity secured him, within the limits set by nature and the enjoyment of similar opportunities by his fellows, to take the action needed in order to ensure that these requirements are satisfied.

It is not my intention to add yet another catalogue of essential rights to the libraries of such lists which already exist; but two observations apply to all of them. In the first place, if the rights are to be an effective guarantee of freedom, they must not be merely formal, like the right of all who can afford it to dine at the Ritz. They must be such that, whenever the occasion arises to exercise them, they can in fact be exercised. The rights to vote and to combine, if not wholly valueless, are obviously attenuated, when the use of the former means eviction and of the latter the sack; the right to education, if poverty arrests its use in mid-career; the right to the free choice of an occupation, if the expenses of entering a profession are prohibitive; the right to earn a living, if enforced unemployment is recurrent; the right to justice, if few men of small means can afford the cost of litigation; the right "to life, liberty, and the pursuit of happiness," if the environment is such as to ensure that, as in a not distant past, a considerable proportion of those born will die within twelve months, and that the happiness-investments of the remainder are a gambling stock.

In the second place, the rights which are essential to freedom must be such as to secure the liberties of all, not merely of a minority. Some sage has remarked that marriage would not be regarded as a national institution if, while five per cent of the population were polygamous, the majority passed their lives unsolaced and unencumbered by husbands or wives. The same is true of freedom. A society in which some groups can do much what they please, while others can do little of what they ought, may have virtues of its own; but freedom is not one of them. It is free in so far, and only in so far, as all the elements composing it are able in fact, not merely in theory, to make the most of their powers, to grow to their full stature, to do what they conceive to be their duty, and—since liberty should not be too austere—to have their fling when they feel like it. In so far as the opportunity to lead a life worthy of human beings is restricted to a minority, what is commonly described as freedom would more properly be called privilege.

As far, therefore, as matters of principle are concerned, the meaning of freedom seems to me pretty simple. The practical interpretation of principles in terms of policy and institutions is, of course, another story. Before values can become a power in everyday life, they need interests as their allies. If they prevail and win general acceptance, they do so with the limitations which those allies impose. They do not, on that account, cease to be values. The idea that they do—the description of honesty and good faith as "bourgeois morality," as though virtues ceased to be virtues when practised (if they are practised) by the middle classes, or the dismissal of political democracy with a shrug of the shoulders as "capitalist democracy," as though in a capitalist society it could be anything else—these and similar inanities had their run in the silly season of the 'thirties, when Bloomsbury awoke to the recondite fact of the existence of a class struggle and announced its discovery with blood-curdling bleats, and invitations to hunt tigers were circulated by sportsmen with whom a brave man might well have hesitated to shoot rabbits. They need no deflating, since they appear, though belatedly, to have deflated themselves. But while values remain values, even when distorted by interests, the perversion which they undergo at the hands of the latter is none the less serious. The conception of freedom commonly held by the well-to-do classes in England, and till recently accepted by the mass of their fellow-countrymen, is a case in point.

It includes some features—tolerance, a respect for personal liberty, a belief in the virtues of representative government, an obstinate determination to hold on our own course and not to be bullied into changing our ways—which are part of the national legend, and which I, at least, admire. But the struggles by which these things were established belong to the past. In the fields where the battles of freedom are still to be won—in matters arising in the economic sphere and in the political regions closest to it—self-congratulation is less easy. As far as such issues are concerned, he must be a charitable man who does not feel that much of the eloquence devoted to applauding freedom, lamenting the menaces to it, and warning the country against surrendering its spiritual treasures for the sake of mere material benefits, is primarily directed to the preservation of the freedom at present possessed by the orators and their friends. Classes already at the top of the ladder may fall, but cannot rise. The construction which they put upon liberty is the result of that position. Whether consciously or not, it is, in large measure, a defence mechanism. Put in a nutshell, it is a doctrine of liberty which regards it as involving, not action to extend opportunities and raise individual faculty to the highest possible level, but the continued enjoyment by individuals and groups of such powers, advantages and opportunities as past history and present social arrangements may happen to have conferred upon them.

If anyone thinks such a picture is overdrawn, let him consider the positions adopted in certain current controversies. Let him study a recent report by an important association of industrialists, with its ingenuous proposal that the State should both give its blessing to the formation of combines and refrain from interfering with their freedom to manage their affairs as they think fit. Let him note the reactions of the body in whose title the words Liberty and Property are so happily united to the programmes of local authorities for the replanning of towns and acquisition of land. Let him mark the reception accorded in influential quarters to the obvious truth that, in the treatment of the controls erected during the war, the only sane course is not to scrap them indiscriminately as incompatible with economic freedom, but to distinguish between them, and, while winding up some of them as soon as circumstances allow, to recognise that there are others without the maintenance of which houses within the reach of families of small means will not be built, necessaries produced before luxuries, tonnage used in the general interest, and the consumer protected against the effects of shortages. Let him observe the successful resistance offered by the children of light in the shape of head masters to the abolition of fees in all secondary schools, on the ground that it would destroy the freedom of parents in selecting schools, though it is perfectly obvious to anyone who knows the facts that, since a large proportion of parents cannot afford the fees charged at the more expensive institutions, the freedom of all but a minority would be increased by their abolition. The premise of all these thinkers—if that word is not too violent—is the same. It is, speaking summarily, that, once emergency restrictions have been buried safely out of sight, such measure of liberty as is either possible or desirable is already secured by the existing social order; that the main menace to liberty consists in the threatened extension of the activities of public bodies into departments of economic and social life which at present escape them; and that a determined resistance to programmes of collective action is the sole safeguard, and a sufficient safeguard, for its continued preservation.

The only sound test of a political doctrine is its practical effect on the lives of human beings. The results of this doctrine we know, and it need not, therefore, be discussed at length. It is perfectly true, of course, that there have been circumstances—those, for example, of a simple economic system combined with political absolutism—in which the chief enemy of freedom was the despotism of an autocrat, and in which, therefore, the obvious way of enlarging freedom was to insist that as many spheres of life as possible should be excluded from his field of action. It should be equally obvious that, in the different conditions of an industrial civilisation, the effect of that alluring formula is precisely the opposite.

It is constantly assumed by privileged classes that, when the State refrains from intervening in any department of economic or social affairs, what remains as the result of its inaction is liberty. In reality, as far as the mass of mankind are concerned, what commonly remains is, not liberty, but tyranny. In urban communities with dense populations, or in great productive undertakings employing armies of workers, someone must make rules and see that they are kept, or life becomes impossible and the wheels do not turn. If public power does not make them, the effect is not that every individual is free to make them for himself. It is that they are made by private power—by landlords interested in increasing rents or by capitalists interested in increasing profits. The result, in either case, is not freedom, but a dictatorship, which is not the less oppressive because largely unconscious, and because those whom it profits regard it, quite sincerely, as identical with liberty.

The classical example in the past, so far as the wage-earners were concerned, was the condition of British workers in the days when trade unions were still feeble, industrial codes crude, social services in their infancy, and measures either to prevent unemployment or to enable its victims to weather the storm not yet in existence. The classical example in the present generation was the condition of many American workers down almost to yesterday. When, just over thirty years ago, I first visited Washington, I was informed on good authority that the miners in West Virginia were in trenches behind barbed wire; that the owners had a corps of snipers and a captive military balloon; and that the only individual enjoying, though precariously, a large measure of liberty, was the officer commanding the owners' troops, who was alleged—doubtless with some poetic licence—to have become a millionaire by threatening to retreat. The apparatus of coercion described long after that by a Senatorial Committee, the La Follette Committee of 1936—black lists, yellow-dog contracts, company unions, spies, undercover men, armed guards, gas-bombs, machine-guns—has since then been either demobilised or stowed safely out of sight; but why has it been demobilised? Because the Federal Government, which down to the 'thirties had no industrial policy, at last, under the brilliant leadership of President Roosevelt, acquired one; made all interference with the right of workers to combine, and the refusal to bargain collectively with them, a criminal offence; and set up administrative machinery to enforce that rule. In both countries it would be absured to exaggerate the results which have been accomplished. In both the parent of such liberty as has been achieved is law, in the form either of trade-union regulations or of legislative enactments.

As far as Great Britain is concerned, that particular issue now seems remote. But what is true of men as producers is equally true of men as consumers. The only intellectually respectable argument against the intervention of the State in the processes of economic life consisted in the statement that the public was protected against exploitation and secured the fruits of economic progress by the mutual rivalry of producers. Each of the latter, it was held, controlled too small a proportion of the output of his industry to be able to affect the market price, which he must accept as a *datum*. Each, if a rival introduced an improvement, would be compelled to follow suit or to go out of business. Thus "greed," in the classical phrase, would be "held in check by greed," and competition would act as an automatic substitute for honesty. Whether competition ever was or can be free in the sense assumed, and whether, if it could, it would be desirable that the welfare of millions of human beings should depend—to borrow the expression of Mr. E. F. M. Durbin—on a system of conditioned reflexes, are questions which need not here be discussed. What is certain is that that state of things, if it ever existed, is today as dead as the theory which purported to be based upon it.

We do not know the extent of monopoly or quasi-monopoly in British industry. The second World War has seen no report on Trusts and Combinations such as appeared in the first. Those best acquainted with the facts refrain from divulging them. If they are in the possession of the Board of Trade, it has not seen fit to take the public into its confidence. What we know is that the movement to combination made astonishing progress in the twenty years between the wars; that as long ago as 1937 an American economist could write that British business opinion was unanimous in favouring organised action to maintain prices; that the movement has received in several industries, such as iron and steel, coal, ship-building, and cotton the encouragement of the State; that it has taken long strides forward since 1939, and that it is now openly applauded in the Press by leading British industrialists as a higher stage of industrial organisation. With the economic consequences of that situation I am not at the moment concerned; but whatever the incidental advantages of monopolistic combines, one thing is certain. It is that, since they limit the consumer's choice to goods of the quality and price supplied by the monopolist, they create semi-sovereignties which are the direct antithesis of anything that can be, or in the past has been, described as freedom. Here, again, the suggestion that capitalism, at the present stage of its history, is the guardian of any liberties but its own is an unplausible affectation. If its pre-war tendencies were to develop unchecked, it would more properly be described as the parent of a new feudalism.

The third point which I would emphasise is equally obvious. It is that, in so far as the immense aggregations of economic power characteristic of the present phase of social history threaten the liberties of men as producers and consumers, they threaten their liberties as citizens as well. Of all paradoxical creeds the most paradoxical is that of those thinkers—a diminishing, but not uninfluential band—who combine an enthusiasm for political and civil freedom with a complacent indifference to the facts, which they ignore, of economic servitude. The economic system is not merely a collection of independent undertakings, bargaining on equal terms with each other. It is also a power system. It is a hierarchy of authority; and those who can manipulate the more important levers are, directly or indirectly, consciously or unconsciously, the real rulers of their fellows.

> All ignorant, they turn an easy wheel
> Which sets sharp racks to pinch and peel.

The livelihood of men working for a small firm depends on the policy of the large firm with which it finds its market; the latter on the cartel with whose rules it must comply; and all three on decisions taken in London or New York by bland, neatly tailored gentlemen who have never seen a colliery or a cotton mill, and who, if they did, would not always know the difference between a loom and a mule or spinning-frame. A firm—to speak of the inter-war period—shuts down a plant without notice, and half a town is ruined. A combine decides on what is euphemistically called a reduction of capacity, and a whole district, like the north-east coast, is paralysed. The capital market sees money in some investment which is the fashion of the moment; coal and cotton remain unmodernised. With the assent of the City, though to the exasperation of many industrialists, sterling is over-valued; there is a miners' stoppage and what is called a general strike. For reasons which I must not now attempt to discuss, a collapse of prices sends industry over a precipice and some Governments with it. No authority exists to steady the ship before it is too late. Where the monster will next break loose, when peace returns, no one can say; but, unless he finds his master, break loose he will. The people to pay the price will be unhappy men and women trembling for their jobs.

Of all emotions the most degrading and the least compatible with freedom is fear. The brutal fact is that, as far as the mass of mankind are concerned, it was by fear, rather than by hope, that the economic system was in the past kept running—fear of unemployment, fear of losing a house, fear of losing savings, fear of being compelled to take children from school, fear of what one's wife would say when these agreeable events all happened together. If you wish to see how, before the days of full employment, the thing worked in practice, ask an employer when it was that men were easiest to drive. He will tell you that they might be awkward when times were good, but that they sweated like slaves at the very moment when a decline in trade made it uncertain whether their output would find a market, because it was then that they were frightened for their jobs. And he, poor devil, with an over-draft at his bank, was often in his heart as frightened as they were.

Whatever might be the merits of such arrangements, they were certainly incompatible with the freedom of all but the minority who profited by them, and, on any but the shortest view, with political, as well as with economic, freedom. The war should have taught us one lesson, if it has taught us nothing else. It is that it is idle to blazon Liberty, Equality, and Fraternity on the façades of public buildings, if to display the same motto in factories and mines would arouse only the cynical laughter that greets a reminder of idealisms turned sour and hopes unfulfilled. What men desire is, not paragraphs in constitutions, but results, in the form of arrangements which ensure them the essentials of a civilised existence and show a proper respect for their dignity as human beings. If they do not get them in one way, they will try to get them in another. If the interpretation given to freedom reduces it to a formal phrase, they will not fight for it against an alternative which pretends, at least, to offer them substance, not a shadow. We are not ignorant what that alternative is. Should some gentlemanly version of Fascism—it will be called, of course, not Fascism, but True Democracy—ever arrive in this country, it will be established, not by the tyranny of a ruthless minority, but as the result of the indifference of an apathetic majority, so sickened by shams as to yield to any regime which promises them the practical conditions of a tolerable life, without which freedom is a phantom.

If Socialists are to restore to the idea of freedom the magic which once belonged to it, they must bring it down to earth. They must state its meaning in realistic and constructive terms, not as a possession to be defended, but as a goal to be achieved. They must prove that it is they, not the interests that use it as a stalking-horse, who are the true champions of the faith. They must make it evident that their policy is to end economic, as well as political, tyranny, by making economic, as well as political, power responsible to authorities acting for the nation. To discuss in detail the contents of such a programme is not within my present province. Whatever else it may imply, it clearly involves, not merely—essential though that is—the wide extension of communal services needed to make available for all advantages which at present are the privilege of the few, but a genuine and decisive transference of economic sovereignty. It does not necessarily mean indiscriminate nationalisation, which is merely one method, though an important method, of achieving that result. It does mean that the key-points and strategic positions of the economic system shall be removed from the sphere of private interests and held by public bodies. It means that the State shall be equipped with the machinery needed to enable it to regulate, stimulate and direct the flow of capital into different undertakings; that the foundation services, such as banks, transport, coal and power, steel—to mention no others—shall be vested in public ownership; that monopolies shall either be treated in the same way or be strictly controlled; and that the mass of industries which continue to be carried on outside the nationalised sector shall be required to work within a framework of policy laid down by a national authority. The particular methods to be employed for effecting that transformation will be, no doubt, of great diversity, and I must not now dwell on them. The essential thing is that private interests should be subordinated to those of the majority of the nation, and that the State should be equipped with such powers and organs as may be needed to guide economic development on lines conducive to the general well-being.

Were such a policy methodically pursued, few would deny, I imagine, that the range of opportunities open to ordinary men, their control over their environment, their power of initiative in matters concerning their economic and social welfare—in short, their freedom—would be far greater than in the past it was. But it is precisely at this point, of course, in the debatable land between economics and politics, that the counter-attack is launched. I do not, I am ashamed to say—as doubtless you have discerned—study the works of economic theorists with the assiduity they deserve, for the reason—if it is a reason, and not mere weakness of the flesh— explained to her pupil by the governess in that ancient, but admirable, play, *The Importance of Being Ernest*: "Do not read Mill's chapter on the fall of the rupee, my dear; it is too exciting for a young girl." If my former much-respected colleague, Professor F. A. Hayek, who has offered in his interesting book, *The Road to Serfdom*, a recent warning against Socialism, had confined himself to a forecast of the economic catastrophes prepared by it, I cannot say that, like the devils, I should have believed and trembled, but I should certainly have trembled, even while I disbelieved. He chose as his target, however, not the economics of Socialism, but the political nemesis which, he is convinced, it entails. And here, perhaps, one of the prospective serfs will not be thought presumptuous if he hazards an opinion on the destiny awaiting him.

The villain in Professor Hayek's tragedy is, of course, Planning; and Planning he defines as the "central direction of all economic activity according to a single plan, laying down how the resources of society shall be 'consciously directed' to serve particular ends in a particular way." This demon, once out of his bottle, reveals criminal potentialities which seem almost illimitable. His career begins with the discovery that no society and no assembly can conceivably agree on any major matter of economic policy. He next proceeds to remedy this unfortunate defect of democratic institutions by appointing himself and his fellow-demons as dictators. Once firmly in the saddle, he substitutes administrative decrees for the rule of law, and uses them to abolish both the workers' choice of occupations and the consumers' choice of goods. Having conquered the economic sphere, he launches a campaign against the realm of the spirit, where freedom might be expected to make its last stand. He employs violence and deceit—the concentration camp and the Press—to secure the appearance of an illusory unanimity. The curtain falls on a world in which tolerance, freedom of thought and speech, personal liberty, objective science, private and public morality, have alike been extinguished. Universal darkness covers all.

Professor Hayek's book has been composed with genuine emotion and a sincerity which commands respect. He writes, as Burke was said to speak, with the expression of a man confronted by assassins. His honesty and competence are both beyond question, and I have no wish to treat his warnings lightly. His history—his account, for example, of German influences on British social thought and of the causes of the British movement to monopoly—is not always, in my judgment, according to light; nor does experience seem to me to confirm the view, which I understand him to hold, that the major issues of economic policy are of their nature such that a democracy, when faced by them, is incapable of reaching sufficient agreement to permit of action. These points, however, are merely the out-works of his argument; and, even were they abandoned, its citadel would still stand. Let me, before reconnoitring it, present him with an admission. Human institutions are merely instruments. All of them—law-courts and police, armies and navies, churches and schools—can be, and have been, used for bad ends. It is perfectly true that public control over the processes of economic life can be used in the same way. It is perfectly true, again, that authority armed with coercive power has often been, and in some countries still is, the enemy of freedom. But to make much of these points is, it seems to me, to labour truisms. The question which matters is not whether, as everyone admits, the abuses feared *may* in certain circumstances occur. It is whether they must necessarily occur, whatever the circumstances and whatever the precautions taken against them—or, at any rate, whether the probability of their occurrence is so great that the only prudent course is to acquiesce in the continuance of existing evils, in order to avoid the more appalling *débâcle* foretold by Professor von Hayek. If my answer to that question differs from his, the principal reason is, I suppose, that I disagree with him on two points. I do not accept his conception of planning, and I do not accept his view of the State.

On the first point, having no pretensions to speak as an economist, I touch with diffidence. Planning, like Capitalism or Socialism, is obviously a genus with several different species. Professor Hayek appears to me to identify it with one species and one alone, and that, to my mind, the least attractive member of the family. He means by it, if I understand him rightly, a comprehensive programme, embracing the whole range of economic activities, under which the quantity and quality of all articles to be produced, from steel plants to pins, and the occupation and payment of every individual, are prescribed in advance for a term of years by a central authority—an authority uninfluenced by the views of consumers and producers, acknowledging no responsibility, however indirect, to a representative assembly, and conducting its affairs by the issue of orders the infringement of which is a criminal offence. Given those assumptions, it is not surprising that a totalitarian monster should emerge as his conclusion, for the author has been at pains to include totalitarianism among his premises. Whether, and in what degree, such a picture of planning corresponds with the Russian or German varieties, I have not the knowledge to say. The version of planning suggested by Professor von Hayek is, doubtless, a possible one, and his readers should be grateful to him for developing its implications. To imply, however, as he appears to do, that the procedure whose horrifying consequences he portrays with such force alone needs to be considered; or that all other procedures must necessarily lead to the same fatal goal, is to beg all questions. It is as fanciful as to dismiss parliamentary institutions as futile on the strength of their futility in certain countries which have tried them, or to suggest that a public system of education—itself an example of planning on a large scale—is necessarily corrupting, because some states have employed it as an engine of corruption.

Planning, like parliaments and public education, is not a simple category. Its results depend, not on the label attached to it, but on the purposes which it is designed to serve, the methods which it employs in order to realise them, and the spirit which determines the choice of both. If, for example, the essential characteristic of a planned economy be regarded as consisting, not as Professor Hayek seems to suggest, in a detailed budget of production, but in the transference of responsibility for the higher ranges of economic strategy from profit-making entrepreneurs to a national authority, his mystery of iniquity is attenuated to a mare's-nest, and his bloodthirsty Leviathan becomes a serviceable drudge.

On that more modest view, it is not necessary that a single central body should intervene in every corner of economic life; it is enough that the sector controlled by it should be sufficiently important to enable the State to take or to determine the major decisions on matters such as investment, credit policy and employment, on which the general welfare depends. It is not necessary that it should plan every detail of production; it is sufficient that it should issue to the public utility corporations, or other productive units responsible to it, instructions as to the general policy which they are to pursue—for example, with regard to output, costs, prices, and the erection of new plants—and that they should conduct their operations within that framework, which itself, of course, would be made after consultation with them and would be subject to public criticism. It is not necessary that it should conscribe workers, assign them their occupations, and dictate their movements; it can leave those concerned to engage them in the ordinary way, by the offer of such inducements as are needed to attract them. It would not have the same motives as the private monopolist for maintaining prices at a level higher than that needed to cover costs, and it might find it convenient in particular cases—for example, on grounds of health—to sell at a loss; but the consumer would remain as free as he is today to suit his own tastes. It could hardly acquiesce in a group of workers in a strong strategic position forcing an advance at the expense of their fellows merely in virtue of their bargaining power; and the Trade Union Movement would have to decide whether, in refusing to exploit to the full that particular advantage of capitalism, it lost more than it gained. Apart from that case, it is not easy to specify what, if any, economic freedoms would disappear as a result of the substitution of a public authority, pursuing a deliberate production and investment policy, for a group of large private combines or a welter of small firms. In so far as economic freedom depends on the removal of the fear of unemployment, fair standards of remuneration, opportunities of promotion uninfluenced by pull and favouritism, the abolition of private monopoly and the contraction of the area of life where the battle is to the strong, it seems reasonable to say that it would be substantially increased.

The conventional retort to such a statement—I do not suggest that it is Professor von Hayek's—is to charge those who make it with a sordid materialism. The serfs, it is said, might be less uncomfortable; but their gains in one sphere would be more than counterbalanced by their losses in another. As cogs in the impersonal mechanism of an authoritarian state, they would have bartered their dignity as citizens and men—their initiative, their responsibility, their right to lead their own lives and make a mess of them if they pleased—for a shot of morphia in the soul.

It is obvious that, if a despotic Government enlarges its control over economic affairs, it will use the only methods which it understands, and manage them as a despot. But why assume despotism? It is as possible to plan for freedom as for tyranny. The idea that there is an entity called "the State," which possesses, in virtue of its title, uniform characteristics existing independently of the varying histories, economic environments, constitutional arrangements, legal systems, and social psychologies of particular states, and that these characteristics necessarily combine the manners of a Japanese customs officer with the morals of a human tiger, is a pure superstition. It is a piece of mysticism, which is pardonable in persons brought up on their knees before some mortal god, but which is none the less a bluff. Half a century ago, when we were informed by philosophers fed on Hegel that the State represented our higher selves, it was an optimistic bluff. Today, when we are sometimes told that the State is the product of one of the nastier Freudian complexes, it is liable to be a pessimistic bluff. But it is a bluff in either case.

The State is an important instrument; hence the struggle to control it. But it is an instrument, and nothing more. Fools will use it, when they can, for foolish ends, and criminals for criminal ends. Sensible and decent men will use it for ends which are decent and sensible, and will know how to keep fools and criminals in their place. What exactly, moreover, does the State in this connection include? Are the Metropolitan Water Board and the London Passenger Board part of it? Is it suggested that public liberties were imperilled when the former succeeded the eight water companies which preceded it, and the latter introduced a measure of unity into the passenger service, and both were made responsible to the appropriate departments? If not, why should they be threatened merely because a group of banking, transport, colliery, power, and steel undertakings go the same way, or because all of them are required to account for their proceedings to a central authority, with power to issue instructions as to the policy they shall pursue?

The truth is that, in the matter of civil and political liberties, the real issue lies, at any rate in this country, on a different plane from that where some prophets of the coming slavery are disposed to seek it. The former depend principally on freedom of speech and writing; freedom of worship; freedom of meeting; freedom in the choice of occupations; and freedom to combine. The latter depend partly on the former, partly on the existence of constitutional arrangements for the maintenance of representative and responsible government. The sole security for the preservation of either is a public opinion which is determined to preserve them. There is no reason whatever why that security should be weakened merely because certain industries are owned and administered by public bodies, and those bodies are guided in their procedure by instructions from a further body, which can take a more comprehensive view of the national needs than is practicable for any one of them. On the contrary, given such an arrangement, it would be both possible and desirable for the ability of the citizen to make his wishes known and his criticisms felt to be a good deal more effective than it commonly is today. When industries are nationalised, there is much to be said for attaching to each a council representative of the principal groups of consumers using their output, with powers of investigation, criticism, and publicity from which private monopolists are at present immune. Associations of producers would naturally be represented on the bodies directing different services, and would add to their present protective functions that of consultants and advisers as to the staffing of works and improvements of productive processes. Regular reports would dispel the atmosphere of artificial darkness in which a good many economic matters, which ought to be common knowledge, are at present shrouded.

The truth is, of course, that the transference of property to public hands is a means, not an end. Its success depends, not on the mere change of ownership, which, though the first step, is no more, but on the degree to which advantage is taken of the opportunity offered by it to carry through measures of reorganisation which private enterprise was unable or unwilling to undertake, to enlist the active co-operation of employees, and to secure first-class management. Such reforms require time. Criticism on the initial phases of a process which must necessarily be lengthy is, therefore, to be welcomed. The essential point is that a Government should not, in nationalising an industry, regard the first step as the last, but should have a clear conception of the subsequent stages. Its aim should be, not merely to keep the undertakings concerned rubbing along rather better than under private ownership, but to make them a model on which the workers in them look with pride, those in other industries with admiration and envy, and the public with confidence. In some cases, such as coal-mining, it should take steps to reconstruct, not only economic organisation, but the social environment as well. In all it must attempt to create a new *moral* by devolving increased responsibilities on the workers, even if at first they are reluctant to assume them, and must ensure that experiments with that end in view are pressed steadily forward. Nor must it forget the necessity for improving management standards. Thirty years ago, Lord Haldane argued that the human qualifications required by managers were not less important than the technical, and urged, in connection with the coal industry, the establishment of a staff college to cultivate the necessary *esprit de corps*, initiative, and capacity for leadership. His proposals have wider applications than those contemplated by him. A Socialist Government might do worse than explore them.

As far, therefore, as mere questions of machinery are concerned, anticipations of the eclipse of political and civil liberty by any form of Socialism probable in this country seem to me to contain more emotion than reason. The serious danger is the opposite. It is not that democracy may be sacrificed to the reckless pursuit of economic freedom. It is that the establishment of the conditions of such freedom may be too long delayed, and that the failure to achieve it may discredit democracy. Socialists ought to recognise the reality of that danger, and plan their strategy to anticipate it. Economic freedom involves a transference of the authority required in order to plan and direct certain major economic activities from the agents of property-owners to organs acting on behalf of the nation and responsible to it. In an industrial society it can be achieved in that way, and it can be achieved in no other.

"FREEDOM COMES IN A
MARXIST ECONOMIC SOCIETY"

Friedrich Engels

The materialist conception of history starts from the principle that production, and with production the exchange of its products, is the basis of every social order; that in every society which has appeared in history the distribution of the products, and with it the division of society into classes or estates, is determined by what is produced and how it is produced, and how the product is exchanged. According to this conception, the ultimate causes of all social changes and political revolutions are to be sought, not in the minds of men, in their increasing insight into eternal truth and justice, but in changes in the mode of production and exchange; they are to be sought not in the *philosophy* but in the *economics* of the epoch concerned. The growing realisation that existing social institutions are irrational and unjust, that reason has become nonsense and good deeds a scourge is only a sign that changes have been taking place quietly in the methods of production and forms of exchange with which the social order, adapted to previous economic conditions, is no longer in accord. This also involves that the means through which the abuses that have been revealed can be got rid of must likewise be present, in more or less developed form, in the altered conditions of productions. These means are not to be *invented* by the mind, but *discovered* by means of the mind in the existing material facts of production.

Where then, on this basis, does modern socialism stand?

The existing social order, as is now fairly generally admitted, is the creation of the present ruling class, the bourgeoisie. The mode of production peculiar to the bourgeoisie—called, since Marx, the capitalist mode of production—was incompatible with the local privileges and privileges of birth as well as with the reciprocal personal ties of the feudal system; the bourgeoisie shattered the feudal system, and on its ruins established the bourgeois social order, the realm of free competition, freedom of movement, equal rights for commodity owners, and all the other bourgeois glories. The capitalist mode of production could now develop freely. From the time when steam and the new tool-making machinery had begun to transform the former manufacture into large-scale industry, the productive forces evolved under bourgeois direction developed at a pace that was previously unknown and to an unprecedented degree. But just as manufacture, and the handicraft industry which had been further developed under its influence, had previously come into conflict with the feudal fetters of the guilds, so large-scale industry, as it develops more fully, comes into conflict with the barriers within which the capitalist mode of production holds it confined. The new forces of production have already outgrown the bourgeois form of using them; and this conflict between productive forces and mode of production is not a conflict which has risen in men's heads, as for example the conflict between original sin and divine justice; but it exists in the facts, objectively, outside of us, independently of the will or purpose even of the men who brought it about. Modern socialism is nothing but the reflex in thought of this actual conflict, its ideal reflection in the minds first of the class which is directly suffering under it—the working class.

In what, then, does this conflict consist?

Previous to capitalist production, that is to say, in the Middle Ages, small-scale production was general, on the basis of the private ownership by the workers of their means of production; the agricultural industry of the small peasant, freeman or serf, and the handicraft industry of the towns. The instruments of labour—land, agricultural implements, the workshop and tools—were the instruments of labour of individuals, intended only for individual use, and therefore necessarily puny, dwarfish, restricted. But just because of this they belonged, as a rule, to the producer himself. To concentrate and enlarge these scattered, limited means of production, to transform them into the mighty levers of production of the present day, was precisely the historic role of the capitalist mode of production and of its representative, the bourgeoisie. In Part IV of *Capital* Marx gives a detailed account of how, since the fifteenth century, this process has developed historically through the three stages of simple co-operation, manufacture and large-scale industry. But as Marx also points out, the bourgeoisie was unable to transform those limited means of production into mighty productive forces except by transforming them from individual means of production into *social* means of production, which could be used only *by a body of men as a whole.* The spinning wheel, the hand loom and the blacksmith's hammer were replaced by the spinning machine, the mechanical loom and the steam hammer; and the factory, making the co-operation of hundreds and thousands of workers necessary, took the place of the individual work-room. And, like the means of production, production itself changed from a series of individual operations into a series of social acts, and the products from the products of individuals into social products. The yarn, the cloth and the metal goods which now came from the factory were the common product of many workers through whose hands it had to pass successively before it was ready. No individual can say of such products: I made it, that is *my* product.

But where the natural spontaneous division of labour within society is the basic form of production, it imprints upon the products the form of *commodities*, the mutual exchange, purchase and sale of which enables the individual producers to satisfy their manifold needs. And this was the case during the Middle Ages. The peasant, for example, sold agricultural products to the artisan and purchased from him in exchange the products of his craft. Into this society of individual producers, producers of commodities, the new mode of production thrust itself, setting up, in the midst of the spontaneous *planless* division of labour which then existed throughout society, the *planned* division of labour organised in the individual factory; alongside of *individual* production, *social* production made its appearance. The products of both were sold on the same market, and consequently at prices which were at least approximately the same. But the planned organization was stronger than the natural division of labour; the factories in which labour was socially organised produced their commodities more cheaply than the separate small producers. Individual production was vanquished on one field after another; social production revolutionised the whole former mode of production. But this, its revolutionary character, was so little understood that, on the contrary, it was introduced as a means of stimulating and accelerating the production of commodities. In its origin, it was directly linked with certain levers of commodity production and exchange which were already in existence: merchant's capital, handicraft, wage labour. Inasmuch as it itself came into being as a new form of commodity production, the forms of appropriation characteristic of commodity production remained in full force also for it.

In commodity production as it had developed in the Middle Ages, the question could never arise of who should be the owner of the product of labour. The individual producer had produced it, as a rule, from raw material which belonged to him and was often produced by himself, with his own instruments of labour, and by his own manual labour or that of his family. There was no need whatever for the product to be appropriated by him; it belonged to him as an absolute matter of course. His ownership of the product was therefore based *upon his own labour.* Even where outside help was used, it was as a rule subsidiary, and in many cases received other compensation in addition to wages; the guild apprentice and journeyman worked less for the sake of their board and wages than to train themselves to become master craftsmen. Then came the concentration of the means of production in large workshops and manufactories, their transformation into means of production that were in fact social. But the social means of production and the social products were treated as if they were still, as they had been before, the means of production and the products of individuals. Hitherto, the owner of the instruments of labour had appropriated the product because it was as a rule his own product, the auxiliary labour of other persons being the exception; now, the owner of the instruments of lobour continued to appropriate the product, although it was no longer *his* product, but exclusively the product of *other's labour*. Thus, therefore, the products, now socially produced, were not appropriated by those who had really set the means of production in motion and really produced the products, but by the *capitalists*. Means of production and production itself had in essence become social. But they were subjected to a form of appropriation which has its presupposition private production by individuals, with each individual owing his own product and bringing it on to the market. The mode of production is subjected to this form of appropriation, although it removes the presuppositions on which the latter was based.[1] In this contradiction, which gives the new mode of production its capitalist character, *the whole conflict of today is already present in germ*. The more the new mode of production gained the ascendancy on all decisive fields of production and in all countries of decisive economic importance, supplanting individual production except for insignificant relics, the *more glaring necessarily became the incompatibility of social production with capitalist appropriation.*

The first capitalists found, as we have said, the form of wage labour already in existence; but wage labour as the exception, as an auxiliary occupation, as a supplementary, as a transitory phase. The agricultural labourer who occasionally went to work as a day labourer had a few acres of his own land, from which if necessary he could get his livelihood. The regulations of the guilds ensured that the journeyman of today became the master craftsman of tomorrow. But as soon as the means of production had become social and were concentrated in the hands of capitalists, this situation changed. Both the means of production and the products of the samll, individual producer lost more and more of their value; there was nothing left for him to do but to go to the capitalist, and work for wages. Wage labour, hitherto an exception and subsidiary, became the rule and the basic form of all production; hitherto an auxiliary occupation, it now became the labourer's exclusive activity. The occasional wage worker became the wage worker for life. The number of lifelong wage workers was also increased to a colossal extent by the simultaneous disintegration of the feudal system, the dispersal of the retainers of the feudal lords, the eviction of peasants from their homesteads, etc. The separation between the means of production concentrated in the hands of the capitalists, on

---

[1] There is no need here to explain that although the form of appropriation remains the same, the *character* of the appropriation is revolutionised by the process described above, to no less a degree than production. My appropriation of my own product and my appropriation of another person's product are certainly two very different forms of appropriation. It may be noted in passing that wage labour, in which the whole capitalist mode of production is already present in embryo form, is a very old institution; in isolated and scattered form it developed alongside slavery for centuries. But the germ could only develop into the capitalist mode of production when the necessary historical conditions had come into existence. [*Note by F. Engels.*]

the one side, and the producers now possessing nothing but their labour power, on the other, was made complete. *The contradiction between social production and capitalist appropriation became manifest as the antagonism between proletariat and bourgeoisie.*

We saw that the capitalist mode of production thrust itself into a society of commodity producers, individual producers, whose social cohesion resulted from the exchange of their products. But every society based on commodity production has the peculiarity that in it the producers have lost control of their own social relationships. Each produces for himself, with the means of production which happen to be at his disposal and in order to satisfy his individual needs through the medium of exchange. No one knows how much of the article he produces is coming onto the market, or how much demand there is for it; no one knows whether his individual product will meet a real need, whether he will cover his costs or even be able to sell it at all. Anarchy reigns in social production. But commodity production, like all other forms of production, has its own laws, which are inherent in and inseparable from it; and these laws assert themselves in spite of anarchy, in and through anarchy. These laws are manifested in the sole form of social relationship which continues to exist, in exchange, and enforce themselves on the individual producers as compulsory laws of competition. At first therefore, they are unknown even to these producers, and have to be discovered by them gradually only through long experience. They assert themselves therefore apart from the producers and against the producers, as the natural laws of their form of production, working blindly. The product dominates the producers.

In mediaeval society, especially in the earlier centuries, production was essentially for the producer's own use; for the most part its aim was to satisfy only the needs of the producer and his family. Where, as in the countryside, personal relations of dependence existed, it also contributed towards satisfying the needs of the feudal lord. No exchange was involved, and consequently the products did not assume the character of commodities. The peasant family produced almost everything it required—utensils and clothing as well as food. It was only when it succeeded in producing a surplus beyond its own needs and the payments in kind due to the feudal lord—it was only at this stage that it also began to produce commodities; these surplus products, thrown into social exchange, offered for sale, became commodities. The town artisans, it is true, had to produce for exchange from the very beginning. But even they supplied the greatest part of their own needs themselves; they had gardens and small fields; they sent their cattle out into the communal woodland, which also provided them with timber and firewood; the women spun flax, wool, etc. Production for the purpose of exchange, the production of commodities, was only in its infancy. Hence, restricted exchange, restricted market, stable methods of production, local isolation from the outside world, and local unity within: the Mark in the countryside, the guild in the town.

With the extension of commodity production, however, and especially with the emergence of the capitalist mode of production, the laws of commodity production, previously latent, also began to operate more openly and more potently. The old bonds were loosened, the old dividing barriers broken through, the producers more and more transformed into independent, isolated commodity producers. The anarchy of social productions became obvious, and was carried to further and further extremes. But the chief means through which the capitalist mode of production accentuated this anarchy in social production was the direct opposite of anarchy: the increasing organisation of production on a social basis in each individual productive establishment. This was the lever with which it put an end to the former peaceful stability. In whatever branch of industry it was introduced, it could suffer no older method of production to exist alongside it; where it laid hold of a handicraft, that handicraft was wiped out. The field of labour became a field of battle. The great geographical discoveries and the colonisation which followed on them multiplied markets and hastened on the transformation of handicraft into manufacture. The struggle broke out not only between the individual local producers; the local struggles developed into national struggles, the trade wars of the seventeenth and eighteenth centuries. Finally, large-scale industry and the creation of the world market have made the struggle universal and at the same time given it an unparalleled intensity. Between individual capitalists, as between whole industries and whole countries, advantages in natural or artificial conditions of production decide life or death. The vanquished are relentlessly cast aside. It is the Darwinian struggle for individual existence, transferred from Nature to society with intensified fury. The standpoint of the animal in Nature appears as the last word in human development. The contradiction between social production and capitalist appropriation reproduces itself as *the antithesis between the organisation of production in the individual factory and the anarchy of production in society as a whole.*

The capitalist mode of production moves in these two forms of manifestation of the contradiction immanent in it from its very nature, without hope of escaping from that "vicious circle" which Fourier long ago discovered in it. But what Fourier in his day was as yet unable to see is that this circle is gradually narrowing; that the motion is rather in the form of a spiral and must meet its end, like the motion of the planets, by collision with the centre. It is the driving force of the social anarchy of production which transforms the immense majority of men more and more into proletarians, and it is in turn the proletarian masses who will ultimately put an end to the anarchy of production. It is the driving force of the social anarchy of production which transforms the infinite perfectibility of the machine in large-scale industry into a compulsory commandment for each individual industrial capitalist to make his machinery more and more perfect, under penalty of ruin. But the perfecting of machinery means rendering human labour superfluous. If the introduction and increase of machinery meant the displacement of millions of hand workers by a few machine workers, the improvement of machinery means the displacement of larger and larger numbers of the machine workers themselves, and ultimately the creation of a mass of available wage workers exceeding the average requirements of capital for labour—a complete industrial reserve army, as I called it as long ago as 1845[2]—a reserve that would be available at periods when industry was working at

---

[2] *The Condition of the Working Class in England*, p. 109. German edition [Note by F. Engels.]

high pressure, but would be thrown out onto the streets by the crash inevitably following the boom; a reserve that would at all times be like a leaden weight on the feet of the working class in their fight for existence against capital, a regulator to keep wages down to the low level which suits the needs of capital. Thus it comes about that machinery, to use Marx's phrase, becomes the most powerful weapon in the war of capital against the working class, that the instruments of labour constantly tear the means of subsistence out of the hands of the labourer, that the very product of the labourer is turned into an instrument for his subjection. Thus it comes about that the economising of the instruments of labour becomes from the outset a simultaneous and absolutely reckless waste of labour power and robbery of the normal conditions necessary for the labour function; that machinery, "the most powerful instrument for shortening labour time, becomes the most unfailing means for placing every moment of the labourer's time and that of his family at the disposal of the capitalist for the purpose of expanding the value of his capital."[3]

Thus it comes about that the excessive labour of some becomes the necessary condition for the lack of employment of others, and that large-scale industry, which hunts all over the world for new consumers, restricts the consumption of the masses at home to a starvation minimum and thereby undermines its own internal market. "The law that always equilibrates the relative surplus population, or industrial reserve army, to the extent and energy of accumulation, this law rivets the labourer to capital more firmly that the wedges of Vulcan did Prometheus to the rock. It establishes an accumulation of misery, corresponding with accumulation of capital. Accumulation of wealth at one pole is, therefore, at the same time accumulation of misery, agony of toil, slavery, ignorance, brutality, mental degradation, at the opposite pole, *i.e.*, on the side of the class that *produces its own products in the form of capital.*"[4]

And to expect any other distribution of the products from the capitalist mode of production is like expecting the electrodes of a battery, while they are in contact with the battery, not to decompose water, not to develop oxygen at the positive pole and hydrogen at the negative.

We have seen how the perfectibility of modern machinery, pushed to an extreme point, through the medium of the anarchy of production in society is transformed into a compulsory commandment for the individual industrial capitalist constantly to improve his machinery, constantly to increase its productive power. The mere possibility of extending his field of production is transformed for him into a similar compulsory commandment. The enormous expanding power of large-scale industry, compared with which the expanding power of gases is mere child's play, now appears to us as a *necessity* for both qualitative and quantitative expansion that laughs at all counteracting pressure. Such counteracting pressure comes from consumption, sale, markets for the products of large-scale industry. But the capacity of the market to expand, both extensively and intensively, is controlled directly by quite other and far less effective laws. The expansion of the market cannot keep

[3] *Capital*, Vol. I, p. 445 (Kerr edition).
[4] *Capital*, Vol. I, p. 709 (Kerr edition).

pace with the expansion of production. The collision becomes inevitable, and as it can yield no solution so long as it does not burst the capitalist mode of production itself, it becomes periodic. Capitalist production brings into being a new "vicious circle."

And in fact, since 1825, when the first general crisis broke out, the whole industrial and commercial world, the production and exchange of all civilised peoples and of their more or less barbarian dependent people have been dislocated practically once in every ten years. Trade comes to a standstill, the markets are glutted, the products lie in great masses, unsalable, ready money disappears, credit vanishes, the factories are idle, the working masses go short of the means of subsistence because they have produced too much of them, bankruptcy follows upon bankruptcy, forced sale upon forced sale. The stagnation lasts for years, both productive forces and products are squandered and destroyed on a large scale, until the accumulated masses of commodities are at last disposed of at a more or less considerable depreciation, until production and exchange gradually begin to move again. By degrees the pace quickens; it becomes a trot; the industrial trot passes into a gallop, and the gallop in turn passes into the headlong onrush of a complete industrial commercial, credit and speculative steeplechase, only to land again in the end, after the most breakneck jumps—in the ditch of a crash. And so on again and again. We have now experienced it five times since 1825, and at this moment (1877) we are experiencing it for the sixth time. And the character of these crises is so clearly marked that Fourier hit them all off when he described the first as *crise pléthorique*, a crises of superabundance.

In these crises, the contradiction between social production and capitalist appropriation comes to a violent explosion. The circulation of commodities is for the moment reduced to nothing; the means of circulation, money, becomes an obstacle to circulation; all the laws of commodity production and commodity circulation are turned upside down. The economic collision has reached its culminating point: *the mode of production rebels against the mode of exchange; the productive forces rebel against the mode of production, which they have outgrown.*

The fact that the social organisation of production within the factory has developed to the point at which it has become incompatible with the anarchy of production in society which exists alongside it and above it—this fact is made palpable to the capitalists themselves by the violent concentration of capitals which take place during crises through the ruin of many big and even more small capitalists. The whole mechanism of the capitalist mode of production breaks down under the pressure of the productive forces which it itself created. It is no longer able to transform the whole of this mass of means of production into capital; they lie idle, and for this very reason the industrial reserve army must also lie idle. Means of production, means of subsistence, available labourers, all the elements of production and of general wealth are there in abundance. But "abundance becomes the source of distress and want" (Fourier), because it is precisely abundance that prevents the conversion of the means of production and subsistence into capital. For in capitalist society the means of production cannot begin to function unless they have first been converted into capital, into means for the exploitation of human labour power. The necessity for the means of production and subsistence to take on the form of capital stands like a ghost between them and the workers. It alone prevents the coming together of the material and personal levers of production; it alone forbids the means of production to function, the workers to work and to live. Thus on the one hand the capitalist mode of production stands convicted of its own incapacity any longer to control these productive forces. And on the other hand these productive forces themselves press forward with increasing force to put an end to the contradiction, to rid themselves of their character as capital, *to the actual recognition of their character as social productive forces.*

It is this pressure of the productive forces, in their mighty upgrowth, against their character as capital, increasingly compelling the recognition of their social character, which forces the capitalist class itself more and more to treat them as social productive forces, in so far as this is at all possible within the framework of capitalist relations. Both the period of industrial boom, with its unlimited credit inflation, and the crises itself through the collapse of great capitalist establishments, urge forward towards that form of the socialisation of huge masses of means of production which we find in the various kinds of joint-stock companies. Many of these means of production are from the outset so colossal that, like the railways, they exclude all other forms of capitalist exploitation. At a certain stage of development even this form no longer suffices; the official representative of capitalist society, the state, is constrained to take over their management.[5] This necessity of conversion into state property makes itself evident first in the big institutions for communication: the postal service, telegraphs and railways.

If the crises revealed the incapacity of the bourgeoisie any longer to control the modern productive forces, the conversion of the great organisations for production and communication into joint-stock companies and state property shows that for this purpose the bourgeoisie can be dispensed with. All the social functions of the capitalists are now carried out by salaried employees. The capitalist has no longer any social activity save the pocketing of revenues, the clipping of coupons and gambling on the Stock Exchange, where the different capitalists fleece each other of their capital. Just as at first the capitalist mode of production displaced the

---

[5] I say *is constrained* to. For it is only when the means of production or communication have *actually* outgrown management by share companies, and therefore their transfer to the state has become inevitable *from an economic standpoint*—it is only then that this transfer to the state, even when carried out by the state of today, represents an economic advance, the attainment of another preliminary step towards the taking over of all productive forces by society itself. Recently, however, since Bismarck adopted state ownership, a certain spurious socialism has made its appearance—here and there even degenerating into a kind of flunkeyism—which declares that *all* taking over by the state, even the Bismarckian kind, is in itself socialistic. If, however, the taking over of the tobacco trade by the state was socialistic, Napoleon and Metternich would rank among the founders of socialism. If the Belgian state, for quite ordinary political and financial reasons, constructed its own main railway lines; if Bismarck, without any economic compulsion, took over the main railway lines in Prussia, simply in order to be better able to organise and use them for war, to train the railway officials as the government's voting cattle, and especially to secure a new source of revenue independent of Parliamentary votes— such actions were in no sense socialist measures, whether direct or indirect, conscious or unconscious. Otherwise, the Royal Maritime Company, the Royal Porcelain Manufacture, and even the regimental tailors in the army, would be socialist institutions. [*Note by F. Engels.*]

workers, so now it displaces the capitalists, relegating them, just as it did the workers, to the superfluous population, even if in the first instance not to the industrial reserve army.

But neither the conversion into joint-stock companies nor into state property deprives the productive forces of their character as capital. In the case of joint-stock companies this is obvious. And the modern state, too, is only the organisation with which bourgeois society provides itself in order to maintain the general external conditions of the capitalist mode of production against encroachments either by the workers or by individual capitalists. The modern state, whatever its form, is an essentially capitalist machine; it is the state of the capitalists, the ideal collective body of all capitalists. The more productive forces it takes over as its property, the more it becomes the real collective body of all the capitalists, the more citizens it exploits. The workers remain wage-earners, proletarians. The capitalist relationship is not abolished; it is rather pushed to an extreme. But at this extreme it is transformed into its opposite. State ownership of the productive forces is not the solution of the conflict, but it contains within itself the formal means, the key to the solution.

This solution can only consist in the recognition in practice of the social nature of the modern productive forces, in bringing, therefore, the mode of production, appropriation and exchange into accord with the social character of the means of production. And this can only be brought about by society, openly and without deviation, taking possession of the productive forces which have outgrown all control other than that of society itself. Thereby the social character of the means of production and of the products—which today operates against the producers themselves, periodically breaking through the mode of production and exchange and enforcing itself only as a blind law of Nature, violently and destructively—is quite consciously asserted by the producers, and is transformed from a cause of disorder and periodic collapse into the most powerful lever of production itself.

The forces operating in society work exactly like the forces operating in Nature: blindly, violently, destructively, so long as we do not understand them and fail to take them into account. But when once we have recognised them and understood how they work, their direction and their effects, the gradual subjection of them to our will and the use of them for the attainment of our aims depends entirely upon ourselves. And this is quite especially true of the mighty productive forces of the present day. So long as we obstinately refuse to understand their nature and their character—and the capitalist mode of production and its defenders set themselves against any such attempt—so long do these forces operate in spite of us, against us, and so long do they control us, as we have shown in detail. But once their nature is grasped, in the hands of the producers working in association they can be transformed from demoniac masters into willing servants. It is the difference between the destructive force of electricity in the lightning of a thunderstorm and the tamed electricity of the telegraph and the arc light; the difference between a conflagration and fire in the service of man. This treatment of the productive forces of the present day, on the basis of their real nature at last recognised by society, opens the way to the replacement of the anarchy of social production by a socially planned regulation of production in accordance with the needs both of society as a whole and of each individual. The capitalist mode of appropriation, in which the product enslaves first the producer, and then also the appropriator, will thereby be replaced by the mode of appropriation of the products based on the nature of the modern means of production themselves: on the one hand direct social appropriation as a means to the maintenance and extension of production, and on the other hand direct individual appropriation as a means to life and pleasure.

By more and more transforming the great majority of the population into proletarians, the capitalist mode of production brings into being the force which, under penalty of its own destruction, is compelled to carry out this revolution. By more and more driving towards the conversion of the vast socialised means of production into state property, it itself points the way for the carrying through of this revolution. *The proletariat seizes the state power, and transforms the means of production in the first instance into state property*. But in doing this, it puts an end to itself as the proletariat, it puts an end to all class differences and class antagonisms, it puts an end also to the state as the state. Former society, moving in class antagonisms, had need of the state, that is, an organisation of the exploiting class at each period for the maintenance of its external conditions of production; that is, therefore, for the forcible holding down of the exploited class in the conditions of oppression (slavery, villeinage or serfdom, wage labour) determined by the existing mode of production. The state was the official representative of society as a whole, its embodiment in a visible corporation; but it was this only in so far as it was the state of that class which itself, in its epoch, represented society as a whole; in ancient times, the state of the slave-owning citizens; in the Middle Ages, of the feudal nobility; in our epoch, of the bourgeoisie. When ultimately it becomes really representative of society as a whole, it makes itself superfluous. As soon as there is no longer any class of society to be held in subjection; as soon as, along with class domination and the struggle for individual existence based on the former anarchy of production, the collisions and excesses arising from these have also been abolished, there is nothing more to be repressed which would make a special repressive force, a state, necessary. The first act in which the state really comes forward as the representative of society as a whole—the taking possession of the means of production in the name of society—is at the same time its last independent act as a state. The interference of the state power in social relations becomes superfluous in one sphere after another, and then ceases of itself. The government of persons is replaced by the administration of things and the direction of the processes of production. The state is not "abolished," *it withers away*. It is from this standpoint that we must appraise the phrase "free people's state"—both its justification at times for agitational purposes, and its ultimate scientific inadequacy —and also the demand of the so-called anarchists that the state should be abolished overnight.

Since the emergence in history of the capitalist mode of production, the taking over of all means of production by society has often been dreamed of by individuals as well as by whole sects, more or less vaguely and as an ideal of the future. But it could only become possible, it could only become a historical necessity, when the material conditions for its realisation had come into existence. Like every other social advance, it becomes realisable not through the perception that the existence of classes is in contradiction with justice, equality, etc., not through the mere will to abolish these classes, but through certain new economic conditions. The division of society into an exploiting and an exploited class, a ruling and an oppressed class, was the necessary outcome of the low development of production hitherto. So long as the sum of social labour yielded a product which only slightly exceeded what was necessary for the bare existence of all; so long, therefore, as all or almost all the time of the great majority of the members of society was absorbed in labour, so long was society necessarily divided into classes. Alongside of this great majority exclusively absorbed in labour there developed a class, freed from direct productive labour, which managed the general business of society: the direction of labour, affairs of state, justice, science, art, and so forth. It is therefore the law of the division of labour which lies at the root of the division into classes. But this does not mean that this division into classes was not established by violence and robbery, by deception and fraud, or that the ruling class, once in the saddle, has ever failed to strengthen its domination at the cost of the working class and to convert its social management into the exploitation of the masses.

But if, on these grounds, the division into classes has a certain historical justification, it has this only for a given period of time, for given social conditions. It was based on the insufficiency of production; it will be swept away by the full development of the modern productive forces. And in fact the abolition of social classes has as its presupposition a stage of historical development at which the existence not merely of some particular ruling class or other but of any ruling class at all, that is to say, of class difference itself, has become an anachronism, is out of date. It therefore presupposes that the development of production has reached a level at which the appropriation of means of production and of products, and with these, of political supremacy, the monopoly of education and intellectual leadership by a special class of society, has become not only superfluous but also economically, politically and intellectually a hindrance to development.

This point has now been reached. Their political and intellectual bankruptcy is hardly still a secret to the bourgeoisie themselves, and their economic bankruptcy recurs regularly every ten years. In each crisis society is smothered under the weight of its own productive forces and products of which it can make no use, and stands helpless in face of the absurd contradiction that the producers have nothing to consume because there are no consumers. The expanding force of the means of production bursts asunder the bonds imposed upon them by the capitalist mode of production. Their release from these bonds is the sole condition necessary for an unbroken and constantly more rapidly progressing development of the productive forces, and therewith of a practically limitless growth of production itself. Nor is this all. The appropriation by society of the means of production puts an end not only to the artificial restraints on production which exist today, but also to the positive waste and destruction of productive forces and products which is now the inevitable accompaniment of production and reaches its zenith in crises. Further, it sets free for society as a whole a mass of means of production and products by putting an end to the senseless luxury and extravagance of the present ruling class and its political representatives. The possibility of securing for every member of society, through social production, an existence which is not only fully sufficient from a material standpoint and becoming richer from day to day, but also guarantees to them the completely unrestricted development and exercise of their physical and mental faculties—this possibility now exists for the first time, but it *does exist*.[6]

The seizure of the means of production by society puts an end to commodity production, and therewith to the domination of the product over the producer. Anarchy in social production is replaced by conscious organisation on a planned basis. The struggle for individual existence comes to an end. And at this point, in a certain sense, man finally cuts himself off from the animal world, leaves the conditions of animal existence behind him and enters conditions which are really human. The conditions of existence forming man's environment, which up to now have dominated man, at this point pass under the dominion and control of man, who now for the first time becomes the real conscious master of Nature, because and in so far as he has become master of his own social organisation. The laws of his own social activity, which have hitherto confronted him as external, dominating laws of Nature, will then be applied by man with complete understanding, and hence will be dominated by man. Men's own social organisation which has hitherto stood in opposition to them as if arbitrarily decreed by Nature and history, will then become the voluntary act of men themselves. The objective, external forces which have hitherto dominated history, will then pass under the control of men themselves. It is only from this point that men, with full consciousness, will fashion their own history; it is only from this point that the social causes set in motion by men will have, predominantly and in constantly increasing measure, the effects willed by men. It is humanity's leap from the realm of necessity into the realm of freedom.

To carry through his world-emancipating act is the historical mission of the modern proletariat. And it is the task of scientific socialism, the theoretical expression of the proletarian movement, to establish the historical conditions and, with these, the nature of this act, and thus to bring to the consciousness of the now oppressed class the conditions and nature of the act which it is its destiny to accomplish.

---

[6] A few figures may given an approximate idea of the enormous expansive power of modern means of production, even under the weight of capitalism. According to Giffen's latest estimates, the total wealth of Great Britain and Ireland was as under in round figures:

1814	£2,200,000,000
1865	6,100,000,000
1875	8,500,000,000

An indication of the waste of means of production and products resulting from crises is the estimate given at the Second German Industrial Congress (Berlin, Feb. 21, 1878) that the total loss to the *German iron industry* alone in the last crisis amounted to 455 million marks [£22,750,000]. [*Note by F. Engels.*]

Social Freedom

Although issues concerning man's political and economic freedom have drawn the most attention in recent years, there is another dimension to man's freedom in society which has been long recognized and which is now increasingly occupying the minds of those concerned with individual freedom. This dimension concerns the effect of culture, tradition, and the general organization of society upon the individual's ability to determine for himself what he is to do and to become. When men are confronted with dictatorial political authority, it is easy to perceive and to dramatize the issues of political freedom. When there are economic exploitation and large-scale economic depressions, it is understandable that men will focus their reforming energies on economic freedom. In those societies where a considerable measure of political and economic stability has been achieved, attention is turning to the subtler influences of traditions and social organization that constrain and limit.

Beginning the discussion of social freedom with basic considerations concerning the impact of culture upon freedom, our first author, Freud, contends that as cultural institutions become more complex and as civilization advances, individual liberty is restricted. Disagreeing with Freud, Malinowski, a noted anthropologist, points out that it is only through culture that man rises above the animals and achieves control of his environment—a control that provides both the birth and growth of human freedom.

Closely related to the question of whether culture enhances man's freedom are questions concerning other aspects of man's life in society which are important in providing the conditions of individual freedom. Thus, John Stuart Mill's essay "On Liberty," though written in 1859, has a remarkably contemporary ring as he notes that there can be a tyranny of the majority more enslaving than any tyranny of a political dictator. Majority rule has more than governmental authority at its disposal, for it can bring to bear upon an individual all the pressures of prevailing opinion and feeling to impose ideas of proper conduct. To defend ourselves against such pressure for conformity, Mill urges that we recognize that "the sole end for which mankind are warrented, individually or collectively, in interfering with the liberty of action of any of their number, is self-protection."

Russell Kirk, a leading contemporary American conservative, calls attention to the importance of custom and authority in creating a free society. For him, those who would defy tradition and authority are asking for "anarchic freedom"—the liberty possessed by the shark and the wolf. What we must seek to establish is "ordered freedom"—a freedom which can exist only when the members of a society have respect for the collective wisdom and experience embodied in their own traditions.

In the next selection, a leading radical of the New Left, Herbert Marcuse, finds little freedom in the traditions and organization of modern industrialized societies. He believes that our technologically integrated society has suppressed individuality on behalf of the efficiency demanded by the system. The facts that individuals may not feel oppressed and may like the satisfaction of needs which modern technology makes possible only indicate that social forces are molding and manipulating even the feelings and likes of individuals. So thoroughly does the system place its stamp upon the individuals within it that we are witnessing the creation of one-dimensional men—men incapable of thinking or behaving in any other dimension than the established order.

Christian Bay seeks first to clarify what is meant in speaking of "social freedom." He distinguishes two meanings of the term: "the relative absence of perceived external restraints on individual behavior," and "the relative absence of unperceived external restraints on individual behavior." According to these definitions, an individual being manipulated by another person without being aware of the manipulation would have social freedom in the first sense of the term but not in the second sense. Bay then goes on to urge that each of these social freedoms has high value. With some qualifications, he contends that we should maximize each of these freedoms and calls attention to some of the factors which must be considered in achieving such a goal.

Taking the Marxist position that democracy and freedom are relative to the economic base of society, Mao Tse-tung, the leader of Communist China, contrasts the capitalist notions of democracy and freedom with those of his own society. Making clear that tolerance does not extend to "reactionaries" nor to those who oppose socialist construction, Mao contends that the centralized guidance of his society provides a wider democracy and more freedom than is to be found in Western parliamentary democracies.

Thus far, the readings in this section have been concerned with some of the general conditions that affect man's social freedom. Little has been said of the particular protests against the restrictions of society which are daily voiced in the news by individuals and groups. Yet a book on the issues of freedom would hardly be complete if it did not note the views of at least some of those in our society who are either fighting to gain their rightful share of accepted freedoms or working for the recognition of new freedoms.

Lerone Bennett, Jr., senior editor of Ebony magazine, calls attention to the presence of racism as the best index of the failure of American society to create freedom for both blacks and whites. Generalizing his concern for blacks to the underprivileged of all races and classes, Bennett calls upon Americans to make the revolutionary changes in the organization and spirit of society that are required to move freedom from lip-service ideal to living reality.

Protest against the existing order of quite a different type is exemplified by the hippie movement. To learn about their outlook on life, Leonard Wolf interviewed a number of hippies in the Haight-Ashbury district of San Francisco. In the selection drawn from Wolf's record of those interviews, three hippies, Lenore Kandel, Peter Cohon, and Peter Berg give their opinions on sex, drugs, work, and freedom. Wolf himself concludes that "the greatest contribution the movement will have made to American life will be the new emphasis their self-expression has brought to the question of personal freedom." Fred Davis, a sociologist who also has studied the hippie community in the Haight-Ashbury district, states in the next reading what he finds to be the distinctive values of this group. Noting their reaction to middle-class standards, he suggests that they are reacting with particular vigor to three features of contemporary American life: compulsive consumption of material goods, passive spectatorship as opposed to active participation, and the constant pursuit of temporally distant goals—a pursuit that neglects the meaningfulness of present activity.

Our final selection provides a sample of thinking from some of the radical activists of the New Left. In 1962, the Students for a Democratic Society (S.D.S.) adopted the "Port Huron Statement" as an expression of beliefs widely accepted by its members. Largely written by Tom Hayden, the statement details criticisms of our existing society, presents the values toward which the group intends to work, and explains the importance of the university as a focal point for influencing social change. In the years that have elapsed since the publication of this document, S.D.S. has added many new members and the thinking of the older members has changed. Accordingly, the statement should not be taken as representative of the organization's present official position. Nevertheless, the document is still regarded as expressing the general outlook on values shared not only by many members of the group but by other young radicals as well.

"CULTURE RESTRICTS MAN'S FREEDOM"

Sigmund Freud

Our discussion of happiness has so far not taught us much that is not already common knowledge. Nor does the prospect of discovering anything new seem much greater if we go on with the problem why it is so hard for mankind to be happy. We gave the answer before, when we cited the three sources of human sufferings, namely, the superior force of nature, the disposition to decay of our bodies, and the inadequacy of our methods of regulating human relations in the family, the community and the state. In regard to the first two, our judgement cannot hesitate: it forces us to recognize these sources of suffering and to submit to the inevitable. We shall never completely subdue nature; our body, too, is an organism, itself a part of nature, and will always contain the seeds of dissolution, with its limited powers

of adaptation and achievement. The effect of this recognition is in no way disheart-
ening; on the contrary, it points out the direction for our efforts. If we cannot
abolish all suffering, yet a great deal of it we can, and can mitigate more; the
experience of several thousand years has convinced us of this. To the third, the
social source of our distresses, we take up a different attitude. We prefer not to
regard it as one at all; we cannot see why the systems we have ourselves created
should not rather ensure protection and well-being for us all. To be sure, when we
consider how unsuccessful our efforts to safeguard against suffering in this particular
have proved, the suspicion dawns upon us that a bit of unconquerable nature lurks
concealed behind this difficulty as well—in the shape of our own mental constitution.

When we start to consider this possibility, we come across a point of view which
is so amazing that we will pause over it. According to it, our so-called civilization
itself is to blame for a great part of our misery, and we should be much happier if
we were to give it up and go back to primitive conditions. I call this amazing,
because—however one may define culture—it is undeniable that every means by
which we try to guard ourselves against menaces from the several sources of human
distress is a part of this same culture.

How has it come about that so many people have adopted this strange attitude of
hostility to civilzation? In my opinion, it arose from a background of profound
long-standing discontent with the existing state of civilization, which finally crystallized into this judgement as a result of certain historical happenings. I believe I can
identify the last two of these; I am not learned enough to trace the links in the
chain back into the history of the human species. At the time when Christianity
conquered the pagan religions some such antagonism to culture must already have
been actively at work. It is closely related to the low estimation put upon earthly
life by Christian doctrine. The earlier of the last two historical developments was
when, as a result of voyages of discovery, men came into contact with primitive
peoples and races. To the Europeans, who failed to observe them carefully and
misunderstood what they saw, these poeple seemed to lead simple, happy lives—
wanting for nothing—such as the travellers who visited them, with all their superior
culture, were unable to achieve. Later experience has corrected this opinion on
many points; in several instances the ease of life was due to the bounty of nature
and the possibilities of ready satisfaction for the great human needs, but it was
erroneously attributed to the absence of the complicated conditions of civilization.
The last of the two historical events is especially familiar to us; it was when people
began to understand the nature of the neuroses which threaten to undermine the
modicum of happiness open to civilized man. It was found that men become
neurotic because they cannot tolerate the degree of privation that society imposes
on them in virtue of its cultural ideals, and it was supposed that a return to greater
possibilities of happiness would ensue if these standards were abolished or greatly
relaxed.

And there exists an element of disappointment, in addition. In the last generations
man has made extraordinary strides in knowledge of the natural sciences and
technical application of them, and has established his dominion over nature in a

way never before imagined. The details of this forward progress are universally known: it is unnecessary to enumerate them. Mankind is proud of its exploits and has a right to be. But men are beginning to perceive that all this newly won power over space and time, this conquest of the forces of nature, this fulfilment of age-old longings, has not increased the amount of pleasure they can obtain in life, has not made them feel any happier. The valid conclusion from this is merely that power over nature is not the only condition of human happiness, just as it is not the only goal of civilization's efforts, and there is no ground for inferring that its technical progress is worthless from the standpoint of happiness. It prompts one to exclaim: is it not then a positive pleasure, an unequivocal gain in happiness, to be able to hear, whenever I like, the voice of a child living hundreds of miles away, or to know directly a friend of mine arrives at his destination that he has come well and safely through the long and troublesome voyage? And is it nothing that medical science has succeeded in enormously reducing the mortality of young children, the dangers of infection for women in childbirth, indeed, in very considerably pro-longing the average length of human life? And there is still a long list one could add to these benefits that we owe to the much-despised era of scientific and practical progress—but a critical, pessimistic voice makes itself heard, saying that most of these advantages follow the model of those 'cheap pleasures' in the anecdote. One gets this enjoyment by sticking one's bare leg outside the bedclothes on a cold winter's night and then drawing it in again. If there were no railway to make light of distances my child would never have left home and I should not need the telephone to hear his voice. If there were no vessels crossing the ocean my friend would never have embarked on his voyage and I should not need the telegraph to relieve my anxiety about him. What is the use of reducing the mortality of children when it is precisely this reduction which imposes the greatest moderation on us in begetting them, so that taken all round we do not rear more children than in the days before the reign of hygiene, while at the same time we have created difficult conditions for sexual life in marriage and probably counteracted the beneficial effects of natural selection? And what do we gain by a long life when it is full of hardship and starved of joys and so wretched that we can only welcome death as our deliverer?

It seems to be certain that our present-day civilization does not inspire in us a feeling of well-being, but it is very difficult to form an opinion whether in earlier times people felt any happier and what part their cultural conditions played in the question. We always tend to regard trouble objectively, *i.e.* to place ourselves with our own wants and our own sensibilities in the same conditions, so as to discover what opportunities for happiness or unhappiness we should find in them. This method of considering the problem, which appears to be objective because it ignores the varieties of subjective sensitivity, is of course the most subjective possible, for by applying it one substitutes one's own mental attitude for the unknown attitude of other men. Happiness, on the contrary, is something essentially subjective. However we may shrink in horror at the thought of certain situations, that of the galley-slaves in antiquity, of the peasants in the Thirty Years' War, of the victims of the Inquisition, of the Jews awaiting a pogrom, it is still impossible for us to feel ourselves into the position of these people, to imagine the differences which would be brought about by constitutional obtuseness of feeling, gradual stupefaction, the cessation of all anticipation, and by all the grosser and more subtle ways in which insensibility to both pleasurable and painful sensations can be induced. Moreover, on occasions when the most extreme forms of suffering have to be endured, special mental protective devices come into operation. It seems to me unprofitable to follow up this aspect of the problem further.

It is time that we should turn our attention to the nature of this culture, the value of which is so much disputed from the point of view of happiness. Until we have learnt something by examining it for ourselves, we will not look round for formulas which express its essence in a few words. We will be content to repeat[1] that the word 'culture' describes the sum of the achievements and institutions which differentiate our lives from those of our animal forebears and serve two purposes, namely, that of protecting humanity against nature and of regulating the relations of human beings among themselves. . . .

Beauty, cleanliness and order clearly occupy a paculiar position among the requirements of civilization. No one will maintain that they are as essential to life as the activities aimed at controlling the forces of nature and as other factors which we have yet to mention; and yet no one would willingly relegate them to the background as trivial matters. Beauty is an instance which plainly shows that culture is not simply utilitarian in its aims, for the lack of beauty is a thing we cannot tolerate in civilization. The utilitarian advantages of order are quite apparent; with regard to cleanliness we have to remember that it is required of us by hygiene, and we may surmise that even before the days of scientific prophylaxis the connection between the two was not altogether unsuspected by mankind. But these aims and endeavours of culture are not entirely to be explained on utilitarian lines; there must be something else at work besides.

According to general opinion, however, there is one feature of culture which characterizes it better than any other, and that is the value it sets upon the higher mental activities—intellectual, scientific and aesthetic achievement—the leading part it concedes to ideas in human life. First and foremost among these ideas come the religious systems with their complicated evolution, on which I have elsewhere endeavoured to throw a light; next to them come philosophical speculations; and last, the ideals man has formed, his conceptions of the perfection possible in an individual, in a people, in humanity as a whole, and the demands he makes on the basis of these conceptions. These creations of his mind are not independent of each other; on the contrary, they are closely interwoven, and this complicates the attempt to describe them, as well as that to trace their psychological derivation. If we assume as a general hypothesis that the force behind all human activities is a striving towards the two convergent aims of profit and pleasure, we must then acknowledge this as valid also for these other manifestations of culture, although it can be plainly recognized as true only in respect of science and art. It cannot be doubted, however, that the remainder, too, correspond to some powerful need in

[1] Cf. *The Future of an Illusion.*

human beings—perhaps to one which develops fully only in a minority of people. Nor may we allow ourselves to be misled by our own judgements concerning the value of any of these religious or philosophical systems or of these ideals; whether we look upon them as the highest achievement of the human mind, or whether we deplore them as fallacies, one must acknowledge that where they exist, and especially where they are in the ascendant, they testify to a high level of civilization.

We now have to consider the last, and certainly by no means the least important, of the components of culture, namely, the ways in which social relations, the relations of one man to another, are regulated, all that has to do with him as a neighbour, a source of help, a sexual object to others, a member of a family or of a state. It is especially difficult in this matter to remain unbiased by any ideal standards and to ascertain exactly what is specifically cultural here. Perhaps one might begin with the statement that the first attempt ever made to regulate these social relations already contained the essential element of civilization. Had no such attempt been made, these relations would be subject to the wills of individuals: that is to say, the man who was physically strongest would decide things in accordance with his own interests and desires. The situation would remain the same even though this strong man should in his turn meet with another who was stronger than he. Human life in communities only becomes possible when a number of men unite together in strength superior to any single individual and remain united against all single individuals. The strength of this united body is then opposed as 'Right' against the strength of any individual, which is condemned as 'brute force'. This substitution of the power of a united number for the power of a single man is the decisive step towards civilization. The essence of it lies in the circumstance that the members of the community have restricted their possibilities of gratification, whereas the individual recognized no such restrictions. The first requisite of culture, therefore, is justice—that is, the assurance that a law once made will not be broken in favour of any individual. This implies nothing about the ethical value of any such law. The further course of cultural development seems to tend towards ensuring that the law shall no longer represent the will of any small body—caste, tribe, section of the population—which may behave like a predatory individual towards other such groups perhaps containing larger numbers. The end-result would be a state of law to which all—that is, all who are capable of uniting—have contributed by making some sacrifice of their own desires, and which leaves none—again with the same exception—at the mercy of brute force.

The liberty of the individual is not a benefit of culture. It was greatest before any culture, though indeed it had little value at that time, because the individual was hardly in a position to defend it. Liberty has undergone restrictions through the evolution of civilization, and justice demands that these restrictions shall apply to all. The desire for freedom that makes itself felt in a human community may be a revolt against some existing injustice and so may prove favourable to a further development of civilization and remain compatible with it. But it may also have its origin in the primitive roots of the personality, still unfettered by civilizing influences, and so become a source of antagonism to culture. Thus the cry for freedom is directed either against particular forms or demands of culture or else against culture itself. It does not seem as if man could be brought by any sort of influence to change his nature into that of the ants; he will always, one imagines, defend his claim to individual freedom against the will of the multitude. A great part of the struggles of mankind centres round the single task of finding some expedient (*i.e.* satisfying) solution between these individual claims and those of the civilized community; it is one of the problems of man's fate whether this solution can be arrived at in some particular form of culture or whether the conflict will prove irreconcilable.

We have obtained a clear impression of the general picture presented by culture through adopting the common view as to which aspects of human life are to be called cultural; but it is true that so far we have discovered nothing that is not common knowledge. We have, however, at the same time guarded ourselves against accepting the misconception that civilization is synonymous with becoming perfect, is the path by which man is ordained to reach perfection. But now a certain point of view presses for consideration; it will lead perhaps in another direction. The evolution of culture seems to us a peculiar kind of process passing over humanity, of which several aspects strike us as familiar. We can describe this process in terms of the modifications it effects on the known human instinctual dispositions, which it is the economic task of our lives to satisfy. Some of these instincts become absorbed, as it were, so that something appears in place of them which in an individual we call a character-trait. The most remarkable example of this process is found in respect of the anal erotism of young human beings. Their primary interest in the excretory function, its organs and products, is changed in the course of their growth into a group of traits that we know well—thriftiness, orderliness and cleanliness—valuable and welcome qualities in themselves, which, however, may be intensified till they visibly dominate the personality and produce what we call the anal character. How this happens we do not know; but there is no doubt about the accuracy of this conclusion.[2] Now, we have seen that order and cleanliness are essentially cultural demands, although the necessity of them for survival is not particularly apparent, any more than their suitability as sources of pleasure. At this point we must be struck for the first time with the similarity between the process of cultural development and that of the libidinal development in an individual. Other instincts have to be induced to change the conditions of their gratification, to find it along other paths, a process which is usually identical with what we know so well as sublimation (of the aim of an instinct), but which can sometimes be differentiated from this. Sublimation of instinct is an especially conspicuous feature of cultural evolution; this it is that makes it possible for the higher mental operations, scientific, artistic, ideological activities, to play such an important part in civilized life. If one were to yield to a first impression, one would be tempted to say that sublimation is a fate which has been forced upon instincts by culture alone. But it is better to reflect over this a while longer. Thirdly and lastly, and this seems most important of all, it is impossible to ignore the extent to which civilization is built up on renunciation of instinctual gratifications, the degree to which the

[2] Cf. 'Character and Anal Erotism' (1908), *Collected Papers*, vol. ii.; also numerous contributions to the subject by Ernest Jones and others.

existence of civilization presupposes the non-gratification (suppression, repression or something else?) of powerful instinctual urgencies. This 'cultural privation' dominates the whole field of social relations between human beings; we know already that it is the cause of the antagonism against which all civilization has to fight. It sets hard tasks for our scientific work, too; we have a great deal to explain here. It is not easy to understand how it can become possible to withhold satisfaction from an instinct. Nor is it by any means without risk to do so; if the deprivation is not made good economically, one may be certain of producing serious disorders.

"CULTURE IS A CONDITION OF MAN'S FREEDOM"

Bronislaw Malinowski

Culture from its very beginnings consists in the organized exploitation by human intelligence of environmental opportunities, and in the disciplining of drives, skills, and nervous reactions in the service of collective and implemented action. The earliest human groups, and the individuals which form them, achieve a much greater integral freedom of mobility and environmental adaptation, freedom of security and prosperity, by the use of tools, by following the principles of knowledge, and by loyalty to a system of activities started with a purpose and carried out concertedly.

In its earliest beginnings, as well as in its fundamental function throughout evolution, culture satisfies first and foremost man's basic needs. Culture thus means primarily the freedom of survival to the species under a variety of environmental conditions for which man is not equipped by nature. This freedom of survival can be analyzed into freedom of security and freedom of prosperity. By freedom of security we mean the protective mechanisms which culture gives through artifacts and co-operation and which endow the species with a much wider margin of safety. Freedom of prosperity refers to the increased, widened, and diversified power of exploiting environmental resources, allowing man to prepare for periods of scarcity, accumulate wealth, and thus obtain leisure for many types of activities which man as an animal would never have undertaken.

The advent of culture changes man the animal into man the artificer, man the organizer, and man the thinker, talker, and planner. Man the animal lives within an environment to which, like any other animal, he became adapted in the course of organic development. Like any animal he is subject to the determinisms of his environment and to the requirements of his organism. Precultural man enjoys as much freedom as any animal and he is subject to the same bondage of his own flesh and its needs, and of the environment with its gifts and potentialities which have to be exploited, as well as its dangers against which any animal has to protect itself.

Culture implies directly and immediately an initial installment in freedom. For culture can be defined as the artifical, secondary, self-made environment which gives man an additional control of certain natural forces. It also allows him to adjust his own responses in a manner which makes the new readaptation by habit and organization more elastic and efficient than the adaptation by reflex and instinct. This initial installment of freedom becomes then gradually developed, and increases into that extensive control of environment, the manipulation of natural forces, and the development of physical and mental faculties which have now made man into the master of this globe, as well as the slave of his own mechanisms and stupidities. The integral increment in freedom, as well as its denials, we can realize by comparing man's place within his physical universe with that from which he started at the birth of culture. The anthropoid species from which man started on his cultural career lived within a limited habitat, probably a tropical jungle. The original man-ape satisfied his needs, feeding on a narrow and definite range of foodstuffs, protected from environmental dangers by a small margin of adjustment. The species was anatomically rather defenseless. Like all anthropoid apes, pre-cultural man has no natural weapons, no fangs, claws, or horns. Nor is he protected by a thick skin or great speed of movement. The ape man was thus vulnerable in his own body and exposed to many dangers because of the long maturation of the young.

Starting from such a somewhat unfavorable position, man, through his cultural development, has now overrun the globe and conquered all climes and all habitats. He is able to adapt to arctic climates as well as to tropical jungles. He lives on mountain slopes and inhabits small islands surrounded by an enormous expanse of ocean. He has developed means to irrigate the desert and to find his subsistence on wide steppes and prairies. Thus taking freedom as the range of adaptive possibilities, we see that it has extended man's control as far as the surface of the earth allows and into the various elements where man was originally unable to penetrate.

This was made possible through the development of instrumentalities and co-operative actions, which gave man control of elements and means of locomotion to which he was originally not adapted. By the use of dug-outs, rafts, canoes, and later on of sailing and power vessels, man has conquered the surface of the water. He has developed means of diving and remaining under the water through the diver's outfit and through the extremely complex instrumentality of the submarine. Even more recently man has also conquered the air, and through this has reduced space in a manner almost incredible to those born in the last century.

The integral freedom given to man as an animal species through the development of his cultural instrumentality is thus objective, tangible and specific. It consists in a more efficient and better-founded way of satisfying the innate biological desires of man, and in the indefinite extension in the range of human mobility. It is a new type of environmental adaptation. It is brought about by the use of tools, artifacts, machines, and weapons; by the organization of human beings in relation to the apparatus, and co-ordinating their actions through rules of concerted behavior; and by the development of symbolic means of communication, more especailly of language, which allows man to cumulate his tradition and to transmit it from generation to generation.

Culture in its initial state grants the freedom to live in security and with a margin of surplus, while at the same time it implies obedience and submission to certain restraints. These restraints consist in the rules of technique and of knowledge how to exploit the environment and avoid its dangers. Bound up with these are the laws of custom and of social give and take. Ethical principles, partly implicit in submission to the supernatural, partly arising out of organized emotional reactions, impose also certain restraints from the very beginning of culture.

All such laws are as indispensable even to the most primitive forms of cultural behavior as they are inevitable. It is important to keep in mind that earliest man was as bound by his rules as is the member of our highly differentiated cultures of to-day. Neither ontogenetically nor phylogenetically is "man born free". The new-born infant is supremely dependent for his very life on the social and cultural setting of his family. As he grows up, the very essence of training and education consists in disciplining certain freedoms, in substituting habit for reflex, skill for random behavior, and in imparting symbolically the full range of technical, social, and moral tradition. Phylogenetically, man begins with culture, and culture begins with trammels. Man is thus not born free, as Jean Jacques Rousseau wanted us to believe. He is born to a new freedom which he can only achieve by taking up the chains of tradition and using them, for, paradoxically, these very chains are the instruments of freedom.

Earliest man also was unable to produce a single artifact by his own devices, to carry out the simplest activity alone, or yet to enjoy the fruits of his labors—to have his share when others got theirs—except under the guarantees of primitive customary law, of property and privilege. This statement may seem exaggerated only to those who forget that all the benefits of tradition as well as all the guarantees of well-being are social. The use of fire as well as its production had to be learned. Stone implements may be produced by one man as well as used by him, but the quarrying of stone, the knowledge where to find and how to use the materials and the techniques, and the principles of private property in tools and goods produced, imply the existence of early customary law, co-operation and tradition.

In all this man establishes a new self-made environment, to which in turn he readapts his own organism. This new artificial environment obeys a determinism of its own. There exist laws of cultural process, of the constitution of culture, and of the efficiency of concerted activities. Hence culture inevitably becomes a source of new constraints imposed upon man. The laws of cultural process are less rigid than those of nature or of the living organism, and are to be found in the relation between artifact, skill, idea, and rule of conduct. They also control as laws of economics the production, distribution, and consumption of goods. As laws of educational process they determine the mechanism of developing and training the young and transforming an infant into a tribal or national citizen. We find also a number of general laws of structure and function in the study of organized systems of behavior, or institutions as we call them.

Within the really existing human societies, no man ever acts alone. He is always a member of a group, or rather of several groups: the family, the neighborhood group, his professional associates, his municipality, his nation and his sovereign state. This applies to the most primitive savages, to university professors, bricklayers and party members of a Communist, Nazi or Fascist totalitarium. A culture functions therefore by means of a system of related institutions. The values of a culture are embodied in its ideals, mythologies, political constitution and economic ideology; its instrumentalities function through the balanced co-ordination and working of institutions. The standard of existence and quality of living depend on the scope, range, distribution and enjoyment of wealth, rights, power, art, science, and religion. Each member of an institution enjoys his own differential freedom in the measure to which he has a part in the planning, a full access to the means of execution, and a share in the rewards. Even in its smallest and most insignificant manifestations, freedom gives any and every member of a society the sense of achievement, and through this the sense of personal value. In a free culture people can form their purpose, undertake activities and enterprises, and enjoy the gains from work thus undertaken.

The leitmotif of all our arguments will be that all those constraints which are dictated by cultural determinism are as indispensable to successful behavior as are the laws of nature and of the organism. Freedom, indeed, consists in the lead and guidance which the rules and laws of culture give man. At the same time we shall see that most of those rules of cultural determinism imply the element of power, placed in the hands of one or of a few. This power can be abused in the form of wealth, of physical violence, and of spiritual intimidation, with regard to initiative and planning, or to the control of cultural instrumentalities, or else to the distribution of the benefits. In every case the distinction between the differential freedom of social organization and minor or major cases of bondage, slavery or oppression turns round the question whether the constraint is necessary for the successful execution of the activity, or whether it is exercised to the advantage of a few and at the expense of others.

As humanity advances, there open up new vistas for human desire, interest, knowledge, and belief. In this, the symbolic aspect of culture—the power to embody tradition into communicable texts; the power to tell tales about past events, past miracles and past achievements; the power to plan, to foresee, and to foretell— becomes the means of invention of new devices, planning of new activities, and the maturing of purpose and motive. From this is derived freedom of conscience, thought and speech.

Freedom also gives man the power to anticipate, and to establish values by the guidance of which man can engage in co-operative activities and does reach new goals and enjoy them under his guarantees of tribal or national citizenship. This type of freedom embraces legal and political planning as well as the shackles and leeways of tradition. Here enter the domains of knowledge, technology, religion, art, and organized recreation, which from their humble beginnings gradually develop and engage more and more of human interests, human ambitions, and human abilities.

Thus it seems clear, first and foremost, that the concept of freedom must always be referred to the increase in range, diversity and power in human planning. The ability to foresee and to plan ahead, that is, the ability to use past experience in order to establish future conditions corresponding to the needs, the desires and the aspirations of man, is the first essential prerequisite of freedom. All planning, however, all visions, aspirations, discoveries or inventions remain idle, insignificant, and, to the science of human behavior, irrelevant, if the instrumentalities for their realization are not present. The freedom of the spirit is either an empty phrase, or it means some definite change in the world of matter, of flesh, and of human circumstances. Finally, and as the anthropologist and the historian know only too well, all human endeavor, all hard work and effort can either be worthwhile or, once more, vain, irrelevant and unreal. This yes-or-no condition of human enterprise depends clearly on its integral success, and on the value of its success to the community, to the institution, and to its component members. The final results of human activities, the satisfaction which they bring to the group and its component individuals, can either be realized or set at naught. To discuss freedom without considering the gratifications and enjoyments of the results obtained is to confuse the work of a slave with that of a free man. Freedom in terms of the standard of living, of the enjoyments and gratifications brought by culture to its carriers, is as important as the freedom of purpose and the freedom of equipment in efficient action.

Thus the maintenance, the management, and the development of the psychological mainsprings in inspiration, invention, and contribution are the first and foremost conditions of freedom. The formation of social loyalties, on which every institution is built, is the second condition. The way in which the cultural values, that is, the enjoyment of economic, social, political, moral, and spiritual benefits, are distributed—in other words, freedom in the pursuit of happiness—is the last and perhaps the main condition of liberty.

This brief outline of the cultural background of our problem in evolutionary perspective was given to show first and foremost that not a single human act, relevant to the science of man, occurs outside the context of culture. In this sense freedom can only be discussed as an attribute of the cultural process. In its very beginnings and throughout evolution, culture grants certain leeways and opportunities, and imposes certain restrictions.

Freedom, therefore, is always a relative concept which implies balance and relation. It is the surplus value in integral achievement, over and above the unavoidable submissions to rule, norm, and restriction. It lies in the relation between the prerogatives of self and of others, for man is dependent on others both through tradition and through co-operation. To start the analysis of freedom by considering how an individual behaves within a short-range phase of activities, a phase arbitrarily cut out, must always lead to error. The error becomes even more serious when we rely on the subjective feeling of the individual under such conditions and try to imagine how he feels. It is essential to start from the objective and real context of freedom rather than to train a psychic telescope or microscope on that unobservable entity, the human soul in its emotional iridescences, as it observes itself in its own private microcosm.

Thus our concept of freedom is an induction from the concrete and specific manifestations thereof. It is an asset given to humanity through the organization of human beings into co-operative groups, who have to obey certain norms, who have to use implements and machines, who have to co-operate for a determined end. In all this they achieve the integral freedom of their purpose at the price of partial submissions and renunciations. The sacrifice is small for their share in such great results. To the extent that these submissions and renunciations deprive some members of an institution—whether this be slavery or serfdom, a military regiment, or the crew of a galley—from either the participation in planning and the building up of the purposes and decisions, or else in the enjoyment of the results, such a denial of initiative and of a fair share in the standard of living means a total or partial, a temporary or chronic abrogation of freedom.

Right through our analysis there runs the thesis that freedom is the successful unimpeded course of the cultural process, bringing full satisfaction of all needs. Freedom is neither more nor less but full success in action. It is activity spontaneously planned, efficiently executed, and enjoyed in its results by all those who have contributed. In all this we shall see that the integral constitution of a culture, whether for peace or war, for collective robbery or the internal development of arts, crafts, and industries, for a religion of cruelty and aggression or for a faith essentially humane and ethical, is the primary determinant of freedom or bondage.

Thus the distribution of freedom within society, the distribution which has to be referred to purpose, activity, and standard of living alike, is one of the concrete and specific problems which cannot be neglected. The use of power in physical constraint, in economic pressure, and in spiritual intimidation has to be studied at any level of human development. Our approach shows that freedom is essentially a positive quality of human behavior, the quality of the smooth, efficient satisfying of all, within the context of a given culture.

"THE TYRANNY OF THE MAJORITY ENDANGERS FREEDOM"

John Stuart Mill

The subject of this Essay is not the so-called Liberty of the Will, so unfortunately opposed to the misnamed doctrine of Philosophical Necessity; but Civil, or Social Liberty: the nature and limits of the power which can be legitimately exercised by society over the individual. A question seldom stated, and hardly ever discussed, in general terms, but which profoundly influences the practical controversies of the age by its latent presence, and is likely soon to make itself recognized as the vital question of the future. It is so far from being new, that, in a certain sense, it has divided mankind, almost from the remotest ages, but in the stage of progress into which the more civilized portions of the species have now entered, it presents itself under new conditions, and requires a different and more fundamental treatment.

The struggle between Liberty and Authority is the most conspicuous feature in the portions of history with which we are earliest familiar, particularly in that of Greece, Rome, and England. But in old times this contest was between subjects, or some classes of subjects, and the government. By liberty, was meant protection against the tyranny of the political rulers. The rulers were conceived (except in some of the popular governments of Greece) as in a necessarily antagonistic position to the people whom they ruled. They consisted of a governing One, or a governing tribe or caste, who derived their authority from inheritance or conquest; who, at all events, did not hold it at the pleasure of the governed, and whose supremacy men did not venture, perhaps did not desire, to contest, whatever precautions might be taken against its oppressive exercise. Their power was regarded as necessary, but also as highly dangerous; as a weapon which they would attempt to use against their subjects, no less than against external enemies. To prevent the weaker members of the community from being preyed upon by innumerable vultures, it was needful that there should be an animal of prey stronger than the rest, commissioned to keep them down. But as the king of the vultures would be no less bent upon preying on the flock than any of the minor harpies, it was indispensable to be in a perpetual attitude of defence against his beak and claws. The aim, therefore, of patriots, was to set limits to the power which the ruler should be suffered to exercise over the community; and this limitation was what they meant by liberty. It was attempted in two ways. First, by obtaining a recognition of certain immunities, called political liberties or rights, which it was to be regarded as a breach of duty in the ruler to infringe, and which, if he did infringe, specific resistance, or general rebellion, was held to be justifiable. A second, and generally a later expedient, was the establishment of constitutional checks; by which the consent of the community, or of a body of some sort supposed to represent its interests, was made a necessary condition to some of the more important acts of the governing power. To the first of these modes of limitation, the ruling power, in most European countries, was compelled, more or less, to submit. It was not so with the second; and to attain this, or when already in some degree possessed, to attain it more completely, became everywhere the principal object of the lovers of liberty. And so long as mankind were content to combat one enemy by another, and to be ruled by a master, on condition of being guaranteed more or less efficaciously against his tyranny, they did not carry their aspirations beyond this point.

A time, however, came, in the progress of human affairs, when men ceased to think it a necessity of nature that their governors should be an independent power, opposed in interest to themselves. It appeared to them much better that the various magistrates of the State should be their tenants or delegates, revocable at their pleasure. In that way alone, it seemed, could they have complete security that the powers of government would never be abused to their disadvantage. By degrees, this new demand for elective and temporary rulers became the prominent object of the exertions of the popular party, wherever any such party existed; and superseded, to a considerable extent, the previous efforts to limit the power of rulers. As the struggle proceeded for making the ruling power emanate from the periodical choice of the ruled, some persons began to think that too much importance had been attached to the limitation of the power itself. *That* (it might seem) was a resource against rulers whose interests were habitually opposed to those of the people. What was now wanted was, that the rulers should be identified with the people; that their interest and will should be the interest and will of the nation. The nation did not need to be protected against its own will. There was no fear of its tyrannizing over itself. Let the rulers be effectually responsible to it, promptly removable by it, and could afford to trust them with power of which it could itself dictate the use to be made. Their power was but the nation's own power, concentrated, and in a form convenient for exercise. This mode of thought, or rather perhaps of feeling, was common among the last generation of European liberalism, in the Continental section of which, it still apparently predominates. Those who admit any limit to what a government may do, except in the case of such governments as they think ought not to exist, stand out as brilliant exceptions among the political thinkers of the Continent. A similar tone of sentiment might by this time have been prevalent in our own country, if the circumstances which for a time encouraged it had continued unaltered.

But, in political and philosophical theories, as well as in persons, success discloses faults and infirmities which failure might have concealed from observation. The notion, that the people have no need to limit their power over themselves, might seem axiomatic, when popular government was a thing only dreamed about, or read of as having existed at some distant period of the past. Neither was that notion necessarily disturbed by such temporary aberrations as those of the French Revolution, the worst of which were the work of an usurping few, and which, in any case, belonged, not to the permanent working of popular institutions, but to a sudden and convulsive outbreak against monarchical and aristocratic despotism. In time, however, a democratic republic came to occupy a large portion of the earth's surface, and made itself felt as one of the most powerful members of the community of nations; and elective and responsible government became subject to the observations and criticisms which wait upon a great existing fact. It was now perceived that such phrases as "self-government," and "the power of the people over themselves," do not express the true state of the case. The "people" who exercise the power, are not always the same people with those over whom it is exercised, and the "self-government" spoken of, is not the government of each by himself, but of each by all the rest. The will of the people, moreover, practically means, the will of the most numerous or the most active *part* of the people; the majority, or those who succeed in making themselves accepted as the majority: the people, consequently, *may* desire to oppress a part of their number: and precautions are as much needed against this, as against any other abuse of power. The limitation, therefore, of the power of government over individuals, loses none of its importance when the holders of power are regularly accountable to the community, that is, to the strongest party therein. This view of things, recommending itself equally to the intelligence of thinkers and to the inclination of those important classes in European society to whose real or supposed interests democracy is adverse, has had no difficulty in establishing itself; and in political speculations "the tyranny of the majority" is now generally included among the evils against which society requires to be on its guard.

Like other tyrannies, the tyranny of the majority was at first, and is still vulgarly, held in dread, chiefly as operating through the acts of the public authorities. But reflecting persons perceived that when society is itself the tyrant—society collectively, over the separate individuals who compose it—its means of tyrannizing are not restricted to the acts which it may do by the hands of its political functionaries. Society can and does execute its own mandates: and if it issues wrong mandates instead of right, or any mandates at all in things with which it ought not to meddle, it practises a social tyranny more formidable than many kinds of political oppression, since, though not usually upheld by such extreme penalties, it leaves fewer means of escape, penetrating much more deeply into the details of life, and enslaving the soul itself. Protection, therefore, against the tyranny of the magistrate is not enough; there needs protection also against the tyranny of the prevailing opinion and feeling; against the tendency of society to impose, by other means than civil penalties, its own ideas and practices as rules of conduct on those who dissent from them; to fetter the development, and, if possible, prevent the formation, of any individuality not in harmony with its ways, and compel all characters to fashion themselves upon the model of its own. There is a limit to the legitimate interference of collective opinion with individual independence; and to find that limit, and maintain it against encroachment, is as indispensable to a good condition of human affairs, as protection against political despotism.

But though this proposition is not likely to be contested in general terms, the practical question, where to place the limit—how to make the fitting adjustment between individual independence and social control—is a subject on which nearly everything remains to be done. All that makes existence valuable to any one, depends on the enforcement of restraints upon the actions of other people. Some rules of conduct, therefore, must be imposed, by law in the first place, and by opinion on many things which are not fit subjects for the operation of law. What these rules should be, is the principal question in human affairs; but if we except a few of the most obvious cases, it is one of those which least progress has been made in resolving. No two ages, and scarcely any two countries, have decided it alike; and the decision of one age or country is a wonder to another. Yet the people of any given age and country no more suspect any difficulty in it, than if it were a subject on which mankind had always been agreed. The rules which obtain among themselves appear to them self-evident and self-justifying. This all but universal illusion is one of the examples of the magical influence of custom, which is not only, as the proverb says, a second nature, but is continually mistaken for the first. The effect of custom, in preventing any misgiving respecting the rules of conduct which mankind impose on one another, is all the more complete because the subject is one on which it is not generally considered necessary that reasons should be given, either by one person to others, or by each to himself. People are accustomed to believe, and have been encouraged in the belief by some who aspire to the character of philosophers, that their feelings, on subjects of this nature, are better than

reasons, and render reasons unnecessary. The practical principle which guides them
to their opinions on the regulation of human conduct, is the feeling in each person's
mind that everybody should be required to act as he, and those with whom he
sympathizes, would like them to act. No one, indeed, acknowledges to himself that
his standard of judgment is his own liking; but an opinion on a point of conduct,
not supported by reasons, can only count as one person's prefence; and if the
reasons, when given, are a mere appeal to a similar preference felt by other people,
it is still only many people's liking instead of one. To an ordinary man, however,
his own preference, thus supported, is not only a perfectly satisfactory reason, but
the only one he generally has for any of his notions of morality, taste, or propriety,
which are not expressly written in his religious creed; and his chief guide in the
interpretation even of that. Men's opinions, accordingly, on what is laudable or
blameable, are affected by all the multifarious causes which influence their wishes in
regard to the conduct of others, and which are as numerous as those which
determine their wishes on any other subject. Sometimes their reason—at other times
their prejudices or superstitions: often their social affections, not seldom their
antisocial ones, their envy or jealousy, their arrogance or contemptuousness: but
most commonly, their desires or fears for themselves—their legitimate or illegitimate
self-interest. Wherever there is an ascendant class, a large portion of the morality of
the country emanates from its class interests, and its feelings of class superiority.
The morality between Spartans and Helots, between planters and negroes, between
princes and subjects, between nobles and roturiers, between men and women, has
been for the most part the creation of these class interests and feelings: and the
sentiments thus generated, react in turn upon the moral feelings of the members of
the ascendant class, in their relations among themselves. Where, on the other hand,
a class, formerly ascendant, has lost its ascendency, or where its ascendency is
unpopular, the prevailing moral sentiments frequently bear the impress of an
impatient dislike of superiority. Another grand determining principle of the rules of
conduct, both in act and forbearance which have been enforced by law or opinion,
has been the servility of mankind towards the supposed preferences or aversions of
their temporal masters, or of their gods. This servility, though essentially selfish, is
not hypocrisy; it gives rise to perfectly genuine sentiments of abhorrence; it made
men burn magicians and heretics. Among so many baser influences, the general and
obvious interests of society have of course had a share, and a large one, in the
direction of the moral sentiments: less, however, as a matter of reason, and on their
own account, than as a consequence of the sympathies and antipathies which grew
out of them: and sympathies and antipathies which had little or nothing to do with
the interests of society, have made themselves felt in the establishment of moralities
with quite as great force.

The likings and dislikings of society, or of some powerful portion of it, are thus
the main thing which has practically determined the rules laid down for general
observance, under the penalties of law or opinion. And in general, those who have
been in advance of society in thought and feeling, have left this condition of things
unassailed in principle, however they may have come into conflict with it in some
of its details. They have occupied themselves rather in inquiring what things society

ought to like or dislike, than in questioning whether its likings or dislikings should be a law to individuals. They preferred endeavoring to alter the feelings of mankind on the particular points on which they were themselves heretical, rather than make common cause in defence of freedom, with heretics generally. The only case in which the higher ground has been taken on principle and maintained with consistency, by any but an individual here and there, is that of religious belief: a case instructive in many ways, and not least so as forming a most striking instance of the fallibility of what is called the moral sense: for the *odium theologicum*, in a sincere bigot, is one of the most unequivocal cases of moral feeling. Those who first broke the yoke of what called itself the Universal Church, were in general as little willing to permit difference of religious opinion as that church itself. But when the heat of the conflict was over, without giving a complete victory to any party, and each church or sect was reduced to limit its hopes to retaining possession of the ground it already occupied; minorities, seeing that they had no chance of becoming majorities, were under the necessity of pleading to those whom they could not convert, for permission to differ. It is accordingly on this battle-field, almost solely, that the right of the individual against society have been asserted on broad grounds of principle, and the claim of society to exercise authority over dissentients openly controverted. The great writers to whom the world owes what religious liberty it possesses, have mostly asserted freedom of conscience as an indefeasible right, and denied absolutely that a human being is accountable to others for his religious belief. Yet so natural to mankind is intolerance in whatever they really care about, that religious freedom has hardly anywhere been practically realized, except where religious indifference, which dislikes to have its peace disturbed by theological quarrels, has added its weight to the scale. In the minds of almost all religious persons, even in the most tolerant countries, the duty of toleration is admitted with tacit reserves. One person will bear with dissent in matters of church government, but not of dogma; another can tolerate everybody, short of a Papist or an Unitarian; another, every one who believes in revealed religion; a few extend their charity a little further, but stop at the belief in a God and in a future state. Wherever the sentiment of the majority is still genuine and intense, it is found to have abated little of its claim to be obeyed.

In England, from the peculiar circumstances of our political history, though the yoke of opinion is perhaps heavier, that of law is lighter, than in most other countries of Europe; and there is considerable jealousy of direct interference, by the legislative or the executive power with private conduct; not so much from any just regard for the independence of the individual, as from the still subsisting habit of looking on the government as representing an opposite interest to the public. The majority have not yet learnt to feel the power of the government their power, or its opinions their opinions. When they do so, individual liberty will probably be as much exposed to invasion from the government, as it already is from public opinion. But, as yet, there is a considerable amount of feeling ready to be called forth against any attempt of the law to control individuals in things in which they have not hitherto been accustomed to be controlled by it; and this with very little discrimination as to whether the matter is, or is not, within the legitimate sphere of legal control; insomuch that the feeling, highly salutary on the whole, is perhaps quite as often misplaced as well grounded in the particular instances of its application. There is, in fact, no recognized principle by which the propriety or impropriety of government interference is customarily tested. People decide according to their personal preferences. Some, whenever they see any good to be done, or evil to be remedied, would willingly instigate the government to undertake the business; while others prefer to bear almost any amount of social evil, rather than add one to the departments of human interests amenable to governmental control. And men range themselves on one or the other side in any particular case, according to this general direction of their sentiments; or according to the degree of interest which they feel in the particular thing which it is proposed that the government should do; or according to the belief they entertain that the government would, or would not, do it in the manner they prefer; but very rarely on account of any opinion to which they consistently adhere, as to what things are fit to be done by a government. And it seems to me that, in consequence of this absence of rule or principle, one side is at present as often wrong as the other; the interference of government is, with about equal frequency, improperly invoked and improperly condemned.

The object of this Essay is to assert one very simple principle, as entitled to govern absolutely the dealings of society with the individual in the way of compulsion and control, whether the means used by physical force in the form of legal penalties, or the moral coercion of public opinion. That principle is, that the sole end for which mankind are warranted, individually or collectively, in interfering with the liberty of action of any of their number, is self-protection. That the only purpose for which power can be rightfully exercised over any member of a civilized community, against his will, is to prevent harm to others. His own good, either physical or moral, is not a sufficient warrant. He cannot rightfully be compelled to do or forbear because it will be better for him to do so, because it will make him happier, because, in the opinions of others, to do so would be wise, or even right. There are good reasons for remonstrating with him, or reasoning with him, or persuading him, or entreating him, but not for compelling him, or visiting him with any evil, in case he do otherwise. To justify that, the conduct from which it is desired to deter him must be calculated to produce evil to some one else. The only part of the conduct of any one, for which he is amenable to society, is that which concerns others. In the part which merely concerns himself, his independence is, of right, absolute. Over himself, over his own body and mind, the individual is sovereign.

It is, perhaps, hardly necessary to say that this doctrine is meant to apply only to human beings in the maturity of their faculties. We are not speaking of children, or of young persons below the age which the law may fix as that of manhood or womanhood. Those who are still in a state to require being taken care of by others, must be protected against their own actions as well as against external injury. For the same reason, we may leave out of consideration those backward states of society in which the race itself may be considered as in its nonage. The early difficulties in the way of spontaneous progress are so great, that there is seldom any choice of means for overcoming them; and a ruler full of the spirit of improvement is warranted in the use of any expedients that will attain an end, perhaps otherwise unattainable. Despotism is a legitimate mode of government in dealing with barbarians, provided the end be their improvement, and the means justified by actually effecting that end. Liberty, as a principle, has no application to any state of things anterior to the time when mankind have become capable of being improved by free and equal discussion. Until then, there is nothing for them but implicit obedience to an Akbar or a Charlemagne, if they are so fortunate as to find one. But as soon as mankind have attained the capacity of being guided to their own improvement by conviction or persuasion (a period long since reached in all nations with whom we need here concern ourselves), compulsion, either in the direct form or in that of pains and penalties for non-compliance, is no longer admissible as a means to their own good, and justifiable only for the security of others.

It is proper to state that I forego any advantage which could be derived to my argument from the idea of abstract right, as a thing independent of utility. I regard utility as the ultimate appeal on all ethical questions; but it must be untility in the largest sense, grounded on the permanent interests of man as a progressive being. Those interests, I contend, authorize the subjection of individual spontaneity to external control, only in respect to those actions of each, which concern the interest of other people. If any one does an act hurtful to others, there is a *primâ facie* case for punishing him, by law, or, where legal penalties are not safely applicable, by general disapprobation. There are also many positive acts for the benefit of others, which he may rightfully be compelled to perform; such as, to give evidence in a court of justice; to bear his fair share in the common defence, or in any other joint work necessary to the interest of the society of which he enjoys the protection; and to perform certain acts of individual beneficence, such as saving a fellow creature's life, or interposing to protect the defenceless against ill-usage, things which whenever it is obviously a man's duty to do, he may rightfully be made responsible to society for not doing. A person may cause evil to others not only by his actions but by his inaction, and in either case he is justly accountable to them for the injury. The latter case, it is true, requires a much more cautious exercise of compulsion than the former. To make any one answerable for doing evil to others, is the rule; to make him answerable for not preventing evil, is, comparatively speaking, the exception. Yet there are many cases clear enough and grave enough to justify that exception. In all things which regard the external relations of the individual, he is *de jure* amenable to those whose interests are concerned, and if need be, to society as their protector. There are often good reasons for not holding him to the responsibility; but these reasons must arise from the special expediencies of the case: either because it is a kind of case in which he is on the whole likely to act better, when left to his own discretion, than when controlled in any way in which society have it in their power to control him; or because the attempt to exercise control would produce other evils, greater than those which it would prevent. When such reasons as these preclude the enforcement of responsibility, the conscience of the agent himself should step into the vacant judgment-seat, and protect those interests of others which have no external protection; judging himself all the more rigidly, because the case does not admit of his being made accountable to the judgment of his fellow-creatures.

But there is a sphere of action in which society, as distinguished from the individual, has, if any, only an indirect interest; comprehending all that portion of a person's life and conduct which affects only himself, or, if it also affects others, only with their free, voluntary, and undeceived consent and participation. When I say only himself, I mean directly, and in the first instance: for whatever affects himself, may affect others *through* himself; and the objection which may be grounded on this contingency, will receive consideration in the sequel. This, then, is the appropriate region of human liberty. It comprises, first, the inward domain of consciousness; demanding liberty of conscience, in the most comprehensive sense; liberty of thought and feeling; absolute freedom of opinion and sentiment on all subjects, practical or speculative, scientific, moral, or theological. The liberty of expressing and publishing opinions may seem to fall under a different principle, since it belongs to that part of the conduct of an individual which concerns other people; but, being almost of as much importance as the liberty of thought itself, and resting in great part on the same reasons, is practically inseparable from it. Secondly, the principle requires liberty of tastes and pursuits; of framing the plan of our life to suit our own character; of doing as we like, subject to such consequences as may follow; without impediment from our fellow-creatures, so long as what we do does not harm them, even though they should think our conduct foolish, perverse, or wrong. Thirdly, from this liberty of each individual, follows the liberty, within the same limits, of combination among individuals; freedom to unite, for any purpose not involving harm to others: the persons combining being supposed to be of full age, and not forced or deceived.

No society in which these liberties are not, on the whole, respected, is free, whatever may be its form of government; and none is completely free in which they do not exist absolute and unqualified. The only freedom which deserves the name, is that of pursuing our own good in our own way, so long as we do not attempt to deprive others of theirs, or impede their efforts to obtain it. Each is the proper guardian of his own health, whether bodily, or mental and spiritual. Mankind are greater gainers by suffering each other to live as seems good to themselves, than by compelling each to live as seems good to the rest.

Though this doctrine is anything but new, and, to some persons, may have the air of a truism, there is no doctrine which stands more directly opposed to the general tendency of existing opinion and practice. Society has expended fully as much effort in the attempt (according to its lights) to compel people to conform to its notions of personal, as of social excellence. The ancient commonwealths thought themselves entitled to practise, and the ancient philosophers countenanced, the regulation of every part of private conduct by public authority, on the ground that the State had a deep interest in the whole bodily and mental discipline of every one of its citizens; a mode of thinking which may have been admissible in small republics surrounded by powerful enemies, in constant peril of being subverted by foreign attack or internal commotion, and to which even a short interval of relaxed energy and self-command might so easily be fatal, that they could not afford to wait for the salutary permanent effects of freedom. In the modern world, the greater size of political communities, and above all, the separation between the spiritual and temporal authority (which placed the direction of men's consciences in other hands than those which controlled their worldly affairs), prevented so great an interference by law in the details of private life; but the engines of moral repression have been wielded more strenuously against divergence from the reigning opinion in self-regarding, than even in social matters; religion, the most powerful of the elements which have entered into the formation of moral feeling, having almost always been governed either by the ambition of a hierarchy, seeking control over every department of human conduct, or by the spirit of Puritanism. And some of those modern reformers who have placed themselves in strongest opposition to the religions of the past, have been noway behind either churches or sects in their assertion of the right of spiritual domination: M. Comte, in particular, whose social system, as unfolded in his *Traité de Politique Positive*, aims at establishing (though by moral more than by legal appliances) a despotism of society over the individual, surpassing anything contemplated in the political ideal of the most rigid disciplinarian among the ancient philosophers.

Apart from the peculiar tenets of individual thinkers, there is also in the world at large an increasing inclination to stretch unduly the powers of society over the individual, both by the force of opinion and even by that of legislation: and as the tendency of all the changes taking place in the world is to strengthen society, and diminish the power of the individual, this encroachment is not one of the evils which tend spontaneously to disappear, but, on the contrary, to grow more and more formidable. The disposition of mankind, whether as rulers or as fellow-citizens, to impose their own opinions and inclinations as a rule of conduct on others, is so energetically supported by some of the best and by some of the worst feelings incident to human nature, that it is hardly ever kept under restraint by anything but want of power; and as the power is not declining, but growing, unless a strong barrier of moral conviction can be raised against the mischief, we must expect, in the present circumstances of the world, to see it increase.

"FREEDOM COMES THROUGH
TRADITION AND ORDER"

Russell Kirk

Civilized man lives by authority; without some reference to authority, indeed, no form of human existence is possible. Also man lives by prescription—that is, by ancient custom and usage, and the rights which usage and custom have established.

Without just authority and respected prescription, the pillars of any tolerable civil social order, true freedom is not possible.

For some time it has been fashionable to deride authority and prescription—though a good many people have been experiencing a change of heart recently. "Authority," in the vocabulary of what has been called "the Freudian ethic," has meant arbitrary restraint; and prescription has been equated with cultural lag and superstition. But the consequences of these emancipated notions have been unpalatable. A generation of young people reared according to "permissive" tenets has grown up bored, sullen, and in revolt against the very lack of order which was supposed to ensure the full development of their personalities. And a world lulled by slogans about absolute liberty and perpetual peace has found itself devoured by thoroughgoing tyranny and increasing violence. If men are to exist together at all, some authority must govern them; if they throw off traditional authority, the authority of church and precept and old educational disciplines and parents, then very soon they are compelled to submit to some new and merciless authority. "If you will not have God—and he is a jealous God—" Mr. T. S. Eliot observes, "then you should pay your respects to Hitler or Stalin." Authority and prescription lacking, order cannot subsist. If the authority is unjust, and the prescription merely the decree of some new domination, then the social order will have small place for freedom. Genuinely ordered freedom is the only sort of liberty worth having: freedom made possible by order within the soul and order within the state. Anarchic freedom, liberty defiant of authority and prescription, is merely the subhuman state of the wolf and the shark, or the punishment of Cain, with his hand against every man's.

So if people really desire genuine freedom, they need to know genuine authority. "Authority" is not the policeman's baton. "Conscience is an authority," Newman writes in his essay on John Keble; "the Bible is an authority; such is the Church; such is Antiquity; such are the words of the wise, such are historical memories, such are legal saws and state maxims; such are proverbs; such are sentiments, presages, and prepossessions." Authority, in fine, is the ground upon which prudent action must be performed. If a man acknowledges no authority, he sets himself up as Cain, and before long he is struck down by nemesis, which follows upon *hubris*.

Political authority, the claims and powers of a legitimate state, though an important part of this complex of authority which rules our lives, is no more than a part. Sometimes authorities conflict; indeed, most of the great disputes of history have been, in essence, controversies over the higher source of authority. And such debates never are wholly and finally resolved. Now and again, for instance, the authoritative claims of church and state cannot well be reconciled, and then great trouble results. Similarly, the authority of faith and the authority of reason collide from age to age. In such clashes, the conscientious man endeavors, according to what light is given him, to determine what representatives of authority have claimed too much; but he is foolish if, despairing, he forsakes authority altogether.

Human nature being irremediably flawed, so that all of us in some degree rebel against the people and the institutions to which we owe most, there is in every man a certain impulse to make himself God: that is, to cast of all authority but his own lust and whim. From this vice comes the corrupting influence of total power upon even the best of natures. The rebellion of Lucifer is the symbol of this ancient anarchic impulse—the passion for overthrowing the just authority of God, that upon the vacant throne of authority the rebel may make himself absolute. Yet the doom of such risings is as sure as Lucifer's. For a grown man to rebel against all authority is as ludicrous as for a three-year-old child to defy his parents: whether they are good parents or bad, he can live scarcely a day without them.

From its beginnings, the liberal movement of the nineteenth century had within it this fatuous yearning for the destruction of all authority. Liberalism also possessed some good qualities; but it never has recovered from this congenital defiance of authority and prescription. The early liberals were convinced that once they should overthrow established governments and churches, supplanting them by rational and egalitarian and purely secular institutions, the principal problems of the human condition would be near solution. Poverty, ignorance, disease, and war might then be terminated, once enlightened self-interest, popular suffrage, and utilitarian public policies had triumphed. One had only to fight clear of the Bad Old Days and the dead weight of superstition. Abolish the old Authorities, and sweetness and light will reign.

Yet the triumph of liberalism endured little more than half a century; by the 1880's, the individualism of the early liberals was being transmuted into socialism, a process easily traced in the life of John Stuart Mill. Liberalism had begun, defying authority and prescription, by breaking all sorts of ancient ties and obligations, but the latter-day Liberal, in Santayana's phrase, relaxes no bond except the marriage knot. Increasingly, though implicitly, Liberals came to accept a new authority, that of the omnicompetent welfare state; they continued to repudiate authority only in the sphere of private life.

Just how archaic and unreal, politically, latter-day Liberalism has become is sufficiently illustrated by a conference of the English Liberal Party in the summer of 1961. Three principal resolutions were proposed: to abolish the monarchy, to abolish the hereditary element in the House of Lords, and to expand the welfare state. Though the first proposal was defeated after discussion, the other two were adopted enthusiastically; and so the conference adjourned, its members satisfied that they had shown the English nation how to solve its difficulties in the twentieth century. To anyone but a Liberal ideologue, it is clear enough that abolition of the British monarchy would accomplish nothing but to destroy the symbol of justice and order in Britain; that to destroy the hereditary element in the House of Lords would only injure the most serious deliberative body in the world; and that to extend the British welfare state would do no less than to finish Liberalism altogether, since that would mean certainly complete socialism, and probably the end of the British constitution and of British prosperity. So much for the eccentricities of a dying party.

Though they have abandoned nearly all their original political program, still the Liberals of the twentieth century cling to their general detestation of authority; but this detestation has shifted from the political sphere to the moral and social. The writings of an American latter-day Liberal, a disciple of J. S. Mill, Mr. David

Riesman, illustrate this. Professor Riesman recognizes the decay of authority among us and is confusedly disturbed by it. He gives up for lost the "tradition-directed individual"—that is, the man with some respect for authority and tradition—and sheds few tears at his passing. What worries Mr. Riesman more, the "inner-directed individual"—that is, the typical active nineteenth-century liberal—also seems to be not long for this world. So there remain the "other-directed"—that is, the modern masses who take for their norms whatever their neighbors seem to be doing—and some scattered and harebrained dissidents, "anomics," masterless men who meaninglessly and futilely defy the great tendencies of their time. Mr. Riesman's only hope is in the possibility of a number of "autonomous" men, uncontrolled by tradition, liberal "inner direction," or the fads and foibles of the hour: rootless persons who somehow, by wishing it, may become superior to the crowd of other-directed about them. No hope could be more ridiculous than this last. Also Mr. Riesman would like to see women "deprivatized"—that is, more footloose—and to see all who would be autonomous spend much time upon "consumership" and other diversions.

One may as well laugh as cry. To such an intellectual and moral bankruptcy have come even the most intelligent of twentieth-century Liberals. Having denied the very existence of sound and just authority, having scoffed at the wisdom of our ancestory, Liberalism is altogether cut loose from such moorings as once it had. Without some principle of authority, life becomes meaningless, and political and intellectual factions slip into the dust-bin of history.

If authority, then—however unfashionable in recent years—remains ineluctable for civilization and for any truly human existence, how do men find such authority? In a number of ways; but of these, the means for most men is what we call prescription or tradition.

Prescription, socially and politically speaking, means those ways and institutions and rights prescribed by long—sometimes immemorial—usage. Tradition (a word until the end of the eighteenth century applied almost exclusively to Christian beliefs not set down in Scripture) means received opinions, convictions religious and moral and political and aesthetic passed down from generation to generation, so that they are accepted by most men as a matter of course. I have discussed the nature of tradition and prescription at some length in my book *Beyond the Dreams of Avarice.*

Fulbert of Chartres and Gerbert of Rheims, those two grand Schoolmen, said that we moderns are dwarfs standing upon the shoulders of giants. We see so far only because we are elevated upon the accomplishment of our ancestors; and if we break with ancestral wisdom, we at once are plunged into the ditch of ignorance. All that we have and know is founded upon the experience of the race. As Burke put it, "The individual is foolish, but the species is wise." Men have no right, Burke said, to risk the very existence of their nation and their civilization upon experiments in morals and politics; for each man's private capital of intelligence is petty; it is only when a man draws upon the bank and capital of the ages, the wisdom of our ancestors, that he can act wisely. Without resort to tradition and prescription, we are left with merely our vanity and the brief and partial experience of our evanescent lives. "What shadows we are, and what shadows we pursue!"

G. K. Chesterton expressed much the same truth when he wrote of "the democracy of the dead." When we decide great questions in our time, he held, we ought to count not merely the votes of our contemporaries, but the opinions of many generations of men—and particularly the convictions of the wise men who have preceded us in time. By trial and error, by revelation, by the insights of men of genius, mankind has acquired, slowly and painfully, over thousands of years, a knowledge of human nature and of the civil social order which no one individual possibly can supplant by private rationality.

This is true especially in matters of morals, politics, and taste; but in considerable degree it is true also even in modern science and technology. Once a student objected to me that surely enlightened modern man could work out rationally a much better system of morals and politics than the hodgepodge we have inherited from blundering ancestors. But I asked this student if, without consulting senior technicians, books, and authority generally, he thought he could construct, unaided, an automobile—if, indeed, he thought that he personally, even with all sorts of advice, could make an automobile at all. He confessed that he could not; and it began to be borne in upon him to construct, *carte blanche*, a system of morals and politics that really would work might be an undertaking more difficult still.

So even the most gifted of men, and always the great mass of human beings, must fall back upon tradition and prescription if they are to act at all in this world. At the very least, it saves a great deal of time. It is conceivable that, if I set myself to it, I might calculate for myself the circumference of the earth, quite independently of previous calculations. But since I have no strong mathematical gifts, it is improbable that my calculations would be more accurate than those of the present authorities; and it seems almost certain that my result would be quite the same as the present calculation of the earth's circumference; so I would have spent months or years of a brief life in trying to gain what I could have had for the asking. If we are to accomplish anything in this life, we must take much for granted; as Newman said, if one had to make the choice, it would be better to believe all things than to doubt all things. In the matter of the earth's circumference, nearly all of us are much better off if we simply accept the "traditional" or "authoritative" calculation.

This is even more true of moral and social first principles. Only through prescription and tradition, only by habitual acceptance of just and sound authority, can men acquire knowledge of the norms for humanity. Authority tells us that murder is wrong; prescription immemorially has visited severe punishments upon murderers; tradition presents us with an ancient complex of tales of the evil consequences of murder. Now a man who thinks his private petty rationality superior to the wisdom of our ancestors may undertake experiments in murder, with a view to testing these old irrational scruples; but the results of such experiments are sure to be disagreeable for everyone concerned, including the researcher; and that experimenter has no right to be surprised if we hang him by the neck until he is quite dead. For if men flout norm and convention, life becomes intolerable. It is through respect for tradition and prescription, and recourse to those sources of knowledge, that the great mass of men acquire a tolerable understanding of norms and conventions, of the rules by which private and social existence is made tolerable.

A norm is an enduring standard. It is a law of our nature, which we ignore at our peril. It is a rule of human conduct and a measure of public virtue. The norm does not signify the average, the median, the mean, the mediocre. The norm is not the conduct of the average sensual man. A norm is not simply a measure of average performance within a group. There exists law for man, and law for thing; the late Alfred Kinsey notwithstanding, the norm for the wasp and the snake is not the norm for man. A norm has an objective existence: though men may ignore or forget a norm, still that norm does not cease to be, nor does it cease to influence men. A man apprehends a norm or fails to apprehend it, but he does not create or destroy norms.

The sanction for obedience to norms must come from a source other than private advantage and rationality—from a source more than human, indeed. Men do not submit long to their own creations. Standards erected out of expediency will be demolished soon enough, also out of expediency. Either norms have an existence independent of immediate utility, or they are mere fictions. If men assume that norms are merely the pompous fabrications of their ancestors, got up to serve the interests of a faction or an age, then every rising generation will challenge the principles of personal and social order and will learn wisdom only through agony. For half a century, we have been experiencing the consequences of a moral and social neoterism.

"Goodnatured unambitious men are cowards when they have no religion." So, in *Back to Methuselah*, writes Bernard Shaw. "They are dominated and exploited not only by greedy and often halfwitted and half-alive weaklings who will do anything for cigars, champagne, motor cars, and the more childish and selfish uses of money, but by able and sound administrators who can do nothing else with them than dominate and exploit them. Government and exploitation become synonymous under such circumstances; and the world is finally ruled by the childish, the brigands, and the blackguards." (One may acknowledge the acuteness of this insight without subscribing to the curious religion, or quasi-religion, which Shaw sets forth—half soberly, half facetiously—in *Back to Methuselah*.)

As a gloss upon this, one may say also that the average good-natured unambitious man is a coward also if he lacks—even though retaining some religious feelings— "that wise prejudice" by which "a man's virtue becomes his habit," in Burke's phrase. If his life is regulated, almost unconsciously, upon certain received opinions concerning justice and injustice, charity and selfishness, freedom and servitude, truth and falsehood, he will behave habitually with some degree of resolution and courage; but if he is all at sea in a latter-day Liberalism and moral relativism, in which any point of view or mode of conduct has something to be said for it, then he will be unnerved when the test comes. Acting customarily upon tradition and prescription, he will not feel alone; the democracy of the dead will endorse him. But acting without norms, he must be, ordinarily, either a coward or a brute in any personal or civic crisis.

A man who accepts tested authority, and acknowledges the beneficent influence of prescription and tradition, is conventional; but he is not servile. Conventions are the means by which obedience to norms is inculcated in society. Conventions are compacts by which we agree to respect one another's dignity and rights. A high degree of respect for convention is quite consonant with a high development of individual personality, and even of eccentricity. Many of the great "characters," indeed, are the great champions of convention; the names of Samuel Johnson and Benjamin Disraeli, of John Adams, John Randolph, and Theodore Roosevelt may suffice for illustration. There exists no necessary opposition between strong outward indifference to foible and strong inward loyalty to norms. A man of strong character who accepts just authority and its works will be meek—but meek only as Moses: that is, obedient to the will of God, but unflinching against human tyrants.

The good citizen is a law-abiding traditionalist: so the politics of Virgil have been summed up. If men are courageous or virtuous, ordinarily this is because they are persons of good moral *habits*: that is, they act habitually, and almost unthinkingly, upon certain premises they have learnt from infancy, through force of example and through formal instruction. This is what Burke meant when he wrote that prejudice is the wisdom of unlettered men. They draw their strength from acceptance of tradition and prescription.

Now it does not follow that an unquestioning acceptance of received opinions and long-established usage will of itself suffice to solve all personal and public problems. The world does change; a certain sloughing off of tradition and prescription is at work in any vigorous society, and a certain adding to the bulk of received opinion goes on from age to age. We cannot live precisely by the rules of our distant forefathers, in all matters. But, again to employ a phrase of Burke's, the fact that a belief or an institution has long been accepted by men, and seems to have exerted a beneficent influence, establishes in its favor "a legitimate presumption." If we feel inclined to depart from old ways, we ought to do so only after very sober consideration of ultimate consequences. Authority, prescription, and tradition undergo in every generation a certain filtering process, by which the really archaic is discarded; yet we ought to be sure that we actually are filtering, and not merely letting our heritage run down the drain.

Similarly, the general principles and valuable institutions which we have inherited from past generations must be applied and utilized with prudence; there the exercise of right reason by the leaders of any society sets to work. We possess moral norms, the Decalogue, for instance, but the way in which we observe those norms must be determined in our time by the circumstances in which we find ourselves, so that wise men in our age must reconcile exigency and enduring standard. We possess tested political institutions; but for those institutions to endure, now and then reform is essential, lest the institutions atrophy. Thus Burke's model of a statesman is one who combines with an ability to reform a disposition to preserve.

Prescription and tradition, then, cannot stand forever if the living do not sustain them by vigorous application and prudent reform. But it is equally true that lively action and ingenious reform are mere ropes of sand, unless linked with the wisdom of the ages.

One instance of the abiding value of inherited convictions—beliefs that have their origin both in the experience of the race and in the reasoning of men of genius, but have acquired through subtle processes the status of popular prejudices—is the idea of justice, as expressed by Plato and Cicero. The great classical philosophers of politics argued that justice resides in this: to each his own. Every man, ideally, ought to receive the things that best suit his own nature. Men's talents and appetites vary greatly from individual to individual; therefore a society is unjust which treats all men as if they were uniform, or which allots to one sort of nature rights and duties that properly belong to other sorts of human beings.

This concept of justice has entered deeply into the ethics, the jurisprudence, and even the imaginative literature of what is called "Western civilization." It still is a profound influence upon many men and women who never have read Cicero or Plato. It creates a prejudice against radical egalitarianism, which would reduce all men to a single mode of existence. It has inculcated a sound prejudice in favor of *order*: that is, a society marked by a variety of rewards and duties, a commonwealth in which, as Burke said, all men "have equal rights; but not to equal things." This theory underlies, for example, the British and American constitutions.

Nowadays this classical idea of justice is challenged by the Marxist doctrine that order should be abolished: all human beings should be treated as identical units, and compulsory equality of condition enforced. When the average American or Englishman is brought face to face with Marxist demands for the overthrow of prescriptive order and the establishment of a society without demarcations, he may not be able to meet the Marxist propagandist with a privately reasoned defense of variety and constitutionalism; but he resists the Marxist doctrine out of a feeling that what the Communist proposes somehow is fundamentally unjust. The average American or Englishman remains a law-abiding traditionalist, even in this day of giddy technological and industrial alteration; he takes it for granted that we were not born yesterday; that we have no right to cast away our tested civil social order; that monotonous uniformity of condition is contrary to deep ancient human aspirations; that Communism flies in the face of the nature of things. And because he is the heir to a great tradition, he knows something of the character of justice, and he is resolute despite the threats and seductions of the radical innovator.

"The great mysterious incorporation of the human race" is, as Burke said, a contract of sorts: but a contract between the divine and the human natures, and among the dead, the living, and those yet unborn. We know something of the terms of that eternal contract of society through traditions and prescriptions. Our obedience to norms, to true and just authority in morals and politics, keeps that immortal contract alive. And that obedience secures us all in ordered freedom.

Government is instituted to secure justice and order, through respect for legitimate authority; and if we ask from government more than this, we begin to imperil justice and order. It is one of the saddest illusions of the Liberal era, the notion that political manipulation can make men happy. But some forms of government can succeed in making men miserable. So I venture to suggest here the general lineaments of the kind of government which seems reasonably consonant with the general welfare. I think that here we need to refer to two principles. The first principle is that a good government allows the more energetic natures among a people to fulfill their promise, while ensuring that these persons shall not tyrannize over the mass of men. The second principle is that in every state the best possible—or least baneful—form of government is one in accord with the traditions and prescriptive ways of its people. Beyond these two general principles, there is no rule of politics which may be applied, uniformly and universally, with safety.

Even Mr. Riesman has rediscovered the old truth that men are not created equal; they are created different. Variety, not uniformity, gives any nation vigor and hope. Thus my first principle of good government—for which I am much indebted to Professor Eric Voegelin—has a hearing once more, though the overmastering tendency of the past century and a half has been social egalitarianism. "One man is as good as another, or maybe a little better": this secular dogma has done mischief to the preservation or establishment of good government. Equality in political power has tended to lead to equality of condition. "Everybody belongs to everybody else"—this is the motto of society in Huxley's *Brave New World*; and that society is a life in death. For these assumptions are thorough falsehoods. One man is not as good as another, and everyone does not belong to everyone else. The first fallacy is the denial of Christian morals, the second the denial of the Christian idea of personality.

Aye, men are created different; and a government which ignores this law becomes an unjust government, for it sacrifices nobility to mediocrity; it pulls down the aspiring natures to gratify the inferior natures. This degradation injures humanity in two ways. First, it frustrates the natural longing of talented persons to realize their potentialities; it leaves the better men dissatisfied with themselves and their nation, and they sink into boredom; it impedes any improvement of the moral, intellectual, and material condition, in terms of quality, of mankind. Second, it adversely affects the well-being, late or soon, of the mass of men; for, deprived of responsible leadership and example, the innumerable men and women destined to walk in the routine ways of life suffer in the tone of their civilization, and in their material condition. A government which converts into a secular dogma the Christian mystery of moral equality, in short, is hostile towards human existence.

Remember that there are two parts to this political principle: not only should a just government recognize the rights of the more talented natures, but it should recognize the right of the majority of men not to be agitated and bullied by these aspiring talents. The prudent statesman endeavors to maintain a balance between these two claims. There have been ages in which the aristocracy, natural or hereditary, has usurped the whole governance of life, demanding of the average man a tribute and an obedience which deprive the majority of their desire to live by custom and prescription and often damage their material interests. Such a regime, indifferent to the welfare of the majority, is as bad a government as a domination indifferent to the claims of the talented minority. But nowadays the danger is not that the stronger natures—and I refer to moral and intellectual qualities, not merely to domineering and acquisitive abilities—will lord it over an abused majority; rather, the curse of our time is what Ortega called "the revolt of the masses," the threat that mediocrity may trample underfoot every just elevation of mind and character, every hopeful talent for leadership and improvement. Therefore the sagacious statesman of our age must be more acutely concerned with the preservation of the rights of the talented minority than with the extension of the rights of the crowd.

A domination which confounds popular government with equality of moral worth, equality of intellect, or equality of condition is a bad government. For a good government respects the claims of extraordinary character. It respects the right of the contemplative to his solitude. It respects the right of the practical leader to take an honest initiative in the affairs of the commonwealth. It respects the right of the inventor to his ingenuity, the right of the manufacturer or merchant to the rewards of his industry, the right of the thrifty man to keep his savings and bequeath them to his heirs. It respects such claims and rights, this good government, because in the enjoyment of these rights, and in the performance of the duties to which these rights are joined, men fulfill themselves; and a considerable measure of justice—"to each his own"—is attained.

Today the balance between the claims of the unusual natures and the ordinary natures, in some ages overthrown to the advantage of aspiring talents, is injured rather by the extortionate demands of a doctrinaire egalitarianism. Communist Russia is the most thorough example of the triumph of this degradation of the democratic dogma. I am aware that Soviet Russia is governed by a clique of party intriguers and successful administrators, paying little more than lip service to their own secular dogma of egalitarianism; yet this does not alter the fact that, obedient to the ideology of dialectical materialism, the Soviets have suppressed the claims of the nobler natures to do the work natural to them. What we see in the new élite of Communism is not a predominance of the higher natures, but a domination of Jacobin fanatics, devoid, nearly all of them, of high moral endowments. This is the regime of a host of squalid oligarchs. Among them are no prophets, and no poets; the only qualification for entry into this élite is ruthless cunning in the struggle for pure power. Not the higher natures, but the lower, in terms of moral attainment and independence of mind, are recognized and rewarded by the Soviets.

Now it is not American "democracy," as such, that stands at the antipodes from the Soviet undertaking; American moral and political tradition, rather, and American constitutionalism are the forces of resistance. A political democracy may attain a tolerable balance between the rights of the talented natures and the claims of the average natures. But it also is possible for a monarchy to achieve that balance, or an aristocracy, or some other frame of government. Respect for natural and prescriptive rights is peculiar to no single set of political institutions.

Yet the kind of government which seems most likely to appreciate and defend the claims of either interest in the commonwealth is what Aristotle called a "polity," a balancing and checking of classes in society. The United States remain, in considerable degree, a polity; *pure* democracy was not intended by the founders of this Republic, and it has not yet triumphed among us. It ought not to triumph. For the good government does not grow up from mere protection of entrenched property, nor yet from the victory of the proletariat.

A prudent government, within the bounds set by decency and good order, leaves every man to consult his own humor. It does not attempt to force the happiness of the statistical Bentham upon the romantic Coleridge; for one man's happiness, even among the talented natures, is another man's misery. By a salutary neglect, this government allows private happiness to take care of itself. One may call this prudent and tolerant government "democracy," if one wishes, though I think that is twisting the word. I call it simply a government which prefers principle to ideology, variety to uniformity, balance to omnipotence.

Now for my second principle of good government: that a government should accord with the traditions and the prescriptive ways of a people. This is the view of Montesquieu and of Burke. A good government is no artificial contrivance, no invention of coffeehouse philosophers, got up upon *a priori* abstractions to suit the intellectual mood of an hour. Governments hastily designed upon theories of pure reason ordinarily are wretched dominations. The longest-lived of these poor governments has been that of modern France, which never has recovered from the hacking and chopping that the constitution of French society received at the hands of rigid metaphysicians from 1789 onward. Much more evanescent, because they had a smaller reservoir of tradition to exhaust, were the artificial governments set up in central and southern Europe after the First World War. Now the good government, very different from these, is the growth of centuries of social experience. It has been called organic; I prefer the analogy "spiritual." Trusting to the wisdom of our ancestors and the experience of the nation, it puts its faith in precedent, prescription, historical trial and error, and consensus of opinion over the generations. Not infatuated with neatness, it prefers the strength and majesty of the Gothic style. The government of Britain, because of its age and success, is our best example of this type. And the government of the United States is nearly as good an instance of the triumph of this principle that society is an august continuity and essence, held together by veneration, prescription, and tradition.

Nominally, of course, we Americans created our Federal Constitution by deliberate action, within the space of a few months. But in actuality that formal constitution, and our state constitutions, chiefly put down on paper what already existed and was accepted in public opinion: beliefs and institutions long established in the colonies, and drawn from centuries of English experience with parliaments, the common law, and the balancing of orders and interests in a realm. Respect for precedent and prescription governed the minds of the Founders of the Republic. We appealed to the prescriptive liberties of Englishmen, not to *liberté, egalité, fraternité*; and the philosophical and moral structure of our civil order was rooted in the Christian faith, not in the worship of Reason.

The success of the American and British governments, I am suggesting, is produced by their preference for growth, experience, tradition, and prescription over a closet-metaphysician's grand design. The great lessons of politics are taught a people through their historical experience; no nation can sever itself from its past and still prosper, for the dead alone give us energy; and whatever constitution has been long accepted in a nation, that constitution—amended, perhaps, but essentially the same—is as good as a people can expect. True, that constitution may be improved, or restored; but if it is discarded altogether, like wastepaper, every order in society suffers terribly.

The American and British constitutions have worked well; but, being living essences, they cannot easily be transplanted to other states. One of the cardinal errors of the French revolutionaries was their endeavor to remake France upon the model of what they thought English politics to be. Though any people have something to learn from the experiences of any other, still there exists no single constitution calculated to work successfully everywhere. For the political institutions of a people grow out of their religion, their moral habits, their economy, even their literature; political institutions are but part of an intricate structure of civilization, the roots of which go infinitely deep. Attempts to impose borrowed institutions upon an alien culture generally are disastrous, though some decades, or even generations, may be required for the experiment to run its unlucky course. Randolph of Roanoke, in opposing Clay's design for encouraging revolutions upon the American pattern, cried out in his sardonic way, "You can no more make liberty out of Spanish matter than you can make a frigate out of a bundle of pine saplings." Though this is somewhat hard upon the Spaniards, it remains true that parliamentary government, Anglo-American style, rarely has been secure in Spanish lands; Spaniards' liberty, when they enjoy it, is secured by different institutions and customs.

Yet still our political theory and our foreign policy are plagued by the delusion that some domination of American constitutions and manners will be established universally—the American Liberal's conviction, in Santayana's sentence, that "the nun must not remain a nun, and China shall not keep its wall." This fond hope never will be realized. For individuals, as Chesterton said, are happy only when they are their own potty little selves; and this is as true of nations. To impose the American constitution upon all the world would not render all the world happy; to the contrary, our constitution would work in few lands and would make many men miserable in short order. States, like men, must find their own paths to order and justice and freedom; and usually those paths are ancient and winding ways, and their signposts are Authority, Tradition, Prescription. Without the legal institutions, rooted in common and Roman law, from which it arose, the American constitutional system would be unworkable. Well, take up this constitutional system, abstractly, and set it down, as an exotic plant, in Persia or Guinea or the Congo, where the common law (English style) and the Roman law are unknown, and where the bed of justice rests upon the Koran or upon hereditary chieftainship—why, the thing cannot succeed. Such an undertaking may disrupt the old system of justice, and may even supplant it, for a time; but in the long run, the traditional morals, habits, and establishments of a people, confirmed by their historical experience, will reassert themselves, and the innovation will be undone—if that culture is to survive at all.

The Asiatic or African who attempts to convert himself and his nation, abruptly and wholesale, to Western ways must end disillusioned; we will be fortunate if he does not end in violent reaction. Like the Lebanon Arab in Cunninghame-Graham's story *Sidi bu Zibbula*, he will crouch upon his dunghill, saying, "I have seen your Western cities; and the dung is better."

Good government is no mass-produced article. Order and justice and freedom are found in divers ways, but they cannot be divorced from the historical experience of a people. Theory divorced from experience is infinitely dangerous, the plaything of the ideologue, the darling dagger of the energumen. Though their social functions may be similar, the justice of the peace cannot supplant the *cadi*; and no James Mill, however learned, can rightfully make laws for India.

I am saying this: far from being right to revolt against the past, a people are fortunate if their political order maintains a tolerable degree of freedom and justice for the different interests in society. We are not made for perfect things, and if ever we found ourselves under the domination of the "perfect" government, we would make mincemeat of it, from sheer boredom. From just authority, from respect for our cultural and moral and political heritage, comes genuine civil freedom. It was something of this sort, I suppose, that St. Paul meant when he declared, "The powers that be are ordained of God." With authority and prescription, a people may work their way towards the freedom of the true polity. Without authority and prescription, they are afflicted by the devastating "freedom" of the Congo.

"CONTEMPORARY TECHNOLOGICAL SOCIETY IS REMOVING MAN'S FREEDOM"

Herbert Marcuse

A comfortable, smooth, reasonable, democratic unfreedom prevails in advanced industrial civilization, a token of technical progress. Indeed, what could be more rational than the suppression of individuality in the mechanization of socially necessary but painful performances; the concentration of individual enterprises in more effective, more productive corporations; the regulation of free competition among unequally equipped economic subjects; the curtailment of prerogatives and national sovereignties which impede the international organization of resources. That this technological order also involves a political and intellectual coordination may be a regrettable and yet promising development.

The rights and liberties which were such vital factors in the origins and earlier stages of industrial society yield to a higher stage of this society: they are losing their traditional rationale and content. Freedom of thought, speech, and conscience were—just as free enterprise, which they served to promote and protect—essentially *critical* ideas, designed to replace an obsolescent material and intellectual culture by a more productive and rational one. Once institutionalized, these rights and liberties shared the fate of the society of which they had become an integral part. The achievement cancels the premises.

To the degree to which freedom from want, the concrete substance of all freedom, is becoming a real possibility, the liberties which pertain to a state of lower productivity are losing their former content. Independence of thought, autonomy, and the right to political opposition are being deprived of their basic critical function in a society which seems increasingly capable of satisfying the needs of the individuals through the way in which it is organized. Such a society may justly demand acceptance of its principles and institutions, and reduce the opposition to the discussion and promotion of alternative policies *within* the status quo. In this respect, it seems to make little difference whether the increasing satisfaction of needs is accomplished by an authoritarian or a non-authoritarian system. Under the conditions of a rising standard of living, non-conformity with the system itself appears to be socially useless, and the more so when it entails tangible economic and political disadvantages and threatens the smooth operation of the whole. Indeed, at least in so far as the necessities of life are involved, there seems to be no reason why the production and distribution of goods and services should proceed through the competitive concurrence of individual liberties.

Freedom of enterprise was from the beginning not altogether a blessing. As the liberty to work or to starve, it spelled toil, insecurity, and fear for the vast majority of the population. If the individual were no longer compelled to prove himself on the market, as a free economic subject, the disappearance of this kind of freedom would be one of the greatest achievements of civilization. The technological processes of mechanization and standardization might release individual energy into a yet uncharted realm of freedom beyond necessity. The very structure of human existence would be altered; the individual would be liberated from the work world's imposing upon him alien needs and alien possibilities. The individual would be free to exert autonomy over a life that would be his own. If the productive apparatus could be organized and directed toward the satisfaction of the vital needs, its control might well be centralized; such control would not prevent individual autonomy, but render it possible.

This is a goal within the capabilities of advanced industrial civilization, the "end" of technological rationality. In actual fact, however, the contrary trend operates: the apparatus imposes its economic and political requirements for defense and expansion on labor time and free time, on the material and intellectual culture. By virtue of the way it has organized its technological base, contemporary industrial society tends to be totalitarian. For "totalitarian" is not only a terroristic political coordination of society, but also a non-terroristic economic-technical coordination which operates through the manipulation of needs by vested interests. It thus precludes the emergence of an effective opposition against the whole. Not only a specific form of government or party rule makes for totalitarianism, but also a specific system of production and distribution which may well be compatible with a "pluralism" of parties, newspapers, "countervailing powers," etc.

Today political power asserts itself through its power over the machine process and over the technical organization of the apparatus. The government of advanced and advancing industrial societies can maintain and secure itself only when it succeeds in mobilizing, organizing, and exploiting the technical, scientific, and mechanical productivity available to industrial civilization. And this productivity mobilizes society as a whole, above and beyond any particular individual or group interests. The brute fact that the machine's physical (only physical?) power surpasses that of the individual, and of any particular group of individuals, makes the machine the most effective political instrument in any society whose basic organization is that of the machine process. But the political trend may be reversed; essentially the power of the machine is only the stored-up and projected power of man. To the extent to which the work world is conceived of as a machine and mechanized accordingly, it becomes the *potential* basis of a new freedom for man.

Contemporary industrial civilization demonstrates that it has reached the stage at which "the free society" can no longer be adequately defined in the traditional terms of economic, political, and intellectual liberties, not because these liberties have become insignificant, but because they are too significant to be confined within the traditional forms. New modes of realization are needed, corresponding to the new capabilities of society.

Such new modes can be indicated only in negative terms because they would amount to the negation of the prevailing modes. Thus economic freedom would mean freedom *from* the economy—from being controlled by economic forces and relationships; freedom from the daily struggle for existence, from earning a living. Political freedom would mean liberation of the individuals *from* politics over which they have no effective control. Similarly, intellectual freedom would mean the restoration of individual thought now absorbed by mass communication and indoctrination, abolition of "public opinion" together with its makers. The unrealistic sound of these propositions is indicative, not of their utopian character, but of the strength of the forces which prevent their realization. The most effective and enduring form of warfare against liberation is the implanting of material and intellectual needs that perpetuate obsolete forms of the struggle for existence.

The intensity, the satisfaction and even the character of human needs, beyond the biological level, have always been preconditioned. Whether or not the possibility of doing or leaving, enjoying or destroying, possessing or rejecting something is seized as a *need* depends on whether or not it can be seen as desirable and necessary for the prevailing societal institutions and interests. In this sense, human needs are historical needs and, to the extent to which the society demands the repressive development of the individual, his needs themselves and their claim for satisfaction are subject to overriding critical standards.

We may distinguish both true and false needs. "False" are those which are superimposed upon the individual by particular social interests in his repression: the needs which perpetuate toil, aggressiveness, misery, and injustice. Their satisfaction might be most gratifying to the individual, but this happiness is not a condition which has to be maintained and protected if it serves to arrest the development of the ability (his own and others) to recognize the disease of the whole and grasp the chances of curing the disease. The result then is euphoria in unhappiness. Most of the prevailing needs to relax, to have fun, to behave and consume in accordance with the advertisements, to love and hate what others love and hate, belong to this category of false needs.

Such needs have a societal content and function which are determined by external powers over which the individual has no control; the development and satisfaction of these needs is heteronomous. No matter how much such needs may have become the individual's own, reproduced and fortified by the conditions of his existence; no matter how much he identifies himself with them and finds himself in their satisfaction, they continue to be what they were from the beginning—products of a society whose dominant interest demands repression.

The prevalence of repressive needs is an accomplished fact, accepted in ignorance and defeat, but a fact that must be undone in the interest of the happy individual as well as all those whose misery is the price of his satisfaction. The only needs that have an unqualified claim for satisfaction are the vital ones—nourishment, clothing, lodging at the attainable level of culture. The satisfaction of these needs is the prerequisite for the realization of *all* needs, of the unsublimated as well as the sublimated ones.

For any consciousness and conscience, for any experience which does not accept the prevailing societal interest as the supreme law of thought and behavior, the established universe of needs and satisfactions is a fact to be questioned—questioned in terms of truth and falsehood. These terms are historical throughout, and their objectivity is historical. The judgment of needs and their satisfaction, under the given conditions, involves standards of *priority*—standards which refer to the optimal development of the individual, of all individuals, under the optimal utilization of the material and intellectual resources available to man. The resources are calculable. "Truth" and "falsehood" of needs designate objective conditions to the extent to which the universal satisfaction of vital needs and, beyond it, the progressive alleviation of toil and poverty, are universally valid standards. But as historical standards, they do not only vary according to area and stage of development, they also can be defined only in (greater or lesser) *contradiction* to the prevailing ones. What tribunal can possibly claim the authority of decision?

In the last analysis, the question of what are true and false needs must be answered by the individuals themselves, but only in the last analysis; that is, if and when they are free to give their own answer. As long as they are kept incapable of being autonomous, as long as they are indoctrinated and manipulated (down to their very instincts), their answer to this question cannot be taken as their own. By the same token, however, no tribunal can justly arrogate to itself the right to decide which needs should be developed and satisfied. Any such tribunal is reprehensible, although our revulsion does not do away with the question: how can the people who have been the object of effective and productive domination by themselves create the conditions of freedom?

The more rational, productive, technical, and total the repressive administration of society becomes, the more unimaginable the means and ways by which the administered individuals might break their servitude and seize their own liberation. To be sure, to impose Reason upon an entire society is a paradoxical and scandalous idea—although one might dispute the righteousness of a society which ridicules this idea while making its own population into objects of total administration. All liberation depends on the consciousness of servitude, and the emergence of this consciousness is always hampered by the predominance of needs and satisfactions which, to a great extent, have become the individual's own. The process always replaces one system of pre-conditioning by another; the optimal goal is the replacement of false needs by true ones, the abandonment of repressive satisfaction.

The distinguishing feature of advanced industrial society is its effective suffocation of those needs which demand liberation—liberation also from that which is tolerable and rewarding and comfortable—while it sustains and absolves the destructive power and repressive function of the affluent society. Here, the social controls exact the overwhelming need for the production and consumption of waste; the need for stupefying work where it is no longer a real necessity; the need for modes of relaxation which soothe and prolong this stupefication; the need for maintaining such deceptive liberties as free competition at administered prices, a free press which censors itself, free choice between brands and gadgets.

Under the rule of a repressive whole, liberty can be made into a powerful instrument of domination. The range of choice open to the individual is not the decisive factor in determining the degree of human freedom, but *what* can be chosen and what *is* chosen by the individual. The criterion for free choice can never be an absolute one, but neither is it entirely relative. Free election of masters does not abolish the masters or the slaves. Free choice among a wide variety of goods and services does not signify freedom if these goods and services sustain social controls over a life of toil and fear—that is, if they sustain alienation. And the spontaneous reproduction of superimposed needs by the individual does not establish autonomy; it only testifies to the efficacy of the controls.

Our insistence on the depth and efficacy of these controls is open to the objection that we overrate greatly the indoctrinating power of the "media," and that by themselves the people would feel and satisfy the needs which are now imposed upon them. The objection misses the point. The preconditioning does not start with the mass production of radio and television and with the centralization of their control. The people enter this stage as preconditioned receptacles of long standing; the decisive difference is in the flattening out of the contrast (or conflict) between the given and the possible, between the satisfied and the unsatisfied needs. Here, the so-called equalization of class distinctions reveals its ideological function. If the worker and his boss enjoy the same television program and visit the same resort places, if the typist is as attractively made up as the daughter of her employer, if the Negro owns a Cadillac, if they all read the same newspaper, then this assimilation indicates not the disappearance of classes, but the extent to which the needs and satisfactions that serve the preservation of the Establishment are shared by the underlying population.

Indeed, in the most highly developed areas of contemporary society, the transplantation of social into individual needs is so effective that the difference between them seems to be purely theoretical. Can one really distinguish between the mass media as instruments of information and entertainment, and as agents of manipulation and indoctrination? Between the automobile as nuisance and as convenience? Between the horrors and the comforts of functional architecture? Between the work for national defense and the work for corporate gain? Between the private pleasure and the commercial and political utility involved in increasing the birth rate?

We are again confronted with one of the most vexing aspects of advanced industrial civilization: the rational character of its irrationality. Its productivity and efficiency, its capacity to increase and spread comforts, to turn waste into need, and destruction into construction, the extent to which this civilization transforms the object world into an extension of man's mind and body makes the very notion of alienation questionable. The people recognize themselves in their commodities; they find their soul in their automobile, hi-fi set, split-level home, kitchen equipment. The very mechanism which ties the individual to his society has changed, and social control is anchored in the new needs which it has produced.

The prevailing forms of social control are technological in a new sense. To be sure, the technical structure and efficacy of the productive and destructive appratus has been a major instrumentality for subjecting the population to the established social division of labor throughout the modern period. Moreover, such integration has always been accompanied by more obvious forms of compulsion: loss of livelihood, the administration of justice, the police, the armed forces. It still is. But in the contemporary period, the technological controls appear to be the very embodiment of Reason for the benefit of all social groups and interests—to such an extent that all contradictions seems irrational and all counteraction impossible.

No wonder then that, in the most advanced areas of his civilization, the social controls have been introjected to the point where even individual protest is affected at its roots. The intellectual and emotional refusal "to go along" appears neurotic and impotent. This is the socio-psychological aspect of the political event that marks the contemporary period: the passing of the historical forces which, at the preceding stage of industrial society, seemed to represent the possibility of new forms of existence.

But the term "introjection" perhaps no longer describes the way in which the individual by himself reproduces and perpetuates the external controls exercised by his society. Introjection suggests a variety of relatively spontaneous processes by which a Self (Ego) transposes the "outer" into the "inner." Thus introjection implies the existence of an inner dimension distinguished from and even antagonistic to the external exigencies—an individual consciousness and an individual unconscious *apart from* public opinion and behavior.[1] The idea of "inner freedom" here has its

[1]The change in the function of the family here plays a decisive role: its "socializing" functions are increasingly taken over by outside groups and media. See my *Eros and Civilization* (Boston: Beacon Press, 1955), p. 96 ff.

reality: it designates the private space in which man may become and remain "himself."

Today this private space has been invaded and whittled down by technological reality. Mass production and mass distribution claim the *entire* individual, and industrial psychology has long since ceased to be confined to the factory. The manifold processes of introjection seem to be ossified in almost mechanical reactions. The result is, not adjustment but *mimesis*: an immediate identification of the individual with *his* society and, through it, with the society as a whole.

This immediate, automatic identification (which may have been characteristic of primitive forms of association) reappears in high industrial civilization; its new "immediacy," however, is the product of a sophisticated, scientific management and organization. In this process, the "inner" dimension of the mind in which opposition to the status quo can take root is whittled down. The loss of this dimension, in which the power of negative thinking—the critical power of Reason—is at home, is the ideological counterpart to the very material process in which advanced industrial society silences and reconciles the opposition. The impact of progress turns Reason into submission to the facts of life, and to the dynamic capability of producing more and bigger facts of the same sort of life. The efficiency of the system blunts the individuals' recognition that it contains no facts which do not communicate the repressive power of the whole. If the individuals find themselves in the things which shape their life, they do so, not by giving, but by accepting the law of things—not the law of physics but the law of their society.

I have just suggested that the concept of alienation seems to become questionable when the individuals identify themselves with the existence which is imposed upon them and have in it their own development and satisfaction. This identification is not illusion but reality. However, the reality constitutes a more progressive stage of alienation. The latter has become entirely objective; the subject which is alienated is swallowed up by its alienated existence. There is only one dimension, and it is everywhere and in all forms. The achievements of progress defy ideological indictment as well as justification; before their tribunal, the "false consciousness" of their rationality becomes the true consciousness.

This absorption of ideology into reality does not, however, signify the "end of ideology."On the contrary, in a specific sense advanced industrial culture is *more* ideological than its predecessor, inasmuch as today the ideology is in the process of production itself.[2] In a provocative form, this proposition reveals the political aspects of the prevailing technological rationality. The productive apparatus and the goods and services which it produces "sell" or impose the social system as a whole. The means of mass transportation and communication, the commodities of lodging, food, and clothing, the irresistible output of the entertainment and information industry carry with them prescribed attitudes and habits, certain intellectual and emotional reactions which bind the consumers more or less pleasantly to the producers and, through the latter, to the whole. The products indoctrinate and

[2] Theodor W. Adorno, *Prismen. Kulturkritik und Gesellschaft*. (Frankfurt: Suhrkamp, 1955), p. 24 f.

manipulate; they promote a false consciousness which is immune against its false-hood. And as these beneficial products become available to more individuals in more social classes, the indoctrination they carry ceases to be publicity; it becomes a way of life. It is a good way of life—much better than before—and as a good way of life, it militates against qualitative change. Thus emerges a pattern of *one-dimensional thought and behavior* in which ideas, aspirations, and objectives that, by their content, transcend the established universe of discourse and action are either repelled or reduced to terms of this universe. They are redefined by the rationality of the given system and of its quantitative extension.

The trend may be related to a development in scientific method: operationalism in the physical, behaviorism in the social sciences. The common feature is a total empiricism in the treatment of concepts; their meaning is restricted to the represen-tation of particular operations and behavior. The operational point of view is well illustrated by P. W. Bridgman's analysis of the concept of length:[3]

We evidently know what we mean by length if we can tell what the length of any and every object is, and for the physicist nothing more is required. To find the length of an object, we have to perform certain physical operations. The concept of length is therefore fixed when the operations by which length is measured are fixed: that is, the concept of length involves as much and nothing more than the set of operations by which length is determined. In general, we mean by any concept nothing more than a set of operations; *the concept is synonymous with the corresponding set of operations.*

Bridgman has seen the wide implications of this mode of thought for the society at large:[4]

To adopt the operational point of view involves much more than a mere restriction of the sense in which we understand 'concept,' but means a far-reaching change in all our habits of thought, in that we shall no longer permit ourselves to use as tools in our thinking concepts of which we cannot give an adequate account in terms of operations.

Bridgman's prediction has come true. The new mode of thought is today the predominant tendency in philosophy, psychology, sociology, and other fields. Many of the most seriously troublesome concepts are being "eliminated" by showing that no adequate account of them in terms of operations or behavior can be given. The radical empiricist onslaught (I shall subsequently, in chapters VII and VIII, examine

[3]P. W. Bridgman, *The Logic of Modern Physics* (New York: Macmillan, 1928), p. 5. The operational doctrine has since been refined and qualified. Bridgman himself has extended the concept of "operation" to include the "paper-and-pencil" operations of the theorist (in Philipp J. Frank, *The Validation of Scientific Theories* [Boston: Beacon Press, 1954], Chap. II). The main impetus remains the same: it is "desirable" that the paper-and-pencil operations "be capable of eventual contact, although perhaps indirectly, with instrumental operations."
[4]P. W. Bridgman, *The Logic of Modern Physics*, loc. cit., p. 31.

its claim to be empiricist) thus provides the methodological justification for the debunking of the mind by the intellectuals—a positivism which, in its denial of the transcending elements of Reason, forms the academic counterpart of the socially required behavior.

Outside the academic establishment, the "far-reaching change in all our habits of thought" is more serious. It serves to coordinate ideas and goals with those exacted by the prevailing system, to enclose them in the system, and to repel those which are irreconcilable with the system. The reign of such a one-dimensional reality does not mean that materialism rules, and that the spiritual, metaphysical, and bohemian occupations are petering out. On the contrary, there is a great deal of "Worship together this week," "Why not try God," Zen, existentialism, and beat ways of life, etc. But such modes of protest and transcendence are no longer contradictory to the status quo and no longer negative. They are rather the ceremonial part of practical behaviorism, its harmless negation, and are quickly digested by the status quo as part of its healthy diet.

One-dimensional thought is systematically promoted by the makers of politics and their purveyors of of mass information. Their universe of discourse is populated by self-validating hypotheses which, incessantly and monopolistically repeated, become hypnotic definitions or dictations. For example, "free" are the institutions which operate (and are operated on) in the countries of the Free World; other transcending modes of freedom are by definition either anarchism, communism, or propaganda. "Socialistic" are all encroachments on private enterprises not undertaken by private enterprise itself (or by government contracts), such as universal and comprehensive health insurance, or the protection of nature from all too sweeping commercialization, or the establishment of public services which may hurt private profit. This totalitarian logic of accomplished facts has its Eastern counterpart. There, freedom is the way of life instituted by a communist regime, and all other transcending modes of freedom are either capitalistic, or revisionist, or leftist sectarianism. In both camps, non-operational ideas are non-behavioral and subversive. The movement of thought is stopped at barriers which appear as the limits of Reason itself.

Such limitation of thought is certainly not new. Ascending modern rationalism, in its speculative as well as empirical form, shows a striking contrast between extreme critical radicalism in scientific and philosophic method on the one hand, and an uncritical quietism in the attitude toward established and functioning social institutions. Thus Descartes' *ego cogitans* was to leave the "great public bodies" untouched, and Hobbes held that "the present ought always to be preferred, maintained, and accounted best." Kant agreed with Locke in justifying revolution *if and when* it has succeeded in organizing the whole and in preventing subversion.

However, these accommodating concepts of Reason were always contradicted by the evident misery and injustice of the "great public bodies" and the effective, more or less conscious rebellion against them. Societal conditions existed which provoked and permitted real dissociation from the established state of affairs; a private as well as political dimension was present in which dissociation could develop into effective opposition, testing its strength and the validity of its objectives.

With the gradual closing of this dimension by the society, the self-limitation of thought assumes a larger significance. The interrelation between scientific-philosophical and societal processes, between theoretical and practical Reason, asserts itself "behind the back" of the scientists and philosophers. The society bars a whole type of oppositional operations and behavior; consequently, the concepts pertaining to them are rendered illusory or meaningless. Historical transcendence appears as metaphysical transcendence, not acceptable to science and scientific thought. The operational and behavioral point of view, practiced as a "habit of thought" at large, becomes the view of the established universe of discourse and action, needs and aspirations. The "cunning of Reason" works, as it so often did, in the interest of the powers that be. The insistence on operational and behavioral concepts turns against the efforts to free thought and behavior *from* the given reality and *for* the suppresed alternatives. Theoretical and practical Reason, academic and social behaviorism meet on common ground: that of an advanced society which makes scientific and technical progress into an instrument of domination.

"Progress" is not a neutral term; it moves toward specific ends, and these ends are defined by the possibilities of ameliorating the human condition. Advanced industrial society is approaching the stage where continued progress would demand the radical subversion of the prevailing direction and organization of progress. This stage would be reached when material production (including the necessary services) becomes automated to the extent that all vital needs can be satisfied while necessary labor time is reduced to marginal time. From this point on, technical progress would transcend the realm of necessity, where it served as the instrument of domination and exploitation which thereby limited its rationality; technology would become subject to the free play of faculties in the struggle for the pacification of nature and of society.

Such a state is envisioned in Marx's notion of the "abolition of labor." The term "pacification of existence" seems better suited to designate the historical alternative of a world which—through an international conflict which transforms and suspends the contradictions within the established societies—advances on the brink of a global war. "Pacification of existence" means the development of man's struggle with man and with nature, under conditions where the competing needs, desires, and aspirations are no longer organized by vested interests in domination and scarcity—an organization which perpetuates the destructive forms of this struggle.

Today's fight against this historical alternative finds a firm mass basis in the underlying population, and finds its ideology in the rigid orientation of thought and behavior to the given universe of facts. Validated by the accomplishments of science and technology, justified by its growing productivity, the status quo defies all transcendence. Faced with the possibility of pacification on the grounds of its technical and intellectual achievements, the mature industrial society closes itself against this alternative. Operationalism, in theory and practice, becomes the theory and practice of *containment*. Underneath its obvious dynamics, this society is a thoroughly static system of life: self-propelling in its oppressive productivity and in its beneficial coordination. Containment of technical progress goes hand in hand with its growth in the established direction. In spite of the political fetters imposed by the statue quo, the more technology appears capable of creating the conditions for pacification, the more are the minds and bodies of man organized against this alternative.

The most advanced areas of industrial society exhibit throughout these two features: a trend toward consummation of technological rationality, and intensive efforts to contain this trend within the established institutions. Here is the internal contradiction of this civilization: the irrational element in its rationality. It is the token of its achievements. The industrial society which makes technology and science its own is organized for the ever-more-effective domination of man and nature, for the ever-more-effective utilization of its resources. It becomes irrational when the success of these efforts opens new dimensions of human realization. Organization for peace is different from organization for war; the institutions which served the struggle for existence cannot serve the pacification of existence. Life as an end is qualitatively different from life as a means.

Such a qualitatively new mode of existence can never be envisaged as the mere by-product of economic and political changes, as the more or less spontaneous effect of the new institutions which constitute the necessary prerequisite. Qualitative change also involves a change in the *technical* basis on which this society rests—one which sustains the economic and political institutions through which the "second nature" of man as an aggressive object of administration is stabilized. The techniques of industrialization are political techniques; as such, they prejudge the possibilities of Reason and Freedom.

To be sure, labor must precede the reduction of labor, and industrialization must precede the development of human needs and satisfactions. But as all freedom depends on the conquest of alien necessity, the realization of freedom depends on the *techniques* of this conquest. The highest productivity of labor can be used for the perpetuation of labor, and the most efficient industrialization can serve the restriction and manipulation of needs.

When this point is reached, domination—in the guise of affluence and liberty—extends to all spheres of private and public existence, integrates all authentic opposition, absorbs all alternatives. Technological rationality reveals its political character as it becomes the great vehicle of better domination, creating a truly totalitarian universe in which society and nature, mind and body are kept in a state of permanent mobilization for the defense of this universe.

"PERCEIVED AND UNPERCEIVED RESTRAINTS
ON MAN'S FREEDOM"

Christian Bay

Social Freedom

"Freedom" means the relative absence of perceived external restraints on individual behavior. In essence, this definition is equivalent to the formulations of Hobbes

and Locke, which were never departed from, in any important respect, in the empiricist-utilitarian tradition. A principal point at issue between these philosophers was whether a powerful, active state was desirable to protect the individual against restraints instituted by his neighbors or whether a circumscribed, passive state should be preferred, to keep down the scope of restraints imposed by law and government.

What the empiricists tended to overlook is that the individual as a social being demands restraints, if this word is taken in a wide sense, as much as he demands freedom, if not much more. Life in groups and in society implies and necessitates many kinds of restraints on the individual, but they are not all perceived as restraints. Some are internalized and are consequently either taken for granted as part of the situation in which the individual acts or are incorporated in his personality as a part of his superego or ego.[1] Others are adhered to with pleasure; they push in the direction the individual wished to go anyway. Others again are complied with as matters of necessity or as lesser evils; or they are not complied with, resulting in some kind of damage for the individual.

Let us note that "restraint" is used in a broad and objective sense, referring to all the potential obstacles that limit the possibilities of individual choice or put penalties on alternatives. Anything that pushes or punishes the individual is a restraint, but so is also anything that hypothetically and probably *would* push or punish him, should he be inclined to a certain kind of behavior at a given time and place.

Restraints are necessary in any society, and they are not emerging at random. This book proceeds on the general assumption that social facts, including social restraints, have functions. To explain institutional regularities and predict their further development one must develop hypotheses about the kinds of needs they serve, individual and social.

When social restraints on individual behavior are studied in terms of their probable functions in social interaction, I shall prefer to call them "sanctions." A *sanction*, then, is any type of restraint on individual behavior that is viewed as an inducement toward or away from a certain kind of behavior.[2] The inducement can consist in the possibility of either rewards or punishments and usually implies both, depending on which side of the coin is looked at. Every kind of sanction, whether light or heavy, is assumed to serve at least one function, either for one or more individuals and/or for one or more social institutions in a social system.

In this context no dynamic discussion of sanctions will be attempted; I am here only interested in a clarification of the concept of social freedom, and in making some tentative suggestions about the extent to which social freedom should be considered desirable.

---

[1] I am speaking of internalization in a wider sense than is usual in psychological literature; internalization in a narrower, more strictly psychological sense would refer to the incorporation in superego or ego only.

[2] This is in substance a widely used definition. Margaret Mead, for example, defines sanctions as "mechanisms by which conformity is obtained, by which desired behavior is induced and undesired behavior prevented." *Cooperation and Competition among Primitive Peoples*, p. 493.

"Restraint" is not the only very broad term in my definition of social freedom. "External" hardly is much of a delimitation, since it includes everything that is external to the individual personality. A body defect, for example, is considered an external restraint, especially, but not only, if it interferes with the individual's ability to enjoy normal social relationships. In fact, even the physical limitations on what a healthy body can do are external restraints on the personality.[3] Yet, my focus of interest is on interpersonal restraints.

"Behavior," again, is no limitation on the concept of social freedom. This term, too, is understood in its very broadest sense, covering attitudes and actions; opinions, emotions, perceptions, cognitions, and motivations; verbal and nonverbal expression; actual and intended activity and passivity.

The one saving circumstance that allows me to delimit this freedom concept is the qualification that the restraints must be *perceived as restraints*. If a government follows Rousseau's advice and is able to succeed in redirecting the wills of the people, it does to this extent not interfere with their social freedom. If a minority is penalized for trying to oppose this manipulation of minds, then this minority is deprived of social freedom. But the majority whose opinions have changed as a result of skillful manipulation are as free as before in this sense; what they have suffered is a reduction in potential freedom.

Let me take one more example to clarify the difference between social and potential freedom. A law prohibiting interracial marriages in a given state curbs the social freedom of a given individual only to the extent that he is aware of the possibility of such a marriage, for himself or for others. Only to the extent that such an idea is completely outside his psychological field—as a biological possibility or as a social arrangement that anybody could want—would it follow from my definition that such a law does not interfere with this particular individual's social freedom.[4]

The *intention* of the restraining agent is irrelevant for determining whether or not an individual is being subjected to restraint. A good husband, for example, may either intentionally or unintentionally impose considerable restraints on his wife, and the same goes the other way.

Even if a given obstacle may not suffice to change the individual's attitudes or overt behavior, it is still limiting his social freedom to the extent that it has been brought to his awareness or half-awareness as a restraint and thus has influenced his motivational behavior. Only if the relevance or seriousness of a possible threat or obstacle to a given individual or to his plans is totally unperceived by him, may it properly be said that his social freedom is wholly unaffected by the event.

If external circumstances become completely internalized, they cease to interfere with the individual's social freedom as defined here. In heroic moments a man may

---

[3] I am here following Talcott Parsons: "The actor is an ego or a self, not an organism, and . . . his organism is part of the 'external world' from the point of view of the subjective categories of the theory of action." *The Structure of Social Action*, p. 49, note 3.

[4] It surely interferes with the social freedom of other people, however, as it is hardly conceivable that such a law would be called for unless there was a widespread awareness that interracial marriage is biologically and socially possible.

identify so completely with his cause or country that even a mission involving death as a certain consequence does not interfere with his social freedom; a call to action may in fact liberate him from the intolerable restraints of enforced passivity "in times that try men's souls."[5]

Problems of social freedom are intimately connected with problems of power. In this context a few remarks must be made on the surface relationship between these two concepts.

"Power" has preliminarily been defined as an individual's degree of control over his security. The power of an individual refers to the probable difference his own effort will make in his access to or advancement of values (including more power) in desired amounts and kinds.[6]

It is useful to distinguish between *independent* and *dependent* power: independent power means autonomous control over values, while dependent power means a kind of control that depends on carrying out obligations in deference to a superior power center. This power center may be one or more individuals (for example, an organization) or an institution, meaning a sanctioned pattern of expected behavior. Very often power is exercised in part independently and in part dependently. A bureaucrat, for example, is independent within a certain sphere, the sphere of his own discretion, while he is dependent on rules and regulations and on the orders of his superiors in many other spheres of his exercise of power.

Power is conceived as a *potential*, to be distinguished from the *process* of *exercising power*. We speak of a *power subject* with reference to the source of independent power; a *power agent* is a holder of dependent power; and a *power object* is an individual over whom power is exercised.

Probably all human beings living in society at all times are both subjects, agents, and objects of power, in proportions differing among individuals and varying from one situation to another for each individual. Nobody is or ever was all-powerful; even a despot needs some cooperation in order to control certain values. And nobody is or ever was completely without power; even a slave is not entirely without at least a subtle bargaining power, unless he is about to be put to death. Every power agent is at the same time a subject and an object of power.

Power as a potential does not necessarily limit anybody's freedom. Even the exercise of power—actual, predicted or expected—does not *necessarily* interfere with anybody's freedom; it depends on the means by which power is exercised. These can for present purposes be sketchily listed as: physical force or threats of force; other value deprivations (or indulgences) or threats (promises) of such; fraud; and persuasion.[7]

---

[5] Needless to say, the enemy, or whatever poses the prospect of death, is necessarily a restraint, in threatening to take away all his social freedom forever.

[6] "Influence" is in this study synonymous with "power."

[7] "Manipulation" is a term that overlaps with both "fraud" and "persuasion." This typology is similar to Russell's: "An individual may be influenced: A. By direct physical power over his body, e.g., when he is imprisoned or killed; B. By rewards and punishments as inducements, e.g., in giving or withholding employment; C. By influence on opinion, i.e., propaganda in its broadest sense." *Power: A New Social Analysis*, p. 36.

The ends of power exercise, or the ends-in-view, may be deliberate or nondeliberate. This is the distinction between rational and institutional exercise of power, corresponding to the distinction between rational and institutional behavior.[8]

It is the means and not the ends of power exercise that determine the extent to which social freedom is interfered with. The intention of the power subject or power agent is irrelevant; it does not necessarily make any difference whether he is acting deliberately or merely by habit of convention, or even in the mistaken belief that he is just helping the power object. What does matter is the means he employs. Threats of physical force or other value deprivations, down to mere withdrawal of approval—all serve to reduce the social freedom of the power object, to the extent that he perceives the sanctions and considers them at all significant as threats. Promises of indulgence conditional on performance can usually be seen as threats of deprivations conditional on nonperformance, and thus as a rule fall in the same category of interfering with social freedom by way of negative sanctions.

If, on the other hand, fraud is employed, it is not the social but the potential freedom of the power object that is affected. And to the extent that pure persuasion is utilized, free of elements of fraud, power can be exercised without anybody's loss of freedom in any sense. In both the latter cases there are no perceived external restraints on individual behavior occasioned by the exercise of power.

Let us now consider whether and to what extent social freedom is desirable. Clearly, it follows from my general position favoring a maximal freedom of expression in the fullest sense that social freedom is desirable, generally speaking. On the other hand, it is quite clear also that many limitations on social freedom are desirable, for the simple reason that life in society necessitates many kinds of restraints. To a certain extent, one man's freedom means another man's restraints, which is almost the same as saying that one man's power often means another man's oppression.

Is it possible to draw a line between desirable and undesirable restraints on social freedom? This is basically an empirical problem, once the value premise of freedom maximization is given. But it involves some further value assumptions as well: one must take at least some general position on the hierarchy of importance of freedom demands. In other words, one has to formulate some criteria on the relative importance for human freedom as a whole of different types of human rights. Once it has been decided which rights are more basic, it becomes an empirical question, though perhaps a complex one, to decide what privileges and what less basic rights have to be curbed in order to extend the more basic rights to all and, first of all, to those who are the most deprived to begin with.

An almost universal consensus can be expected in support of the proposition that murder is a worse deprivation for the victim than is a not fatal blow. It will be less universally but still widely agreed that physical assault is a worse interference with freedom and dignity than is verbal scolding, on the whole. Beyond this it is hard to

[8] "Rational" is here used in a broad sense.

achieve consensus on more specific hierarchies of values in the realm of social freedom (which is the same as hierarchies of negative values in the realm of damages to social freedom).

My general position is intentionally simple in the hope of qualifying it for a wide support: I consider *coercion* the supreme political evil. I desire for the individual and for society, first of all, the maximization of freedom from coercion, and consequently I consider all other freedom values second-priority goals.

The utility of this formula evidently hinges on what is understood by "coercion." It is well-nigh impossible, I believe, to find a very specific definition that is at the same time generally acceptable. But this is perhaps not a crucial obstacle: it may well be desirable to use a coercion concept with somewhat flexible limits toward the border area of the neighboring concept of noncoercive restraint, provided there is general agreement on what constitutes the more central areas of coercion. A natural and desirable consequence of social and cultural growth may be that the reference of "coercion" gradually is extended to include new and somewhat subtler kinds of sanctions, parallel to the gradual reduction in occurrences of the more brutal and direct ones.

Lasswell and Kaplan define coercion simply as "a high degree of constraint and/or inducement."[9] Loosely delimited as this concept is, it nevertheless at first seems to depart from common sense and thus from the probability of consensus in one respect: inducements (rewards) are not ordinarily thought of as coercive. Yet, I believe it is in the interest of clear thinking to admit that they can be, if strong enough. If a man in dire poverty is offered a very large sum of money to perform some deed on the shady side of the law, and this appears to him his only chance ever to get into the money, he may yield to the temptation against his principles. The high degree of inducement has for him created a new perspective of the future, and from that moment on the necessity of either performing the deed or letting go of the new perspective may be psychologically equivalent to a high degree of constraint.[10]

Following the general approach of Lasswell and Kaplan, *coercion* in this study means *(a) the application of actual physical violence,* or *(b) the application of sanctions sufficiently strong to make the individual abandon a course of action or inaction dictated by his own strong and enduring motives and wishes.* A man who conforms willingly, abandoning his earlier desires, is no longer coerced. The more repugnant the induced course of action is to the power object, the more it presumably takes of pressure to make him comply, and still more it would take to make him conform willingly. Among two men whose initial wishes endure, a timid man is more easily coerced toward compliance than is a courageous man. Institutions can be just as coercive on the individual as the exercise of power in the service of deliberate plans.

[9] *Power and Society,* p. 97.
[10] The example has been suggested by Harold D. Lasswell in conversation.

Degrees of coercion are determined according to the power of the coercive sanctions toward making the individual abandon important intentions in order to comply. Judged on a social scale, coercive pressures are more severe the more of the average man's individuality they are able to suppress. Judged in the individual case, coercion is more severe the stronger the motives and wishes that the power object abandons in order to comply. Actual physical violence is considered coercive regardless of whether the victim succumbs and complies—and coercive to the highest degree.

Coercion can take place without being intended; the perennial overprotecting mother is a case in point. On the other hand, intentions of even the most flagrant coercion are not always successful. It depends on whether or not the victim succumbs to the pressures.

The means of power are insufficient as criteria for determining whether coercion is accomplished; the decisive criterion is the outcome. Yet, one particular means, the actual application of physical violence, is for my purposes considered coercive even if the victim does not comply or does not even try to comply. Physical violence is usually a potent means of making potential victims take heed, and it always interferes with the actual victim's own strong motives and wishes. With the possible exception of confirmed masochists, we may assume that every human being strongly desires physical integrity and inviolability.

Now let me return to the value question. My position is that coercion is the supreme political evil, or the supreme evil that results from power processes and that can be reduced by political means. A maximal amount of freedom from coercion is supremely desirable. Coercion can be justified only if it serves to reduce the occurrence of worse kinds of coercion. And the worst kind of coercion is the actual application of substantial physical violence; degrees of violence are determined medically in the consequences for the victim's health, physical and mental.[11] Degrees of violent *intent* are, of course, judged by the intended or expected consequences of the act of violence.

The total abolition of coercion is an ideal that can possibly never be fully vindicated in practice, but it can be approached in practice and is not unattainable in principle. It is not inconceivable that psychologically free individuals can be made to endure willingly all the restraints that an enlightened, self-restraining government and public opinion may impose. A society within which all children go to school motivated by a spontaneous quest for knowledge, in which there are no criminals to lock up, and in which reasonable taxes are paid willingly—such a conception strains the imagination but does not surpass it.

---

[11] Poisoning usually involves fraud but is also a specimen of physical violence, to be judged by its outcome, just as other kinds of violence. Confinement or imprisonment is considered physical violence only if and to the extent that it damages the individual's health, physical or mental.

Let me assert, therefore, not only that a maximal freedom of expression for all should be the supreme goal of a civilized society, but also this: among all freedom goals, the goal of maximizing everyone's freedom from coercion should take first priority.[12]

Beyond this, I shall not assert that external restraints on individual behavior in general are undesirable or, for that matter, desirable. The extent to which social restraints are required in social life, for purposes such as social solidarity, division of labor, prevention of anomie, mental health, and cultural growth, will become clearer in Chapters 5 and 6, where determinants of social and potential freedom will be discussed in the context of a theory of social systems.

Potential Freedom

"Freedom" means the relative absence of unperceived external restraints of individual behavior.

I observed earlier that Plato and Aristotle in some ways understood better than Bentham did the extent to which human nature, including minds and motives, is subject to change by legislative and other institutional means. Plato, for example, attributes to Socrates the view that the rulers of the state, "in their dealings either with enemies or with their own citizens, may be allowed to lie for the public good."[13] The maxim of Karl Marx that religion is the opiate of the people is only an extreme statement of a very old discovery. J. B. Bury, writing on the later Roman Republic and the early Empire, says: "Most of the leading men were unbelievers in the official religion of the State, but they considered it valuable for the purpose of keeping the uneducated populace in order."[14] Machiavelli in his turn observes that ecclesiastical principalities can endure without much ability or fortune on the part of their princes. Their rule is

sustained by ancient religious customs, which are so powerful and of such quality, that they keep their princes in power in whatever manner they proceed and live. These princes alone have states without defending them, have subjects without governing them, and their states, not being defended, are not taken from them; their subjects not being governed do not resent it, and neither think nor are capable of alienating themselves from them. Only these principalities, therefore, are secure and happy.[15]

Rousseau was clear and forceful on this point. In his *Discourse on the Origin of Inequality*, he explains the origin of political society in the invention by rich men of "the profoundest plan that ever entered the mind of man: this was to employ in

[12]My human rights approach means that the liberation of the more coerced individuals takes precedence over the liberation of those who are less coerced, even if the latter are more numerous. Kenneth Boulding sees a possibility for consensus on a more moderate version of this value position: "It should be possible to agree that coerciveness *in itself* is an evil, and that any development in society toward less coercive forms of social organization that have survival value is desirable." *The Organizational Revolution*, p. 217.

[13]*The Republic*, pp. 86–87.

[14]*A History of Freedom of Thought*, p. 39.

[15]"The Prince" in *The Prince and The Discourses* (Modern Library), pp. 41–42.

his favour the forces of those who attacked him, to make allies of his adversaries, to inspire them with different maxims, and to give them other institutions as favourable to himself as the law of nature was unfavourable." And in his *Discourse on Political Economy* he offers the following advice: "that government which confines itself to mere obedience will find difficulty in getting itself obeyed. It is good to know how to deal with men as they are, but it is much better to make them what there is need that they should be."[16] The tradition of "totalitarian democracy,"[17] of which Soviet communism is the foremost example today, has followed Rousseau's advice: the way toward a more secure and a "better" social order is evidently seen as leading through thoroughly organized efforts to make men "what there is need that they should be."

In liberal democracy, on the other hand, in so far as a highly developed individuality and thus a wide diversity among men is hoped for, the problem of political manipulation must be approached from the opposite angle: How can we insure conditions under which men can develop into what they have it *in themselves* to become? How can the growth of individuality be sheltered against institutional and reformist pressures—against being pushed into whatever harness is adapted toward the improvement and perfection, in some sense, or preservation, of social and political institutions?

Tocqueville, who was an aristocrat in the best sense of the word, was keenly aware of this problem and was for this reason apprehensive about the extreme majoritarianism in the United States, as this country looked to him more than a century ago:

The authority of a king is physical and controls the actions of men without subduing their will. But the majority possesses a power that is physical and moral at the same time, which acts upon the will as much as upon the actions and represses not only all contest, but all controversy. I know of no country in which there is so little independence of mind and real freedom as in America.[18]

Speaking of the contemporary American scene, Phillips Bradley declares:

The "tyranny" we have to fear today, especially as to our legislatures, is not the defeat of majority demands, however transitory. It is rather the distortion of majority concern—the promotion of the general welfare—by the organized and concentrated minorities pursuing special interests.[19]

The literature focusing on potential freedom is as scant as the literature on social freedom is plentiful. Even the very concept of potential freedom, or any approximate equivalent, has to my knowledge never been given much attention. The problem has been perceived by many writers, some of whom have just been cited. But none of them has attempted to place this problem in the systematic context of

[16]*The Social Contract and Discourses*, pp. 250 and 297.
[17]In Talmon's phrase.
[18]*Democracy in America* (Vintage), I, 273.
[19]"A Historical Essay," Appendix II in Tocqueville, *Democracy in America*, II, 454.

a study of freedom, whether philosophically or empirically. Philosophers throughout history and behavioral scientists in recent times have been much concerned with problems of how people in societies ought to live and how they can be influenced toward living that way. How to help people resist the manipulation of their benefactors, or would-be benefactors, is a relatively new problem of freedom, however. Its significance, at least, has not been as apparent until recent times.[20]

The concept of potential freedom is a difficult one to delimit. Human behavior is restrained by innumerable circumstances, and the great majority of these are not perceived as restraints. Factors in childhood backgrounds, conventions, biological and social needs, interpersonal relations, aspirations and expectations for the future —all these aspects of life can be said to imply numerous restraints on the individual, restraints that as a rule either are taken for granted as part of the self or the situation or are unperceived parts of the unconscious ego, id, or superego.

Such a broad concept is not of much use as it stands. A goal of maximizing potential freedom in this sense would be difficult to conceptualize. It might well turn out to be a nonsensical goal, somewhat like a goal of maximizing everybody's power over everybody else or of maximizing everybody's prestige and fame.

When discussing social freedom, a much narrower concept, I found it convenient to limit the scope of my concern to the freedom from coercion and to refrain from asserting in general that it is desirable to maximize individual freedom from perceived restraints that are no longer coercive. When it comes to potential freedom, some corresponding kind of a limitation is even more evidently necessary.

My value position with respect to potential freedom can be stated in general terms as follows: *I wish to see maximized the ability and potential incentive of every man to resist manipulation, whether institutional or deliberate, in so far as the manipulation serves other interests at the expense of his own.*

"Interest" is to be understood in an objective sense. It is assumed to be in a man's interest: (1) to achieve a maximum of health, physical and mental, and a maximum of psychological freedom; (2) to develop his talents and potentialities toward maturity and achievement; (3) to gain an adequate access to other values according to freely expressed preferences; (4) to have security that circumstances will continue to favor his freedom, growth, and value position; and (5) to gain access to information bearing on alternatives of behavior including value choices, that are or can become open to him. Manipulation serving other interests *at the expense of* his own means manipulation that interferes with one or more of these five basic interests of man without demonstrably serving one or more of them. I shall call this phenomenon *special interest manipulation*, assuming that all manipula-

---

[20]It must be said that Thoreau recognized the practical significance of the problem when he wrote: "If I knew for a certainty that a man was coming to my house with the conscious design of doing me good, I should run for my life."

tion going on it in *somebody's* special interest if it is not in the interest of the objects of manipulation.[21]

I consider it as part of the total goal of a maximal freedom of expression, in other words, that man should become as *autonomous* as possible, roughly in David Riesman's sense:

The "autonomous" are those who on the whole are capable of conforming to the behavioral norms of their society ... but are free to choose whether to conform or not. ... The person here defined as autonomous may or may not conform outwardly, but whatever his choice, he pays less of a price, and he *has* a choice: he can meet both the culture's definitions of adequacy and those which (to a still culturally determined degree) slightly transcend the norm for the adjusted.[22]

Many social institutions operate as essential supports for freedom and security in civilized societies. Large sections of criminal law tend to serve this end as their main function. Many other institutions derive their main independent support[23] from limited groups in society, and it can frequently be demonstrated that such institutions benefit these groups more than others. The young Rousseau believed that all political institutions, at any rate in the first political societies, fell into this category. For my own part, I might suggest the institution of racial segregation as a relatively clear example of this second kind. Let me for brevity's sake talk about *nonspecially supported* as opposed to *specially supported* institutions. Both may in fact be generally supported, but only in the latter case do certain necessarily limited interest groups have a special stake as power subjects in supporting them.

It may be objected that criminal laws according to this logic should be considered specially supported institutions, since governmental agencies have a special stake in supporting them. However, governments in their role of upholding the laws are not in principle acting as power subjects. They are, particularly in democracies, supposed to act on behalf of the people, the parliament, and the laws themselves. Secondly, democratic governments are not in principle limited interest groups. Their interest is supposedly diffusely defined as equivalent with the nation's interest, as they see it, and the composition of the governing group is in principle flexible, offering openings to those who can gain sufficient amounts of public support. Criminal laws in democratic countries are emphatically to a considerable extent nonspecially supported institutions. Only certain kinds of laws, say "class laws"

[21]If manipulation is in the general interest, it is also in the interest of the object of manipulation. Provided, of course, that he would agree and provided, also, that humanitarian but personally detached observers, relying on the best available psychological knowledge, would not disagree. As an objective condition, I would add: provided his psychological freedom is not reduced. Note that I assume in this context the existence of some hierarchy of basic human needs.

[22]*The Lonely Crowd: A Study of the Changing American Character* (Anchor Books), pp. 278–79.

[23]By independent support is meant the support of men as power subjects, not as power agents.

such as those prohibiting strikes, may be considered specially rather than non-specially supported institutions, marking the preponderance of a limited class interest in the legislature. In some nondemocratic countries the impact of specially supported institutions in defining and dealing with crime is likely to be much more pronounced. The ruling group in such countries is sometimes more of a limited special interest group, and revisions of criminal law can be made in support of their special interests.

"Manipulation" in this book means the process of regulating the supply of information in the interest of encouraging or discouraging certain types of behavior. All education is manipulative to a certain extent, at least in its earlier stages, but advanced education may approach the ideal type of neutrality, in the sense that the teacher may strive to present all facts and opinions pertaining to certain problems without partiality.

It does not follow from my value position that education *ought to* approach the ideal type of impartiality, however, even at the advanced stage. On the contrary, note that I am not posing a reduction in the amounts of manipulation as a part of my freedom goal. Manipulation produces restraints only to the extent that it is effective. It is the ability to resist manipulation I wish to see increased, and this ability can best be developed in institutions in which not impartiality but controversy is fostered. Genuine controversy implies manipulation of the same audience from opposite sides at the same time, and on this general level of analysis I know of no better type of incentive toward autonomous or independent thinking than direct exposure to lively controversy. On this score I swear to the wisdom of Socrates.

If I assert that cross-pressures of manipulation in the educational process can stimulate the growth of potential freedom, I am also saying, of course, that education itself can promote freedom in this sense. But I wish to say more than this: education is essential to accomplish this purpose. Man's ability and potential incentive to resist manipulation hinges on his access to knowledge. The merits of manipulative persuasion can be judged only by placing its contents in a context of a relatively systematically organized knowledge, or in relation to knowledge about facts and opinions that are relevant to but not manipulatively related to the purposes for which persuasion is being employed.

The process of manipulation can be either *institutional* or *deliberate*, or both at the same time, in varying proportions. As a power subject, a manipulator is deliberately pursuing purposes of his own, though his goals may be public or private, and in either of these cases they may be narrowly selfish or include a concern for the interests of others. As a power agent, a manipulator may be pursuing the deliberate purposes of his superior, or he may act in support of institutional expectations, without conscious considerations about the impact of each institution on values in which he believes. It is probable that consciousness takes a relatively larger part than unconsciousness in deliberate manipulation, while institutional manipulation is carried on unconsciously to a greater extent.

Note that it is man's ability or potential incentive to resist manipulation that I wish to see maximized. As Riesman's discussion of autonomy makes clear, there is no value in nonconformity as such.[24] In fact, every society demands a lot of conformity, and every individual needs the kind of relationships to groups that implies conformity and submission to some manipulation, both institutional and deliberate.

The ability to resist manipulation is ideally put to use whenever the individual is pushed toward behavior detrimental to his own interests. To the extent that he enjoys psychological freedom, he knows what his own goals are, and to the extent that he has potential freedom, he knows his situation and prospects, including the various action alternatives that in fact are open to him. To the same extent he knows when it is in his interest to resist manipulation.

But ability is not enough. There must also be some incentive to act unconventionally when the time comes, regardless of inconvenience or other consequences. If, for example, a war scare is contrived in a given country, potential freedom is not demonstrated by moments of individual insight into the phoniness of the propaganda avalanche. It requires also an incentive for the individual to achieve detachment and to protect his detachment—by actually resisting the manipulation in one way or another, even if it may be more convenient to glide along with most other people. Manipulation may be resisted either by independent thinking, by a stubborn memory, by seeking access to unorthodox information, or by a general distrust of certain leaders, to give a few examples only. These are examples of resistance within the personality. Resistance within the social system would, of course, require overt expression of attitudes and insights acquired by these means. For example, when Tocqueville in the 1830s deplores the extent of uniformity of opinion in the United States, he is in effect referring to deficiencies in potential freedom: "I found very few men who displayed that manly candor and masculine independence of opinion which frequently distinguished the Americans in former times, and which constitutes the leading feature in distinguished characters wherever they may be found. It seems at first sight as if all the minds of the Americans were formed upon one model, so accurately do they follow the same route." People who are without incentive to develop independence of opinion and to express it with candor are potentially unfree. If they have the incentive but are inhibited by the anticipation of sanctions, they are socially unfree. If they lack the capacity of caring for goals and issues beyond the requirements of ego defense, they are psychologically unfree.

---

[24] *The Lonely Crowd*, Part III. General pleas for nonconformity, says William H. Whyte, Jr., "have an occasional therapeutic value, but as an abstraction, nonconformity is an empty goal, and rebellion against prevailing opinion merely because it is prevailing should no more be praised than acquiescence to it." Cf. *The Organization Man*, p. 11.

"FREEDOM THROUGH DICTATORSHIP
OF THE PEOPLE"

Mao Tse-tung

Our general subject is the correct handling of contradictions among the people. For convenience's sake, let us discuss it under twelve sub-headings. Although reference will be made to contradictions between ourselves and our enemies, this discussion will center mainly on contradictions among the people.

Two Different Types of Contradictions. Never has our country been as united as it is today. The victories of the bourgeois-democratic revolution and the socialist revolution, coupled with our achievements in socialist construction, have rapidly changed the face of old China. Now we see before us an even brighter future. The days of national disunity and turmoil which the people detested have gone forever. Led by the working class and the Communist party, and united as one, our 600 million people are engaged in the great work of building socialism. Unification of the country, unity of the people, and unity among our various nationalities—these are the basic guarantees for the sure truimph of our cause. However, this does not mean that there are no longer any contradictions in our society. It would be naive to imagine that there are no more contradictions. To do so would be to fly in the face of objective reality. We are confronted by two types of social contradictions—contradictions between ourselves and the enemy and contradictions among the people. The two types of contradictions are totally different in nature. . . .

In the conditions existing in China today, what we call contradictions among the people include the following:

Contradictions within the working class, contradictions within the peasantry, contradictions within the intelligentsia, contradictions between the working class and the peasantry, contradictions between the working class and the peasantry on the one hand and the intelligentsia on the other, contradictions between the working class and other sections of the working people on the one hand and the national bourgeoisie on the other, contradictions within the national bourgeoisie, and so forth. Our People's Government is a government that truly represents the interests of the people and serves the people, yet certain contradictions do exist between the Government and the masses. These include contradictions between the interests of the state, collective interests and individual interests; between democracy and centralism; between those in positions of leadership and the led, and contradictions arising from the bureaucratic practices of certain state functionaries in their relations with the masses. All these are contradictions among the people;

generally speaking, underlying the contradictions among the people is the basic identity of the interests of the people. . . .

Ours is a people's democratic dictatorship, led by the working class and based on the worker-peasant alliance. What is this dictatorship for? Its first function is to suppress the reactionary classes and elements and those exploiters in the country who range themselves against the socialist revolution, to suppress all those who try to wreck our socialist construction; that is to say, to solve the contradictions between ourselves and the enemy within the country—for instance, to arrest, try and sentence certain counter-revolutionaries, and for a specified period of time deprive landlords and bureaucrat-capitalists of their right to vote and freedom of speech—all this comes within the scope of our dictatorship. To maintain law and order and safeguard the interests of the people, it is likewise necessary to exercise dictatorship over robbers, swindlers, murderers, arsonists, hooligans and other scoundrels who seriously disrupt social order.

The second function of this dictatorship is to protect our country from subversive activities and possible aggression by the external enemy. Should that happen, it is the task of this dictatorship to solve the external contradiction between ourselves and the enemy. The aim of this dictatorship is to protect all our people so that they can work in peace and build China into a socialist country with a modern industry, agriculture, science and culture.

Who is to exercise this dictatorship? Naturally, it must be the working class and the entire people led by it. Dictatorship does not apply in the ranks of the people. The people cannot possibly exercise dictatorship over themselves; nor should one section of them oppress another section. Lawbreaking elements among the people will be dealt with according to law, but this is different in principle from using the dictatorship to suppress enemies of the people. What applies among the people is democratic centralism. Our constitution lays it down that citizens of the People's Republic of China enjoy freedom of speech, of the press, of assembly, of association, of procession, of demonstration, of religious belief and so on. Our constitution also provides that state organs must practice democratic centralism and must rely on the masses, that the personnel of state organs must serve the people. Our socialist democracy is democracy in the widest sense, such as is not to be found in any capitalist country. Our dictatorship is known as the people's democratic dictatorship, led by the working class and based on the worker-peasant alliance. That is to say, democracy operates within the ranks of the people, while the working class, uniting with all those enjoying civil rights, the peasantry in the first place, enforces dictatorship over the reactionary classes and elements and all those who resist socialist transformation and oppose socialist construction. By civil rights, we mean political freedom and democratic rights.

But this freedom is freedom with leadership, and this democracy is democracy under centralized guidance, not anarchy. Anarchy does not conform to the interests or wishes of the people.

Certain people in our country were delighted when the Hungarian events took place. They hoped that something similar would happen in China, that thousands upon thousands of people would demonstrate in the streets against the People's

Government. Such hopes ran counter to the interests of the masses and therefore could not possibly get their support. In Hungary, a section of the people deceived by domestic and foreign counter-revolutionaries made the mistake of resorting to acts of violence against the People's Government, with the result that both the state and the people suffered for it. The damage done to the country's economy in a few weeks of rioting will take a long time to repair.

There were other people in our country who took a wavering attitude toward the Hungarian events because they were ignorant about the actual world situation. They felt that there was too little freedom under our people's democracy and that there was more freedom under Western parliamentary democracy. They ask for the adoption of the two-party system of the West, where one party is in office and the other out of office. But this so-called two-party system is nothing but a means of maintaining the dictatorship of the bourgeoisie; under no circumstances can it safeguard the freedom of the working people. As a matter of fact, freedom and democracy cannot exist in the abstract; they only exist in the concrete.

In a society where there is class struggle, the exploiting classes are free to exploit the working people while the working people have no freedom from being exploited; where there is democracy for the bourgeoisie, there can be no democracy for the proletariat and other working people. In some capitalist countries, the Communist parties are allowed to exist legally, but only to the extent that they do not endanger the fundamental interests of the bourgeoisie; beyond that, they are not permitted legal existence.

Those who demand freedom and democracy in the abstract regard democracy as an end and not a means. Democracy sometimes seems to be an end, but it is in fact only a means. Marxism teaches us that democracy is part of the superstructure and belongs to the category of politics. That is to say, in the last analysis it serves the economic base. The same is true of freedom. Both democracy and freedom are relative, not absolute, and they come into being and develop under specific historical circumstances. . . .

This is how things stand today: The turbulent class struggles waged by the masses on a large scale characteristic of the revolutionary periods have, in the main, concluded, but class struggle is not entirely over. While the broad masses of the people welcome the new system, they are not yet quite accustomed to it. Government workers are not sufficiently experienced and should continue to examine and explore ways of dealing with questions relating to specific policies.

In other words, time is needed for our socialist system to grow and consolidate itself, for the masses to get accustomed to the new system, and for Government workers to study and acquire experience. It is imperative that at this juncture we raise the question of distinguishing contradictions among the people from contradictions between ourselves and the enemy, as well as the question of the proper handling of contradictions among the people, so as to rally the people of all nationalities in our country to wage a new battle—the battle against nature—to develop our economy and culture, enable all our people to go through this transition period in a fairly smooth way, make our new system secure, and build up our new state.

"FREEDOM AND THE BLACK MINORITY"

Lerone Bennett, Jr.

There has never been a free people, a free country, a real democracy on the face of this earth.

In a city of some 300,000 slaves and 90,000 so-called free men, Plato sat down and praised freedom in exquisitely elegant phrases.

In a colony of 500,000 slaves and thousands of white indentured servants, Thomas Jefferson, a wealthy slaveowner, sat down and wrote the memorable words of the Declaration of Independence.

In a country with 10 million second-class citizens and millions on millions of poverty-stricken whites, Woodrow Wilson segregated the toilets in Washington, D. C., and went forth to make the world safe for democracy.

There has never been a free people, a free country, a real democracy in the recorded history of man.

The great masses of men have always lived in suburbs of hell.

The great masses of men and almost all women have always been anvils for the hammers of the few.

We have gathered therefore to talk about a subject which has no past, insofar as mankind is concerned, and which can have no future, unless it is visualized and made concrete in the body of mankind. And it seems to me that one forfeits the right to talk about freedom unless one is prepared to face that fact and to do something about it.

Almost 200 years ago, at a time of revolutionary turbulence not unlike the present, Tom Paine held that unpalatable truth up to the unseeing eyes of his contemporaries. "Freedom," he said, hath been hunted around the Globe ... O! receive the fugitive, and prepare in time an asylum for mankind." Today, after a thousand evasions, after a thousand proclamations and manifestoes, freedom is still a fugitive—in America as well as in Russia, in Portugal as well as in Angola, in England as well as in Rhodesia, in Boston as well as in Mississippi.

We live in a world where two-thirds of the people are hungry.

We live in a world where most of the peoples are diseased and illiterate.

In such a world, who has the effrontery—who has the gall—to praise the state of freedom?

The whole problem of freedom in the white and nonwhite worlds must be placed first in this larger context, for henceforth it will be impossible to speak of freedom in terms of the concerns of the tiny minority of men who live in Europe and North

America. We must note, moreover, that freedom in Western Europe and North America is abstract, negative and largely illusory. And even in these areas, millions live on the edge of despair, and millions more are slaves to their skin or to their omnivorous machines.

It will be my argument here that the truth of freedom in the world is the truth of the truly disinherited. And by that I mean that the state of freedom is most accurately reflected in the lives of the men on the bottom. The men on the top and the men in the middle can remain ignorant of what they do and of what they are. But the men on the bottom experience the truth of society irremediably. They are the truth of every society. In them, we can see what we are, and what we have become. In the mirror of their eyes, we can measure the depth of our alienation from freedom and from man.

To be even more explicit and to bring the matter closer to home, I intend to maintain here that racism is the best index of the failure of American society to create a human and equitable society *for white people*. My argument here is the very simple one that the depth of racism is a measure of the unfreedom in the white community. And from that premise, we can conclude that black men are not free because white men are not free. And by all this we must understand that when the Emancipation Proclamation finally comes it will be most of all an emancipation of white people from the fears and frailties that cruelly twist and goad their lives.

Before pursuing that argument, let us pause for a moment and examine the meaning and implications of the word that everybody praises and few people live. As we all know, freedom lends itself to numerous interpretations. In the white Western world, it is usually defined negatively as "freedom from." This definition finds its truth in certain abstract liberties: freedom of speech, freedom of association, *et cetera*. To define freedom thusly, and to stop there, is, in my opinion, a perversion of freedom, for freedom also means "freedom to." And this positive definition finds its truth in concrete possibilities created in the social field, in the right to work, in the right to eat, in the right to shelter, in the right to be.

There is still another definition of freedom, a psychological one, which stresses the act of willing or choosing. And this definition, in turn, is linked to a fourth one which contends that man—by his ability to rise above or transcend a situation, any situation, by his ability to say No—is the measure and the meaning of freedom in the world.

In my opinion, no definition of freedom is adequate in today's world which does not embrace all these meanings—freedom from, freedom to transcendence—in a concrete context linked to conditions that open or close real possibilities to concrete men in their social and historical situation. Such a definition would recognize the existentialist truth that man *is* freedom and would recognize that the alienation of the world from freedom is a measure of its alienation from man and the possibilities of man. It would also recognize the truth that man has not yet been created and that the creation of man—black man as well as white man—awaits the winning of real, concrete freedom for all men.

Here and there, across the great wastelands of time, little knots of men have glimpsed the terrifying possibilities of that paradox. I think particularly of African village democracy and other free forms developed by American Indians and other communal groups. But these groups were hemmed in by material limitations and it was left to Western Europe to free man from feudal restrictions and to hoist high the standards of individuality and personal autonomy. But Europe, in its lunge toward freedom, made three fatal errors. First of all, and most important of all, Europe experienced its newfound freedom as the untrammelled exercise of the ego. And in pursuit of the goal of possessive individualism, it drew a circle around itself, excluding and enslaving three-fourths of mankind.

Second, out of sheer terror, Europe cut freedom into two parts, separating man into positive and negative poles, the mind and the body, reason and emotion, sex and the soul. Refusing to recognize the full force of freedom, which manifests itself in sex as well as in prayer, Europe facilitated that manic process by which men project their rejected freedom onto the scapegoats and outcasts of society.

In the third place, Europe refused to admit the full logic of its own idea. With few exceptions, Europeans and the sons of Europeans found it difficult to extend the idea of freedom to poor whites and impossible to extend it to nonwhites. In Europe and in the extensions of Europe, freedom became a function of the skin and of property.

Despite the huge achievements of European technology and science, European freedom, beautiful as it was, was not freedom. Or better still: it was not yet freedom. Having freed man from arbitrary restraints, Europe stopped halfway, leaving man tied to the chains of caste, class and passion. Having expelled man from his tribal and feudal Eden, Europe retreated, in terror, from Nietzsche's lucid question:

"Not free from what, but free for what?"

America inherited Europe's immense achievements and its immense failures—and extended both. The history of America, like the history of Europe, has been a history of a magnificent evasion of the multiple meanings of freedom. The most obvious example of that failure is the black American. But the failure to integrate black people into the American community is only a part of our culture's general inability to create a just and human environment.

Despite our alleged affluence, 30 to 40 million Americans, many of them white, live in abject poverty, and millions more live lives of harrowing economic insecurity.

Despite our extraordinary mechanical ability, which cannot be praised too highly, we have failed to create a truly human community. Machines are more real here than human beings—and vastly more important. In a society of machines, by machines and for machines, we are increasingly powerless, and a nihilistic individualism has made conformists—and cowards—of us all. Dehumanized, depersonalized, distracted by bread and television, we have almost lost sight of man. Mystified by an ethic which confuses the verb to be with the verb to have, we try to staunch the running wound of our lives by adding layers and layers of mechanical band-aids. We lack passion, we lack purpose, and we decide nothing. The great alternatives are formulated by others, and in our name and without our assent men, women, and little children are killed in poverty-stricken countries. Increasingly irresponsible as our choices become fewer, and as the world becomes more threatening, we whirl around and in a materialistic inferno between collective madness and collective self-destruction.

And we are afraid.

We are afraid of our neighbors, of Negroes, of Chinese, of Communists, of four-letter words, sex, fluoridation—we are afraid, in a word, of ourselves.

Because we fear ourselves and others, because we are dominated by machines and things, because we are not in control of our destiny, we are neither happy nor free.

"If one probes beneath the chrome-plated surface," Senator J. W. Fulbright says, "he comes inescapably to the conclusion that the American people by and large are not happy. . . . I believe . . . that America's trouble is basically one of aimlessness at home and frustration abroad."

As you have probably guessed by now, I believe America's trouble is at a deeper level. The problem, in my opinion, is structural, that is, institutional. We have not created a single community here. We have not even created a single community for white people. Men tell me that white people ought to love black people. But it is clear to me that white people don't love each other, not to speak of the fact that an incredibly large number of white Americans don't love themselves.

Racism in America is a reflection of this structural problem. As I have said elsewhere, we misunderstand racism completely if we do not see it as a confused and alienated protest against a suffocating reality. On the level of power, racism is used by men to effect magical solutions of the unresolved social problems in the white community. On a personal level, particularly among lower-income and middle-income whites, racism is an avenue of flight, a cry for help from desperate men stifling in the prisons of their skins. Viewed in this perspective, racism is a flight from freedom, a flight from the self, a flight from the intolerable burdens of being a man in a mechanized world.

There is considerable evidence that America's stress on possessive individualism induces exaggerated anxieties which are displaced onto the area of race relations. The fear of failure, the fear of competitors, the fear of losing status, of not living in the right neighborhood, of not having the right friends or the right gadgets: these fears weigh heavily on the minds of millions of Americans and lead to a search for avenues on the escape. And so the factory worker or the poor farmer who finds himself at a dead end with a nagging wife, a problem child and a past-due bill uses the black man as a screen to hide himself from himself and intolerable reality.

To adapt the perceptive words of Richard Wright, social discontent assumes many guises, and the social commentator who focuses on the police blotter misses the real clues to contemporary reality. By this I mean that it is possible to know, *before it happens*, that certain forms of violence will occur. It can be known, *before it happens*, that a native-born American, educated, healthy, with a pretty wife, a split-level house and two cars, with all the abstract liberties *but devoid of basic human satisfactions*, will seize upon a powerless black man and derive deep feelings of pleasure from hacking him to death with a chain. "But," as Wright said, "to know that a seemingly normal, ordinary American is capable of such brutality implies making a judgment about the nature and quality of our everyday American experiences which most Americans simply cannot do, FOR, TO ADMIT THAT OUR INDIVIDUAL EXPERIENCES ARE OF SO LOW A QUALITY ... AS TO PRECLUDE THE DEEP, ORGANIC SATISFACTIONS NECESSARY FOR CIVILIZED, PEACEFUL LIVING, IS TO CONDEMN THE SYSTEM THAT PROVIDES THOSE EXPERIENCES."

The real question in America is how we build a society in which apparently normal people do not need scapegoats or whipping boys to build their egos and to maintain their dignity?

How can we build a society that will enhance freedom and integrity and obviate the need for racism?

First of all, we have to condemn the system.

And we have to condemn the system in the name of that America, of that Commonwealth of Silence, which was written, which was promised, and which has never existed. I am suggesting here that we must initiate a sustained dialogue on the foundations of our society. And we must demand the right to subject every institution to the claims of freedom.

Let me say immediately that I don't have all the answers. The only thing I know is that everything must be rethought again. We need a new definition of work embracing any act of value that a man brings to society and a new definition of politics embracing the full and effective participation of all men in formulating the alternatives and choosing between the alternatives of the political, economic and social decisions that affect their lives. We also need a new definition of sex which would free women for equal roles in the church, in labor unions, in the professions and every other institution of our society. I often say to my wife that women, not Negroes, are the most brainwashed people in the Western world. Of course, in this regard, I am very much like Thomas Jefferson. I want women to have absolute freedom everywhere right now—but I hope that the revolution starts with somebody else's wife.

But wherever the revolution starts, I am prepared to welcome it, for I believe that the future of freedom in America is dependent upon the formulation of a broader definition of freedom and of man and of woman than our society is based upon. And it seems to me that it is necessary to set liberty in the context of equality with the understanding that every individual is entitled to the space and the chance to fulfill himself, which is only another way of saying that every individual is entitled to the instruments that will permit him to go to the boundaries of himself.

This, I believe, is a precondition for black and white freedom in America. For if we want black men and white men to cooperate, we must create conditions that will make it possible for them to cooperate. In other words, we must change the conditions that lead white men to see black men as threats to their homes, to their jobs, to their masculinity. And to do this we must modify the situation of the white man from top to bottom. For to demand that white men give up their irrational responses to black reality is to demand that a situation which requires irrational responses be abolished.

We must conceive and organize in this country programs that will make it impossible for one man to profit by another man's fall.

We must conceive and organize in this community, and in every other community, programs that will relieve the economic pressures on all men so that some men will not find it to their short-term economic interest to keep other men down.

In other words, we must take the profit out of bigotry.

The first steps in this direction would be a guaranteed annual income, the extension of Medicare to all citizens, the elimination of regressive taxes, and housing and educational subsidies to lower-and middle-income groups.

Ultimately, however, such an effort would require a reevaluation of our dominant myths, including the myth of possessive individuality, which is the greatest single obstacle to individuality, and the myth of property, which is the greatest single obstacle to the free enjoyment of property by all men.

Let there be no misunderstanding here: I am not saying that property in itself is evil—what I'm saying is that property masquerading as God is the major roadblock to freedom in the world today. Men need a certain amount of property to validate themselves and their freedom, but freedom becomes unfreedom and life loses its meaning when property becomes an inhuman idol, when anything and everything is sacrificed to an abstract Thing.

There was an interesting article on this subject in the New York Post which I would like to quote at some length. The article referred to the summer marches by Dr. Martin Luther King Jr., and his supporters through the Gage Park area of Chicago. Peter Hamill visited the neighborhood and wrote the following words:

"This was the way the Hollywood hustlers used to put their cardboard America together, in a time more innocent than ours.

"Children played in the streets, or burbled from baby carriages. Young boys mowed lawns which still smelled sweetly from the morning rains. Housewives pushed strollers to the grocery stores, or drove the family cars to the supermarkets. A man on vacation nailed a brass numeral to his front door. A lot of people seemed to be polishing automobiles with an almost reverent devotion. Gage Park on Monday afternoon seemed as innocuous as anyplace where Doris Day had ever lived on film.

"But underneath, past the front doors of those two-story houses, in the secret places behind those lawns and those automobiles and those smiling children, Gage Park was like a tray of summer worms. By the time the thing that is crawling through Gage Park has hooked its last inhabitant, that neighborhood is almost certainly going to murder someone. It is going to murder someone because of the accident of color. It is going to murder someone over the combination of wood, metal and concrete which the inhabitants fondly describe as their property."

The same animal is crawling through the Gage Parks of Boston and New York and California. And if we don't confront it soon, an unspeakably horrible disaster is going to happen here. It's going to happen because our churches and schools have not taught people that no thing is higher than man. It's going to happen because our civilization has not yet learned that men are important, whether they own property or not.

To a great extent, racism in America is grounded on the whole sick syndrome surrounding real estate, status, greed, and human pettiness. If we are serious about freedom, we are going to have to come to grips with that syndrome.

We hear a great deal about freedom and property, but we must have the courage to say that words cannot be prostituted with impunity. Freedom is a fine word, but it has its boundaries. Men who say the community is free when it is enslaved, men who say the sky is black when it is blue, are debasing reality and preparing the way for tyranny.

We can respect freedom only when it is intended for freedom. A freedom that denies freedom must be denied in the name of freedom. For to be free is not to have the power to do anything you want to do. I am oppressed if I am denied the right of free movement, but I am not oppressed if I am denied the right to deny my neighbor freedom of movement.

Beyond all that, we must note that the idea of one-class, one-kind neighborhoods is in and of itself a clear and present danger to American democracy. The standardized neighborhoods, the standardized houses, the standardized minds and the standardized fears which stretch from one end of America to another is a denial of the movement of life which advances by integrating differences. As Chardin has said: "Joy lies not in exclusiveness and isolation, but in variety which is the reservoir of experience and emotion." On the other hand, uniformity, sameness, standardization make for cultural stagnation and, as sure as night follows day, regimentation and eventually neo-Fascism.

In order to deal with the anti-democratic ideas, which have made deep inroads in American life, we must make revolutionary changes at every level of our lives. We confront, in a word, the need for not a law here or a law there but for a vital change in the whole spirit of our civilization.

All signs indicate that we are moving toward a critical point in American history. The rise of the Radical Right, the deepening despair in the ghetto, the deepening fear in the white community, the explicit avowals of *apartheid* in the recent elections: all these bespeak the seriousness of the moment.

This is an important moment in the history of the Commonwealth. There stretch out before us now two roads and two roads only. America must now become America or something else, a Fourth Reich perhaps or a Fourth Reich of the spirit. To put the matter bluntly—we must become what we say we are or give in to the secret dream that blights our hearts.

Let us rejoice that it has come to this.

Now that freedom is dangerous, perhaps men will stop prostituting it. Now that freedom is exploding in broad open daylight in the streets of America and Vietnam, perhaps we will be able to recognize her true friends.

As individuals, we are called upon to make a creative response to this challenge by assuming our own freedom and validating it in social acts designed to create spaces in which the seeds of freedom can grow.

In a very real sense, the struggle in America is a struggle to free white Americans or, to be quite precise, it is a struggle to put them in the presence of their freedom. And it seems to me that it is the duty of this convocation to send abroad the good news that one can be free, even in Boston or Chicago or New York.

Freedom isn't something you can buy on the installment plan. It is not a gift from anybody—it is a priceless possession that must be reclaimed and rewon every day. As Silone has said: "One can be free even under a dictatorship. All you have to do is to struggle against it." He who thinks with his own head and acts with his own heart is free. He who is not afraid of his neighbors is free. He who struggles for what he believes in is a free man. On the other hand: If you live in the richest Boston suburb and if you are lazy, timid, conformist, you are not free, but a slave.

Because men deny the tiny bit of psychological freedom at their disposal, it is necessary to awaken them by social movements in which wills confront each other. This is the meaning of the Black Revolution, which is inviting us to become ourselves by going to the limits of ourselves. This revolution defines the state of freedom in America today, and it tells us that freedom has no future in America if the black man does not have a future in freedom.

More than 100 years ago, Walt Whitman told Ralph Waldo Emerson:

"Master, I am a man who has perfect faith. But Master, we have not come through centuries, caste, heroism, fables, to halt in this land today."

The spirit of Walt Whitman is marching today in the Harlems of our mind. Men and women made in Whitman's image are saying to us: "Fellow Americans, we have perfect faith. But Fellow Americans, we have not come through slavery, segregation, degradation, blood, cotton, roaches, rats, to halt in this land today."

Black Americans, by daring to claim their freedom, are daring us to claim our own.

And the movement which expresses that thrust will continue despite the recent revelations of the depth and extent of racism in America. Whatever the problems, whatever the setbacks, whatever the dangers, oppression must be rejected at any cost. For, as Du Bois said, the price of freedom is always less than the cost of oppression.

In the Black Revolution, America comes hard up against a new fact: *the color of the world has changed*. And with that change, a terrifying freedom has become the burden of all men, especially those men who were tyrannized for so long by the arbitrary limitations of their skin. If white men come forward now to claim their own freedom and individuality, if they abandon their trenches and come out into the open, America will become the America that was dreamed.

This is the real meaning of the Black Revolution, which is a desperate attempt to place before our freedom the burning alternatives history is offering us.

Walt Whitman said:

"We have not come through centuries, caste, fables, to halt in this land today."

Black Americans are saying:

"We have not come through slavery, segregation, degradation to halt in this land today."

And the question now is:

What do you say?

"FREEDOM: VOICES FROM
THE LOVE GENERATION"

Leonard Wolf

Lenore Kandel

Lenore: The culture is crumbling faster and faster. The hypocrisies are more and more apparent. [Young people] look at their parents—they're lying to each other. They're married for thirty years, they go out and fuck other people and lie about it to each other. They know it doesn't work, but there's a lot of exterior pressure. There's war. There's the fear of death. And if you don't want it to happen, you've got to have another direction. If you don't want the world you're pushed into, you have to find another world. You can't sit back and say it's all going to work out. No exterior movement can function unless it's composed of people whose interior is fit. . . . The first place that it has to happen is inside. You learn where you are. You learn if you want to make it here or in the trees. You learn if you want to make it with men or make it with women or play with yourself. You learn, not because this is the way it's supposed to be, but truthfully, in yourself it's what you want.

Q: Acid is said to be a tool for reaching this point.

Lenore: It can be a tool. My particular direction was such that I went along that trip through meditation. All these things are guideposts, no one of them is an end in itself. The reason one sits in Zen is to connect, connect yourself and that which you are surrounded by interiorly and exteriorly. If you lose that, the whole thing doesn't work. When you take acid, it is a guidepost. If you forget that and get hung up taking acid and playing games, you'll be just as clearly a loser as any other way.

Q: You don't find acid that illuminating?

Lenore: It hasn't been to me, but I had already done an awful lot of the groundwork.

Q: Have you taken other drugs?

Lenore: I've tried peyote. I had a very strong trip on it some years ago. It gave me a lot to work on. It's a very similar thing. It can be an instant revelation if you let it. If you've got guilt, despairs, and lies inside of you, they're very likely to come up and hit you in the face. If you do meditation, it's not just sitting cross-legged. There's sitting meditation, walking meditation, scrubbing-floors medita-tion, dishwashing meditation. It's a way of life, a consciousness. Now if you start living this kind of life where you really move with awareness, acid's a great help. Meditation is a help. Talking truthfully to another human being can be a help. And being truthful to yourself can be the greatest help of all. Acid helps people talk truthfully to themselves. I wouldn't say it does it one hundred per cent of the time, because sometimes people are so terrified of themselves that all they do is run screaming in circles. Now that can help too, because if they admit that they're terrified of what happens if they run screaming in circles, they can do something.

Q: What about psychiatry, the old-fashioned way?

Lenore: One of the troubles with psychiatry is that its direction was to adjust the person to the norm. The norm is sick. I don't think any of the people I'm involved with care to be adjusted to the sick.

Q: What, besides the hypocrisy, are the signs of the sickness?

Lenore: First of all, any nation that sits and says, well, we have to destroy this food, because it keeps the economy up, has a sickness in it. Because to me, there's no valid reason for destroying food when there are people hungry. Any group of people who can easily accept murder as a way of life is sick. . . . It's no longer functional to continue on that level . . . I feel that the forces toward survival are very strong. I don't feel it's necessary for everybody to explode and everybody die. The only way I know that we can move in a life-centered direction is to tell the truth. The first place you start telling the truth is within yourself. Then you carry on to all phases of life, including the nation as a whole. I don't know how this works in politics. . . . I'm not a politician so I don't know how that's going to resolve.

Q: What about the emergence of sexual awareness?

Lenore: Well, I've always been pretty sensual myself. I think all this thing about original sin and guilt and Adam's fall is passing. I think the main thing is not to hurt people unnecessarily. I don't believe in inflicting physical or mental pain on someone, though there are people who dig it. But I don't think they should put their trip on someone who doesn't.

Q: What about the sexual mores?

Lenore: That's what's really getting worked over right now. And nobody's really got the answers yet. It's all in process. [As it is], if a man and a woman are together, and one of them cheats on the other, well, that's a betrayal if they're doing it behind [each] other's back. But they're going to do it anyway, and try to sneak. But if they come out straight and say, "Look I love you, but I can't help it, I'll make it with somebody else sometime," [then] that's the way it is. It may be painful, but it can be worked out because it's right up front, [and those] people involved are going to have to deal with it. There's no general proscription.

All I know is that people have to tell the truth to each other. One of the things that leads to the whole cheating process is fake morality. "Kids, I know that your bodies are all bright and pounding, but don't do anything. You just cross your legs, dear." Of course, if you're a boy, boys are different. "Why don't you go downtown and visit the local whore?" A lot of fathers take their sons to the local whore.

That's one thing this book of mine has done. I've learned a whole lot about what's going on in all kinds of different groups of people. [Fake morality] is still going on. It's still extant, but it's beginning to die out, because people are going through so much pain because of it. I think that kids develop at differing times. . . .

I think it's really wrong if someone is really ready and wants [to make love] and doesn't. Because then they get all hung up from it. And so many women turn frigid because they spend all their lives being a commodity. "Don't make it with anybody, because if you're a virgin, you'll marry somebody with a lot of money, and this is what you have to do. It's as easy to fall for a rich man as a poor man." That's one of the slogans of the country. By the time she marries, she's going to take it all out on the cat she marries. . . .

Q: Do you think that across the country young people are working out a new sense of what they'll accept as truth?

Lenore: That goes back to what I've been saying. You start from the inside and tell the truth to yourself. Find out where you are. And then you do everything working outward from there. They're working on the assumption that you get married to someone and you're supposed to be faithful to them physically. So if one of them has desires toward another person, this immediately sets up a whole thing. Guilt. Now when you get guilt going you usually take it out on those that are near you. Why. There's immediately a straining pressure thing going on there. This is what's been going on in this country for a long time.

Q: How will things change?

Lenore: Each two people will have to work it out for themselves.

Peter Cohon

Q: What is your sense of work in the culture?

Peter: Well, you know work used to be the only means by which one participated in the wealth of the nation. The problem was a problem of scarcity . . . and the means of portioning out wealth and food was work. Consequently all sorts of moral and ethical structures came up relative to work. Well, technological innovations can occur very rapidly and wipe out the premise of those ethical/social relations. Cybernation turns the problem of scarcity into the problem of surplus. Machines can go on and on creating more than anyone needs. So if there's enough for everyone, everyone should have it. . . . Everyone should have food. Why should you have to work for it? In other words, you used to say, "Well, you work so that you can get the good things in life. You work so you can get certain kinds of pleasures. You work so that you can do what you want." The way it seems to have turned out is that now when you work eight hours a day at something that's not relevant to your life and doesn't interest you, [you] wind up working to support a host of things society offers you as substitutes for your life. Meaning television, nightclubs, movies, bowling, etcetera. . . . I really think that those things are absolutely vital to anyone who does something he doesn't like. . . . And then you end up supporting those diversions, instead of living the way you want to from in front. . . .

Q: You're a Digger. That implies a point of view about ownership and property. Do you want to—

Peter: I think the Diggers should be killed. I think the word has gotten out of hand already. All it means is *free* and *do your thing.*

Q: You still hold to that: *free* and *do your thing?*

Peter: Yes. Which is not to say that I don't deal in money. It's impossible to avoid it, living in this culture. But being free draws a line. . . . It puts you outside the premises of this culture, no matter where you want to start. The premises of this culture are profit and private property and power. There's nothing wrong with the logic. The logic is absolutely consistent. That's what's so threatening about it. Once you leave the premises, then the whole thing becomes very clear. You understand a lot of things. If you live in this society, you're put in the position of using the society's evils as excuses for perpetuating it. If you're a doctor, you *need* a modern office or people won't think you're up to date and won't trust you. You *need* malpractice insurance because pinched people might sue. Those kinds of things are reflected in the patient's bill. The patient then has to go out and hustle somebody else. So most everybody knows it's a crummy system but they say, "Well, I just want to get mine out of it for me and the people I love." When a union goes on strike, they don't care that their strike is going to up prices for the consumer . . . all they want is their slice of the pie. Nowhere do people just stop and say, "That's not the way I want to live."

Peter Berg

Peter: That's where we start, man. Now, do it. Now, do it, shit, now, go ahead, drop out now. What, now what, what now, now, what, whatever you want, go ahead, do it, do it. . . . . You doin' what you want to? Uh-huh? *Sure* it's what you want to do? Do what you want to do, right? Can't do what you want to do? Uh-oh. Now things get very real. . . . Go do what you want to do. You tell me you're free, you tell me you're free, man. Tell me you're free, man, you do whatever you want to do, you tell me that. Now what. What happens now? Got busted? Did what? Free store, free food, wow, beautiful! Free theater, free poems, like that, we got busted! Yeah. You assume freedom? *Assume* freedom. Now what? It's pure intuition, man. Come on, we're talking about freedom. . . . You sit on the floor. You tell me what you can do tomorrow. You tell me what you can do, what you can get away with. . . . And then we find it's necessary to bail each other out.

There are internal contradictions in the society that have been heightened to such a degree that the country has become the equivalent of fascist. It's General Motors fascism. That's out front. Our lives are in fact revolutionary within the context of General Motors fascism. We expect to live our lives and to defend them. We have been cultural outsiders in this civilization. We will become the political dynamic of the new society because we are *living* a new civilization. My life is now political, it's ultimately political. . . .

The internal contradictions in this country are creating a void that one would have to be blind not to see. The void is rushing at us so fast now that Zen is breakfast. Within a short time, the general cultural movement will become more social. The issue is being forced by the black people. . . . We are in the middle, we people, and we find our vanity can no longer be a shield. So we have to adopt the state of mind that's proper to the world that's opening for us. Our life style is the mode of existence for free men, a new vision of freedom that is bought at the price that freedom has always been bought. Our people are in jails. What we do now will be called treason. . . . It is necessary to take the responsibility for being. . . . There is no escape; there can only be confrontation. . . . And there's every chance that we won't be allowed the opportunity to carry it out without an interim period where there's going to be a great deal of death. We've passed the meridian. . . . We're passing now into a time of death, and we have to confront death with the vision of life.

Q: What do you foresee?

Peter: Civil war. Civil war with some attendant trips.

Leonard Wolf, Editor

Whether hippies as such survive or not seems to me irrelevant. In the long run, the greatest contribution the movement will have made to American life will be the new emphasis their self-expression has brought to the question of personal freedom. With all of its outrageousness, its occasional affectation, its political innocence, its neurotic flavor, the movement will have startled the rest of us into asking what we do mean by freedom. The Diggers are not wrong when they ask, "Free what? What free?" John Donne's question, "Alas, alas, who's injured by my love?" may well be asked about all the qualities and styles of love that human hunger is capable of. How indeed *is* the structure of American society threatened by adult embraces that an outworn legal code still forbids? What in fact, compared with the Vietnam war or race hatred, *is* the national calamity that will overtake us if men or women or children choose to be naked? Why *must* our young people rush to be useful in the terms of a utility which had meaning at the beginning of the Industrial Revolution? How deep is our national hypocrisy when we forbid the use of drugs no more harmful than the cocktails we drink or the tranquilizers and cigarettes we consume that we take by the billion?

The hippie movement becomes historically relevant just because it poses for us the question of freedom as youth sees it. Not freedom someday, but now. Do it, they tell us. Now.

"FREEDOM: THE LOVE GENERATION VS. THE MIDDLE CLASS"

Fred Davis

And thus in love we have declared the purpose of our hearts plainly, without flatterie, expecting love, and the same sincerity from you, without grumbling, or quarreling, being Creatures of your own image and mould, intending no other matter herein, but to observe the Law of righteous action, endeavoring to shut out of the Creation, the cursed thing, called Particular Propriety, which is the cause of all wars, bloud-shed, theft, and enslaving Laws, that hold the people under miserie. Signed for and in behalf of all the poor oppressed people of England, and the whole world.

Gerrard Winstanley and others
June 1, 1649

This quotation is from the leader of the Diggers, a millenarian sect of communistic persuasion that arose in England at the time of Oliver Cromwell. Today in San Francisco's hippie community, the Haight-Ashbury district, a group of hippies naming themselves after this sect distributes free food to fellow hippies (and all other takers, for that matter) who congregate at about four o'clock every afternoon in the district's Panhandle, an eight-block strip of urban green, shaded by towering eucalyptus trees, that leads into Golden Gate Park to the west. On the corner of a nearby street, the "Hashbury" Diggers operate their Free Store where all—be they hip, straight, hostile, curious, or merely in need—can avail themselves (free of charge, no questions asked) of such used clothing, household articles, books, and second-hand furniture as find their way into the place on any particular day. The Diggers also maintained a large flat in the district where newly arrived or freshly dispossessed hippies could stay without charge for a night, a week, or however long they wished—until some months ago, when the flat was condemned by the San Francisco Health Department. Currently, the Diggers are rehabilitating a condemned skid-row hotel for the same purpose.

Not all of Haight-Ashbury's 7500 hippies are Diggers, although no formal qualifications bar them; nor, in one sense, are the several dozen Diggers hippies. What distinguishes the Diggers—an amorphous, shifting, and sometimes contentious amalgam of ex-political radicals, psychedelic mystics, Ghandians, and Brechtian avant-garde thespians—from the area's "ordinary" hippies is their ideological brio, articulateness, good works, and flair for the dramatic event. (Some are even rumored to be over 30.) In the eyes of many Hashbury hippies, therefore, the Diggers symbolize what is best, what is most persuasive and purposive, about the surrounding, more variegated hippie subculture—just as, for certain radical social critics of the American scene, the hippies are expressing, albeit elliptically, what is best about a seemingly ever-broader segment of American youth: its openness to new experience, puncturing of cant, rejection of bureaucratic regimentation, aversion to violence, and identification with the exploited and disadvantaged. That this is not the whole story barely needs saying. Along with the poetry and flowers, the melancholy smile at passing and ecstatic clasp at greeting, there is also the panicky incoherence of the bad LSD trip, the malnutrition, a startling rise in V.D. and hepatitis, a seemingly phobic reaction to elementary practices of hygiene and sanitation, and—perhaps most disturbing in the long run—a casualness about the comings and goings of human relationships that must verge on the grossly irresponsible.

But, then, social movements—particularly of this expressive-religious variety—are rarely of a piece, and it would be unfortunate if social scientists, rather than inquiring into the genesis, meaning, and future of the hippie movement, too soon joined ranks (as many are likely to, in any case) with solid burghers in an orgy of research into the "pathology" of it all: the ubiquitous drug use (mainly marihuana and LSD, often amphetamines, rarely heroin or other opiates), the easy attitudes toward sex ("If two people are attracted to each other, what better way of showing it than to make love?"), and the mocking hostility toward the middle-class values of pleasure-deferral, material success, and—ultimately—the whole mass-media-glamorized round of chic, deodorized, appliance-glutted suburban existence.

The Hip Scene Is the Message. Clearly, despite whatever real or imagined "pathology" middle-class spokesmen are ready to assign to the hippies, it is the middle-class scheme of life that young hippies are reacting against, even though in their ranks are to be found some youth of working-class origin who have never enjoyed the affluence that their peers now so heartily decry. To adulterate somewhat the slogan of Marshall McLuhan, one of the few non-orientalized intelluctuals whom hippies bother to read at all, *the hip scene is the message*, not the elements whence it derives or the meanings that can be assigned to it verbally. (Interestingly, this fusion of disparate classes does not appear to include any significant number of the Negro youths who reside with their families in the integrated Haight-Ashbury district or in the adjoining Negro ghetto, the Fillmore district. By and large, Negroes view with bewilderment and ridicule the white hippies who flaunt, to the extent of begging on the streets, their rejection of what the Negroes have had scant opportunity to attain. What more revealing symbol of the Negro riots in our nation's cities than the carting off of looted TV sets, refrigerators, and washing machines? After all, aren't these things what America is all about?)

But granting that the hippie scene is a reaction to middle-class values, can the understanding of any social movement—particularly one that just in the process of its formation is so fecund of new art forms, new styles of dress and demeanor, and (most of all) new ethical bases for human relationships—ever the wholly reduced to its reactive aspect? As Ralph Ellison has eloquently observed in his critique of the standard sociological explanation of the American Negro's situation, a people's distinctive way of life is never solely a reaction to the dominant social forces that have oppressed, excluded, or alienated them from the larger society. The cumulative process of reaction and counterreaction, in its historical unfolding, creates its own ground for the emergence of new symbols, meanings, purposes, and social discoveries, none of which are ever wholly contained in embryo, as it were, in the conditions that elicited the reaction. It is, therefore, less with an eye toward explaining "how it came to be" than toward explaining what it may betoken of life in the future society that I now want to examine certain facets of the Hashbury hippie subculture. (Of course, very similar youth movements, subcultures, and settlements are found nowadays in many parts of the affluent Western world— Berkeley's Telegraph Avenue teeny-boppers; Los Angeles' Sunset Strippers; New York's East Village hippies; London's mods; Amsterdam's Provos; and the summer *Wandervögel* from all over Europe who chalk the pavements of Copenhagen's main shopping street, the Strøget, and sun themselves on the steps of Stockholm's Philharmonic Hall. What is culturally significant about the Haight-Ashbury hippies is, I would hazard, in general significant about these others as well, with—to be sure—certain qualifications. Indeed, a certain marvelous irony attaches itself to the fact that perhaps the only genuine cross-national culture found in the world today builds on the rag-tag of beards, bare feet, bedrolls, and beads, not on the cultural-exchange programs of governments and universities, or tourism, or—least of all—ladies' clubs' invocations for sympathetic understanding of one's foreign neighbors.)

What I wish to suggest here is that there is, as Max Weber would have put it, an *elective affinity* between prominent styles and themes in the hippie subculture and certain incipient problems of identity, work, and leisure that loom ominously as Western industrial society moves into an epoch of accelerated cybernation, staggering material abundance, and historically-unprecedented mass opportunities for creative leisure and enrichment of the human personality. This is not to say that the latter are the *hidden causes* or tangible *motivating forces* of the former. Rather, the point is that the hippies, in their collective, yet radical, break with the constraints of our present society, are—whether they know it or not (some clearly do intuit a connection)—already rehearsing *in vivo* a number of possible cultural solutions to central life problems posed by the emerging society of the future. While other students of contemporary youth culture could no doubt cite many additional emerging problems to which the hippie subculture is, willy-nilly, addressing itself (marriage and family organization, the character of friendship and personal loyalties, the forms of political participation), space and the kind of observations I have been able to make require that I confine myself to three: the problems of *compulsive consumption*, of *passive spectatorship*, and of the *time-scale of experience*.

Compulsive Consumption. What working attitude is man to adopt toward the potential glut of consumer goods that the new technology will make available to virtually all members of the future society? Until now, modern capitalist society's traditional response to short-term conditions of overproduction has been to generate—through government manipulation of fiscal devices—greater purchasing power for discretionary consumption. At the same time, the aim has been to cultivate the acquisitive impulse—largely through mass advertising, annual styling changes, and planned obsolescence—so that, in the economist's terminology, a high level of aggregate demand could be sustained. Fortunately, given the great backlog of old material wants and the technologically-based creation of new wants, these means have, for the most part, worked comparatively well—both for advancing (albeit unequally) the mass standard of living and ensuring a reasonably high rate of return to capital.

But, as Walter Weisskopf, Robert Heilbroner, and other economists have wondered, will these means prove adequate for an automated future society in which the mere production of goods and services might easily outstrip man's desire for them, or his capacity to consume them in satisfying ways? Massive problems of air pollution, traffic congestion, and waste disposal aside, is there no psychological limit to the number of automobiles, TV sets, freezers, and dishwashers that even a zealous consumer can aspire to, much less make psychic room for in his life space? The specter that haunts post-industrial man is that of a near worker-less economy in which most men are constrained, through a variety of economic and political sanctions, to frantically purchase and assiduously use up the cornucopia of consumer goods that a robot-staffed factory system (but one still harnessed to capitalism's rationale of pecuniary profit) regurgitates upon the populace. As far back as the late 1940s sociologists like David Riesman were already pointing to the many moral paradoxes of work, leisure, and interpersonal relations posed by a then only nascent society of capitalist mass abundance. How much more perplexing the paradoxes if, using current technological trends, we extrapolate to the year 2000?

Hippies, originating mainly in the middle classes, have been nurtured at the boards of consumer abundance. Spared their parents' vivid memories of economic depression and material want, however, they now, with what to their elders seems like insulting abandon, declare unshamefacedly that the very quest for "the good things of life" and all that this entails—the latest model, the third car, the monthly credit payments, the right house in the right neighborhood—are a "bad bag." In phrases redolent of nearly all utopian thought of the past, they proclaim that happiness and a meaningful life are not to be found in things, but in the cultivation of the self and by an intensive exploration of inner sensibilities with like-minded others.

Extreme as this antimaterialistic stance may seem, and despite its probable tempering should hippie communities develop as a stable feature on the American landscape, it nonetheless points a way to a solution of the problem of material glut; to wit, the simple demonstration of the ability to live on less, thereby calming the acquisitive frenzy that would have to be sustained, and even accelerated, if the present scheme of capitalist production and distribution were to remain unchanged. Besides such establishments as the Diggers' Free Store, gleanings of this attitude are even evident in the street panhandling that so many hippies engage in. Unlike the street beggars of old, there is little that is obsequious or deferential about their manner. On the contrary, their approach is one of easy, sometimes condescending casualness, as if to say, "You've got more than enough to spare, I need it, so let's not make a degrading charity scene out of my asking you." The story is told in the Haight-Ashbury of the patronizing tourist who, upon being approached for a dime by a hippie girl in her late teens, took the occasion to deliver a small speech on how delighted he would be to give it to her—provided she first told him what she needed it for. Without blinking an eye she replied, "It's my menstrual period and that's how much a sanitary napkin costs."

Passive Spectatorship. As social historians are forever reminding us, modern man has—since the beginnings of the industrial revolution—become increasingly a spectator and less a participant. Less and less does he, for example, create or play music, engage in sports, dance or sing; instead he watches professionally-trained others, vastly more accomplished than himself, perform their acts while he, perhaps, indulges in Mitty-like fantasies of hidden graces and talents. Although this bald statement of the spectator thesis has been challenged in recent years by certain social researchers—statistics are cited of the growing numbers taking guitar lessons, buying fishing equipment, and painting on Sunday—there can be little doubt that "doing" kinds of expressive pursuits, particularly of the collective type, no longer bear the same *integral* relationship to daily life that they once did, or still do in primitive societies. The mere change in how they come to be perceived, from what one does in the ordinary course of life to one's "hobbies," is in itself of profound historical significance. Along with this, the virtuoso standards that once were the exclusive property of small aristocratic elites, rather than being undermined by the oft-cited revolutions in mass communications and mass education, have so diffused through the class structure as to even cause the gifted amateur *at play* to apologize for his efforts with some such remark as, "I only play at it." In short, the cult of professionalism, in the arts as elsewhere, has been institutionalized so intensively in Western society that the ordinary man's sense of expressive adequacy and competence has progressively atrophied. This is especially true of the college-educated, urban middle classes, which—newly exposed to the lofty aesthetic standards of high culture—stand in reverent, if passive, awe of them.

Again, the problem of excessive spectatorship has not proved particularly acute until now, inasmuch as most men have had other time-consuming demands to fill their lives with, chiefly work and family life, leavened by occasional vacations and mass-produced amusements. But what of the future when, according to such social prognosticators as Robert Theobald and Donald Michael, all (except a relatively small cadre of professionals and managers) will be faced with a surfeit of leisure time? Will the mere extension of passive spectatorship and the professional's monopoly of expressive pursuits be a satisfactory solution?

Here, too, hippies are opening up new avenues of collective response to life issues posed by a changing socio-technological environment. They are doing so by rejecting those virtuoso standards that stifle participation in high culture; by substituting an extravagantly eclectic (and, according to traditional aestheticians, reckless) admixture of materials, styles, and motifs from a great diversity of past and present human cultures; and, most of all, by insisting that every man can find immediate expressive fulfillment provided he lets the socially-suppresed spirit within him ascend into vibrant consciousness. The manifesto is: All men are artists, and who cares that some are better at it than others; we can all have fun! Hence, the deceptively crude antisophistication of hippie art forms, which are, perhaps, only an apparent reversion to primitivism. One has only to encounter the lurid *art nouveau* contortions of the hippie posters and their Beardsleyan exoticism, or the mad mélange of hippie street costume—Greek-sandaled feet peeking beneath harem pantaloons encased in a fringed American Indian suede jacket, topped by pastel floral decorations about the face—or the sitar-whining cacophony of the folk-rock band, to know immediately that one is in the presence of *expressiveness* for its own sake.

In more mundane ways, too, the same readiness to let go, to participate, to create and perform without script or forethought is everywhere evident in the Hashbury. Two youths seat themselves on the sidewalk or in a store entranceway; bent beer can in hand, one begins scratching a bongo-like rhythm on the pavement while the other tattoos a bell-like accompaniment by striking a stick on an empty bottle. Soon they are joined, one by one, by a tambourinist, a harmonica player, a penny-whistler or recorder player, and, of course, the ubiquitous guitarist. A small crowd collects and, at the fringes, some blanket-bedecked boys and girls begin twirling about in movements vaguely resembling a Hindu dance. The wailing, rhythmic beating and dancing, alternately rising to peaks of intensity and subsiding, may last for as little as five minutes or as long as an hour, players and dancers joining in and dropping out as whim moves them. At some point—almost any—a mood takes hold that "the happening is over"; participants and onlookers disperse as casually as they had collected.

Analogous scenes of "participation unbound" are to be observed almost every night of the week (twice on Sunday) at the hippies' Parnassus, the Fillmore Auditorium, where a succession of name folk-rock bands, each more deafening than the one before, follow one another in hour-long sessions. Here, amidst the electric guitars, the electric organs, and the constantly metamorphizing show of lights, one can see the gainly and the graceless, the sylph bodies and rude stompers, the crooked and straight—all, of whatever condition or talent, *dance* as the flickering of a strobe light reduces their figures in silhouette to egalitarian spastic bursts. The recognition dawns that this, at last, is dancing of utterly free form, devoid of fixed sequence or step, open to all and calling for no Friday after-school classes at Miss Martha's or expensive lessons from Arthur Murray. The sole requisite is to tune in, take heart, and let go. What follows must be "beautiful" (a favorite hippie word) because it is *you* who are doing and feeling, not another to whom you have surrendered the muse.

As with folk-rock dancing, so (theoretically, at least) with music, poetry, painting, pottery, and the other arts and crafts: expression over performance, impulse over product. Whether the "straight world" will in time heed this message of the hippies is, to be sure, problematical. Also, given the lavish financial rewards and prestige heaped upon more talented hippie artists by a youth-dominated entertainment market, it is conceivable that high standards of professional performance will develop here as well (listen to the more recent Beatles' recordings), thus engendering perhaps as great a participative gulf between artist and audience as already exists in the established arts. Despite the vagaries of forecasting, however, the hippies—as of now, at least—are responding to the incipient plenitude of leisure in ways far removed from the baleful visions of a Huxley or an Orwell.

The Time-Scale of Experience. In every society, certain activities are required to complete various tasks and to achieve various goals. These activities form a sequence —they may be of short duration and simple linkage (boiling an egg); long duration and complex linkage (preparing for a profession); or a variety of intermediate combinations (planting and harvesting a crop). And the activity sequences needed to complete valued tasks and to achieve valued goals in a society largely determine how the people in that society will subjectively experience *time*.

The distinctive temporal bent of industrial society has been toward the second of these arrangements, long duration and complex linkage. As regards the subjective experience of time, this has meant what the anthropologist Florence Kluckhohn has termed a strong "future orientation" on the part of Western man, a quality of sensibility that radically distinguishes him from his peasant and tribal forebears. The major activities that fill the better part of his life acquire their meaning less from the pleasure they may or may not give at the moment than from their perceived relevance to some imagined future state of being or affairs, be it salvation, career achievement, material success, or the realization of a more perfect social order. Deprived of the pursuit of these temporally distant, complexly modulated goals, we would feel that life, as the man in the street puts it, is without meaning.

This subjective conception of time and experience is, of course, admirably suited to the needs of post-18th century industrial society, needs that include a stable labor force; work discipline; slow and regular accumulation of capital with which to plan and launch new investments and to expand; and long, arduous years of training to provide certain people with the high levels of skill necessary in so many professions and technical fields. If Western man had proved unable to defer present gratifications for future rewards (that is, if he had not been a future-oriented being), nothing resembling our present civilization, as Freud noted, could have come to pass.

Yet, paradoxically, it is the advanced technology of computers and servo-mechanisms, not to overlook nuclear warfare, that industrial civilization has carried us to that is raising grave doubts concerning this temporal ordering of affairs, this optimistic, pleasure-deferring, and magically rationalistic faith in converting present effort to future payoff. Why prepare, if there will be so few satisfying jobs to prepare for? Why defer, if there will be a superabundance of inexpensively-produced goods to choose from? Why plan, if all plans can disintegrate into nuclear dust?

Premature or exaggerated as these questions may seem, they are being asked, especially by young people. And merely to ask them is to prompt a radical shift in time-perspective—from what *will be* to what *is*, from future promise to present fulfillment, from the mundane discounting of present feeling and mood to a sharpened awareness of their contours and their possibilities for instant alteration. Broadly, it is to invest present experience with a new cognitive status and importance: a lust to extract from the living moment its full sensory and emotional potential. For if the present is no longer to hold hostage to the future, what other course than to ravish it at the very instant of its apprehension?

There is much about the hippie subculture that already betokens this alteration of time-perspective and concomitant reconstitution of the experienced self. Hippie argot—some of it new, much of it borrowed with slight connotative changes from the Negro, jazz, homosexual, and addict subcultures—is markedly skewed toward words and phrases in the active present tense: "happening," "where it's at," "turn on," "freak out," "grooving," "mind-blowing," "be-in," "cop out," "split," "drop acid" (take LSD), "put on," "uptight" (anxious and tense), "trip out" (experience the far-out effects of a hallucinogenic drug). The very concept of a happening signifies immediacy: Events are to be actively engaged in, improvised upon, and dramatically exploited for their own sake, with little thought about their origins, duration, or consequences. Thus, almost anything—from a massive be-in in Golden Gate Park to ingesting LSD to a casual street conversation to sitting solitarily under a tree—is approached with a heightened awareness of its happening potential.

Similarly, the vogue among Hashbury hippies for astrology, tarot cards, I Ching, and other forms of thaumaturgic prophecy (a hippie conversation is as likely to begin with "What's your birthday?" as "What's your name?") seems to be an attempt to denude the future of its temporal integrity—its unknowability and slow unfolding-ness—by fusing it indiscriminately with present dispositions and sensations. The hippie's structureless round-of-day ("hanging loose"), his disdain for appointments, schedules, and straight society's compulsive parceling out of minutes and hours, are all implicated in his intense reverence for the possibilities of the present and uninterest in the future. Few wear watches, and as a colleague who has made a close participant-observer study of one group of hippies remarked, "None of them ever seems to know what time it is."

It is, perhaps, from this vantage point that the wide-spread use of drugs by hippies acquires its cultural significance, above and beyond the fact that drugs are easily available in the subculture or that their use (especially LSD) has come to symbolize a distinctive badge of membership in that culture. Denied by our Protestant-Judaic heritage the psychological means for experiencing the moment intensively, for parlaying sensation and exoticizing mundane consciousness, the hippie uses drugs where untutored imagination fails. Drugs impart to the present—or so it is alleged by the hippie psychedelic religionists—an aura of aliveness, a sense of union with fellow man and nature, which—we have been taught—can be apprehended, if not in the afterlife that few modern men still believe in, then only after the deepest reflection and self-knowledge induced by protracted experience.

A topic of lively debate among hippie intellectuals is whether drugs represent but a transitory phase of the hippie subculture to be discarded once other, more self-generating, means are discovered by its members for extracting consummatory meaning from present time, or whether drugs are the *sine qua non* of the subcul-ture. Whatever the case, the hippies' experiment with ways to recast our notions of time and experience is deserving of close attention. . . .

It is difficult to foresee how long they will remain there and what the conse-quences for later stages of their careers will be, inasmuch as insufficient time has passed for even a single age cohort of hippies to make the transition from early to middle adulthood. However, even among those youths who "remain in" conven-tional society in some formal sense, a very large number can be expected to hover so close to the margins of hippie subculture as to have their attitudes and outlooks substantially modified. Indeed, it is probably through some such muted, gradual, and indirect process of social conversion that the hippie subculture will make a lasting impact on American society, if it is to have any at all.

At the same time, the hippie rebellion gives partial, as yet ambiguous, evidence of a massiveness, a universality, and a density of existential texture, all of which promise to transcend the narrowly-segregated confines of age, occupation, and residence that characterized most bohemias of the past (Greenwich Village, Blooms-bury, the Left Bank). Some hippie visionaries already compare the movement to Christianity sweeping the Roman Empire. We cannot predict how far the movement can go toward enveloping the larger society, and whether as it develops it will—as have nearly all successful social movements—significantly compromise the visions that animate it with the practices of the reigning institutional system. Much depends on the state of future social discontent, particularly within the middle classes, and on the viable political options governments have for assuaging this discontent. Judging, however, from the social upheavals and mass violence of recent decades, such options are, perhaps inevitably, scarce indeed. Just possibly, then, by opting out and making their own kind of cultural waves, the hippies are telling us more than we can now imagine about our future selves.

"FREEDOM AND THE NEW LEFT"

S.D.S.

Introduction: Agenda For a Generation

We are people of this generation, bred in at least modest comfort, housed now in universities, looking uncomfortably to the world we inherit.

When we were kids the United States was the wealthiest and strongest country in the world; the only one with the atom bomb, the least scarred by modern war, an initiator of the United Nations that we thought would distribute Western influence throughout the world. Freedom and equality for each individual, government of, by, and for the people—these American values we found good, principles by which we could live as men. Many of us began maturing in complacency.

As we grew, however, our comfort was penetrated by events too troubling to dismiss. First, the permeating and victimizing fact of human degradation, symbolized by the Southern struggle against racial bigotry, compelled most of us from silence to activism. Second, the enclosing fact of the Cold War, symbolized by the presence of the Bomb, brought awareness that we ourselves, and our friends, and millions of abstract "others" we knew more directly because of our common peril, might die at any time. We might deliberately ignore, or avoid, or fail to feel all other human problems, but not these two, for these were too immediate and crushing in their impact, too challenging in the demand that we as individuals take the responsibility for encounter and resolution.

While these and other problems either directly oppressed us or rankled our consciences and became our own subjective concerns, we began to see complicated and disturbing paradoxes in our surrounding America. The declaration "all men are created equal . . ." rang hollow before the facts of Negro life in the South and the big cities of the North. The proclaimed peaceful intentions of the United States contradicted its economic and military investments in the Cold War status quo.

We witnessed, and continue to witness, other paradoxes. With nuclear energy whole cities can easily be powered, yet the dominant nation-states seem more likely to unleash destruction greater than that incurred in all wars of human history.

Although our own technology is destroying old and creating new forms of social organization, men still tolerate meaningless work and idleness. While two-thirds of mankind suffers undernourishment, our own upper classes revel amidst superfluous abundance. Although world population is expected to double in forty years, the nations still tolerate anarchy as a major principle of international conduct and uncontrolled exploitation governs the sapping of the earth's physical resources. Although mankind desperately needs revolutionary leadership, America rests in national stalemate, its goals ambiguous and tradition-bound instead of informed and clear, its democratic system apathetic and manipulated rather than "of, by, and for the people."

Not only did tarnish appear on our image of American virtue, not only did disillusion occur when the hypocrisy of American ideals was discovered, but we began to sense that what we had originally seen as the American Golden Age was actually the decline of an era. The worldwide outbreak of revolution against colonialism and imperialism, the entrenchment of totalitarian states, the menace of war, overpopulation, international disorder, supertechnology—these trends were testing the tenacity of our own commitment to democracy and freedom and our abilities to visualize their application to a world in upheaval.

Our work is guided by the sense that we may be the last generation in the experiment with living. But we are a minority—the vast majority of our people regard the temporary equilibriums of our society and world as eternally-functional parts. In this is perhaps the outstanding paradox: we ourselves are imbued with urgency, yet the message of our society is that there is no viable alternative to the present. Beneath the reassuring tones of the politicians, beneath the common opinion that America will "muddle through," beneath the stagnation of those who have closed their minds to the future, is the pervading feeling that there simply are no alternatives, that our times have witnessed the exhaustion not only of Utopias, but of any new departures as well. Feeling the press of complexity upon the emptiness of life, people are fearful of the thought that at any moment things might be thrust out of control. They fear change itself, since change might smash whatever invisible framework seems to hold back chaos for them now. For most Americans, all crusades are suspect, threatening. The fact that each individual sees apathy in his fellows perpetuates the common reluctance to organize for change. The dominant institutions are complex enough to blunt the minds of their potential critics, and entrenched enough to swiftly dissipate or entirely repel the energies of protest and reform, thus limiting human expectancies. Then, too, we are a materially improved society, and by our own improvements we seem to have weakened the case for further change.

Some would have us believe that Americans feel contentment amidst prosperity—but might it not be better be called a glaze above deeply-felt anxieties about their role in the new world? And if these anxieties produce a developed indifference to human affairs, do they not as well produce a yearning to believe there *is* an alternative to the present, that something *can* be done to change circumstances in the school, the workplaces, the bureaucracies, the government? It is to this latter yearning, at once the spark and engine of change, that we direct our present appeal.

The search for truly democratic alternatives to the present, and a commitment to social experimentation with them, is a worthy and fulfilling human enterprise, one which moves us and, we hope, others today. On such a basis do we offer this document of our convictions and analysis: as an effort in understanding and changing the conditions of humanity in the late twentieth century, an effort rooted in the ancient, still unfulfilled conception of man attaining determining influence over his circumstances of life.

Values

Making values explicit—an initial task in establishing alternatives—is an activity that has been devalued and corrupted. The conventional moral terms of the age, the politician moralities—"free world," "people's democracies"—reflect realities poorly, if at all, and seem to function more as ruling myths than as descriptive principles. But neither has our experience in the universities brought us moral enlightenment. Our professors and administrators sacrifice controversy to public relations; their curriculums change more slowly than the living events of the world; their skills and silence are purchased by investors in the arms race; passion is called unscholastic. The questions we might want raised—what is really important? can we live in a different and better way? if we wanted to change society, how would we do it?—are not thought to be questions of a "fruitful, empirical nature," and thus are brushed aside.

Unlike youth in other countries we are used to moral leadership being exercised and moral dimensions being clarified by our elders. But today, for us, not even the liberal and socialist preachments of the past seem adequate to the forms of the present. Consider the old slogans: Capitalism Cannot Reform Itself, United Front Against Fascism, General Strike, All Out on May Day. Or, more recently, No Cooperation with Commies and Fellow Travellers, Ideologies are Exhausted, Bipartisanship, No Utopias. These are incomplete, and there are few new prophets. It has been said that our liberal and socialist predecessors were plagued by vision without program, while our own generation is plagued by program without vision. All around us there is astute grasp of method, technique—the committee, the ad hoc group, the lobbyist, the hard and soft sell, the make, the projected image—but, if pressed critically, such expertise is incompetent to explain its implicit ideals. It is highly fashionable to identify oneself by old categories, or by naming a respected political figure, or by explaining "how we would vote" on various issues.

Theoretic chaos has replaced the idealistic thinking of old—and, unable to reconstitute theoretic order, men have condemned idealism itself. Doubt has replaced hopefulness—and men act out a defeatism that is labelled realistic. The decline of utopia and hope is in fact one of the defining features of social life today. The reasons are various: the dreams of the older left were perverted by Stalinism and never recreated; the congressional stalemate makes men narrow their view of the possible; the specialization of human activity leaves little room for sweeping thought; the horrors of the twentieth century, symbolized in the gas-ovens and concentration camps and atom bombs, have blasted hopefulness. To be idealistic is to be considered apocalyptic, deluded. To have no serious aspirations, on the contrary, is to be "toughminded."

In suggesting social goals and values, therefore, we are aware of entering a sphere of some disrepute. Perhaps matured by the past, we have no sure formulas, no closed theories—but that does not mean values are beyond discussion and tentative determination. A first task of any social movement is to convince people that the search for orienting theories and the creation of human values is complex but worthwhile. We are aware that to avoid platitudes we must analyze the concrete conditions of social order. But to direct such an analysis we must use the guideposts of basic principles. Our own social values involve conceptions of human beings, human relationships, and social systems.

We regard *men* as infinitely precious and possessed of unfulfilled capacities for reason, freedom, and love. In affirming these principles we are aware of countering perhaps the dominant conceptions of man in the twentieth century: that he is a thing to be manipulated, and that he is inherently incapable of directing his own affairs. We oppose the depersonalization that reduces human beings to the status of things—if anything, the brutalities of the twentieth century teach that means and ends are intimately related, that vague appeals to "posterity" cannot justify the mutilations of the present. We oppose, too, the doctrine of human incompetence because it rests essentially on the modern fact that men have been "competently" manipulated into incompetence—we see little reason why men cannot meet with increasing skill the complexities and responsibilities of their situation, if society is organized not for minority, but for majority, participation in decision-making.

Men have unrealized potential for self-cultivation, self-direction, self-understanding, and creativity. It is this potential that we regard as crucial and to which we appeal, not to the human potentiality for violence, unreason, and submission to authority. The goal of man and society should be human independence: a concern not with image of popularity but with finding a meaning in life that is personally authentic; a quality of mind not compulsively driven by a sense of powerlessness, nor one which unthinkingly adopts status values, nor one which represses all threats to its habits, but one which has full, spontaneous access to present and past experiences, one which easily unites the fragmented parts of personal history, one which openly faces problems which are troubling and unresolved; one with an intuitive awareness of possibilities, an active sense of curiosity, an ability and willingness to learn.

This kind of independence does not mean egotistic individualism—the object is not to have one's way so much as it is to have a way that is one's own. Nor do we deify man—we merely have faith in his potential.

Human relationships should involve fraternity and honesty. Human interdependence is contemporary fact; human brotherhood must be willed, however, as a condition of future survival and as the most appropriate form of social relations. Personal links between man and man are needed, especially to go beyond the partial and fragmentary bonds of function that bind men only as worker to worker, employer to employee, teacher to student, American to Russian.

Loneliness, estrangement, isolation describe the vast distance between man and man today. These dominant tendencies cannot be overcome by better personnel management, nor by improved gadgets, but only when a love of man overcomes the idolotrous worship of things by man. As the individualism we affirm is not egoism, the selflessness we affirm is not self-elimination. On the contrary, we believe in generosity of a kind that imprints one's unique individual qualities in the relation to other men, and to all human activity. Further, to dislike isolation is not to favor the abolition of privacy; the latter differs from isolation in that it occurs or is abolished according to individual will.

We would replace power rooted in possession, privilege, or circumstance by power and uniqueness rooted in love, reflectiveness, reason, and creativity. As a *social system* we seek the establishment of a democracy of individual participation, governed by two central aims: that the individual share in those social decisions determining the quality and direction of his life; that society be organized to encourage independence in men and provide the media for their common participation.

In a participatory democracy, the political life would be based in several root principles:

that decision-making of basic social consequence be carried on by public groupings;

that politics be seen positively, as the art of collectively creating an acceptable pattern of social relations;

that politics has the function of bringing people out of isolation and into community, thus being a necessary, though not sufficient, means of finding meaning in personal life;

that the political order should serve to clarify problems in a way instrumental to their solution; it should provide outlets for the expression of personal grievance and aspiration; opposing views should be organized so as to illuminate choices and facilitate the attainment of goals; channels should be commonly available to relate men to knowledge and to power so that private problems—from bad recreation facilities to personal alienation—are formulated as general issues.

The economic sphere would have as its basis the principles:

that work should involve incentives worthier than money or survival. It should be educative, not stultifying; creative, not mechanical; self-directed, not manipulated, encouraging independence, a respect for others, a sense of dignity and a willingness to accept social responsibility, since it is this experience that has crucial influence on habits, perceptions and individual ethics;

that the economic experience is so personally decisive that the individual must share in its full determination;

that the economy itself is of such social importance that its major resources and means of production should be open to democratic participation and subject to democratic social regulation.

Like the political and economic ones, major social institutions—cultural, educational, rehabilitative, and others—should be generally organized with the well-being and dignity of man as the essential measure of success.

In social change or interchange, we find violence to be abhorrent because it requires generally the transformation of the target, be it a human being or a community of people, into a depersonalized object of hate. It is imperative that the means of violence be abolished and the institutions—local, national, international—that encourage non-violence as a condition of conflict be developed.

These are our central values. . . .

The University and Social Change

. . . From where else can power and vision be summoned? We believe that the universities are an overlooked seat of influence.

First, the university is located in a permanent position of social influence. Its educational function makes it indispensable and automatically makes it a crucial institution in the formation of social attitudes. Second, in an unbelievably complicated world, it is the central institution for organizing, evaluating, and transmitting knowledge. Third, the extent to which academic resources presently are used to buttress immoral social practice is revealed first, by the extent to which defense contracts make the universities engineers of the arms race. Too, the use of modern social science as a manipulative tool reveals itself in the "human relations" consultants to the modern corporations, who introduce trivial sops to give laborers feelings of "participation" or "belonging," while actually deluding them in order to further exploit their labor. And, of course, the use of motivational research is already infamous as a manipulative aspect of American politics. But these social uses of the universities' resources also demonstrate the unchangeable reliance by men of power on the men and storehouses of knowledge: this makes the university functionally tied to society in new ways, revealing new potentialities, new levers for change. Fourth, the university is the only mainstream institution that is open to participation by individuals of nearly any viewpoint.

These, at least, are facts, no matter how dull the teaching, how paternalistic the rules, how irrelevant the research that goes on. Social relevance, the accessibility to knowledge, and internal openness—these together make the university a potential base and agency in a movement of social change.

1. Any new left in America must be, in large measure, a left with real intellectual skills, committed to deliberativeness, honesty, reflection as working tools. The university permits the political life to be an adjunct to the academic one, and action to be informed by reason.

2. A new left must be distributed in significant social roles throughout the country. The universities are distributed in such a manner.

3. A new left must consist of younger people who matured in the post-war world, and partially be directed to the recruitment of younger people. The university is an obvious beginning point.

4. A new left must include liberals and socialists, the former for their relevance, the latter for their sense of thoroughgoing reforms in the system. The university is a more sensible place than a political party for these two traditions to begin to discuss their differences and look for political synthesis.

5. A new left must start controversy across the land, if national policies and national apathy are to be reversed. The ideal university is a community of controversy, within itself and in its effects on communities beyond.

6. A new left must transform modern complexity into issues that can be understood and felt close-up by every human being. It must give form to the feelings of helplessness and indifference, so that people may see the political, social, and economic sources of their private troubles and organize to change society. In a time of supposed prosperity, moral complacency, and political manipulation, a new left cannot rely on only aching stomachs to be the engine force of social reform. The case for change, for alternatives that will involve uncomfortable personal efforts, must be argued as never before. The university is a relevant place for all of these activities.

But we need not indulge in illusions: the university system cannot complete a movement of ordinary people making demands for a better life. From its schools and colleges across the nation, a militant left might awaken its allies, and by beginning the process towards peace, civil rights, and labor struggles, reinsert theory and idealism where too often reign confusion and political barter. The power of students and faculty united is not only potential; it has shown its actuality in the South, and in the reform movements of the North.

The bridge to political power, though, will be built through genuine cooperation, locally, nationally, and internationally, between a new left of young people, and an awakening community of allies. In each community we must look within the university and act with confidence that we can be powerful, but we must look outwards to the less exotic but more lasting struggles for justice.

To turn these possibilities into realities will involve national efforts at university reform by an alliance of students and faculty. They must wrest control of the educational process from the administrative bureaucracy. They must make fraternal and functional contact with allies in labor, civil rights, and other liberal forces outside the campus. They must import major public issues into the curriculum— research and teaching on problems of war and peace is an outstanding example. They must make debate and controversy, not dull pedantic cant, the common style for educational life. They must consciously build a base for their assault upon the loci of power.

As students for a democratic society, we are committed to stimulating this kind of social movement, this kind of vision and program in campus and community across the country. If we appear to seek the unattainable, as it has been said, then let it be known that we do so to avoid the unimaginable.

FURTHUR READINGS FOR PART 5.

Political Freedom
Abraham, Henry J., *Freedom and the Court: Civil Rights and Liberties in the United States* (New York: Oxford U.P., 1967) Considers where a democratic

society must draw the line between the rights of the individual and the rights of the community. Examines the role that the judiciary has played in the evolution and implementation of civil rights and liberties.

Anshen, Ruth Nanda (ed.), *Freedom: Its Meaning* (New York: Harcourt, 1940). Forty-two essays by outstanding persons in a variety of fields on topics concerned with the history, meaning, and conditions of freedom. See especially Section 3, "Freedom in the Body Politic."

Benn, S. I., and R. S. Peters, *Social Principles and the Democratic State* (London: George Allen and Unwin, 1959), Chap. 10. Also published under the title *The Principles of Political Thought* (New York: Free Press, 1965). A general treatment of freedom as a political ideal. In addition, provides a critical evaluation of some of the central ideas expressed by John Stuart Mill in *On Liberty*.

Brinton, Crane, *The Anatomy of Revolution*, rev. ed. (New York: Prentice-Hall, 1952). Seeks to discover uniformities in four revolutions: the English Revolution of the 1640's and the American, French, and Russian Revolutions.

Bryson, Lyman, Louis Finkelstein, R. M. MacIver, and Richard McKeon, (eds.), *Freedom and Authority in Our Time*: Twelfth Symposium of the Conference on Science, Philosophy, and Religion (New York: Harper, 1953). A collection of fifty-seven papers on various aspects of freedom and authority, together with comments on the papers from other participants in the symposium.

Dowden, Wilfrid S., and T. N. Marsh (eds.), *The Heritage of Freedom: Essays on the Rights of Free Men* (New York: Harper, 1962). A book of readings dealing with political freedom in general and some particular varieties, such as freedom of the press, speech, and religion.

Friedrich, Carl J. (ed.), *Nomos IV: Liberty* (New York: Atherton, 1962). A collection of essays on liberty, with several authors devoting their primary attention to a critical evaluation of John Stuart Mill's *On Liberty*.

————, *Nomos VIII: Revolution* (New York: Atherton, 1966). Eleven essays on general theories of revolution, on Marxist revolution, and on the relations of revolution to ideology and international order.

Konvitz, Milton R., *Bill of Rights Reader: Leading Constitutional Cases*, 4th ed., rev. and enl., (Ithaca: Cornell U.P., 1968). A comprehensive collection of Supreme Court cases dealing with civil rights and civil liberties. Helpful background notes are provided for each case.

————, *First Amendment Freedoms: Selected Cases on Freedom of Religion, Speech, Press, Assembly* (Ithaca: Cornell U.P., 1963). A comprehensive collection of Supreme Court cases dealing with First Amendment freedoms. Helpful background notes are provided for each case.

Meyer, Frank S. (ed.), *What Is Conservatism?* (New York: Holt, 1964). A collection of essays by contemporary conservatives stating their views about the conditions of a free society.

Mill, John Stuart, *On Liberty*. A classic discussion of political liberty and defense of freedom of discussion.

Milton, John, *Areopagitica: A Speech for the Liberty of Unlicenc'd Printing*. A classic defense of freedom of press.

Neumann, Franz, "The Concept of Political Freedom," *Columbia Law Review*, LIII (1953), pp. 901-935. A general treatment of political freedom and its conditions.

Spitz, David, *Essays in the Liberal Idea of Freedom* (Tucson, Ariz.: Arizona U.P., 1964). A collection of essays treating the nature of freedom, its limits, and its relation to power. Defends liberalism against contemporary conservatism and radicalism.

Economic Freedom

Boulding, Kenneth E., *Principles of Economic Policy* (Englewood Cliffs, N.J.: Prentice-Hall, 1958), Chap. 5. Discusses the nature of economic freedom and its conditions.

The Conservative Papers, Intro. by Rep. Melvin R. Laird (Chicago: Quadrangle, 1964). Fourteen papers by contemporary conservatives on domestic and international problems.

Dunayevskaya, Raya, *Marxism and Freedom . . . From 1776 Until Today*, with a Preface by Herbert Marcuse (New York: Bookman Associates, 1958). A reinterpretation of the significance of Marx's thought by an author who believes in Marxism as a theory of liberation but rejects the totalitarianism of Russian and Chinese Communism.

Finer, Herman, *Road to Reaction* (Boston: Little, Brown, 1945). An answer to Hayek's *The Road to Serfdom* from which one of the reading selections in this text is taken.

Friedman, Milton, *Capitalism and Freedom* (Chicago: Chicago U.P., 1962). Argues that competitive capitalism provides economic freedom and is a necessary condition for political freedom. Author is sympathetic to, and amplifies, the type of position taken by Hayek in the selection presented in this text.

Hale, Robert L., *Freedom Through Law: Public Control of Private Governing Power* (New York: Columbia U.P., 1952). Taking economic liberty to be freedom from restrictions on one's economic activities as consumer or as producer, Hale studies the relationship of government and law to the distribution of economic liberty.

Hayek, Friedrich A., *The Constitution of Liberty* (Chicago: Chicago U.P., 1960). A leading proponent of free enterprise discusses the value of freedom, its relation to law, and its status in the welfare state.

Hoover, Calvin B., *The Economy, Liberty, and the State* (Garden City, N.Y.: Doubleday, 1961). Analyzes the relationships among the major national economies, the liberties enjoyed by their citizens, and the extent of the states' control over the lives of their citizens.

Knight, Frank H., *Freedom and Reform: Essays in Economics and Social Philosophy* (New York: Harper, 1947). A collection of essays by a critic of socialism who defends a modified economy of free enterprise.

Mannheim, Karl, *Freedom, Power, and Democratic Planning*, Edited by Hans Gerth and Ernest K. Bramstedt (London: Routledge and Kegan Paul, 1950). Urges that democratic social planning is the key to increasing freedom.

Petit, Thomas A., *Freedom in the American Economy* (Homewood, Ill.: Irwin, 1964). Deals with the changing relationship between freedom and order in the

American economy. Points out that the greater economic role of government has reduced freedom of business but not necessarily the total level of economic freedom in American society.

Petrović, Gajo, *Marx in the Mid-twentieth Century* (Garden City, N.Y.: Doubleday, 1967). A reinterpretation of Marx in the light of modern developments by a leading Yugoslavian philosopher. See Part II especially for his view of freedom.

Rostow, Eugene V., *Planning for Freedom: The Public Law of American Capitalism* (New Haven: Yale U.P., 1959). Reviews and synthesizes the impact of the "Keynesian Revolution" on the relations of government and economic life. Seeks to appraise the legal system for governing and directing the economy of the United States as one of the means through which we seek the goals of personal and social freedom under law without altering the property base of modern capitalism.

Selsam, Howard, *Socialism and Ethics* (New York: International Publishers, 1943). An orthodox Marxist presents his view of the ethical implications of capitalism and socialism. See Chapter VII especially for his position concerning the nature of freedom and its conditions.

Theobald, Robert, *Free Men and Free Markets* (New York: Potter, 1963). Argues that the provision of a constitutionally guaranteed right to an income is the only way to prevent the emergence of a technologically dehumanized consumer society.

Social Freedom

Bidney, David (ed.), *The Concept of Freedom in Anthropology* (The Hague: Mouton, 1963). A collection of papers focusing attention on the problem of freedom from the perspective of anthropological theory.

Farmer, James, *Freedom—When?* (New York: Random House, 1965). A black civil rights leader puts forward his views of what needs to be done in the United States to bring freedom to the minorities.

Fromm, Erich (ed.), *Socialist Humanism: An International Symposium* (Garden City, N.Y.: Doubleday, 1965). Thirty-six essays on contemporary social problems by an international group of authors, most of whom write from a humanist and socialist point of view.

Gettleman, Marvin E., and David Mermelstein (eds.), *The Great Society Reader: The Failure of American Capitalism* (New York: Random House, 1967). A Collection of articles and documents by major American public figures and their critics. Seeks to provide a critique of the basic assumptions, values, and aims of the Great Society.

Grant, Joanne (ed.), *Black Protest: History, Documents, and Analyses: 1619 to the Present* (New York: Fawcett, 1968). A collection of essays and documents dealing with the history and present state of black protest in the United States.

Jacobs, Paul, and Saul Landau, *The New Radicals: A Report with Documents* (New York: Random House, 1966). An analytical report of the young radical activists who have repudiated traditional liberalism and who seek a new vision of America through civil rights, university reform, and antiwar and antipoverty activities.

Josephson, Eric and Mary (eds.), *Man Alone: Alienation in Modern Society* (New

York: Dell, 1962). A collection of forty-four readings on the causes of, and possible solutions for, man's alienation in contemporary society.

Lee, Dorothy, *Freedom and Culture* (Englewood Cliffs, N.J.: Prentice-Hall, 1959). An anthropologist describes how different cultures vary in their concepts of individuality and personal freedom.

MacIver, Robert M., *Academic Freedom in Our Time* (New York: Columbia U.P., 1955). An analysis of the status and problems of academic freedom in the United States.

Marcel, Gabriel, *Man Against Mass Society*, trans. by G. S. Fraser (Chicago: Regnery, 1962). Focuses on the "mass man," who has been dehumanized in a society which reduces the person to the functions he performs, in which as an individual he has no distinctive worth and cannot claim to be unique and irreplaceable.

Simmons, J. L., and Barry Winograd, *it's happening: a portrait of the youth scene today* (Santa Barbara, Calif.: Marc-Laird Publications, 1966). Describes the happening world of the young. The authors find a unifying philosophy in "the hang-loose ethic," which embodies in a new way the old ideals of individualism, self-determination, and self-realization.

Westin, Alan F. (ed.), *Freedom Now! The Civil-Rights Struggle in America* (New York: Basic Books, 1964). An anthology of fifty-one selections dealing with various aspects of the contemporary struggle for civil rights in the United States.

Whyte, William H., Jr., *The Organization Man* (New York: Simon and Schuster, 1956). A study of the life and values of Americans who work in large organizations.

Wolff, Robert Paul, Barrington Moore, Jr., and Herbert Marcuse, *A Critique of Pure Tolerance* (Boston: Beacon, 1965). Three essays, written from different points of view, which agree that the prevailing theory and practice of tolerance are hypocritical masks to cover appalling political realities.

Biographical Notes

JOHN EMERICH EDWARD DALBERG ACTON (1834–1902) served as Regius Professor of Modern History at Cambridge University and was one of the outstanding Catholic liberals of the nineteenth century. Among his works are *The History of Freedom and Other Essays* (1907) and *Essays on Church and State* (1953).

MORTIMER JEROME ADLER (1902–   ) has been President and Director of the Institute for Philosophical Research since 1952. Included in his numerous works on educational, social, and philosophical problems is the two-volume *The Idea of Freedom* (1958–61).

ST. AUGUSTINE (354–430) synthesized Neoplatonic thought with Christianity. His most famous books are the *Confessions*, an autobiography describing his conversion to Christianity, and *The City of God*, which contrasts the world views of Christianity and paganism.

CHRISTIAN BAY (1921–   ) is Professor and Head of the Department of Political Science at the University of Alberta. His major published work is *The Structure of Freedom* (1958).

LERONE BENNETT, JR. (1928–   ) is senior editor of *Ebony* magazine. His numerous works on the Negro in America include *Before the Mayflower: A History of the Negro in America, 1619–1966* (3rd ed., 1966), *The Negro Mood* (1964), and *Confrontation: Black and White* (1965).

SIR ISAIAH BERLIN (1909–   ) is President of Wolfson College, Oxford. From 1957 to 1967, he was Chichele Professor of Social and Political Theory at Oxford. Among his major works are *The Hedgehog and the Fox* (1953), *Two Concepts of Liberty* (1958), and *Studies in the Philsosphy of History* (1968).

HUGO LA FAYETTE BLACK (1886–   ) is an associate justice of the U.S. Supreme Court—a position to which he was appointed in 1937 by Franklin D. Roosevelt.

BERNARD BOSANQUET (1848–1943) taught at Oxford and was a leader of the British Hegelian idealist school of philosophy. Among his books are *The Philosophical Theory of the State* (1899), *The Principle of Individuality and Value* (1912), and *The Value and Destiny of the Individual* (1913).

WILLIAM JOSEPH BRENNAN, JR. (1906–   ) is an associate justice of the U.S. Supreme Court—a position to which he was appointed in 1956 by Dwight D. Eisenhower.

CHARLES ARTHUR CAMPBELL (1897–   ) is Professor Emeritus at the University of Glasgow. His major publications include *On Selfhood and Godhood* (1957) and *In Defence of Free Will with Other Philosophical Essays* (1967).

FRED DAVIS (1925–   ), Professor of Sociology at the University of California Medical Center in San Francisco, is studying the interaction of Haight-Ashbury's hippie community with the larger San Francisco community. He is the author of *Passage Through Crisis: A Study of Polio Victims and Their Families* (1963).

JOHN DEWEY (1859–1952), one of America's outstanding philosophers, wrote upon topics in all of the major fields of philosophy and was also widely influential for his treatment of problems in education, social psychology, and politics. His major works include *Democracy and Education* (1916), *Reconstruction in Philosophy* (1920; enl. ed., 1948), *Liberalism and Social Action* (1935), and *Freedom and Culture* (1939).

FYODOR MIKHAILOVICH DOSTOEVSKY (1822–81) was one of the two or three greatest Russian novelists. Some of his famous novels are *Crime and Punishment* (1866), *The Idiot* (1868), and *The Brothers Karamazov* (1880).

WILLIAM ORVILLE DOUGLAS (1898–   ) is an associate justice of the U.S. Supreme Court—a position to which he was appointed in 1939 by Franklin D. Roosevelt.

FRIEDRICH ENGELS (1820–1895) was a close friend and collaborator of Karl Marx. Together, the two men wrote *The Communist Manifesto* (1848). Engels also edited and completed the last two volumes of Marx's *Capital* (1885–1894) and wrote numerous works developing the doctrine of dialectical materialism.

EPICTETUS (c. 50–138) was a freed slave who became one of the major Stoic philosophers. The two most famous records of his thought are the *Discourses* and the *Manual*.

SIGMUND FREUD (1856–1939) was the founder of psychoanalysis. Among his major works are *A General Introduction to Psychoanalysis* (1920), *Civilization and Its Discontents* (1930), and *New Introductory Lectures on Psycho-Analysis* (1933).

ERICH FROMM (1900–   ) is Professor of Psychoanalysis at the Medical School of the National Autonomous University of Mexico and adjunct Professor at New York University. Writing widely upon problems of ethics, social philosophy, and religion, his books include *Escape from Freedom* (1941), *The Sane Society* (1955), and *The Revolution of Hope* (1968).

FRIEDRICH AUGUST VON HAYEK (1899–   ), Professor of Economics at the University of Freiburg, has taught previously at the Universities of Vienna, London, and Chicago. A critic of economic planning, he is well known for such works as *The Road to Serfdom* (1944) and *The Constitution of Liberty* (1960).

PAUL HENRI THIRY, BARON D'HOLBACH (1723–89) was one of the most outspoken materialists and atheists during the Enlightenment. In addition to contributing to Diderot's *Encyclopedia*, he wrote *The System of Nature* (1770) and *Good Sense* (1772).

DAVID HUME (1711–76), outstanding British empiricist, wrote not only upon philosophical subjects but also became famous as a historian. Among his major works are *A Treatise of Human Nature* (1739–40), *Essays, Moral and Political* (1741–42), and *The History of England* (1754–62).

THOMAS JEFFERSON (1743–1826) was the third President of the United States, 1801–09. He wrote in the epitaph for his tombstone that he wished to be remembered as the author of the Declaration of Independence, of the statute of Virginia for religious freedom, and father of the University of Virginia.

IMMANUEL KANT (1724–1804) synthesized rationalism and empiricism in one of the most original and influential systems of Western philosophy. His major works include *Critique of Pure Reason* (1781; 2d. ed., 1787), *Fundamental Principles of the Metaphysics of Morals* (1785), *Critique of Practical Reason* (1788), *Critique of Judgment* (1790), and *Perpetual Peace* (1795).

RUSSELL AMES KIRK (1918–   ) is Research Professor of Politics at C. W. Post College and University Professor at Long Island University. He writes a syndicated daily newspaper column. Included among his several books are *The Conservative Mind* (1953), *A Program for Conservatives* (1954), and *Edmund Burke* (1967).

HAROLD JOSEPH LASKI (1893–1950) was a Professor of Political Science at the University of London and a leader of the British Labour Party. Among his books are *A Grammar of Politics* (1925), *Liberty in the Modern State* (1930), *The*

State in Theory and Practice (1935), and *The Rise of European Liberalism* (1936).

JOHN LOCKE (1632–1704), English empiricist and political philosopher, wrote two major works regarded as classics, *Two Treatises of Government* (1689) and *An Essay Concerning Human Understanding* (1690).

MARTIN LUTHER (1483–1546) led the Protestant Reformation in Germany. He translated the Bible into German and wrote numerous treatises, including *An Address to the Christian Nobility of the German Nation* (1520), *The Babylonian Captivity of the Church* (1520), and *The Liberty of a Christian Man* (1520).

BRONISLAW KASPAR MALINOWSKI (1884–1942), a social anthropologist, taught for many years at the University of London. Making a major contribution to the transformation of nineteenth-century speculative anthropology into a modern science of man, his works include *A Scientific Theory of Culture, and Other Essays* (1944), *Freedom and Civilization* (1944), and *Magic, Science and Religion, and Other Essays* (1948).

MAO TSE-TUNG (1893–   ) is Chairman of the Communist Party of the People's Republic of China and the leader of some 700 million Chinese. His numerous writings include *New Democracy* (1944), *The Fight for a New China* (1945), and *Quotations from Chairman Mao Tse-Tung* (1966).

HERBERT MARCUSE (1898–   ), one of the intellectual leaders of the New Left, taught at Brandeis University for several years and is currently Professor of Philosophy at the University of California at San Diego. Among his major works are *Reason and Revolution* (1941), *Eros and Civilization* (1955), and *One-Dimensional Man* (1964).

JOHN STUART MILL (1806–73) was the most influential British philosopher in the nineteenth century. His major works include *On Liberty* (1859), *Considerations on Representative Government* (1861), *Utilitarianism* (1863), and *The Subjection of Women* (1869).

HERBERT JOSEPH MULLER (1905–   ) is Distinguished Service Professor at Indiana University. Among other major works, he has written a trilogy on the history of freedom in Western civilization: *Freedom in the Ancient World* (1961), *Freedom in the Western World* (1963), and *Freedom in the Modern World* (1966).

PERCY HERBERT PARTRIDGE (1910–   ) is Director of the Research School of Social Sciences and Professor of Social Philosophy at the Australian National University. He is the author of *Society, Schools, and Progress in Australia* (1968) and numerous papers on topics in social philosophy.

HENDRIK JOSEPHUS POS (1898–1955) served as President of the International Federation of Philosophical Societies in 1952. He taught philosophy at Amsterdam University and was editor of the Dutch *Journal of Philosophy*. Author of several publications in philosophy and philology, his works have not been translated into English.

JEAN-PAUL SARTRE (1905–   ), French existentialist, was Professor of Philosophy at Lycée Condorcet from 1935 to 1942. A successful playwright and novelist, as well as a philosopher, Sartre has given up teaching to devote his time to writing. His major works include *Being and Nothingness* (1943) and *Existentialism and Humanism* (1946).

POTTER STEWART (1915–   ) is an associate justice of the U.S. Supreme Court—a position to which he was appointed in 1958 by Dwight D. Eisenhower.

STUDENTS FOR A DEMOCRATIC SOCIETY (S.D.S.) was founded in 1960. "The Port Huron Statement," largely written by Tom Hayden in 1962, expresses some of the basic beliefs shared by many of the members.

DAISETZ TEITARO SUZUKI (1870–1966) was a Buddhist scholar who wrote many works interpreting Eastern religious ideas for the West and Western religious ideas for the East. He is best known in the English-speaking world for his works on Zen Buddhism, which include *An Introduction to Zen Buddhism* (1948), *Essays in Zen Buddhism* (1949–53), and *A Manual of Zen Buddhism* (1950).

RICHARD HENRY TAWNEY (1880–1962) was an English social and economic historian who taught at the University of London. Some of his major books are *The Acquisitive Society* (1920), *Religion and the Rise of Capitalism* (1926), and *Equality* (1931).

FREDERICK MOORE VINSON (1890–1953) was appointed Chief Justice of the United States by Harry S. Truman in 1946 and served in that capacity until 1953.

LEONARD WOLF (1923–   ), Professor of English at San Francisco State College, has been involved with the Haight-Ashbury hippie community as an observer and as director of Happening House, a communications center in the district. In collaboration with his wife, Deborah, he recorded and edited interviews with fifteen hippies, publishing them in *Voices from the Love Generation* (1968).

INDEX